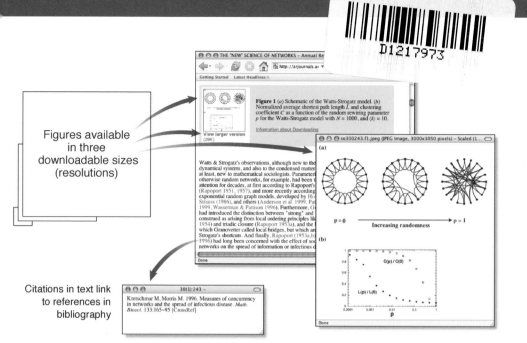

Figures available in three downloadable sizes (resolutions)

Citations in text link to references in bibliography

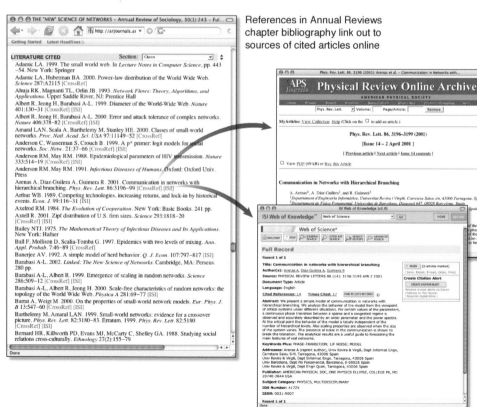

References in Annual Reviews chapter bibliography link out to sources of cited articles online

ANNUAL REVIEW OF LAW AND SOCIAL SCIENCE

ANNUAL REVIEW OF LAW AND SOCIAL SCIENCE

VOLUME 1, 2005

JOHN HAGAN, *Editor*
Northwestern University

KIM LANE SCHEPPELE, *Associate Editor*
Princeton University

TOM R. TYLER, *Associate Editor*
New York University

www.annualreviews.org   science@annualreviews.org   650-493-4400

ANNUAL REVIEWS
4139 El Camino Way • P.O. Box 10139 • Palo Alto, California 94303-0139

ANNUAL REVIEWS
Palo Alto, California, USA

International Standard Serial Number: 1550-3585
International Standard Book Number: 0-8243-4101-5

TYPESET BY TECHBOOKS, FAIRFAX, VA
PRINTED AND BOUND BY MALLOY INCORPORATED, ANN ARBOR, MI

PREFACE

The *Annual Review of Law and Social Science* will advance theory and research on law by providing a forum in which emerging and leading scholars review and debate the important work of our field. The first volume of this series pursues this purpose through several kinds of chapters. One set of chapters provides a staple of *Annual Review* volumes—contributions that survey and assess in comprehensive fashion the notable recent research of a well-established domain. For example, in the current volume, Whitman reviews comparative studies of capital punishment; Smith considers work on plea bargaining in relation to the jury system; Weisberg analyzes studies linking the death penalty to issues of deterrence and jury behavior; MacCoun addresses the literature on procedural fairness; Diamond & Rose update us on research with real juries; and Simon critiques the resurgence of individual risk assessment in the field of criminal justice.

Another kind of chapter that is well represented in this volume explores ways interconnected fields intersect with one another. These chapters bridge and link contributions from different disciplines. Here, they include Fligstein & Choo, who bring together work on law and corporate governance; Lucas & Paret, who synthesize studies of law, race, and education; Uggen, Behrens, and Manza, who connect studies of criminal disenfranchisement and the analysis of political behavior; Hadfield, who combines the insights of feminist law and economic understandings of fairness and welfare policy; and Williamson, who fuses the study of law with economics and organization.

A third kind of chapter informs readers about theoretical and methodological developments. Daughety & Reinganum reprise economic theories of settlement bargaining; Silbey recharts the terrain of legal consciousness; while Saks & Faigman bring us into the world of expert evidence after *Daubert*. We are anxious to provide space as well for topics that are still new, changing, and in the process of formation or reformation. For example, Klug provides an overview of the persistence and globalization of human rights, and Stinchcombe explores the modes and meanings of law facts. These chapters will map new territory and may often challenge existing boundaries of social and legal scholarship.

We also adopt a tradition of a number of *Annual Review* volumes in honoring one of our field's most distinguished scholars with an invited prefatory essay. Laurence Friedman inaugurates this tradition with his customary charm and grace, providing a rich overview of the law and society tradition of theory and research that he concludes "comes of age" with the initiation of this series of volumes.

So how did the contents of this volume emerge and how were their authors chosen for the topics we have covered? The largest number of topics and authors were suggested and vetted at an annual meeting by the editors and the membership of the editorial committee that is listed at the outset of this volume. Prospectively, we will rely on our growing stable of present and past authors to suggest additional areas and topics for review. Finally, we are pleased to receive unsolicited suggestions, and encourage that these suggestions be accompanied with a brief outline or abstract that can be taken to our board for its annual meeting.

All proposals are brought to a fall weekend meeting where the board joins together in an only modestly regulated free-for-all discussion of the merits of the many suggestions. A priority is attached to achieving a balance and diversity of topics, and the nature of the give-and-take exchange assures that each participant in the annual board meeting is likely to see no more than two or three proposals approved.

The prospective authors of chapters receive mailed invitations to undertake their chapters at year's end or in the beginning of the new year, and their manuscripts are due for review by board or external readers about a year later. The writing time is designed to allow our "high demand" authors to schedule their work and assure their timely completion. Our initial experience and that of other *Annual Review* volumes is that a very high proportion of prospective authors accept and complete their charge. Rejections of invited chapters are infrequent, but all chapters are reviewed, and some undergo significant revision before publication.

Looking forward, we anxiously anticipate and welcome the input of our readers. For now, we extend our gratitude to all who have contributed to the launch of this series, and we thank all who join us in this intellectual adventure.

John Hagan
Editor

Annual Review of Law and Social Science
Volume 1, 2005

CONTENTS

RELATED ARTICLES

Annu. Rev. Law Soc. Sci. 2005. 1:1–16
doi: 10.1146/annurev.lawsocsci.1.041604.115951
First published online as a Review in Advance on April 20, 2005

COMING OF AGE: Law and Society Enters an Exclusive Club

Lawrence M. Friedman

Stanford University School of Law, Stanford, California 94305; email: lmf@stanford.edu

Key Words legal culture, legal system, sociology of law, impact studies

■ **Abstract** Law and society, though not a field in itself, is the object of a growing movement that studies legal systems using tools of social science. Founded by sociologists, the movement now includes representatives of all the social sciences. It has developed strong organizations in the United States and in a number of other countries. Its adherents share a number of basic assumptions; they reject extreme ideas of legal autonomy and stress instead the dependence of law on its social context. Key components of the legal order, and thus key objects of study, are substance, procedures, structures, and legal culture. Scholars focus on the actual forces that produce law and on the impact of legal interventions. Sanctions, the peer group, and the internal moral sense are among the factors that determine actual impact. Much has been accomplished in the field, although much remains to be done, and translating findings into policy is often quite problematic.

INTRODUCTION

It was an honor to be asked to write an introduction to the first volume of an *Annual Review* that is devoted to work in law and society. It is a red-letter day for the field as a whole. Getting an *Annual Review* of its own is definitely a sign that a field is coming of age—it is a kind of rite of passage. Law and society studies have now, symbolically at least, made the transition from infancy to a seat among the elders.

But what *is* the field? It is not easy to give a definition or assign boundaries to law and society scholarship. Law itself, as studied in law faculties, may be a field, but it is most certainly not a discipline, and certainly not a social science. In civil-law countries, people talk about legal science, but hardly anybody in the United States, or in other common-law countries, uses the term; and nobody in the law and society business thinks of law as a science at all. Yet law can be studied scientifically or, if you will, studied rigorously. Not, however, from the inside, so to speak. Most orthodox legal scholarship asks whether some result or finding is right or wrong, legally. To most of us, this is a meaningless question, or at least a question that cannot be answered with the tools we have in our tool chest. There is nothing unusual about this situation. Sociologists of religion cannot answer questions of theology, nor do they want to. They have no way to decide which is the true religion and which is not, and no particular interest in the question. Sociologists of medicine have never cured patients of any known disease, and sociologists of sport have never won a game of tennis. But these branches of sociology are all, of course, valid fields of inquiry.

Law and society can be compared, in a way, to area studies. Russia or the Far East are not disciplines, and there is no such thing as the science of Latin America. Rather, they are or can be objects of science—a University Center for Latin American studies (for example) might house sociologists, anthropologists, historians, economists, and others. What they have in common is an interest in a particular geographical area. They bring their own discipline to bear on issues relating to that area. Law and society studies have something of the same quality. The field brings together social scientists who are, each in their own way, and with their own skills and methods, concerned with the legal system, how it works, and what it does. They are anthropologists and psychologists and political scientists and sociologists, with a scattering of historians and economists, and people from miscellaneous other fields.

Law and society is, in short, not a discipline but the application of other disciplines to a specific social system. Hence, it borrows its assumptions, on the whole, from the other social sciences. It borrows their methods as well. Some scholars do survey research, some look at archival material, some squeeze out findings from masses of quantitative data. Some do experiments—with mock juries, for example, or with the usual guinea pigs, psychology students. Some canvas the scene to find natural or quasi-experiments. Some carefully analyze legal language and legal rhetoric. A few might travel to tropical islands to watch the elders resolve quarrels in the shade of a coconut palm. Some use game theory, regression equations, advanced statistics. Others spin out socio-legal theory, sometimes from nothing more solid than intuition. Law and society is thus a very big tent, and getting bigger all the time.

In many ways, of course, the analogy to area studies is very imperfect. Every scholar who focuses on Russia agrees, in some basic way, on what Russia is, where its borders are, and perhaps even on some basic facts and propositions. But law and society scholars have in one sense little common ground. Each country—each society, each community—has its own legal system. Presumably, sociology and economics and psychology are much the same whether taught in Canada or the Chad Republic. But a legal system begins and ends at national borders, or in some cases at the borders of states or provinces. One can study French law, Icelandic law, the law of Honduras or Vanuatu; no two are exactly alike. It is hard, or maybe impossible, to formulate general statements that cut across all these jurisdictions—statements that also apply, or might apply, to the scores and scores of extinct legal systems, to the code of Hammurabi or classical Roman law, or to the hundreds of different "law-ways" of preliterate peoples. Of course, in the modern global village, a lot of legal activity spills over national borders. And the study of almost any foreign system of law, like the study of almost any foreign language, sheds a lot of light on one's own legal system or language. Moreover, science demands control groups, whenever possible, and what could be a better control for your study of your own legal system, today, than to compare it to other systems, either now or in the past.

Let me add a word about the definition of law. There is, as we said, no general agreement about a definition, nothing that commands a general consensus. Nor can there be. Law is not a thing in the real world that can be described with any precision. There is no such thing as a purely objective definition of law. What we call law depends on why we want to call something law. Most definitions presuppose two basic functions of the legal system: the process of making authoritative rules, and the process of enforcing or carrying out these rules. Carrying out the rules means enforcing them or dealing with disputes and conflicts about rules and rights. But every term here is a problem in itself: What is a rule, what makes a rule authoritative, what is a dispute, what does it mean to enforce a rule, and so on. None of these questions has an obvious answer. None has an answer that can possibly be valid for everybody, everywhere, and for every study.

To be sure, there is no lack of definitions of law, legal systems, or the legal order; or, perhaps we should say, no lack of attempts at definitions. Attempts at definitions do fall into a few big categories. They all seem to agree, more or less, on the notion of law as the process of making and enforcing rules (whatever that might mean). Some definitions emphasize the official or state nature of the rules and the process of enforcement. Law, in other words, is government. The penal code of Wyoming is part of the state's legal system; the rules of an Elks club chapter, meeting in Laramie, Wyoming, is not. Black (1972) defines law as governmental social control. Social control that is not connected to some aspect of the state is thus not part of Black's idea of law.

One may also define law in such a way as to emphasize formality or institutional organization. If the Elks club has rules and ways of enforcing them, and if the process is reasonably formal, then we can speak about the law of the Elks club. In Schwartz's (1956) classic study of two Israeli settlements, one settlement had a judicial committee; the other lacked any specialized legal institution. Schwartz defined legal control as control carried out by "specialized functionaries who are socially delegated the task of intragroup control." He placed his emphasis on formality and the existence of an institution. Both settlements, of course, were part of the state of Israel, and the judicial committee he described was a nonstate institution; it would no doubt fail Black's test. But if what we want to study is the whole process of social control or social behavior, broadly defined, we will probably want to include the rules of the Elks club and almost certainly the actions of the judicial committee. If we define our goal broadly enough, we will want to include what went on in both of Schwartz's settlements. Again, this is not an issue confined to studies of law. A social study of education can focus (quite legitimately) on schools. Schools are very important institutions, very worthy of study. But for other purposes, we might want to study education in a broader sense—including what people learn or mislearn from television, what they get out of newspapers and books, and even how parents inculcate norms and ideas into children's little heads.[1]

From the two factors mentioned—formality and connection with a government—we can construct a nice four-box matrix. There is to begin with law that is both formal and official. Any statute of any modern country would qualify. There is also law that is official but completely or partly informal. Official actions often operate within zones of discretion and leeway. Administrative government and criminal justice are shot through with such zones. A policeman stops a driver, starts to write a ticket, listens to an argument or a sob story, and tears the ticket up; he might give the driver a mild lecture and let her drive away. The police officer's behavior is official, but highly informal. Then there is law that is unofficial but quite formal. Most large organizations—hospitals, universities, big businesses—operate what look like miniature legal systems. They make rules, they enforce them, and they have regular procedures. A private university holds formal disciplinary proceedings when it catches a student cheating on an exam. If the student is convicted, he or she can be suspended or expelled. The student may even be entitled to a lawyer. As Macaulay (1986) has pointed out, "[m]uch of what we would call governing" is carried out by groups that are not part of the government at all, but by private individuals and organizations. Lastly, there are actions that are both informal and unofficial; most people would not consider most of these law at all. For some purposes, however, it might be useful to think of them as law, so that, say, the way a family makes and applies rules about how the children should behave could be looked at as a kind of law within the family.

LAW AND SOCIETY STUDIES: A BRIEF HISTORICAL SKETCH

The field—law and society—does not have a particularly long history as such; neither does modern social science in general. It is, of course, a kind of intellectual game to look for and find precursors here and there, as far back as one wants to go. And, of course, perceptive jurists in the early nineteenth century were hardly blind to the fact that laws did not execute themselves and that politics played a role in the passage of statutes. But systematic study really begins, essentially, in the late nineteenth century. Social theorists, including Karl Marx and Emile Durkheim, had a lot to say about the legal system. A true pioneer was Eugen Ehrlich, who investigated "living law" in the corners of the Austro-Hungarian empire where he lived.

By far the most important founding father was Max Weber. Weber had been trained as a lawyer; his brilliant and erudite explorations of legal systems,

---

[1]The same, one might point out, is true for legal education; it can be studied at the level of law faculties or law schools, but people also learn a lot (or think they learn a lot) about law in school, at home, and from watching television (Macaulay 1987, Friedman 1989).

particularly in the West, are still important sources of socio-legal theories and still provide scholars with insights and hypotheses. Max Rheinstein edited an English edition of Weber's writings on the sociology of law that was published in 1954 (Rheinstein 1954).

In the United States, there was a flurry of interest, and some research, in the 1920s and 1930s; but it soon petered out. Real progress, and a genuine law and society movement, really came into being only after the Second World War (on the history and nature of the movement, see Garth & Sterling 1998, Friedman 1986). The prime movers were not law professors but sociologists. Soon, of course, some law professors did join in. The little band of scholars founded a Law and Society Association in 1964 and incorporated it in the state of Colorado; its first president was Robert Yegge of the University of Denver Law School. The association began publishing a journal, the *Law and Society Review*, in 1966.[2] It holds annual meetings; at first these meetings were adjuncts of other professional meetings (sociology, for example), but since 1975 it has held meetings on its own. These have become quite large: Today, typically, more than 1000 scholars from all sorts of disciplines attend. Scores of papers are presented. Some subgroups have their own organizations: law and economics, for example. Groups of political scientists who study courts get together at annual meetings of political science associations and peddle their wares.

There are law and society associations in other countries as well. The Japanese society is particularly large and has a history going back even further than the Law and Society Association. Canada, Great Britain, and Germany have or had their own associations. There are also journals published abroad—the *Zeitschrift für Rechtssoziologie* in Germany and *Sociologia del Diritto* in Italy, for example. The Law and Society Association is, in one regard, unique. It is not formally a national association. Most members are from the United States, but almost a quarter of the members are not. Non-Americans have served on the board of trustees and are well represented at the annual meetings. Nonetheless, this is primarily an American institution, although it has a certain international flavor and is eager to have more. The meetings are ordinarily in the United States, but a few have taken place outside the boundaries as well—in Vancouver, British Columbia, and also in Amsterdam, Glasgow, and Budapest. The European meetings have had a cosponsor: the Research Committee on the Sociology of Law, an organ of the International Sociological Association. This body *is* formally international. It, too, holds annual meetings (much smaller than those of the Law and Society Association). Despite its name, most of its members are not sociologists: They are law and society scholars from a variety of disciplines and institutions, including law faculties.[3]

---

[2]There are now other journals as well, particularly *Law and Social Inquiry*, published by the American Bar Foundation (and formerly called the *American Bar Foundation Research Journal*). In 2004, a *Journal of Empirical Legal Studies* was launched.

[3]I am the current (2005) president of this organization.

BASIC ASSUMPTIONS

As we said, every social science is represented in the law and society movement (including history). Are there any beliefs, assumptions, axioms, or points of view that everyone in the movement shares? Probably not. But there are some core ideas or notions that would command, I believe, if not unanimous agreement, at least something close to consensus.

To begin with, people in the field have to make some sort of assumption about the autonomy of the legal system. More accurately, about the lack of autonomy. An autonomous system is a system that operates under its own rules, that grows, changes, and develops according to its own inner program. Living things, in this sense, have a great deal of autonomy. They have genetic programs that govern the way they grow and the way they live. A mouse is programmed to become a mouse, a flatworm is programmed to become a flatworm. Of course, no system is totally autonomous. The mouse and the flatworm do not automatically grow from a fertilized cell into a full-grown mouse or flatworm. They need, like every living thing, some sort of food or way of making food. An organism must, in short, take in material from the outside world. But the genetic program itself is, in essence, fully autonomous.

No social scientist who studies law thinks the legal system is as autonomous as the genetic program of the flatworm. It would mean that culture, the economy, politics, tradition, and social norms would have little or no effect on the way the system functions. That seems obviously wrong. There are, to be sure, many law and society scholars who feel that law is at least somewhat autonomous, or that it is partly or mostly self-referential. Probably most law and society scholars are willing to concede at least a little bit of autonomy. How much is a difficult question. There might be a slightly different answer for every society or community. In any event, I think most scholars who work in the field feel that the legal system is basically not autonomous, that it always bears the deep imprint of the society in which it is imbedded. Whether this is so or not is essentially an empirical question (but not an easy one to answer with any sort of rigor). Some scholars argue that it makes little or no sense even to talk about law and society as if they were separate entities. They are so enmeshed that they "constitute" each other. Such concepts as marriage, property, contract, and crime are legal concepts, but they also lie at the very core of social life. Relationships such as parent and child, husband and wife, boss and worker, landlord and tenant are both legal statuses and part of the very warp and woof of everyday life (Gordon 1984, p. 103).

There are a few propositions or assumptions that almost all law and society scholars seem to share, propositions or assumptions that are basic to their thought and research. Conventional legal scholarship is obsessed with rules, codes, procedures, and decisions. It pays very little attention to actual impact, or it more or less assumes away the whole issue of impact. But to law and society scholars, impact is always an empirical question. Whether some rule or decision makes a difference, and what difference it makes, is a matter for investigation and research. This is the case whether we are talking about overtime parking regulations, rules of tort or contract, or the Supreme Court's abortion decision.

A second proposition, closely linked to the first, is that the impact of some rule or other form of legal behavior depends almost entirely on events, situations, or configurations from outside, that is, from society itself. If Mexican cab drivers break traffic rules and rules about how much to charge customers more often than Finnish cab drivers, if more couples in Iceland have children without bothering to get married than do couples in Greece or Iran, the reasons have probably little or nothing to do with differences in the traffic laws, or laws about cabs or marriages in these countries. They have to do, above all, with aspects of Mexican, Finnish, Icelandic, Greek, and Iranian society. Of course, levels of enforcement of laws, methods of enforcement, and incentives and deterrents make a real difference in the level of compliance; it is not purely a matter of configurations in local society. But levels of enforcement and the like are themselves matters that always bear the imprint of their society.

A third proposition is this: Any major change in society will surely lead to some sort of legal reaction. Wars, plagues, earthquakes, the invention of computers, the so-called sexual revolution, the rise of fundamentalism, everything that goes on leaves its mark on some part of the legal system, or all of it. Many lay people think of legal systems as slow, or conservative, or affected by inertia or drag, or as harboring archaic features. What they really mean is that they disapprove of something the system is doing. If something seems archaic or behind the times, this merely means that some concrete interest group is fighting (successfully) to keep it from changing. Many people who have some vague idea about the common-law doctrine of precedent imagine that the common law, in particular, worships the past; they may imagine it is a kind of museum of ancient legal forms and practices. But this is a myth. Law is an intensely practical affair. It has no sentimental attachment to the past. In fact, it prunes away quite ruthlessly anything that does not serve the present. If something survives for centuries, it is because it is useful right now. The jury, the mortgage, and the trust all have medieval roots. But their utility is anything but medieval, and they are, after all, lonely survivors. The rest of medieval law is gone with the wind. The people who ultimately call the shots in the legal system are the people with power and influence, and they too are hardly sentimentalists.

Despite this, I have to be careful not to fall into the trap of assuming that legal systems always work, that because they fit their societies, they are all equally efficient and adaptive. This may be true, as a matter of theory and at some exalted level of abstraction. After all, somebody benefits even from a corrupt, bureaucratic system, a system tied up in miles of red tape and roundly disliked by the general public. Structural impediments (from some point of view) in the legal system correspond to structural impediments in the society at large. An autocratic society, a viciously corrupt and brutal society, will have a viciously corrupt and brutal legal system. It works, but not for the society as a whole.

Moreover, even if the legal system is incredibly plastic, it would be wrong to say that legal tradition never matters. The common law was neatly adapted to a feudal system, then neatly adapted to capitalism, and then to the modern welfare state, but it adapted in its own inimitable style. The English language is so totally different from the language of *Beowulf* that a modern American cannot read *Beowulf* at all, even with a dictionary. But English is still English and not Chinese.

The discussion thus far has already implied the fourth proposition. A particular type of society produces a particular type of legal system. The legal system of the United States is geared to a welfare-regulatory state, more or less democratic. A tribe in the Amazon jungle will have an entirely different system. The legal system of the United States is also extremely different from the legal system of medieval England. Legal tradition, as I said, makes some difference. But how much? There are enormous similarities in the legal systems of all developed modern countries. Each one is, of course, unique, and the study of what makes each of them unique is of great sociological interest (see, for example, the work of Blankenburg 1997, Feldman & Bayer 1999). Still, the legal systems of modern Japan, France, England, or Norway are much more like each other than any of these systems is like its own remote ancestor. Neither the Tokugawa Shogun nor Edward II nor Charlemagne would recognize most of what goes on in the legal world of today.[4] There is, I have argued, a modern legal culture that all these countries share (Friedman 1994). Lawyers in these countries can talk to each other quite intelligibly about the rights of shareholders, copyrighting computer software, antitrust law, air traffic control, and a whole host of other issues. Ordinary people can talk about divorce and custody, health insurance and old age pensions, and all sorts of matters that are legal but also of everyday interest and would be total gibberish to an ancestor who somehow came back to life.

ON LEGAL BEHAVIOR

Law and society studies are, of course, studies of human behavior. Each branch—psychology of law, anthropology of law, sociology of law, and so on—works on the basis of certain assumptions about human behavior. Human behavior is complex and mysterious; each science slices off a different part of the whole to focus on.

In principle, the work of economists should be at the heart of the law and society enterprise. It is impossible to fathom modern societies without paying some attention to money, markets, and economic behavior. Yet, in fact, few economists are members of the Law and Society Association, and few identify as law and society scholars. There are some very notable exceptions. Why is the movement

---

[4]In the case of Japan, there was, of course, a sharp break in the middle of the nineteenth century; but even without importing European law, Japan today would undoubtedly have a modern legal system, one way or another.

unattractive to economics? Not because no economist is interested in the legal system; actually, many of them are. But economists, historically, have tended to stand somewhat apart from other social scientists. This situation is very unfortunate. Why it is so is another question. I choose to dodge it for now.

Economics has achieved a great deal of success, made a lot of progress, and gotten itself invited to sit at the tables of power. The federal government has a Council of Economic Advisers; there is no Council of Social Science Advisers. There is no formal body to give advice on crime, delinquency, family life, or, indeed, on noneconomic issues involving markets, money, and risks. Economists even have a kind of ersatz Nobel Prize. No other social science gets this kind of high-class treatment. It is hard not to be at least a little bit jealous.

How did economics achieve all this success? Economists would say: because it is a real science and because they get results. Economics became a science, basically, by doing what all science must do: Economists chose a slice of life and tried to study it with absolute rigor. In doing so, they pruned away almost everything that would interfere with the formal and even mathematical beauty of the field. Essentially, economists tend to ignore most human motives. They have placed rational, self-interested behavior, maximizing behavior, at the core of their work. Rational self-interest is not all there is, and everybody knows this, including economists. Recent work in behavioral economics has, to be sure, chipped away at some of the edges of the basic assumption. Still, for most economists, rational, self-interested behavior is the default position. The result is a structure that other social scientists have often admired, and even copied, because of its clarity and rigor. This has been notably true of some forms of political science. Even in sociology, economics can cast a long shadow.

No other social science has had the same success in trying to get agreement on a set of basic, fundamental propositions. If economics is Euclid, nobody has invented a satisfying non-Euclidean sociology or psychology. Yet, implicitly, some work (in anthropology, for example) does seem to start from a different angle and use a different default position. It puts at the core of human behavior custom, norms, habits, and traditions; rational self-interest is then the exception, not the rule.

This may seem an exaggerated, unrealistic, or even delusional way of looking at the world. It may seem particularly silly in the United States (as compared to the Trobriand Islands). But consider the behavior of most people, ordinary people, on a typical day in a typical place, even in a modern society, far removed from any of the jungles and islands of classical anthropology. A person gets up in the morning, gets dressed, takes a shower, brushes teeth, eats, talks, interacts with family and friends, goes to work, has lunch, plays, has fun, makes love, goes to sleep. The ways these are done vary enormously from society to society, in every possible way; almost none of it is reckoned, planned, or calculated. Most of it follows familiar ruts and grooves.[5] Most of it is unthinking, habitual, and responsive to hidden and unconscious cues. Of course, I am talking about people,

---

[5]This, of course, might make it quite rational and even efficient; but that is another issue.

not stock exchanges or business firms. But even for businesses, a lot of what goes on can probably be explained not solely in terms of efficiency or rational self-interest, but in terms of habit, custom, and norms. This was, for example, the message of Macaulay's (1963) famous article on the behavior of Wisconsin businessmen. Indeed, these habits, customs, and norms form the template within which rational maximizing can and must take place. In any event, the motives underlying business behavior are complex; purely instrumental reasons are part of the picture, but certainly not all of it (see Gunningham et al. 2004). Markets, as Edelman (2004) has pointed out, are themselves cultural, and they are also political in the sense that "economic institutions are often the outcome of political contests and power struggles" (p. 192). Of course, the market ruthlessly prunes away firms and businesses that do not compete effectively, but this, too, takes place within a framework that cannot be explained solely in market terms. To be sure, it cannot be explained solely in nonmarket terms either.

Free choice itself is culturally determined, and is often an illusion. When I buy a pair of shoes, I think of the purchase as entirely my own decision. And part of it is: the color, for example, and the price range. But I never stop to ask why I, an American male, will wear pants and not a dress or a toga, why orange or purple are not acceptable colors for shirts or shoes, why one cut or style is fashionable and another will strike me (and everybody else) as hopelessly out of date, why sandals are acceptable in some situations and not in others. In some ways, people are like animals born and raised in zoos; they are not aware that their world of cages and enclosures is highly artificial, that their range of behavior is limited by conditions they did not create for themselves. There is, to be sure, a sphere of active and deliberate choice in all our lives; and it is an important sphere (Friedman 1990). Nor is there any reason to assume that the sphere of choice is the same in all societies. It is certainly bigger in democratic societies than in autocratic societies, bigger in modern societies than in traditional societies. But in all societies it is strictly limited, and in ways that most people are not conscious of. Very few people, after all, are trained anthropologists or sociologists. They are ignorant of how fashion, custom, and habit act as unseen puppet masters, pulling the strings.

This is true for legal behavior as much as for any other form of behavior. Sociologists, for example, should be able to tell us a lot about why people react to rules in particular ways, and even which kinds of norms, rules, and procedures they find emotionally or otherwise satisfying, as well as which kinds of norms, rules, and procedures particular kinds of society are likely to adopt. Criminologists, I think, can tell us more about crime—about why armed robbers rob, and how armed robbers think (see Wright & Decker 1997)—than formal models can. This is because they are more willing than most economists to talk to people, snoop around their lives, and sniff out their attitudes and motives. But my purpose here is not to trash economics. There are, as I said, first-rate economists who are part of the law and society movement, and their work, and the work of other empirical and behavioral economists, has been of enormous value. My purpose is rather to argue for more collaboration. All the social sciences that are interested in legal behavior—in human behavior—should work together and learn from each other. They have, after all, a common enemy: orthodox legal scholarship and its cavalier blindness to real-world concerns. Perhaps another common enemy is the ordinary public, which is woefully uninformed, and even misinformed, about issues of policy and law.

PAST AND FUTURE

On the whole, our field, law and society studies, has shown and continues to show a lot of vitality. It has grown tremendously in the past 40 years. As we said, the number of members of the Law and Society Association keeps increasing, and the volume of law and society work in the United States and elsewhere has increased as well. Most of the work has been done, and will continue to be done, by social scientists, but professors at a number of law schools have been major figures in the field. Canada, the United Kingdom, and Australia have respectable movements of their own, and scholars in these countries have been more and more willing to put their own systems under the microscope of the social sciences. In continental Europe, there are or have been important centers of scholarship: Germany, Italy, the low countries, Spain, Poland, and Scandinavia. Scholars such as the late Vilhelm Aubert (Norway), Adam Podgorecki (Poland), and Renato Treves (Italy) were catalytic scholars in their countries. In Asia, Japanese scholars have taken the lead in the field, but there has also been work in India, Hong Kong, Taiwan, and Korea, among other countries.

There are, however, all sorts of blank spots on the map. We can talk about growth spurts, but we must remember, too, that the work started more or less from a zero base. How far has the movement gotten? In some ways, not very far. Every country has a legal system, but not every country has a law and society movement. Most of the world has little or nothing to show for itself in this field. Law and society work seems to be a luxury good that Third World countries, for the most part, cannot afford. The work is critical and skeptical, and it has a hard time in autocratic countries. Even in richer and more hospitable countries, young scholars can find the prospects of building a career in the field somewhat daunting. Looking and measuring, and other kinds of empirical work, are costly and time-consuming. Nor is this work particularly valued in many law schools, compared with more orthodox kinds of scholarship. In the social sciences, looking and measuring are, on the contrary, at the very heart of these endeavors; but even here, law and society studies seem somehow outside the mainstream.

I am not overwhelmingly optimistic about the future of law and society studies in the law schools and law faculties. In most of these, law and society studies are probably doomed to be at best a frill. After all, in common-law countries, the main job of law schools and law faculties, quite naturally, is to train men and women for the professional practice of law. Some law schools, to be sure, were particularly hospitable to law and society studies: Denver, Northwestern, Wisconsin, and

Berkeley. At Wisconsin, J. Willard Hurst was an especially powerful influence. His field was American legal history, but not conventional legal history; rather, it was legal history that stressed the importance of the economic and political context. In civil-law countries, the faculties are obsessed with legal science, a pursuit that to some of us seems about as scientific as astrology or phrenology. In any event, career patterns and prestige structures in European and Asian universities seem to leave little room for empirical research on the legal system. In some countries, the field seems to be stagnant or even moving backward.

Despite the gaps and obstacles, we can and should celebrate the solid and rigorous work that scholars are doing. The contents of this volume make this point clear. Of course, as in all fields, there are trends and fashions. An interest in poverty rises and falls. Alternative dispute resolution comes to the fore, then fades a bit. Neglected subjects, like gender discrimination, burst on the scene and demand their share of attention. Some topics seem perennial: juries, the police, the legal profession, courts and how they behave. Trends and fashions, in part, reflect what is happening in society at large. If privacy and surveillance become social issues, scholars will pick up on that fact and turn their attention to it. In part, trends are responses to intellectual fads. In part, they are like fashions generally, that is, they pop up for mysterious reasons, then die back in an equally mysterious way.

There have been hundreds, perhaps thousands, of studies that we can classify as law and society studies. (Some of the authors of these studies would be surprised to be classified this way.) The existing studies deal with a huge range of subjects. Analytically, any legal system consists of substance (the actual rules, formal and informal, official and unofficial, that are in effect), procedures (ways of settling disputes, passing laws, appealing cases, and so on), structures (the bony skeleton of the legal system: organization of courts and administrative agencies, composition of legislatures), and legal culture. This last is a much disputed term. I have defined it, and used it, to mean attitudes, expectations, and opinions about law (Friedman 1975). Other scholars have had their own definitions. Whatever you want to call it, legal culture in the sense of values and attitudes is vitally important. Think of the law as a kind of machine. The machine has a structure. It also has a program of outputs. And it has directions: how to turn it on and off, how to make it run smoothly, and so on. But the decision, whether to turn it on or off, how to use it, whether to fix it or smash it with a hammer, depends on the decisions of actual people—the workers and bosses in the factory. And their attitudes, values, and opinions are what make them decide what to do. It would be hard to deny that culture in this sense is a crucial element in any legal system. Every person has his or her own legal culture, and perhaps no two are the same. But there are undoubtedly measurable patterns as well—the legal culture of men as opposed to women, of Chinese people as opposed to South Africans, of cab drivers as opposed to programmers, young people as opposed to old. All this is a legitimate, though difficult, area of study. The volume of work is, alas, not large.

There is another rather important use of the term culture. People talk about Japanese culture or American culture to mean long-term, persistent, traditional traits and habits—culture in an anthropological sense. Are there also long-term, persistent, traditional legal traits and habits? In one sense, the answer seems obvious: There are common-law countries, and civil-law countries, and sometimes the twain seem never to meet. Some scholars—James Whitman comes to mind—have tried to show that legal tradition has had a lasting effect on behavior and thought in, say, France, Germany, and the United States (Whitman 2000, 2003). There are also notions—much disputed—that some peoples are more litigious or claims-conscious, and that others are more disposed to harmony and conciliation. Americans are supposed to be the big, bad litigators, and the Japanese occupy the opposite pole. Kagan (2001) has argued that the United States is rather different from other countries of the West in its devotion to what he has called adversarial legalism. But there is also scholarly skepticism about American litigiousness, and the idea that there is a litigation explosion in America rests on fairly shaky empirical grounds. Some scholars, too, have been skeptical about the Japanese end of this cultural continuum (see, for example, Haley 1978). Perhaps legal systems today are, in a way, pretty much the same, and yet, at the same time, quite different, depending on the lens through which you look. But this is also true of human beings in general: all basically alike—arms, legs, brains, power of speech, genetic makeup—yet each one a distinct and unique individual.

Much of the research concerns itself with a simple and elementary question: How do legal institutions actually work? What do the police really do? How do courts actually decide cases? What is life like inside the Food and Drug Administration? In court cases, do the "haves" come out ahead, and if they do, why is this so (Galanter 1974)? There is also work on how law in the broadest sense gets made. If we start from the premise that social forces mold and shape the legal order, for the most part, we still have to ask the more interesting questions: which social forces, and how do they do the job? These are the underlying issues in studies, for example, of interest groups and lobbying, or of the work of public interest lawyers, or of what led California to adopt a no-fault divorce statute (Jacob 1988), or of how scandals, incidents, and horrifying crimes lead to changes in the criminal justice system.

Equally important is the study of impact. One of the main sins of conventional legal scholarship is that it neglects this matter almost entirely. The law student studies cases but is never asked: Did it make any difference? Did behavior change? What actually happened after the Supreme Court decided *Brown v. Board of Education*? Has a plague of malpractice suits really made doctors practice defensive medicine? There are surprisingly few studies of the effect of laws and decisions on society in general, or on some audience in particular. The question, at the most general level, is this: What factors monitor, control, and shape the actual impact of some legal intervention? A legislature passes a law. What happens next, if anything? The answer clearly depends on a whole cluster of factors. One of these factors is sanctions: rewards and punishments. This is probably the most densely researched impact issue. Especially rich is the literature on deterrence. Deterrence studies are impact studies in criminal justice. They examine whether ratcheting up punishment, or putting more muscle into enforcement, has an effect on levels of compliance. Common sense tells us that it does, but if so, how much? For example, do tough sanctions have an effect on the number of people who drive under the influence (Ross 1982)? The deterrent effect, if any, of the death penalty has been a particularly salient issue, an issue that people feel passionately about, one way or another. Does capital punishment deter crime—does it have an impact above and beyond, say, life imprisonment (see, for example, Archer et al. 1983)? Some studies say yes; some say no.

There is no question that human beings do react to the carrot and the stick. However, people are not blindly mechanical cost-benefit machines. The effect of the peer group has not received very much systematic study, but it is surely powerful. What our friends, family, coworkers, and other people think has an effect on what we do. Schwartz (1956), in his study of the two Israeli settlements, argued that informal sanctions—peer sanctions—in small, tight communities have enormous strength. Hagan et al. (1979) argued that strong, informal controls constitute one reason why women commit fewer crimes than men. The moral sense—conscience and the sense of legitimacy, the feeling that we ought to obey the law (see Tyler 1990, Friedman 1975)—is also a significant cluster of motives that surely affect how people behave. Here, too, a lot remains to be done.

I mentioned hundreds, perhaps thousands of studies: What, on the whole, have they accomplished? Not much, in one sense: no sweeping general laws, no breakthrough that would make somebody's heart pound, no magic discoveries that change the face of the earth. But in another sense a great deal has been accomplished. Small insights, careful studies of particular institutions—there is no reason to look down on these. If two researchers show that there really is plea bargaining in England, despite official denials (Baldwin & McConville 1979), that is no small thing. If a team examines what effect a California tort case had on how psychiatrists and social workers thought and acted, that, too, is important (Givelber et al. 1984). In general, law and society scholars have been like archaeologists, digging patiently into the soil, uncovering bits and pieces of pottery, exposing fragments of buried cities.

Spreading the word about our work is something of a problem. What we do and what we find is not usually sensational enough to make the headlines. An even bigger problem is getting people in power—or people, period—to listen to what we say. Unfortunately, many issues that are the subjects of our research are also issues about which people have already made up their minds. They already know, or think they know, whether pornography causes sex crimes or whether tort cases are driving businesses to the wall. With regard to some issues, the people who count hear what we have to say, but it has no effect on policy, for both good and bad reasons. For example, *McCleskey v. Kemp* (1987), a death penalty case from Georgia, went to the United States Supreme Court on a race discrimination issue. The defense relied on the so-called Baldus study (Baldus et al. 1983). The Baldus study suggested that, in Georgia, killers whose victims were white were far more likely to be sentenced to death than those whose victims were black. This meant, said the defense, that McCleskey's death sentence was fatally flawed.

A bare majority of the Supreme Court turned this argument aside. Georgia later put McCleskey to death.

Was the Supreme Court wrong? That, of course, depends on policy considerations, on political and social judgments. The Baldus study could address the facts, the data. It could pose a problem. But it could not resolve the issue. At least the Supreme Court took the Baldus study seriously. An intelligent and honest policy maker would want to consider the data and conclusions that law and society scholars can provide. But policy is policy. Ideally it should be based on sound foundations: facts, data, knowledge. Still, data and facts are tools; they never dictate an answer. And law and society scholars, above all, should be skeptical about how many "intelligent and honest policy makers" there really are in the government. The "intelligent and honest policy maker" is probably always a rare beast—if the phrase means someone who makes decisions solely on the basis of "merit," and not on political considerations or who exists in some rarefied world where his or her own norms and values play no part in decisions, consciously or unconsciously.

Of course, in close cases, data do make a difference. And people do change their minds. Perhaps not about deeply held beliefs, but surely about marginal issues where their attitudes are close to the edge. Here the field can make a contribution. A modest one, to be sure. But the same can be said for the other social sciences— the established ones, the ones that have had their own *Annual Reviews* for quite a while. In any event, it is a great day for us to be admitted as full members of the club of *Annual Reviews*. A great honor. But, on the whole, I think we deserve it.

The *Annual Review of Law and Social Science* is online at
http://lawsocsci.annualreviews.org

LITERATURE CITED

Archer D, Gartner R, Beittel M. 1983. Homicide and the death penalty: a cross-national test of a deterrence hypothesis. *J. Crim. Law Criminol.* 74:991

Baldus DC, Pulaski C, Woodworth G. 1983. Comparative review of death sentences: an empirical study of the Georgia experience. *J. Crim. Law Criminol.* 74:661

Baldwin J, McConville M. 1979. Plea bargaining and plea negotiation in England. *Law Soc. Rev.* 13:287

Black D. 1972. The boundaries of legal sociology. *Yale Law J.* 81:1086, 1096

Blankenburg E. 1997. *Patterns of Legal Culture: The Netherlands Compared to Neighboring Germany.* Amsterdam: Duitsland Inst., Univ. Amsterdam

Edelman L. 2004. Rivers of law and contested terrain: A law and society approach to economic rationality. *Law Soc. Rev.* 38:181

Feldman EA, Bayer R, eds. 1999. *Blood Feuds: AIDS, Blood, and the Politics of Medical Disaster.* New York: Oxford Univ. Press

Friedman LM. 1975. *The Legal System: A Social Science Perspective.* New York: Russell Sage Found.

Friedman LM. 1986. The law and society movement. *Stanford Law Rev.* 38:763

Friedman LM. 1987. Popular legal culture: law, lawyers, and popular culture. *Yale Law J.* 98:1579

Friedman LM. 1990. *The Republic of Choice: Law, Authority, and Culture.* Cambridge, MA: Harvard Univ. Press

Friedman LM. 1994. Is there a modern legal culture? *Ratio Juris* 7:117

Galanter M. 1974. Why the haves come out ahead: speculations on the limits of legal change. *Law Soc. Rev.* 9:95

Garth B, Sterling J. 1998. From legal realism to law and society: reshaping law for the last stages of the activist state. *Law Soc. Rev.* 32: 409

Givelber DJ, Bowers WJ, Blitch CL. 1984. *Tarasoff*, myth and reality: an empirical study of private law in action. *Wis. Law Rev.* 1984: 443

Gordon RW. 1984. Critical legal histories. *Stanford Law Rev.* 36:57

Gunningham N, Kagan RA, Thornton D. 2004. Social license and environmental protection: why businesses go beyond compliance. *Law Soc. Inq.* 29:307

Hagan J, Simpson JH, Gillis AR. 1979. The sexual stratification of social control: a gender-based perspective on crime and delinquency. *Brit. J. Sociol.* 30:25

Haley JO. 1978. The myth of the reluctant litigants. *J. Jpn. Stud.* 4:359

Jacob H. 1988. *Silent Revolution: The Transformation of Divorce Law in the United States.* Chicago: Univ. Chicago Press

Kagan RA. 2001. *Adversarial Legalism: The American Way of Law.* Cambridge, MA: Harvard Univ. Press

Macaulay S. 1963. Non-contractual relations in business: a preliminary study. *Am. Sociol. Rev.* 28:55

Macaulay S. 1986. Private government. In *Law and the Social Sciences*, ed. L Lipson, S Wheeler, p. 445. New York: Russell Sage Found.

Macaulay S. 1987. Images of law in everyday life: the lessons of school, entertainment, and spectator sports. *Law Soc. Rev.* 21:185

McCleskey v. Kemp, 481 U.S. 279 (1987)

Rheinstein M, ed. 1954. *Max Weber on Law in Economy and Society.* Chicago: Univ. Chicago Press

Ross HL. 1982. Interrupted time series studies of deterrence of drinking and driving. In *Deterrence Reconsidered: Methodological Innovations*, ed. J Hagan, pp. 71–97. Beverly Hills, CA: Sage

Schwartz RD. 1956. Social factors in the development of legal control: a case study of two Israeli settlements. *Yale Law J.* 63:471

Tyler T. 1990. *Why People Obey the Law.* New Haven, CT: Yale Univ. Press

Whitman JQ. 2000. Enforcing civility and respect: three societies. *Yale Law J.* 109:1279

Whitman JQ. 2003. *Harsh Justice: Criminal Punishment and the Widening Divide Between America and Europe.* New York: Oxford Univ. Press

Wright RT, Decker SH. 1997. *Armed Robbers in Action: Stickups and Street Culture.* Boston: Northeastern Univ. Press

Annu. Rev. Law Soc. Sci. 2005. 1:17–34
doi: 10.1146/annurev.lawsocsci.1.041604.115833
First published online as a Review in Advance on June 14, 2005

THE COMPARATIVE STUDY OF CRIMINAL PUNISHMENT

James Q. Whitman

Yale University Law School, New Haven, Connecticut 06520;
email: james.whitman@yale.edu

Key Words   penality, comparative law, modernity

■ **Abstract**   This article reviews some of the literature on comparative criminal pun-ishment and suggests possible directions for future research. It focuses on four topics. First is the sociology of modernity found in such authors as Foucault, Durkheim, Gar-land, Feeley and Simon, and others. While studies of modernity tend to downplay dif-ferences in modern societies, the work of these sociologists offer many starting points for valuable research. Second, the article discusses possible approaches to explaining differing degrees of harshness in criminal punishment. Third, the article surveys some of the approaches to the problem of explaining differing rates of violence in different cultures. Fourth, it explores some issues in the intersection between comparative crim-inal law and the comparative sociology of punishment. The article is intended to be suggestive rather than exhaustive.

INTRODUCTION

The literature on comparative punishment is one of the oldest and richest in social science. Lawyers in the Western world have been actively studying, and borrow-ing from, the criminal justice systems of other countries for many generations. As a result, comparative criminology got an early start. The early nineteenth century was already a period of vigorous comparative scholarship, in particu-lar among continental Europeans who were eager to import both the common-law jury and the American penitentiary (Padoa-Schioppa 1987, Schmidt 1965). Early journals of comparative law were disproportionately concerned with problems of punishment. By the later nineteenth century, international associations and con-gresses of criminology were already flourishing. There is no corner of comparative law with a longer or more distinguished history. Criminology maintains a strong comparative bent today: Comparative criminologists, including figures of the first importance like Michael Tonry, continue to produce a body of work that ought to be the envy of scholars studying other subjects (Tonry 2001, Tonry & Frase 2001).

Moreover, the criminologists are not alone among distinguished students of punishment. The theoretical sociology of punishment is superb. As new approaches to punishment spread in the late eighteenth and early nineteenth centuries, they stimulated theoretical reflection among figures like Bentham and Tocqueville. Thereafter the problems of criminal punishment never lost their place at the heart of theoretical sociology. The core research of sociologists like Durkheim and Foucault concerned punishment. There is also the memorable work of Rusche and Kirchheimer, Pitirim Sorokin, Gustav Radbruch, of leading social thinkers today like David Garland, Jonathan Simon, Loïc Wacquant, and more. There are very few fields in any part of the modern university that can claim achievements of such varied brilliance.

Indeed, the accomplishments in the existing literature are so impressive that the student might easily conclude that there was nothing left to be said about comparative criminal punishment. That would be a mistake. There remain real opportunities for innovative research. The statistical literature produced by criminologists, while it offers a fund of powerful insights, has some weaknesses. The literature of theoretical sociology, despite its nearly unmatched brilliance, has weaknesses, too: In particular, theoretical sociologists have often succumbed to the temptation of speaking about a uniform modernity in ways that tend to obscure comparative differences. Many aspects of comparative punishment have been neglected. The study of comparative criminology remains too isolated from the study of comparative criminal law. There is plenty of work to do.

This review is not intended as an encyclopedic survey of the field. Instead, it offers one view, singling out certain topics that seem to this author to deserve more investigation. Inevitably any particular view is somewhat idiosyncratic, and interested readers should also consult other accounts (e.g., Tonry & Frase 2001, Feeley 1997, Savelsberg 1994, Nelken 1994). Nevertheless, even an idiosyncratic view may serve to stimulate further argument and research.

Of the many topics that might be discussed, I focus on four. The first section of this report addresses the high theoretical sociology of modernity that we find in authors like Foucault and his many imitators and competitors. The sociology of modernity has a great deal to offer students of comparative punishment, but it must be used with care. The second section discusses a variety of approaches to one of the cardinal problems facing comparatists today: differences in the harshness of punishment from society to society. The third section discusses briefly one of the most challenging problems we face: explaining differences in cultures of violence. The last section turns to the uses of comparative criminal law. Well-trained lawyers, able to compare the criminal law of different countries, are in a position to do much-needed work in the field. Many other topics could also be discussed: For example, it would be valuable to investigate systematically some of the pitfalls in the interpretation of comparative statistical data. Such other topics must left for another day, though.

HOW TO USE THE SOCIOLOGY OF MODERNITY

The theoretical sociology of modernity, from Durkheim and Weber to the present, is rich in analytic insights that could be used to explain differences in criminal punishment from society to society. Comparatists should approach the work of the theoretical sociologists with considerable caution, though.

This is because the very concept of modernity is full of intellectual danger for comparatists. It is certainly the case that contemporary societies resemble each other in a host of ways, many of which can usefully be called modern. Nevertheless, it is difficult to reconcile the idea of a modernity with the work of comparative law. Modernity is, by hypothesis, the same everywhere it is found. This means that scholars who set out to plumb the mysteries of modernity inevitably tend to lose sight of the significant differences among contemporary societies. Differences are not what such scholars are looking for, and so they have at least a mild bias against finding them. The danger of bias is particularly acute among intellectually ambitious theoretical sociologists, who often hope to make their academic mark by crossing swords with the great theorists of modernity, from Durkheim and Weber on. A sociologist whose aim is to create a novel theory of modernity is unlikely to focus squarely on the differences among putatively modern punishment orders.

This danger has dogged the study of comparative criminal punishment from the beginning. The intellectual origins of the field date to the nineteenth century, and in particular to two great periods of international borrowing. In the early nineteenth century, the borrowings involved the Anglo-American penitentiary model, which was proclaimed as the wave of the future in many parts of continental Europe (Schmidt 1965, Petit 1991). In the later nineteenth century, the borrowings involved the theory of individualization in punishment, especially as advocated by continental thinkers such as Franz von Liszt, Raymond Saleilles, and Cesare Lombroso, all of whom held that punishment should be tailored to the individual characteristics of the offender (Saleilles 1911, Wetzell 2000).[1] Like the penitentiary, the theory of individualization was proclaimed as the wave of the future.

Wave-of-the-future theories tend, by their nature, to rest on claims about the necessary, and uniform, evolution of modern society. Yet of course sociologists rarely succeed in predicting the necessary and uniform future of punishment, let alone the necessary and uniform future of society in general. It is not easy to distinguish a wave of the future from a vogue of the present. Despite the difficulties of prediction, though, from an early date there was a modernist school of criminology (the school favoring, in various ways, individualization in punishment), and theoretical sociology has continued on much the same hunt ever since. Students of

---

[1] Lombroso's biologizing orientation was rather different from the individualizing approaches of Saleilles and von Liszt. Nevertheless, we can think of all these late-nineteenth-century thinkers as sharing a common goal in rejecting the formal equality of classical criminal law.

criminal justice continue to search for one or another form of "the new penology," to borrow a phrase used by two important and influential scholars who believe that the modernist project has not come to an end (Feeley & Simon 1992).

This hunt for the modern has produced a literature full of authentic brilliance, with insights that comparatists ought to be eager to exploit. As they read this literature, though, comparatists must be on their guard. The task of the comparatist is to explain differences—which means that the comparatist must be prepared to engage in an intellectually risky enterprise. The comparatist must be prepared to exploit the insights of theoretical sociology in ways that theoretical sociologists themselves rarely intended. The challenge is to use the theoretical sociology of a uniform modernity to explain how modern societies can differ.

This challenge is not an impossible one to meet. If we read the work of theoretical sociology carefully, we can find many analytical insights that can be used to explain why criminal punishment differs from society to society. My purpose in this section is to do exactly that: To explore how some insights of modernist sociology can be exploited to explain differences.

At the risk of overgeneralization, we can say that the best theoretical sociologists have commonly taken more or less the same analytic tack: They have tried to relate the practices of criminal punishment, in one way or another, to other social practices. Thus, some of our literature is about the relationship between criminal punishment, on the one hand, and the structures of workplace and household discipline, on the other. Some is about the relationship between the system of criminal punishment and the organization of labor markets. Some is about the relationship between the system of criminal punishment and the organization of the welfare state, or the management of prisons and the management of insane asylums. Some, most recently, is about the relationship between criminal punishment and risk management. This style of analysis promises a great deal for comparatists: If criminal punishment is related to other social practices, like household discipline or the functioning of the social welfare state or the practices of risk management, then we can potentially relate transnational differences in criminal punishment to transnational differences in those other social practices.

Let us turn, then, to how sociologists relate criminal punishment to other social practices. Much of our most interesting literature explores the structural relationships between the criminal punishment and other forms of social discipline. The widest-ranging effort of this kind is the most famous modern study of punishment, Foucault's 1975 *Surveiller et Punir*, which aimed to show that the forms of nineteenth-century criminal punishment were intimately related to the forms of discipline in the workplace and the schools. Foucault saw the same forms of regimentation and surveillance appearing in a wide range of nineteenth-century social institutions. Criminal punishment, Foucault argued, could only be understood if we recognized its structural affinities with broader patterns of disciplinary behavior (Foucault 1977).

Although few studies are as ambitious as Foucault's, many have taken a similar tack, analogizing the structure of criminal punishment to other social practices of discipline. Scholars have put particular emphasis on the analogy between criminal punishment and the discipline of low-status workers, especially in the context of historical studies. Thus, Gustav Radbruch argued that the forms of criminal punishment were borrowed, historically, from the forms of workplace discipline administered to slaves. Such practices as flogging and head shaving were first used on the unfree labor force, before being transposed into the world of penal institutions (Radbruch 1950). Thorsten Sellin expanded on Radbruch's argument in a wide-ranging book that linked centuries of the history of criminal punishment to the treatment of slaves (Sellin 1976). Similarly, several historians have demonstrated that the nineteenth-century American penitentiary borrowed its practices, in large measure, from the slave plantation. American prisoners were disciplined like slaves, and indeed they had the technical status of "slaves of the state" into the late twentieth century (Hindus 1980, Hirsch 1992, Whitman 2003). Other studies have related the treatment of criminal offenders to the treatment of nonenslaved low-status workers. Pieter Spierenburg, in work that provides an important historical corrective to the claims of Foucault, has explored the connections between the prison and the workhouse in early modern Europe. From a very early date, prisoners were subjected to a harsh work regime and commingled with the destitute in houses of forced labor (Spierenburg 1991).

The implication of these studies is much the same: The way we punish criminals is often closely related to the way we discipline low-status workers, whether free or unfree. Criminal punishment borrows its structures, at least in part, from the structures of labor discipline.

There are also other studies that relate practices of criminal punishment to the treatment of low-status laborers. In particular, scholars have seen important connections between the management of prisons and the management of the low-wage economy. Some of those connections follow directly from the fact that prisons remain institutions of labor. Inmates work, in most modern prisons, and their labor is generally priced very cheaply. This means that prison labor competes with low-wage labor in the outside world. But the place of prisons in the economy of low-wage labor goes beyond that. Indeed, some powerful arguments have been made by scholars who believe that the deep structures of criminal punishment have to do precisely with the economics of low-wage labor and unemployment.

The pioneering effort to link criminal punishment to the dynamics of the low-wage labor market was made in the 1930s by Georg Rusche and Otto Kirchheimer. Drawing on analyses proposed by the Fabian socialists, Rusche and Kirchheimer emphasized the principle of less eligibility. This principle, which assumed the truth of a Marxist theory of economics, described the relationship between prison and the economic opportunities of the least advantaged workers in society. If conditions in prison were insufficiently harsh, workers might have no incentive not to commit criminal offenses. Such a situation would be intolerable in a capitalist economy, which could maintain low wages only so long as a large number of workers were seeking employment rather than accepting incarceration. The logic of capitalism thus demanded that conditions of imprisonment be at least somewhat harsher than the conditions of civilian life for the average unemployed or low-wage worker (Rusche & Kirchheimer 1939).

Rusche and Kirchheimer's argument is very elegant. Indeed, the principle of less eligibility deserves serious attention, even in an age in which Marxist economic theory has been generally discredited. To be sure, Rusche and Kirchheimer probably paid too little attention to the dynamic of stigma, which also affects the incentives of potential offenders. Nevertheless, the core claim of Rusche and Kirchheimer is clearly correct, and it remains provocative: Prisons are not just institutions in which punishment is administered. They are also institutions that distribute social resources, including food, shelter, medical care, and more. This means that there is always some possibility, in every society, that imprisonment may serve in part as means of providing social support and social services to disadvantaged segments of the population.

Some of the most important recent literature has pursued exactly that insight. David Garland, in his earlier work, emphasized the structural connections between imprisonment and the social welfare state. Prison administrators tend to think of themselves as in the business of providing social services to a population of inmates made up of poorly integrated and poorly socialized individuals. Although punishment, of course, plays some role in prison, it does not necessarily dominate in the way one might expect (Garland 1985). A similar argument has recently been made by Loïc Wacquant, who sees modern prisons as institutions increasingly devoted to housing the desperately poor in societies that have given up on maintaining a social welfare state. As Wacquant presents it, prisons are playing an increasingly important role: From being one of many institutions oriented toward the management of the lowest social orders, the prison is gradually evolving into the primary institution serving that purpose. This does not necessarily mean, however, that they have lost their punishment function. On the contrary, it may be that, in our use of prisons, we have substituted punishment for the provision of social services. In a dire and depressing return to the world of early modern Europe, our prisons are once again becoming workhouses (Wacquant 1999).

Kindred arguments have been made about the relationship between the management of prisons and the treatment of one disadvantaged population in particular: the mentally ill. Early modern prison/workhouses also served as insane asylums, and scholars have often seen a connection between penal and mental institutions. Foucault began as a student of insanity before moving to the related topic of criminal punishment. In an influential argument, Erving Goffman related criminal punishment to the social structures of the insane asylum (Goffman 1970). And today some reformers, such as Human Rights Watch, observe that a stunning proportion of incarcerated persons in the United States is mentally ill (Human Rights Watch 2003). This suggests that American prisons are becoming the institution of last resort, or in many localities the only available institution, for the confinement of the mentally ill. Again, one fears that we are experiencing a dire and depressing return to the world of early modern Europe.

Thus, we have a rich and complex body of literature, all of which offers variations on the same basic claim. Criminal punishment is only one aspect of a much larger realm of social life: the realm of the management of low-wage, low-status, and disadvantaged populations. This claim is not all that surprising, but it is developed with tremendous panache and insight in the literature.

Now, most of the sociologists who have produced this rich literature have brought a strongly modernist orientation to their work: They have generally written as though all the world were evolving in the same direction. (I do not mean to imply that these scholars are unaware of difference. I mean only that their modernist orientation has generally diminished their interest in difference.) This should not discourage comparatists from reading these sociologists, though. Quite the contrary: Properly understood, this is a literature that can well be exploited for comparative studies, and indeed illuminated by comparative studies.

The critical point, of course, is that low-wage, low-status, and disadvantaged populations are treated quite differently around the world. This suggests a natural agenda for comparative study. For example, comparative lawyers could be investigating whether the practices of criminal punishment are different in countries with relative well-financed social welfare states, as compared with relatively poorly financed ones. The same is true of the provision of social and medical services to the mentally ill. Other issues deserve exploration, too. Labor discipline is not administered in the same way everywhere in the world. Continental Europe, for example, imposes relatively stringent limits on the forms of discipline that may be administered in the workplace. Is there something similar that can be seen in practices of continental criminal punishment? [This author has argued that there are indeed similarities between prison discipline and workplace discipline in contemporary Europe (Whitman 2003)]. These sorts of studies are much needed. They are not at all inconsistent with the work of the sociologists I have just reviewed. On the contrary, if properly executed, such studies can lend great support to the claims of those sociologists. Most of all, such studies promise something of real importance for public policy.

There are other ways, too, in which comparatists can investigate the relationship between criminal punishment and other forms of discipline and punishment in a given society. One of Foucault's claims was the discipline in schools was related to discipline in prisons. This, too, points toward another large and important topic: The punishment of children, both within and without schools, is a part of the larger system of punishment, and one that deserves careful comparative study. Corporal punishment of children is accepted in some societies and rejected in others. These differences are indeed of major policy importance today, notably in Europe: Continental efforts to ban all corporal punishment of children have been resisted in England. The comparative problems are not limited to Europe, though. Societies worldwide differ in their toleration of corporal punishment. Studies of these differences are badly needed. The punishment of children is perhaps the primary social locus in which punishment behaviors are defined and transmitted. Much the same can be said about spousal beating, which is tolerated (or encouraged) to widely different degrees in different societies.

The punishment of workers, both in the workplace and at home, is also badly in need of comparative study. Corporal punishment of workers mostly ended in the Western world in the nineteenth century. It has not ended everywhere, though. Moreover, the issues are not limited to corporal punishment. There are also significant differences in the extent to which workers are subject to verbal abuse and, perhaps most importantly, great differences in the extent to which workers may be freely discharged. Employment at will is, after all, a tool of discipline itself. Discipline in the workplace is another supremely important locus of social relations. Military punishment also deserves study. All of these aspects of punishment cry out for systematic study alongside, and in conjunction with, the study of criminal punishment.

Other aspects of the sociology of modernity should also be mentioned. One is the theory of punishment developed by Emile Durkheim, which raises the important question of the relationship between criminal and civil law. Durkheim's starting point was much that of the other thinkers discussed here. He assumed that criminal punishment was simply one of a variety of social mechanisms for steering individual behavior. Behavior could also be controlled through less directly coercive mechanisms—in particular through the incentive mechanisms of the developed market. As Durkheim saw it, the need for criminal punishment in a given society was thus correlated with the complexity of its markets. Durkheim was especially concerned with "solidarity": that is, with the mechanisms for inducing individuals to behave as members committed to the values and goals of society. As he saw it, a high degree of reliance on criminal punishment was particularly characteristic of relatively simple "segmented" societies, with little division of labor. In such societies, solidarity was created through penal legislation, especially penal legislation targeting the sorts of morals offenses that draw strong communal disapproval. In more complex, market-oriented societies, the division of labor itself was adequate to create social bonds, and criminal punishment was *pro tanto* less necessary (Durkheim 1984, 1992).

Durkheim's theory is perhaps the classic example of an account of modernity that is plainly wrong. The example of punishment in the contemporary United States is sufficient to undermine Durkheim's claims. Market forces play a larger role in steering American society than they do anywhere else in the industrialized world. Yet America has unusually harsh criminal punishment and considerable penalization of morals offenses. Nevertheless, there is a core insight in Durkheim that merits serious attention from comparatists. It is true that individual behavior may be steered through more than one mechanism. Criminal sanctions are one way of governing behavior; the civil law of obligations is another. A given society may use either or both of these mechanisms, and different societies rely on these different mechanisms in strikingly distinctive ways. For example, many matters that are dealt with through the tort system in the United States could be dealt with by the criminal justice system instead—and in fact other countries make much heavier use of light criminal sanctions in place of tort recoveries. Thus, sexual harassment is a criminal offense in France, whereas it is a strictly civil offense in the United States. How should we interpret these differences? To put it most generally: How should we understand a given social system of steering mechanisms as a system, in which criminal punishment plays only one, variable, role? This is a fundamental question, one that was first posed by the sociology of modernity but one to which only comparative lawyers can give convincing answers.

Before leaving the sociology of modernity behind, I devote a few words to one of the most recent, and most stimulating, efforts: the theory of the "new penology," proposed by Malcolm Feeley and Jonathan Simon. Feeley and Simon have argued that modern punishment is oriented toward actuarial risk management. Penal practice has departed fundamentally from the orthodoxies of the early nineteenth century, which viewed offenders as individuals who merit punishment on account of the decisions they have freely made. It has also departed from the style of individualization that dominated until 1970 or so. Instead, it engages in risk analysis, subjecting individuals to a kind of statistical punishment regime aimed at incapacitation (Feeley & Simon 1992). Like other leading theories, the "new penology" thus places criminal punishment within the context of a larger domain of social practices. Criminal punishment is akin to the insurance system, social welfare state systems, workplace safety regimes, environmental regulation, and the whole range of risk minimization devices used in the modern "risk society."

This theory deserves much more extended discussion than I can give it here. Let me only observe that the "new penology," like so much of what I have described, may overgeneralize the uniformity of the modern world. Risk-minimization practices differ dramatically from society to society. For example, some forms of risk-seeking behavior are much more widespread in the United States than they are in Western Europe. Levels of consumer indebtedness are an illustrative example: American consumers are willing to live with much higher levels of financial risk than are consumers elsewhere. The diminishing level of financial security for the unemployed and elderly in the United States may be another example: The American polity seems less committed to minimizing risk than are other polities. It is simply not clear that the United States offers a good example of a risk society of the kind we find in Germany. How then does American penal policy fit in? Why do we see different mixes of socially accepted risk in different societies? These are, once again, questions that only careful comparative study can address.

EXPLAINING HARSHNESS

Some of the most urgent problems in the comparative study of punishment involve comparative harshness or punitiveness. Some societies have markedly harsher punishment than others. Rates of incarceration are one measure of this. Another, much more problematic measure is the use of the death penalty. Beyond these easily ascertainable measures of harshness there are also others that are more elusive but of great importance. Conditions within carceral institutions are an important measure of harshness, for example. So is the range of behavior criminalized and the severity of the application of alternative sanctions. It is clear that, by these measures, some industrialized and industrializing societies are far harsher than others. Toward the mild end of the spectrum are the Scandinavian countries, the countries of northern continental Europe, and Japan. Toward the harsh end we find the United States, Russia, South Africa, and China.

It is a matter of pressing public importance to determine why these differences exist. Nevertheless, despite the excellent work of such scholars as Tonry and Frase, close comparative study of harshness remains relatively rare (Tonry & Frase 2001). Once again, this arguably has something to do with our theoretical sociology, with its inveterate tendency to speak in terms of a modernity. Nevertheless, not all is dark. Our literature does offer some analytic tools that could be employed by comparatists to shed new light on differences in harshness. In particular, in this section, I suggest four promising avenues of investigation: First, that harshness in criminal punishment can be correlated with the relative heterogeneity of a given society; second, that it can be correlated with religious traditions; third, that it can be correlated with patterns of political economy; and fourth, that it can be correlated with patterns of social hierarchy.

Studies of the relative heterogeneity of societies are particularly promising. The hypothesis that harshness in criminal punishment is a function of social hetero-geneity was best stated by Pitirim Sorokin, a Russian emigré working at Harvard during the 1930s and 1940s and into the cold war. Those decades were a period of sharp ideological conflicts between communism, fascism, and democracy, of course. It may have been the intensity of those conflicts that encouraged sociolo-gists like Sorokin to suppose that modern societies might take strongly divergent forms. At any rate, in the effort to explain differences in the harshness of crim-inal punishment from society to society, Sorokin formulated his rather clumsily named "law of ethnojuridical heterogeneity," which held that more heterogeneous societies tend to punish more harshly (Sorokin 1962). However we formulate it, the fundamental approach of Sorokin has an obvious appeal: It is indeed possible that the harshness of criminal punishment in a given society depends in some way on the degree of heterogeneity in the population. Let us call this the heterogeneity hypothesis.

The heterogeneity hypothesis has obvious power. It is particularly well suited to explaining the harshness of countries with histories of racial exclusion and dis-crimination, of which the three paradigmatic examples are the United States, Nazi Germany, and South Africa. Punitive criminal punishment in all three countries has of course been particularly visited on historically disfavored racial minorities. Elsewhere, too, racial minorities are typically the targets of particularly harsh treat-ment. But of course racial heterogeneity need not be the only form of heterogeneity that matters.

Nevertheless, any broad claim that the harshness of a given society is a function of its social heterogeneity would have to be stated with extreme care. It is certainly true that we find relatively mild punishment in some societies that are homogeneous in the sense that they have a population of an overwhelmingly common ancestry. The Scandinavian countries and Japan come immediately to mind. It is plausible that criminal punishment in these countries is tempered by a sense of identity, or at least fraternity, among citizens. Nevertheless, it is also the case that we find relatively mild punishment in societies, like those of France and the Netherlands, that lack common ancestry but that have a long history of integrating outsiders: The relative homogeneity of a country like France, founded on the acquisition of certain cultural knowledge, linguistic capabilities, and a kind of daily habitus, is quite different from the homogeneity of a country like Finland or Japan. Countries like postwar Germany or postwar Austria present even more complex cases. So does the case of China, a country with a strong cultural tradition of asserting a common Han identity, but one with quite harsh punishment. In most or all of these countries, ethnic and racial outsiders are treated comparatively harshly. Nevertheless, in all of them the definition of the ethnic and racial outsider depends on exceedingly complex social traditions of exclusion and integration.

The case for the heterogeneity hypothesis thus must be presented with great care. Homogeneity can sometimes belong more to the realm of constitutive national mythology than to the realm of common ancestry—to the realm of the "imagined community" (Anderson 1991). This means that it will rarely do simply to seek easily verifiable statistical measures of social heterogeneity. A careful scholar will always have to take account of qualitatively elusive and complex cultural traditions. That said, though, studies of the relationship between social heterogeneity (as carefully defined) and harshness are among the most promising areas of comparative investigation. A good study of developments in the Netherlands, for example, could offer great and generalizable insight: That country is currently wrestling painfully with punishment traditions that seem to assume national homogeneity in the face of an incontrovertibly heterogeneous population.

Alongside the heterogeneity hypothesis are several other important and appealing analytic possibilities. I single out three in particular: religious traditions; political structures; and, briefly, traditions of social hierarchy, which I have discussed at length elsewhere (Whitman 2003).

The idea that religious traditions might account for differences in the harshness of the criminal justice system has become especially intriguing as a result of the recent decades of increasing harshness in the United States. Viewed on a state-by-state basis, it seems probable that American harshness correlates with Christian fundamentalist sentiment. The rhetoric of American harshness is also frequently Christian in coloration. This suggests the intuitively plausible hypothesis that American harshness is in some way the product of what is sometimes called an Old Testament strain of severity in some American sects—a strain marked most particularly by its fondness for the talionic "eye for an eye, tooth for a tooth."

Outside the United States, too, the same hypothesis has real attractions. We might well expect harshness in punishment to be connected to religious tradition. All the world religions are founded on some account of just deserts. This is true of the major schools of Buddhism, for example, just as it is true of Islam and Christianity. It would not be surprising to learn that social attitudes toward punishment were closely connected to the historically prevailing religious values of a given society.

This is another hypothesis that can be tested—although again, testing it requires real finesse. We can do regional studies of the United States. We can also do transnational studies that attempt to relate harshness to religious tradition. These are difficult projects that can only be undertaken by scholars willing and able to master challenging problems in the theology and practice of different religions. Nevertheless, they cry out to be done. Cross-regional studies of Catholic and Protestant areas of Europe, for example, may prove revealing. The same is true of studies of harshness in countries marked by the Islamic revival.

Studies of differences in political traditions are also much needed. Indeed, the comparative political economy of punishment may be the single most neglected area in the field. This author has argued that the harshness of American punishment is in part the product of a pernicious pattern in American political economy. Criminal punishment in the United States is the subject of democratic politics. Politicians often run on tough-on-crime platforms. Judges and prosecutors are often elected officials, who in effect also run for office on tough-on-crime platforms. In these respects, criminal punishment is significantly more politicized in the United States than it is in countries such as France or Germany, where judges and prosecutors pursue advancement strictly through bureaucratic career paths, and where the criminal justice profession maintains better control both of the penal code and of the process of criminal punishment (Whitman 2003). That claim could be tested against examples of other countries in which criminal punishment is comparatively more or less democratized.

More broadly, the place of criminal punishment within the larger political system deserves study. Simon (1997) has written provocatively about "governing through crime." Comparatists could profitably extend his approach. How often do governments attempt to create or cement popular support through highly visible punishments? Such practices are familiar from the histories of both fascism and communism. Are they common? What determines their nature, and the extent of their use? These are questions that lend themselves to a Durkheimian approach: Criminal punishment can be used to create forms of social solidarity. High-profile criminal cases in particular may be used to stir up the voting public in ways useful both to democratic politicians and to authoritarian states.

Indeed, fundamental questions about dictatorship and democracy deserve study. Do dictatorships use harsh punishments to intimidate their populations? Are democracies more or less prone to harshness? These are large and important questions that have not always been dealt with carefully. (For an example of careful political science research, see Shapiro 1981.) In treating authoritarian regimes in particular, it is important to distinguish between political offenders and common criminals. If we exclude the category of political offenses, do we discover that punishment is systematically harsher or milder in authoritarian regimes?

Finally, let me turn to another possible causal factor in the harshness of criminal punishment, one that I have explored at length elsewhere (Whitman 2003). Harshness in punishment may have something to do with traditions of hierarchical ordering in a given society. Punishment, as the philosopher Jean Hampton (1992) and others have argued, has an inherently degrading component: The sting of punishment tends to have something to do with the fact that the person punished is treated like an inferior. This means that the system of criminal punishment in any society has to be seen in the context of its forms of social hierarchy. Hierarchical behavior is learned, culturally conditioned behavior. Punishment as a form of hierarchical behavior thus has a cultural context.

As I have tried to show, attention to traditions of hierarchical behavior help explain why criminal punishment is milder in contemporary Germany and France than it is in the United States. Over the last two centuries, the German and French cultures have developed strong norms against degrading treatment. These have norms have affected punishment culture in those countries just as they have affected other aspects of German and French law. American culture does not have such strong norms against degrading treatment, and its punishment is correspondingly rough (Whitman 2003).

These, too, are claims that could be tested against other examples. Is it the case that we can link punishment culture to traditions of social hierarchy—for example, in countries like Japan, China, India, or Brazil? The arguments I have presented about continental Europe and the United States will, of course, only be fully convincing if they are examined in such other settings.

CRIMINAL PUNISHMENT AND SOCIAL TRADITIONS OF VIOLENCE

Traditions and rates of violence differ from society to society. This raises questions of fundamental importance for the study of comparative criminal punishment in part because the harshness of criminal punishment is clearly affected in some way by the rate of violent crime, or at least by the perceived rate of violent crime. For this reason alone, no account of punishment in a given society can be complete without some attention to patterns of violent crime. Patterns of violence matter for another reason, too: The practices of criminal punishment are likely to reflect the patterns of violence in the surrounding society. A society that is generally given to violence is also likely to be a society that deploys violence in its criminal punishment. Zimring (2003) has recently argued, for example, that the use of the death penalty in American states can be linked to histories of lynch violence.

Because patterns of violence are linked to practices of criminal punishment, explaining why some societies are more violent than others is fundamentally important. Why are American cities, for example, more dangerous than northern European ones? Why (to come back to a question raised earlier) have the continental European countries embarked on a campaign to criminalize the corporal punishment of children? What explains cultural patterns of violence?

We have no persuasive answers to these questions. Bodies of literature may point us in the right direction, though. Particularly noteworthy is the growing literature on the "civilizing process." This is a literature inspired by the sociology of Norbert

Elias. Elias, a dévoté both of the sociology of Max Weber and of the psychology of Sigmund Freud, argued that the decline of violence in human society could be linked to the rise of other cultural patterns of self-control. In particular, the forms of self-control inculcated through courtly forms of etiquette tended to damp violent instincts. Thus, as human beings became more "civilized," whether in their table manners or in their forms of verbal *politesse*, they became less violent (Elias 2000).

Elias's sociology has inspired a large literature (e.g., Spierenburg 1998). It does seem to offer a means of explaining some of the pattern of continental European history. It remains quite unclear, however, whether Elias's arguments can be easily extended beyond northern Europe. To date, though, Elias has few competitors among social scientists aiming to explain how rates of violence can differ so dramatically from society to society.

This subject needs careful, sustained study. There are interesting starting points in the literature of psychology. Scholars have argued, for example, that violent impulses can be traced to cultural patterns of attachment to personal honor. This suggests an interesting avenue for the explanation of differing levels of violence, for example, between the northern and southern United States (Nisbett & Cohen 1996). Further study might produce further examples.

Whatever approach scholars take, though, they must make some effort to explain the differing pattern of human violence. In the end, no account of comparative criminal justice will be adequate without some elucidation of this fundamental problem.

COMPARATIVE CRIMINAL LAW AND COMPARATIVE PUNISHMENT

Some of the most promising, and least studied, topics in comparative punishment involve comparative criminal law, of a kind that only trained lawyers can do well. Lawyers willing to deploy their expertise in technical criminal law can make important contributions to our understanding of comparative punishment.

For comparative purposes, criminal law can be usefully broken down into three broad subject areas. First is penalization: that is, the range and type of human behaviors subject to potential criminal liability in a given society. Second is doctrinal criminal law: the details of the doctrinal manipulation of questions of criminal responsibility. Third is the law of punishment: the law of the nature and severity of punishments.

All three of these subject areas are of interest for comparatists. With regard to the first, we want to know what different sorts of behavior are forbidden in different societies. For example, are drugs and prostitution penalized? How are nonviolent property crimes treated? How do different societies approach the relationship between civil remedies and criminal remedies? With regard to the second, we want to know how different societies determine criminal responsibility. In particular, we want to understand when different societies excuse or justify nominally criminal acts, and how willing different societies are to criminalize collective and unintentional acts. Third, we want to know how different societies regulate the process of punishment.

Work has been done in all of these areas, but there is room for much more. The penalization of morals offenses has certainly attracted some attention. There are comparative studies of the treatment of intoxicants and prostitution, for example. Beyond morals offenses, however, there are numerous neglected topics that deserve careful study. Take the treatment of nonviolent property offenses. Such offenses are generally no longer subject to imprisonment in Western European countries, whereas in the United States the imprisonment of property offenders has contributed considerably to high comparative incarceration rates. What explains the difference in attitude? Why are certain forms of behavior formally criminalized in some societies and not others? Some of the most important contemporary problems in comparative penalization have to do with the business sector. In which societies are business executives exposed to the serious danger of prosecution, and why? When and why are antitrust violations subject to criminal prosecution? Prosecution of politicians is another example of great current importance: Politicians are much more actively prosecuted in some countries, such as Italy, than in others, such as Germany. Why?

Topics in comparative penalization need to be pursued with great care. It is especially important not to put too much faith in the text of the Criminal Code: The investigator must make careful efforts to determine whether behaviors that are nominally forbidden are in fact prosecuted. Pursued with proper care, though, these are among the most important, and most neglected, topics in comparative law.

Doing comparative studies of doctrinal criminal law is somewhat more difficult because it demands a particularly good command of juristic technique and a willingness to look closely at the details of criminal decision making. Nevertheless, the study of comparative doctrinal criminal law is also full of opportunity for the serious student of comparative law.

Doctrinal criminal law is a body of rules about the limits of criminal liability. Different societies establish those limits in strikingly different ways. Doctrines of justification and excuse in the law of homicide offer a fine example. Many traditions excuse or justify "crimes of passion"—classically, homicides committed by spouses who discover their mates *in flagrante delicto* with a third party. The approach of criminal justice systems to such classic crimes of passion, and to others as well, such as homicides committed by men who have been homosexually propositioned, is a beckoning topic for comparatists. (The full study of this class of offenses would also include so-called "honor killings.") The attitude of different societies to crimes of passion and to matters of sexual honor can tell us a great deal about comparative social organization, and comparative sexual relations. Indeed, there are few more promising avenues for exploring differences in the role of male sexual honor in different societies. Yet, although we have many studies of particular societies, good comparative studies are wanting.

There are many other examples of revealing topics in comparative doctrinal criminal law. One that has been well explored by George Fletcher involves differences in rules about the imputation of collective criminal responsibility. American criminal law permits considerable imputation of collective responsibility through its law of conspiracy and such doctrines as felony murder. European legal systems are currently under some pressure to follow the American lead, partly to deal with terrorism but also in the face of the international trade in drugs and cultural property. Nevertheless, Europeans continue to resist, holding the classic nineteenth-century view that criminal responsibility is exclusively individual (Fletcher 1994). What explains these fundamental differences in approach? Which societies countenance the imposition of collective criminal responsibility, and which do not? These are questions of pressing public interest that go the heart of the culture of criminal law in different societies. There are many other such topics in comparative substantive criminal law—for example, differences in the willingness of different systems to accept entrapment defenses, a topic recently investigated by Jacqueline Ross (2005). For the good lawyer, willing to learn about the practices of foreign systems, comparative substantive criminal law has a wealth of research opportunities to offer.

The comparative law of punishment is also of immense interest—although again it is a subject that may require some juristic adeptness. There are simple questions of great significance about the nature of the punishments inflicted. We possess a vast literature on the death penalty but too few studies of lesser punishments. When do societies incarcerate, and when do they use alternative sanctions? Which alternative sanctions do they use? Why do some societies use dayfine systems, geared to ability to pay, while others have a fixed schedule? Why do some use suspension of privileges, such as the driver's license, as a routine sanction? Why do some societies sentence offenders to public service, while others do not?

Individualization in punishment is especially important today. The United States has moved dramatically toward determinate sentencing over the past 25 years or so. A system oriented toward determinate sentencing aims to impose exactly the same sentence on every individual who has committed the same offense, without regard to individual circumstances. Punishment systems that favor individualization, by contrast, aim to tailor sentences to the individual needs and circumstances of the offender. It is probably the case that all systems individualize punishment to some extent and through some means. For example, prosecutorial discretion plays an important role in the United States, as prosecutors aim to individualize the effective sentence faced by an individual offender through manipulating the charge brought against that offender. A deep understanding of these issues would require, however, comparative studies that we lack as yet.

CONCLUSION

The topics discussed here are hardly the only ones that might be mentioned. There are rich literatures in criminology and comparative cultural studies that suggest other approaches. Readers should read on.

The *Annual Review of Law and Social Science* is online at
http://lawsocsci.annualreviews.org

LITERATURE CITED

Anderson B. 1991. *Imagined Communities: Reflections on the Origin and Spread of Nationalism.* London/New York: Verso. Rev. ed.

Durkheim E. 1984. *The Division of Labor in Society.* Trans. WD Halls. New York: Free Press

Durkheim E. 1992. Two laws of penal evolution. In *The Radical Sociology of Emile Durkheim*, ed. M Gane, pp. 21–49. London: Routledge

Elias N. 2000. *The Civilizing Process: Sociogenetic and Psychogenetic Investigations.* Trans. E Jephcott. Oxford: Blackwell. Rev. ed.

Feeley M. 1997. Comparative criminal law for criminologists: comparing for what purpose? In *Comparing Legal Cultures*, ed. D Nelken, pp. 93–104. Aldershot, Hants, UK/Brookfield, VT: Dartmouth

Feeley M, Simon J. 1992. The new penology: notes on the emerging strategy of corrections and its implications. *Criminology* 30(4):449–74

Fletcher G. 1994. Is conspiracy unique to the common law? *Am. J. Comp. Law* 43:171

Foucault M. 1977. *Discipline and Punish: The Birth of the Prison.* Trans. A Sheridan. New York: Pantheon

Garland D. 1985. *Punishment and Welfare: A History of Penal Strategies.* Aldershot, Hants, UK/Brookfield, VT: Gower

Goffman E. 1970. *Asylums: Essays on the Social Situation of Mental Patients and Other Inmates.* Chicago: Aldine

Hampton J. 1992. An expressive theory of retribution. In *Retributivism and Its Critics*, ed. W Cragg, pp. 1–25. Stuttgart: Steiner

Hindus M. 1980. *Prison and Plantation: Crime, Justice, and Authority in Massachusetts and South Carolina, 1767–1878.* Chapel Hill: Univ. N. C. Press

Hirsch AJ. 1992. *The Rise of the Penitentiary: Prisons and Punishment in Early America.* New Haven, CT: Yale

Human Rights Watch. 2003. Ill-equipped: U.S. prisons and offenders with mental illness. *HRW Rep. 1564322904*, Human Rights Watch, New York, NY. http://www.hrw.org/reports/2003/usa1003/usa1003.pdf

Nelken D. 1994. Whom can you trust?: The future of comparative criminology. In *The Futures of Criminology*, ed. D Nelken, pp. 220–43. London: Sage

Nisbett R, Cohen D. 1996. *Culture of Honor: The Psychology of Violence in the South.* Boulder, CO: Westview

Padoa-Schioppa A, ed. 1987. *The Trial Jury in England, France and Germany.* Berlin: Duncker & Humblot

Petit J-G. 1991. Politiques, modèles et imaginaires de la prison (1790–1875). In *Histoire des Galères, Bagnes et Prisons*, ed. JG Petit, N Castan, C Faugeron, M Pierre, pp. 109–37. Toulouse: Privat

Radbruch G. 1950. Der Ursprung des Strafrechts aus dem Stande des Unfreien. In *Elegantiae Juris Criminalis; Vierzehn Studien zur Geschichte des Strafrechts*, ed. G Radbruch, pp. 17–30. Basel: Verlag für Recht und Gesellschaft. 2nd ed.

Ross J. 2005. Impediments to transnational cooperation in undercover policing: a comparative study of the United States and Italy. *Am. J. Comp. Law.* In press

Rusche G, Kirchheimer O. 1939. *Punishment and Social Structure.* New York: Columbia Univ. Press

Saleilles R. 1911. *The Individualization of Punishment.* Trans. R Jastrow. Boston: Little, Brown

Savelsberg J. 1994. Knowledge, domination, and criminal punishment. *Am. J. Sociol.* 99: 911–43

Schmidt E. 1965. *Einführung in die Geschichte*

der deutschen Strafrechtspflege. Göttingen: Vandenhoeck & Ruprecht. 3rd ed.

Sellin JT. 1976. *Slavery and the Penal System.* New York: Elsevier

Shapiro M. 1981. *Courts: A Comparative and Political Analysis.* Chicago: Univ. Chicago Press

Simon J. 1997. Governing through crime. In *The Crime Conundrum*, ed. G Fisher, L Friedman, pp. 171–90. Boulder, CO: Westview

Sorokin P. 1962. *Social and Cultural Dynamics: A Study of Change in Major Systems of Art, Truth, Ethics, Law, and Social Relationships.* 4 Vols. New York: Bedminster

Spierenburg P. 1991. *The Prison Experience: Disciplinary Institutions and Their Inmates in Early Modern Europe.* New Brunswick: Rutgers

Spierenburg P, ed. 1998. *Men and Violence: Gender, Honor and Rituals in Modern Europe and America.* Columbus: Ohio State Univ. Press

Tonry M, ed. 2001. *Penal Reform in Overcrowded Times.* Oxford: Oxford Univ. Press

Tonry M, Frase R, eds. 2001. *Sentencing and Sanctions in Western Countries.* Oxford: Oxford Univ. Press

Wacquant L. 1999. *Les Prisons de la misère.* Paris: Raisons d'agir

Wetzell R. 2000. *Inventing the Criminal: A History of German Criminology, 1880-1945.* Chapel Hill: Univ. N. C. Press

Whitman J. 2003. *Harsh Justice: Criminal Punishment and the Widening Divide Between America and Europe.* New York: Oxford Univ. Press

Zimring F. 2003. *The Contradictions of American Capital Punishment.* New York: Oxford Univ. Press

Annu. Rev. Law Soc. Sci. 2005. 1:35–59
doi: 10.1146/annurev.lawsocsci.1.041604.115856
First published online as a Review in Advance on June 14, 2005

ECONOMIC THEORIES OF SETTLEMENT BARGAINING

Andrew F. Daughety and Jennifer F. Reinganum

*Department of Economics and Law School, Vanderbilt University, Nashville, Tennessee
37235; email: andrew.f.daughety@vanderbilt.edu, jennifer.f.reinganum@vanderbilt.edu*

Key Words   multiple litigants, externalities, asymmetric information

■ **Abstract**   We briefly review two basic models of settlement bargaining based on
concepts from information economics and game theory. We then discuss how these
models have been generalized to address issues that arise when there are more than
two litigants with related cases. Linkages between cases can arise because of exogenous factors such as correlated culpability or damages, or they can be generated by
discretionary choices on the part of the litigants themselves or by legal doctrine and
rules of procedure.

INTRODUCTION

This review provides a selective survey of recent work on the economics of settlement bargaining, emphasizing settings in which there are multiple (more than two)
litigants. The research on multiple-litigant settlement bargaining has built on previous work on bilateral settlement bargaining and employs the tools used therein.
Thus, we first provide a brief review of the salient concepts from information
economics in the bilateral settlement bargaining context.

The essential feature of multilateral bargaining is the creation or presence of
externalities that arise when bargaining between two litigants is influenced by
the possibility, or necessity, of simultaneous or subsequent bargaining by a litigant
with other parties. For example, a confidential settlement between an early plaintiff
and a defendant is likely to affect the information and case viability of a later
plaintiff suing the same defendant if the defendant's culpability is, to some extent,
correlated across the cases. Thus, in the section below entitled Externalities Induced
by Litigant Discretionary Choice, we consider recent papers that examine how
discretionary choices by one or more litigants (to create or capitalize on possible
linkages among yet other litigants) generate such externalities. The preferences of
the litigants concerning the use of such devices need not directly conflict; that is,
the litigants need not have preferences such that one litigant's payoff improves if
the other's payoff is reduced (i.e., as in diametrically opposed preferences). In the
case of confidential settlement, early plaintiffs and a defendant (who is common

1550-3585/05/1209-0035$20.00

to the early and to later plaintiffs) may agree that employing the device is mutually advantageous (but this may or may not be true for later plaintiffs).

However, sometimes existing legal doctrine (for example, the doctrine of joint and several liability) or rules of procedure (such as collateral estoppel) may induce bargaining externalities. Of course, as stated above, the choice by one or another of the litigants to make use of the relevant legal doctrines or procedural rules may be voluntary, but in this case preferences of the individual litigants over the use of such doctrines and procedures are usually diametrically opposed; such rules exist to provide recourse when agreement is not possible. We discuss this possibility in the final section, entitled Externalities Induced by Doctrines or Procedural Rules.

BILATERAL SETTLEMENT BARGAINING

Hay & Spier (1998) and Daughety (2000) provide detailed reviews of settlement bargaining between two parties in which disagreement may lead to trial. This section provides a very brief review of the bilateral settlement bargaining literature, with special emphasis on the models used in the rest of the discussion. Early papers on this topic, such as those by Landes (1971), Gould (1973), Posner (1973), and Shavell (1982), considered settings in which both litigants knew all relevant information. In such cases, because trial is costly, both litigants are better off avoiding trial and agreeing to split the avoided costs. Thus, this literature provided models that predicted that no trials would occur when information was symmetric (that is, either everything was commonly known or all assessments of unknowns were shared). These papers also provided models in which bargaining might collapse, thereby resulting in a trial. In this approach, trials occur when there are irreconcilable conflicts between the litigants as to assessments over the likely outcome in court; these irreconcilable conflicts reflect differences the parties could not eliminate even if all information were commonly known. Analyses with irreconcilable assessments that drive the possibility of settlement failure are known as inconsistent priors analyses. Thus, the decision-theoretic models provide the possibility of inefficient settlement bargaining, but the cause of the inefficiency lies in intransigence on the part of the litigants.

Models of settlement bargaining that employ game theory and information economics have developed over the past 20 years. In these models, bargaining agents may possess different information (called private information); if the information were common knowledge to both bargainers, there would be no barrier to settlement, but the asymmetry in what each agent knows may result in bargaining failure. The presence of private (that is, asymmetric) information affects the strategic behavior of the bargainers; thus, such models rely on strategic response to informational differences, rather than on intransigence, to provide a range of outcomes, some of which involve inefficiency. More precisely, if A and B are bargaining and A possesses some information that is relevant to the transaction (and B does not have this information but knows that A does), then in choosing bargaining strategies, both A and B have to account for how their opponent will modify their bargaining strategies in the light of this asymmetry. For example, a plaintiff is likely to know more about the actual damages she has suffered owing to a harm from a product than is the product's manufacturer. Knowing this, and recognizing that plaintiffs have an incentive to inflate their demands, the game's equilibrium may involve the manufacturer being more resistant to higher demands than to lower ones: His willingness to go to trial increases as the plaintiff's settlement demand increases. Alternatively, a manufacturer is likely to be better informed as to his likely liability. Thus, in bargaining, defendants might understate their culpability, and plaintiffs will be more resistant to accepting lower offers. This feeds back to influence the plaintiff's decision about what demand to make, recognizing that higher demands are likely to elicit a higher chance of bargaining failure, leading to a costly trial. Thus, in contrast with the early (full information) literature and in contrast with the inconsistent priors literature, trial may occur not because of intransigence but because of rational wariness. Moreover, the equilibrium prediction provides the likelihood of trial as a specific function of the distribution of damages (and/or the degree of culpability) and the attributes of the parties involved.

Bebchuk (1984) and Reinganum & Wilde (1986) provided what are now viewed as the canonical models of settlement bargaining, employing tools from game theory and information economics. Both models assume that one party is better informed about a salient fact (or facts) than is the other party.[1] Continuing with the earlier example, assume a consumer bought a product from a manufacturer and has been harmed by the product. The consumer (as plaintiff, denoted P) sues the manufacturer (as defendant, denoted D) for damages. Moreover, for ease of discussion, assume that the parties agree that D will be found liable with probability p, but that damages (denoted d) are P's private information. This is not unreasonable because P is likely to be better informed as to her damages than is D; here, P is the informed party and D is the uninformed party. P's possible levels of damages (alternatively, the possible values of her private information) are called P's types. To fill in the details of the model, assume

1. D's conjecture as to the possible values of the actual damages follows a distribution $F(d)$, with d ranging between a lowest possible value, d_L, and a highest possible value, d_H;
2. this distribution is commonly known to P and D and has an associated density denoted $f(d)$;
3. each party must pay their own court costs, denoted t_P for P and t_D for D (respectively), if bargaining fails and they go to trial (for convenience, let aggregate court costs be $T = t_P + t_D$), and that these trial costs are commonly known; and

---

[1]We discuss one-sided models below; two-sided asymmetric information models combine aspects of the one-sided models; for details see Schweizer (1989) and Daughety & Reinganum (1994).

4. at trial the court can correctly determine the true level of damages (which is the private information P possesses).[2]

To understand the Bebchuk analysis,[3] assume that the bargaining follows an ultimatum structure: D makes a settlement offer, s, to P, who then either accepts the offer (resulting in s dollars transferred from D to P) or rejects the offer (thereby going to trial, where the court awards damages d with probability p).[4] For P's threat to go to trial to be credible, we require that $pd_L \geq t_P$; that is, the net expected payoff for the type with the lowest possible damages is nonnegative (this last assumption can be relaxed, but doing so complicates the exposition unnecessarily). Such bargaining games in which the uninformed player moves first are called screening (or sorting) models because the demand made by the uninformed player acts to screen the second-mover's types into those who will accept the offer and those who will reject it. This means that whatever the initial distribution of possible damage levels (the distribution of possible types of P, denoted above as F), the model can provide a prediction of the resulting likelihood of settlement or trial and the expected returns and costs associated with the bargaining process.

D's objective is to make an offer that minimizes total expected trial and settlement costs. Because there is a continuum of P's types between d_L and d_H, an offer s that screens these types into two groups will make some type, denoted $\tilde{d}$ (called the marginal type), just indifferent between the offer s and going to trial; at trial this type would obtain $p\tilde{d} - t_P$. That is, the offer s selects the marginal type $\tilde{d} = (s + t_P)/p$. However, if this type of P were to choose to go to trial, D's cost at trial would be $p\tilde{d} + t_D$. Therefore, we can think of D's problem as making an offer (that is accepted by some type $\tilde{d}$, and by all those types with lesser damages than $\tilde{d}$) so that expected costs are minimal. This is formalized as the following optimization problem:

$$\min_{\tilde{d}} \int_{\tilde{d}}^{d_H} (px + t_D) f(x)\, dx + F(\tilde{d})(p\tilde{d} - t_P). \qquad 1.$$

The first term is the expected cost to D of going to trial, because all types above $\tilde{d}$ will reject the offer $s = p\tilde{d} - t_P$ (they can do better at trial). In the integral, D's cost at trial for any such type is weighted by the likelihood that D is of that type.

---

[2] A variety of papers in the literature weaken or manipulate some of these assumptions.

[3] In Bebchuk's paper, the private information was about liability, whereas in Reinganum & Wilde's (1986) paper the private information concerned damages. To make the comparisons between the models straightforward, we pose both applied to the case of privately known damages.

[4] More complex models with counter-proposals are possible, but if we focus on the last stage of any such finite-horizon process, it has the form of an offer/demand followed by a response, followed either by settlement or trial. Note that, in contrast with the standard bargaining literature, it is plausible to posit a last stage because defendants have an incentive to delay, thereby necessitating that courts set a deadline.

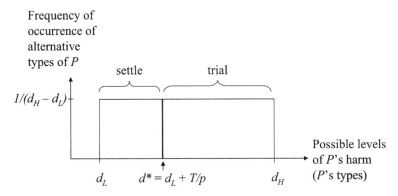

Figure 1   Equilibrium in a screening model.

The second term above is the expected cost of settlement to D because all types at and below $\tilde{d}$ accept the offer $p\tilde{d} - t_P$ (they do no better, and most do worse, at trial). The term $F(\tilde{d})$ weights the offer by the fraction of types who will accept it. Once the marginal type $\tilde{d}$ that minimizes this total expected cost is found (denoted as d^*, the solution to Equation 1), the optimal offer by D is $s^* = pd^* - t_P$. This is an equilibrium as long as the limits on the integral are not violated, so d^* must be less than d_H and greater than d_L.

Figure 1 illustrates the equilibrium in a screening model for the case where possible damage levels are uniformly distributed [that is, all values of d are equally likely, so $f(d) = 1/(d_H - d_L)$]. By solving the problem in Equation 1 above, one can show that the equilibrium marginal type is $d^* = d_L + T/p$ (as shown in the Figure), so the equilibrium offer is $s^* = pd^* - t_P = pd_L + T - t_P = pd_L + t_D$.[5] Thus, the likelihood of settlement is $F(d^*) = (d^* - d_L)/(d_H - d_L) = (T/p)/(d_H - d_L) < 1$, the likelihood of trial is $(d_H - d_L - T/p)/(d_H - d_L) > 0$, and the expected total trial cost is $T(d_H - d_L - T/p)/(d_H - d_L)$. This last item is the social cost associated with the presence of asymmetric information. Notice also that the distribution of types going to trial is just a truncated version of the original distribution of types, F. Thus, the model predicts that cases with low levels of damages will settle, whereas only those with sufficiently high levels of damages will proceed to trial.

This model provides a number of other implications; we list a few here. First, an increase in the range of expected stakes (that is, an increase in $d_H - d_L$ or an increase in p) or a decrease in either litigant's court costs leads to a reduction in the likelihood of settlement. Second, redistribution of court costs from one litigant to the other (that is, adjustments in t_P and t_D, holding T fixed) has no impact on the likelihood of settlement or on the magnitude of the social cost. Third, a cap on damages (if modeled as a reduction in d_H) leads to a reduction in the

---

[5]The requirement that $d^* < d_H$ means that, for screening to be an equilibrium, we require $p(d_H - d_L) > T$. That is, the range of the expected stakes should exceed the total court costs.

likelihood of trial and a reduction in the social costs associated with bargaining (of course, this does not account for the fact that Ps with very high damages would be undercompensated).

In the Reinganum & Wilde (1986) model, the informed party moves first and the uninformed party then considers the demand and decides whether to accept or reject the demand (again, rejection leads to trial). This type of model is called a signaling model because the first mover signals information via their settlement demand. Returning to the example outlined earlier, P makes a demand, with higher demands reflecting a P with greater damages. Now D must be wary of high demands from P, as a low-damaged P would also like to make a high demand if D would naively infer that damages awarded at trial would be high. Thus, D rationally rejects higher demands more frequently (that is, D is willing to go to trial with a higher likelihood for demands that are higher). It is the equilibrium wariness of D that deters mimicry and results in the signal being informative (that is, the signal provides useful information about P's type to D when D is trying to decide what is likely to happen at trial, and whether to reject the demand from P).

While somewhat more technically demanding [see Reinganum & Wilde (1986) for details], the basics of the model are that P makes a demand and D uses the demand to update his assessment of which type of P he is likely to go to trial against, should bargaining break down. Thus, for any demand S, D forms beliefs $b(S)$ as to which type (or types) would have made such a demand. D then decides whether to accept or reject the demand employing these beliefs: D accepts the demand S if and only if $S \leq pb(S) + t_D$. Let D's probability of rejecting demand S be denoted as $r(S)$. Because P must choose S, recognizing that she will go to trial against D if he rejects her demand, P's problem is to choose S to maximize her return:

$$\max_S S(1 - r(S)) + (pd - t_P)r(S), \qquad\qquad 2.$$

where the first term reflects settlement at S, which occurs with probability $1 - r(S)$, and the second term reflects P's return if she goes to trial. Under mild conditions there is a revealing equilibrium in which a P of type d makes the equilibrium demand $S^*(d) = pd + t_D$ and D's beliefs are correct. Furthermore, D's equilibrium rejection function, $r^*(S)$, is zero at the lowest type's revealing demand, $S_L \equiv S^*(d_L) = pd_L + t_D$; is increasing and concave in S; and reaches a maximum value, which is less than 1, at the highest type's revealing demand, $S_H \equiv S^*(d_H) = pd_H + t_D$. This rejection function is displayed in Figure 2, illustrating the earlier example involving a continuum of uniformly distributed types of possible damage levels for P.

In contrast with the screening model, notice that one implication of the signaling model is that (except for $d = d_L$) all types have a positive chance of going to trial, with that chance increasing with the level of damages (because the settlement demand is increasing in the true level of damages). Moreover, the distribution of types who go to trial is different from the distribution of types who have been harmed: In the example, the initial distribution of types was a uniform distribution,

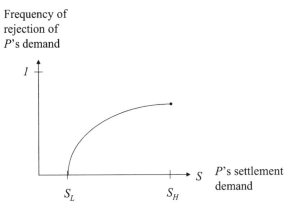

Figure 2 D's equilibrium strategy in a signaling model.

but the resulting distribution implied by the rejection function shown in Figure 2 is weighted toward higher types. We can obtain comparative statics results similar (in direction) to those found in the screening model as well.

EXTERNALITIES INDUCED BY LITIGANT DISCRETIONARY CHOICE

Confidential Settlement

Imagine that a plaintiff, P_1, has been harmed by a product[6] produced by a defendant, D. P_1 may suspect that others have been harmed as well (that is, there may be other plaintiffs, P_2, P_3, etc.), but these harmed individuals might have suffered their losses at other times and places, so perhaps there is little or no chance for P_1 to find these other plaintiffs so as to pursue, say, a class action suit [suppressing the ability of plaintiffs to share information, such as might be obtained via discovery, appears to be a major purpose of protective orders used in a variety of cases; see Hare et al. (1988)]. Moreover, even if there were some way to locate others who may have been harmed, the existence of substantial issues of law might preclude the formation of a class.[7] Instead, when P_1 and D bargain, a confidential settlement, in which the details (and possibly even the existence) of the agreement are kept secret, might be mutually advantageous. The law provides for such secrecy either

---

[6]We restrict discussion to the product's liability context for concreteness of the analytical results, but as has become apparent in the popular press, confidentiality has figured into a variety of other concerns (e.g., public health and sexual abuse of minors).

[7]See Judge Richard Posner's majority opinion in *In re Rhone-Poulenc Rorer Inc.*, in which the court decertified a class action lawsuit partly because of problems of discerning a common set of negligence standards across multiple jurisdictions.

via court-authorized sealing, or through contracts of silence that specify stipulated damages should the plaintiff violate the confidentiality agreement.

The central economic questions are (*a*) how does the possibility of bargaining over both money and confidentiality affect the likelihood of settlement and the settlement amounts (if agreement is reached), and (*b*) how does the availability of confidentiality, as a bargaining option, influence the welfare of all litigants (including that of possible future plaintiffs). The basic results are threefold. First, confidentiality improves the likelihood of settlement and raises the expected settlement amount between P_1 and D. In this sense, the early plaintiff obtains hush money to help the defendant suppress information if so doing helps reduce the likelihood of suits by later plaintiffs. Second, the degree of correlation of D's culpability (and, therefore, liability) across the individual plaintiffs' cases influences the degree to which confidentiality may reinforce or undermine deterrence. Such a correlation is weak when D's actions may have led to conditions contributing to the separate harms but each case may have substantially different issues of causation to prove. Thus, for example, D's chemical spill may have contributed to P_1's stomach cancer and to P_2's brain tumor, but informationally the only value P_2 obtains from knowing about the case between P_1 and D is that the spill may have a role in P_2's harm. In contrast, suppose that D is a national gasoline retailer, with a chain of gas stations around the country, all employing the same design for underground tanks for gasoline storage. Thus, although precise local geological conditions might affect the likelihood of a gasoline leakage into the water table, a high likelihood of liability in one case (a community P_1 versus D) implies a high likelihood of liability in any other case (another community P_2 versus D; see *Ashcraft v. Conoco*). We refer to this as strong correlation.[8]

Suppose D has private information regarding his culpability in two cases. As shown in Daugherty & Reinganum (1999, 2002), if, on the one hand, the cases are weakly correlated, then even though D has private information regarding his culpability in P_1's case, both P_1 and D have the same expected value for D's future expenditures due to settlement negotiations or trial with future plaintiffs. Thus, it is possible for the early plaintiff's bargain to extract (as hush money) enough of a payment from D so as to make D face the same expected costs for potential harms as would occur without confidentiality: Under weak correlation, deterrence need not be reduced. On the other hand, in the case of strong correlation, the fact that D's culpability is common to the two cases makes D's costs in the continuation game (the future suits) dependent on this information, which means that P_1 cannot efficiently extract the full value of confidentiality she provides to D. Therefore, under strong correlation, deterrence is undermined. If correlation is weak, the average plaintiff (that is, a plaintiff who is equally likely to be early or

---

[8]The early case is assumed not to be fully determinative of what will occur in a later case. If it were, then we would think in terms of collateral estoppel, wherein liability in one case means liability in the next; see Externalities Induced by Doctrines or Procedural Rules, below.

late) may prefer the availability of confidentiality as a bargaining option, but if case correlation is strong, the average plaintiff is strictly worse off when confidentiality is available than when it is forbidden.

We briefly consider some of the details of the strong correlation case. Daughety & Reinganum (2002) consider a model in which D sequentially bargains with two plaintiffs (P_1 followed by P_2) over both the amount of each plaintiff's settlement and (in the case of P_1) whether to keep the settlement details confidential.[9] Assume that P_1 has already filed suit against D, and that although P_2 has not yet filed a suit, she is more likely to do so if she becomes aware of P_1's suit. For example, P_2 may not initially be aware that the harm she has suffered might be due to D's product or to D's culpability. The analysis considers three possible outcomes for the bargaining game between P_1 and D: (a) a confidential settlement specifying that both parties will keep all details secret, (b) an open settlement in which the details of the agreement are publicly available, and (c) a trial with a publicly available record. Associated with each possible outcome is a probability that P_2 will become aware that she, too, should sue D, with this probability being lowest under confidentiality and highest under trial. Moreover, because the cases are strongly correlated, to the degree that the outcome of the first suit provides information about D's culpability in the second case, this information will influence P_2's beliefs about the type of D she faces as well, possibly influencing the demand she might make in her own settlement bargaining process. Alternatively put, the first case generates a positive externality to P_2 (and a negative externality to D) by raising her awareness of D's involvement in her harm. Because P_1 cannot directly charge P_2 for this service, she instead charges D for reducing the size of the negative externality (that is, his expected losses due to a suit from P_2) by agreeing to provide confidentiality.

Sequential bargaining is modeled as a series of screening games, but now the outcome of the first screening game potentially signals information to the participants in the second screening game. Let p denote the probability that D is liable; assume that p is distributed uniformly on $[p_L, p_H]$ and that it is the same for both cases (this is strongly correlated culpability); moreover, assume that only D knows p. In each screening bargaining game, the plaintiff makes a demand, which is accepted by D types with sufficiently high values of p and rejected by those with lower values of p. Applying the screening analysis discussed above (see Bilateral Settlement Bargaining), we define settlement demands and marginal types associated with an open settlement and a confidential settlement in the first case (denoted s_O and p_O, and s_C and p_C, respectively). These expressions can be ordered as follows: $s_C > s_O$ and $p_C < p_O$. That is, the equilibrium settlement demand and the likelihood of settlement are both higher under confidentiality than under openness. This is because confidentiality creates a gain for D in which P_1

---

[9]Yang (1996) reports results from a model of correlated damages in which the settlement amount is (exogenously) sealed and finds that if the litigation costs are high, then D is willing to offer even more to settle the first suit (and deter the filing of the second suit), while if litigation costs are low, then confidentiality results in less settlement.

can share: Despite P_1's higher confidential settlement demand, more D types are willing to accept it. However, because confidentiality also suppresses publicity (relative to an open settlement and, especially, to trial) that might have triggered P_2's suit, P_2 is worse off when P_1 and D settle confidentially. Finally, a plaintiff behind the veil of ignorance (with an equal chance of becoming P_1 or P_2) is worse off under confidentiality, so the gain to P_1 is more than offset by the loss to P_2. Nevertheless, it can be shown that total expected litigation costs are lower when confidential settlement is permitted.

In sum, the foregoing analysis suggests that confidentiality should be expected to lower overall litigation costs, but it is not Pareto superior to openness. Furthermore, this analysis has not accounted for privacy considerations (such as valid privacy concerns for individual plaintiffs, or valid trade secrecy issues for firms), which undoubtedly make some confidential agreements welfare-enhancing. However, the fact that confidentiality is available as a bargaining tool makes the early negotiating parties better off at the expense of later plaintiffs. This suggests that one cannot rely on the arguments that the early parties might make for maintaining secrecy without examining how likely it is that a sequence of cases exists, and whether any culpability by the defendant in such a sequence is likely to be strongly correlated.

Most-Favored-Nations Clauses

A second linkage across seemingly bilateral settlement negotiations occurs when settlement bargains may use a most-favored-nations (MFN) clause, meaning that early settling plaintiffs are entitled to retroactive increases in their settlements should the defendant settle with later plaintiffs at better terms.[10] Such clauses have shown up in settlement agreements in a variety of settings, including cases involving antitrust violations, copyright infringement, bankruptcy, and racial discrimination, as well as the tobacco cases to be discussed below. The implications for settlement bargaining and a variety of examples of the use of MFNs have been explored in papers by Spier (2003a,b) and Daughety & Reinganum (2004).

The agreements reached between the tobacco industry and the states in the mid- to late 1990s [see Viscusi (2002) on the agreements] provide examples of two different (but related) uses of an MFN clause in a collection of settlement agreements. Over a period of a few years, four states reached agreements with the tobacco industry: Mississippi settled in 1997 for $3.6 billion, Florida settled in 1997 for $11.3 billion, Texas settled in 1998 for $15.3 billion, and Minnesota settled in 1998 for $6.6 billion. All four states had pursued a novel legal theory that the firms in the industry owed the states restitution for past health expenditures made by each state on behalf of smokers, and all four agreements contained MFN clauses. The MFN clauses in the Mississippi, Florida, and Texas agreements were triggered by

---

[10]The term most-favored nations derives from tariff agreements in international trade. Most-favored-customer clauses provide the parallel notion in consumer markets such that a customer is promised the lowest price offered to any other customer.

the Minnesota settlement (yielding MFN payments of $550 million, $1.8 billion, and $2.3 billion, respectively). The remaining 46 states shortly thereafter signed the Master Settlement Agreement (MSA), which also contained an MFN clause, now to make sure that all the states would join the one agreement (the MSA did not trigger the earlier MFN clauses for the first four states). This suggests two possible motivations that we explore briefly below. One is that early (noncommon) litigants (e.g., the individual states) may propose MFN clauses as a means of obtaining later payments; for reasons made clear below, we refer to this as a leverage motive. The other motive is that the common litigant may propose an MFN clause to reduce delay and to improve commitment power on its behalf; we refer to this as the delay-reduction motive, and we discuss it first.

Spier (2003a,b) considers the following multiple-litigant bargaining scenario. Consider a defendant, D, facing a large number of plaintiffs who have individually suffered harms of different magnitudes due to the use of D's product. Thus, the rectangular density shown in Figure 1 might represent the different harms of a large number of plaintiffs (rather than representing alternative levels of harm for a single plaintiff). Here, the harm each plaintiff has suffered is her own private information and D is uninformed with respect to this information (although D knows the distribution of plaintiffs' harms). D is contemplating settling with some of these plaintiffs and going to trial against the remainder, so the problem is one of screening. Moreover, bargaining in this model may occur over time, and delay in reaching an agreement is costly to all; for convenience, assume that there are now two possible rounds of bargaining. Consider the following strategy for D: D makes an offer to settle, perhaps making the offer s^* shown in Figure 1. In the screening analysis discussed in the section on Bilateral Settlement Bargaining, such an offer is a one-time, take-it-or-leave-it offer. However, if some plaintiffs settle at s^* and others do not, then D's second offer will be higher than s^*, so as to further screen those plaintiffs who might go to trial under s^* (in Figure 1, those to the right of d^*). Of course, if the first group of plaintiffs recognizes that D will subsequently raise the offer, then they will not agree to s^*, but will instead wait for the improved offer. This results in delay, which is costly. Without the commitment power implicit in the one-time-only structure of the original Bebchuk-style screening analysis, D faces the possibility of having to make an increasing sequence of offers, which clearly would be inferior to the one-time-only offer that minimized overall cost, namely s^*.

Spier (2003a) shows that an MFN clause eliminates the incentive for D to make the higher second offer. To see why, note that an offer of s^* with an MFN clause means that any plaintiff who accepts s^* now will also obtain any increase associated with any later, better offer accepted by other plaintiffs, so no plaintiff has an incentive to wait. If D subsequently made a higher offer, he would have to make MFN payments to all those who previously settled; thus, he does not make a higher second offer. An MFN allows D to commit to his cost-minimizing offer s^*, thereby eliminating delay in reaching an agreement (hence, the delay-reduction motive); the MFN provides D with a degree of monopoly power, as he no longer competes for settling plaintiffs with his future (second-round) self. Spier also compares the likelihood of settlement, the welfare of plaintiffs, and the total costs of litigation between a setting in which an MFN is allowed and one in which it is not. In keeping with the notation in the earlier section on bilateral bargaining, let the probability density describing the expected damages be denoted as $f(\cdot)$; Figure 1 shows an f that is constant. Spier (2003a) shows that the likelihood of settlement and plaintiff welfare improves (respectively: declines; stays constant) if f is increasing (respectively: decreasing; constant) in value at the point of the first-period marginal type when an MFN clause is precluded.[11] Thus, Figure 1 illustrates a type of watershed example, as f is constant everywhere. Distributions with rising densities imply that an MFN improves the settlement rate and is preferred by plaintiffs, whereas those distributions with declining densities yield the reverse results.

Daughety & Reinganum (2004) analyze the second motivation for using an MFN, which we refer to as a leverage motivation, when there is asymmetric information.[12] Consider a version of Spier's setup (a defendant who is uninformed about the damages individual plaintiffs have suffered), but now limit the number of plaintiffs to two, and assume there is an early plaintiff (P_1) and a later plaintiff (P_2). Furthermore, assume that the bargaining between each plaintiff and the common defendant is modeled as a signaling game (see Bilateral Settlement Bargaining). In period one, the informed P_1 makes a settlement demand of D, and there is either agreement or trial, followed by period two, in which the informed P_2 makes a demand of D, which again may result in agreement or trial. Without an MFN, the sequential pair of signaling games behaves just like a sequence of signaling games as illustrated in Figure 2 above.

Assume that P_1 and D conclude an agreement that contains an MFN and that the settlement amount was S_1. This agreement now affects what P_2 can hope to obtain in her settlement negotiations with D. P_2, who might have suffered a greater harm than P_1, knows that if D were to pay P_2 her full damages plus D's court costs (i.e., the amount that would be demanded in the no-MFN case), then this would generate an MFN payment to P_1, and D might be better off simply going to trial because a judgment at trial does not trigger an MFN payment (whereas a higher settlement does). Thus, D's rejection function is now progressively higher for all demands by P_2 above S_1. Hence, for demands she might make above S_1, P_2 moderates her demand to account for the higher likelihood of rejection that the MFN has now created. When P_2 does make a (moderated) demand above S_1, sometimes it is accepted by D and an MFN payment is made to P_1 as well, and

---

[11]More limited results hold for total litigation and trial costs: These are decreasing when the settlement rate is increasing or constant, but may move in either direction if the settlement rate is decreasing.

[12]Spier (2003b) explores the leverage motivation in an example with symmetric information. In such a setting the probability of trial is either one or zero, so the use of an MFN is predicted to raise total trial costs.

sometimes it is rejected by D. So P_1 is distinctly better off because of the expected MFN payment. But P_1's benefit from an MFN does not stop there because the possibility of the MFN payment means that there is a lower incentive for types of P_1 with low damages to try to mimic the types with higher damages because they have more to lose if they are rejected by D. This lower incentive, in turn, means that the probability that D will reject P_1's demand is not as high as it would be if there were no MFN payment possibility. Thus, P_1 can make the same demand as she would have before, and D will reject this demand with a lower likelihood.

In sum, the expected value of an MFN clause to P_1 reflects two effects: (*a*) the expected MFN payment and (*b*) the reduced likelihood of bargaining failure. This is referred to as a leverage motive because the first plaintiff is able to use an MFN clause and her role as an early settling player to leverage an advantage, extracting money owing to the presence of the later plaintiff. Not surprisingly, P_2 is always worse off (in expectation) because of the demand-moderating effect of the MFN and the potential increased likelihood of bargaining breakdown.[13] However, as Daughety & Reinganum show, overall litigation costs may fall with the use of an MFN. Thus, although not Pareto superior (because it would be opposed by the later plaintiff), the use of an MFN may be welfare-enhancing when viewed from the perspective of reducing total litigation costs.

As is illustrated by the settlements between the states and the tobacco industry, MFNs may reflect both leverage and delay-reduction purposes, and different multilateral bargaining settings may result in agreements using such clauses for one or both reasons. Significantly, as both analyses have shown, the use of an MFN may improve welfare (at least in a litigation-cost reduction sense) and might be Pareto improving (under the conditions discussed earlier in the delay-reduction setting). Use of the MFN in settlement bargaining contrasts with the use of most-favored-customer clauses in monopoly and oligopoly pricing, which have generally been found to be welfare-reducing (because their use generally enhances monopoly or cartel power).

EXTERNALITIES INDUCED BY DOCTRINES OR PROCEDURAL RULES

Collateral Estoppel and Precedent

Collateral estoppel makes a ruling in one case binding in subsequent related cases. For instance, if a driver is found liable for the injuries to the driver of another car, the passenger in the victim's car may argue that she need not separately establish the first driver's liability; rather, she may assert that collateral estoppel already

---

[13]Note that second plaintiffs with harms that are less than those suffered by the first plaintiff will make smaller demands than S_1, and face the no-MFN rejection probability, and therefore will not be affected by the presence of an MFN clause.

establishes liability, and only the passenger's damages remain to be determined. It is a matter of judicial discretion to determine whether collateral estoppel applies in a given situation. This doctrine thus establishes a link between cases brought by different plaintiffs that might otherwise not exist.

Another example is a government antitrust prosecution that establishes a firm's liability for the harms associated with its anticompetitive behavior. According to Briggs et al. (1996, p. 770), "Section 4 of the Clayton Act permits a private plaintiff to use findings from a prior antitrust suit brought by the government to pursue a treble damage suit against the same defendant for the same conduct." In this case, the statute specifically authorizes the application of collateral estoppel. Subsequent civil suits for damages need only demonstrate and document the extent of their harms.

Briggs et al. (1996) examine equilibrium settlement behavior in a sequence of suits. First, there is a government suit in which the defendant's type (a violator, denoted V, or nonviolator, denoted NV) is his private information. The defendant has an opportunity to make a settlement offer, to which the government may respond with settlement, with a trial, or by dropping the case; thus, this is a signaling game as discussed in the section on Bilateral Settlement Bargaining. If the government suit goes to trial and establishes the defendant's liability, or if the defendant settles (which is taken as an admission of liability in their model), then a private plaintiff will file suit and settle (because her damages are also assumed to be common knowledge). However, if the government drops its suit, then the defendant's liability has not been established; indeed, a rational (Bayesian) private plaintiff will lower her posterior belief that the defendant will be found liable in the future, which may deter the filing of her suit. So the question is how the possibility of a follow-on suit by a private plaintiff affects the defendant and the government's settlement behavior in the first suit.

First, consider a single suit between the government (G) and the defendant (D). D is in violation of antitrust laws (that is, he is of type V) with probability p; D's type is his private information, whereas p is commonly known by D and G. Let d_G represent the damages that G will receive if she prevails at trial. Let t denote the cost of trial for each litigant; for simplicity, we assume this is the same for D, G, and the private plaintiff P. The following parameter restriction is maintained: (A1) $pd_G - t > 0$; that is, the ex ante expected value of G's suit is positive. The equilibrium takes the following form. G files suit; a D of type NV makes no offer to settle while a D of type V mixes between making no offer and making the lowest offer that would be acceptable to G if D were known to be liable ($s = d_G - t$; we will call this a serious offer). G responds to a serious offer by accepting it and responds to no offer by mixing between trial and dropping the case.

Let τ_G denote $Pr\{\text{trial}|\text{no offer}\}$ and let η_G denote $Pr\{\text{no offer}|V\}$. For G to be willing to randomize between trial and dropping the case following no offer, then $[p\eta_G/(1 - p + p\eta_G)]d_G - t = 0$. The left-hand side is $Pr\{V|\text{no offer}\}$ (which is found using Bayes' Rule) times the amount collected (d_G) from a D of type V, minus G's trial costs, whereas the right-hand side is the value of dropping the case (i.e., zero). Similarly, for a D of type V to be willing to randomize between making no offer and offering d_G, then $\tau_G(d_G + t) = d_G - t$. The left-hand side is $Pr\{\text{trial}|\text{no offer}\}$ times the award D must pay plus his trial costs, whereas the right-hand side is the value of making a serious settlement offer, which is accepted for sure. Solving yields $\tau_G^* = (d_G - t)/(d_G + t)$ and $\eta_G^* = t(1 - p)/p(d_G - t)$; these are fractional given (A1). Now consider the filing decision. Calculating G's equilibrium payoff using the equilibrium values τ_G^* and η_G^* allows us to verify that this equilibrium payoff reduces to $pd_G - t$, which is positive by (A1). Thus, anticipating that the game will play out in an equilibrium fashion, it is optimal for G to file suit.

Now suppose that there is a potential follow-on suit by a private plaintiff P; let d_P denote P's damages. Many of the properties of the previous case continue to hold; in particular, η_G^* is unchanged. However, D's payoffs are now adjusted by the additional costs (of the second suit) that accompany both settlement and trial. If P would not file suit following a dropped suit by G, then for D to be indifferent between making no offer and settling (first with G and then with P), it must be that $\tau_G^{**}(d_G + t + d_P) = d_G - t + d_P$, or $\tau_G^{**} = (d_G - t + d_P)/(d_G + t + d_P)$. Note that $\tau_G^{**} > \tau_G^*$; in equilibrium, G will go to trial more often (following no offer) when there is a potential follow-on suit by a private plaintiff.

Che & Yi (1993) provide a model in which settlement does not imply an admission of liability. A defendant faces a sequence of two plaintiffs, and the decision regarding the defendant's liability in the second case is positively correlated with the decision in the first case. Although relitigation of a common issue is either estopped or not based on judicial discretion, the model of correlated decisions might be viewed as a situation in which both litigants in the first suit have symmetric but imperfect information about whether the judge in the second suit will find the first decision precedential. Che & Yi ask how this correlation of outcomes in a sequence of trials affects litigants' incentives to settle. They find that a defendant with a high likelihood of being found liable in the first case will be more eager to settle so as to avoid setting an unfavorable precedent, whereas a defendant with a low likelihood of being found liable in the first case will be more eager to go to trial so as to set a favorable precedent for the next case.

In each suit, it is assumed that the plaintiff has private information about her damages, that the probability that the plaintiff will prevail is common knowledge, and that the defendant makes a take-it-or-leave-it settlement offer; thus, this is a screening game in the taxonomy of the Bilateral Settlement Bargaining section. Let p_1 denote the probability that P_1 will prevail at trial. Then the probability that P_2 will prevail at trial, denoted p_2, is some base probability p_0 (independent of p_1), which is potentially modified by the outcome of the first suit. In particular, assume that: (a) $p_2 = p_0 + \epsilon$ if P_1 won her suit; (b) $p_2 = p_0$ if P_1 settled her suit; and (c) $p_2 = p_0 - \epsilon$ if P_1 lost her suit, where $\epsilon > 0$. Che & Yi refer to this as a mutual and symmetric precedential effect; they consider alternative versions in their paper. This probability structure is common knowledge to all the litigants.

Consider settlement negotiations in the second suit, conditional on the first suit's outcome. Using the analysis from the section on Bilateral Settlement Bargaining, we know that the marginal type in the second suit will be defined by $d_2^* = d_L + T/p_2$, and the associated likelihood of settlement will be $F(d_2^*) = T/p_2(d_H - d_L)$. From this, we see that the likelihood that the second suit will settle is highest when P_1 lost her suit and lowest when P_1 won her suit. Notice that if P_1 settled her suit, then P_2 faces the same probability of prevailing as if there were no P_1; that is, P_1's suit has no precedential effect. In addition, D's expected costs in the second suit are highest when P_1 won her suit and lowest when P_1 lost her suit.

Let $C_H > C_S > C_L$ denote D's expected cost in the second suit when P_1 won, settled, or lost, respectively, the first suit. In considering what offer to make to P_1, D recognizes the impact that P_1's decision regarding settlement will have on D's continuation payoff in his suit with P_2. Because P_1 is a nonrepeat litigant, a P_1 with damages of d_1 will accept any settlement offer $s \geq p_1 d_1 - t_P$. However, D now anticipates future costs of C_S if P_1 accepts his offer and future costs of $p_1 C_H + (1 - p_1)C_L$ if P_1 rejects his offer and trial occurs. These future costs are added to the usual costs associated with settlement and trial, respectively. Modifying the objective function given in the section on Bilateral Settlement Bargaining to reflect these continuation costs implies that the probability that the first case settles is given by $F(d_1^*) = (T + p_1 C_H + (1 - p_1)C_L - C_S)/p_1(d_H - d_L)$.

To determine the effect of the second suit on settlement behavior in the first suit, we compare the equilibrium probabilities of settlement in the first suit with and without the second suit. Recall that (using the section on Bilateral Settlement Bargaining) the probability of settlement in the first suit when there is no P_2 is given by $F(d^*) = T/p_1(d_H - d_L)$. It follows that $F(d_1^*) \geq F(d^*)$ if and only if $p_1 C_H + (1 - p_1)C_L \geq C_S$. Given the ordering of D's expected costs in the second suit, the left-hand side is an increasing function of p_1, which starts out below C_S and ends up above C_S. Thus, there is a unique value $p^* \in (0, 1)$ such that the presence of P_2 results in a greater likelihood of settlement when $p_1 > p^*$ (because D would then like to reduce his exposure to trial where he faces a relatively high risk of establishing an unfavorable precedent) and a lower likelihood of settlement when $p_1 < p^*$ (because D is then more willing to risk trial, where he faces a relatively high chance of establishing a favorable precedent).[14]

Class Action Lawsuits

Rule 23 of the Federal Rules of Civil Procedure authorizes the formation of a class action lawsuit. In a class action lawsuit, a small number of named (representative)

---

[14]Choi (1998) provides a model in which two imitators consider entering the market of an incumbent patent holder. A finding of patent validity (or invalidity) in an infringement suit against the first entrant is presumed to apply equally to the second entrant. He finds that the patent holder may accommodate (rather than sue) the first entrant to avoid a finding of patent invalidity. Accommodation plays the same role as settlement, as it avoids the setting of any precedent.

plaintiffs litigate on behalf of a very large number of harmed plaintiffs. Whether the individuals' cases are sufficiently similar so as to be aggregated into a class (i.e., whether the class will be certified) is a matter of judicial discretion. For instance, if a defendant's product has injured many consumers, then the issue of liability may be the same in each case. Pursuit of judicial economy and stability of the law suggests that this issue should be litigated once and for all. Moreover, the scale economies achievable for plaintiffs, whose individual harms might otherwise not rationalize a suit, can help ensure that victims receive compensation and defendants face the costs generated by their behavior, thus inducing more appropriate precaution.

If the extent of harm is also similar, then this too could be determined once and for all. If the extent of harm differs widely among the victims, then the class may be certified only for the issue of liability determination, but each individual must pursue a separate suit for damages. In most cases, participation in the class is voluntary; that is, individuals can opt out of the class and pursue their claims directly against the defendant. Thus, an interesting question arises when damages are somewhat heterogeneous, but nevertheless a class action has been certified to determine both liability and damages for the entire class. In this case, the award at trial may result in damages averaging; that is, a lump-sum amount may be awarded to the plaintiff class to be distributed in equal shares. In this event, those class members with relatively high damages will be undercompensated, while those with relatively low damages will be overcompensated. Thus, a potential class member who anticipates that she will be undercompensated may be tempted to opt out; on the other hand, by doing so she will have to bear the full costs of her suit against the defendant. Moreover, if a class member with comparatively high damages opts out, this lowers the average damages within the class and (assuming scale economies in litigation) raises the costs of each remaining member. Thus, multiple externalities are involved when individual suits are aggregated into a single suit. Scale economies in litigation costs represent a positive externality, but high-damaged plaintiffs suffer a negative externality from the presence of low-damaged plaintiffs in the class, and low-damaged plaintiffs enjoy a positive externality from high-damaged plaintiffs in the class. Finally, because each member is bound by the same liability decision at trial, there may be similar externalities if there is some heterogeneity in the probability of each plaintiff prevailing in an individual suit.

Che (1996) provides a formal model of the formation of a class action and the subsequent settlement negotiations between the class (or an opt-out) and a single defendant. The timing of the model is as follows. First, each plaintiff simultaneously and noncooperatively decides whether to join the class action or to opt out and pursue an individual suit; once made, this decision is irreversible. Moreover, it is assumed that no plaintiff can be excluded from the class. The defendant makes a take-it-or-leave-it settlement offer that the plaintiff either accepts or rejects. At trial, the court learns the average harm of the plaintiff class and awards this amount to each plaintiff. Che assumes that any settlement obtained by the class will also be shared equally among its members. Thus, all class members will agree about whether to accept or reject a given settlement offer. He first examines a model in which the strength of individual claims (which may be viewed as a product of the likelihood of prevailing and the extent of damages), though heterogeneous, are observable. For simplicity, he considers only two plaintiff types, those with high stakes (H) and those with low stakes (L). If plaintiffs' types are observable, he finds that (under moderate scale economies in litigation) there is always a Nash equilibrium in which all H-type plaintiffs opt out, while all L-type plaintiffs join the class. This is because it is a dominant strategy for all L-types to join, but whether an H-type P joins the class depends on the anticipated behavior of the other H-type Ps. If a P of type H expects that no other H-types will join, then she will not join either because she will suffer greatly from damages averaging. Thus, there is always an equilibrium in which only L-type Ps join the class.

Next, Che considers a model in which each plaintiff's type is her private information vis-à-vis the defendant and other plaintiffs (the court still learns, and awards, the average class damages at trial). Incomplete information has a substantial effect on the kinds of participation equilibria that can exist. In particular, it is no longer possible for an equilibrium to exist in which all L-type Ps join the class and all H-type Ps opt out (recall that this kind of equilibrium always exists when information is complete) because if all L-type Ps (and no H-type Ps) are expected to join the class, then *not* joining the class is a clear signal of type H and would elicit a high settlement offer; but then any P of type L would want to defect from joining the class to opting out. Similarly, there cannot be an equilibrium in which all H-types (and no L-types) join the class because then L-types are revealed by opting out and would want to defect to joining the class, both to receive a higher settlement offer and to enjoy the lower litigation costs. Instead, some, but not all, plaintiffs of each type join the class. It is also possible that the class fails to form.

In a subsequent paper, Che (2002) considers a model that is quite similar to the preceding one, except that each member of a class will receive her correct damages at trial and the members of the class can decide internally (and contract over) how to allocate money received in settlement. The defendant only knows the distribution of plaintiffs' damages, but each plaintiff knows her own damages. The incentives for collective negotiation are then examined under two different assumptions about the information regime within the class: (*a*) all members costlessly observe all other members' damages, and (*b*) each member's damages remain her private information within the class as well.

Under the assumption that members' damages are costlessly observed within the class and that they can contract on the internal allocation of a settlement, each member will insist on receiving at least what she would receive at trial. Knowing this, all H-type Ps will join. But then, as argued above, not joining is taken by D as a clear signal of weakness (and would be followed by a low offer), so L-types will join as well. Thus, the equilibrium involves all Ps joining their cases. Notice how different this is from the result above in which, under the same informational circumstances, damages averaging could generate an equilibrium in which a class fails to form. This does not happen here because H-types' payoffs are not dragged down by the participation of L-types.

When damages are private information even within the class, then every P will be tempted to claim to be of type H. The class can resolve this issue by using a mechanism that specifies whether to accept a settlement offer s, and how to divide it among the members of the class, based on their reported types (for details, see Che 2002). In brief, this entails the L-types receiving information rents to induce them to forebear claiming to be of type H and to truthfully reveal that they are of type L; H-types do not have an incentive to claim to be L-types, so they receive no information rents. Only settlement offers that are high enough to cover both the aggregate expected payoff from trial plus the required information rents will be accepted. Thus, the class will be a tougher bargainer (i.e., will require a higher settlement offer) when it faces this internal allocation problem under asymmetric information. When the choice regarding participation is considered, it remains an equilibrium for all Ps to join the class.

Joint and Several Liability

Joint and several liability (JSL) may apply when multiple tortfeasors act concurrently or in concert to cause a plaintiff's injury. For example, two firms that dump hazardous waste into a single waterway may harm the health of people living downstream. Under JSL, a plaintiff suing both defendants may collect the full amount of the damages if she prevails against either or both of the defendants at trial. In contrast, under nonjoint liability (NJL), a plaintiff can collect from each defendant only that portion of the harm that is attributable to that defendant. Thus, JSL introduces externalities between the defendants that would not exist under NJL; these externalities manifest themselves both at trial and in settlement negotiations.

The classic analysis of the impact of JSL on incentives to settle was provided by Kornhauser & Revesz (1994a). They consider a model in which a single plaintiff sues two defendants under complete, but imperfect, information about whether the defendants will be found liable. The assumption of complete information immediately suggests that there should be no trials in equilibrium, but this turns out to be false. Rather, they show that both cases will go to trial when the correlation between the defendants' likelihoods of being found liable is sufficiently low, but will settle when the correlation is high.

Assume that there are two defendants, each of whom has contributed equally to the plaintiff's harm; let the plaintiff's total harm be denoted $2d$. Each defendant suffers a trial cost of t, while the plaintiff suffers a trial cost of t per defendant; thus, there are no scale economies for the plaintiff in going to trial against both defendants. Finally, assume that each defendant is capable of paying the full damages $2d$.[15] Let p denote the probability that the plaintiff prevails when she goes to

---

[15]Their general model allows unequal contributions by the defendants to the plaintiff's harm, scale economies in the plaintiff's trial costs, different setoff rules, and a different selection rule when multiple equilibria exist. In Kornhauser & Revesz (1994b) they consider partially insolvent defendants and find that (for the case of equal contribution) this increases the parameter range over which settlement occurs.

trial against a single defendant, and let δp denote the probability that the plaintiff prevails against the second defendant, having prevailed against the first, when she goes to trial against both defendants. The parameter δ varies between $\delta = 1$ and $\delta = 1/p$. When $\delta = 1$ the probability of prevailing against both defendants is p^2 (that is, the case outcomes are uncorrelated), whereas when $\delta = 1/p$ the probability of prevailing against both defendants is p (that is, the case outcomes are perfectly correlated). In general, when the plaintiff goes to trial against both defendants, she has a probability δp^2 of prevailing against both defendants, and a probability $2p(1 - \delta p)$ of prevailing against one defendant; in either case, she collects the full amount $2d$.

The timing of the game is as follows: The plaintiff makes a settlement demand of the pair of defendants, denoted (s_1, s_2). Simultaneously and noncooperatively, each defendant decides whether to accept or reject the settlement demand made of him. Finally, any defendant who rejects his demand is taken to trial by the plaintiff. We assume the unconditional pro tanto setoff rule, which specifies that if one defendant settles, then the amount of the settlement is deducted from what the plaintiff can hope to obtain from trial against the remaining defendant. We first characterize the Nash equilibrium strategies in the subgame following receipt of the settlement demands, and then determine the plaintiff's optimal demands. In the sequel, we denote the plaintiff by P and the defendants by D_1 and D_2.

Given a pair of demands (s_1, s_2), it is a Nash equilibrium for both D_1 and D_2 to accept their respective demands if and only if $s_i \leq p(2d - s_j) + t$, for $i = 1, 2$. This is because, given that D_j is expected to accept s_j, D_i can expect to pay the total harm less the amount of the settlement with D_j, should D_i be found liable at trial (which occurs with probability p); in addition, D_i will pay trial costs of t. Thus, D_i will prefer to accept any settlement demand $s_i \leq p(2d - s_j) + t$.

Given a pair of demands (s_1, s_2), it is a Nash equilibrium for D_i to accept s_i and D_j to reject s_j if and only if $s_i \leq .5\delta p^2(2d) + p(1 - \delta p)(2d) + t$ and $s_j \geq p(2d - s_i) + t$. This is because, given that D_j is expected to reject s_j and go to trial, D_i can choose to go to trial as well, in which case D_i can expect to pay his share (half) of the total damages if both defendants are found liable (which occurs with probability δp^2), and D_i can expect to pay all the total damages if he is found liable while his codefendant is found not liable [which happens with probability $p(1 - \delta p)$]. In addition, D_i will pay trial costs of t. If s_i is less than this amount, then D_i prefers to settle. On the other hand, if D_i is expected to settle for s_i, then D_j can expect to pay the full amount of the damages offset by the amount of the settlement with D_i if D_j is found liable, which occurs with probability p; in addition, D_j will pay trial costs of t. If s_j exceeds this amount, then D_j will indeed prefer trial.

Finally, given a pair of demands (s_1, s_2), it is a Nash equilibrium for both D_1 and D_2 to reject their respective demands if and only if $s_i \geq .5\delta p^2(2d) + p(1 - \delta p)(2d) + t$, for $i = 1, 2$. In this case, each defendant prefers to go to trial (given that the other defendant is expected to go to trial as well) rather than to acquiesce to the plaintiff's demand.

We now consider P's optimal settlement demand pair (s_1, s_2). We assume that whenever it is a Nash equilibrium for both D_1 and D_2 to accept their respective demands, they do so.[16] This simplifies the exposition and ensures that any trials that occur are not the result of coordination failure. Moreover, it can be shown that, from P's point of view, a pair of settlement demands that induces acceptance by only one D is always dominated by either a demand pair that induces both Ds to accept or by a demand pair that induces both Ds to reject. Thus, we need only ask (a) what settlement demand pair maximizes P's expected payoff from settlement with both Ds, and (b) when is the resulting expected payoff better than what she expects from trial against both Ds?

To answer the first question, we define P's maximized return from inducing both Ds to accept their respective settlement demands as $V^P(A, A) = \max s_1 + s_2$ subject to: $s_i \leq p(2d - s_j) + t$, for $i = 1, 2$. P's most-preferred settlement pair consists of $(s_1, s_2) = (s^*, s^*)$, where the two constraints intersect. This settlement demand is $s^* = (2pd + t)/(1 + p)$, which yields the payoff $V^P(A, A) = 2(2pd + t)/(1 + p)$. Alternatively, if P induces both Ds to choose trial, she can expect to receive $V^P(R, R) = \delta p^2(2d) + 2p(1 - \delta p)(2d) - 2t$. This payoff reflects the fact that P collects the full damages $2d$ if she prevails against either D, or both; however, she pays the trial costs $2t$.

To answer the second question, we compare the payoffs $V^P(A, A)$ and $V^P(R, R)$. It is straightforward to show that $V^P(A, A) \gtreqqless V^P(R, R)$ as $\delta \gtreqqless \delta^* \equiv (2p^2d - t(2 + p))/p^2(1 + p)$. Notice that $\delta^* < 1/p$ always holds, but $\delta^* > 1$ if and only if $t < p^2d(1 - p)/(2 + p)$. Thus, we conclude that if $t \geq p^2d(1 - p)/(2 + p)$, then all cases will settle under JSL. However, if $t < p^2d(1 - p)/(2 + p)$, then cases whose outcomes are sufficiently highly correlated will settle, but P will go to trial against both Ds if the case outcomes are sufficiently uncorrelated.

Two related strands of literature have been developed, but they are outside the purview of this survey. Klerman (1996) and Feess & Muehlheusser (2000) discuss how alternative setoff rules affect settlement incentives. Spier (1994) and Kahan (1996) discuss the effect of settlement under JSL on care taken in the primary activity.

Insolvency

Spier (2002) describes another settlement negotiation scenario that involves externalities and has a formal structure quite similar to the one just described. This situation arises when a single defendant has harmed two plaintiffs but does not have enough wealth to compensate both plaintiffs; indeed, we consider the case in which the defendant does not have enough wealth to fully compensate even one plaintiff because the commonalities with the Kornhauser & Revesz model are most

---

[16]For some parameters, there may be two symmetric equilibria (e.g., one in which both defendants accept and one in which both reject), or two asymmetric equilibria (in which one defendant accepts and the other rejects). Kornhauser & Revesz discuss this issue in detail; in a related paper to be discussed below, Spier (2002) uses risk dominance to select among equilibria.

evident when the defendant's insolvency problem is extreme [see Spier (2002) for the more general model, as well as several extensions]. In particular, we retain all the notation used above, but the defendant's wealth, denoted w, replaces the total damages $2d$ from above. In addition, Spier assumes that the defendant, denoted D, makes simultaneous settlement offers to the plaintiffs, denoted P_1 and P_2, who simultaneously and noncooperatively decide whether to accept or reject the offers. Of course, if P_i accepts her offer, this reduces the amount that P_j can expect to obtain at trial, just as in the unconditional pro tanto setoff rule.

Given a pair of offers (s_1, s_2), it is a Nash equilibrium for both P_1 and P_2 to accept their respective offers if and only if $s_i \geq p(w - s_j) - t$, for $i = 1, 2$. This is because, given that P_j is expected to accept s_j, P_i can expect to receive the defendant's total wealth less the amount of the settlement with P_j should P_i prevail at trial (which occurs with probability p); in addition, P_i will pay trial costs of t. Thus, P_i will prefer to accept any settlement demand $s_i \geq p(2d - s_j) - t$.

Given a pair of offers (s_1, s_2), it is a Nash equilibrium for P_i to accept s_i and P_j to reject s_j if and only if $s_i \geq .5\delta p^2 w + p(1 - \delta p)w - t$ and $s_j \leq p(w - s_i) - t$. This is because, given that P_j is expected to reject s_j and go to trial, P_i can choose to go to trial as well, in which case P_i can expect to receive her share (half) of the defendant's wealth if both plaintiffs prevail (which occurs with probability δp^2), and P_i can expect to receive all the defendant's wealth if P_i prevails but P_j does not [which happens with probability $p(1 - \delta p)$]. However, P_i will pay trial costs of t. If s_i exceeds this amount, then P_i will prefer to settle. On the other hand, if P_i is expected to settle for s_i, then P_j can expect to receive the defendant's total wealth offset by the amount of the settlement with P_i if P_j prevails at trial, which occurs with probability p; however, P_j will pay trial costs of t. If s_j is less than this amount, then P_j will indeed prefer trial.

Finally, given a pair of offers (s_1, s_2), it is a Nash equilibrium for both P_1 and P_2 to reject their respective offers if and only if $s_i \leq .5\delta p^2 w + p(1 - \delta p)w - t$, for $i = 1, 2$. In this case, each plaintiff prefers to go to trial (given that the other plaintiff is expected to go to trial as well) rather than to accept the defendant's offer.

As before, we assume that whenever there is a Nash equilibrium in which both plaintiffs accept their offers, this equilibrium is selected. Also as before, it can be shown that a settlement offer pair that induces P_i to accept and P_j to reject is always dominated by either an offer pair that induces both to accept or by an offer pair that induces both to reject. Thus, we need only ask (*a*) what settlement offer pair minimizes D's expected cost from settlement with both Ps, and (*b*) when is the resulting expected cost lower than what he expects from trial against both Ps?

D's minimized expected cost from inducing both Ps to accept their respective settlement offers is $V^D(A, A) = \min s_1 + s_2$ subject to $s_i \geq p(w - s_j) - t$, for $i = 1, 2$. D's least-cost offer pair consists of $(s_1, s_2) = (s^{**}, s^{**})$, where the two constraints intersect. This settlement offer is $s^{**} = (pw - t)/(1 + p)$, which yields the payoff $V^D(A, A) = 2(pw - t)/(1 + p)$. Alternatively, if D induces both Ps to reject his demands, he can expect to pay the amount $V^D(R, R) = \delta p^2 w +$

$2p(1 - \delta p)w + 2t$. This payoff reflects the fact that D forfeits his entire wealth w if either P prevails, or both; in addition, he pays the trial costs $2t$.

We now compare the payoffs $V^D(A, A)$ and $V^D(R, R)$. It is straightforward to show that $V^D(A, A) \gtreqless V^D(R, R)$ as $\delta \gtreqless \delta^{**} \equiv (2p^2w + 2t(2 + p))/p^2w(1 + p)$. Notice that $\delta^{**} > 1$ always holds, but $\delta^{**} < 1/p$ holds if and only if $t < pw(1 - p)/2(2 + p)$. Thus, we conclude that if $t \geq pw(1 - p)/2(2 + p)$, then all cases will settle when D is insolvent. However, if $t < pw(1 - p)/2(2 + p)$, then cases whose outcomes are sufficiently highly correlated will go to trial, but D will settle with both Ps if the case outcomes are sufficiently uncorrelated.

Note the similarities to (and differences from) the Kornhauser & Revesz (1994a,b) model: Here, the acceptance versus rejection constraints involve (a) a reversed inequality; (b) the substitution of w for $2d$; and (c) the subtraction, rather than the addition, of t. The defendant's payoff differs from that of the plaintiff in Kornhauser & Revesz by the substitution of w for $2d$ and by the addition, rather than the subtraction, of the trial costs $2t$; moreover, the defendant wants to minimize his expected costs, whereas the plaintiff in Kornhauser & Revesz wants to maximize her expected payoff. Finally, settlement negotiations fail when the case outcomes are sufficiently correlated, whereas in Kornhauser & Revesz they fail when the case outcomes are sufficiently uncorrelated.

SUMMARY

Recent work on the economics of settlement bargaining has emphasized multiple-litigant settlement negotiation. The essential feature of such bargaining is that seemingly bilateral negotiations affect, and are affected by, simultaneous or sequential settlement possibilities with other litigants. We subdivided this sampling of the literature into two groupings. In the first grouping, we considered papers in which discretionary choices by one or more of the litigants (to create, or capitalize on, possible linkages among yet other litigants) generate such externalities. In that section, the preferences of the litigants over the use of such devices need not be directly opposed.

The second grouping emphasized examples in which employing existing legal doctrine or rules of procedure may induce bargaining externalities. We noted that the choice by one or another of the litigants to use the relevant legal doctrines or procedural rules may be voluntary, but in this second grouping preferences of the individual litigants over using such doctrines and procedures are usually diametrically opposed; such rules exist to provide recourse when agreement is not possible.

In both types of analysis, formal models relying on game theory and information economics have been used to understand which attributes of such multiple-litigant bargaining are privately and/or socially advantageous (or disadvantageous), and when such devices, doctrines, or rules lead to a greater or lesser likelihood of settlement.

ACKNOWLEDGMENTS

We thank the National Science Foundation for support via NSF grant SES-0239908. We also thank Kathryn Spier for comments on an earlier draft.

The *Annual Review of Law and Social Science* is online at http://lawsocsci.annualreviews.org

LITERATURE CITED

Ashcraft v. Conoco, Inc. 1998. U.S. Dist. LEXIS 4092

Bebchuk LA. 1984. Litigation and settlement under imperfect information. *RAND J. Econ.* 15:404–15

Briggs HC III, Huryn KD, McBride ME. 1996. Treble damages and the incentive to sue and settle. *RAND J. Econ.* 27:770–86

Che YK. 1996. Equilibrium formation of class action suits. *J. Public Econ.* 62:339–61

Che YK. 2002. The economics of collective negotiation in pretrial bargaining. *Int. Econ. Rev.* 43:549–75

Che YK, Yi JG. 1993. The role of precedents in repeated litigation. *J. Law Econ. Organ.* 9:399–424

Choi JP. 1998. Patent litigation as an information transmission mechanism. *Am. Econ. Rev.* 88:1249–63

Daughety AF. 2000. Settlement. In *Encyclopedia of Law and Economics*, ed. B Bouckaert, G De Geest, 5:95–158. Cheltenham, UK: Edward Elgar

Daughety AF, Reinganum JF. 1994. Settlement negotiations with two-sided asymmetric information: model duality, information distribution, and efficiency. *Int. Rev. Law Econ.* 14:283–98

Daughety AF, Reinganum JF. 1999. Hush money. *RAND J. Econ.* 30:661–78

Daughety AF, Reinganum JF. 2002. Informational externalities in settlement bargaining: confidentiality and correlated culpability. *RAND J. Econ.* 33:587–604

Daughety AF, Reinganum JF. 2004. Exploiting future settlements: a signalling model of most-favored-nation clauses in settlement bargaining. *RAND J. Econ.* 35:467–85

Feess E, Muehlheusser G. 2000. Settling multidefendant lawsuits under incomplete information. *Int. Rev. Law Econ.* 20:295–313

Gould JP. 1973. The economics of legal conflicts. *J. Legal Stud.* 2:279–300

Hare FH, Gilbert JL, Remine WH. 1988. *Confidentiality Orders.* New York: Wiley

Hay BL, Spier KE. 1998. Settlement of litigation. In *The New Palgrave Dictionary of Economics and the Law*, ed. P Newman, 3:442–51. New York: Stockton

In re Rhone-Poulenc Rorer Inc., 51 F.3d. 1293 (7th Cir. 1995)

Kahan M. 1996. The incentive effects of settlements under joint and several liability. *Int. Rev. Law Econ.* 16:389–95

Klerman D. 1996. Settling multidefendant lawsuits: the advantage of conditional setoff rules. *J. Legal Stud.* 25:445–62

Kornhauser LA, Revesz RL. 1994a. Multidefendant settlements: the impact of joint and several liability. *J. Legal Stud.* 23:41–76

Kornhauser LA, Revesz RL. 1994b. Multidefendant settlements under joint and several liability: the problem of insolvency. *J. Legal Stud.* 23:517–42

Landes WM. 1971. An economic analysis of the courts. *J. Law Econ.* 14:61–107

Posner RA. 1973. An economic approach to legal procedure and judicial administration. *J. Legal Stud.* 2:399–458

Reinganum JF, Wilde LF. 1986. Settlement, litigation, and the allocation of litigation costs. *RAND J. Econ.* 17:557–66

Schweizer U. 1989. Litigation and settlement under two-sided incomplete information. *Rev. Econ. Stud.* 56:163–77

Shavell S. 1982. Suit, settlement and trial: a theoretical analysis under alternative methods for the allocation of legal costs. *J. Legal Stud.* 11:55–81

Spier KE. 1994. A note on joint and several liability: insolvency, settlement, and incentives. *J. Legal Stud.* 23:559–68

Spier KE. 2002. Settlement with multiple plaintiffs: the role of insolvency. *J. Law Econ. Organ.* 18:295–323

Spier KE. 2003a. The use of most-favored-nation clauses in settlement of litigation. *RAND J. Econ.* 34:78–95

Spier KE. 2003b. Tied to the mast: most-favored-nation clauses in settlement contracts. *J. Legal Stud.* 32:91–120

Viscusi WK. 2002. *Smoke-Filled Rooms—A Postmortem on the Tobacco Deal.* Chicago: Univ. Chicago Press

Yang BZ. 1996. Litigation, experimentation, and reputation. *Int. Rev. Law Econ.* 16:491–502

Annu. Rev. Law Soc. Sci. 2005. 1:61–84
doi: 10.1146/annurev.lawsocsci.1.041604.115944
First published online as a Review in Advance on June 14, 2005

LAW AND CORPORATE GOVERNANCE

Neil Fligstein and Jennifer Choo

*Department of Sociology, University of California, Berkeley, California 94720;
email: fligst@uclink4.berkeley.edu*

Key Words   comparative capitalism, agency theory, economic development

■ **Abstract**   Corporate governance concerns three sets of issues: property rights, relationships between firms and financial markets, and labor relations. Our literature review shows that the system of corporate governance that emerges within a particular country reflects the outcome of political, social, and economic struggles in that country and that it does not reflect efficiency considerations focused on managing agency relations between owners and managers. Despite these facts, much research has been done in recent years attempting to analyze whether a superior matrix of institutional arrangements or a set of best practices of corporate governance exists to produce greater economic growth. Our review shows that there does not appear to be a single set of best practices, but rather that what is important are stable institutions that are legitimate and prevent extreme rent seeking on the part of governments and capitalists.

INTRODUCTION

One of the great intellectual divides in modern social science is the gap between economics and sociology. Classically, economists have seen the rise of modern society as the reduction of the role of governments and of the influence of rent-seeking actors and their replacement with calculating individuals who seek profits by producing for markets (Smith 1904). By being forced to compete with others, the "invisible hand of the market" pushed producers to create the efficient allocation of societal resources, and, of course, they became the source of the "wealth of nations." While classical sociology saw the rise of modern society as deeply connected with markets, it also maintained that social elements like law, norms, religion, social classes, and politics play crucial roles in the development of firms and markets (Durkheim 1997; Marx 1977; Weber 1978, 2001). Both Marx and Weber foresaw many of the problems markets would create, such as the economic instability caused by ruinous competition, the attempts by producers to obtain monopolies and enlist the state on their behalf in these efforts, and the possibility that governments would be rent seekers in their own right.

More recently, economic sociology has pushed forward the view that action in markets is less about anonymous firms competing over the price of goods and more about firms creating social structures for particular markets (Fligstein 2001, Granovetter 1985, White 2002). For economic sociology, the degree to which these social structures are efficient from a neoclassical perspective is an empirical question. Indeed, much of sociology has been agnostic on the question of whether social institutions (including markets) are efficient. Sociologists have argued that under some conditions one set of arrangements might be more profitable than another. But sociologists are equally prepared to believe that social institutions and markets are artifacts of historical accidents whereby one social group has benefited over others and that the link between particular institutional and market arrangements and optimal economic outcomes is highly complex [see Granovetter (1985) for an argument to this effect].

The gap between sociology and economics has narrowed significantly in the past 15 years. For example, Douglass North, a Nobel Prize–winning economist, has argued that legal, political, and social institutions played a fundamental role in the rise of the West (North 1981, 1990). A whole branch of historical and institutional economics has begun to explore the role of social factors in the relative performance of the developed and less-developed societies (Acemoglu et al. 2001; Amsden 2001; Djankov et al. 2003; Greif 1994; La Porta et al. 1998, 1999a,b, 2002a; Rodrik 2003; Shleifer & Vishny 1993, 1994a,b, 1997; Wade 1990). Bodies of literature in sociology, law, and political science have always considered social and political factors as fundamental to firms and economic growth. Scholars have attributed differences in capitalist systems to varying degrees and types of state interventions into the economy, legal systems, structures of capitalist enterprises, and processes of economic growth (Albert 1993; Cioffi 2000; Coffee 2001a,b; Crouch & Streeck 1997; Evans 1995; Fligstein 1990; Hall & Soskice 2001; Mahoney 2001; Roe 1994, 2003; Streeck 1992). Efforts to understand these links have grown even more intense with the collapse of communism, the continued bad economic times in Africa, and the rapid economic growth of the Asian economies (Evans 1995, Eyal et al. 1998, Guthrie 1999, Nee 1992, Radaev 2002, Stark 1996). Economists, sociologists, legal scholars, and political scientists have converged on an old, deep question: How do social and legal arrangements affect firms, markets, and economic growth?

The purpose of this paper is to review the recent literature that surrounds the comparative and historical study of law and corporate governance. We accept Cioffi's (2000) definition of corporate governance as a "nexus of institutions defined by company law, financial market regulation, and labor law" (p. 574). Our review begins by elaborating upon this definition. Then, we consider how the problem of efficiency was introduced into discussions of law and corporate governance by agency theory. We suggest that much of the current literature has offered both a theoretical and an empirical critique of the agency theory perspective on the evolution of systems of corporate governance. The literature now agrees that there is variation in systems of corporate governance across societies and that most of this difference reflects national political, social, and cultural trajectories that have created and continuously shaped the laws that define corporate governance. Despite these noneconomic processes dominating the structuring of law and markets, scholars have continued to wonder if certain systems of corporate governance might even accidentally prove to be more efficient at producing long-term economic growth. This leads us to consider the literature on how political and legal institutions affect the economic performance of societies. We end with some observations about what we do and do not know in this contentious field.

DEFINITION OF CORPORATE GOVERNANCE

It is useful to propose a general framework to organize the literature. The first step is to define the three relevant types of laws for understanding the comparative structuring of corporations. First, company law defines the legal vehicles by which property rights are organized (Hansmann & Kraakman 2000). It defines the legal standing of publicly and privately held corporations. It also specifies the legal liability of owners. In the case of publicly held corporations, company law helps define the relationships among owners, boards of directors, managers, and workers. The main variable that is of interest in the literature is the degree to which there is a separation of ownership from control in publicly held corporations. One main way to index this separation is the degree to which shareholding of firms is widespread or concentrated (either in banks, other financial institutions, or families).

Second, financial market regulation refers to how firms obtain capital for their operations, and in doing so it specifies firms' relationships to banks, other financial institutions, and public equity and debt markets. All firms need to raise capital to fund their operations. Owners traditionally have supplied their own funds to do this. But, as the scale of enterprise has grown in the past 150 years, firms have needed to borrow larger sums of money. Historically, banks and private individuals were the main source of these funds. Since the 1950s, firms (particularly in the United States) have increasingly turned to the public markets to raise money. The equity markets allow firms to sell additional stock in the firm, while the bond markets allow firms to borrow money and issue bonds that will be repaid eventually. Financial market regulations refer to the laws that govern all these transactions, both private and public. In the case of the sale of equity and debt, they also force firms to disclose information in order for potential lenders and investors to understand the financial situation of the firm.

Third, labor law defines how labor contracts will operate in a particular society. Such laws include the rights of labor to organize, the conditions under which labor is hired and fired, and how and to what degree workers participate in corporate governance. These issues are paramount for corporate governance because they greatly affect the structure of the firm and how decisions are made regarding the allocation of corporate resources. In societies like the United States where labor law is weak, corporate boards make decisions to maximize shareholder value without regard to its effects on labor. In Germany, where labor law is well developed, workers have representatives on boards of directors and are viewed as partners in business decision making. Obviously, these differing arrangements could greatly affect corporate strategies in the deployment of capital.

CORPORATE GOVERNANCE AND THE PROBLEM
OF EFFICIENCY

At the heart of the literature on law and corporate governance is the question of whether some sets of rules promote economic efficiency more than others. This claim is somewhat vague. Neoclassical economists view efficiency as the outcome of the optimal allocation of land, labor, and capital by a firm given the various prices of these resources. Economies of scale and scope represent how firms make investments to produce the most goods for the lowest prices. Economists have considered other ways in which efficiency might emerge. They have focused attention on the minimization of transaction costs (Williamson 1975, 1985), the minimization of agency costs (Jensen & Meckling 1976), and the process of reaching a Nash equilibrium in a game (Tirole 1988). To assess efficiency empirically, economists study the performance of firms (profits, return on capital) or whole national economies (where the dependent variable is frequently measured by changes in GDP).

Historically, economists have been skeptical of the claim that political, legal, or cultural factors affect efficiency. Most economists think that price signals are central to the efficient allocation of resources and most responsible for making things efficient. But economists have shifted away from their position that efficiency is purely about rational actors making decisions about the allocation of productive assets and have begun focusing on social arrangements like contracts in the context of, for example, firm governance, as we discuss more below. Their attempt to view institutions like contracting and the construction of the boundaries of the firm as efficiency enhancing moves them toward sociology and organizational theory. Economists have gone from this focus on contracting to a more expansive view of the kinds of institutions, like law, trust, and good government, that might affect market outcomes (Berkowitz et al. 2003; Carlin & Mayer 2003; La Porta et al. 1997a,b, 1998, 1999b; Mahoney 2001; North 1990).

The institutionalist position within law and economics that has dominated discussions of efficiency and corporate governance in the past 25 years is agency theory. Here, we use agency theory as a foil to explore how other social, political, and legal factors might affect corporate governance. Agency theory views the firm as a nexus of contracts and as such sees the firm as a "useful fiction" [see Jensen & Meckling (1976) for the classic statement of this position and Fama & Jensen (1983a,b) for a more didactic explication; see Hansmann (1996) for a longer excursus on the evolution of ownership forms and the ultimate domination of the public corporation in the United States].

One can conceive of all relationships within the firm and between the firm and other firms as being bound by contracts. These contracts frequently have a hierarchical structure in which a principal delegates responsibility to an agent to perform some task. The contract that is written specifies rights, duties, and compensation of agents and frequently provides some mechanism by which the principal can monitor the agent. The problem that agency theory set out to solve in the 1970s was why there appeared to be a separation of ownership from control over the large corporation in the United States.

Beginning with Berle & Means (1932), a long history of scholarship had argued that this separation was inefficient. It suggested that managerial control led firms to make investments that stabilized the firms by preferring growth over profits (i.e., managers pursued less risky investments to preserve their jobs) and producing perks for the managers themselves (Marris 1968, Penrose 1959). The problem with this theory was that all available evidence suggested that firms controlled by managers performed at least as well as owner-controlled firms [for a review, see Short (1994)]. It should be noted that efficiency in this case was usually measured by comparing profit rates across firms with different ownership types. These consistent empirical results caused some economists to rethink the problem and attempt to figure out why the separation of ownership and control was efficient.

Agency theory began by arguing that in modern capitalist economies, firms need to raise sufficient money to produce complex products and to take advantage of economies of scale and scope. On the one side, the managers who ran these firms lacked the capital to do so. On the other side, there existed people with money who could be owners but who lacked either the expertise or the interest to run the firm. To solve this problem, the principals (i.e., the investors) would give their money to agents (the managers) in order for those managers to make profits and assure those principals of maximum returns on their investments. The main problem was that the owners of capital who lacked information about how to produce the product were potentially at the mercy of the managers, the agents, which led to the problem of monitoring those agents. The cost of this monitoring is called agency cost. A number of solutions to this problem purportedly exist: Boards of directors are charged with a fiduciary duty to shareholders to monitor the managers; managers' compensation is tied to firm performance, thereby aligning their interests with the interests of owners; and disclosure laws require timely filing of operational and performance results to current and prospective investors. Agency theory posited that if managers still behaved badly and boards of directors ducked their fiduciary responsibility, the existence of a market for corporate control would provide the final check on managerial opportunism (Fama & Jensen 1983a,b).

In this story, corporate law and financial market regulation make it possible for minority shareholders who have little access to the internal workings of the firm to gain knowledge of how firms are doing financially. In essence, these laws solve the agency problem by specifying rules governing the disclosures and governance of public corporations. In exchange for being able to raise capital publicly, teams of managers must make information available to the public and be governed by a board of directors (Hansmann 1996). Thus, the separation of ownership and control in large U.S. corporations is thought to efficiently satisfy the needs of firms for capital as well as the needs of investors to be guaranteed a fair shake by teams of managers. Note that for agency theorists, these laws and arrangements are created to meet the functional needs of owners who prefer not to administer firms directly.

These arrangements are deemed efficient because they maximize the returns to these owners by lowering agency costs.

For agency theorists (mostly economists, but a few law professors as well), history, culture, and politics are irrelevant for the issue of how to get the right (i.e., efficient) mix of investments made in a particular economy. In essence, societies that discover this complex but elegant solution to the problem of raising large sums of capital by separating ownership from control and insuring that managers use capital wisely (i.e., minimize agency costs) will prosper precisely because the shareholder wealth-maximizing investments will get made. Societies that try to pursue goals other than shareholder wealth maximization through their corporate governance structures or that ignore the problem of agency costs entirely are doomed to underperformance because their capital markets will not be deep enough to allow the most profitable (efficient) investments for owners [see Jensen (1989) for a rhetorical defense of the American system along these lines].

This clean story has lots of power, and it has captured the intellectual imagination of many scholars in economics departments and law schools. But the story has a significant flaw. The theory argues that the functional needs of owners of capital drive the creation of institutions and that therefore whichever institutions survive are by definition efficient. However, this argument ignores the fact that the creation of these markets, even in the United States, was a political and historical accident (Roe 1994). Roe documents that in the 1930s, the U.S. government passed a series of laws forbidding banks and other financial institutions from controlling industrial corporations. These laws were passed for populist reasons, and their intention was to prevent the concentration of economic power in the hands of a few powerful financial institutions. They were not passed to produce efficient capital markets or to solve agency problems of firms. The argument also ignores the fact that these institutions did not emerge anywhere else in the developed world (with the exception of Great Britain, which began to develop these institutions by mimicking the U.S. case during the 1980s; see Vitols 2001). Moreover, Japan, Germany, France, Italy, the countries in Scandinavia, and more recently Taiwan, Singapore, and South Korea have attained high levels of industrial development without producing American-style institutions or deep capital markets (Hall & Soskice 2001, La Porta et al. 1998, Roe 2003), suggesting that the U.S.-style of public firms may be a localized phenomenon generated by elements of historical and political forces unique to the United States.

The empirical failure of agency theory to account for varieties of successful systems of corporate governance presents two problems for efficiency analysis. First, systems of corporate governance result from political and historical processes rather than from efficient solutions to the functional needs of the owners of capital who seek to maximize profits for themselves. Second, the fact that many societies appear to have experienced comparable economic growth without converging on a single form of corporate governance (i.e., that of the United States) suggests that there is no set of best practices of corporate governance but rather many sets of best practices, and that the relationship linking these institutions to good societal outcomes like economic growth is more complex than agency theory would allow.

The scholarship can be broken down into two camps around these issues. In the first camp are some institutional economists who have recognized that political, cultural, and legal factors might indeed operate as independent variables to affect the organization of firms (Demirgüç-Kunt & Maksimovic 1998; La Porta et al. 1997a,b, 1998). They have been joined by a number of political scientists who have been interested in the question of how public policy might be harnessed to produce better economic growth (Albert 1993, Berger & Dore 1996, Boyer & Drache 1996, Crouch & Streeck 1997, Streeck 1992). These scholars have engaged in an ambitious project to document what these differences in political and legal systems are and what kinds of capital markets and corporate governance systems they tend to produce. Although they are prepared to believe that the creation of these institutions related to how firms are financed and owned and did not solely involve efficiency considerations, these scholars continue to maintain that some institutions might be more efficiency enhancing than others.

Their approach is to argue that the same set of agency problems (i.e., the problems of owners and managers) and the need for firms to obtain capital are solved differently in different societies because of the opportunities and constraints of the existing political and legal systems. This has produced an interesting literature on the study of comparative capitalist systems that focuses on how the particular relationships among owners, managers, and workers evolved (La Porta et al. 1997a, 1998). The literature is willing to accept that there may be more than one path to development. But economists and political scientists would still like to believe that even if corporate governance structures are largely shaped by the political and legal context, there still may be ways to resolve problems of external finance and optimal monitoring of managers that ultimately are more efficient and thereby produce more economic growth than other institutional arrangements. They have produced a large number of interesting papers that try to quantify these differences and to show that they are consequential for societal economic growth.

The second camp is more agnostic about the ultimate linkage among institutions, efficiency, and economic growth (Bebchuk & Roe 1999; Fligstein 1990, 2001; Hall & Soskice 2001; Maier 1987; Roe 1994, 2003). These scholars document how political, cultural, and legal systems interact with firms and over time produce a system that reflects less efficiency considerations and more the outcomes of particular political, social, and economic struggles. An interesting subtext in this literature (sometimes more explicit, sometimes less so) is that economic growth, at least in developed countries, is more likely to come about because stable political institutions exist to enable such growth rather than because some exact configurations of laws and institutions are generated. Scholars who have studied less-developed countries have drawn similar conclusions. Developing societies need stable governments that do not rent seek too much (i.e., that are not so corrupt that payoffs, bribes, and extortion are regular ways of doing business), help resolve class struggle, let private actors accumulate wealth, and generally provide for public order (Evans 1995, Evans & Rauch 1999, Wade 1990, Weiss 1998). In other words, it seems less important that specific sets of laws or specific solutions to societal problems like class struggle be implemented to create economic growth than that stable societal conditions exist more generally.

A CONCEPTUAL APPROACH TO POLITICS, SOCIETY, CULTURE, LAW, AND CORPORATE GOVERNANCE

To explore more fully the tensions produced by these different scholarly positions, we now turn to Figure 1. Institutionalists in economics, sociology, and political science all agree that societal conditions give rise to governance structures of firms (defined as corporate law, financial market regulation, and labor law). They identify a number of societal institutions as potentially important.

First, the political system of a particular society (i.e., democracy versus dictatorship) and the existence of the rule of law are important preconditions for understanding corporate governance structures. The cultural tradition of the legal systems, such as whether they have civil or common law legal systems, is part of

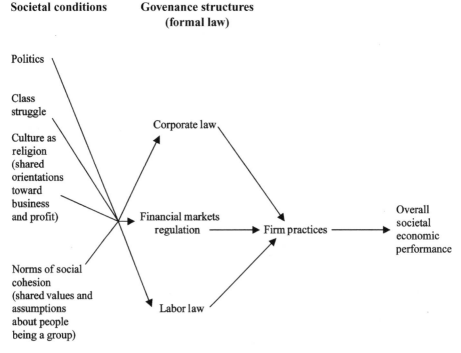

Figure 1   An institutionalist model of the relationship linking social and political factors to law and corporate governance.

this apparatus as well. Some scholars (La Porta et al. 1997a, 1998, 2000b; Shleifer & Vishny 1997) have identified the most important feature of the common law systems for corporate governance as the protection of minority shareholder rights.

Second, class struggle, defined here as the conflict between owners and workers, plays out in the politics of societies (Roe 2003). These conflicts and their resolution greatly affect the nature of ownership relations (including the rights of minority stockholders), the development of financial markets, and labor law.

Third, the religion of various societies plays into the political system in several ways. Some religious traditions are more tolerant and promoting of wealth generation than others. Another source of social solidarity is the shared values and assumptions that people hold about one another. In societies that are homogeneous, people exhibit a great deal of trust, which presumably shapes the types of corporate governance that exist (Coffee 2001a).

The general argument in both camps is that these more general, contextual factors of politics and culture shape and produce the legal institutions of corporate governance in a given society and, by implication, firm practices. All the institutionalist literature agrees that the larger, contextual factors of politics and culture shape corporate governance institutions. The main difference of opinion is that the more sociological and historical approaches see these national differences in corporate governance systems as generated by historical accidents and larger social processes, and they discount the role of microeconomic processes involving agency costs.

Some institutional economists and law and economics scholars, in contrast, treat political and legal institutions as exogenous variables that affect the size of agency costs. The resulting sets of corporate governance institutions, therefore, reflect how rational economic actors deal with agency costs created under differing political, societal, and legal contexts. Here, then, rational economic actors choose corporate governance arrangements that minimize agency costs to them. For example, the common law system of the United States has led to strong protection of minority shareholder rights. These in turn have reduced agency costs of monitoring and thus, some have argued, opened up capital markets to firms and reduced the influence of majority shareholders (La Porta et al. 1997a, 1998). We consider these arguments in some detail.

SOCIETAL CONDITIONS AND THE COMPARATIVE STUDY OF GOVERNANCE

The starting point of discussion for institutional economists, political scientists, and legal scholars who study corporate governance systems is the acknowledgment that there exist multiple systems of corporate governance around the world (Berger & Dore 1996; Blair & Roe 1999; Boyer & Drache 1996; Cioffi 2002; Coffee 1999; Gourevitch 2003; Hall & Soskice 2001; La Porta et al. 1997a, 2000b; Roe 2003). Scholars have tended to cluster corporate governance models around four paradigms, while acknowledging that national and regional characteristics are also apparent. The U.S. model contains dispersed shareholders who provide the bulk of the financing to large, public firms. These firms are directed by management teams that are constrained by boards of directors. Workers have few rights and no representation on boards. In the United States, outside directors, private watch-dog entities (such as accountants, securities analysts, and bond-rating agencies), and government authorities like the Securities and Exchange Commission keep information flow open and play a role in keeping managers in check. Incentive compensation for managers and takeovers and proxy fights also provide compet-itive market mechanisms designed to align management interests more closely to those of the shareholders. The U.S. model (which has been called the model of shareholder capitalism) characterizes corporate governance in Great Britain, Canada, Australia, and New Zealand.

The German model has large stock shareholders, often composed of founding families, banks, insurance companies, or other financial institutions who own the bulk of the shares. This close ownership structure enables large shareholders to internally monitor the day-to-day operation of the firm. Cross-shareholding among insiders is common, and information flow is controlled and opaque. Stakeholders such as organized labor play a substantially greater role in the governance of corporate firms under the German model. In Germany, a codetermination system exists that provides representation of workers on boards of directors (Roe 2003). Norms of shareholder capitalism do not automatically prevail over the claims of other corporate stakeholders in countries that exhibit the concentrated ownership model. The German model (or variants of it) dominate across continental Europe and parts of Asia, including Japan.

A third model is government ownership of firms. Here, large firms and the financial sector are owned and operated by the government. Although there has been substantial privatization of state-owned firms in the past 20 years, in many developed and developing societies, there is still substantial government ownership of firms. This is particularly true in sectors like banking, natural resources, utilities, and transportation. Because employees are government employees, they tend to have careers guided by bureaucratic rules and fixed benefits.

A final model, one that dominates in most of the developing world, is the model of family-owned business (La Porta et al. 1999a). Here, owners are managers. Firms are private, and equity and debt markets tend to play minor roles in the provision of capital. Workers generally have less power.

Of overriding interest is what accounts for this variation in corporate governance regimes. Figure 1 presents some of the political, social, and cultural mechanisms that scholars have thought structured the institution of corporate governance. It is useful to go through some of the empirical literature to highlight how scholars have conceptualized the ways in which these factors have had causal effects on governance structures. Mahoney (2001) suggests that politics played an important role in the construction of a common law system in Great Britain and civil law system in France. He argues that in England the common law system resulted from the victory of private landholders over the king and nobility. Here, the law worked to prevent arbitrary seizure of land by the sovereign. In France, Napoleon created a civil law system precisely because he did not want judges to have the discretion to restore feudal privileges after the French Revolution. The German civil law system generally provides for the independence of judges and the protection of individual property rights and, Mahoney suggests, operates as a kind of hybrid system that has proven effective in promoting economic growth. One proof of the efficacy of the German system is that it succeeded in helping German development and was borrowed by Japan and Korea (two societies that have as a result also experienced economic success).

A large number of studies have shown that common and civil law systems appear to correlate with certain features of property rights and financial markets. La Porta et al. (1998) show that legal origins affect creditor rights, shareholder rights, and bank and stock market developments. Subsequent research links these systems to corporate valuations and ownership concentration (La Porta et al. 2000a,b, 2002b) and firm access to external finance (Demirgüç-Kunt & Maksimovic 1998).

Roe (1994, 2003) argues that the main form of politics relevant to understanding corporate governance is class struggle, i.e., the conflict between managers and owners and workers. Where managers and owners have the upper hand, corporate governance institutions favor shareholders over stakeholders. There is frequently a separation of ownership from control in publicly held corporations, and stock ownership is dispersed. Workers have little formal power over boards of directors. The United States is an extreme example of this. Where workers have more power, as they do in many of the European social democracies, corporate governance institutions tend to favor concentrated ownership of firms. Workers are frequently represented on boards of directors or at the very least have mechanisms in place to communicate with top management. Germany provides an extreme example of such a corporate governance structure.

Shleifer & Vishny (1989, 1993, 1994a,b) argue that government officials can potentially affect corporate governance institutions if they are able to rent seek. This will result in official corruption that is likely to negatively affect corporate governance institutions. Djankov et al. (2003) refine this argument and suggest that developing societies sometimes face a trade-off between political disorder and dictatorship. In a situation of political disorder, there are few stable institutions, low investment, and low economic growth. But a dictatorship may be able to create political and social order. Although there are many cases in which dictators use their power for rent-seeking behavior, there are also examples in which dictators pursue good economic policies and actually aid economic growth.

Another kind of historical accident that has had a profound effect on corporate governance is the transplantation of corporate governance institutions. Because of colonialization, many societies were forced to take the corporate governance system of their respective colonizers. Acemoglu et al. (2001) make a provocative case that societies where Europeans actually settled (like the United States, Canada, Australia, and New Zealand) fared better than societies that were colonized and exploited mainly for mineral wealth (like most of the societies in Africa and Latin America). Berkowitz et al. (2003) show that the legitimacy of a legal system was affected by the conditions under which it was transplanted, and this legitimacy had a big effect on the subsequent efficacy of the legal system. They argue that where institutions were forced on populations, they enjoyed less legitimacy and failed to produce an effective rule of law. Beck et al. (2003) show that both the extent of European settlements in various colonies and the type of legal system (i.e., civil versus common law) that was adopted have affected property rights regimes and the evolution of financial institutions.

War, revolution, invasion, colonialization, class struggle, and politics have been at the heart of how societies have differentially structured their economies and the organization of their corporate governance institutions (Roe 2003). Ethnic and religious differences also appear to account for why some governments work better, have more legitimacy, and produce more effective systems of corporate governance (Coffee 2001a; Easterly & Levine 1997; La Porta et al. 1997b, 1999b; Stulz & Williamson 2003). There is little evidence that these corporate governance institutions arose as a result of efficiency considerations (Djankov 2003, La Porta et al. 2000b, Shleifer & Vishny 1997). Most societal rules and laws are products of political processes, processes that reflect the relative power of various organized social groups. Incumbent groups work to produce benefits for themselves and costs and constraints for their challengers. Culture, indexed by religious traditions and solidarity that generates trust in a population, also appears to affect such laws.

SOCIAL AND POLITICAL INSTITUTIONS, LAW, AND ECONOMIC GROWTH

This analysis of the origins of corporate governance systems presents us with a puzzle. Despite the use of political and legal systems to forward the interests of particular groups and cultural barriers that make markets more difficult to organize, market society has advanced in Western Europe, the United States, and now parts of Asia. Despite obvious rent seeking by governments and capitalists, there has been amazing growth in incomes and wealth. Somehow, political, legal, and social institutions were able to create enough social space such that private actors were able to organize firms, production, and markets. This has led scholars across disciplines (Djankov et al. 2003, Evans & Rauch 1999, Fligstein 2001, Glaeser et al. 2004, La Porta et al. 1999b) to suggest that having institutions that produce stable laws and peaceful governments without too much rent seeking on the part of any group of social actors may be the necessary and sufficient condition by which development occurs.

Still, scholars cannot help but wonder if there is some set of political and legal institutions that produce corporate governance structures that might in the long run prove more efficient than other institutions. In other words, even if actors did not rationally set institutions into place to produce efficient outcomes for firms and investors, it still might be the case that there are distinct advantages to one system of corporate governance over another. If policy makers could pinpoint what these are, so the story goes, they could encourage countries who want to improve their economic performance to adopt this set of best institutions. The search for the single best set of institutions has been the holy grail of the economics and political science literature for the past 20 years. Scholars have chased the chimera of institutional causes of economic growth as first Japan (Johnson 1982) and Germany (Albert 1993, Streeck 1992), and then Italy (Locke 1995), the so-called Asian tigers (Amsden 2001, Orru et al. 1997, Wade 1990), and now China (Guthrie 1999, Nee 1992) have all embarked on rapid economic growth. Scholars have researched and debated whether each of these societies has somehow discovered the right configuration of institutions.

In this section, we review some of the literature that attempts to show how particular corporate governance institutions have performed over time. It should be noted that efficiency in this literature is mostly indexed by growth in GDP per capita. The rationale animating this research is that the purpose of corporate governance is to produce the right set of incentives for investors by helping them procure finance, solve their agency problems, and contract with their workers. Those societies that manage to establish governance systems that solve these problems get people to make investments and grow their firms. This growth virtuously combines across firms and economic sectors to produce economic growth for the society as a whole. The literature tries to compare these institutional arrangements across societies and across time to assess their relative effects on economic growth. Some of the literature uses aggregate data and sophisticated econometric techniques, and other parts of the literature use case studies.

One must be cautious about this literature. To believe that a system of governance affects long-run economic performance, one has to assume that on average all firms in a society do better with a particular set of governance institutions. Moreover, institutions change very slowly, while firms frequently rise and fall, indicating that to adjudicate among various sets of corporate governance institutions one must undertake an analysis of economic performance in various societies over long stretches of time. Finally, many factors affect economic performance of economies, and separating out the effects of institutions from these other causes is difficult. To view long-run economic growth as the outcome of a stable set of corporate governance institutions seems a remarkably heroic assumption.

There is a deeper problem as well. Firms compete in various industries, and the industrial mix of societies varies. The sectoral mix of industries and the organizing capacities of those industries will profoundly affect economic growth over time independent of corporate governance institutions. Equating general economic performance with overall firm performance and attributing this to the broader legal conditions in a society does not take this differential distribution and performance of industrial sectors into account. Instead, it makes the strong assumption that these do not matter; only the legal arrangements of firms matter. But the evidence for this assertion is quite circumstantial. No studies to date have set forth the relationship between firm performance in different political-legal environments and overall economic performance. Having sounded this cautionary note, it is useful to consider some of the literature on political and legal institutions and economic growth.

The issue of property rights concerns whether or not ownership rights are assigned to individuals. Ownership rights imply that if a person makes investments, he or she will be able to reap profits from those investments. There are several mechanisms by which this affects economic growth. First, if individuals do not have ownership rights over the returns on their investments, they will not invest. Second, even if they do have these property rights, if profits are subject to seizure either by governments or by other private actors (legally or illegally), they will not make investments. Finally, governments that own property will crowd out private economic actors. Governments will do this because they will create monopolies for themselves. They will also likely make investments that are not efficient but instead reward their friends by giving them jobs and opportunities to rent seek.

There is substantial evidence to support the importance of property rights in the rise of the West (North & Weingast 1989). Hurst (1977) and Friedman (1973) have argued that the creation of the modern corporate form endowed with ownership rights over goods and assets allowed economic development to proceed in the United States. Research by de Soto (1989) has documented how defining property rights in developing societies is an important mechanism to produce economic growth. The literature on state ownership of firms has demonstrated that generally government-owned firms perform less well than their private sector counterparts (Barberis et al. 1996, Boycko et al. 1996, Frydman et al. 1999, Lopez-de-Silanes et al. 1997, Megginson et al. 1994). When governments privatize firms, firms generally begin to perform better.

One of the largest bodies of literature in the field of corporate governance concerns the role of financial markets in economic development (Demirgüç-Kunt & Maksimovic 1998, King & Levine 1993, Rajan & Zingales 1998). The consensus is that the existence of a developed banking system and stock market is generally positively related to subsequent economic growth [for a review, see Levine (1997)]. The literature begins with the idea that if financing is not available, people will not be able to raise money to build firms that might produce economic growth. Thus, one of the central problems of economic development for any country is matching people who have money with people who need financing to build firms. Gerschenkron (1962), an economic historian, is most frequently credited with coming up with this insight. One of the most interesting questions for developing and developed societies is how financial services are provided.

We earlier discussed how banks, corporations, and financial markets embed the four ideal typical models of corporate governance (Roe 2003, Shleifer & Vishny 1997). The Anglo-American model is one in which corporations rely on corporate equity (i.e., stock markets) and debt (i.e., bond markets) for most of their financing. In the German and Japanese models, banks own shares in firms and tend to loan those same firms money. In these societies, equity and debt markets are much less developed. Not surprisingly, ownership is more concentrated in these societies. The third model is state ownership of banking systems, like in Korea and France (until recently). The fourth model is one in which owners and their families provide the capital to finance the expansion of closely held firms.

The empirical literature presents mixed results regarding which model produces the most economic growth. Although there is some evidence that government ownership of banks is detrimental to growth (La Porta et al. 2002a), there is also evidence that such support played an important role in the development of Korea, Taiwan, and perhaps China (Amsden 2001, Wade 1990). Although some scholars believe that the American system of dispersed stock ownership and deep equity and bond markets is most conducive to efficient investment (Hansmann 1996, Hansmann & Kraakman 2001, for example), the empirical evidence is more mixed (see Levine 1997). Indeed, there is evidence that banks and financial markets independently produce economic growth. Levine (1997) argues that in modern, advanced industrial societies, banks and financial markets actually serve different functions in the economy.

The literature on how labor laws affect economic outcomes is the least developed. There is evidence that less-developed societies have labor laws that make hiring and firing workers more difficult than in advanced industrial societies (Botero et al. 2003). But advanced industrial societies have broader welfare state policies such as unemployment insurance, welfare, and social security (Garrett 1998, Hicks 1999). These offset the insecurity produced by looser laws regarding hiring and firing by cushioning workers from unemployment spells.

There is no systematic evidence that shows that workers' organizations, workers' rights, and welfare state expansion have influenced long-run economic growth (Garrett 1998, Hicks 1999, Rodrik 2003). The evidence shows that the social democratic countries of Western Europe did offer more social protection and higher benefits than did the Anglo-American countries (the United States, Great Britain, Australia, New Zealand, Canada). These employment and labor protection measures also helped reduce income inequality in those countries. An OECD (1997) report on jobs examines how various forms of collective bargaining have affected economic growth and job creation in OECD countries in the past 20 years. The results are worth quoting: "While higher unionization and more coordinated bargaining lead to less earnings inequality, it is more difficult to find consistent and clear relationships between those key characteristics of collective bargaining systems and aggregate employment, unemployment, or economic growth" (OECD 1997, p. 2).

To summarize these results, the literature shows that having well-defined property rights that grant ownership of profits to individuals is generally positive for economic growth. It also shows that well-developed financial institutions offer would-be entrepreneurs the opportunity to grow new firms. The literature is less clear on whether one particular system of organizing financial markets is superior to any other and even suggests that banks, stock markets, and bond markets all generate comparable economic growth. Finally, there is little evidence that labor laws that provide more extensive worker rights and welfare provisions inhibit economic growth. One could conclude that rent seeking on the part of either firms or governments is detrimental for economic growth. But there is little evidence that rent seeking on the part of labor (i.e., getting the government to create welfare states) does anything more than redistribute income and produce social justice. This leads us to an interesting conclusion. Rather than looking for a single way to organize economies to maximize economic growth, we might more sensibly try to understand what general sorts of economic problems a wide variety of institutions solve.

This leads us to consider more broadly several claims in the literature: first, that common law systems are better than civil law systems at producing market-enhancing environments, and second, that how Western-style law and governance were adopted by and inserted into various societies affected economic growth around the world. In a provocative series of papers, La Porta, Lopez-de-Silanes, Shleifer, and Vishny (hereafter LLSV) have tried to document how countries with common law systems have offered better growth prospects for countries than those with civil law (especially French civil law) systems.

The argument is that civil law systems evolved, first in France but later in Germany, that were "top down" in the sense that lawmakers provided laws that gave judges very little discretion and preserved state power over the rights of individuals. Common law systems evolved "bottom up." In England, local courts protected the rights of the landed gentry from infringement by the king. Later, merchants used these same courts to enforce contracts and prevent the expropriation of their property. Scholars have argued that this protection of individuals under common law systems produces greater property protection and more stable conditions for contracting and thus promotes economic growth (Mahoney 2001, North & Weingast 1989). In a series of papers, LLSV try to evaluate this claim by producing econometric models for a wide variety of countries with a large number of controls. They end up arguing that common law systems do produce superior economic growth. They claim that the main mechanism for this growth is the laws that protect minority shareholders, which common law countries provide more extensively and enforce more effectively (La Porta et al. 1997a, 1998). Laws that protect minority investors promote diffuse ownership of large public firms and the separation of owners from managers. These developments, in turn, allow for the growth of deep and liquid capital markets that generate a more extensive source of external financing for firms.

This claim has sparked an outpouring of research. There are several problems with the basic result. First, legal scholars have tended to dispute the validity of the legal index LLSV generated to measure what they claim are critical minority shareholder rights around the world (La Porta et al. 1998). Some scholars have voiced doubts as to whether LLSV have constructed an accurate legal index that meaningfully measures different degrees of investor protection in their sample of countries (Coffee 2001a, footnote 6; Roe 2003). In the United States, for example, corporate law provisions that provide for shareholder rights and compensation for corporate losses limit judges to considering only managerial malfeasance that involves fraud or self-dealing. Incompetence or shirking on the job that results in massive shareholder losses is not open to judicial review (Roe 2003). The legal index may obscure the degree to which legal provisions that it highlights are truly relevant for measuring effective protection of minority shareholders in different countries. Second, the practical impact of formal laws is difficult to gauge from a reading of the laws on the books. Local practices, functional substitutes, and business norms bolster, shape, attenuate, or even eviscerate the actual impact of formal laws.

Lamoreaux & Rosenthal (2004) argue that the civil law system, in fact, provided greater latitude in forms of business organizations and in contracting to individual investors in the nineteenth century and through most of the twentieth century in France compared with the common law system in the United States. They also hint at a particularly important problem for evaluating LLSV's hypothesis. LLSV assume that institutions, like the common or civil law systems, once laid down, never change, either in their meaning or impact. In fact, as conceptualized by LLSV, legal regimes are exogenously established in a one-time event of colonization or conquest, and their effects remain static. Yet, Cioffi (2000) shows that in fact corporate governance institutions changed in France, the United States, Germany, and Great Britain during the 1980s and 1990s. Coffee (1999) indicates that formal legislation follows rather than precedes business practices.

Another criticism of the LLSV measures (especially the measure for civil or common law systems) is that they are stand-ins for other variables. For example, common law systems tend to be in societies that are peaceful and democratic (like the United States), whereas civil law societies tend to be wracked by war and poor economic conditions (as in Africa). This has led scholars to offer alternative explanations for the differential institutional structures that affect economic performance. For instance, Acemoglu et al. (2001) have argued that in countries where settlers were able to homestead, live, and expand (like in the United States, Canada, Australia, and New Zealand), institutions that guaranteed private property rights and checks on government were transplanted, which promoted economic growth. Where conditions were more difficult, like sub-Saharan Africa and much of Latin America, colonial powers chose more extractive strategies. They set in place repressive regimes that mostly maximized the extraction of mineral and other forms of wealth. These institutions persisted and hindered the growth of a postcolonial political economy that restrained government and protected private property.

Others have tried to use variables that measure both common/civil law systems and measures of settler mortality to test these competing hypotheses set forth by LLSV and Acemoglu et al. by putting these variables into equations that predict economic growth. Beck et al. (2003) find some evidence to support both theories but conclude that Acemoglu et al.'s explanation seems the stronger of the two. In a recent paper, Berkowitz et al. (2003) argue that the mode of insertion of these systems is critical. In countries that were forced to accept institutions that were not indigenous or that were poorly adapted to local circumstances, economic growth was slower. These scholars were able to make the effects of civil/common law systems disappear once they controlled for the mode of insertion of such institutions.

One big criticism of much of this empirical literature is the constant misspecification of models. Scholars rarely control for many factors. So, for example, in a paper analyzing the role of institutions in economic growth compared with investments in physical and human capital, Glaeser et al. (2004) show that human capital is a much stronger predictor of economic growth than institutions. Because many of the earlier papers failed to include controls for human and physical capital investments, their results may be suspect.

Papers rarely pit all the variables from the different perspectives against one another to do a fair evaluation of those variables. When such models are run, they frequently provide evidence to support multiple hypotheses. It seems more probable that economic growth is a multidimensional process that reflects many social and political institutions. Many factors enter into such growth, and many institutional paths to growth exist. These lively debates show the difficulty of trying to assess the effects of a particular set of social or economic institutions on economic growth.

CONCLUSIONS

In the past 20 years, there has been a great deal of interest in comparing the evolution of institutions across market societies over time. Some of the impetus came from economists who wanted to prove that the American system of corporate governance was the best because it evolved from the functional needs of investors. Others wanted to understand how Japan, Germany, Italy, the countries in Scandinavia, Korea, Taiwan, and now China have managed to produce incredible economic growth in the past 40 years. Still others have been concerned about the causes of economic stagnation in Africa, Latin America, and Russia. In the past few years, globologists (Castells 1996, Strange 1996) have argued that political, social, and economic institutions were bound to converge as firms sought out efficient ways to organize.

Our survey of the literature analyzing the relationships among law, corporate governance, and economic outcomes produces a different picture. Generally, most scholars agree that corporate governance institutions like property rights, the organization of financial markets, and labor laws reflect the politics, culture, and history of particular societies. Most systems of governance were not produced by investors seeking out laws and institutions to reduce agency costs, but instead arose out of struggles over the rights and roles of capitalists and workers in democratic and authoritarian societies. The legal systems that evolved reflect the outcomes of these struggles and have had a profound effect on the national structures of corporate governance.

Despite the view that economic institutions did not evolve for efficiency reasons, scholars have been quite interested in understanding how institutions have, in the end, played an important role in capitalist development. Here, there is little controversy. Stable property rights and evolved financial systems play a key role in economic development. Labor laws figure into economic growth because they buy labor peace. In societies that mediate class struggles, either by repressing the working class (like America or China) or by empowering them (like the social democratic countries in Europe), economic development is facilitated.

Controversy revolves around the degree to which different legal regimes are more or less efficient than other systems. The differential role of civil and common law systems on stable economic growth is still being debated and explored. There are a number of conflicting opinions. First and foremost, scholars debate the possible reasons why common versus civil law systems may have differential impacts on development. Some believe that common law systems protect individual rights more than civil law systems and that this has a bearing on economic growth. Others think that common versus civil law measures index other features of societal development like how these societies were settled, how the institutions were inserted, and the degree to which they were considered legitimate. Another big debate concerns the role of politics, religion, ethnicity, and culture in the economic evolution of societies. Again, the causal mechanisms by which these factors foster economic growth are hotly debated. Finally, some scholars think that there are many paths to economic development. Others argue that there is one best way to organize the political economy of a society. The empirical literature, on the contrary, suggests that the relative advantages of particular legal institutions are difficult to tease out, and even where they can be discerned, they do not suggest the dominance of one best system.

This controversy suggests some clear and interesting paths for subsequent research. First, we think that comparative studies in institutions and economic growth must be analyzed longitudinally within countries, as they evolve over time. Linking institutions, institutional change, and economic growth together more carefully in some societies might reveal more closely when and why institutions matter. Such research will also begin to untangle the kinds of feedback that are possible between institutions and economic actors. As societies develop and new interest groups appear, for example, such developments may alter institutions. We also know that institutions that exist set up the possibilities for new institutions. It seems useful to tease out such trends and dynamics over long historical periods. Finally, scholars ought to take seriously the possibility that there may be many paths to economic growth (including ones not yet discovered) and that solving certain kinds of broad societal problems, like class struggle and ethnic and religious conflict, may be as or more important to economic development as adopting a particular set of legal institutions.

One also needs to be aware that institutional components of national corporate governance appear to work together as a system. The literature clearly shows that institutional features of property law, financial market regulation, and labor law tend to hang together in various societies. This understanding is somewhat in opposition to much of the empirical literature, which tends to treat these legal elements as discrete variables. The variable approach implies that importing some institutional facet linked to economic growth will work like a panacea to cure inefficiency and generate high growth. But the importation of another country's corporate governance institutions is not likely to work unless the whole system is borrowed or the borrowed element fits in with what already exists in a given society. So, for example, protecting minority shareholder rights in societies dominated by dictators, war, and famine (like in some places in Africa) is not likely to make much of a difference in economic performance. Scholars need to be more modest in their claims for a particular law or set of practices and more attuned to the fact that societal institutions tend to be national systems.

What seems to be clear is that Weber, Marx, and Durkheim all picked up important aspects of the development of a market society. States that create social stability by mediating class struggle and that engage in protecting property rights appear to be pivotal to economic development. Legal systems that support contracting and financial systems that provide access to capital to entrepreneurs are both critical ingredients for modern development. Multiple paths to solving these social and economic problems exist. The plurality of capitalist systems (what is called the study of comparative capitalisms) shows both the multiple ways in which these various systems have evolved and their robustness in generating economic growth.

ACKNOWLEDGMENT

We thank Robert Gordon for comments on an earlier draft.

**The *Annual Review of Law and Social Science* is online at
http://lawsocsci.annualreviews.org**

LITERATURE CITED

Acemoglu D, Johnson S, Robinson JA. 2001. The colonial origins of comparative development: an empirical investigation. *Am. Econ. Rev.* 91(5):1369–401

Albert M. 1993. *Capitalism Against Capitalism.* London: Whurr

Amsden A. 2001. *The Rise of "The Rest": Challenges to the West from Late-Industrializing Economies.* Oxford/New York: Oxford Univ. Press

Barberis N, Boycko M, Shleifer A, Tsukanova N. 1996. How does privatization work? Evidence from the Russian shops. *J. Polit. Econ.* 104(4):764–90

Bebchuk LA, Roe MJ. 1999. A theory of path dependence in corporate ownership and governance. *Stanford Law Rev.* 52(1):127–70

Beck T, Demirgüç-Kunt A, Levine R. 2003. Law, endowments, and finance. *J. Finan. Econ.* 70:137–81

Berger S, Dore R, eds. 1996. *National Diversity and Global Capitalism.* Ithaca, NY: Cornell Univ. Press

Berkowitz D, Pistor K, Richard J. 2003. Economic development, legality, and the transplant effect. *Eur. Econ. Rev.* 47:165–95

Berle AA Jr, Means GC. 1932. *The Modern*

Corporation and Private Property. Chicago: Commerce Clearing House

Blair MM, Roe MJ, eds. 1999. *Employees and Corporate Governance.* Washington, DC: Brookings Inst.

Botero J, Djankov S, La Porta R, Lopez-de-Silanes F, Shleifer A. 2003. *The regulation of labor.* Work. Pap. 9756, Nat. Bur. Econ. Res.

Boycko M, Shleifer A, Vishny RW. 1996. A theory of privatisation. *Econ. J.* 106 (435):309–19

Boyer R, Drache D, eds. 1996. *States Against Markets: The Limits of Globalization.* New York: Routledge

Carlin W, Mayer C. 2003. Finance, investment, and growth. *J. Finan. Econ.* 69:191–226

Castells M. 1996. *The Information Age: Economy, Society, and Culture,* Vol. 1: *The Rise of the Network Society.* Cambridge, MA: Blackwell

Cioffi JW. 2000. Governing globalization? The state, law, and structural change in corporate governance. *J. Law Soc.* 27(4):572–600

Cioffi JW. 2002. *Public law and private power: the comparative political economy of corporate governance in the United States and Germany.* PhD thesis. Univ. Calif., Berkeley. 578 pp.

Coffee JC Jr. 1999. The future as history: the prospects for global convergence in corporate governance and its implications. *Northwestern Univ. Law Rev.* 93:641–707

Coffee JC Jr. 2001a. Do norms matter? A cross-country evaluation. *Univ. Penn. Law Rev.* 149(6):2151–77

Coffee JC Jr. 2001b. The rise of dispersed ownership: the roles of law and the state in the separation of ownership and control. *Yale Law J.* 111:1–82

Crouch C, Streeck W, eds. 1997. *Political Economy of Modern Capitalism: Mapping Convergence and Diversity.* London: Sage

Demirgüç-Kunt A, Maksimovic V. 1998. Law, finance, and firm growth. *J. Finan.* 53(6):2107–37

de Soto H. 1989. *The Other Path: The Invisible Revolution in the Third World.* New York: Harper & Row

Djankov S, Glaeser E, La Porta R, Lopez-de-Silanes F, Shleifer A. 2003. The new comparative economics. *J. Comp. Econ.* 31:595–619

Durkheim E. 1997. *The Division of Labor in Society.* New York: Free Press

Easterly W, Levine R. 1997. Africa's growth tragedy: policies and ethnic divisions. *Q. J. Econ.* 112(4):1203–50

Evans P. 1995. *Embedded Autonomy: States and Industrial Transformation.* Princeton, NJ: Princeton Univ. Press

Evans P, Rauch R. 1999. Bureaucracy and growth: a cross-national analysis of the effects of "Weberian" state structures on economic growth. *Am. Sociol. Rev.* 64(5):748–65

Eyal G, Szelenyi I, Townsley E. 1998. *Making Capitalism Without Capitalists: Class Formation and Elite Struggles in Post-Communist Central Europe.* London/New York: Verso

Fama EF, Jensen MC. 1983a. Agency problems and residual claims. *J. Law Econ.* 26:327–49

Fama EF, Jensen MC. 1983b. Separation of ownership and control. *J. Law Econ.* 26:301–25

Fligstein N. 1990. *The Transformation of Corporate Control.* Cambridge, MA: Harvard Univ. Press

Fligstein N. 2001. *The Architecture of Markets: An Economic Sociology of Twenty-First-Century Capitalist Societies.* Princeton, NJ: Princeton Univ. Press

Friedman LM. 1973. *A History of American Law.* New York: Simon & Schuster

Frydman R, Gray C, Hessel M, Rapaczynski A. 1999. When does privatization work? The impact of private ownership on corporate performance in the transition economies. *Q. J. Econ.* 114(4):1153–91

Garrett G. 1998. *Partisan Politics in the Global Economy.* New York: Cambridge Univ. Press

Gerschenkron A. 1962. *Economic Backwardness in Historical Perspective: A Book of Essays.* Cambridge, MA: Belknap

Glaeser EL, La Porta R, Lopez-de-Silanes F, Shleifer A. 2004. Do institutions cause growth? *J. Econ. Growth* 9:271–303

Gourevitch P. 2003. Political determinants of corporate governance: political context, corporate impact. *Yale Law J.* 112(7):1829–80

Granovetter M. 1985. Economic action and social structure: the problem of embeddedness. *Am. J. Sociol.* 91(3):481–510

Greif A. 1994. Cultural beliefs and the organization of society: a historical and theoretical reflection on collectivist and individualist societies. *J. Polit. Econ.* 102(5):912–50

Guthrie D. 1999. *Dragon in a Three Piece Suit: The Emergence of Capitalism in China.* Princeton, NJ: Princeton Univ. Press

Hall PA, Soskice D, eds. 2001. *Varieties of Capitalism: The Institutional Foundations of Comparative Advantage.* Oxford/New York: Oxford Univ. Press

Hansmann H. 1996. *The Ownership of Enterprise.* Cambridge, MA: Belknap

Hansmann H, Kraakman R. 2000. The essential role of organizational law. *Yale Law J.* 110(3):387–440

Hansmann H, Kraakman R. 2001. The end of history for corporate law. *Georgetown Law J.* 89:439–68

Hicks AM. 1999. *Social Democracy and Welfare Capitalism: A Century of Income Security Politics.* Ithaca, NY: Cornell Univ. Press

Hurst JW. 1977. *Law and Social Order in the United States.* Ithaca, NY: Cornell Univ. Press

Jensen MC. 1989. Eclipse of the public corporation. *Harvard Bus. Rev.* 67(5):61–74

Jensen MC, Meckling WH. 1976. Theory of the firm: managerial behavior, agency costs, and ownership structure. *J. Finan. Econ.* 3:305–60

Johnson C. 1982. *MITI and the Japanese Miracle: The Growth of Industrial Policy, 1925–1975.* Stanford, CA: Stanford Univ. Press

King RG, Levine R. 1993. Finance and growth: Schumpeter might be right. *Q. J. Econ.* 108(3):717–37

La Porta R, Lopez-de-Silanes F, Shleifer A. 1999a. Corporate ownership around the world. *J. Finan.* 54(2):471–517

La Porta R, Lopez-de-Silanes F, Shleifer A. 2002a. Government ownership of banks. *J. Finan.* 57(1):265–301

La Porta R, Lopez-de-Silanes F, Shleifer A, Vishny RW. 1997a. Legal determinants of external finance. *J. Finan.* 52(3):1131–50

La Porta R, Lopez-de-Silanes F, Shleifer A, Vishny RW. 1997b. Trust in large organizations. *Am. Econ. Rev.* 87(2):333–38

La Porta R, Lopez-de-Silanes F, Shleifer A, Vishny RW. 1998. Law and finance. *J. Polit. Econ.* 106(6):1113–55

La Porta R, Lopez-de-Silanes F, Shleifer A, Vishny RW. 1999b. The quality of government. *J. Law Econ. Organ.* 15(1):222–79

La Porta R, Lopez-de-Silanes F, Shleifer A, Vishny RW. 2000a. Agency problems and dividend policies around the world. *J. Finan.* 55(1):1–33

La Porta R, Lopez-de-Silanes F, Shleifer A, Vishny RW. 2000b. Investor protection and corporate governance. *J. Finan. Econ.* 58:3–27

La Porta R, Lopez-de-Silanes F, Shleifer A, Vishny RW. 2002b. Investor protection and corporate valuation. *J. Finan.* 57(3):1147–70

Lamoreaux N, Rosenthal J. 2004. *Legal regime and business's organizational choice: a comparison of France and the United States during the mid-nineteenth century.* Work. Pap. 10288, Nat. Bur. Econ. Res.

Levine R. 1997. Financial development and economic growth: views and agenda. *J. Econ. Lit.* 35(2):688–726

Locke RM. 1995. *Remaking the Italian Economy.* Ithaca, NY: Cornell Univ. Press

Lopez-de-Silanes F, Shleifer A, Vishny RW. 1997. Privatization in the United States. *RAND J. Econ.* 28(3):447–71

Mahoney PG. 2001. The common law and economic growth. *J. Legal Stud.* 30:503–25

Maier CS. 1987. *In Search of Stability: Explorations in Historical Political Economy.* New Rochelle, NY: Cambridge Univ. Press

Marris R. 1968. *The Economic Theory of "Managerial" Capitalism*. New York: Basic Books

Marx K. 1977. *Capital*, Vol. 1. New York: Vintage Books

Megginson WL, Nash RC, Van Randenborgh M. 1994. The financial and operating performance of newly privatized firms: an international empirical analysis. *J. Finan.* 49(2): 403–52

Nee V. 1992. Organizational dynamics of market transition: hybrid forms, property rights, and mixed economy in China. *Admin. Sci. Q.* 37(1):1–27

North DC. 1981. *Structure and Change in Economic History*. New York: WW Norton

North DC. 1990. *Institutions, Institutional Change, and Economic Performance*. Cambridge, UK: Cambridge Univ. Press

North DC, Weingast BR. 1989. Constitutions and commitments: the evolution of institutional governing public choice in seventeenth-century England. *J. Econ. Hist.* 49(4):803–32

OECD. 1997. *OECD Jobs Report*. Paris: OECD

Orru M, Biggart NW, Hamilton GG. 1997. *The Economic Organization of East Asian Capitalism*. Thousand Oaks, CA: Sage

Penrose ET. 1959. *The Theory of the Growth of the Firm*. New York: Wiley

Radaev V. 2002. Entrepreneurial strategies and the structure of transaction costs in Russian business. In *The New Entrepreneurs of Europe and Asia: Patterns of Business Development in Russia, Eastern Europe, and China*, ed. V Bonnell, T Gold, pp. 68–92. Armonk, NY: M.E. Sharpe

Rajan RG, Zingales L. 1998. Financial dependence and growth. *Am. Econ. Rev.* 88(3): 559–86

Rodrik D, ed. 2003. *In Search of Prosperity: Analytic Narratives on Economic Growth*. Princeton, NJ: Princeton Univ. Press

Roe MJ. 1994. *Strong Managers, Weak Owners: The Political Roots of American Corporate Finance*. Princeton, NJ: Princeton Univ. Press

Roe MJ. 2003. *Political Determinants of Corporate Governance: Political Context, Corporate Impact*. Oxford/New York: Oxford Univ. Press

Shleifer A, Vishny RW. 1989. Management entrenchment: the case of manager-specific investments. *J. Finan. Econ.* 25:123–39

Shleifer A, Vishny RW. 1993. Corruption. *Q. J. Econ.* 108(3):599–617

Shleifer A, Vishny RW. 1994a. Politicians and firms. *Q. J. Econ.* 109(4):995–1025

Shleifer A, Vishny RW. 1994b. The politics of market socialism. *J. Econ. Perspect.* 8(2): 165–76

Shleifer A, Vishny RW. 1997. A survey of corporate governance. *J. Finan.* 52(2):737–83

Short H. 1994. Ownership, control, financial structure and the performance of firms. *J. Econ. Surveys* 8(3):203–49

Smith A. 1904. *An Inquiry into the Nature and Causes of the Wealth of Nations*. London: Methuen

Stark D. 1996. Recombinant property in East European capitalism. *Am. J. Sociol.* 101(4): 993–1027

Strange S. 1996. *The Retreat of the State: The Diffusion of Power in the World Economy*. New York: Cambridge Univ. Press

Streeck W. 1992. *Social Institutions and Economic Performance: Studies of Industrial Relations in Advanced Capitalist Economies*. Newbury Park, CA: Sage

Stulz RM, Williamson R. 2003. Culture, openness, and finance. *J. Finan. Econ.* 70(3):313–49

Tirole J. 1988. *The Theory of Industrial Organization*. Cambridge, MA: MIT Press

Vitols S. 2001. Varieties of corporate governance: comparing Germany and the UK. In *Varieties of Capitalism: The Institutional Foundations of Comparative Advantage*, ed. P Hall, D Soskice, 10:337–60. Oxford/New York: Oxford Univ. Press

Wade R. 1990. *Governing the Market: Economic Theory and the Role of Government in East Asian Industrialization*. Princeton, NJ: Princeton Univ. Press

Weber M. 1978. *Economy and Society.* Berkeley: Univ. Calif. Press

Weber M. 2001. *The Protestant Ethic and the Spirit of Capitalism.* New York: Routledge

Weiss L. 1998. *The Myth of the Powerless State.* Ithaca, NY: Cornell Univ. Press

White HC. 2002. *Markets from Networks: Socioeconomic Models of Production.* Princeton, NJ: Princeton Univ. Press

Williamson OE. 1975. *Markets and Hierarchies.* New York: Free Press

Williamson OE. 1985. *The Economic Institutions of Capitalism: Firms, Markets, Relational Contracting.* New York: Free Press

Annu. Rev. Law Soc. Sci. 2005. 1:85–103
doi: 10.1146/annurev.lawsocsci.1.041604.115903
First published online as a Review in Advance on June 14, 2005

TRANSNATIONAL HUMAN RIGHTS: Exploring the Persistence and Globalization of Human Rights

Heinz Klug

Law School, University of Wisconsin, Madison, Wisconsin 53706; University of the Witwatersrand, School of Law, Johannesburg, South Africa; email: Klug@wisc.edu

Key Words humanitarian law, constitutional rights, international norms, national sovereignty

■ **Abstract** This review considers how a socio-legal approach may be used to explore the relationship between human rights and law in the new century. Drawing on the classic traditions of law and society research, including gap studies, rights consciousness, public interest lawyering, and legal resource mobilization, as well as more recent approaches to legal globalization and epistemic communities or nongovernment networks, this paper begins to define a field of transnational human rights. The review traces the idea of transnational human rights to the struggles between social movements, in national and international fora, and the impact these struggles have had on the relationship between state power or sovereignty and the quest for legitimate and effective forms of governance. A key element of this endeavor, the paper concludes, is the need to integrate and understand the interaction between three traditionally separate domains of rights: international human rights, humanitarian law, and constitutional rights. It is this focus that defines the emerging field of transnational human rights.

INTRODUCTION

Human rights, some have argued, have simply become a fact of life (see Rorty 1993). But the hegemony of human rights discourse coexists with persistent violation and even impunity (Hoffmann 2003). Despite the general rhetoric condemning torture, exposed in digital camera shots from Iraq, Afghanistan, and other fronts in the "war on terror," the practice of human rights has remained highly contextual. Although the U.S. military has conducted hundreds of investigations into allegations of torture and other human rights abuses, most have been inconclusive because victims cannot be located or evidence is not forthcoming. Thus, the practice of human rights is located between the formal requirements of a highly technical legal process and the realities of power and confrontation in the world. In this context, we must first look beyond the formal claims of human rights law and doctrine and consider how socio-legal approaches may help to produce a more deeply textured understanding of the relationship between human rights and law in the early twenty-first century.

A socio-legal approach to human rights addresses questions of individual and social emancipation from a historical view, recognizing that a link exists between the interaction of claims to citizenship, national emancipation, and individual and collective rights and the demand for law. The aim of this review is to draw together different strands of the law and society project to construct and reveal an emerging field of research in the tradition of law and social science that is building a new understanding of the relationship between law and human rights. In addition to recent discussions of human rights in the law and society tradition (Hajjar 2004), the construction of this field requires drawing upon the now classic law and society studies of public interest lawyering (Sarat & Scheingold 2001), legal resources and mobilization (Epp 1998, Rosenberg 1991), and rights consciousness (Williams 1991, Hartog 1988). To these approaches must be added areas of research and analysis that are new to, or have remained on the fringes of, law and society work. First is the work on new forms of transnational governance, from the transmission of new global orthodoxies (Dezalay & Garth 2002a), the construction of counter-hegemonic movements (Santos 1995), and new forms of global ordering (Slaughter 2004) to epistemic communities (Canan & Reichman 2002) and networks (Keck & Sikkink 1998). Second, we must relate these international studies to the work of those who are building a scholarship around the development of new constitutional orders while linking these domestic or national processes to broader global trends (Scheppele 2004, Klug 2000a, Arjomand 1992).

DEFINING A FIELD OF TRANSNATIONAL HUMAN RIGHTS

To understand the important contribution law and society scholarship brings to the field of human rights, we must begin by reconsidering the traditional approach to human rights. Premised on the history of Western philosophical thought and legal doctrine, the traditional approach to human rights focuses first on the emergence of particular human rights claims and their incorporation through international legal processes into binding legal norms (Cranston 1973, Henkin 1990, Ishay 2004). Second, there is a focus on the international legal and institutional machinery that is designed to monitor human rights violations and pursue strategies for the greater recognition and implementation of human rights (Shelton 2002, Thornberry 1989). A socio-legal approach must take a more holistic view of human rights, not only linking the emergence and implementation or enforcement of human rights to continuing social, political, and professional struggles, but also understanding the essential continuity between struggles for rights and the control of power—at the international, national, and local levels. Finally, the emerging field of human rights within the socio-legal tradition must not only apply the existing socio-legal strategies of research and analysis, such as gap studies, public interest lawyering, questions of resources, or the impact on social mobilization; it must also endeavor to break down the traditional distinctions between humanitarian law, international human rights, and constitutionalism to reveal the interconnections that make up the field of transnational human rights.

The field of law and society has already produced an extraordinarily rich empirical scholarship on the question of rights, from the nature and basic function of rights in legal conflicts, "toward understanding how rights operate in the social world" (Nielsen 2004, p. 64). This debate has extended beyond the traditional law and society focus on national law and particularly U.S. law (Abel 1995b), showing that the deployment of legal rights is neither a "uniquely American phenomenon" (Nielsen 2004, p. 73), nor limited to national legal systems. Instead, the "rights explosion" (Epp 1998) has become a central part of the phenomena of globalization (Boyle & Meyer 2002), whether through the rising hegemony of global cultural forces in the form of corporate capital, global finance and related professional elites, and the global campaign to establish the "rule of law," or through colonial encounters (Benton 2002, Chanock 2001, Merry 2000, Badie 2000) and struggles for human rights (Hajjar 1997, Abel 1995a, Sikkink 1993). A major contribution to a socio-legal understanding of the international human rights movement has been made by Yves Dezalay and Bryant Garth, who apply their method of relational biography to trace the creation of the field of international human rights "through the careers of individuals in law and politics" (Dezalay & Garth 2001, p. 355). Although their research reveals the crucial and symbiotic linkages between struggles over human rights in the global South, intra-elite contestations over political power in the North, and the politics of major philanthropic foundations in the United States, their presentation of the construction of the international human rights movement is confined by the tendency in law and society to focus on private power and law outside of the state. Even though they highlight the movement of human rights lawyers into positions of power in the newly democratized states of the South, they do not consider the independent role of states and state-dominated international institutions in facilitating the creation of the international human rights movement. Instead, their analysis leads them to recognize the relative autonomy of international human rights and yet to argue that "the field of human rights expertise is dominated by the influence and prestige of the U.S.-based multinationals" (Dezalay & Garth 2001, p. 357).

Building on their contribution requires us to consider a period before the domestic palace wars so central to their argument (Dezalay & Garth 2002b). First, we must understand how major obstacles, such as the notion of state sovereignty, protected by the United Nations Charter, were overcome, thus creating the legal terrain and space within which an expertise could develop and an international movement flourish. Although this exercise has been traditionally done through a description of changes in legal doctrine, a socio-legal approach should both focus on the broader context, such as the process of decolonization (Wilson 1994), and pay attention to the individual steps through which international diplomats and their allies in national liberation movements—precursors to the international human rights movement—undermined and challenged state assertions of exclusive authority (Von Eschen 1997). A key example is the struggle to place the question of racial discrimination in South Africa onto the agenda of the newly established United Nations (Thomas 1996, Sohn 1994). This is the story of a transformed world in which newly emerging postcolonial states began to link the issue of racial discrimination, revealed and discredited by the Holocaust, with the question of colonialism and foreign domination. Recognition of the right to self-determination became not only the lodestar of the international human rights framework but also the means to question the authority of states over peoples, and eventually over individuals.

STATE SOVEREIGNTY, ARTICLE 2(7), AND THE ANTI-APARTHEID MOVEMENT

The international campaign against South Africa's policy of apartheid and the anti-apartheid movement that mobilized people across the globe provide a useful lens through which to view the transformation of human rights from the state-based system of international legal norms to what might more accurately be thought of as a normative and institutional system of transnational human rights. This transformation occurs not only in the elaboration of human rights norms, on which most human rights discourse is focused, but also in the changing relationship between states in the international system, as well as in the evolution of a plethora of national and international institutions, organizations, and campaigns designed to oppose and overcome particular human rights problems. A number of different human rights problems—from slavery, to the system of forced labor in the Belgian Congo in the years before the Universal Declaration, to torture in Latin America, to political repression in the former state socialist societies—all play a part in the story of human rights and their emergence in global law and politics. The international response to apartheid, however, played a unique role in the early struggles over the legitimate form and scope of international intervention.

South Africa's assertion of domestic jurisdiction as a defense against United Nations concern over racial discrimination marks the first salvo, even before the adoption of the Universal Declaration, in the struggle over the post–World War II commitment to human rights. In June 1946, in response to the passage of the Asiatic Land Tenure and Indian Representation Act, which both prohibited people of Indian descent from acquiring land and excluded them from the political process in South Africa, the South African Indian Congresses launched a passive resistance campaign. At the same time, the Indian government lodged a complaint against the South African government's increasingly discriminatory policies toward South African nationals of Indian descent, thus raising the issue of racial discrimination in South Africa for the first time in the UN General Assembly. In response, Field-Marshall Smuts, one of the initiators of the League of Nations and, as prime minister of South Africa, a founding member of the United Nations, objected, arguing that "within the domain of its domestic affairs a State is not subject to control or interference, and its actions could not be called into question by any other state" (Sohn 1994, p. 49). Smuts asserted that Article 2(7) of the United Nations Charter "embodied an over-riding principle qualifying. . .all the other provisions of the Charter," and threatened that if it was decided that a recommendation by the General Assembly on such an issue was not an intervention in the domestic affairs of a member state under Article 2(7), then "every domestic matter could be taken through every stage in the procedure of the Assembly" (Sohn 1994, p. 50).

Rejecting this claim, the UN General Assembly initially argued that the pre-existing bilateral agreements between South Africa and India provided a basis for the assembly's jurisdiction. As the conflict over South Africa's discriminatory policies continued, the assembly argued that the situation in South Africa was "a humanitarian question of international importance," and that under Article 14 of the charter, the assembly "had the necessary competence to recommend measures to ensure the peaceful adjustment of a situation which had, in the Assembly's opinion, led to the impairment of friendly relations" (Sohn 1994, p. 55). This assertion of jurisdiction relied in part on the advisory opinion in the case of the Permanent Court of International Justice (PCIJ) in the Nationality Decrees Issues in Tunis and Morocco (PCIJ 1923, p. 24[1]), in which the court held that "the question whether a certain matter is or is not solely within the jurisdiction of a State is an essentially relative question; it depends upon the development of international relations." This formulation allowed the General Assembly to claim fealty to the notion of a "reserved domain" of domestic jurisdiction and to argue that "the right of a State to use its discretion may nevertheless be 'restricted by obligations which it may have undertaken towards other States'" and thus, "jurisdiction which, in principle, belongs solely to the State, is limited by rules of international law" (Sohn 1994, p. 51).

Despite continued objections from the South African government and concern by others, such as the Canadian delegation who emphasized the "necessity of making a distinction between the right of the Assembly to discuss the problem under the terms of the Charter and its competence to intervene," which they argued depended on "the kind of action the Assembly might be invited to take" (Sohn 1994, p. 54), the assembly proceeded to strengthen the legal basis of its jurisdiction. This was achieved in practice by, on the one hand, suggesting the weakest form of intervention by merely inviting the parties, India, South Africa, and Pakistan, "to enter into discussion," while, on the other hand, extending the grounds upon which concern could be raised by stating that the discussion should take into consideration the "purposes and principles of the Charter of the United Nations and the Declaration of Human Rights" (Sohn 1994, p. 55).

In September 1952, 13 Asian and African countries requested that the issue of apartheid be placed on the General Assembly's agenda on the grounds that these policies created a "dangerous and explosive situation, which constitutes both a threat to international peace and a flagrant violation of the basic principles of

---

[1]See Appendix A for a list of national constitutions, human rights documents, and cases.

human rights and fundamental freedoms which are enshrined in the Charter of the United Nations." In response, the South African government argued that it was "completely unfounded and quite preposterous" to view apartheid as a threat to international peace and that the only exception to the prohibition against interference in the domestic affairs of a member state is when the Security Council is authorized to intervene under Chapter VII of the charter and then only in situations specified in Article 39. Furthermore, South Africa argued, the General Assembly is not authorized to intervene in any manner—including by resolutions, recommendations, or even discussion—as the charter provides no other exceptions outside of Article 39, and certainly contains no "additional exception with respect to questions of human rights" (Sohn 1994, p. 64). This position is still maintained by South Africa's last apartheid state president, F.W. de Klerk. In his submissions and appearances before the Truth and Reconciliation Commission in 1997, de Klerk continued to reject the description of apartheid as a crime against humanity, arguing that the international declaration that apartheid is a crime against humanity was invalid as it was merely a General Assembly resolution and not a resolution of the UN Security Council, which in his view was the only body with the authority to intervene in the domestic affairs of a member state.

Addressing the issue of apartheid for the first time in 1952, the UN General Assembly adopted two resolutions in which the assembly affirmed that governmental policies of member states that are not directed toward the goal of "ensuring equality before the law of all persons regardless of race, creed or color," but that instead "are designed to perpetuate or increase discrimination, are inconsistent with the pledges of Members under Article 56 of the Charter" [UN Gen. Assem. Resolution 616(VII) B (1952)[2]]. In response, the South African government refused to cooperate with the commission established by the General Assembly to study and report on the racial situation in South Africa. Reviewing South Africa's objections to the exercise of jurisdiction by the General Assembly, the commission argued that the General Assembly was authorized by the charter "to undertake any studies and make any recommendations to Member States which it may deem necessary in connection with the application and implementation of the principles to which the Member States have subscribed by signing the Charter" [UN Commission Report (1953), paragraph 893(i)]. Furthermore, the commission concluded that this "universal right of study and recommendation is absolutely incontestable with regard to general problems of human rights and particularly of those protecting against discrimination for reasons of race, sex, language or religion" [UN Commission Report (1953), pp. 16–22, 114–19].

The outcome of this process was to slowly disconnect human rights claims from the strictures of Article 2(7) and the standard of noninterference, in effect favoring international or transnational human rights standards over local claims. Over the

---

[2]See Appendix B for a list of United Nations documents related to apartheid. Many of these documents have been reprinted in *The United Nations and Apartheid 1948–1994* (United Nations 1994).

next 40 years, the international community, driven by struggles in South Africa and the emergence of an international anti-apartheid movement, continued to extend its jurisdiction over the issue of apartheid, moving from recommendation to condemnation [UN Gen. Assem. Resolution 1761 (1962)]; from encouraging discussion of racial discrimination to the rejection of the apartheid government's credentials to represent South Africa in the General Assembly [Bouteflika 1974; UN Gen. Assem. Resolution 3206 (1974); UN Gen. Assem. Resolution 3207 (1974)]; and from support for the victims of apartheid [UN Gen. Assem. Resolution 3411 (1975)] to the imposition of a mandatory arms embargo in response to the 1976 student uprisings and the apartheid regime's brutal response [UN Secur. Counc. Resolution 418 (1977)]. Even then, as UN Secretary General Kurt Waldheim told the Security Council on the adoption of Resolution 418, "[t]he adoption of this resolution marks the first time in the 32-year history of the Organization that action has been taken under Chapter VII of the Charter against a Member State" (Waldheim 1977). In fact, each step of the way was marked by a combination of internal resistance to apartheid and the development of an international social movement opposed to South Africa's racial policies of overt de jure discrimination.

The initial assertion of General Assembly jurisdiction "to study and recommend" in the field of human rights provided the stepping stones over which activists and states maneuvered in building an international human rights system during the last half of the twentieth century. This was not merely the construction of a normative framework but rather a globalizing process that only came to prominence through the struggles of national and international social movements, from the civil rights movement in the United States to the mothers of the Plaza de Mayo in Argentina and the international anti-apartheid movement itself. Despite the old formal doctrine that states are the sole or primary subjects of international law, by the end of the twentieth century the reality of a constant renegotiation of state sovereignty was well established, providing a smorgasbord of subjects—international organizations, nongovernment organizations, transnational corporations and movements, as well as individuals—and a fragmentation of jurisdiction in which the nation-state provides the locus for constant renegotiation, realignment, and reassignment of jurisdictional powers. Although many of the participants may have thought that apartheid in South Africa presented an exceptional case, these developments were important markers in the renegotiation of state sovereignty and the exercise of supranational jurisdiction over fundamental political choices and decisions. This then is the "terrain of international human rights" (Dezalay & Garth 2002b, p. 129) upon which the participants in domestic U.S. palace wars, identified by Dezalay and Garth, could operate, simultaneously reconstructing an international human rights movement while focusing "on the state at home" (Dezalay & Garth 2002b, p. 132).

By the end of the cold war, the realm of international human rights—formally constituted through regional treaty systems, international institutions, and a machinery of annual reports and reviews, supplemented by ad hoc commissions and even the adjudication of some cases—was being supplemented by a more proscriptive set of declarations and commitments that aimed at shaping the future development of intrastate political and social arrangements, captured in the rubric of good governance. In the South African case, this was evidenced in the shift from the rejection and condemnation of the 1983 constitution [UN Secur. Counc. Resolution 554 (1984)]—which represented an attempt at internal reform based on racial power sharing but still dominated by the white minority—to the adoption of a declaration establishing a set of principles for a democratic transition and constitutional framework that would be acceptable to the international community [UN Gen. Assem. Resolution S-16 (1989)]. The idea of constitutional principles that was at the center of this new form of intervention represents an extraordinarily bold assertion of international norms in the context of the exercise of domestic self-determination. Although this may be considered proof of the complete demise of the notion of sovereignty and the guarantee of noninterference contained in Article 2(7) of the charter, in fact it is again bolstered by a series of international declarations by states committing themselves to the principles of democracy and constitutionalism reflected in these principles (see Warsaw Declaration 2000).

BREAKING THE TRADITIONAL HUMAN RIGHTS MOLD

The Universal Declaration of Human Rights is the paradigmatic representation of international human rights—a comprehensive list of rights to be held up as a standard of civilized behavior. At the same time, it reflects the popular experience of human rights, on the one hand realized most often in their repeated violation (Barnett 2002) and, on the other hand, existing at best as a weak form of customary international law, a "soft law" not much more effective than a set of aspirations toward which we must constantly strive. Although international human rights law is grounded most directly in the "hard law" of binding international treaties, particularly in the regional human rights conventions such as the European Convention on Human Rights, the effective implementation of human rights has been achieved either through domestic law or more recently through the exercise of humanitarian intervention and the enforcement of international criminal law. Despite debates over the different philosophical and legal sources of human rights (Rubin 2003), at the local level the assertion of rights comes through experiences of resistance and of mass violation. Human rights thus find their expression, regardless of their formal legal embodiment at any particular level—national or international—in violation, resistance, and struggles for recognition and social emancipation (Santos 1995).

The contours of the relationship between law and human rights may be revealed through a number of different research strategies employed by socio-legal scholars. One classic approach applied to the field of international human rights by Lisa Hajjar is "gap studies," which provides an essential additive to the range of autobiographies that are beginning to define our understanding of the human rights movement (Mandela 1994, Laber 2002, Neier 2003). Although Hajjar recognizes that the question of a gap between human rights principles and practice has been a traditional issue of concern among human rights scholars, her analysis goes further than the traditional bemoaning of the realities of international law and the fate of human rights. Instead, she traces how the negotiation and implementation of particular human rights agreements—from the Genocide Convention and Geneva Conventions to the Torture Convention—reflect the tension between the pressures to adopt these norms and yet concern among elites that these commitments not be extended to apply to their own domestic or international human rights violations (Hajjar 2004, p. 596). Nevertheless, she argues that the creation of this legal and normative field, and the failure to uphold these commitments, stimulated the emergence of a global human rights movement that today fulfills "a panoptic function of international surveillance by documenting and protesting violations" (Hajjar 2004, p. 597). By combining both the traditional law and society approach to the empirically based "gap problem" with a postrealist conception of rights and legal consciousness, Hajjar demonstrates how "pluralization and fragmentation" (Sarat 2004, p. 8) in the field of law and society offer new methods and insights into the relationship between law and human rights. The effect is to demonstrate how, despite obvious legal limitations and failures, human rights have transformed the global order.

To fulfill the promise of scholarly understanding and engagement that a law and society approach to human rights offers, we must now go further and question the traditional legal divisions that have characterized the evolution of human rights in the transnational context. Instead of approaching the question of human rights through the prism of legal distinctions, between natural and positive law or between humanitarian law, international human rights law, and constitutional rights, it is important to recognize, as Jurgen Habermas has suggested, that "the revolutionary moment of turning natural into positive law has been worn out during the long process of the democratic integration of basic rights," thus creating "both political space and a legal framework for citizen's participation in democratic decision-making procedures" (Savic 1999, p. 5). Building on this insight, a socio-legal approach should trace the linkages and increasing interconnections in state and nonstate legal practice and activism between different notions of human rights in the diverse arenas in which the claims and tools of human rights are brought to bear. Although original claims against sovereign power may have been constituted as privileges won in the battle to create domestic constitutional orders, today this process has come full circle. Domestic constitutional orders are now shaped in part by demands that state reconstruction be negotiated within a framework that recognizes and implements particular forms of the range of available transnational human rights. The task, then, is both to connect the different legal realms in which transnational human rights operate and to trace their slow consolidation as these rights are formulated and given increasing effect through the marshaling of resources and exchange of meanings.

Humanitarian Law

Attempts to codify standards of treatment, based on the recognition that individual humans have inviolable rights over and above those granted or recognized by specific national communities or sovereign authorities, began with the emergence of humanitarian law in the nineteenth century. Humanitarian law, first codified comprehensively at the international level in the Hague Conventions, recognized the worth of individual human beings in the context of armed conflict, but the standards of treatment guaranteed by humanitarian law were closely tied to the particular individual's status—as combatant, noncombatant, injured, or captured—and did not apply universally (De Lupis 1987). Although a series of negotiated agreements extended the protections of humanitarian law, particularly after World War II, the specific context of this law—the realm of international armed conflict—has limited the scope of its effective protections. Attempts to overcome this limitation through the extension of the rules of humanitarian law to civil wars and nontraditional combatants through the Geneva Convention protocols received limited support, and the law of occupation, a significant part of the core 1949 Geneva Conventions, has been consistently avoided or denied (Benvenisti 1993, p. vii) in those circumstances and conflicts where it seemed to be most urgently required—from Namibia to Iraq.

Violations of humanitarian law, including crimes against humanity, war crimes, and genocide, have since the end of the cold war led to the most direct enforcement of international human rights norms, most recently through the work of the international tribunals for the former Yugoslavia (ICTY) and Rwanda (ICTR). At the same time, the impact of human rights law on the evolution of humanitarian law is evident in the judicial interpretation of the Geneva Conventions; for example, in the *Tadic* case the appeals chamber of the ICTY adopted an approach to the fourth Geneva Convention. The appeals chamber held that the applicability of the law of occupation is not "dependent upon formal bonds and purely legal relations," but rather upon its primary purpose, which "is to ensure the safeguards afforded by the Convention to those civilians who do not enjoy diplomatic protection... of the state in whose hands they might find themselves" (*Tadic*, para 168). The coming into force of the Rome Treaty and the establishment of the International Criminal Court offer further promise that international human rights norms—in the form of humanitarian law in particular—might increasingly be enforced in the international arena. Yet resistance remains, and even amid scenes of major human rights violations, such as the conflict in the Darfur region of Sudan, the debate over whether to characterize events as genocide or gross violations of human rights and the refusal of the United States to recognize the jurisdiction of the International Criminal Court all effect the form and effectiveness of the global response. The form these debates take, such as the identification and claiming of specific and at times minute distinctions between factual settings, distinguishes humanitarian law from the broader diffuse claims of human rights, simultaneously limiting the scope of effective humanitarian rules and denying the applicability of broader human rights claims in conflict zones. Embedded in these debates and disputes are continuing political tensions over the reach of international human rights law and its relationship to ideas of sovereign equality, nonintervention in internal affairs, and other legal underpinnings of the community of states that is reflected in the United Nations Charter.

International Human Rights

The universal status of human rights immediately distinguishes this body of law from humanitarian law, which remains primarily based on the status of those falling within its ambit. Although claims of universalism have broadened the scope of human rights law, they have also led to the undermining of specific human rights claims in the name of culture and context. International human rights, particularly in their post–World War II guise, also facilitated the arrival of a host of new subjects into the traditional realm of public international law (Slaughter 2002). Scholars readily recognize that the emergence of international human rights law introduced individuals as subjects of public international law, which before had applied solely to relations between sovereign states with international organizations having a particular and exceptional status. Less often recognized is the fact that the emergence of the individual subject also dramatically enhanced the status of nongovernment organizations. Even though nongovernment bodies such as the International Committee of the Red Cross had managed to transform themselves into international organizations in the post–World War II era, the emergence of international human rights brought forth a new generation of nongovernment organizations, from Amnesty International to Doctors Without Borders, who both represent the organized embodiment of emergent global social movements and articulate networks of human rights defenders independent of, but increasingly engaged with, state actors (Sikkink 2002).

The Challenge of 9/11, the War on Terror, and the Iraq War

Although the ICTY and ICTR provide examples of the enforcement of international human rights, they also reflect the continuing tension between the promise of human rights and the realities of power asserted through claims of national interest, state sovereignty, and the principle of noninterference in the domestic affairs of a member state of the United Nations. Unlike an earlier era in which states simply asserted that domestic human rights issues were insulated from international intervention by Article 2(7) of the United Nations Charter, today most states, and particularly the more powerful states such as the United States and the United Kingdom, simply claim that their actions are consistent with their human rights obligations. Alternatively, there has been a move since the September 11, 2001, terrorist attacks in the United States to claim, in the name of the war on terrorism, that certain categories of people are cast outside of the normally applicable protections, such as the Geneva Conventions (Klug 2003). Despite the power of those arguing for this exception, the discourse of human rights has nevertheless reasserted itself, and even as violations continue, the executive branch in the United States is once again claiming fealty to international human rights standards.

The power of human rights discourse lies not only in the depth of institutional organization, from the United Nations system to transnational nongovernment organizations, but most significantly in the process of internalization that has fundamentally linked the claims of human rights to domestic political arrangements, thus transforming violations against others into a potential threat to domestic constituencies. This transformation has been achieved through the domestic constitutionalization of human rights, either through the interpretation of existing provisions in bills of rights—as happened in the post–World War II interpretation of the rights guaranteed in the U.S. Constitution (Amar 1998)—or through the adoption of new charters of rights in the post–World War II and post–cold war processes of state reconstruction, in which justiciable bills of rights have been adopted by an increasing number of countries (Klug 2000a). This development truly marks the emergence of transnational human rights, claims to rights that are institutionalized at multiple levels in the global system, and where struggles over rights in any particular context both transform the content of these rights and serve as immediate examples to others who then employ these new arguments and claims from other jurisdictions—national or international—to further their local campaigns for rights (Amann 2004, Klug 2000b).

Constitutional Rights

In the last decade of the twentieth century, well over $1 billion was spent on rule of law projects in every conceivable corner of the globe. This rule of law movement accompanied the enormous political reconstructions of the post–cold war era. More than 56% of the 185 member states of the United Nations made major amendments to their constitutions in the decade between 1989 and 1999, and of these at least 70% adopted completely new constitutions (Klug 2000a, pp. 11–14). As a result, about half the member states of the United Nations had, by the beginning of the new millennium, incorporated bills of rights, fundamental rights, or some form of individual and/or collective rights into their constitutional orders. Although the content of these rights varies dramatically in form as well as application, one may nevertheless argue that the notion of human rights, whether individual or collective, had become a central aspect of constitutionalism by the early twenty-first century.

Despite the apparent contradiction between the adoption of universal norms and the particularism of each country's institutional arrangements and even differing understandings of the obligations that flow from these universal commitments, it is precisely the ways in which the particular is bounded by the universal that marks the process of a globalized constitutionalism. Unlike the debates between law and justice, between positive law and natural law, or over universal human rights, a globalized constitutionalism has introduced a dynamic in which the idealism of universal principles both limits the range of local variation and is simultaneously enhanced by incorporating the specific attributes that emerge from viewing the universal through the prism of local conditions. Although this leaves open the possibility of seemingly opposite outcomes—such as the acceptance or rejection of affirmative action as a necessary attribute of equality—it is precisely the dynamic character of this process that precludes an absolute answer to any human rights problem. Instead, this interaction between global norms and local conditions introduces a dynamic and continuing debate about both the nature of the right and the degree of acceptable action in seeking its implementation, such as, for example, acceptable options in implementing a policy to achieve a more equitable distribution of resources in a democratic society. The outcome in any particular circumstance may produce a hybrid form, simultaneously pushing the boundaries of interpretation and offering a new example of how the norm may be shaped to address particular conditions.

The legalization of political conflict (Kogacioglu 2004) inherent in this turn to judicial decision making and the courts marks a central shift in the structure of constitutionalism around the globe. Even though many constitutions had incorporated some form of constitutional review prior to this period, the application of this power by judiciaries has been so limited in many jurisdictions that it is extremely difficult to argue that an effective system of constitutional review existed even when given formal constitutional status. So, for example, although the Malaysian constitution of 1957 explicitly provided for judicial review, during the first 30 years that the constitution was in force "no single legislative enactment. . . [was] held to be void for being unconstitutional" (Ibrahim & Jain 1992, p. 528). Thus, before 1989 only about 10 countries around the globe had effective systems of constitutional review in which a constitutional court or the courts in general regularly struck down proposed or validly enacted legislation as contrary to the state's constitution. A decade after the end of the cold war, at the dawn of the twenty-first century, at least 70 states, or approximately 38% of all member states of the United Nations, had adopted some form of constitutional review.

Although this embrace of rights and the constitutionalization of politics has been heralded as the rise of world constitutionalism (Ackerman 1997), the jury is still out when it comes to judging either the meaningful implementation or effectiveness of these new institutions. In some cases, the decisions of constitutional courts have already been explicitly rejected by executive authorities or the courts themselves disbanded (Trochev 2004). In other cases, despite the explicit inclusion of a power of constitutional review in the constitution, the judiciary has declined or very rarely exercised this power to strike down a legislative act. In more extreme cases, the constitutional developments so heralded in the first half of the 1990s have already been swept aside by military coups or have been ignored in the face of protracted civil wars. However, for those states where there is an attempt to consolidate the process of political reconstruction that swept the globe at the end of the cold war, the balance between adherence to a globally defined constitutionalism and the imperatives of local political dynamics remains a central legacy of this latest wave of state reconstruction (Maveety & Grosskopf 2004).

The continuing relevance of the local context is most evident in the expansion of what might be considered an anomaly in the field of transnational human rights.

At exactly the moment when claims of human rights are being most successfully pursued and institutionalized, we are also witnessing at the domestic level
an explosion of alternative ways to address past violations that are in many ways
inconsistent with a traditional human rights perspective. On the one hand, in the
face of massive violations of human rights, countries undergoing democratic tran-
sitions have relied on truth commissions as an alternative to prosecutions, while on
the other hand government officials and political party members in former state socialist countries in eastern Europe and most recently Baath party members in Iraq
have been denied civil rights, employment, and other opportunities because of their
prior connections to authoritarian regimes. These processes of amnesty and lustration are justified under theories of transitional justice (Teitel 2000, Mendez 1997),
yet they raise the specter of impunity on the one hand and the fear of unjustified
exclusion and punishment without adequate legal process on the other hand. These
processes have also opened extremely fruitful avenues of socio-legal research that
explore the relationship between law, human rights, and the promise of reconciliation (Gibson 2004, Wilson 2001) and other means of addressing past injustice
(Halmai & Scheppele 1997). Once again, only by recognizing the emerging field
of transnational human rights is it possible to highlight and adequately theorize
the relationship between the promise of domestic civil rights and the obligations
of international human rights.

Although the constitutional protection of political and civil rights remains the
dominant form of human rights at the national level, more recent constitutional
bills of rights have been infiltrated by claims for socio-economic and other even
more aspirational rights. Likewise, the understanding of the purpose of constitutional rights—to protect the individual or distinct minorities against state power
or unbridled majoritarianism—has been broadened through attempts to expand
the application of rights into arenas of power beyond the state. Although earlier
recognition of socio-economic rights was implicit in the constitutional definition
of the state as a social state (Basic Law of the Federal Republic of Germany 1949),
more explicit recognition occurred in the constitutionalization of policy goals in the
form of directives of social or state policy (Constitution of India 1950). Unlike the
effervescence of the declaratory statement of socio-economic rights that characterized the state socialist constitutions, these directives of state policy have developed
into interpretative guides (Constitution of the Republic of Namibia 1990), giving
socio-economic rights a jurisprudential reality that provides a basis for their inclusion in more recent bills of rights as enforceable constitutional rights (Constitution
of the Republic of South Africa 1996). Here we see a convergence of traditional
international human rights and the domestic development of constitutional rights.

Significantly, there has been a similar trend in the expanded application of
rights. From the interpretative expansion of the state action requirement to include
privately formulated, racially discriminatory contracts by the U.S. Supreme Court,
to the notion of *drittwirkung* in the jurisprudence of the German Constitutional
Court, there has been a constant struggle over the impact of constitutional rights
on the private exercise of power. Although the requirement of state action has

remained largely constrictive in the United States, the German Constitutional Court has long recognized the radiating effect constitutional rights have on private actions impugning the rights of other private parties. Although this horizontal application of the bill of rights was at first rejected by the South African Constitutional Court in its interpretation of the 1993 constitution, the reaction of the constitutional assembly was to rewrite the application clause in the final 1996 constitution to explicitly apply the Bill of Rights to relevant private action.

CONCLUSION

Although formal distinctions exist between humanitarian law, human rights, and constitutional rights, a historical link exists between them that gives meaning to the idea of a field of transnational human rights. This link is revealed most clearly in the prosecution of war crimes, genocide, and crimes against humanity in which the substantive meaning of the rights violated are being increasingly informed by developments in human rights law and national constitutional rights. In the field of humanitarian law, this trend may be seen most clearly in the incorporation of understandings of gender and the crime of rape in the jurisprudence of the ICTY and ICTR. Transnational human rights are reflected also in the increasing assertion of rights by communities and individuals in a growing range of places and circumstances. Here the assertion of rights is accompanied by the wholesale borrowing of arguments, as well as the specification of rights by analogizing to similar claims and distinguishing others. These practices are most visible in the arguments of nongovernment organization networks and in the jurisprudence of constitutional and supreme courts in many countries. At the same time, the articulation of the particular field of study within the law and society tradition will help us to understand how the mobilization of resources and the formation of common understandings, networks, epistemic communities, and social movements facilitate the practical or effective evolution of human rights claims across different jurisdictions and legal regimes. It is precisely this interaction that the field of transnational human rights is designed to address. Whether through ethnographies or other more traditional law and society methods, studies focused on the processes that create, or the effects of the practice of, transitional human rights promise to provide insight into the persistence and increasingly global spread of rights, despite vast cultural, economic, and political differences.

APPENDIX A: NATIONAL CONSTITUTIONS, HUMAN RIGHTS DOCUMENTS, AND CASES

African Charter on Human and People's Rights, adopted June 26, 1981, O.A.U. Doc. CAB/LEG/67/3 Rev. 5. Reprinted in 21 I.L.M. 58

American Convention on Human Rights. San Jose, Nov. 22, 1969. Entered into force, July 18, 1978. O.A.S. Treaty Ser. No. 36, at 1, O.A.S. Off.

Rec. OEA/Ser. L/V/II.23 doc. 21 rev. 6 1979. Reprinted in 9 I.L.M. 673 1970

Basic Law of the Federal Republic of Germany. 1949

Charter of the United Nations. San Francisco, June 26, 1945. Entered into force for the United States, Oct. 24, 1945. 59 Stat. 1031, T.S. No. 993, 3 Bevans 1153, 1976 Y.B.U.N. 1043

Constitution of India. 1950

Constitution of the Republic of Namibia. 1990

Constitution of the Republic of South Africa. 1996

European Convention for the Protection of Human Rights and Fundamental Freedoms. Rome, Nov. 4, 1950. Entered into force, Sept. 3, 1953. Eur. T.S. No. 5

Permanent Court of International Justice. 1923: *Advisory opinion in the nationality decrees issued in Tunis and Morocco Case.* P.C.I.J. Rep., Ser. B, No. 4

Prosecutor v. Dusko Tadic. 1995. ICTY Appeals Chamber, 1995. Case No. IT-94-1-AR72 (Oct. 2). Decision on the Defense Motion for Interlocutory Appeal on Jurisdiction

UN Gen. Assem. Resolution 217 A (III). 1948. *Universal Declaration of Human Rights*, Dec. 10. UN Doc. A/810, at 71

Warsaw Declaration. 2000. *Towards a Community of Democracies*, June 27. 39 ILM 1306

APPENDIX B: UNITED NATIONS DOCUMENTS ON APARTHEID

Bouteflika A. 1974. Ruling by the President of the General Assembly, Mr. Abdelaziz Bouteflika (Algeria), concerning the credentials of the delegation of South Africa. (See United Nations 1994.)

Letter dated 12 September 1952 addressed to the Secretary-General by the permanent representatives of Afghanistan, Burma, Egypt, India, Indonesia, Iran, Iraq, Lebanon, Pakistan, the Philippines, Saudi Arabia, Syria and Yemen, A/2183

UN Gen. Assem. Resolution A/RES/44 (I). 1946. *Treatment of Indians in the Union of South Africa*, Dec. 8. Article 2

UN Gen. Assem. Resolution 616(VII) B. 1952. 7 GAOR, Suppl. No. 21 (A/2361), at 8–9, establishing the UN Commission on the Racial Situation in the Union of South Africa

UN Commission on the Racial Situation in the Union of South Africa. 1953. *Report on the United Nations Commission on the Racial Situation in the Union of South Africa.* 8 GAOR, Suppl. No. 16 (A/2505 and Add. 1)

UN Gen. Assem. Resolution 1761, A/RES/1761 (XVII). 1962. *The policies of apartheid of the Government of the Republic of South Africa*, Nov. 6

UN Gen. Assem. Resolution 3206, A/RES/3206 (XXIX). 1974. *Credentials of Representatives to the twenty-ninth session of the General Assembly*, Sept. 30

UN Gen. Assem. Resolution 3207, A/RES/3207 (XXIX). 1974. *Relationship between the United Nations and South Africa*, Sept. 30

UN Gen. Assem. Resolution 3411, A/RES/3411 C (XXX). 1975. *Policies of apartheid of the Government of South Africa—special responsibility of the United Nations and the international community towards the oppressed people of South Africa*, Nov. 28

UN Gen. Assem. Resolution S-16, A/RES/S-16/1. 1989. *Declaration on apartheid and its destructive consequences in southern Africa*, Dec. 14

UN Secur. Counc. Resolution 418, S/RES/418. 1977. *The question of South Africa*, Nov. 4

UN Secur. Counc. Resolution 554, S/RES/554. 1984. *The question of South Africa*, Aug. 17

Waldheim K. 1977. *Statement by Secretary-General Kurt Waldheim in the Security Council after the adoption of resolution 418 1977 concerning mandatory arms embargo against South Africa S/PV.2046*, Nov. 4

The *Annual Review of Law and Social Science* is online at
http://lawsocsci.annualreviews.org

LITERATURE CITED

Abel RL. 1995a. *Politics by Other Means: Law in the Struggle Against Apartheid, 1980–1994.* New York: Routledge

Abel RL. 1995b. What we talk about when we talk about law. In *The Law and Society Reader*, ed. RL Abel, pp. 1–10. New York: NY Univ. Press

Ackerman B. 1997. The rise of world constitutionalism. *Va. Law Rev.* 83:771

Amann DM. 2004. "Raise the flag and let it talk": on the use of external norms in constitutional decision making. *Int. J. Const. Law* 2(4):597–610

Amar AR. 1998. *The Bill of Rights: Creation and Reconstruction.* New Haven, CT: Yale Univ. Press

Arjomand SA. 1992. Constitutions and the struggle for political order: a study in the modernization of political traditions. *Arch. Eur. Soc.* 23:39

Badie B. 2000. *The Imported State: The Westernization of the Political Order.* Stanford CA: Stanford Univ. Press

Barnett M. 2002. *Eyewitness to a Genocide: The United Nations and Rwanda.* Ithaca, NY: Cornell Univ. Press

Benton L. 2002. *Law and Colonial Cultures: Legal Regimes in World History, 1400–1900.* Cambridge UK: Cambridge Univ. Press

Benvenisti E. 1993. *The International Law of Occupation.* Princeton NJ: Princeton Univ. Press

Boyle EH, Meyer JW. 2002. Modern law as a secularized and global model: implications for the sociology of law. See Dezalay & Garth 2002a, pp. 65–95

Canan P, Reichman N. 2002. *Ozone Connections: Expert Networks in Global Environmental Governance.* Sheffield, UK: Greenleaf

Chanock M. 2001. *The Making of South African Legal Culture 1902–1936: Fear, Favour and Prejudice.* Cambridge, UK: Cambridge Univ. Press

Cranston M. 1973. *What Are Human Rights?* New York: Taplinger

De Lupis ID. 1987. *The Law of War.* Cambridge/New York: Cambridge Univ. Press

Dezalay Y, Garth BG. 2001. Constructing law out of power: investing in human rights as an alternative political strategy. See Sarat & Scheingold 2001, pp. 354–81

Dezalay Y, Garth BG, eds. 2002a. *Global Prescriptions: The Production, Exportation, and Importation of a New Legal Orthodoxy.* Ann Arbor: Mich. Univ. Press

Dezalay Y, Garth BG. 2002b. *The Internationalization of Palace Wars: Lawyers, Economists, and the Contest to Transform Latin American States.* Chicago: Chicago Univ. Press

Epp CR. 1998. *The Rights Revolution: Lawyers, Activists and Supreme Courts in Comparative Perspective.* Chicago: Univ. Chicago Press

Gibson JL. 2004. Truth, reconciliation, and the creation of a human rights culture in South Africa. *Law Soc. Rev.* 38(1):5–40

Hajjar L. 1997. Cause lawyering in transnational perspective: national conflict and human rights in Israel/Palestine. *Law Soc. Rev.* 31:473–504

Hajjar L. 2004. Human rights. See Sarat 2004, pp. 589–604

Halmai G, Scheppele KL. 1997. Living well is the best revenge: the Hungarian approach to judging the past. See McAdams 1997, pp. 155–84

Hartog H. 1988. The constitution of aspiration and "the rights that belong to us all." In *The Constitution and American Life,* ed. D Thelen, pp. 353–74. Ithaca, NY: Cornell Univ. Press

Henkin L. 1990. *The Age of Rights.* New York: Columbia Univ. Press

Hoffmann FF. 2003. Human rights and political liberty. *Int. Legal Theory* 9(1):105–22

Ibrahim A, Jain MP. 1992. The constitution of Malaysia and the American constitutional influence. In *Constitutional Systems in Late Twentieth Century Asia,* ed. LW Beer, pp. 507–70. Seattle: Univ. Wash. Press

Ishay MR. 2004. *The History of Human Rights: From Ancient Times to the Globalization Era.* Berkeley: Univ. Calif. Press

Keck M, Sikkink K. 1998. *Activists Beyond Borders.* Ithaca, NY: Cornell Univ. Press

Klug H. 2000a. *Constituting Democracy: Law, Globalism and South Africa's Political Reconstruction.* Cambridge, UK: Cambridge Univ. Press

Klug H. 2000b. Model and anti-model: the United States Constitution and the "rise of world constitutionalism." *Wis. Law Rev.* 2000(3):597–616

Klug H. 2003. The rule of law, war, or terror. *Wis. Law Rev.* 2003(2):365–84

Kogacioglu D. 2004. Progress, unity, and democracy: dissolving political parties in Turkey. *Law Soc. Rev.* 38(3):433

Laber J. 2002. *The Courage of Strangers: Coming of Age with the Human Rights Movement.* New York: Public Affairs

Mandela NR. 1994. *Long Walk to Freedom: The Autobiography of Nelson Mandela.* New York: Little Brown

Maveety N, Grosskopf A. 2004. "Constrained" constitutional courts as conduits for democratic consolidation. *Law Soc. Rev.* 38(3):463

McAdams AJ, ed. 1997. *Transitional Justice and the Rule of Law in New Democracies.* Notre Dame/London: Univ. Notre Dame Press

Mendez JE. 1997. In defense of transitional justice. See McAdams 1997, pp. 1–26

Merry SE. 2000. *Colonizing Hawai'i: The Cultural Power of Law.* Princeton, NJ: Princeton Univ. Press

Neier A. 2003. *Taking Liberties: Four Decades in the Struggle for Rights.* New York: Public Affairs

Nielsen LB. 2004. The work of rights and the work rights do: a critical empirical approach. See Sarat 2004, pp. 63–79

Rorty R. 1993. Human rights, rationality and sentimentality. In *On Human Rights: The Oxford Amnesty Lectures 1993,* ed. S Shute, S Hurley, pp. 111–34. New York: Basic Books

Rosenberg GN. 1991. *The Hollow Hope:*

Can Courts Bring About Social Change? Chicago: Chicago Univ. Press

Rubin EL. 2003. Rethinking human rights. *Int. Legal Theory* 9(1):5–78

Santos BdS. 1995. *Toward a New Common Sense: Law, Science and Politics in the Paradigmatic Transition.* New York: Routledge

Sarat A, ed. 2004. *The Blackwell Companion to Law and Society.* Malden, MA/Oxford: Blackwell

Sarat A, Scheingold S, eds. 2001. *Cause Lawyering and the State in a Global Era.* Oxford: Oxford Univ. Press

Savic O. 1999. Introduction. In *The Politics of Human Rights*, ed. The Belgrade Circle, pp. 3–15. London/New York: Verso

Scheppele KL. 2004. Constitutional ethnography: an introduction. *Law Soc. Rev.* 38(3): 389–406

Shelton D. 2002. Protecting human rights in a globalizing world. *Boston Coll. Int. Comp. Law Rev.* 25:273–322

Sikkink K. 1993. Human rights, principled issue-networks and sovereignty in Latin America. *Int. Organ.* 47:411–41

Sikkink K. 2002. Transnational advocacy networks and the social construction of legal rules. See Dezalay & Garth 2002a, pp. 37–64

Slaughter A-M. 2002. Breaking out: the proliferation of actors in the international system. See Dezalay & Garth 2002a, pp. 12–36

Slaughter A-M. 2004. *A New World Order.* Princeton, NJ: Princeton Univ. Press

Sohn LB.1994. *Rights in Conflict: The United Nations & South Africa.* Irvington, NY: Transnational

Teitel RG. 2000. *Transitional Justice.* Oxford/New York: Oxford Univ. Press

Thomas S. 1996. *The Diplomacy of Liberation: The Foreign Relations of the African National Congress since 1960.* London/New York: Tauris Acad. Stud.

Thornberry P. 1989. Self-determination, minorities, human rights: a review of international instruments. *Int. Comp. Law Q.* 30: 867

Trochev A. 2004. Less democracy, more courts: a puzzle of judicial review in Russia. *Law Soc. Rev.* 38(3):513

United Nations. 1994. *The United Nations and Apartheid 1948–1994*, Vol. I, *The United Nations Blue Book Series.* New York: Dep. Public Inf. UN

Von Eschen PM. 1997. *Race Against Empire: Black Americans and Anticolonialism, 1937–1957.* Ithaca, NY: Cornell Univ. Press

Williams PJ. 1991. *The Alchemy of Race and Rights.* Cambridge, MA: Harvard Univ. Press

Wilson HS. 1994. *African Decolonization.* New York: Edward Arnold

Wilson RA. 2001. *The Politics of Truth and Reconciliation in South Africa: Legitimizing the Post-Apartheid State.* Cambridge, UK: Cambridge Univ. Press

Annu. Rev. Law Soc. Sci. 2005. 1:105–30
doi: 10.1146/annurev.lawsocsci.1.041604.115907
First published online as a Review in Advance on June 28, 2005

EXPERT EVIDENCE AFTER *DAUBERT*

Michael J. Saks[1] and David L. Faigman[2]

[1]*College of Law and Department of Psychology, Arizona State University, Tempe,
Arizona 85287;* [2]*Hastings College of the Law, University of California, San Francisco,
California 94102; email: Michael.Saks@asu.edu, faigmand@uchastings.edu*

Key Words law and science, admissibility, philosophy of science, courts

■ **Abstract** *Daubert* stands for a trilogy of Supreme Court cases as well as revisions of the Federal Rules of Evidence. Together they represent American law's most recent effort to filter expert evidence offered at trial. This review begins by placing the *Daubert* trilogy in the context of earlier judicial efforts to solve the screening problem, which began well before the twentieth century, and then provides a brief explication of evidence law under *Daubert*. Next, we discuss several aspects of the jurisprudence of expert evidence: its connection to debates in the philosophy of science, the practical legal problems courts are trying to solve, and procedural implications. Then we review and discuss varied impacts of *Daubert*: changes in law, marked increases in cases and scholarship relating to expert evidence, and research examining judicial gatekeeping under *Daubert* (civil defendants appear to benefit greatly and criminal defendants hardly at all). We conclude by offering several predictions and prescriptions for the future of expert evidence.

INTRODUCTION

The law of expert testimony provides a lens through which many aspects of modern legal practice can be studied. Every jurisdiction that confronts devising a rule of admission for expert evidence must resolve two basic matters. First, how strict should the rule be? Should it be liberal and allow testimony from virtually all who claim expertise, stopping short perhaps of astrologers and tea-leaf readers? Or should it be conservative and demand rigorous proof of experts' claims of expertise? The second matter that a jurisdiction must resolve is where the real axis of decision making will be. Should courts defer to the professionals in the field from which the experts come, or should they evaluate the quality of the expert opinion for themselves? Implicit in the answers that a particular jurisdiction gives to these two, largely independent, matters are numerous beliefs about legal process and beyond, including its faith in the adversarial process, its confidence in judicial competence, its trust of the jury system, and even its philosophy and sociology of science and empirical knowledge.

Yet, the particular admissibility rules that a jurisdiction adopts might not be reflected in the results reached by the courts that employ them. A jurisdiction, for example, might set forth a restrictive test that obligates courts to evaluate for themselves the quality of proffered expertise. Such a rule might in theory apply to all cases yet in practice be applied only to civil matters; in criminal prosecutions, perhaps, these same courts, ostensibly applying the same rule, might actually employ a permissive threshold and be highly deferential to the professional field from which the asserted expertise comes.

The study of expert evidence, therefore, must consider both theory and practice. The rules on the books might reflect one set of choices about the legal process, and in practice a wholly different set might operate. In this review of the contemporary state of expert evidence, we consider how the law of expert testimony developed into its current incarnation, describe the processes of and justification for the current state of the law, and examine how it is applied in daily practice.

THE ADMISSIBILITY OF EXPERT EVIDENCE

Courts have long struggled to develop a test to guide their gatekeeping of expert testimony, scientific or otherwise. The task is easily framed: How is a judge to determine which kinds of opinions from which areas of asserted expertise are dependable enough to be permitted at trial? But the task presents what may be an insuperable dilemma: Courts need expert evidence to assist them in making decisions on issues about which they by definition know far less than the expert, yet for that very same reason courts are in a poor position to assess the expertise. The history of rules and procedures for screening expert witnesses represents successive responses to that dilemma.

Before the *Frye* Test

Most discussions of the admissibility of scientific expert testimony begin with *Frye v. U.S.* (1923). This is an odd custom, first because judges had been screening expert evidence for centuries before *Frye*, and second because for decades after *Frye* was decided the case was ignored by both courts and scholars (Faigman et al. 1994). Its influence emerged only when the adoption of the Federal Rules of Evidence drew near, the very time when *Frye* should have become obsolete.

The earliest record of the use in trial of what were then called skilled witnesses was the 1678 trial of the Earl of Pembroke for the murder of Nathaniel Cony (Cobbett 1810), although the use of such witnesses was not regarded as a novelty even in that case. The earliest reported decision affirming the propriety of using expert witnesses proffered by a party occurred in 1782 in *Folkes v. Chadd* (Golan 2004). When such experts did testify, courts were not clear or explicit about the legal principles governing their qualifications or their use. One of the few efforts to discern what test gatekeeping judges (in the nineteenth century) were using (beyond the witness's qualifications) suggests that the courts employed what could be termed a marketplace test (Faigman et al. 1994). The courts seemed to ask themselves whether expertise had been of value to consumers in the commercial marketplace. If consumers spent their money on an expert or an expertise, then it was presumed to be sound enough for courts as well.

The marketplace test had virtues, but it also had drawbacks (Faigman et al. 2005). The market does not always select for validity. Much that is false, junky, or harmful may nevertheless sell well. The marketplace test honestly applied is unable to distinguish between astronomy and astrology and thus would admit both. In addition, the marketplace test conflates the expert and the expertise. The body of knowledge and the people who purport to possess it tend to be treated as one. A final problem, which ultimately gave rise to the *Frye* test, is that some fields have little or no life in any commercial marketplace. In particular, there are fields that have no function outside of their possible courtroom utility. The courtroom is their marketplace. Where then were judges to look for evaluation help?

Frye and Its Aftermath

The court in *Frye* was confronted with a technology for which there was at the time no commercial market—early polygraph examination. To help it evaluate the admissibility of that testimony, the *Frye* court devised a variation of the marketplace test. It substituted an intellectual marketplace for the commercial one. The court asked whether the principles that underlie the proffered testimony had "gained general acceptance in the particular field in which it belongs."

The *Frye* variant changed the law's perspective regarding experts in several substantial ways. Principally, by changing the marketplace from the consumers of the expertise to the experts themselves, *Frye* helpfully separated the expertise from the expert. This innovation divided the issue of admissibility more clearly into two parts: (*a*) the credentials of the expert and (*b*) the body of knowledge the expert sought to impart. But the *Frye* innovation also, and counterproductively, replaced buyers with sellers as the principal evaluators of the value of what was being offered. Specifically, the test leads the courts to adopt the standards of the field that is the subject of scrutiny. Thus, rigorous scientific fields are judged using strict admissibility standards (because that is how they judge themselves), whereas fields lacking a rigorous tradition are judged using lax admissibility standards (Evett 1993, Saks & Koehler 1991). Even tea-leaf reading is generally accepted if the reference field is composed of practicing tea-leaf readers. Although this transfer of power from consumers to producers may appear peculiar, it was entirely consistent with one of the defining notions of professionalism extant during much of the twentieth century (Haber 1991, Pavalko 1988).

The *Frye* test eventually became a trope for one major notion of the proper criterion for the admissibility of scientific evidence: general acceptance of particular expertise within its field. The test was seemingly easy to apply, required little scientific sophistication on the part of judges, and was to be applied only to evidence that presented a novel scientific issue, allowing much expert evidence to be scrutinized minimally, if at all.

Offsetting these advantages were limitations: The *Frye* test is vague, is easily manipulated, obscures the relevant inquiry, imposes a protracted waiting period on the use of sound new evidence and techniques, and lacks any definition of when a scientific proposition has become generally accepted. Some products of the most rigorous fields with the healthiest scientific discourse might fail the *Frye* test, while the work of shoddy fields with a great deal of uncritical internal acceptance would easily pass. Moreover, no standards defined what constituted the particular field to which a technique belonged (to one or many fields, and which ones?). Although often criticized for being the most conservative test of admissibility, the *Frye* test could produce the most liberal standards of admission. The more narrowly a court defines the pertinent field, the more agreement it is likely to find. The general acceptance test degenerated into a process of deciding whose noses to count, as well as how many (Black 1988; Faigman et al. 2005, chapter 1; Giannelli 1980; Horrobin 1990; Maletskos & Speilman 1967).

Despite *Frye's* defects, it remains the standard by which expert evidence is evaluated by courts in many jurisdictions. Increasingly, however, the alternative perspective articulated by the U.S. Supreme Court in *Daubert v. Merrell Dow Pharmaceuticals* (1993), and now the standard codified in the Federal Rules of Evidence, is gaining ascendance.

The *Daubert* Trilogy

The Supreme Court's gatekeeping revolution came in three cases, each of them essentially unanimous. *Daubert v. Merrell Dow Pharmaceuticals* (1993) held that the admissibility of scientific evidence depends mainly on its evidentiary reliability (its scientific merit)—suggesting that courts consider whether the scientific basis has been tested empirically, the methodological soundness of that testing, and the results of that testing. These were flexible criteria, so that if courts thought of more appropriate criteria they could use the alternatives. Lower courts were later cautioned, however, against taking flexibility as a license to scrutinize sloppily or not at all: "Though. . .the *Daubert* factors are not holy writ, in a particular case the failure to apply one or another of them may be unreasonable and hence an abuse of discretion" [*Kumho Tire Co. v. Carmichael* (1999), Scalia concurring]. *General Electric v. Joiner* (1997) held that appellate courts must review trial court admission decisions under *Daubert* deferentially and that the logic by which the expert traveled from principles and evidence to a conclusion also is subject to appraisal by the court. Finally, *Kumho Tire Co. v. Carmichael* (1999) held that *Daubert's* essential evidentiary reliability requirement applies to all fields of expert evidence, not only to science. *Daubert* retained the general acceptance criterion, though in downgraded status, and *Kumho Tire* demoted it further.

Although the standards set forth in the *Daubert* trilogy were ostensibly mere interpretations of the applicable Federal Rules of Evidence, those rules were amended in 2000 to reflect trial courts' obligations to insure the soundness of expert evidence as prescribed in these cases. Specifically, three rules governing opinion testimony—Rules 701, 702, and 703—were amended. Rule 701, which permits lay witness opinions under certain circumstances, was strengthened to ensure that testimony that should be evaluated under Rule 702 did not slip in through the back door of Rule 701. Rule 702 essentially codified *Daubert* by adding three new numbered clauses. The rule now states:

> If scientific, technical, or other specialized knowledge will assist the trier of fact to understand the evidence or to determine a fact in issue, a witness qualified as an expert by knowledge, skill, experience, training, or education, may testify thereto in the form of an opinion or otherwise, if (1) the testimony is based upon sufficient facts or data, (2) the testimony is the product of reliable principles and methods, and (3) the witness has applied the principles and methods reliably to the facts of the case.

Rule 703 had often been used to import otherwise inadmissible hearsay statements into evidence (Carlson 1992). The rule has now been amended to prevent this. The new Rule 703 provides, in relevant part: "Facts or data that are otherwise inadmissible shall not be disclosed to the jury by the proponent of the opinion or inference unless the court determines that their probative value in assisting the jury to evaluate the expert's opinion substantially outweighs their prejudicial effect."

The federal courts have averaged about 500 decisions per year on *Daubert*-related issues, and law journals have published thousands of articles at least touching on the subject. The states also are actively involved in this area, with more than half the state courts now following the basic *Daubert* approach (though not all of them the full trilogy) (Bernstein & Jackson 2004), and many other state courts are deeply influenced by *Daubert* (Faigman et al. 2005). Some *Frye* states have on occasion interpreted their test in ways that bear a strong resemblance to *Daubert* principles (Florida and New York are the most notable).

The Meaning of *Daubert*

In essence, the *Daubert* trilogy adopts a changed perspective and relocates the axis of decision. With the old commercial marketplace test, judges piggy-backed onto what consumers seemed to think about a proffered expertise and expert. Under *Frye's* general acceptance test, judges took a rough nose count and deferred to what the producers of knowledge thought about the knowledge they had to offer. *Daubert* finally places the obligation to evaluate the evidence where one might have expected it to be all along: on the judges themselves. For empirical or scientific proffers, *Daubert* requires judges to evaluate the research findings and methods supporting expert evidence and the principles used to extrapolate from that research to the task at hand (Risinger 2000a). And for nonscience expertise (that is, expertise on questions that are seldom the topic of systematic empirical investigation), courts might have to develop new criteria for evaluating the soundness of proffered expert evidence. [But see Sanders (2001), discussed below, who argues that the basic principles of *Daubert* can be applied, if only by analogies still to be worked out, to all expert knowledge.] This obligation on the part of judges is daunting. It may be more apparent now than it was for centuries before why judges sought ways to avoid such responsibility (and why, notwithstanding the commands of *Daubert*, many of them still do).

Daubert, in many respects, appeared to be a revolutionary decision. Certainly judges', scholars', and lawyers' reactions to it support this view (see, e.g., *Weisgram v. Marley* 2000). The core principle of *Daubert* is its changed focus from *Frye's* deference to the experts to a more active judicial evaluation of a particular field's claims of expertise. Under *Frye*, judges did not need to understand research methodology because it was sufficient to inquire into the conclusions of professionals in the pertinent fields. *Daubert* mandates that judges query which methods support the scientific opinions that experts seek to offer as testimony, and this requires that they understand those methods and data. In *Daubert v. Merrell Dow Pharmaceuticals*, for instance, questions about testing and error rate led to responses about comparison groups, standard deviations, relative risk, statistical significance, and many other concepts foreign to the average lawyer. The revolutionary core of *Daubert* is in this call for judges to become knowledgeable about basic research methods. *Daubert*, in effect, brought the scientific revolution into the courtroom.

Revolutions inevitably produce partisans having widely varying views, including some who defend the old regime, others who seek to justify the new order, and still others on either side of the barricades, who determine its ultimate fate. Many of the battles over the *Daubert* revolution have been carried out in the law review literature, where the debate moved quickly from whether a revolution had occurred at all to the nature of that revolution, and, even more so, to the philosophical justifications for it. For instance, some commentators argue that in *Daubert*, "the U.S. Supreme Court took it upon itself to solve, once and for all, the knotty problem of the demarcation of science from pseudoscience" (Goodstein 2000), or that the Court adopted and imposed a specifically experimental or Newtonian or Popperian view of science. But, in the legal context in which the *Daubert* trilogy arose and to which it pertains, the Court can be seen as trying to solve more flexibly a more modest (though similarly enduring and knotty) problem of trial evidence, namely, how to filter proffered expert opinion testimony so that reliable evidence is admitted and unreliable evidence is not. *Daubert* confronted a particular type of expertise, empirical claims, that lends itself to evaluation by scientific methods. *Daubert's* answer, in essence, is that if the proponent of such evidence cannot supply good grounds for concluding that the expert opinion is sufficiently trustworthy—cannot supply appropriate validation—then the testimony should be excluded. It added that the obligation to test the soundness of expert proffers is applicable to timeworn as well as to novel testimony. Given that *Daubert* itself was a case about epidemiological (correlational) data, the charge that it wrongheadedly demands experimental data is hard to support. Still, one can debate whether the best filter has been chosen. In addition, one can debate the philosophical justifications for the revolution itself. How long this philosophical debate will endure only time can reveal, but it certainly occupied a prominent place in the *Daubert* era's first decade.

JURISPRUDENCE OF EXPERT EVIDENCE

In the course of writing *Daubert*, the Court, perhaps somewhat improvidently, cited Sir Karl Popper and his notion of falsifiability as the defining criterion of a scientific statement. As a consequence, the Court seemed to step into the quagmire of the philosophy of science. Justice Blackmun's citation to Popper has been roundly criticized, beginning with the concurring opinion of Chief Justice Rehnquist. The chief justice complained that neither he nor, he supposed, most federal judges understood what falsifiability was. Moreover, the majority opinion, he complained, appeared to call upon judges to be amateur scientists, a role for which they were not trained and in which they were not likely to excel. Scholars also have challenged Blackmun's conception of the philosophy of science, alternating between pointing out that by 1993 Popper was no longer *au courant* among philosophers and that, in any case, Popper's philosophy was largely inapposite to the Court's ultimate holding. Not surprisingly, no citations to Popper are to be found in the subsequent two legs of the *Daubert* trilogy. Despite the protestations and general hand-wringing among courts and scholars, the Popperian perspective offers useful insights into the regime enacted by *Daubert* and provides a basic justification for the Court's decision.

The *Daubert* Court's Philosophy of Practicality

As is true in many legal contexts, especially when it comes to Supreme Court opinion construction, Blackmun's citation to Popper was meant to be more illustrative than necessary to understanding or applying the opinion. For Blackmun, Popperianism was a synecdoche for the Court's desire to distinguish proper scientific inquiry from the perceived detritus of "junky science" (Edmond & Mercer 2002). Good science, according to the Court, follows certain methodological conventions. Bad science does not. Accordingly, the Court suggested guideposts for lower courts in their new obligations to admit good science and exclude the junk. The vaunted *Daubert* four factors—(*a*) testing, (*b*) peer review and publication (which Blackmun suggested mainly as a means of assisting judges in evaluating research methodology), (*c*) error rate, and (*d*) general acceptance—are essentially aspects of the ordinary conduct of scientific investigation.

The *Daubert* Court, therefore, was engaged in the rather pedestrian activity of articulating a test by which lower courts could make decisions regarding the admissibility of expert evidence. The decision must be understood in those terms. Unlike philosophers of science, trial courts must make concrete decisions in particular cases. But in articulating this evidentiary standard, Justice Blackmun effectively entered the science wars (Haack 2003a). By citing Popper, rather than, say, Thomas Kuhn (1996), the Court was signing on to scientific realism. Indeed, it is not terribly surprising that the Court, in seeking to establish standards for decisions in concrete cases, would reject relativism in favor of a more positivistic and objective form of realism.

Although commentators' criticisms of the Court's seeming philosophy are not illegitimate, they are largely beside the point (Leiter 1997). Popper's notion of falsification was concerned with a fairly narrow philosophical issue involving the problem of demarcating science from pseudoscience. Only peripherally was Popper's analysis relevant to demarcating admissible from inadmissible expertise (O'Connor 1995). And this was precisely how the Court used Popper. Falsifiability was shorthand for how scientists largely understand their jobs (Lewontin 1994), and the Court was trying to incorporate scientific sensibilities into the legal culture (Faigman 1999, Haack 2003b). The four factors the Court chose are immediately recognizable as central to the scientific enterprise. Few scientists would disagree that their task is to test hypotheses with a view to describing quantitatively the world around them, whether it is the effects of Vioxx® or the causes and effects of global warming. Moreover, virtually all scientists are concerned with the quality of research design and methods, and they understand peer review and publication as a standard component of the process of checking methodology before disseminating research. Finally, general acceptance of one's findings is the hoped-for end result of the process. Thus, the Popper reference in *Daubert* can be seen to be more a synecdoche for good science than a literal answer to some unasked question in the philosophy of science.

Interestingly, when the Court eventually reached the legal question that was more synonymous with the one for which Popper is so closely associated—demarcating science and pseudoscience—the Court neither cited him nor attempted to draw a bright line around which statements count as scientific. In *Kumho Tire*, the Eleventh Circuit, as had several other circuits, concluded that *Daubert's* gatekeeping standard applied only to scientific testimony and did not pertain to "technical or other specialized knowledge" that constitutes the other kinds of expert testimony contemplated by Rule 702. The Supreme Court in *Kumho Tire*, however, held that *Daubert* applied to all expert testimony, not just the determinedly scientific variety. Whereas Popper had good philosophical reasons for trying to define those statements that qualify as scientific, the Court had good legal reasons for eschewing that task (Jonakait 1997).

The basic challenge for trial courts in the area of expert testimony is to define the boundary between admissible and inadmissible evidence. As the *Kumho Tire* Court understood, the definition of adequate science is only a subpart of this greater task. Expertise comes to court in myriad forms, ranging from the most traditionally rigorous fields, such as physics, to the most traditionally lax, such as clinical medicine. Some experts dress in the guise of science, such as forensic document examiners, whereas others claim expertise by virtue of experience alone, such as police officers. The one thing all these ostensible experts have in common is their claim to opinions that are relevant and sufficiently accurate to be helpful to the trier of fact.

Daubert's holding, in fact, was limited to this helpfulness assessment. *Daubert* described trial courts as gatekeepers whose responsibility is to preliminarily assess whether proffered expert testimony is relevant and whether its basis is reliable. Many courts and commentators, however, have confused this basic holding with the factors that Justice Blackmun suggested might be useful to carrying out this gatekeeping duty (see, e.g., Crump 2003). Consequently, these scholars have accused the Court of naively applying a positivistic model of science onto all expert testimony. Reading *Daubert* as requiring the application of the very same criteria to any and all expert evidence is plainly absurd. Auto mechanics, for example, are not likely to publish their ideas in peer-reviewed journals or know what error rates apply to the technology they rely upon. But the so-called four-factor test of *Daubert* was never more than a set of suggested criteria by which to evaluate ostensibly scientific evidence. As the Court has repeatedly said, including in the *Daubert* opinion itself, no one set of criteria would be useful to assess the validity of every kind of science (from physics to biology), much less every kind of expertise (from engineering to real estate appraisals).

The holding of *Daubert*, as made clear in *Kumho Tire*, applies to all expert testimony. It provides, simply enough, that trial courts are obligated to determine whether the basis for proffered expert testimony is, more likely than not, reliable and valid. The four *Daubert* factors will often help courts make that determination, and sometimes they will not. In *Kumho Tire*, the Court declined any attempt to set forth a single set of criteria that might be useful in assessing the myriad kinds of expertise the courts hear. The point is that trial judges are obligated to carry out the gatekeeping function; how they do so is a separate question. Therefore, in the *Daubert* trilogy, the Court was engaged in the task of defining a rule of procedure that would apply to all forms of expertise. Philosophers and sociologists of science could offer insights into the difficulty of the task, but their views have limited relevance to whether the Court chose the correct rule for its purposes.

The *Daubert* trilogy, however, has left much that still needs to be done. The four *Daubert* factors offer some guidance regarding a large proportion of experts, particularly those from professional fields in which quantitative empirical methods can be, and ordinarily are, employed. The Court in *Kumho Tire*, however, made no attempt to offer similar sorts of criteria for evaluating experts for whom some or all of the *Daubert* criteria might not be decisive or sufficient. Auto mechanics, historians, accountants, clinical medical doctors, and scores of others have traditionally testified but would not be able to meet one or more *Daubert* criteria. Clearly, the Court and the Rules of Evidence contemplate that many experts from these fields would still be permitted to testify, but, at the same time, trial courts must in some way determine if the bases for the opinions they intend to offer are sufficiently valid to admit.

Evaluating Expertise

Commentators have suggested various ways for courts to evaluate this wide variety of expert opinion. The first challenge is to establish expectations regarding the testing that should have been done. In making the necessary validity assessment, should courts consider whether an opinion could be rigorously tested, or should they simply accept the standard practice of the particular field, which might include relying on experience as a basis of expertise? For example, perfume testers might believe they gain expertise through long experience with different kinds of perfumes, and it might not occur to them to carry out validity tests to measure this belief. Clearly, such testing could be easily done, but just as clearly professional perfume testers generally do not do so. Should a court demand that these tests be done, or that a particular perfume tester undergo proficiency testing before his or her opinion will be admitted into evidence (Faigman 2002)?

In addition to the level of rigor to be expected, courts must determine how (or pursuant to what criteria) they should evaluate the numerous expertises that rely on a wide variety of methods, from casual experience to controlled experiment (Seton Hall Symposium 2003). Scholars have begun to address this issue, with several setting forth taxonomies that might be employed for different categories of expertise (Gross & Mnookin 2003, Risinger 2005). Sanders (2001) argues for a different approach. He suggests that "[t]he judicial task will be made more manageable if in both scientific and nonscientific testimony, the courts assess the expert's reasoning from an objective, rational processing perspective with a single test" (p. 409). In favoring this rational form of information processing, Sanders rejects as undependable the basic alternative foundation of most expert opinion: experientially based information processing. As a practical matter, he states that this approach means that courts "should focus on the first *Daubert* criterion" (Sanders 2001, p. 409). The testing criterion, he explains, has at its core a concern with methodology. It asks the expert to describe objectively how the hypothesis at issue can be tested and how the expert put the hypothesis to the test (Sanders 2001, p. 409).

Social Construction and Gatekeeping

Implicit in much of the debate about the nature of scientific knowledge is another controversial matter that concerns whether judges as gatekeepers usurp the role of jurors in the trial process. Scholars who reject the scientific realism of *Daubert*, preferring a more Kuhnian-based relativism, have also bemoaned what they believe to be *Daubert's* conferral of excessive power on judges. For instance, sociologists of science who believe that scientific knowledge is largely socially constructed have generally doubted the wisdom of the gatekeeper function at the core of *Daubert*. However, the tenets associated with a social constructionist view of science are not necessarily inconsistent with the gatekeeping role defined in *Daubert*. Consider, for example, the views of Jasanoff (1992), a particularly influential sociologist of science, who has questioned the wisdom of adopting a restrictive rule of admissibility, such as that of *Daubert*. According to Jasanoff (1992, p. 347),

> [t]he most significant insight that has emerged from sociological studies of science in the past 15 years or so is the view that science is socially constructed. . . . [T]he "facts" that scientists present to the rest of the world are not simply reflections of nature; rather, these "facts" are produced by human agency, through the institutions and processes of science, and hence they invariably contain a social component.

This insight leads ineluctably to the conclusion that judges should exercise their power to exclude expert evidence with restraint. When judges exclude experts,

> [t]hey help shape an image of reality that is colored in part by their own preferences and prejudices about how the world should work. Such power need not always be held in check, but it should be exercised sparingly. Otherwise, one risks substituting the expert authority of the black robe and the bench for that of the white lab coat—an outcome that poorly serves the causes of justice or of science (Jasanoff 1992, p. 359).

The view that science might be socially constructed is not foreign to courts' understanding, and, indeed, the *Daubert* Court cited Jasanoff when it cautioned that peer review and publication are not the *sine qua non* of good science. At the same time that the Court's reliance on Popper and Hempel reflected its scientific realism, its acknowledgment of a role for social construction reflected courts' traditional, cautious approach to experts and advocates. Nor is social construction foreign to the understanding of scientists. The very purpose of scientific method is to try to minimize the contribution of bias (borne of social or personal construction) and maximize the contribution of evidence of the phenomenon under study. This reflects what is probably the dominant view among thoughtful scientists, scholars, and courts: a realist-constructionist view of science (social construction constrained by the empirical world) (Cole 1992, Haack 2003a, Sanders et al. 2002).

But assessing whether research methodology is successful, and therefore whether scientific knowledge, or empirical knowledge more generally, is socially constructed, does not answer the question of what standard of admissibility should apply to expert testimony. Indeed, from a legal-structural perspective, *Daubert's* gatekeeping standard is entirely consistent with at least the nonradical version of the social construction of science. Jasanoff, for example, cites the fear that the "preferences and prejudices" of the "black robe and bench" will replace "the white lab coat." But the more that science is socially constructed, the less the black robe should defer to the white lab coat. Judges have the institutional and, in most respects, the constitutional obligation to ensure due process and fair and balanced trial procedures. To the extent that expert testimony is infused with "preferences and prejudices," they should be those of the judge and not the expert. The responsibility to exercise such preferences and sometimes impose such prejudices devolves upon judges in our constitutional system. Jasanoff, in contrast, would invest this authority first in experts who are not accountable in the way that judges are and, second, in juries to judge whether the evidence given them is worth any consideration. Experts are fact witnesses, and their value to the trial process lies exclusively in their capacity to assist jurors to adjudicate disputed facts. Judges are charged with the discretion to interpret the law and apply the values inherent in these interpretations to particular disputes. If anyone's preferences and prejudices are going to infuse the trial process, it should be those of the judges, whose biases (such as they are) are imposed with political legitimacy. And, if we hope to limit the effect of bad, biased, or seriously misleading testimony, judicial gatekeeping is our best hope.

Law uses expertise (whether scientifically, technically, or experientially based) as a tool for its own purposes. A philosophy of science answers only a small portion of the questions involved in developing a philosophy of expert evidence. Whereas science strives for truth, truth is only one component of the law's mission.

Expertise and Procedural Considerations

Ordinarily, rulings regarding the admissibility of evidence are firmly within the trial court's discretion. The principal reason for this is that trial courts are in a better position than appellate courts to screen evidence, an essential part of conducting a trial. In *Joiner* and *Kumho Tire*, the Supreme Court followed the conventional wisdom and held that appellate courts owe substantial deference to the trial court, both in the criteria used to assess the validity of proffered expertise (*Kumho Tire*) and the ultimate admissibility decision (*Joiner*). Under the *Daubert* trilogy, rulings on expert evidence, like other evidentiary rulings, can be overturned on appeal only for an abuse of discretion. This approach makes jurisprudential sense if expert evidence is like other kinds of evidence, but it is not.

Some questions are case specific, whereas others are relevant across a broad spectrum of cases. For example, whether or not a car in a particular case went though a red light has no implications for what color a traffic light was in other cases. But if "Which color grants a driver the right of way?" has a different answer from case to case, that would be arbitrary and lawless. Questions of fact, which typically affect only the case before the court and do not have meaning for other future cases, can be altered on appeal only when clear error is found. In contrast, matters of law, which apply across cases, are reviewed de novo. This differential treatment grants deference on some kinds of questions and consistency on other kinds, and facilitates judicial efficiency along with the rule of law: Once green is declared by a legislature or appellate court to indicate go, that question is decided for all trial courts in the jurisdiction.

Similarly, in most evidentiary contexts, admissibility decisions are case specific. Scientific evidence, however, does not conform to this traditional wisdom. Many scientific findings transcend individual cases. Questions such as whether Bendectin is a teratogen, smoking causes lung cancer, or polygraphs detect lying do not, in principle, vary from case to case. (Conversely, such questions as the fit of a body of knowledge to issues in a particular case or whether a given expert has correctly applied a technique in a given instance are case specific.)

Monahan and Walker, writing before the *Daubert* decisions, were the first to explore the implications of this insight (Monahan & Walker 1986; Walker & Monahan 1987, 1988). Monahan and Walker argue that although facts and law differ in that one is positive and the other normative, facts sometimes share an important similarity with law: Some factual issues are case specific and some transcend individual cases. The Monahan-Walker analysis has procedural implications. Facts that are trans-case in nature should be treated much as law is treated: Subject to de novo review on appeal, courts are not obligated to rely on the record developed by the parties but can engage in their own inquiries, and the holdings of higher courts should be binding on lower courts.

To allow issues such as whether smoking increases the risk of lung cancer to be decided one way in one case in one trial court and differently in another case in another trial court in the same jurisdiction would strike most observers as plainly irrational. Moreover, to require appellate courts to declare that contradictory answers to such questions by lower courts are, in the absence of clear error, both right, as the holding in *Joiner* requires, merely highlights the problem. Were courts to make such rulings, scientists, editorial writers, and the general public would wonder out loud about how courts can possibly believe that two contradictory propositions about unchanging general phenomena can both be regarded by the law as true. When the problem presents itself starkly, courts certainly see the implications. Thus, for example, when confronted by two different district courts reaching opposite conclusions about whether billboard advertising of alcohol increases auto accidents (and would therefore be subject to regulation), the U.S. Court of Appeals for the Fifth Circuit ruled that it had no choice but to examine the underlying empirical question for itself and reach one decision for both cases below (*Dunagin v. City of Oxford* 1983).

Of course, the scientific questions and their answers are not always, or ever, straightforward. The procedural suggestions of Monahan and Walker work best when the answers are reasonably well studied and accessible to the courts, which may require allowing the science and judicial experience with the matter to ripen before an appellate court rules as a matter of law. Even then, an appellate court might get the science wrong, so that courts at all levels need to be ready to revisit issues they thought had been resolved (whenever a party makes a sufficient showing)—just as they do when an error of law has been made. Moreover, we might expect scientific conclusions to be more subject to change than are normative conclusions because the former are more vulnerable to the growth of knowledge and convincing demonstrations of past errors than normative conclusions generally are.

The preceding discussion about the law-likeness of some scientific questions applies to decisions whether or not to admit expert evidence. A certain kind of medical knowledge, applied to a certain class of problems, cannot be valid in some jurisdictions and invalid in others. Basic principles of microscopic hair comparison evidence or the identification of handprinting or fragmentary fingerprints cannot be invalid in some places and valid in others.

THE IMPACT OF *DAUBERT*

What difference does *Daubert* actually make? The answer is multifaceted. Although changes in the gatekeeping behavior of judges might be the kinds of effects that first come to mind, one ought not to overlook changes in the behavior of lawyers, litigants, and expert witnesses—either in anticipation of or in reaction to changes in judicial treatment of expert evidence—or the discussions that scholars and those in the legal system generally have about expert evidence.

Anticipation of Increased Scrutiny

The most unmistakable impact of *Daubert* has been the changes in federal evidence law, changes that have been radiating into state law. Another unmistakable impact has been the production of many hundreds of scholarly articles on the admissibility of expert testimony, most of them clearly undertaken in the wake of *Daubert*, concerning the meaning and role of the *Daubert* trilogy and their application by lower courts. The federal courts alone have recently averaged about 500 decisions per year on *Daubert*-related issues. Many of those decisions involved *Daubert* hearings at which scrutiny was given to proffers of expert evidence, many of which, before *Daubert*, entered court with little if any scrutiny. If nothing more, one can certainly say that the law has changed and that people have been talking about those changes.

Some courts and commentators assumed that *Daubert*, like *Frye*, applied only to novel scientific evidence. Those who thought so were wrong. The *Daubert* opinion explicitly mentions (though only in a footnote) that the Court did "not read the requirements of Rule 702 to apply specially or exclusively to unconventional evidence." It continues that "well-established propositions are less likely to be challenged than those that are novel, and they are more handily defended." This plainly suggests that long veneration was no protection from scrutiny. And, as the Court later taught in *Kumho Tire*, *Daubert* was not even limited to science.

Many courts and commentators were unsure or disagreed about whether *Daubert*, in contrast to *Frye*, raised or lowered the threshold of admission. Gatowski and colleagues' (2001) survey of judges found that 32% believed the intent was to raise the threshold of admissibility for scientific evidence, 23% believed the intent was to lower the threshold, and 36% believed the intent was neither to raise nor to lower but instead to articulate a framework for admissibility. Numerous courts have expressed surprise to discover that their application of a supposedly more liberal test led them to the brink of excluding evidence that had never before appeared so excludable. The better answer probably is that "it depends."

Permit us to oversimplify here to illustrate an essential point. The *Frye* and *Daubert* tests look at different attributes of scientific propositions. *Frye* asks how

TABLE 1 Outcomes of scrutiny of expert evidence under the *Frye* and *Daubert* tests

Frye: General acceptance in scientific community	*Daubert*: Valid scientific foundation	
	Strong	**Weak**
High	Both admit	*Frye* admits *Daubert* excludes
Low	*Frye* excludes *Daubert* admits	Both exclude

generally accepted the proposition is in a reference community or communities. *Daubert*, in contrast, inquires directly into the proposition's scientific foundations. As Table 1 illustrates, these two questions should usually lead to the same answer about admissibility. That which has a strong scientific foundation usually will be generally accepted; that which has a weak scientific foundation usually will not be widely accepted. In either situation, both tests should lead to the same decision to admit or to exclude.

But there are circumstances in which the underlying attributes of the expert evidence diverge. When a scientific proposition is sound but not generally accepted, *Daubert* should admit while *Frye* should exclude. This is the category of cases that most commentators and courts had in mind when they suggested that *Daubert* is more liberal than *Frye*. But when a scientific proposition has not been shown to be sound yet nevertheless has gained general acceptance in its field, then *Daubert* excludes even though *Frye* admits. This latter category is not a null set; it contains, perhaps most notably, many of the forensic sciences.

The anticipated impact of *Daubert's* filtering of expert evidence prompted concern, litigation, and even empirical research in fields that had done little previous testing of their theories. For a time, some fields tried to evade scrutiny by redefining themselves as nonscience or by emphasizing their art over their science. Pursuing this strategy, a consortium of law enforcement organizations—fearing that the assertedly expert testimony of forensic scientists and police officers would be excluded if they were to be required to prove that what they were saying had a sound basis—submitted an amicus brief to the Supreme Court in *Kumho Tire*. The brief urged the Court to exempt from *Daubert* scrutiny prosecution expert evidence, "the great bulk of [which] does not involve scientific theories, methodologies, techniques, or data in any respect..." but instead offers opinions "about such things as accident reconstruction, fingerprint, footprint and handprint [identification], handwriting analysis, firearms markings and toolmarks and the unique characteristics of guns, bullets, and shell casings, and bloodstain pattern identification" (Am. Eff. Law Enforc. et al. 1997). Nevertheless, the decision in *Kumho Tire* extended *Daubert* scrutiny to all fields of asserted expertise.

Daubert and *Kumho Tire* prompted expectations that if fields such as the forensic sciences that lacked a basis in sound research were to survive scrutiny they would need to undertake the necessary research. Such thinking led the National Institute of Justice to launch several funding initiatives, inviting researchers to begin to fill the considerable gaps in the knowledge claims of these fields that they were sure the courts would now discover in the glare of *Daubert* and *Kumho Tire* scrutiny (e.g., Natl. Inst. Justice 2000).

Similarly, civil litigants, especially tort plaintiffs, anticipated that *Daubert* would raise barriers to their proffered expert evidence—although less dramatically than the prosecution sciences because most civil plaintiff experts come from fields such as medicine and engineering, where research and education are better established and more systematic. Plaintiffs' attorneys were advised to choose their experts more carefully and prepare their experts (and themselves) more thoroughly to meet *Daubert* scrutiny; some were advised to avoid filing their cases in the federal courts to avoid *Daubert* scrutiny entirely (Assoc. Trial Lawyers Am. 2004).

One can find articles by practitioners and scholars in various fields reflecting anxieties about the prospect of having their offerings challenged and tested under *Daubert*. Some scholars and researchers point out that the Supreme Court's decision in *Daubert* has had the salutary effect of precipitating improvements in their own fields (e.g., Shuman & Sales 1999). Yet others argue that some fields are unlikely to make any improvements if not impelled to do so by the threat of exclusion or limitation (e.g., Faigman et al. 2005, chapter 1).

Admissibility on the Books versus Admissibility in Action

That the law in action can sometimes be quite different from the law on the books is something legal realists noted decades ago. The implementation of the *Daubert* trilogy can be viewed as an immense case study of this phenomenon. But the picture is not a simple one.

Several studies have examined the patterns of admissibility decisions in cases decided prior to and after the adoption of *Daubert*, casting at least some light on the behavior of both federal and state courts in several categories of cases. The patterns of change and nonchange provoke one to think about the nature of courts and the society in which they are embedded.

Comparisons of the rate of pretrial challenges to the admissibility of expert evidence before and following *Daubert* found, overall, a marked increase [Risinger (2000b), both civil and criminal case samples in both federal and state courts; Dixon & Gill (2001), federal civil cases; Krafka et al. (2002), federal civil cases]. But, in the civil arena, Risinger (2000b) found that nearly 90% of the challenges were raised by defendants against plaintiffs' expert evidence. Among the criminal cases, where the overwhelming bulk of expert evidence is offered by the government, defendants are far less active in bringing challenges, often failing to raise objections that would have been reasonable and available, and which presumably would have been raised in a civil case involving evidence with similarly weak foundations. In federal courts, fewer than 10% of the challenges to expert evidence were in criminal cases. Of those, the prosecution brought more challenges to defense evidence than vice versa by a ratio of 7:2, even though the government presents the far larger target for attack.

When a challenge is mounted, how do the courts respond? In civil cases, post-*Daubert* courts are more likely to exclude challenged expert evidence than they had been before. Dixon & Gill (2001) found that challenged expert evidence was excluded about 50% of the time pre-*Daubert*; that figure rose to as much as 70% in years post-*Daubert*. In surveys conducted by Krafka et al. (2002) before and after *Daubert*, federal judges reported excluding or limiting challenged expert evidence 25% of the time pre-*Daubert*, compared with 41% of the time post-*Daubert*. But the data on excluded evidence reveal a notable lack of symmetry between the success of plaintiffs compared with defendants. Risinger (2000b) found that defendants succeeded about two thirds of the time in the many federal cases in which they challenged plaintiff experts. In the smaller set of cases in which plaintiffs challenged defense-proffered expertise, the challenges succeeded less than half the time. This pattern was repeated on appeal. In state civil cases, Risinger found that challenges by plaintiffs and by defendants succeeded at about the same 40% rate, but of course defendants were more active in bringing challenges (82% of the challenges on appeal were by defendants). A reading of the cases confirms that courts have become more aggressive in their scrutiny and exclusion of evidence in civil cases. The reader can get a good taste of this from reading the "Notes of Decisions" accompanying chapters on economics, engineering, survey research, epidemiology, toxicology, and medicine in the *Annotated Reference Manual on Scientific Evidence, Second* (Saks et al. 2004).

On the criminal side, the picture is quite different. Risinger found that, post-*Daubert*, in federal district courts defense challenges to government evidence succeeded less than 10% of the time. Government challenges to defense evidence succeeded two thirds of the time. On appeal, defense-proffered expertise was found to have been properly excluded 83% of the time. Prosecution-proffered expertise that had been admitted at trial was excluded only once on appeal. Defendants did somewhat better in state courts than in federal courts, winning a quarter of their challenges. Prosecution challenges to defense expertise succeeded about three quarters of the time.

Groscup and colleagues' (2002) data (criminal cases drawn from federal appellate courts) suggest that patterns of admission and exclusion are unchanged from before *Daubert*, and that this constancy has held true for each category of expert testimony examined. Much of the difference between the conclusions of this study and that of the others can be attributed to the universe of cases on which this study focused. That is, the findings reflect the behavior of the courts in the body of cases examined. As Groscup et al. realized, by focusing on appellate cases they are missing most of the action (or inaction) at the trial court level. The only trial rulings their selection method captures are those that resulted in appeal, meaning cases in which defendants lost *Daubert* challenges and then also lost their trials. However, Groscup et al.'s method allows us to see more precisely how the decisions of appellate courts compare with the decisions of trial courts on the same cases.

"Of course, none of this," as Risinger notes, "goes directly to the validity of any given decision," but the data "are fairly striking in their own right" (Risinger 2000b, p. 108). One possible explanation for the differences between civil and criminal cases is that there are meaningful differences in the quality of the science being offered in the different groups of cases and that there are systematic differences between the factual issues that arise in civil and criminal cases. Or, perhaps, the differential outcomes are attributable to differences in the quality of advocacy (borne of differences in resources) in the two realms. However, some commentators suggest that social and political differences easily explain the differential treatment: As a general proposition, judges disfavor civil plaintiffs and criminal defendants and are more likely to rule against them than against their opposites even when presenting equivalent evidence or arguments. A more definitive explanation of the pattern awaits future research.

Meanwhile, one can ponder some tantalizing hints. Risinger's analyses of decisions by type of expert evidence proffered in criminal cases, as well as other reviews of government science in criminal cases (e.g., Faigman et al. 2005, forensic science chapters), suggest that if *Daubert* gatekeeping were rationally based on the quality of the underlying expert evidence, the exclusion rate pursuant to defense challenges would be higher than it is. The irony is more pronounced in light of data examining the trial evidence in DNA exoneration cases, which find that faulty forensic science is second only to eyewitness errors as the leading cause of erroneous convictions (Saks & Koehler 2005).

What Are Judges Doing When Undertaking *Daubert* Review?

Can we explain the contrast between the success of challenges by civil defendants and lack of success by criminal defendants? Recalling the discussion that accompanied Table 1, for well-developed disciplines the same results should occur whether the filter applied is *Frye* or *Daubert*. No change should occur for most of the evidence proffered in civil cases if *Frye*-like criteria were being employed pre-*Daubert*. Apparently, such criteria were not being employed. Notwithstanding that rules of evidence apply equally to civil and criminal cases (with few exceptions), courts often acted as though *Frye* applied only to criminal cases, whereas many judges understood *Daubert* to apply especially to civil cases. So *Daubert* had much to offer to civil cases, even if logically it should not have. But the cell in Table 1 that would have called for the most dramatic changes in admissibility pre- to post-*Daubert* is the low-validity/high-general-acceptance cell, which is largely populated with weak forensic individualization science. For fields in this category, the move from *Frye* to *Daubert* would (logically) have produced a noticeable (if not dramatic) shift from admission to exclusion. But, as both counts and readings of the cases suggest, it has not. Can this be explained?

A number of studies suggest that judges do not employ *Daubert* as the directive it seems by its terms to be—a directive to conduct meaningful and sincere analyses of the substance of proffered expert evidence, using rational criteria and following them to their logical destination. Instead, judges have taken *Daubert* to be a vague call to arms against junk science in civil cases while keeping hands off of the government's proffers in criminal cases.

Several studies have looked beneath the surface of mere counts of decisions to admit or exclude to find the basis of the courts' less-than-straightforward treatment of admissibility issues in the post-*Daubert* era. Krafka et al.'s (2002) surveys found that in deciding expert admissibility in civil cases, federal judges were far more likely to rest their appraisal of the evidence on considerations that were not new with *Daubert* (e.g., relevance, qualifications, ability to assist trier of fact) than they were to employ the new *Daubert* factors (testing, quality of underlying research, error rates). Thus, in the wake of *Daubert*, judges were excluding more expert evidence, but doing so using legal doctrines that were available before *Daubert*. The new guidance developed in *Daubert* played little role in these courts' analyses of the expert evidence they were now excluding.

Similar conclusions emerged from a very different research approach: Groscup et al. (2002) analyzed the amount of time (word counts, actually) a large sample of federal criminal appellate opinions devoted to discussing the factors they were employing to evaluate the proffered expert evidence in the case. After *Daubert*, appellate opinions concerning the admissibility of expert evidence spent less time discussing general acceptance and more time discussing Rule 702 and the procedures under which pretrial challenges are conducted, but they did not increase the amount of attention paid to the specific factors suggested by *Daubert* for evaluating scientific evidence. "There was no comparable increase in the discussion of the four *Daubert* criteria in evaluating expert testimony. Discussion of *Daubert* was lengthy, but the discussion devoted to the three new criteria was relatively abbreviated" (Groscup et al. 2002, p. 365).

The limited attention actually paid in judicial opinions to the vaunted (or reviled) *Daubert* factors is less surprising once one realizes that judges do not understand what they mean. Gatowski et al. (2001) surveyed and interviewed a large sample of state court judges. Nearly all the respondents strongly supported the gatekeeper role and nearly two thirds asserted that they were in fact active in making expert evidence admissibility decisions, and asserted high regard for *Daubert's* provision of "the basis. . . for justifying or explaining the decision-making process" and for the usefulness of the specific *Daubert* guidelines. But when asked to define or explain each of the *Daubert* factors, and probed further when they had difficulty, only 5% of the respondents demonstrated a working understanding of falsifiability, and only 4% demonstrated an understanding of error rate. And, when presented with specific examples of expert testimony to evaluate, the criterion relied upon most heavily was general acceptance. The authors summed up their findings by suggesting that the judges' "responses reflected more of the rhetoric of *Daubert* than the substance." Other research suggests that judges have difficulty distinguishing good research designs from poor ones (Kovera & McAuliff 2000).

More traditional legal analysis—that is, close reading of cases—generally supports the quantitative findings summarized above. Whether excluding or admitting expert evidence, judicial opinions displaying sophisticated application of *Daubert* or other thoughtful focus on the validity of the proffered expertise are few and far between. The major exceptions to this generalization seem to be toxic tort litigation, where judicial sophistication is more evident, and cases involving economic analysis of damages (compare relevant chapters in Faigman et al. 2005). These exceptions suggest that the evolution of judicial sophistication is associated with increasing sophistication of counsel and with growing experience with debate on a subject.

As an example of judicial casualness about validity, the forensic science area is particularly telling. Logically, many of these fields are highly vulnerable under *Daubert* (Thornton & Peterson 2005). But those fields have endured little other than anxiety. Three examples suffice [but for one notable exception, see *U.S. v. Crisp* (2003), dissenting opinion].

First, a review of cases found that although not a single court could cite any systematic empirical evidence supporting critical propositions underlying fingerprint identification, the courts all nevertheless found the proffered testimony regarding fingerprint evidence not only admissible but often worthy of high praise ["the very archetype of reliable expert testimony under [*Daubert*]," (*U.S. v. Havvard* 2000, p. 855)]. That review summed up the body of cases it examined as little more than "a catalog of evasions" of the duty to scrutinize under *Daubert* (Faigman et al. 2005, chapter 27, p. 432). An explanation might be that the field of fingerprint identification has been so effective in its public mythology that courts cannot suspend their belief long enough to examine the real basis of the claims (Cole 2001).

Second, not long after the Kentucky Supreme Court adopted *Daubert* as that state's standard for testing expert evidence, the same court had occasion to evaluate the admissibility of microscopic hair comparison evidence (*Johnson v. Commonwealth* 1999). Although the court could not cite any studies at all, it nevertheless held the evidence to be fully admissible based on its assumption of general acceptance by past Kentucky cases—even though no prior Kentucky cases had found the evidence to be generally accepted or had even addressed the issue. The *Johnson* court reasoned that silence bespoke general acceptance (Saks 2004).

Third, in the very case by which the Alaska Supreme Court adopted *Daubert* as its admission doctrine (*State v. Coon* 1999), and even though the court remanded to the trial court for the taking of further evidence in anticipation of adopting and applying *Daubert*, no court involved in the case built its holding on a foundation of relevant studies or other data. Voiceprint identification expert evidence was admitted as unthinkingly as ever, even in Alaska's inaugural *Daubert* decision, and even though for this forensic identification science a good bit of relevant data does exist (Faigman et al. 2005).

In sum, *Daubert* has had somewhat paradoxical effects. Judges overwhelmingly say they subscribe to the gatekeeper role and endorse *Daubert's* framework for analyzing scientific (and other) expert evidence. It has precipitated a great increase in judicial examination of expert evidence. Yet judges often appear to have little understanding of the basis of the expertise at issue, and all indications are that they invest little of their scrutiny and decision making in seriously applying *Daubert* or in bringing any other kind of thoughtful examination to bear. Nevertheless, the decisions reveal a pattern of impact: *Daubert* has led to increased exclusion of expert evidence, mostly in civil cases, and most of that excluding plaintiffs' evidence. The questionable sciences of criminal cases, often among the weakest of the scientific evidence that comes to court, are by one device or another usually admitted (or perhaps it is more accurate to say they are granted exemption from serious scrutiny).

Daubert has precipitated a pattern of gatekeeping that is impossible to explain in terms of *Daubert's* doctrinal elements or the relative quality of the underlying science presented for scrutiny. Thus, *Daubert's* impact may have more to do with the sociology of judging than with the law of *Daubert* (Kaye et al. 2004). The future of expert evidence will need to take into account these odd patterns of decision making.

THE FUTURE OF EXPERT EVIDENCE

One can contemplate the future of expert evidence either predictively or prescriptively. The former, of course, is the more challenging and risky.

Predictions

Dramatic national change in the law of expert evidence is unlikely to occur again soon. The Supreme Court rarely changes its mind shortly after making a grand pronouncement. But once the Court becomes aware of problems in the implementation of its earlier rulings, it might adjust the law in ways it thinks will solve those problems. This is especially so if the lower courts split in regard to how they handle certain kinds of evidence. The most likely candidate for high court intervention is clinical medicine, a subject currently dealt with differently in different jurisdictions. Some jurisdictions, for example, allow expert medical opinion with little supporting research (see, e.g., *Heller v. Shaw* 1999), whereas others exclude such opinion pending the completion of sufficient research to support the proffered opinion (see, e.g., *Black v. Food Lion, Inc.* 1999).

The more profound problem in the implementation of *Daubert*, as discussed in the previous section, is the lower courts' apparent inconsistency in applying *Daubert* in civil and criminal cases. If the causes are in any sense sociological or political, and the Court shares in the cultural assumptions and biases that led to that pattern of differential treatment, then the Court may have little desire to alter them.

Although *Daubert* had potential to press various fields toward improvements, including the first serious research they have done on their claims, little of the potential has been realized, and it seems to be declining. Indeed, one scholar has pointed out that once the courts approve shoddy science under the banner of

Daubert, the chances of improvement in those fields, like the chance of judicial re-examination, are less than ever (Berger 2003).

The deferential standard of review announced in *General Electric v. Joiner* cannot survive in the long run. Courts will find ways to fudge, to slow the contradictory or repetitive examinations of the same evidence again and again. Eventually, the Supreme Court can be expected to authorize less deferential review, at least in some classes of cases.

The frequent calls for the increased use of court-appointed witnesses (e.g., Breyer 2000) will go largely unheeded. Although the net use of court-appointed experts and, possibly more so, technical advisers is likely to rise over time, this reform is unlikely to be as transforming as its advocates hope. The power to appoint experts has long been available to the courts, was codified in the Federal Rules of Evidence, and, despite periodic calls for making more use of the power, remains largely unused (Cecil & Willging 1993). This pattern is a testament to the courts' commitment to the adversarial process or to their disinclination to become more managerial. Gross (1991) has offered an impressive analysis of the failure, and continuing failure, of calls for more use of court-appointed experts. And he suggests an alternative for accomplishing much of the good of court appointment while preserving the adversarial imperative: Invite the parties to nominate a certain number of experts to be court-appointed, appoint everyone the parties nominated (who would then understand that their first loyalty is to the court), and then require that all meetings with these experts be open to all parties (and forbid any contact outside of those open meetings). To our knowledge, Gross's suggestions have not yet been followed by any court.

As the fraction of the population of lawyers and judges consisting of people with scientific training slowly grows—due as much as anything else to the advent of more technologies (requiring lawyers to protect or challenge intellectual property claims) or downturns in the market for scientists and engineers—there will be more lawyers and judges who are capable of understanding what *Daubert* is aiming to do and able to see where it has been failing most.

Kumho Tire has potentially deep and demanding implications, as illustrated by the taxonomies of expert evidence that several scholars have started the law thinking about. We suspect that, given the difficulties courts have had in using the essentially ready-made criteria of empirical science handed to them by *Daubert*, the development of nonscience criteria for nonscience fields will be a much steeper and thornier path for the courts to travel.

Prescriptions

In one particular type of case, courts could and might and, we think, should make increased use of experts appointed to serve by (and for the educational benefit of) the court and not by the parties: In consolidated class actions, such as mass toxic torts, the dispute over certain empirical claims is to be resolved in one grand proceeding, rather than in a lengthy stream of individual cases. On such occasions, courts might feel an unusual obligation to reach the best possible answer. On such occasions they can appoint advisory juries (or similar panels composed of experts) to consider the evidence and offer the court suggested findings. Expert panels have been appointed, for example, in the silicone breast implant litigation (*In re SGBI Litigation* 1997) and the Parlodel litigation (*Soldo v. Sandoz* 2003). The use of such panels should be expanded.

Although there have been efforts to teach judges to become better students of natural and social science as well as statistics, crash courses and checklists will probably not accomplish much. To ensure that courts have judges with scientific acumen, the best method is to recruit scientifically educated lawyers to the legal profession and then to the bench. We note above that more such persons are becoming lawyers. Perhaps the process could be accelerated. Perhaps the judiciary—which employs a great many students of the humanities—already has all the personnel it needs to assess the offerings of nonscience expertises.

Judicial gatekeeping has unavoidable effects on the creation of new knowledge. We believe the courts should act in ways that promote the growth of knowledge that is important to resolving major or frequent disputes that come before the courts.

For example, some fields will do no more research than is required of them. If the courts set a low threshold of admission, some fields will develop little or no fundamental new knowledge. They can remain in business with what they already have and, indeed, risk setting themselves back in the eyes of courts by producing real data that can never show them to be as flawless as they have long claimed themselves to be. For these fields, most often seen on the criminal side of the docket, the courts should set higher thresholds, or set time limits (a period of years) for the production of research on fundamental questions about the field. If nothing else, courts should require parties to remain within the bounds of the knowledge they have, forbidding wishful exaggerations, and requiring statements of the limits of what is known, whether those statements are informed by data showing error rates or by the absence of data on error rates. A court could ask parties for briefs on these matters and issue its own instruction to the jury on the limits of expertise.

On the civil side, a similar problem of ignorance-is-bliss exists, but it requires a different solution. A manufacturer, such as a pharmaceutical company, has no inherent incentive to test a product for safety or effectiveness. That is why regulations sometimes exist to compel such testing. Once the product is approved and is in the market, then the less the company learns about it the better. When plaintiffs begin to suspect harmfulness, under *Daubert* their claims will often die with the pretrial *Daubert* hearing because the limited evidence will mean that their experts cannot even testify at trial. (In the past, such suits would sometimes get to juries and, under that scenario, manufacturers had an incentive to conduct additional research in the hope of acquiring evidence with which to defend against the claim.) Thus, *Daubert* ironically acts as a disincentive to improve the body of scientific knowledge about products. To ameliorate this problem, one procedural device might be considered: When one party has a substantially greater ability to collect data about a matter, the burden of producing needed evidence could be placed on that party. In its absence, the other side's experts could be allowed to testify to the limited knowledge that does exist, across some lowered threshold of admission.

Finally, we urge that the serious study of expert evidence by social scientists continue and expand. To understand the interaction of experts and the courts, more research is needed.

The *Annual Review of Law and Social Science* is online at http://lawsocsci.annualreviews.org

LITERATURE CITED

Am. Eff. Law Enforc., et al. 1997. Brief Amici Curiae, submitted in *Kumho Tire Company, Ltd. v. Carmichael*, 526 U.S. 137 (1999)

Assoc. Trial Lawyers Am. 2004. *Annual Convention Reference Materials*, Vol. 2, *Products Liability*. Washington, DC: Assoc. Trial Lawyers Am.

Berger MA. 2003. Expert testimony in criminal proceedings: questions *Daubert* does not answer. *Seton Hall Law Rev.* 34:1125–40

Bernstein DE, Jackson JD. 2004. The *Daubert* trilogy in the states. *Jurimetr. J.* 44:351–66

Black B. 1988. A unified theory of scientific evidence. *Fordham Law Rev.* 56:595–695

Black v. Food Lion, Inc., 171 F.3d 308 (Fifth Cir. 1999)

Breyer S. 2000. Science in the courtroom. *Issues Sci. Technol.* 2000:52–56

Carlson RL. 1992. Experts as hearsay conduits: confrontation abuses in opinion testimony. *Minn. Law Rev.* 76:859–75

Cecil JS, Willging TE. 1993. *Court-Appointed Experts: Defining the Role of Experts Appointed Under Federal Rule of Evidence 706.* Washington, DC: Fed. Judic. Cent.

Cobbett W. 1810. The Trial of Philip, Earl of Pembroke and Montgomery, at Westminster, for the murder of Nathaniel Cony (1678). In *Cobbett's Complete Collection of State Trials*, 6:1310–50. London: R. Bagshaw

Cole S. 1992. *Making Science: Between Nature and Society.* Cambridge, MA: Harvard Univ. Press

Cole SA. 2001. *Suspect Identities: A History of Fingerprinting and Criminal Identification.* Cambridge, MA: Harvard Univ. Press

Crump D. 2003. The trouble with *Daubert-Kumho*: reconsidering the Supreme Court's philosophy of science. *Missouri Law Rev.* 68:1–42

Daubert v. Merrell Dow Pharmaceuticals, Inc., 509 U.S. 579 (1993)

Dixon L, Gill B. 2001. *Changes in the Standards for Admitting Expert Evidence in Federal Civil Cases since the* Daubert *Decision.* Santa Monica, CA: RAND

Dunagin v. City of Oxford, 718 F.2d 738 (5th Cir. 1983)

Edmond G, Mercer D. 2002. Conjectures and exhumations: citations of history, philosophy and sociology of science in U.S. federal courts. *Law Lit.* 14:309–52

Evett IW. 1993. Criminalistics: the future of expertise. *J. Forensic Sci. Soc.* 33:173–78

Faigman DL. 1989. To have and have not: assessing the value of social science to the law as science and policy. *Emory Law J.* 38:1005–95

Faigman DL. 1999. *Legal Alchemy: The Use and Misuse of Science in the Law.* New York: Freeman

Faigman DL. 2002. Is science different for lawyers? *Science* 197:339–40

Faigman DL. 2004. *Laboratory of Justice: The Supreme Court's 200-Year Struggle to Integrate Science and the Law.* New York: Henry Holt (Times Books)

Faigman DL, Kaye DH, Saks MJ, Sanders J. 2005. *Modern Scientific Evidence: The*

Law and Science of Expert Testimony. Minneapolis, MN: West/Thompson. 2nd ed. Republished

Faigman DL, Porter E, Saks MJ. 1994. Check your crystal ball at the courthouse door, please: exploring the past, understanding the present, and worrying about the future of scientific evidence. *Cardozo Law Rev.* 15:1799–835

Folkes v. Chadd, 3 Dougl. 157, 99 Eng. Rep. 589 (K.B. 1782)

Frye v. U.S., 293 F. 1013 (D.C. Cir. 1923)

Gatowski SI, Dobbin SA, Richardson JT, Ginsburg GP, Merlino ML, Dahir V. 2001. Asking the gatekeepers: a national survey of judges on judging expert evidence in a post-*Daubert* world. *Law Hum. Behav.* 25:433–58

General Electric v. Joiner, 522 U.S. 136 (1997)

Giannelli PC. 1980. The admissibility of novel scientific evidence: *Frye v. United States,* a half-century later. *Columbia Law Rev.* 80:1197–250

Golan T. 2004. *Laws of Men and Laws of Nature: The History of Scientific Expert Testimony in England and America.* Cambridge, MA: Harvard Univ. Press

Goodstein D. 2000. How science works. In *Reference Manual on Scientific Evidence, Second,* pp. 67–82. Washington, DC: Fed. Judic. Cent.

Groscup JL, Penrod SD, Studebaker CA, Huss MT, O'Neil KM. 2002. The effects of *Daubert* on the admissibility of expert testimony in state and federal criminal cases. *Psychol. Public Policy Law* 8:339–72

Gross S. 1991. Expert evidence. *Wis. Law Rev.* 1991:1113–232

Gross SR, Mnookin J. 2003. Expert information and expert evidence: a preliminary taxonomy. *Seton Hall Law Rev.* 34:141–89

Haack S. 2003a. *Defending Science—Within Reason: Between Scientism and Cynicism.* New York: Prometheus

Haack S. 2003b. Inquiry and advocacy, fallibilism and finality: culture and inference in science and the law. *Law Probab. Risk* 2:205–14

Haber S. 1991. *The Quest for Authority and Honor in the American Professions, 1750–1900.* Chicago: Univ. Chicago Press

Heller v. Shaw, 167 F.3d 146 (3d Cir. 1999)

Horrobin DF. 1990. The philosophical basis of peer review and the suppression of innovation. *JAMA* 263:1438–41

In re Silicone Gel Breast Implant Product Liability Litigation, 996 F. Supp. 1110 (N.D.Ala. 1997)

Jasanoff S. 1992. What judges should know about the sociology of science. *Jurimetr. J.* 32:345–59

Jasanoff S. 1996. *Science at the Bar: Law, Science, and Technology in America.* Cambridge, MA: Harvard Univ. Press

Johnson v. Commonwealth, 12 S.W. 3d 258 (1999)

Jonakait RN. 1997. The assessment of expertise: transcending construction. *Santa Clara Law Rev.* 37:301–47

Kaye D, Bernstein D, Mnookin J. 2004. *The New Wigmore, A Treatise on Evidence: Expert Evidence.* New York: Aspen

Kovera MB, McAuliff BD. 2000. The effects of peer review and evidence quality on judge evaluations of psychological science: Are judges effective gatekeepers? *J. Appl. Psychol.* 85:574–86

Krafka C, Meghan A, Dunn MA, Johnson MT, Cecil JS, Miletich D. 2002. Judge and attorney experiences, practices, and concerns regarding expert testimony in federal civil trials. *Psychol. Public Policy Law* 8:309–32

Kuhn T. 1996. *The Structure of Scientific Revolutions.* Chicago: Univ. Chicago Press. 3rd ed.

Kumho Tire Ltd. v. Carmichael, 526 U.S. 137 (1999)

Leiter B. 1997. The epistemology of admissibility: why even good philosophy of science would not make for good philosophy of evidence. *BYU Law Rev.* 1197:803–19

Lewontin RC. 1994. Facts and the factitious. In *Questions of Evidence: Proof, Practice, and Persuasion Across the Disciplines,* ed. J Chandler, A Davidson, H Harootunian, pp. 478–91. Chicago: Univ. Chicago Press

Maletskos CJ, Spielman SJ. 1967. Introduction of new scientific methods in court. In *Law Enforcement, Science & Technology*, ed. SA Yefsky, pp. 957–64. Washington, DC: Thompson

Monahan J, Walker L. 1986. Social authority: obtaining, evaluating, and establishing social science in law. *Univ. Penn. Law Rev.* 134:477–517

Natl. Inst. Justice. 2000. *Solicitation for Forensic Friction Ridge (Fingerprint) Examination Validation Studies*. Washington, DC: US Dep. Justice

O'Connor S. 1995. The Supreme Court's philosophy of science: Will the real Karl Popper please stand up? *Jurimetr. J.* 35:263–76

Pavalko RM. 1988. *Sociology of Occupations and Professions*. Itasca, IL: Peacock. 2nd ed.

Popper K. 1989. *Conjectures and Refutations: The Growth of Scientific Knowledge*. New York: Basic Books. 5th ed.

Risinger DM. 2000a. Defining the "task at hand": non-science forensic science after *Kumho Tire v. Carmichael. Wash. Lee Law Rev.* 57:767–800

Risinger DM. 2000b. Navigating expert reliability: Are criminal standards of certainty being left on the dock? *Albany Law Rev.* 64:99–152

Risinger DM. 2005. Preliminary thoughts on a functional taxonomy of expertise for the post-*Kumho* world. See Faigman et al. 2005, 1:69–93

Risinger DM, Saks MJ, Rosenthal R, Thompson WC. 2002. The *Daubert/Kumho* implications of observer effects in forensic science: hidden problems of expectation and suggestion. *Calif. Law Rev.* 90:1–56

Saks MJ. 1998. Merlin and Solomon: lessons from the law's formative encounters with forensic identification science. *Hastings Law J.* 49:1069–141

Saks MJ. 2004. *Johnson v. Commonwealth*: How dependable is identification by microscopic hair comparison. *Advocate [J. Crim. Justice Educ. Res.]* 26:14–23

Saks MJ, Faigman DL, Kaye D, Sanders J. 2004. *Annotated Reference Manual on Scientific Evidence, Second*. Minneapolis, MN: West

Saks MJ, Koehler JJ. 1991. What DNA "fingerprinting" can teach the law about the rest of forensic science. *Cardozo Law Rev.* 13:361–72

Saks MJ, Koehler JJ. 2005. The coming paradigm shift in forensic identification science. *Science.* 309:892–95

Sanders J. 2001. *Kumho* and how we know. *Law Contemp. Probl.* 64:373–415

Sanders J, Diamond SS, Vidmar N. 2002. Legal perceptions of science and expert knowledge. *Psychol. Public Policy Law* 2:139–53

Seton Hall Symposium. 2003. Expert admissibility symposium: What is the question to which standards of reliability are to be applied? *Seton Hall Law Rev.* 34:1–388

Shuman DW, Sales BD. 1999. The impact of *Daubert* and its progeny on the admissibility of behavioral and social science evidence. *Psychol. Public Policy Law* 5:3–15

Soldo v. Sandoz Pharmaceuticals Corp., 244 F. Supp. 2d 434, 534–36 (W.D.Pa. 2003)

State v. Coon, 974 P. 2d 386 (Alaska 1999)

Thornton J, Peterson J. 2005. The general assumptions and rationale of forensic identification. See Faigman et al. 2005, 3:157–222

U.S. v. Crisp, 324 F.3d 261 (4th Cir. 2003)

U.S. v. Havvard, 117 F. Supp. 2d 848, 849 (S.D. Ind. 2000), aff'd, 260 F.3d 597 (7th Cir. 2001)

Walker L, Monahan J. 1987. Social frameworks: a new use of social science in law. *Va. Law Rev.* 73:559–98

Walker L, Monahan J. 1988. Social facts: scientific methodology as legal precedent. *Calif. Law Rev.* 76:877–96

Weisgram v. Marley Co., 528 U.S. 440 (2000)

Annu. Rev. Law Soc. Sci. 2005. 1:131–49
doi: 10.1146/annurev.lawsocsci.1.041604.115948
Copyright © 2005 by Annual Reviews. All rights reserved
First published online as a Review in Advance on June 28, 2005

PLEA BARGAINING AND THE ECLIPSE OF THE JURY

Bruce P. Smith

University of Illinois College of Law, Champaign, Illinois 61820;
email: smithb@law.uiuc.edu

Key Words   criminal trial, summary proceedings, nonjury proceedings, bench trial

■ **Abstract**   The right to criminal jury trial is protected by the U.S. Constitution and the constitutions of all 50 states. In practice, however, roughly 95% of persons convicted of felonies in America waive their right to trial by jury by entering guilty pleas. Most such pleas derive from plea bargaining, whereby defendants plead guilty in exchange for prosecutorial and judicial concessions. Although plea bargaining has generated an extensive scholarly literature, its history, until recently, has remained obscure. This review examines existing legal-historical scholarship on the origins and expansion of plea bargaining in the nineteenth century and explores the range of factors cited by legal historians for plea bargaining's rise. It reveals that plea bargaining was one of several methods employed by Anglo-American criminal justice administrators to dispose of criminal cases without juries. When compared with these other modes of bypassing trial by jury, plea bargaining appears less distinctive—and less distinctively American—than often considered.

INTRODUCTION

Amidst the constellation of rights bounded by America's early state and federal constitutions, the right to criminal jury trial arguably shone the brightest. Viewed as a means to enhance the "public legitimacy of the criminal justice system, to pursue truth, and to protect innocence," and as an embodiment of "popular sovereignty and republican self-government" (Amar 1997, pp. 120–22), the right to trial by jury in criminal cases was the only right included in every state constitution adopted in America between 1776 and 1787 (Alschuler & Deiss 1994). For good measure, the framers of the U.S. Constitution included language protecting criminal jury trial in both Article III ("The Trial of all Crimes, except in cases of Impeachment, shall be by Jury") and the Sixth Amendment ("In all criminal prosecutions, the accused shall enjoy the right to a...public trial, by an impartial jury"), seemingly ensuring that the right to trial by jury in criminal cases would remain inviolable.

But while radiant in constitutional principle, criminal jury trial has long been eclipsed in actual practice. By 1860, less than three generations after the framers' era, most felony cases in New York City—America's largest and most influential jurisdiction—were resolved by guilty pleas rather than by jury verdicts (Moley

1928). By the late 1920s, guilty pleas accounted for over 80% of felony convictions not only in New York, but in cities such as Chicago, Cleveland, and Los Angeles as well (Moley 1928). Recent data reveal that the eclipse of criminal jury trial in America is, by now, virtually complete: Of the roughly 1.05 million adults convicted of felony offenses in American state courts in 2002, 95% pleaded guilty (US Dep. Justice 2004), and the 75,000 or so convicted in federal courts in that year pleaded guilty at even higher rates (Admin. Office US Courts 2004).[1]

What accounts for the near-total eclipse of criminal jury trial over the course of the past 200 years? Much like the ancients, who attributed solar eclipses to sun-devouring devils (Wanner 2005), modern-day scholars have also blamed a "demon" (Alschuler 1983), and one with a seemingly American pedigree: plea bargaining. The practice of plea bargaining, whereby criminal defendants exchange pleas of guilty (and thus waive their right to trial by jury) in exchange for charge- or sentence-related concessions,[2] has been derided as "coercive" (Alschuler 2003), "disastrous" (Schulhofer 1992), "dishonest" (Langbein 1992), and "hypocritical" (Alschuler 1983); compared with poker (Moley 1929), torture (Langbein 1978), and a "Turkish rug market" (Langbein 1992); and even proposed as a fitting subject of "exorcism" (Alschuler 1983).

As a subject of academic study, plea bargaining has also been written about so frequently that two leading scholars of the subject expressed concern—nearly three decades ago—that the academic literature had "become characterized by repetitiousness and even sterility" (Baldwin & McConville 1977, pp. 1–2). Yet the history of plea bargaining—the explanation of when, where, how, and why the phenomenon arose and expanded so dramatically—still remained, by that date, largely unwritten. Commenting in 1979, Lawrence Friedman accurately characterized the then-current legal-historical scholarship on plea bargaining as "a fairly blank chapter in the history of criminal justice" (Friedman 1979, p. 247)—itself, at that time, a rather thin book.

As Friedman well knew, this state of affairs had already begun to change by the time that he offered his characterization. In 1979, *Law and Society Review* published a series of pioneering historical reflections on plea bargaining (Alschuler 1979, Friedman 1979, Langbein 1979) that, collectively, provided an important chronological and theoretical framework for future scholars. In the 1980s and 1990s, a series of studies of criminal justice administration in nineteenth-century American jurisdictions—including Alameda County (Friedman & Percival 1981), Philadelphia (Steinberg 1989), Boston (Ferdinand 1992, Vogel 1999), and

---

[1] Our leading historian of the Anglo-American criminal trial has described the modern-day state of affairs as follows: "Criminal jury trial has all but disappeared in the United States. Can you find it? Of course, you can find it. You can find it in the show trials of the day. . . . But jury trial no longer typifies our system. Can you find a hippopotamus in the Bronx? Yes, there's one in the Bronx Zoo, but it has nothing to do with life in the Bronx. It's a goner. And so, stunningly, is criminal jury trial. . ." (Langbein 1992, p. 121).

[2] Plea bargaining typically takes the form of either charge bargaining (whereby a defendant enters a guilty plea in exchange for a lesser charge) or sentence bargaining (whereby a defendant enters a guilty plea in exchange for an anticipated concession at sentencing).

New York (McConville & Mirsky 1995)—all added considerably to our knowledge of plea bargaining's emergence and expansion. In 2003, George Fisher's *Plea Bargaining's Triumph: A History of Plea Bargaining in America* (Fisher 2003) provided the first book-length treatment of plea bargaining's emergence in any jurisdiction—in this case, nineteenth-century Massachusetts. And interest in the subject has shown little sign of flagging.[3]

Given the richness of the secondary literature and the range of jurisdictions that it surveys, this review seeks to accomplish three discrete goals. First, it canvasses the four principal theories offered for plea bargaining's emergence and expansion: caseload pressure; the increasing complexity of criminal trials; institutional changes in prosecution and policing; and, finally, socio-political pressures exogenous to the courtroom. Next, these theories are assessed by examining the case of Boston, the nineteenth-century American jurisdiction about which we know the most. The review concludes by assessing briefly the degree to which the evidence from Boston can be generalized to other American jurisdictions, to England, and to the administration of civil (as opposed to criminal) cases.

THEORIES OF PLEA BARGAINING'S DEVELOPMENT

Before 1800, plea bargaining in felony cases was virtually nonexistent in both America and England (Fisher 2003, Beattie 1986).[4] By the early decades of the twentieth century, by contrast, guilty pleas disposed of most serious criminal cases in major urban jurisdictions such as New York (Moley 1928), Boston (Fisher 2003), and London (Feeley & Lester 1994). How have scholars explained the emergence and dramatic expansion of plea bargaining in America and England during the nineteenth century?

At the outset, and at the risk of belaboring the obvious, most scholars of plea bargaining—whether they are historians, sociologists, or legal academics—have analyzed plea bargaining as a process by which prosecutors, defendants, and judges seek to secure benefits and avoid costs in the shadow of criminal trial (see, e.g., Alschuler 1968, 1975, 1976; Heumann 1978; Scott & Stuntz 1992; but see Bibas 2004). Although scholars have probed the motivations of these principal legal actors from a variety of perspectives [see, e.g., Heumann 1978 (sociology), Easterbrook 1983 (law and economics), Bibas 2004 (behavioral law and

---

[3] Vogel's *Coercion to Compromise: Plea Bargaining, the Courts, and the Making of Political Authority, 1830–1920* (Vogel 2005) and McConville & Mirsky's *Jury Trials and Plea Bargaining: A True History* (McConville & Mirsky 2005) were in press at the time that this review was substantially complete. For the purposes of this essay, I have cited their previously published works (Vogel 1999, McConville & Mirsky 1995), which develop related themes.

[4] Fisher describes incidents of plea bargaining before "the opening decade of the nineteenth century" as "isolated" and "episodic" (Fisher 2003, pp. 12). On the basis of his study of eighteenth-century Sussex and Surrey, Beattie has concluded that "[t]here was no plea bargaining in felony cases in the eighteenth century" in England (Beattie 1986, pp. 336–37).

economics)], our basic understanding of the respective payoffs to the relevant institutional actors of avoiding trial by jury has remained largely constant through the years.

Writing in 1929, Raymond Moley, professor of law at Columbia University and a participant in several of the era's pioneering studies of urban criminal justice administration [e.g., New York Crime Comm. 1974 (1928), Illinois Assoc. Crim. Justice 1929], summarized the benefits that guilty pleas provided to the relevant actors. For prosecutors, guilty pleas avoided "onerous and protracted" trials whose outcomes—"losing" or "having to oppose an appeal to a higher court"—were both undesirable; more importantly, guilty pleas permitted elected prosecutors to go "before the voters. . .[and] talk in big figures about the number of convictions secured." For criminal defendants, plea bargaining offered the opportunity "to plead guilty to a crime other than the one. . .charged" (i.e., charge bargaining) or to receive "an express or implied assurance of a light sentence by the judge" (i.e., sentence bargaining), without requiring any "abject gesture of confession and renunciation." And for trial judges, plea bargains helped clear space on dockets crowded with criminal and civil business and, moreover, eliminated "the danger of being reversed on some point of law" on appeal (Moley 1929, pp. 157–58).

Of course, the enduring motivations of prosecutors, criminal defendants, and judges ultimately tell us little about why plea bargaining emerged at the times and places that it did. The earliest studies of plea bargaining, which were associated with a series of detailed crime surveys conducted in the late 1920s and early 1930s [e.g., Clevel. Surv. Crim. Justice 1922, Missouri Assoc. Crim. Justice 1926, New York Crime Comm. 1974 (1928)], largely attributed the emergence and expansion of the practice to what has come to be known as caseload pressure. In 1927, Dean Justin Miller of the University of Southern California School of Law attributed the frequent "compromise" of criminal cases before trial to "the great increase in the number of acts" defined as criminal under recently adopted liquor, traffic, financial, and building regulations (Miller 1927, pp. 17–18). The following year, in an influential article on "the vanishing jury," Moley provided support for the thesis of caseload pressure by noting that district attorneys and judges typically justified plea bargaining because it "clears the docket," "saves expense," and makes it "possible to give more attention to the few jury trials that remain" (Moley 1928, p. 123).

As Feeley (1997) has observed, the notion that plea bargaining can best be explained in functional terms "as an adaptation to caseload pressures" has remained an "important commonalty" in most explanations of plea bargaining's origin and development (p. 183). A second, related hypothesis suggests that changes in the character of criminal trial—specifically, its increasing complexity over time—also contributed to plea bargaining's rise.[5]

---

[5]Unfortunately, as Heise (2004) has recently noted, scholars continue to lack "a clear definition of case complexity" and know "little. . .about what makes cases complex for the major actors in criminal trials" (pp. 366–67). For an ambitious attempt to develop a seven-factor test of complexity and apply it to trials at London's Old Bailey in the nineteenth century, see Feeley & Lester (1994).

Seeking to explain the virtual absence of plea bargaining in English felony cases before 1800, Langbein has argued that the streamlined trials of the day provided little incentive for prosecutors, defendants, or judges to bypass trial by jury—which, itself, was essentially a summary process (Langbein 1979, 1992, 2003). Put differently, "when trials were short and rapid, the [state] had no particular incentive to engage in the exchange, and thus the defendant had no bargaining chips" (Langbein 2003, p. 19). Under this theory, routine plea bargaining only developed in England in the middle decades of the nineteenth century, when the "increased presence of lawyers, refinements in the rules of criminal procedure and evidence, and changes in the substantive criminal law" made pleas more desirable for prosecutors to secure and more palatable for judges to accept (Feeley 1997, p. 187).

A third theory of plea bargaining's emergence and expansion focuses on institutional changes in prosecution and policing. Recently, Ramsey (2002) has suggested that district attorneys in late-nineteenth-century New York City increasingly resorted to plea bargaining as a means of dealing with insufficient staffing, a backlog of indictments, heightened oversight by state officials, and the advent of popular elections for prosecutors in 1846. In turn, Friedman & Percival (1981) have suggested that improvements in policing and associated refinements in evidence gathering may have helped encourage pleas by clarifying important facts before trial, thus, presumably, narrowing the gap between the parties' expectations about the likely outcome of the proceedings.[6]

Finally, some scholars have suggested that the emergence and growth of plea bargaining in the nineteenth century can best be explained by examining factors exogenous to the courthouse. Thus, McConville & Mirsky (1995) have argued that "explanations for systemic transformation" in the nature of criminal case disposition in nineteenth-century New York City are likely to be "located in structural changes within the political economy of the state" and shifts in ideological attitudes to crime (p. 468). Noting that crowded dockets and adversarial trials characterized criminal justice administration in New York City from the early decades of the nineteenth century, but that plea bargaining did not become the dominant mode of criminal case disposition in the city until roughly 1860, the authors have suggested that plea bargaining should be understood as part of a broader transformation from individualized to aggregate justice.[7] For her part, Vogel (1999) has contended that the emergence of plea bargaining in nineteenth-century Boston should be understood as a technique of governance instituted by the city's elites to preserve their

---

[6]In a similar vein, a staple aspect of the law-and-economics literature on *civil* dispute resolution holds that "[w]hen relative optimism prevents the parties from settling out of court, they may be able to correct the relative optimism before trial and then settle" (Cooter & Ulen 2004, p. 408).

[7]According to McConville & Mirsky (1995), the era of individualized justice (1800–1845) in New York City focused on "securing individual justice for the private prosecutor (i.e., the victim or the victim's kin) and the defendant." By contrast, the era of aggregate justice (1845–1865) was typified by "a political concern with maximizing the rate of conviction through reliance upon guilty pleas..." (p. 460).

political power by securing the loyalty of the lower classes through displays of "episodic leniency."

How successful are these various theories in explaining the emergence and expansion of plea bargaining in nineteenth-century America and England? In seeking to answer this question, we turn our attention to Boston, whose urban criminal courts have been studied more extensively (Ferdinand 1992; Fisher 2000, 2003; Vogel 1999) than those in any other nineteenth-century jurisdiction.

PLEA BARGAINING IN NINETEENTH-CENTURY AMERICA: THE CASE OF BOSTON

At the threshold, scholars seeking to reconstruct the history of plea bargaining face a pair of methodological problems: first, the selection of the court (or courts) in which plea bargaining is likely to have emerged; and, second, the identification of actual instances of plea bargaining in the surviving contemporary sources. As we shall see, the approaches taken to the questions of where and how plea bargains can be found may have important implications for the corresponding explanations of why plea bargaining emerged.

Finding Plea Bargains

Generalizing broadly, most American jurisdictions in the nineteenth century, whether located in rural or urban settings, featured a multi-tiered structure of criminal courts. At the lower tier, justices of the peace (JPs) or urban magistrates adjudicated cases summarily (i.e., without juries) and referred more serious cases for trial in higher courts. In the middle tier, judges administered jury trials, and prosecutors and defense lawyers appeared with regularity. At the upper tier, a court with jurisdiction over appellate matters often possessed exclusive jurisdiction over a narrow range of serious crimes, such as murder.

Given the challenges involved for historians in mastering the relevant archival records that might bear on the phenomenon of plea bargaining, the selection of the appropriate court (or courts) for study is an important threshold task. Such choices can also shape one's historical assessment of the emergence and expansion of plea bargaining. Focusing on the city of Boston, Ferdinand (1992) and Vogel (1999) both claim that plea bargaining began in the 1830s in the lower-tier police court and spread thereafter to the city's middle-tier municipal court. By contrast, relying on evidence from a major county adjoining Boston, Fisher (2003) contends that plea bargaining began in the county's middle-tier court as early as the 1800s and then spread to the commonwealth's upper-tier court four decades later.

Regardless of the tier (or tiers) chosen for study, historians of plea bargaining face a second challenge: identifying clear instances of the phenomenon. On occasion, nineteenth-century prosecutors candidly described their bargaining practices. In 1844, for example, a district attorney in Essex County, Massachusetts, acknowledged in response to a legislative inquiry that his practice was to induce defendants charged with multiple counts of illegally selling liquor to "enter a plea of nolo contendere," to agree to "abstain from future sales of liquor without [a] license," to "pay at least one penalty [and associated costs] to the Commonwealth," and to let the indictment "stand continued as security that the defendant would fulfill his agreement" (Ferdinand 1992, p. 70; Fisher 2003, p. 31).[8]

Absent these frank (but rare) admissions, scholars seeking to identify plea bargaining in the arcane records of nineteenth-century criminal courts must rely on more recondite evidence. From time to time, clear plea bargains can be identified in the existing archival records, such as where "the clerk's account [explicitly] discloses a concession made in exchange for the defendant's plea" (Fisher 2003, p. 22). Yet, as Fisher concedes, evidence of these types of clear plea bargains in the surviving records of the Massachusetts court system in the first half of the nineteenth century is extremely rare: Of the 770 adjudicated cases in the middle-tier court of Middlesex County, Massachusetts, in which defendants went to trial, pleaded guilty, or pleaded no contest between 1789 and 1849, only 49 (6.4%) resulted from clear plea bargains—and this modest percentage declined to only 2.5% in cases that did not involve liquor-related violations (Fisher 2003, p. 251, footnote 38).[9]

Although, as we shall see, a focus on clear plea bargains sharpens the analysis concerning plea bargaining's emergence, it risks grounding an analysis of plea bargaining's subsequent expansion on a small and idiosyncratic evidentiary base. Other scholars have employed less rigid evidentiary markers designed to chart plea bargaining's advent and ascendancy. Ferdinand (1992), for example, has inferred the presence of systematic plea bargaining in Boston's lower- and middle-tier courts in the 1830s and 1840s from the sheer volume of guilty pleas in those courts, the frequency at which defendants switched their pleas from not guilty to guilty, and the fact that certain categories of defendants who pleaded guilty received lighter sentences than those who went to trial. Vogel (1999), in turn, has sought to establish through statistical analysis that defendants in Boston who pleaded guilty received sentences that were less severe than those meted out to similarly situated defendants who contested their cases at trial. Yet although these analyses purport to find routine evidence of plea bargaining in Boston's lower- and middle-tier courts by the second quarter of the nineteenth century, their parameters for identifying plea bargains are so expansive, and the resulting collection of ostensible bargains so extensive and varied, that the precise dynamics of plea bargaining in actual cases or types of cases become very difficult to explain.

Explaining Plea Bargains

All the main theories of plea bargaining's development—caseload pressure, case complexity, institutional changes, and socio-economic forces—make an

---

[8] A plea of nolo contendere or no contest occurs when a defendant refuses to acknowledge guilt but nonetheless submits to punishment.

[9] I am grateful to John Langbein and Mary Vogel for encouraging me to think carefully about these quantitative issues.

appearance in the leading works on the rise of plea bargaining in Boston. Ferdinand (1992) argues that plea bargaining began in Boston in regulatory and vice cases as a means of "eas[ing] the burdens of prosecution" (p. 65). Vogel (1999), as suggested above, emphasizes factors exogenous to the courtroom, arguing that embattled elites in Boston adopted plea bargaining as a means to maintain political dominance at a time of social, economic, and political crisis (p. 163).

Fisher (2003), for his part, offers a multifaceted account that incorporates theories of caseload pressure, complexity, institutional developments, and, importantly, statutory change. According to Fisher, prosecutors in Massachusetts in the early decades of the nineteenth century engaged in charge bargaining in liquor cases, taking advantage of a sentencing structure that assigned a fixed penalty for various offenses and thus cabined judicial discretion.[10] Later, in the 1840s, plea bargaining emerged in murder cases in which prosecutors could employ a procedural device known as a "partial nol pros" to permit defendants accused of capital murder to plead guilty to the noncapital offense of manslaughter.[11] Although prosecutors in Middlesex County consistently sought to "ease their crushing workloads," to "avoid the risk that wanton juries would spurn their painstakingly assembled cases," and, after 1832, to report favorable rates of conviction to the commonwealth's legislature (Fisher 2003, p. 13), trial judges only began to consent routinely to plea bargains in the last quarter of the nineteenth century, when a rash of complex personal injury cases encouraged them to seek "relief from their out-of-control civil caseloads" (p. 123).

Did plea bargaining emerge in Boston's lower-tier courts or in its middle-tier courts? According to Ferdinand (1992), "the diffusion of plea bargaining was from the Police Court to the Municipal Court—that is, from a lower court to a higher court" (p. 95), a view shared by Vogel (1999). In contrast, Fisher (2003) contends that the city's lower-tier police court "lacked two institutions—jury and prosecutor—whose role in the criminal system looms far too large. . .to think that much can be explained without them" (p. 4). Because the police court was "a nonjury forum that usually operated without a professional prosecutor," and in which defendants lacked the ability to "reject a plea offer in the hope of winning an acquittal from a jury," Fisher holds out little hope that this tribunal can tell us much about the emergence and expansion of plea bargaining in antebellum America (p. 139).[12]

---

[10]By contrast, judges in Massachusetts could punish persons convicted of common law offenses within a broad sentencing range: In cases of petty larceny, punishments could range up to one year in prison or $300; in cases of grand larceny, judges could render sentences of up to five years in prison or $600 (Fisher 2003, p. 24).

[11]In turn, after 1858, defendants charged with intentional murder could avoid the risk of a capital sentence by pleading guilty to second-degree murder (Fisher 2003).

[12]Striking a cautionary note, Feeley, in turn, has warned of the risks of "unwarranted inferences and overgeneralization" in assuming that plea bargaining accounts for the

Yet if plea bargaining emerged in Boston's middle-tier courts before 1850, as Fisher claims, it is curious that historians have found no evidence of plea bargaining in such courts where they might have expected most to find it: in routine, high-volume cases such as those alleging larceny.[13] The failure to find any evidence of such bargains in theft-related cases is particularly surprising not only because such offenses crowded Boston's judicial dockets, but because prosecutors in Massachusetts, after 1838, possessed the ability "to reduce a charge of grand larceny to petty larceny and thereby guarantee defendants. . .a maximum one-year [rather than five-year] sentence" (Fisher 2003, p. 25). Seeking to explain the absence of plea bargains involving accused larcenists, Fisher speculates that "the lowered maximum [of one year]. . .usually was not sufficient to induce a defendant to plead"—although precisely why a reduction from a five- to a one-year maximum term should not have induced more defendants to consummate a plea bargain during this period remains unexplained (Fisher 2003, p. 25).

Might criminal justice administrators who were repeatedly confronted with cases of petty theft have employed a different way of avoiding the expense, delay, and risk of trial by jury rather than by merely consenting to plea bargains in middle-tier courts? Such a prospect is at least suggested by Ferdinand's data, which reveal that the lower-tier police court and middle-tier municipal court shared responsibility for adjudicating cases of larceny, with the police court consistently adjudicating the majority of such cases.[14] Recent studies of nineteenth-century London reveal that magistrates in that city's police courts routinely adjudicated the cases of persons suspected of property theft rather than sending them on to trial in higher courts because summary proceedings permitted convictions to be secured more promptly, cheaply, and easily than in the higher courts (Smith 2005a,b). In London, at least, urban criminal justice administrators did not need to ratify plea bargains to pursue a routine and overt method of jury avoidance; instead, summary proceedings provided them, in many respects, with the functional equivalent of plea bargaining.

How might these dynamics have worked in Boston? As in London, magistrates desired cheap, speedy, and reliable convictions. In both England and America, criminal suspects wished to avoid pretrial detention and obtain the more lenient

---

prevalence of guilty pleas in lower-tier criminal courts, noting that "the classic process of plea bargaining does not take place very frequently" in such venues (Feeley 1979, p. 463; see generally Feeley 1992).

[13]Ferdinand's (1992) evidence from the middle-tier municipal court similarly reveals that very few persons accused of larceny "switched" their pleas from not guilty to guilty, and accused larcenists who pleaded guilty appear to have been awarded "no reduction" for entering such a plea (p. 77).

[14]In 1840, for example, the police court disposed of 325 cases of larceny (Ferdinand 1992, p. 62, table 2.4), whereas the municipal court disposed of 177 cases of minor property crime (Ferdinand 1992, p. 76, table 3.4).

sentences typically dispensed by magistrates sitting in the lower-tier courts.[15] And while persons in Massachusetts lacked the right to a jury trial in summary proceedings before lower-tier magistrates, they did traditionally possess the right to appeal their convictions to a middle-tier tribunal in which the right to trial by jury obtained (Frankfurter & Corcoran 1926, p. 941). Although Fisher's evidence suggests that defendants rarely appealed their convictions from lower-tier courts (Fisher 2000, p. 41), the right to appeal may still have provided people who appeared before magistrates with a bargaining chip by which to secure a comparatively lenient sentence. In short, rather than viewing the process of jury avoidance as the exclusive domain of plea bargaining and a product of the internal dynamics of one level of court, scholars may benefit from considering the varied forms of jury avoidance and the complex interactions between different levels of courts within a single jurisdiction (Smith 2005a,b).

COMPARATIVE PERSPECTIVES

In the remaining portion of this review, I briefly explore three questions that relate not only to the emergence and expansion of plea bargaining, but also to the eclipse of trial by jury more generally: First, can the recent studies of plea bargaining in Boston be generalized across other nineteenth-century American jurisdictions? Second, can studies of plea bargaining in America be generalized across national boundaries? And, finally, can theories about the decline of criminal jury trial be refined by referring to scholarship addressing an equally timely topic, the decline of civil jury trial?

The Varied Mechanisms of Jury Avoidance

Fisher (2003) contends that his "recounting of plea bargaining's rise to dominance would offer little if it explained events in one smallish northeastern state and nowhere else" (p. 16). In his view, "the lessons of Middlesex County apply generally throughout Massachusetts and, with allowances for statutory and regional variances, in several other jurisdictions as well" (p. 6). To what extent does Fisher's important account of the history of plea bargaining in nineteenth-century Massachusetts find support in the experiences of other American jurisdictions? By way of illustration, we focus on America's largest urban jurisdiction in the nineteenth century, New York City.

---

[15]In this regard, *Jones v. Robbins* (1857) is suggestive. In *Jones*, a person who had pleaded guilty in the police court to stealing a gold ring later challenged his conviction by way of a writ of habeas corpus. Sentenced by the police magistrate to six months of hard labor in the house of correction, and apparently dismayed by the harsh sentence, the defendant argued that he had been indicted for an aggravated robbery within the exclusive jurisdiction of the municipal court. The Supreme Judicial Court of Massachusetts granted the writ and discharged the prisoner.

Evidence from New York City corroborates prominent aspects of Fisher's account of the motivations of prosecutors, defendants, and judges. Thus, Ramsey, like Fisher, has drawn attention to the opportunities for plea bargaining created by New York's "statutory grading of crimes" (Ramsey 2002, p. 1333). McConville & Mirsky (1995) have suggested that the requirement in the 1830s that prosecutors submit statistical reports to the New York secretary of state heightened prosecutorial concern for securing high conviction rates—a theme also sounded by Fisher. And Fisher's intriguing hypothesis that guilty pleas were spurred by the commonwealth's decision, in 1866, to abolish the common law rule disqualifying defendants from testifying finds support in accounts of criminal practice in New York from the early twentieth century.[16] For example, in 1906, Arthur Train, an assistant district attorney in New York City, wrote that the traditional rule of testimonial disqualification permitted "the guiltiest of criminals. . ., almost with impunity, [to] shield himself behind his lawyer's eloquent assertion that his client had a 'perfect defense,' but that the law 'had sealed his lips.'" According to Train, after the legislature of New York rendered defendants competent to testify in 1868, defense lawyers concluded that "the prisoner who [did] not take the stand [was] doomed" (Train 1906, p. 163).[17]

Yet the evidence from New York also suggests the possibility of regional variations in practice, even concerning the seemingly mundane issue of where and how guilty pleas were actually secured. In alluding to the tactics of "plea getters," who visited the underground holding cells of New York's courts and "negotiate[d] with the prisoners for pleas" (Train 1906, p. 173), Train reconstructed a typical interaction as follows:

> [T]he [district attorney]. . .is usually depicted as a fierce and relentless prosecutor and the jury as a hardened, heartless crew who would convict their own mothers on the slightest pretext. The joys of Elmira as contrasted with other places of confinement are alluringly described and a somewhat paradoxical

---

[16]At common law, criminal defendants were disqualified from offering sworn testimony. Beginning in Maine in 1864, and following two years later in Massachusetts, the common law disqualification rule was rescinded in numerous American jurisdictions (Allen 1997). Fisher suggests that defendants who were rendered competent to testify likely felt increased pressure to enter into plea negotiations out of fear that their silence at trial would be perceived as a sign of wrongdoing or that their efforts to defend themselves, should they elect to take the stand, would be derailed by skilled cross-examination (Fisher 2003, pp. 104–10).

[17]As Train observed, "a rule originally intended to benefit the innocent defendant by *permitting* him to offer his explanation of the charge against him. . .practically resulted in *compelling* all defendants, guilty or innocent alike, to testify" (Train 1906, p. 163, emphasis in original). Of course, we need not accept at face value Train's conclusion that all defendants were harmed by being made eligible to testify. Certain contemporary commentators associated the abolition of the common law disqualification rules with a rise in the frequency of perjury (Fisher 1997, Schneider 2003). As one American observer declaimed in the early 1880s, "[e]xperience has, beyond all question, proved [the defendant's option to testify under oath] to be the most powerful and the most fruitful incentive to perjury ever devised by the legislator" (Fisher 1997).

readiness to accept any sort of plea, in view of his bull-dog character, is attributed to the [district attorney].[18]

Reflecting on this combination of inducement and threat, Train observed that he was familiar with an "entire population of a prison pen pleading guilty one after another under [such]. . .persuasion" (Train 1906, pp. 73–74).

In New York City, however, summary proceedings before nonjury tribunals diverted far more cases from juries than did the collective efforts of plea getters. Under legislation dating from the 1730s and 1740s, courts of special sessions in New York possessed broad authority to resolve petty larcenies and minor misdemeanors in instances when suspects failed to post bail to appear at a higher court (Frankfurter & Corcoran 1926, Moglen 1994). In the first decade of the 1800s, well before systematic plea bargaining emerged in New York City, criminal justice administrators in New York continued to look to summary proceedings as a means of avoiding, in the words of the English police magistrate Patrick Colquhoun, the "tedious and circuitous process of indictment and trial by jury" (Knapp 1834, p. 194).[19] In the late 1820s, the New York City Common Council successfully received the blessing of retired Chancellor James Kent concerning the constitutionality of the city's Court of Special Sessions, whose failure to meet had resulted in increased work for grand and petty jurors.[20] And by the early years of the twentieth century, Train himself boasted that New York City's misdemeanor court, the successor to the city's Court of Special Sessions, operated as "[o]ne of the most efficient, effective, and important criminal courts in the civilized world," a "huge mill of justice" that decided roughly 10,000 cases per year without juries (Train 1906, p. 62).

If high-volume summary proceedings were an important means by which cases bypassed jury trials in urban jurisdictions such as New York, the distinctly American practice of bench trial, by which defendants charged with felonies could elect to be tried by a judge rather than by a jury (Doran & Jackson 1997, Kalven &

---

[18]The Elmira Reformatory, established in 1876, provided vocational training, rewards for good behavior, and indeterminate sentences—a regime apparently considered less severe than that in place at the state's prisons at Auburn and Sing Sing.

[19]Colquhoun expressed this characterization of criminal jury trial in a letter to Thomas Eddy, a prominent Quaker reformer and inspector of the New York State Prison (Knapp 1834).

[20]It is worth noting that the inconvenience of trial by jury did not merely affect prosecutors, defendants, and judges. Despite de Tocqueville's optimistic observation in *Democracy in America* that jury service was "a burden easy to bear and submitted to without difficulty" [de Tocqueville 1988 (1840), p. 729], evidence from New York suggests otherwise. By the 1840s, New York recognized the following occupational exemptions to trial by jury: "ministers, doctors, firemen, members of uniform companies or paupers; persons in the actual employment of any glass, cotton, linen, woolen or iron manufacturing company. . .; superintendents, engineers, or collectors of any canal. . .and teachers in colleges" [cited in Smith (1996), p. 394; spelling modernized].

Zeisel 1966, Towne 1982), also contributed to the eclipse of trial by jury.[21] In the last quarter of the nineteenth century, for reasons that still remain obscure, several states adopted measures permitting bench trial in cases of serious crime (Towne 1982). Such proceedings now account for roughly 3% of felony convictions in state courts—a modest percentage, to be sure, but one that is higher than the percentage of such convictions meted out by juries (US Dep. Justice 2004).

The Myth of American Exceptionalism

Virtually all scholars who have discussed the historical development of plea bargaining in the nineteenth century have viewed the practice as a predominately American phenomenon (see, e.g., Fisher 2003, Langbein 1979, McConville 2002). According to the received understanding, because England traditionally relied on private prosecutors to initiate and manage prosecutions for felony and did not establish a director of public prosecutions until the 1870s, its system of prosecution for serious crime lacked, for most of the nineteenth century, a necessary institutional actor interested in brokering and accepting pleas.

It is worth noting that recent scholarship on English criminal justice administration has suggested that the long-standing dichotomy between American "public" prosecution and English "private" prosecution may benefit from substantial re-thinking (Smith 2005c). At any rate, research by Randall McGowen has revealed that the Bank of England, after 1801, frequently pursued two-count indictments that charged suspected forgers with the capital offense of forging and the non-capital offense of possessing forged notes. The bank could then employ these two-count indictments to engage in charge bargaining with defendants, offering to drop the capital offense in exchange for the defendant's entry of a guilty plea to the noncapital charge. By so doing, the bank spared itself from both acquittals (which were felt to weaken the bank's ability to deter potential forgers) and capital convictions (which risked exciting criticism from people opposed to the death penalty for nonviolent, monetary offenses) (McGowen 2003).

At the other end of the spectrum, we have already considered how magistrates in London's lower-tier police courts routinely resorted to summary proceedings in theft-related cases that, in theory, were triable as felonies. In a submission to a parliamentary subcommittee in 1837, the London police magistrate James Traill observed that "it [was] well known that magistrates [were] in the practice of applying their summary jurisdiction even beyond the spirit, certainly beyond the words, of the law...assuming to themselves the power of adjudicating in cases of actual felony, by treating them as misdemeanors..." (Smith 2005a,b). As suggested

---

[21] Although certain English criminal defendants accused of minor property-related offenses have, since the 1840s and 1850s, been allowed to choose whether to be tried by a jury or a magistrate, England has traditionally not allowed defendants to waive trial by jury and elect bench trial in more serious felony cases (Doran & Jackson 1997, Jackson 2002).

previously, summary proceedings arguably furnished their participants with the same benefits of American-style plea bargaining: Prosecutors (often the arresting officers) and magistrates secured speedy, cheap, and reasonably certain convictions; defendants, although not always by choice, received penalties less severe than those typically meted out in the higher courts.

Writing of eighteenth-century English felony trials, Langbein has observed that "[i]t should surprise no one that in a system of trial as rough and rapid as this there was no particular pressure to develop nontrial procedure, or otherwise to encourage the accused to waive the right to jury trial" (Langbein 1979, p. 264). Although English prosecutors appear to have engaged in explicit plea bargaining only rarely (for example, in cases of forgery), trials for felony remained sufficiently vexing, costly, and uncertain to encourage magistrates to bypass trial by jury. Thus, although certain English practitioners and commentators expressed shock in the 1970s upon discovering the existence of plea bargaining in the Crown Court (Baldwin & McConville 1977, 1979a,b), efforts to bypass trial by jury, in fact, had characterized English criminal justice administration for nearly 200 years.

The Vanishing Civil Jury

In recent years, considerable attention has been focused on the phenomenon of the vanishing civil jury. In 2004, under the auspices of the American Bar Association Section of Litigation's vanishing trial project, the *Journal of Empirical Legal Studies* published a series of important papers on the decline of civil jury trial in America (e.g., Friedman 2004, Galanter 2004, Heise 2004, Kritzer 2004). In England, scholars have likewise focused attention on recent initiatives designed to streamline the judicial management of civil cases and, in doing so, to alter the traditional responsibilities of judges and juries (Jackson 2002, Lloyd-Bostock & Thomas 2000). Although the findings of these studies lie beyond the scope of this paper, they suggest the benefit of assessing the eclipse of trial by jury across both the criminal and civil realms.

Such an invitation, indeed, is provided by Fisher himself, who, as we have noted, argues that plea bargaining ultimately appealed to American trial judges only after their dockets had become crowded by increasing numbers of tort cases (Fisher 2003). Yet although recent studies have identified the difficult legal and administrative challenges occasioned in the late nineteenth century by injury-causing industrial machines, railways, and streetcars (see, e.g., Karsten 1997, Welke 2001, Witt 2004), it remains less clear, in the words of Fisher, why judges "who faced an explosion in civil litigation. . .[chose] to acquiesce and take part in a prosecutorial initiative that served to limit only their criminal workload" (Fisher 2003, p. 123).

According to Fisher, American trial judges who possessed jurisdiction over both criminal and civil cases "had far greater power to coerce pleas on the criminal side than to induce settlements on the civil side." In criminal cases, "the judge's nearly wide-open sentencing discretion gave him the power to make good on both promise and threat, mediated only by the defendant's power to win acquittal from a jury." In civil cases, by contrast, "the judge's power to promise a palatable outcome to a party who agreed to settle extended only so far as his ability to persuade the opposing party to go along." Hence, although judges in Massachusetts could threaten to reduce the jury verdicts of victorious plaintiffs by invoking the doctrine of remittitur, judges lacked the power to increase jury verdicts under the doctrine of additur (Fisher 2003, pp. 123–24).

Caution is warranted, however, before concluding that trial judges lacked the authority to control their civil dockets effectively. For example, while Fisher's evidence reveals that civil settlements were growing in the postbellum period, "from 15.7% of cases in 1865 to 28.4% in 1895 to 41.9% in 1905," he concedes that "no study...[has] attempt[ed] to discern the judge's role in this increase" (Fisher 2003, p. 124). And while several traditional bars to tort recovery had been substantially weakened in America by the latter decades of the nineteenth century (see, e.g., Karsten 1997), trial judges likely continued to possess the ability to encourage settlements by threatening to rule on dispositive motions or by otherwise adjusting the parties' expectations through formal rulings or informal commentary. If American trial judges did look primarily to plea bargains (rather than civil settlements) as a means of denying certain parties their right to trial by jury, their decisions to do so may have had as much to do with their relative attitudes toward criminal defendants and injured victims as with their relative abilities to manage their criminal and civil dockets.

CONCLUSION

Our leading scholars of plea bargaining in America and England have observed that the dominance of plea bargaining in the modern age has lent an air of inevitability to the practice (Alschuler 1983, McConville 2002). Recent developments on both sides of the Atlantic offer little reason to challenge their somber view: Prosecutors in some American states now engage in habeas bargaining, by which defendants who plead guilty waive their right to collaterally attack their convictions (Malani 2004); functional analogs to plea bargaining have developed in civil law countries such as Italy, Argentina, and Germany (Langer 2004), where, at least in theory, "all offenses of some gravity [traditionally had to] be processed at trial" (Damaška 1986, p. 193); and even the International Court of Justice has turned to plea bargaining in cases of alleged genocide, although to considerable popular outcry (Combs 2002). In the words of one prominent American commentator, "[s]entencing discounts will exist for the foreseeable future, so we might as well make our lemons into lemonade" (Bibas 2003, p. 1428).

More surprising, however, is the tone of determinism in our recent histories of plea bargaining's rise. Fisher (2003), for example, concludes that "plea bargaining possessed a power of its own," implies that institutions antagonistic to plea bargaining could not survive, and refers to the seeming inevitability of the practice. But the variety of modes by which Anglo-American criminal justice administrators sought to bypass trial by jury suggests that plea bargaining's nineteenth-century history was more contingent than Fisher's assessment suggests. Indeed, the range of nonjury modes employed over the course of the nineteenth century—including summary proceedings before single magistrates, courts of special sessions, and bench trials—continues to provide possible models for those commentators who have called for alternatives to plea bargaining that are more transparent and more just (e.g., Alschuler 1983; Schulhofer 1988, 1992).

On a concluding note, a flurry of cases decided by the U.S. Supreme Court in the past few years demonstrates that the constitutional right to trial by jury continues to flicker. In a quartet of important cases—*Apprendi v. New Jersey* (2000), *Ring v. Arizona* (2002), *Blakely v. Washington* (2004), and *U.S. v. Booker* (2005)—the Court has held that juries, not judges, must resolve certain sentencing-related facts, including those that increase a criminal penalty beyond its statutory maximum (*Apprendi*), those that constitute aggravating factors for purposes of imposing the death penalty (*Ring*), and those that support sentences in excess of the relevant ranges imposed by state (*Blakely*) and federal (*Booker*) sentencing guidelines.

In the *Booker* decision, issued in January 2005, Justice Stevens observed that the Court's decisions were "not the product of recent innovations in our jurisprudence, but rather have their genesis in the ideals our constitutional tradition assimilated from the common law" (*Booker*, 125 S.Ct. at 753). No doubt there will be those who argue that the Court's recent decisions, by strengthening the hands of criminal defendants, will induce prosecutors to offer even more deals. Only time will tell. At the very least, the Court's decisions remind us that, although our constitutional right to trial by jury has been obscured, it has not yet been completely eclipsed.

ACKNOWLEDGMENTS

In preparing this article, I benefited from conversations with Howie Erlanger, Margareth Etienne, John Langbein, Richard McAdams, Elizabeth Robischon, and Mary Vogel. I am also grateful to Randy McGowen and Mary Vogel for sharing with me their unpublished work.

The *Annual Review of Law and Social Science* is online at
http://lawsocsci.annualreviews.org

LITERATURE CITED

Admin. Off. US Courts. 2004. *Statistical tables for the federal judiciary, June 30, 2004.* http://www.uscourts.gov/judiciary2004/jun contents.html

Allen CJW. 1997. *The Law of Evidence in Victorian England.* Cambridge, UK: Cambridge Univ. Press

Alschuler AW. 1968. The prosecutor's role in plea bargaining. *Univ. Chicago Law Rev.* 36:50–112

Alschuler AW. 1975. The defense attorney's role in plea bargaining. *Yale Law J.* 84:1179–314

Alschuler AW. 1976. The trial judge's role in plea bargaining, Part I. *Columbia Law Rev.* 76:1059–154

Alschuler AW. 1979. Plea bargaining and its history. *Law Soc. Rev.* 13:211–45

Alschuler AW. 1983. Implementing the criminal defendant's right to trial: alternatives to the plea bargaining system. *Univ. Chicago Law Rev.* 50:931–1050

Alschuler AW. 2003. Straining at gnats and swallowing camels: the selective morality of Professor Bibas. *Cornell Law Rev.* 88:1412–24

Alschuler AW, Deiss AG. 1994. A brief history of the criminal jury in the United States. *Univ. Chicago Law Rev.* 61:867–928

Amar AR. 1997. *The Constitution and Criminal Procedure: First Principles.* New Haven, CT: Yale Univ. Press

Apprendi v. New Jersey, 530 U.S. 466 (2000)

Baldwin J, McConville M. 1977. *Negotiated Justice.* London: Martin Robertson

Baldwin J, McConville M. 1979a. Plea bargaining and plea negotiation in England. *Law Soc. Rev.* 13:287–307

Baldwin J, McConville M. 1979b. Plea bargaining and the research dilemma. *Law Policy Q.* 1:223–33

Beattie JM. 1986. *Crime and the Courts in England, 1660–1800.* Princeton, NJ: Princeton Univ. Press

Bibas S. 2003. Bringing moral values into a flawed plea-bargaining system. *Cornell Law Rev.* 88:1425–32

Bibas S. 2004. Plea bargaining outside the shadow of trial. *Harvard Law Rev.* 117:2463–547

Blakely v. Washington. 542 U.S. __, 124 S.Ct. 2531 (2004)

Clevel. Surv. Crim. Justice. 1922. *Criminal Justice in Cleveland.* Cleveland, OH: Clevel. Found.

Combs NA. 2002. Copping a plea to genocide: the plea bargaining of international crimes. *Univ. Penn. Law Rev.* 151:1–157

Cooter R, Ulen T. 2004. *Law & Economics.* Boston: Pearson Addison Wesley. 4th ed.

Damaška MR. 1986. *The Faces of Justice and State Authority: A Comparative Approach to the Legal Process.* New Haven, CT: Yale Univ. Press

de Tocqueville A. 1988 (1840). *Democracy in America.* Transl. G Lawrence, 1969. New York: Perennial Library

Doran S, Jackson J. 1997. The case for jury waiver. *Crim. Law Rev.* 1997:155–72

Easterbrook FH. 1983. Criminal procedure as a market system. *J. Leg. Stud.* 12:289–332

Feeley MM. 1979. Pleading guilty in lower courts. *Law Soc. Rev.* 13:461–66

Feeley MM. 1992. *The Process Is the Punishment: Handling Cases in a Lower Criminal Court.* New York: Russell Sage Found.

Feeley MM. 1997. Legal complexity and the transformation of the criminal process: the origins of plea bargaining. *Israel Law Rev.* 31:183–222

Feeley MM, Lester C. 1994. Legal complexity and the transformation of the criminal process. In *Subjektivierung des justiziellen Beweisverfahrens,* ed. A Gouron, L Mayali, AP Schioppa, D Simon, pp. 337–75. Frankfurt am Main, Germany: Vittorio Klostermann

Ferdinand T. 1992. *Boston's Lower Criminal Courts, 1814–1850.* Newark: Univ. Delaware Press

Fisher G. 1997. The jury's rise as lie detector. *Yale Law J.* 107:575–713

Fisher G. 2000. Plea bargaining's triumph. *Yale Law J.* 109:857–1096

Fisher G. 2003. *Plea Bargaining's Triumph: A History of Plea Bargaining in America.* Stanford, CA: Stanford Univ. Press

Frankfurter F, Corcoran TG. 1926. Petty federal offenses and the constitutional guaranty of trial by jury. *Harvard Law Rev.* 39:917–1019

Friedman LM. 1979. Plea bargaining in historical perspective. *Law Soc. Rev.* 13:247–59

Friedman LM. 2004. The day before trials vanished. *J. Empir. Leg. Stud.* 1:689–703

Friedman LM, Percival R. 1981. *The Roots of Justice: Crime and Punishment in Alameda County, California, 1870–1910.* Chapel Hill: Univ. N. C. Press

Galanter M. 2004. The vanishing trial: an examination of trials and related matters in federal and state courts. *J. Empir. Leg. Stud.* 1:459–570

Heise M. 2004. Criminal case complexity: an

empirical perspective. *J. Empir. Leg. Stud.* 1:331–69

Heumann M. 1978. *Plea Bargaining: The Experiences of Prosecutors, Judges, and Defense Attorneys.* Chicago: Univ. Chicago Press

Illinois Assoc. Crim. Justice. 1929. *The Illinois Crime Survey.* Chicago: Blakely Printing

Jackson J. 2002. The adversary trial and trial by judge alone. In *The Handbook of the Criminal Justice Process,* ed. M McConville, G Wilson, pp. 335–51. Oxford: Oxford Univ. Press

Jones v. Robbins, 74 Mass. 329 (1857)

Kalven H, Zeisel H. 1966. *The American Jury.* Boston: Little, Brown

Karsten P. 1997. *Heart Versus Head: Judge-Made Law in Nineteenth-Century America.* Chapel Hill: Univ. N. C. Press

Knapp SL. 1834. *The Life of Thomas Eddy.* New York: Conner & Cooke

Kritzer H. 2004. Disappearing trials? A comparative perspective. *J. Empir. Leg. Stud.* 1:735–54

Langbein JH. 1978. Torture and plea bargaining. *Univ. Chicago Law Rev.* 46:3–22

Langbein JH. 1979. Understanding the short history of plea bargaining. *Law Soc. Rev.* 13:261–72

Langbein JH. 1992. On the myth of written constitutions: the disappearance of criminal jury trial. *Harvard J. Law Public Policy* 15:119–27

Langbein JH. 2003. *The Origins of Adversary Criminal Trial.* Oxford: Oxford Univ. Press

Langer M. 2004. From legal transplants to legal translations: the globalization of plea bargaining and the Americanization thesis in criminal procedure. *Harvard Int. Law J.* 45:1–64

Lloyd-Bostock S, Thomas C. 2000. The continuing decline of the English jury. In *World Jury Systems,* ed. N Vidmar, pp. 53–92. Oxford: Oxford Univ. Press

Malani A. 2004. *Habeas bargaining.* Work. Pap., John M. Olin Prog. Law Econ., Univ. Va. Law School

McConville M. 2002. Plea bargaining. In *The Handbook of the Criminal Justice Process,* ed. M McConville, G Wilson, pp. 352–77. Oxford: Oxford Univ. Press

McConville M, Mirsky CL. 1995. The rise of guilty pleas: New York, 1800–1865. *J. Law Soc.* 22:443–74

McConville M, Mirsky CL. 2005 *Jury Trials and Plea Bargaining: A True History.* Oxford: Hart

McGowen R. 2003. *The Bank of England and the death penalty, 1979–1821.* Presented at Annu. Meet. Pac. Coast Conf. Brit. Stud., 31st, Berkeley, CA

Miller J. 1927. The compromise of criminal cases. *South. Calif. Law Rev.* 1:1–31

Missouri Assoc. Crim. Justice. 1926. *The Missouri Crime Survey.* New York: Macmillan

Moglen E. 1994. Taking the fifth: reconsidering the origins of the constitutional privilege against self-incrimination. *Mich. Law Rev.* 92:1086–130

Moley R. 1928. The vanishing jury. *South. Calif. Law Rev.* 2:97–127

Moley R. 1929. *Politics and Criminal Prosecution.* New York: Minton, Balch

New York Crime Comm. 1974 (1928). *Report of the Crime Commission, 1928, State of New York.* New York: Arno

Ramsey CB. 2002. The discretionary power of "public" prosecutors in historical perspective. *Am. Crim. Law Rev.* 39:1309–93

Ring v. Arizona, 536 U.S. 584 (2002)

Schneider WJ. 2003. Perjurious albion: perjury prosecutions and the English trial. In *Law and History: Current Legal Issues 2003,* ed. A Lewis, M Lobban, pp. 343–74. Oxford: Oxford Univ. Press

Schulhofer SJ. 1988. Is plea bargaining inevitable? *Harvard Law Rev.* 97:1037–107

Schulhofer SJ. 1992. Plea bargaining as disaster. *Yale Law J.* 101:1979–2009

Scott RE, Stuntz WJ. 1992. Plea bargaining as contract. *Yale Law J.* 101:1909–68

Smith BP. 1996. *Circumventing the jury: petty crime and summary jurisdiction in London and New York City, 1790–1855.* PhD thesis. Yale Univ.

Smith BP. 2005a. Did the presumption of

innocence exist in summary proceedings? *Law Hist. Rev.* 23:191–99

Smith BP. 2005b. *Summary proceedings and the myth of private prosecution in England, 1790–1850.* Work. Pap., Univ. Ill. Coll. Law

Smith BP. 2005c. The presumption of guilt and the English law of theft. *Law Hist. Rev.* 23:133–71

Steinberg A. 1989. *The Transformation of Criminal Justice: Philadelphia 1800–1880.* Chapel Hill: Univ. N. C. Press

Towne SC. 1982. The historical origins of bench trial for serious crime. *Am. J. Leg. Hist.* 26:123–59

Train A. 1906. *The Prisoner at the Bar: Sidelights on the Administration of Criminal Justice.* New York: Scribner's

U.S. v. Booker, 543 U.S. __, 125 S. Ct. 738 (2005)

US Dep. Justice, Bur. Justice Stat. 2004. *Felony sentences in state courts, 2002.* http://www.ojp.usdoj.gov/bjs/abstract/fssc02.html

Vogel ME. 1999. The social origins of plea bargaining: conflict and the law in the process of state formation, 1830–1860. *Law Soc. Rev.* 33:161–246

Vogel ME. 2005. *Coercion to Compromise: Plea Bargaining, the Courts and the Making of Political Authority, 1830–1920.* New York: Oxford Univ. Press. In press

Wanner N. 2005. *The sun-eating dragon and other ways to think about an eclipse.* http://www.exploratorium.edu/eclipse/dragon.html

Welke BY. 2001. *Recasting American Liberty: Gender, Race, Law, and the Railroad Revolution, 1865–1920.* Cambridge, UK: Cambridge Univ. Press

Witt JF. 2004. *The Accidental Republic: Crippled Workingmen, Destitute Widows, and the Remaking of American Law.* Cambridge, MA: Harvard Univ. Press

Annu. Rev. Law Soc. Sci. 2005. 1:151–70
doi: 10.1146/annurev.lawsocsci.1.051804.082336
Copyright © 2005 by Annual Reviews. All rights reserved
First published online as a Review in Advance on June 30, 2005

THE DEATH PENALTY MEETS SOCIAL SCIENCE:
Deterrence and Jury Behavior Under New Scrutiny

Robert Weisberg

Stanford University, School of Law, Stanford, California 94305;
email: weisberg@stanford.edu

Key Words   capital punishment, econometrics, sentencing, life imprisonment, juries, discrimination

■ **Abstract**   Social science has long played a role in examining the efficacy and fairness of the death penalty. Empirical studies of the deterrent effect of capital punishment were cited by the Supreme Court in its landmark cases in the 1970s; most notable was the 1975 Isaac Ehrlich study, which used multivariate regression analysis and purported to show a significant marginal deterrent effect over life imprisonment, but which was soon roundly criticized for methodological flaws. Decades later, new econometric studies have emerged, using panel data techniques, that report striking findings of marginal deterrence, even up to 18 lives saved per execution. Yet the cycle of debate continues, as these new studies face criticism for omitting key potential variables and for the potential distorting effect of one anomalously high-executing state (Texas). Meanwhile, other empiricists, relying mainly on survey questionnaires, have taken a fresh look at the human dynamics of death penalty trials, especially the attitudes and personal background factors that influence capital jurors.

INTRODUCTION

The endlessly recycling debates in the United States over whether we should have capital punishment tend to mix two entirely different types of discourse: a retributivist discourse about whether certain criminals morally deserve the death penalty, and a utilitarian discourse about whether the death penalty serves to reduce murder and, occasionally, about whether it has been imposed fairly. On the latter score, social science research has played a persistent, if fitful, role in influencing jurists and occasionally legislators and even the lay public. This review focuses almost entirely on the most visible category of social science research and the death penalty—the question of deterrence. In the final section, I briefly allude to other areas of capital punishment policy and law where social science research has played a role, such as racial issues and jury behavior.

Perhaps no question relevant to law and social science has been so salient in American public opinion in the last few decades, and yet has so vexed social scientists, as, "Does the death penalty deter murder?"

The general hypothesis of the deterrent justification for capital punishment is straightforward: Although many potential murderers may not rationally reflect on the consequences of their actions, a considerable number do weigh negative consequences, consciously or instinctively. Indeed, one reason why homicide detectives sometimes have to struggle to find the right suspect is that many murderers go to great lengths to conceal their acts or escape detection. Conversely, some scholars argue that it is common sense to expect the death penalty to *increase* murders. Such an increase might occur because (*a*) there are suicidal killers out there who will only murder if they think they can then achieve the ultimate penalty, or (*b*) there is a brutalization effect—i.e., executions or the willingness to execute lead some potential killers to act out their intents, either inspired by the role model of the state or because in some way the state's willingness to execute cheapens the value of life (Bowers & Pierce 1980). But data supporting any positive correlation between the death penalty and murders are weak. Moreover, for those who doubt the deterrent effect of the death penalty, it may be self-contradictory to claim that criminals are too impulsive to contemplate the negative consequences of their actions but are still sufficiently sensitive to public signals that they are sometimes motivated to kill by social signals modeling killing.

What about direct evidence of deterrence? Certain seemingly direct measures of the deterrent effect of the death penalty are available. For example, once facing prosecution, almost all criminals seek to avoid punishment, and only in about 1% of cases does a capital defendant actually request the death penalty or waive rights of appeal. And then there is the anecdotal evidence, as in the case of one murderer who said he robbed and killed drug dealers in Washington, DC, where he was conscious that there was no death penalty, but specifically chose not to do so in Virginia because he was frightened by memories of Virginia prisoners in the electric chair (Blecker 2005). But such seemingly direct measures are too unsystematic to play an important role in social science research on the death penalty. Thus, the focus of this review is, of course, on more systematic statistical research.

But before examining the undulating history of research on this question, some key qualifications are in order. First, other things being equal, the presence or enforcement of the death penalty obviously will produce fewer homicides than not punishing homicides at all. Thus, the question is one of *marginal* deterrence—i.e., whether the death penalty deters more homicides than the next most severe penalty, which in all jurisdictions is some form of life imprisonment, and in most is the relatively new sentence of life without the possibility of parole. So it is solely for convenience that throughout this review deterrence stands for marginal deterrence.

Second, deterrence is only one way that the death penalty could reduce murders. Another utilitarian justification for punishment is incapacitation, and one might posit that the death penalty reduces the number of murders not by virtue of sending a deterrent message to other potential murderers but simply by preventing the condemned killer from ever killing again. Of course, that issue only arises if, assuming the alternative punishment is always a true life sentence, a convicted murder were able to kill in prison (or perhaps order a killing on the outside). The magnitude of these possibilities lies outside the scope of this review.

Third, the term murder may signify to the lay public any illegal or intentional killing. But of course murder is a complex legal concept covering a number of forms of homicide. Thus, as noted below, statistical analysis of the deterrent effect of capital punishment is somewhat contingent on the question of what type of homicide might be deterred. Most crime data indexes count all homicides explicitly labeled as murder under state law, plus a category called "non-negligent manslaughter" (FBI 2003). In this review, murder is the necessarily imprecise term generally used for the types of homicides covered by the research discussed here.

Fourth, whatever measures of statistical significance one uses, social scientists face a couple of blunt facts about death penalty and deterrence. First, the percentage of people sentenced to death in the United States who actually are executed is minute, so if research is concerned with the actual or perceived likelihood of a death-sentenced murderer suffering the ultimate penalty, the data will always seem insufficient. Second, as discussed below, the executions that do occur are disproportionately centered in a few states—indeed, close to a majority in a single state—so the various effects of skewing hamper sound empirical inference-drawing.

EARLY RESEARCH: THE SELLIN/ERHLICH STANDOFF

Although the issue of the deterrent effect of the death penalty has a long legacy in criminology generally, it began to play a major role in American legal doctrine most notably in *Furman v. Georgia* (1972) and *Gregg v. Georgia* (1976). In *Furman*, the Supreme Court declared all then-operational death penalty laws of the United States unconstitutional. In *Gregg*, it upheld against Eighth Amendment challenges the new type of guided discretion laws that are now used in three fourths of the states and in the federal system. In the years following *Gregg*, important social science evidence of a deterrent effect to which *Gregg* alluded met widespread skepticism and arguably utter refutation in later social science research. And now, 30 years after the restoration of the death penalty in the United States, the state of the research has become roiled again with new claims of proof of that deterrent effect.

Generally, what research existed before 1972 did little to establish any deterrent effect. Most of the early work was done by criminologists or psychologists whose empirical work relied mainly either on comparisons of homicide rates in states with and without capital punishment, or, within a particular jurisdiction, on comparisons of homicide rates before and after executions. But because this research did not employ the statistical technique of multiple regression, it could not meaningfully distinguish the effect of capital punishment on murder from the effects of other factors. One of the oldest studies (Dann 1935) looked at homicides within 60 days of an execution. Two decades later, another study (Savitz 1958) examined murders eight weeks before and after trials ending in death sentences. Working with sparse data, these studies found no deterrent effect. Another 1950s study (Schuessler 1952) compared murder rate changes between states that maintained capital punishment and those that never had capital punishment in the year under study and also measured before-and-after murder rates in states that switched in one direction or another. This study concluded that non–death penalty states have murder rates equal to or lower than those of death penalty states. In a key example, the study noted that South Dakota went from a non–death penalty to a death penalty regime in 1939 and saw in the next decade a modest drop in its murder rate of 16%, but that North Dakota, which was a non–death penalty state before and after 1939, enjoyed a drop of 40% for that same decade. This study also attempted to analyze the effects of actual executions and found no evidence of a deterrent effect.

The most notable figure in this early phase of deterrence research was Thorsten Sellin. Sellin, examining the period from 1920 to 1955, found that states retaining the death penalty exhibited murder rates at least as high as those that had abolished it (Sellin 1959). He also did a rough comparison of contiguous jurisdictions and found that on the whole they exhibited similar murder rates and homicide rate trends even where they differed on capital punishment.

However, Sellin could not explain a few contiguous pairs with dramatic differences—especially Ohio/Michigan and Colorado/Kansas—perhaps because he did not address the possibility that some paired states differ significantly along social, economic, or political dimensions that affect murder rates. Sellin also looked at murder rates in a number of states over time as a way to finesse the initial condition problem. That is, he examined murder rates in particular states when they changed from having the death penalty to abolishing it or from not having it to reinstituting it. And, once again, he found no evidence of deterrence. Sellin acknowledged the problem of recursive effect—the possibility that states abolish capital punishment when and because the murder rate is falling, thus raising a problem of reverse causality—and he performed some tests that yielded results inconsistent with this hypothesis. Finally, Sellin studied killings by life prisoners and discerned that a majority of the small number of prison killers were in death penalty states.

The pivotal moment in the history of death penalty deterrence research came in the mid-1970s with the work of University of Chicago economist Isaac Ehrlich. Indeed, the death penalty deterrence debate might be said to be divisible into two eras: before Ehrlich (BE) and after Ehrlich (AE). Ehrlich was the first to study capital punishment's deterrent effect using multivariate regression analysis (Ehrlich 1975). This approach enabled Ehrlich to distinguish the effects on murder of such different factors as the racial and age composition of the population, average income, unemployment, and the execution rate.

Ehrlich's famous 1975 paper examined time series data for the period 1933–1969. He tested the effect on national murder rates of various potential deterrent variables (probabilities of arrest, conviction, and execution), demographic variables (size of population, percentage of minorities in the population, percentage of people ages 14–24 in the population), economic variables (unemployment rate, per capita permanent income, per capita government expenditures, and per capita expenditures on police), and a time variable. Ehrlich concluded that there was a statistically significant negative relationship between the murder rate and execution rate, i.e., a deterrent effect. Specifically, he estimated that each execution resulted in approximately seven or eight fewer murders. This paper was offered to the Supreme Court in draft form by the solicitor general when *Gregg* was originally litigated. It was then cited in the plurality decision in the *Gregg* decision itself, in which Justice Stewart cited it as part of a mix of studies that, he inferred, established a scholarly standoff on the question of whether the death penalty deterred murder and so justified treating the deterrence issue as essentially irrelevant to the constitutionality of capital punishment.

Ehrlich's second paper (1977) studied cross-sectional data from the 50 states from 1940 to 1950. That is, whereas the first paper tested how the total U.S. murder rate changed across time as the execution rate changed, Ehrlich now explored the relationship, during a single year, between a state's execution rate and its murder rate. Ehrlich again used multivariate regression analysis, including variables similar to those in the 1975 study (for a deterrent variable he added median time spent in prison as well as a dummy variable to distinguish executing states from nonexecuting states, and, for economic variables, median family income and percentage of families with income below half of the median income). Again, he inferred a significant deterrent effect. Ehrlich himself was publicly cautious about trumpeting his conclusions, but immediately his work received both extravagant public praise and sharp academic criticism. It rapidly entered the political sphere as citable proof that each execution could indeed save at least eight innocent lives. But in the ensuing years, many social scientists tried to replicate Ehrlich's results with differing data and methods, and most were unable to confirm Ehrlich's conclusions. Indeed, in 1978, a National Academy of Sciences scholarly panel publicly criticized Ehrlich's work (Blumstein & Cohen 1978).

Because Ehrlich's work was, or seemed, so pivotal in the history of research on the death penalty, a fuller description of the problems in his studies may be useful, and it is supplied by legal sociologist Richard Lempert (1981). As seen by Lempert, Ehrlich could be credited for deploying multivariate regression analysis to study the deterrence hypothesis, but he could be faulted for not using the technique comprehensively or well. First, as Ehrlich himself recognized, his work failed to measure the length of prison sentences in general or the probability of life sentences in particular. Hence, his work is wanting precisely on the question of marginal deterrence. As Lempert suggests, if murderers who would have been executed or sentenced to life imprisonment during periods when execution rates were high often received sentences of *less* than life when execution rates were low (perhaps reflecting generally more lenient sentences in periods of diminished fear of crime), an association between low homicide rates and high execution rates would not necessarily indicate that executions are a greater deterrent than life sentences. The association might exist because executions and life sentences, or indeed just life sentences, are greater deterrents than sentences of less than life. The marginal deterrence issue, which is whether executions are a greater deterrent than life sentences, or in today's sentencing schemes sentences of life without parole, is in these circumstances not necessarily addressed by the data.

Second, replication of Ehrlich's data shows that if we eliminate the years 1965 through 1969, the deterrent effect is statistically insignificant or even reverses itself. As Lempert (1981) explains this problem, the premise of Ehrlich's approach is not in the first instance empirical, but theoretical. It posits an economic model of why punishment deters, then uses empirical evidence to test the soundness of this deterrence theory, and then finds the theory confirmed. But the theory cannot explain why the economic model yields different results for different periods of years because this model assumes something fairly essential about human nature. The only way to accommodate the issue of time sensitivity to sustain Ehrlich's finding is to take account of other factors, such as the state of racial tension, the rate of gun ownership or use, the Vietnam War and political events of other sorts, and then to see if they explained the model's sensitivity to time period. Not only did Ehrlich not do this, but, Lempert argues, no obvious explanations for the time sensitivity come to mind.

Finally, Lempert (1981) suggests a reversal of Ehrlich's technique, treating the results as the statement of a hypothesis and then asking whether that hypothesis jibes with data from various jurisdictions. One researcher did a version of this test on several states and found no support for Ehrlich's hypothesis (Bailey 1978). Lempert himself takes the approach of borrowing from Sellin's idea that fluctuations in homicide rates over time tend to be similar in contiguous states, so that if one state executes and the other does not, the advantage of the executing state in reducing homicides should increase with each additional execution. Looking back to Sellin through the lens of Ehrlich promises better controls on other relevant variables because each state becomes its own control. Lempert tests Ehrlich's data along these lines and finds no support for the Ehrlich hypothesis (Lempert 1983).

THE STATE OF RESEARCH AFTER EHRLICH

The newness of Ehrlich's methods, coupled with his striking findings, brought great attention to his research. Justice Stewart's inference in *Gregg* of an empirical standoff on the deterrence issue, prominently citing Ehrlich for the proposition that the death penalty deters, further spurred researchers to examine the deterrent effect of executions. The papers that immediately followed Ehrlich used his data or similar data sets and the same or related statistical methods. Some of this after-Ehrlich, or AE, research found a deterrent effect of capital punishment (Cloninger 1977, Yunker 1976), but others did not (e.g., Bowers & Pierce 1980, Passel & Taylor 1977), while one study came to mixed conclusions depending on the cross-section year used (Leamer 1983).

A second generation of AE econometric studies in the late 1980s and 1990s extended Ehrlich's national time series data or used more recent cross-sectional data. As before, some papers found deterrence by using, for example, an extension of Ehrlich's national time series data covering up to 1977 (e.g., Layson 1985) or national time series data for 1966–1985 (e.g., Chressanthis 1989). Still, others found no deterrent effect by, for example, using daily data for California during 1960–1963 (e.g., Grogger 1990).

Nevertheless, most of these AE studies suffered from their dependence on either national time series or cross-section data. National time series data created a serious aggregation problem. For example, when the murder rate in a state with no executions happens to increase simultaneously with a decrease in the murder rate in a state with a number of executions, the data might mask a true deterrent effect. In contrast, cross-sectional studies, by definition, do not account for changes in criminal behavior and the operations of the criminal justice system over time, nor can they account for cultural factors that might affect the homicide rate in particular regions.

PANEL STUDIES AND THE NEW DETERRENCE CLAIMS

Recently, an impressive new generation of deterrence studies has promised to overcome these difficulties by relying on panel data—that is, data from numerous units (in terms of American criminal justice, the 50 states or all counties in the United States) for numerous time periods. These data sets allow for comparisons across jurisdictions over time; they typically include information on potentially confounding variables; they have enough observations to ensure that analyses based on them will have reasonable statistical power; and they benefit from the increased rate at which executions occurred during the 1980s and 1990s. And, most dramatically, these recent studies, using modern regression techniques, find that executions have not just a significant but a substantial deterrent effect.

For example, one new study by Hashem Dezhbakhsh, Paul H. Rubin, and Joanna Shepherd draws on 20 years of data from 3054 counties nationwide to test the effect of county differences on murder rates (Dezhbakhsh et al. 2002). The authors conclude that all types of homicide are deterred by the death penalty, and they infer from their results that each execution prevents as many as 18 murders. Another study by Shepherd (2004a) uses monthly data from all 50 states over 22 years to test the short-term effect of the death penalty, and also takes the important extra step of examining different gradations of homicide. The gradation factor is important because some might argue that, for example, so-called heat-of-passion killings are impossible to deter or that other types of killings might even be inspired by executions. The Shepherd (2004a) study finds that the combination of death sentences and executions deters all types of homicide, from impassioned intimate killings to stranger killings and robbery-motivated killings, regardless of the race or ethnicity of the killer or victim. It concludes that on the whole each death sentence deters approximately 4.5 homicides and that each execution deters approximately 3 more. Notably, another recent study by Dezhbakhsh and Shepherd focuses on the flipside of deterrence—that is, the effect on the murder rate of delays in or even moratoria on actual executions (Dezhbakhsh & Shepherd 2003). Delays between death sentence and execution, of course, depend on the vagaries of the state and federal appellate systems, and moratoria may result from judicial decisions in particular jurisdictions that suspend imposition of death sentences or on executive decisions to suspend actual executions. This study, using state-level panel data from 1960–2000, compares the murder rate for each state immediately before and after the state either suspended or reinstated capital punishment. This approach relies on the fact, or assumption, that many factors that might influence the murder rate, i.e., social or cultural factors or operational changes in criminal justice, change only slightly over a short period of time. In addition, and happily for this study, the various suspensions started and ended in different years in different states and were of widely differing durations. The study finds that 90% of states manifest higher murder rates after suspensions, whereas 70% show murder rate drops after reinstatements. More strikingly, this study concludes that every reduction in the average wait between death sentence and execution of 2.75 years deters an extra murder. The authors pronounce, "The results are boldly clear: executions deter murders and murder rates increase substantially during moratoriums. The results are consistent across before-and-after comparisons and regressions regardless of the data's aggregation level, the time period, or the specific variable to measure executions" (Dezhbakhsh & Shepherd 2003, p. 27).

Finally, recent research by a Federal Communications Commission economist, Paul Zimmerman (2004), using state-level panel data from 1978 to 1997, not only finds a deterrent effect but more boldly seeks to distinguish the effects of particular methods of execution (this last effort may be legally moot because virtually all executions now use lethal injection). Using state-level panel data from 1978 to 1997 for all 50 states (excluding Washington, DC), Zimmerman concludes not only that each execution deters an average of 14 murders but that electrocution can push the number closer to the mid-20s.

NEW DETERRENCE STUDIES USING OTHER TECHNIQUES

The new wave of research finding strong evidence of a deterrent effect is not limited to the panel data studies. For example, Cloninger & Marchesini (2001) rely on a portfolio analysis in a type of controlled experiment by examining an unofficial moratorium on executions in Texas during most of 1996. They infer that this hiatus spared few condemned prisoners but caused a significant net increase in lives lost to murder. Another cross-sectional study (Brumm & Cloninger 1996), covering 58 cities in 1985, sought to measure the influence of criminals' perceived risk of punishment. It concluded that this perceived risk, including the perceived probability of execution, is negatively and significantly correlated with the murder rate. Other studies, including a reentry to the fray by Ehrlich himself (Ehrlich & Liu 1999), use state-level and cross-section analysis to reconfirm that executions have a significant deterrent effect. And another study, by Ehrlich's coresearcher, Liu (2004), finds that legalizing the death penalty not only adds capital punishment as a deterrent but also increases the marginal productivity of other deterrence measures in reducing murder rates.

Finally, Yunker (2002) tests the deterrence hypothesis using two sets of post-moratorium data: state cross-section data from 1976 and 1997 and national time series data from 1930–1997. He finds a strong deterrent effect in the time series data, an effect that disappears when the data are limited to the 1930–1976 period. Therefore, he concludes that postmoratorium data are critical to testing the deterrence hypothesis.

Summarizing this new wave of deterrence research, both the panel-based studies and others, one prolific participant in this research confidently draws even a further conclusion:

> [T]he studies that find a deterrent effect of other criminal sanctions give additional support to the deterrent effect of the death penalty, because, if lesser sanctions deter, then we know that more severe sanctions also deter. The studies that find a deterrent effect of 1. increased police presence, or any other levels of security; 2. arrest/arrest rates; 3. criminal sentencing/incarceration terms; and 4. the presence of rules, laws and statutes all provide additional, collateral support for the deterrent effect of the death penalty (Shepherd 2004b).

THE NEW STUDIES UNDER SCRUTINY

The apparent power and unanimity of this new round of studies in proving a deterrent effect has, unsurprisingly, provoked a strong response from skeptics. Although the new round of research has not yet been subjected to the depth and breadth of peer review that ultimately undermined confidence in Ehrlich's early studies, some general points of attack and some specific criticism of certain components of the new studies have emerged.

As summarized by Jeffrey Fagan (2004), two major criticisms stand out. First, all these studies suffer too much from the statistical risk that their overall findings are driven by a few outlier jurisdictions—most notably Texas. Thus, more fine-tuned comparisons between certain states (say, Texas and California) will be needed to retest the results. Next, the studies do not take account of the most important new legal innovation that has arisen in the post-*Gregg* era—namely, the availability of life without the possibility of parole (LWOP) sentences in all death penalty states except two (New Mexico and, ironically, Texas, where a new LWOP law has just been enacted). LWOP sentences are far more numerous than death sentences these days, and beyond their obvious incapacitating effect they may well have a powerful deterrent effect as well. Indeed, LWOP may be the key deterrent even when the potential offender might also somewhat fear a death sentence. The data showing that some death row inmates waive their appeals are at least anecdotal evidence that a criminal code with a maximum sentence of LWOP alone may be more of a deterrent than a code that allows for either LWOP or the death penalty.

Other potential lines of criticism that Fagan suggests include the following:

1. These new studies tend to aggregate several forms of murder, and, as above, the one study that breaks them down purports to find all forms deterrable. This conclusion may be implausible if we believe that heat-of-passion killings are necessarily somewhat harder to deter than other murders. If so, more fine-tuned research will be needed, especially of such specific contextual factors as the availability of guns in certain domestic situations.

2. The new studies do not control for the phenomenon of autoregression, that is, the influence that trends in certain years may exert over longitudinal or time series data covering succeeding years. This problem is especially serious in the context of very rare events like executions.

3. The new studies are only sporadically successful, at best, in accounting for controls supplied by the various operations of the criminal justice system, including such essential factors as the success of police in even identifying offenders. It is a virtual cliché of criminal deterrence that the *certainty* of punishment, of any type, is a more effective deterrent than the *possibility* of severe punishment, contingent on apprehension and conviction. If the cliché is true, then initial police success in catching offenders should be a more effective deterrent than the rarer death sentences or still rarer executions. If high-executing states also have higher-than-average homicide clearance or arrest rates, this fact could explain the apparent deterrent effects. Some of the newer studies try to control for murder or homicide arrest rates (Dezhbaksh et al. 2002, Mocan & Gittings 2005). But because arrest rates are likely to be particularly high for homicides that are not death-eligible or for which the death penalty is seldom given (e.g., fights between friends, crimes of passion), the adequacy of the control is questionable unless arrest rates as well as homicide rates are broken down by the death-eligibility of the crime. Unfortunately, none of the new studies attempts that breakdown.

4. The studies ignore large amounts of missing data in important states such as Florida, thus potentially biasing their conclusions. Fagan suggests that different techniques for restoring missing data should be used to determine whether the lack of available data can explain findings of deterrence.

Finally, to those who tell a deterrence story by using new data and quantitative methods to shore up their findings, Fagan suggests that these researchers look for confirming evidence in actual mechanisms by which deterrence may operate. For example, the deterrence case could find support in evidence that violence-prone people are aware of executions and the relative likelihood of executions in their own states. Studies that use only national data improbably assume that violence-prone people are aware of execution rates in faraway states, and this assumption needs scrutiny. Similarly, researchers might offer an explanation of why executions should deter non-death-eligible homicides. Do potential offenders attend to punishments enough to know that murderers may be executed but not enough to know that only certain kinds of murders are death-eligible? Do they know that executions for murder occur but not know how rare they are in many states? Is there any evidence that murderers rationally decide to forego homicide and use less lethal forms of violence? On all these questions about deterrence, argues Fagan, empiricists should consider the contemporary social science research on the generally bounded rationality of human decision making and attempt to apply it to the even more dubiously rational thinking of violent offenders.

One new deterrence study is worth further attention because its findings have been closely examined, and its data reanalyzed, by a leading quantitative sociologist, Richard Berk. Berk's (2005) article is a sharp critique of work by H. Naci Mocan and R. Kaj Gittings (2005). Mocan & Gittings use state-level panel data from 1977 to 1997 (including information on all 6143 death sentences in this period) to examine the relationship between executions, commutations, and murder. Their study finds a significant deterrent effect, suggesting that each execution deters an average of five murders. More strikingly, it concludes that each commutation results in approximately five extra murders and that each removal from death row generates an additional murder. Finally, it infers that every set of three additional pardons (i.e., commutations of the death sentence) causes 1 to 1.5 additional murders.

Berk's (2005) sharp critique, one with implications beyond the Mocan-Gittings study that is his focus, argues that these new studies show flaws ranging from the "conceptual leap of treating observational data as an experiment to a large number of nuts-and-bolts statistical difficulties." Berk points out that in the Mocan-Gittings study, the mean for the number of executions per state per year is 0.35, implying that each state executes about one prisoner every three years, but he then notes that because the standard deviation is 1.35, skewing is a serious concern. Moreover, Berk notes that in the Mocan-Gittings study, the median is zero, with the mean dominated by a few extreme values (i.e., 29 for Texas in 1997, the last year studied). Thus, statistical leverage becomes a serious problem because extreme values of an explanatory variable are paired with extreme values of the response variable. As Berk says, "The potential impact of leverage on a model's fit becomes a reality," and the problem is especially severe when an extreme value is not just atypical, but also an outlier—that is, located a great distance from the mass of the data. (This is true with respect to the number of homicides per year, for which the mean is 420 but the standard deviation is 607.)

Further, argues Berk, after controlling for potential confounders, we can conclude that once one knows the large number of homicides in a particular state during the 20-year period, knowing the number of executions adds virtually nothing to the analysis. (This phenomenon is especially evident in situations of five executions or fewer.) As for the temporal dimension, when indicator variables for years rather than states are used to account for national trends in the number of homicides and the homicide rate, we gain no new knowledge of any deviance.

Reanalyzing the data, Berk finds that the relationship Mocan & Gittings report seems entirely dependent on the small number of states with more than five executions. If we exclude the 11 observations out of 1000 that involve more than five executions from the analysis, then we find no systematic difference in the average homicide rate between states that have had no executions and those that have had one; we find a slight negative relationship as we move from states executing one individual to states executing three; and we find a slight positive relationship as we move from states with three to those with five.

Berk acknowledges the possible counterargument that states may differ in their inclination and ability to seek the death penalty, so that controlling for state differences is misleading. If so, using just the 1977 homicide rate as a predictor could adjust for that because the factors affecting the homicide rate were hardly stationary over the following 20 years. Nevertheless, Berk concludes that using this factor as a predictor affects the outcome hardly at all. Unsurprisingly, then, if instead of using the number of executions one uses a binary indicator of zero executions versus one or more executions, evidence of a deterrence effect disappears. Equally unsurprisingly, notes Berk, little evidence of deterrence appears when Texas is removed from the analysis. Put another way, if we shuffle the number of executions for all states other than Texas randomly, so that the number is unrelated to any of the other variables for those states, and we then add Texas back into the mix, the result is an apparent deterrent effect similar to the one found in the real data. Still more skeptically, Berk suggests that using monthly time units or county area units cannot solve any of these problems because the number will be zero for the great majority of them. Finally, he questions whether the data from Texas are ample enough to prove a deterrent effect to the death penalty even there.

THE UNCERTAIN FUTURE OF DETERRENCE RESEARCH

Intuitively, the notion that the death penalty deters finds support in some very rough empiricism about recent events in the United States: Murder rates plummeted over the last decade and a half, and some might argue that a steady diet of executions must have played a role. From 1966–1980, the murder rate nearly doubled, from 5.6 to 10.2 per 100,000. During that 1966–1980 period, the United States averaged only one execution every three years, with a maximum of two executions per year, most obviously because that period covers the last national moratorium on executions (June 1967 to January 1976). Conversely, between 1995 and 2000 the national murder rate dropped 46%, from a high of 10.2 per 100,000 to 5.5 per 100,000, while executions for that period averaged 71 per year. But of course those figures, however convincing they might look to some, tell us little about the real relationship, if any, between these parallel rates. Similarly, one of the most striking correlations comes in the nation's most active death penalty jurisdiction, Harris

County (Houston) Texas, where the murder rate dropped 73% between 1982, when executions were resumed, and 2000. But that correlation may just signal that Texas is too anomalous to tell us much about the nation. More generally, while homicide rates were dropping dramatically across the nation, so were rates for other crimes not punishable by death (Levitt 2004).

Data from the multiple regression studies already mentioned are less intuitive than the simple statistics given above but are obviously potentially more meaningful. Nevertheless, some have questioned whether the modern econometric approaches, which most of the new research employ, are as powerful or sophisticated as they might appear. As one harsh critic summarized the econometric approaches, "There is simply too little data and too many ways to manipulate it" (Goertzel 2004). That is, there are too many ways to select model specifications. As a technical matter, notes another critic, to obtain a significant deterrent effect many new studies take the questionable approach of adding a set of data with no executions to a time series and including an executing/nonexecuting dummy in the cross-sectional analysis (Cameron 1994). Thus, we see that the proper specification of econometric approaches is open to controversy, and choices made by researchers, even if defensible, have an inevitable subjective element and could conceivably be more important than the data in determining a study's conclusions.

Recall Justice Stewart's remark in *Gregg* that there is an empirical standoff on the matter of the death penalty's deterrent value. That remark may thus now be true even if, when uttered, it distorted the apparent weight of the studies that had been done to that point. It is certainly difficult for the uninvolved observer to be confident of where the truth lies. The claims of the latest round of empirical research appear strong, and the work is not vulnerable to the relatively simple and convincing refutations that followed Ehrlich's initial foray into these matters. Fagan's critique and Berk's close look at the Mocan-Gittings data suggest, however, that the results of even these sophisticated studies will have to be qualified as the analyses of the capital punishment deterrence data become yet more refined. Whether the effects of further scrutiny will be to support the deterrence hypothesis, while perhaps putting it in more precise context, or will be to provide further evidence of the null hypothesis of no effect remains impossible to say. We can, however, conclude with more confidence, now that critics have begun to weigh in on the most recent research, that the relationship between executions and murders still lacks clear proof.

SOCIAL SCIENCE RESEARCH ON OTHER DEATH PENALTY ISSUES

Some of the most incisive and insightful interventions of social science into the operation of the death penalty have addressed issues other than deterrence. I briefly discuss some of these studies here.

Victim-Race Discrimination

When the Supreme Court temporarily suspended the use of the death penalty in the United States in *Furman* in 1972, a major issue was whether capital punishment was being imposed in a racially discriminatory manner. Many noted that the penalty was imposed on minorities, most notably black Americans, in numbers several times greater than their proportion in the population. But because the disproportion was similar in terms of convictions for murder, it was difficult to argue that the death penalty by itself was inflicted disproportionately on black defendants. The belief that the death penalty did indeed discriminate on the basis of the race of the defendant may have influenced the *Furman* outcome, but soon thereafter in *Gregg* the Court held that the new post-*Furman* death penalty statutes were well designed to prevent any such effects.

After the Court reimposed the death penalty in *Gregg*, the focus of the death penalty discrimination research shifted more substantially from the race of the defendant to the race of the victim. A major study, first published in 1983, by David C. Baldus, George Woodworth, and Charles Pulaski (Baldus et al. 1990) examined over 2000 murder cases that occurred in Georgia during the 1970s. It inferred that defendants charged with killing white persons received the death penalty in 11% of the cases, whereas those charged with killing blacks received the death penalty in only 1% of the cases. Ironically but significantly (given that most killings occur between members of the same race or group), the race-of-defendant numbers revealed a reverse disparity—4% of the black defendants but 7% of white defendants received the death penalty.

Baldus et al. (1990) also divided the cases according to the combination of the race of the defendant and the race of the victim. They found that capital punishment was imposed in 22% of the cases with black defendants and white victims; 8% of the cases with white defendants and white victims; 1% of the cases with black defendants and black victims; and 3% of the cases with white defendants and black victims. As for prosecutorial penalty-seeking decisions, prosecutors asked for capital punishment in 70% of the black-kills-white cases; 32% of the white-kills-white cases; 15% of the black-kills-black cases; and 19% of the white-kills-black cases.

The Baldus study initially used multiple regression techniques to control for 230 variables; its subsequent regressions included only the theoretically or sub-stantively most important explanatory variables. The study concluded that people killing white victims were more than four times as likely to receive death as those killing black victims. A parallel study using newer data and covering other states (Gross & Mauro 1989) came to very similar conclusions. No later research has seriously questioned these results.

The Baldus study was the main evidence used by the defendant in *McCleskey v. Kemp* (1987), a case of a black man charged with killing a white, to argue for a reversal of the death sentence on the basis of racial discrimination. When *McCleskey* went to the Supreme Court, many predicted that the Court would dodge the issue by finding the empirical research unconvincing or not yet sufficient.

To the surprise of many, the Court effectively mooted this line of research by its apparent willingness to concede that the Baldus study was accurate. But on McCleskey's claim that his death sentence therefore violated the equal protection clause, the Court followed established doctrine in requiring proof of intentional discrimination. And the statistical evidence in the Baldus study was not designed to show intent, and except in the case of extreme intentional discrimination in which the inference is inescapable, statistical evidence of discrimination will usually be consistent with a variety of causes. Although discriminatory intent cannot be ruled out in some death penalty cases, the discriminatory effects documented by Baldus may well have resulted from a complex mixture of half-conscious or unconscious decisions by various legal system actors, including judges, juries, and prosecutors. And as for McCleskey's alternative Eighth Amendment claim that the effects themselves rendered the death penalty unconstitutional, McCleskey lost because, paradoxically, the Court found that the implications of the Baldus study were too great for the system to bear: The Court assumed the causes of the discriminatory effect Baldus reported probably infected the entire law enforcement system, but the justices feared that if they recognized the defense in a capital case, the logic of the decision would effectively require that they put our entire criminal justice system into receivership.

Prosecution-Prone Jurors

A year before *McCleskey*, the Court heard and rejected another very dramatic social science–based claim about the death penalty in *Lockhart v. McCree* (1986). The claim specifically rested in large part on the new type of death penalty procedure legislated after *Furman* and approved by *Gregg*. As the post-*Gregg* statutes operate, a jury first determines whether the defendant is guilty of the highest degree of murder. Then, if the prosecutor seeks the death penalty, a second, separate penalty trial occurs, and in the great majority of the cases the decision maker at this second trial is the very same jury that has already convicted the defendant. This jury is always death qualified. That is, in helping choose the jury, the prosecutor can challenge for cause those jurors who state in voir dire that they categorically oppose and would refuse to impose the death penalty. The rationale for such challenges is that a juror who admits to such views implicitly admits that he or she will be unable or unwilling to obey jury instructions on the penalty decision because the instructions will require the juror to at least entertain the possibility of a death sentence.

Several decades ago, defendants began to argue that automatically excluding opponents of the death penalty denied the defendant a fair cross section of eligible jurors and also ensured that the jury would be biased in favor of the prosecution at the guilt phase. Of course, with a separate decision on penalty, rendered after the guilty verdict and following the presentation of evidence bearing solely on the penalty, the court could reconfigure the jury after the guilty verdict to exclude and replace those jurors who earlier stated their categorical refusal or inability to impose death.

The defendant in *Witherspoon v. Illinois* (1968) had made this very argument to the Supreme Court with the support of some empirical evidence. The *Witherspoon* Court, treating a pre-*Gregg* death penalty statute, acknowledged that the claim was plausible in theory, but the Court found insufficient evidence that death-qualified juries would be more prone to convict defendants than juries that had been seated without regard to whether its members supported the death penalty. But rather than shut the door on the issue, the Court seemed to invite death penalty opponents to reopen the issue if they developed more and better evidence.

When the death penalty was reinstated under new statutes that clearly separated the guilt phase of the trial from the penalty phase, death penalty opponents could again argue that there was no need for death qualification of the jury that decided guilt or innocence, and they set about making a firmer social science case for the conviction-proneness of death-qualified juries than the case they been able to present in *Witherspoon.*

Relying on a number of new empirical studies done with sophisticated survey and jury simulation techniques (e.g., Cowan et al. 1984), the defendant in *Lockhart v. McCree* made a compelling claim that jurors who would not impose the death penalty tended on more general questions of guilt or innocence to lean more heavily to the side of leniency or not-guilty verdicts. Moreover, he presented evidence that the very process of death qualification might itself incline jurors toward guilty verdicts (Haney 1984).

But despite the quality of the empirical data, the Court rejected the argument that this phenomenon violated the Sixth Amendment requirement of a fairly selected and impartial jury. The Court criticized most of the research cited by the defendant for problems peculiar to each study but never acknowledged the power of the body of the research taken as a whole nor the fact that all the research presented to it pointed in the same direction. Not only was the Court not persuaded by the claims of unfairness, but it also took the view that the only solution under the new death penalty statutes would be to convene a second, separate jury for the penalty phase, a procedure it regarded as too cumbersome to impose on the states. Since then, the prosecution-proneness argument has itself become less visible; one federal trial judge recently held that newer studies had strengthened the earlier prosecution-proneness arguments enough to warrant requiring a second, separate jury in federal death penalty cases, although this ruling was then reversed by the Court of Appeals (*U.S. v. Green* 2005).

The Vagaries of Jury Behavior

The newest category of application of social science concerns some of the subtler processes by which capital jurors decide whether a defendant shall receive a life or death verdict. This research, even more clearly than the research in *Lockhart*, is a byproduct of the particular procedures mandated by the new post-*Gregg* laws. It also results from a now-healthy amount of data available about the operation of the hundreds of capital trials we have in the United States each year. A decade of new studies, especially a remarkable set of papers done by a group at Cornell Law School (Theodore Eisenberg, Stephen Garvey, and Martin Wells), takes advantage of the opportunity to identify and interview large numbers of people who have actually served on capital juries, most notably in South Carolina, where the information has been developed by the Capital Jury Project. The Cornell researchers have constructed survey/questionnaire instruments to examine a variety of important post-*Gregg* questions, such as how well jurors follow jury instructions and what conscious and perhaps unconscious factors influence their votes in capital cases. The jurors' responses are translated into complex factor-coding, followed by advanced multiple regression analysis.

One paper (Eisenberg et al. 2001a) shows that the personal characteristics of jurors strongly influence their votes on the death penalty, with the dominant factors being race, religion, and general attitudes about the propriety of the death penalty for murder. Moreover, those factors play an especially dominant role on the first vote the jury takes, and that first vote usually determines the final one.

Another study (Eisenberg et al. 2001b) examines jurors who have indicated a willingness to impose the death penalty; it discovers that some of these jurors nevertheless harbor considerable concerns about its potential unfairness and would be prone to decline to impose the death penalty in favor of LWOP. The authors find these concerns especially evident among black jurors and Southern Baptists of both races.

An earlier study by the Cornell group (Eisenberg et al. 1996) examines whether jurors accept responsibility for their decisions. On the one hand, jurors may take the view that when they vote for a death sentence they are, in effect, merely affirming a result that naturally follows from the defendant's egregious actions. On the other hand, they may believe that their vote is just one step, and not necessarily a major step, in a complicated legal process, so that the real responsibility for any ultimate death sentence rests more with, say, a judge or appellate court that will review their vote. But the law contemplates that jurors have primary responsibility and substantial discretion to determine whether the defendant should live or die, and this study sets out to measure jurors' attitudes and understandings about their mandate. This study concludes somewhat optimistically that jurors on the whole appreciate the degree to which the criminal law actually does impose responsibility on them, although it suggests some reforms in the mechanisms by which that message is conveyed.

Still earlier research (Eisenberg & Wells 1993) examined juror understanding of the jury instructions they had received. It concludes that the jurors often do not appreciate the alternatives to a death sentence that state law provides them, and also that they do not understand the special burden-of-proof rules applied at the sentencing phase. On both these scores, this study suggests that the misunderstanding disfavors the capital defendant.

Conversely, a paper examining so-called victim-impact statements and their role in death sentencing (Eisenberg et al. 2003) offers somewhat more reassuring conclusions, at least for those who are dubious about the fairness of these statements.

Although victim-impact statements cause jurors to rate the murder victim higher on an admirability scale, the study finds little evidence that a higher rating on this scale increases the chances of a death sentence for the defendant. Rather, the possible effect of a victim-impact statement is largely mooted by the jurors' reaction to more facts about the killing itself. A parallel study by Sundby (2003), using California data, found somewhat stronger evidence that the perceived character of the victim influences the sentence. When asked fairly abstract questions, surveyed jurors tended to deny that the character of the victim would make much difference. But their descriptions of actual jury deliberations suggested an important victim-evidence effect along two specific dimensions. Jurors are significantly more inclined toward a death verdict when the victim was engaged in ordinary activity and was chosen randomly by the killer, whereas they tilted toward leniency if the victim had exhibited antisocial or deviant behavior, even if that behavior in no way mitigated the killer's culpability for the crime by providing some defense.

Even if these and similar studies do not lead to global constitutional litigation over the legitimacy of the death penalty, they offer the prospect of usefully educating judges and even legislators into ensuring that the promise of the so-called guided discretion statutes approved in *Gregg* is fulfilled.

But regarding the perceived legitimacy of capital punishment, the increasing number of DNA acquittals during the past decade may be more important than these studies. These DNA acquittals include acquittals of many prisoners on death row and prisoners serving life sentences who would have been on death row had their alleged crimes not been committed during the period of the death penalty moratorium (Scheck et al. 2000). It is the sheer number of these cases that is so striking. Although death penalty supporters may have acknowledged, in principle, that mistakes can happen in death penalty cases, the general assumption before these DNA acquittals seems to have been that the legal system took its greatest care in cases in which execution was possible, and the chance of error in capital cases was in fact minimal. We now know this is not so, and we can put faces on people who, but for the system's slowness and their own good luck, might well have been executed for murders they did not commit. This human reality may prove to be more important than masses of social science evidence on deterrence and other issues in determining support for the death penalty in the long run.

The *Annual Review of Law and Social Science* is online at
http://lawsocsci.annualreviews.org

LITERATURE CITED

Bailey W. 1978. Deterrence and the death penalty for murder in Utah: a time-series analysis. *J. Contemp. Laws* 5:1–20

Baldus D, Woodworth G, Pulaski C Jr. 1990.

Equal Justice and the Death Penalty: A Legal and Empirical Analysis. Boston: Northeast. Univ. Press

Berk R. 2005. New claims about executions and general deterrence: déjà vu all over again? *J.*

Empir. Leg. Stud. In press. http://preprints. stat.ucla.edu/396/JELS.pap.pdf

Black T, Orsagh T. 1978. New evidence of the efficacy of sanctions as a deterrent to homicide. *Soc. Sci. Q.* 58:616–31

Blecker R. 2005. *The Worst of the Worst: Who Deserves to Die?* New York: Basic Books

Blumstein A, Cohen J. 1978. *Deterrence and Incapacitation: Estimating the Effects of Criminal Sanctions on Crime Rates.* Washington, DC: Natl. Acad. Sci.

Bowers W, Pierce JL. 1980. Deterrence or brutalization: What is the effect of executions? *Crime Delinq.* 26:453–84

Brumm H, Cloninger D. 1996. Perceived risk of punishment and the commission of homicides: a covariance structural analysis. *J. Econ. Behav. Org.* 31:1–11

Cameron S. 1994. A review of the econometric evidence on the effects of capital punishment. *J. Socio-Econ.* 23:197–214

Chressanthis G. 1989. Capital punishment and the deterrent effect revisited: recent time-series econometric evidence. *J. Behav. Econ.* 18:81–97

Cloninger D. 1977. Deterrence and the death penalty: a cross sectional analysis. *J. Behav. Econ.* 6:87–107

Cloninger DO, Marchesini R. 2001. Executions and deterrence: a quasi-controlled group experiment. *Appl. Econ.* 35(5):569–76

Cowan C, Thompson W, Ellsworth P. 1984. The effects of death qualification on jurors' predisposition to convict and on the quality of deliberation. *Law Hum. Behav.* 8:53–79

Dann R. 1935. *The Deterrent Effect of Capital Punishment.* Philadelphia: Friends Soc. Serv. Ser.

Dezhbaksh H, Rubin P, Shepherd J. 2002. Does capital punishment have a deterrent effect? New evidence from post-moratorium panel data. *Am. Law Econ. Rev.* 5(2):344–76

Dezhbaksh H, Shepherd J. 2003. *The deterrent effect of capital punishment: evidence from a "judicial experiment."* Work. Pap. No. 03–14, Dep. Econ., Emory Univ. http://people. clemson.edu/~jshepe/CaPuJLE·submit.pdf

Ehrlich I. 1975. The deterrent effect of capital punishment: a question of life and death. *Am. Econ. Law Rev.* 65:347–417

Ehrlich I. 1977. Capital punishment and deterrence. Some further thoughts and additional evidence. *J. Polit. Econ.* 85:741–88

Ehrlich I, Liu Z. 1999. Sensitivity analysis of the deterrence hypothesis: let's keep the econ in econometrics. *J. Law Econ.* 41(1):455–88

Eisenberg T, Garvey S, Wells M. 1996. Jury responsibility in capital sentencing: an empirical study. *Buff. Law Rev.* 44:339–80

Eisenberg T, Garvey S, Wells M. 2001a. Forecasting life and death: juror race, religion, and attitude toward the death penalty. *J. Leg. Stud.* 30:277

Eisenberg T, Garvey S, Wells M. 2001b. The deadly paradox of capital jurors. *South. Calif. Law Rev.* 74:371–97

Eisenberg T, Garvey S, Wells M. 2003. Victim characteristics and victim impact evidence in South Carolina capital cases. *Cornell Law Rev.* 88:306–41

Eisenberg T, Wells M. 1993. Deadly confusion: juror instructions in capital cases. *Cornell Law Rev.* 79:1–11

Fagan J. 2005. *Deterrence and the death penalty: a critical review of the new evidence.* Testimony to NY State Assem. Standing Comm. on Codes, Judiciary and Correction. Jan. 21. http://www.deathpenaltyinfo.org/FaganTestimony.pdf

FBI. 2003. *Uniform crime reports.* http://www. fbi.gov/ucr/03cius.htm

Furman v. Georgia 408 U.S. 238 (1972)

Goertzel T. 2004. Capital punishment and homicide: sociological realities and econometric illusions. *Skept. Inq.* July. http://www. csicop.org/si/2004–07/capital-punishment. html

Gregg v. Georgia, 428 U.S. 153 (1976)

Grogger J. 1990. The deterrent effect of capital punishment: an analysis of daily homicide counts. *J. Am. Stat. Assoc.* 85:295–303

Gross S, Mauro R. 1989. *Death and Discrimination.* Boston: Northeast. Univ. Press

Haney C. 1984. On the selection of capital juries: the biasing effects of death qualification. *Law Hum. Behav.* 8:121–32

Layson S. 1985. Homicide and deterrence: a reexamination of the United States evidence. *South. Econ. J.* 52:68–89

Leamer E. 1983. Let's take the con out of econometrics. *Am. Econ. Rev.* 73:31–43

Lempert R. 1981. Desert and deterrence. *Mich. Law Rev.* 79:1177–225

Lempert R. 1983. The impact of executions on homicide: a new look in an old light. *Crime Delinq.* 1983:88

Levitt S. 2004. Understanding why crime fell in the 1990s: four factors that explain the decline and six that do not. *J. Econ. Perspect.* 18:163–90

Liu Z. 2004. Capital punishment and the deterrence hypothesis: some new insights and empirical evidence. *East. Econ. J.* 30(2):237–58

Lockhart v. McCree, 476 U.S. 162 (1986)

McCleskey v. Kemp, 481 U.S. 279 (1987)

Mocan N, Gittings K. 2005. Getting off death row: committed sentences and the deterrent effect of capital punishment. *J. Law Econ.* 46(2):453–78

Passel P, Taylor J. 1977. The deterrent effect of capital punishment: another view. *Am. Econ. Rev.* 67:445–51

Savitz L. 1958. A study in capital punishment. *J. Crim. Law Criminol. Police Sci.* 49:338–41

Scheck B, Neufeld P, Dwyer J. 2000. *Actual Innocence.* New York: Doubleday

Schuessler K. 1952. The deterrent effect of the death penalty. *Annals* 284:54–62

Sellin T. 1959. *The Death Penalty.* Philadelphia: Am. Law Inst.

Sharp D. 2003. *The deterrent effect of the death penalty.* http://www.prodeathpenalty.com/DeterrentEffect.html

Shepherd J. 2004a. Murder of passion, execution delays, and the deterrence of capital punishment. *J. Leg. Stud.* 33(2):283–322

Shepherd J. 2004b. Statement at the Terrorist Penalties Enhancement Act of 2003 hearing before House Judiciary Subcommittee on Crime Terrorism and Homeland Security, April 21, 108th Congr., 2nd sess. http://commdocs.house.gov/committees/judiciary/hju93224.000/hju93224‘0f.htm

Sundby S. 2003. The capital jury and empathy: the problem of worthy and unworthy victims. *Cornell Law Rev.* 88:343–81

U.S. v. Green, U.S. App. LEXIS 8236 (1st Cir. 2005)

Witherspoon v. Illinois, 391 U.S. 510 (1968)

Yunker J. 1976. Is the death penalty a deterrent to homicide? Some time-series evidence. *J. Behav. Econ.* 5(1):45–81

Yunker J. 2002. A new statistical analysis of capital punishment incorporating U.S. post-moratorium data. *Soc. Sci. Q.* 82:297–311

Zimmerman P. 2004. State execution, deterrence, and the incidence of murder. *J. Appl. Econ.* 7:163–93

Annu. Rev. Law Soc. Sci. 2005. 1:171–201
doi: 10.1146/annurev.lawsocsci.1.041604.115958
Copyright © 2005 by Annual Reviews. All rights reserved
First published online as a Review in Advance on July 1, 2005

Voice, Control, and Belonging: The Double-Edged Sword of Procedural Fairness

Robert J. MacCoun

*Goldman School of Public Policy and Boalt Hall School of Law, University of California,
Berkeley, California 94720-7320; email: maccoun@berkeley.edu*

Key Words procedural justice, fairness, psychology of law, litigation, policing,
ADR

■ **Abstract** The procedural justice literature has grown enormously since the early
work of Thibaut and Walker in the 1970s. Since then, the finding that citizens care
enormously about the process by which outcomes are reached—even unfavorable
outcomes—has been replicated a wide range of methodologies (including panel surveys, psychometric work, and experimentation), cultures (throughout North America,
Europe, and Asia), and settings (including tort litigation, policing, taxpayer compliance, support for public policies, and organizational citizenship). We have learned a
great deal about the antecedents and consequences of these judgments. In particular,
the work of Tom Tyler and Allan Lind and their colleagues suggests that people care
about voice, dignity, and respect for relational and symbolic reasons rather than (or in
addition to) instrumental reasons. This finding has benevolent implications for governance and social cooperation, but also some troubling implications, leaving people
susceptible to manipulation and exploitation.

INTRODUCTION

Like many states, in the 1980s New Jersey officials sought a way to manage an
increasingly congested and backlogged civil trial caseload. Their response was
to introduce a program of mandatory but nonbinding court-annexed arbitration,
with simple and informal hearings, for auto negligence cases worth up to $15,000.
The program was premised on a seemingly straightforward argument: Because
trials are costly and slow, diverting cases from the trial calendar will increase
court efficiency. Thus, officials were quite surprised when a quasi-experimental
evaluation revealed a significant increase in time to termination among eligible
cases and a significant increase in the number of suits actually resolved by court
hearings (MacCoun et al. 1988). How could this happen?

Like many observers, New Jersey officials assumed that litigants were motivated primarily by economic concerns—dollar outcomes and transaction costs. Of
course, litigants do care a great deal about these factors. But three decades of socio-
legal research have demonstrated that citizens also care deeply about the process

by which conflicts are resolved and decisions are made, even when outcomes are unfavorable or the process they desire is slow or costly (Thibaut & Walker 1978, Lind & Tyler 1988). Although many aspects of procedure shape this fair process effect—lack of bias, thoroughness, clarity—two particularly important dimensions are voice (the ability to tell one's story) and dignified, respectful treatment (Lind & Tyler 1988).

Interpreted in this light, the New Jersey experience is easier to understand. Surveys showed that arbitration provided litigants with the same desirable procedural dimensions they wanted from trials: the opportunity to present their case, receive a dignified and respectful hearing, and get a verdict on the merits (MacCoun et al. 1988, Lind et al. 1990b). But of course arbitration provides those procedural features more quickly and cheaply than trial. Because few cases went to trial anyway, the program had no significant effect on trial rates. But there was a significant reduction in private, bilateral settlements (from 92% to 45%); arbitration diverted many more cases from settlement than from trial. In surveys, the most popular motivation cited by litigants was to "tell my side of the story." Defendants and plaintiffs alike rated this as more important than winning their case or minimizing transaction costs (also see Lind et al. 1990, Lind 1990). Was the program a failure? From an efficiency perspective, narrowly construed, yes. But by opting for arbitration hearings, citizens were clearly "voting with their feet" in favor of procedural attributes they valued, attributes they could not get in bilateral settlement (see Lind et al. 1990).

The fair process effect was first documented empirically in an innovative program of research psychologist John Thibaut and legal scholar Laurens Walker in the late 1970s (e.g., 1975, 1978) on what they labeled "procedural justice." (In some ways, "procedural fairness" is a better label, but the distinction matters more to academic theorists than to ordinary citizens, and I will use the terms interchangeably; see Van den Bos & Lind 2002, p. 8.) The second decade of procedural justice research centered on the remarkably prolific solo and joint efforts of Tom Tyler and Allan Lind, although many others made major contributions. Although Lind and Tyler remain active, work on the topic exploded in the 1990s as researchers found applications in a remarkably wide range of literatures (law, medicine, politics, business, education, social work, sports, and so on). As of early 2005, the PsychInfo database lists almost 700 articles with the phrase "procedural justice" in the abstract (more than 40 per year since 1995 and more than 70 per year in 2000–2003, and this excludes many articles in socio-legal journals not abstracted there). Astonishingly, more than 600 of these articles were published after Lind & Tyler's (1988) influential review of the literature.

This review cannot hope to do justice to such a large literature, pun intended. But I will survey the major empirical findings across a range of legal and political domains, showing just how central procedural justice has become in the study of law and society. I critically examine our current understanding of the nature and etiology of fair process concerns—especially the voice motive—including the roles played by instrumental control, self-identity and group relational concerns, and cognitive and emotional factors. I give special attention to the moderating effects of diversity and culture and to the sometimes surprising lack of such effects. This raises both normative and empirical concerns about the degree to which procedural justice phenomena reflect "false consciousness" and what that might imply for policy makers on the one hand and political activists on the other.

A Methodological Note

Some methodological practices in the procedural justice literature are common in psychology but less familiar in other disciplines, where they are a source of discomfort if not skepticism. But the key point is the cumulative rigor of the literature as a whole. One can be troubled by the use of college students, simulated conflicts, structural equation causal modeling, or the inherently subjective nature of fairness judgments. But each of these issues has received considerable attention by procedural justice scholars, and the sheer heterogeneity of tasks, domains, populations, designs, and analytic methods provides remarkable convergence and triangulation. Few if any socio-legal topics—perhaps only deterrence theory—have received as much attention using as many different research methods.

The original Thibaut and Walker program was largely experimental, involving college students' reactions to simulated conflict resolution scenarios. These experiments necessarily sacrifice ecological realism in order to increase the internal (causal) validity of the hypothesis testing (Mook 1983), which is essential in a domain where endogenous, reciprocal, or spurious influences are plausible. Most of the major variables of theoretical interest have been experimentally manipulated: the disputants' role (e.g., plaintiff versus defendant); the evidentiary support for each party; the third party's decision; the disputants' process and decision control; the decision maker's bias; the relationship among disputants and their relationship to the third party; etc.

Artificial experiments are vulnerable to threats to external validity, but those threats are not proof of external invalidity, which is ultimately an empirical question. And indeed, most concerns about the external validity of the fair process effect (and its antecedents and consequences) have long since been settled. As documented below, the basic phenomena of procedural justice have been documented across dozens of social, legal, and organizational contexts involving every major demographic category in the United States, and almost every major industrial country in North America, Asia, and Europe. (A meta-analysis of 190 procedural justice studies initially appeared to show significant discrepancies between laboratory and field studies, but this turned out to be a statistical error; Cohen-Charash & Spector 2001, 2002.)

Inevitably, these field studies have purchased external validity at the cost of greater uncertainty about causation. Most of these studies use multivariate statistical analysis to assess whether the data are consistent with causal hypotheses. Some variant of hierarchical regression, path analysis, and/or structural equation modeling is often an attempt to rule out spurious effects and control for endogenous or reciprocal influences (Bollen 2002). Psychologists often use such techniques to test for moderator effects (where variable C modifies the existence, magnitude, or valence of a correlation between A and B) or mediator effects (where A exerts its influence on C through an intermediate causal link: $A \rightarrow B \rightarrow C$; see Baron & Kenny 1986). These methods are very convincing when used with experimental data but more fallible in correlational field research. Many studies (e.g., Lind et al. 2000, Tyler 1990) strengthen correlational designs using multiple waves of data collection, which permit cross-lagged inference. In future work, procedural justice research might benefit from greater use of quasi-experimental design strategies as well as modern econometric techniques for handling identification and selection problems.

Even cross-lagged analyses can lead to incorrect inferences owing to measurement unreliability (Rogosa 1980). But few areas of socio-legal research can boast a comparable level of attention to measurement reliability and construct validity. Almost all procedural justice studies measure key constructs using multiple indicators; inter-item reliabilities are usually reported (and usually reasonably high), and exploratory or confirmatory factor analyses are used to establish that theoretically distinct concepts are, in fact, empirically distinguishable (see Blader & Tyler 2003, Cohen-Charash & Spector 2001, Colquitt 2001, Colquitt et al. 2001, Skitka et al. 2003). Future work would be enriched by the complementary use of other measurement approaches, including qualitative methods, observational coding, content analysis, unobtrusive measures, and so on.

THE INFLUENCE OF PROCEDURAL FAIRNESS ON SOCIETY AND LAW

Procedural Preferences for Dispute Resolution

Most Americans now recognize at least one of the several dozen lawyer jokes long in circulation (see Galanter 1998). But the fact that we rarely tell jokes about physicians, whom we hold in high regard, or child molesters, whom we loathe, suggests that we are ambivalent about lawyers—we decry their ruthless mercenary adversarialism unless they are representing us in a conflict (MacCoun 2001).

The remarkably fruitful (and then still rare) interdisciplinary collaboration between Thibaut & Walker (1975, 1978) helped explain our ambivalent relationship with adversarialism. In doing so, they were the first to systematically document the fair process or voice effect discussed above. But they also launched an empirical research program on the design properties of legal procedure that has been enormously influential in the alternative dispute resolution (ADR) community.

Coming from an instrumental, social exchange theory tradition, Thibaut and Walker analyzed procedures with respect to the distribution of control across parties. Decision control refers to the disputants' ability to directly shape the final outcome. Process control refers to the disputants' ability to influence the presentation of evidence and arguments. This is reminiscent of Thibaut's work with Kelley on interdependence theory, which formally decomposed game theoretic outcome matrices with respect to abstract dimensions of bilateral reflexive control, mutual fate control, and mutual behavior control (Kelley & Thibaut 1978). In bargaining, parties retain both forms of control. In mediation, they cede some process control to a third party while retaining decision control. In an idealized adversarial system, they cede decision control but retain process control. In an idealized autocratic system, the parties cede both process and decision control to a third-party inquisitor.

Thibaut & Walker (1975) asked American students to imagine various hypothetical conflicts and various mechanisms for resolving them—including two-party mediation, third-party investigation and resolution by a neutral inquisitor, and a third-party decision based on investigation and arguments presented by advocates for each side. Importantly, the descriptions were stripped of labels like "lawyer" or "judge" and other overt references to actual legal systems. A strong majority identified the adversarial system as the fairest mechanism. Subsequent studies (see Lind & Tyler 1988) have replicated this finding in European nations with inquisitorial systems, suggesting that it is not an artifact of American socialization or mere familiarity (but see Anderson & Otto 2003). (As discussed further below, citizens in Asian countries tend to divide their support between the adversarial model and two-party mediation.)

It is now clear that this favorable view of adversary procedures is by no means unconditional (Shestowsky 2004, Tyler et al. 1997). There is no particular reason to believe that a taste for adversarial procedures should be universal or evolutionarily hard wired. Thibaut and Walker argued that third parties were most likely to be sought out when a resolution was urgent, in zero-sum situations, when convergent win-win solutions were elusive, or when the parties' relationship seemed unlikely to support cooperative problem solving. We now know that a variety of conditions increase support for nonadversarial procedures. On the one hand, autocratic, inquisitorial-style procedures (with less process control than the adversarial model) are rated more favorably when they provide opportunities for voice (Sheppard 1985, Folger et al. 1996) or when the conflict involves a highly volatile opponent (Morris et al. 2004). On other hand, disputants often prefer to retain decision control (through bilateral bargaining or nonbinding third-party mediation) when they have strong bargaining power, when integrative solutions are apparent, when a more adversary process threatens the disputants' ongoing relationship, or in more collectivist, communitarian cultures (see Heuer & Penrod 1986, Leung & Lind 1986, Lind et al. 1994, Shestowsky 2004). But we lack a comprehensive theory of decision control to match our level of understanding of process control (discussed below). Perhaps because so many political and organizational domains constrain the possibilities for decision control, process control has received much more attention in the literature.

Thibaut and Walker's research program also included two other dimensions that receive less attention here. One is a focus on the objective behavioral and cognitive effects of legal procedure on decision makers and on witnesses. For example, discovery and trial presentation produces a more biased distribution of facts (relative to the fact pool made available in the experiment) in the adversarial format (where each party had a representative) than in the inquisitorial format (where a third party assembled evidence) (Thibaut & Walker 1975). Relative to inquisitorial questioning, adversarial questioning biases witness responses in favor of the party that called them to testify (Sheppard & Vidmar 1980). Empirical study of the consequences of procedural variations (in witness interviewing, in lineup format, in jury trials, and so on) is a flourishing enterprise in the psychology and law literature (and the socio-legal literature more generally), but the term procedural justice is now largely reserved for studies of the evaluations and responses of the recipients of procedure, rather than its enactors. Thibaut & Walker (1978) also offered a normative theory of procedure, arguing that inquisitorial procedures are best suited for truth conflicts and adversarial procedures are best suited for conflicts of interest. This tidy dichotomy seems difficult to sustain in practice; for a critical discussion, see MacCoun (2005).

Americans hold more favorable opinions of the jury system than of the courts more generally (Hans 1993, MacCoun & Tyler 1988). MacCoun & Tyler (1988) found that citizens strongly preferred trial by jury to trial by judge, and the traditional 12-person unanimous jury to smaller or nonunanimous juries. Relative to trial by judge and to smaller or nonunanimous juries, the traditional jury structure was seen as fairer, more accurate, more thorough, and more representative of community viewpoints. This was not blind enthusiasm; citizens preferred more efficient approaches (trial by judge or small nonunanimous juries) for trivial cases like shoplifting.

Satisfaction with Legal Experiences

Citizens do not always have much choice of the procedures they encounter. Speeding drivers get pulled over by the police, civil litigants may be obligated to go to ADR rather than (or before) trial, and criminal suspects must face trial if they want a chance to avoid sanctions. In a number of studies, Tyler and colleagues (1984, 1988; Casper et al. 1988) have examined how criminal defendants assess their day in court, finding that even citizens sentenced to steep prison terms are more satisfied and more positive in their views of authorities when they perceive the decision makers as honest and unbiased and the legal process as fair.

Tyler & Folger (1980) were the first procedural justice researchers to move beyond the court-based simulations of Thibaut and Walker and examine the role of procedural fairness judgments in citizen evaluations of police authority. In doing so, they also launched a focus on less formal, more interpersonal aspects of authority behavior (see also Bies & Tyler 1993, Blader & Tyler 2003, Collie et al. 2002, Vermunt et al. 1998).

Bandura (1986) notes that "almost every urban riot was sparked by a provocative police encounter with a ghetto resident that provoked onlookers to retaliatory violence" (p. 174). Law enforcement experts now view the perceived fairness of police conduct as a crucial aspect of effective policing (see Skogan & Frydl 2003). Tyler & Folger (1980) assessed the reactions of ordinary citizens to encounters with the police during 911 calls for assistance or routine traffic stops. In both contexts, the perceived fairness of the officers' treatment of the citizen had a reliable effect on citizen satisfaction, even after controlling for the actual outcome of the encounter, a finding consistently replicated in later surveys (e.g., Tyler & Huo 2002, Tyler 1990). Interestingly, police performance and satisfaction are themselves influenced by officer evaluations of procedural fairness in departmental assignment decisions (Farmer et al. 2003).

In the civil domain, proponents of ADR have argued that traditional trials are too complex and too alienating, but in fact, disputants who actually participate in trials tend to view the trial process favorably, and again, to a surprising extent this is true of "losers" as well as of those who win their cases (Lind et al. 1990; MacCoun et al. 1988, 1992). These procedural fairness results are not limited to naive or inexperienced citizens. MacCoun et al. (1988) found that although attorneys tended to perceive greater process fairness than their clients, their judgments differed in degree rather than in kind, and attorneys and their clients emphasized similar various procedural attributes in their fairness judgments, with both giving greater weight to ratings of the quality of treatment than to the actual monetary outcome of the case. Lind (1990) found that litigants in very high-stakes arbitration cases in federal court evaluated procedural fairness quite similarly to "one-shot" litigants in low-stakes ADR studies. And Stalans & Lind (1997) found that both taxpayers and their professional representatives were influenced by similar aspects (e.g., dignity) of the procedural fairness of the tax audit process, although the representatives were more sensitive to outcome characteristics.

An inevitable concern with these interview studies is that talk is cheap—little is at stake in the interview, social desirability pressures may encourage good sportsmanship, and fair process ratings may covary with more global satisfaction ratings because of shared semantic content. This concern is mitigated in part by the experimental simulations, which show that people will readily denounce patently bad procedures and outcomes. But in the field, one would like some behavioral manifestations of the process effect. Fortunately, there are an increasing number of examples in the literature. One early behavioral effect was that the perceived fairness of arbitration hearings significantly predicts litigant decisions to accept an arbitration decision, rather than rejecting it in favor of trial de novo (MacCoun et al. 1988). Lind et al. (1993) replicated this effect and showed that it is independent of the arbitration outcome. Using pooled data from civil litigants who participated in mandatory nonbinding arbitration in U.S. District Courts in nine states, they found that the decision to accept the arbitration award was more strongly associated with procedural justice judgments (standardized path coefficient $= .47$) than with the objective size of the arbitration award ($.20$).

Although a detailed discussion is beyond the scope of this essay, procedural justice theory has played an important role in the restorative justice movement (Braithwaite 2002, Strang 2004). Restorative justice draws on the notions of voice and respect from procedural justice, together with Braithwaite's notion of "reintegrative shaming," to design procedures that bring victims and offenders together to seek reconciliation. Proponents suggest that these hearings can help victims emotionally, while providing both rehabilitation and deterrence for the offender.

Compliance with the Law

Empirical research on deterrence theory shows that the correlation between legal sanctioning and legal compliance is surprisingly weak and partially spurious (see MacCoun 1993). Given the impossibility (and, in a democratic society, the undesirability) of absolute surveillance and enforcement, social scientists have long argued that civil order is maintained in large part by citizens' willingness to comply with laws via personal moral beliefs, conformity to social norms, or informal social sanctions (Weber 1968, French & Raven 1959). Tyler (1990) argued that willingness to comply with laws is determined in large part by the perceived fairness of their enforcement. He tested this reasoning using cross-lagged correlational analysis of a panel study of citizens in the Chicago area to test the association between the perceived fairness of the police and the courts and subsequent compliance with the law. Tyler showed that the association between Wave 1 evaluations and Wave 2 compliance was significantly stronger than the lagged association of initial compliance on later evaluations.

Other studies support this procedural justice effect. A re-analysis of data from the Milwaukee Domestic Violence Experiment found that the suspect's evaluation of the police conduct as unfair was a stronger predictor of the suspect's subsequent domestic violence than whether the suspect was arrested or not arrested (Paternoster et al. 1997). Murphy (2004) and Wenzel (2002) each documented a link between procedural fairness judgments and taxpayer compliance. Long (2003) shows procedural effects on compliance with mediation outcomes. Makkai & Braithwaite (1996) found mixed support for a procedural fairness effect on regulatory compliance by business executives. A newer study by Tyler & Huo (2002) presents a somewhat more nuanced picture. California citizens' acceptance of the outcomes of encounters with legal authorities was better predicted by perceptions of trustworthiness and fair treatment by the authorities (standardized path coefficients = .46 and .32, respectively) than by outcome fairness (.09). But for a direct measure of compliance, the effects were much weaker (.12 for trust, .06 for fair treatment, and .07 for outcome fairness). The authors argue that the effects were weaker because, unlike acceptance, "compliance can be induced by the fear of force or punishment" (p. 82). All these studies share a reliance on correlational methods that cannot conclusively establish causality. Experimental simulations confirm the causal influence of procedure on compliance intentions in studies of taxpaying compliance (Casey & Scholz 1991) and of mental health professionals' reactions to malpractice verdicts (Poythress 1994). But an obvious next step would be to deploy quasi-experimental design strategies and modern econometric identification techniques in field research.

Claiming and Litigiousness

In a workplace survey, Bies & Tyler (1993) found that employee perceptions of the fairness of the organization's procedures and rules were the most important correlate of self-reported willingness to consider suing the organization. In a survey of 996 workers who had been fired or laid off, Lind et al. (2000) were able to link such perceptions directly to actual decisions about whether to file a wrongful termination lawsuit. Perceptions of how they had been treated during the termination itself were the strongest correlates of employee claiming—stronger than the expected dollar value of the suit and stronger than their perceptions of how they had been treated during their full career at the firm. Lind and colleagues used 4-month follow-up interviews to show that the treatment ratings were more likely a cause than a consequence of the decision to file a lawsuit. The authors estimate that employers could have saved $13,200 per termination by ensuring that employees perceived their treatment at termination as honest and respectful. Roberts & Markel (2001) report similar results in a study of the decision to file workers' compensation claims.

A number of studies have identified physicians' "bedside manner" to patient decisions to file malpractice lawsuits, including two surveys of medical malpractice claimants (Hickson et al. 1992, Vincent et al. 1994) and a content analysis of plaintiff depositions (Beckman et al. 1994). Hickson et al. (1992) note that mothers of injured or deceased infants complained that "physicians would not listen (13% of sample) [and] would not talk openly (32%)." Vincent et al. (1994) found that "[t]he decision to take legal action was determined not only by the original injury, but also by insensitive handling and poor communication after the original incident. Where explanations were given, less than 15% were considered satisfactory.... Patients taking legal action wanted greater honesty, an appreciation of the severity of the trauma they had suffered, and assurances that lessons had been learnt from their experiences." Seventy-one percent of the plaintiff depositions examined by Beckman et al. (1994) cited problems in the physician-patient relationship, clustering around four themes: "deserting the patient (32%), devaluing patient and/or family views (29%), delivering information poorly (26%), and failing to understand the patient and/or family perspective (13%)."

Unfortunately, by excluding patients who could but did not claim, these studies cannot conclusively establish a correlation between procedural or relational judgments and medical malpractice claiming. But the inference is strengthened by a clever content analysis of audiotaped office visits involving a large sample of physicians with and without lifetime malpractice claims (Levinson et al. 1997). Among primary care physicians, those without claims experience spent more time with patients, used more humor, explained more, and "tended to use more facilitation (soliciting patients' opinions, checking understanding, and encouraging patients to talk)"—i.e., encouraged patient voice. Interestingly, no such differences were found among surgeons who had or had not been sued.

In light of such evidence, many commentators have argued that physicians can and should improve their interpersonal skills, both to reduce their liability exposure and because the ethical principle of beneficence requires it (see Beckman et al. 1994, Forster et al. 2002). As Hickson et al. (1992) note, "Obtaining money may not be the only goal for some families who file suit." Similarly, Vincent et al. (1994) argue that "a no-fault compensation system, however well intended, would not address all patients' concerns. If litigation is viewed solely as a legal and financial problem, many fundamental issues will not be addressed or resolved."

Legitimacy and the Acceptance of Government Policies

Tyler and colleagues have documented the role that procedural fairness plays in citizens' willingness to cooperate with government decisions and policies, including Supreme Court rulings (Tyler & Mitchell 1994), whites' support for affirmative action (Smith & Tyler 1996), California's three strikes law (Tyler & Boeckmann 1997), Californians' response to a 1991 water shortage (Tyler & Degoey 1995), and citizen attributions about whether police stops constitute racial profiling (Tyler 2003). Others have examined the role of fair process in citizen contributions to public goods (De Cremer & van Knippenberg 2003), views of the Kenneth Starr prosecution and the congressional impeachment of President Bill Clinton (Kershaw & Alexander 2003), and reactions to corporate drug-testing policies (Kulik & Clark 1993, Wagner & Moriarty 2002).

Tyler (e.g., Tyler & Lind 1992, Tyler 2003) has long argued that procedural fairness plays a key role in shaping the legitimacy that citizens grant to government authority. Following Weber (1968), Tyler argues that this legitimacy or support for the system is critical to the ability to govern effectively without tyranny and coercion. He has repeatedly documented a pattern of correlations consistent with a causal chain in which procedural fairness leads to perceived legitimacy, which leads to the acceptance of policies. Gibson (1989) disputed Tyler's interpretation of these correlations, arguing that legitimacy is the cause rather than the consequence of perceived fairness. Using the 1987 General Social Survey, Gibson found significant correlations between procedural fairness and legitimacy (.42) and between legitimacy and acceptance (.15), but the association of procedural fairness and acceptance was not significant (.05). (Confusingly, some studies have labeled acceptance "compliance," but unlike the studies discussed above, what is measured is an attitude rather than a behavior.) Tyler & Rasinski (1991) replied that this is exactly what one would expect from a causal model in which procedural fairness affects acceptance indirectly via legitimacy; if so, one would predict a direct effect of. 42 × .15 = .06, almost exactly what Gibson found. Mondak (1993) claimed to support Gibson's causal interpretation by finding no effect on legitimacy of an experimental manipulation of the Supreme Court's procedural fairness. But because Mondak could not actually manipulate the Court's behavior, what he actually varied was whether respondents were told that the Court was scrupulous in its procedures. This method of encouraging new views about actual institutions and outcomes seems much less persuasive than typical experiments that can credibly manipulate information about purely hypothetical scenarios. At any rate, Tyler (2003) has now amassed enough evidence that his interpretation seems sound. There is ample evidence that procedural fairness and legitimacy are correlated, and it is almost surely the case that the correlation reflects causation in both directions.

Organizational Citizenship

In the 1990s, much of the growth in procedural justice studies occurred in the organizational behavior literature. Although only indirectly relevant to the socio-legal focus of this review, these studies conceptually replicate and extend some of the basic findings discussed above. For example, Brockner and colleagues have published a number of large-scale field studies of the reactions of employee survivors of corporate layoffs (e.g., Brockner et al. 1990, 1992; see also Robbins et al. 2000). These studies suggest that the quality of managers' conduct during the layoff—their efforts to explain the rationale for the layoff, and the dignity and respect they afforded to those terminated—influences the morale, commitment, and cooperation of the remaining staff. Bies et al. (1993) found that this good citizenship effect even extended to laid-off employees during the period between notification and termination.

THEORY

Background

Economics, behaviorist psychology, and the public choice and social exchange traditions share a common emphasis on the explanatory power of outcomes and incentives. The mass media and the legal literature tend to perpetuate the view that outcomes—especially monetary outcomes—drive legal behavior, legal judgments, and evaluations of the legal system (see Miller 1999). An early refinement of this view was relative deprivation theory—the notion that what matters to citizens are relative outcomes (mine versus yours or theirs) rather than absolute outcomes (for a review, see Tyler et al. 1997). A related viewpoint was equity theory (e.g., Walster & Walster 1975), which links fairness to the relative ratio of inputs to outcomes across actors.

Each approach had important successes. Relative deprivation theory seems to explain many important historical rebellions (see Crosby 1976) as well as some surprising effects of social class on health and longevity (e.g., Wilkinson 1997). Equity theory provided a good account of many work-based allocation situations (Walster & Walster 1975); even citizens in Eastern and Central Europe (Bulgaria, Hungary, Poland, Russia) apply this equity standard in reactions to job-related conflicts (Cohn et al. 2000). But both models fare poorly in nonmarket contexts and relationships (Fiske 1992). Across various settings, studies have found support for allocation by equality, by need, or by more complex multidimensional decision rules (see Deutsch 1975, Mellers & Baron 1993). And both theories tend to over-predict resentment and rebellion and underpredict citizen acceptance. Of course, citizen acquiescence can stem from simple cost-benefit calculations. Moreover, both theories fail to predict which of many possible comparison standards the citizen will use; citizens do not invariably choose the source (my ingroup, an outgroup, people in the past, myself in the past) that provides the most invidious compar-isons. But a major drawback of this analysis was that the relative deprivation and equity traditions largely ignored procedural considerations.

Thibaut & Walker's (1975) research program demonstrated that the processes by which outcomes are reached matter profoundly to citizens. Thibaut & Walker (1975) adopted an instrumental interpretation of their findings. They contended that procedures matter to citizens because fair procedures produce fair outcomes. From this perspective, process control matters not so much as an end in itself but as a means to an end—a way of improving one's prospects given the inevitability of relinquishing some decision control. The process effects first documented by Thibaut and Walker have proved to be remarkably robust. Their control-based account of voice effects has fared less well.

The Relational Perspective

If Thibaut and Walker's control perspective is tough minded, the dominant per-spective since the late 1980s is the more tender-minded interpretation offered by Tom Tyler and Allan Lind in their group-value model (Lind & Tyler 1988) and their relational model of authority (Tyler & Lind 1992). (The Tyler-Lind relational model extends the earlier model beyond decision procedures to public support for authorities and rules more generally.) They argue that the interdependence of social life creates a fundamental dilemma for people. A trusting, cooperative rela-tionship with our group can provide resources and rewards we would be unable to obtain on our own. But the need to cede control to others puts us at risk—we could be harmed, neglected, discriminated against, or ostracized. Decision making and allocation procedures not only deliver immediate outcomes; they also convey im-portant information about our relationship with the group and its authorities. Thus, Tyler and Lind argue that we are especially attuned to three process dimensions: the neutrality of the procedure, the trustworthiness of the third party, and signals that convey our social standing. Although the first two dimensions were included in an earlier list of procedural desiderata (Leventhal 1980), the third factor, social standing, is the most distinctive contribution of their models. Tyler & Lind (1992, Lind & Tyler 1988) argued that standing is communicated by "dignitary process" features—the perception that one was treated with politeness, dignity, and respect.

Those of a tough-minded bent usually find it almost impossible to believe that politeness could possibly approach the impact of the bottom line, be it a tort award, a criminal sentence, or a job layoff. Nevertheless, citizen ratings of the dignity and respectfulness of their treatment consistently emerge as primary correlates of procedural justice. For example, in a correlational study of tort litigants in three counties, Lind et al. (1990) found that perceived dignity accounted for more variance in litigant outcome satisfaction than did case duration or personal trial costs. Many authorities clearly recognize the importance of dignified treatment (or at least give lip service to it) and are reproached when they do not. In 2004, the Command Joint Task Force listed "Treat civilians with dignity and respect" as one of their key rules for security contractors in Iraq (*New York Times* 2004). The Second District Court of Appeal recently ruled that Los Angeles citizens have a right to "courteous treatment," after Los Angeles City Council members, flamboyantly dressed for their Hawaiian Shirt Day, ruled against the owner of a strip club after visibly ignoring a presentation by his lawyer (Associated Press 2005).

There are now many lines of evidence testing the Tyler-Lind model (see Tyler 1994; Tyler & Lind 1990, 1992; Tyler et al. 1996). For example, those treated poorly by authorities experience some reduction in self-esteem (De Cremer 2003). And stronger procedural justice effects are found when one's status is made salient (van Prooijen et al. 2002), when people feel included rather than excluded from the relevant group (van Prooijen et al. 2004), when the relationships at stake are important to the person (Kwong & Leung 2002), when group identification is strong (Huo et al. 1996, Wenzel 2004), when the person scores high on a "need to belong" scale (De Cremer & Alberts 2004), and when the authority is an ingroup member rather than an outgroup member (Smith et al. 1998; but see Ståhl et al. 2004). An especially interesting finding is that process effects are weaker for citizens who identify strongly with a subordinate group but weakly with a superordinate group, e.g., minority "separatists" as opposed to "assimilationists" (Huo et al. 1996), an effect discussed in greater detail below. Perceived disrespect has also been linked to many other emotional and behavioral reactions, including violence (see Anderson 1999, Miller 2001).

Nonrelational Influences on Procedural Justice

Despite the dominance of the relational perspective, many lines of research suggest that more individualized cognitive and moral factors do influence procedural fairness evaluations. People judge procedures and outcomes relative to their beliefs about what will happen, what could happen, and what should happen. A number of studies have found that justice judgments are influenced by others' ex ante predictions about an allocation decision (Heuer & Penrod 1994) as well as by others' ex post evaluations of an allocation (Folger et al. 1979). Drawing on concepts from social exchange theory and the counterfactual reasoning literature, Folger proposed a referent cognition theory of relative deprivation (e.g., Folger 1984, Folger & Martin 1986, Folger et al. 1983), predicting that discontent is a joint function of low justification for outcomes combined with a readily imaginable better outcome. Van den Bos & van Prooijen (2001) argued that referent cognition theory can contribute to our understanding of the voice effect. In two experiments they found that the lack of voice affected citizens' perceived injustice most strongly when a salient counterfactual outcome (what could have happened) was close to rather than distant from the actual outcome. On the other hand, Tyler & Huo (2002) found little independent influence of expectations in a California survey, but ex post ratings of ex ante expectations tend to be tainted by knowledge of what actually happened—what psychologists call a hindsight bias (e.g., Hawkins & Hastie 1990).

People also bring to a situation various pre-existing personal moral intuitions, and some of these intuitions are about fair process (Cropanzano et al. 2003). In accord with the Kohlberg tradition on moral reasoning, Wendorf et al. (2002) argue that intuitions about procedural justice emerge in a developmental sequence that is preceded by pure self-interest and then concerns about distributive justice. But Gold et al. (1984) found that American first graders were already sensitive to procedural justice, reacting negatively to a mother who punished her child for a broken vase if she failed to first consult a witness to the event.

But of course people also have other moral intuitions that may conflict with, or override, fair process concerns. For example, in a laboratory work simulation, Hegtvedt & Killian (1999) found that rising pay increased pay satisfaction but at the price of guilt over unfairness to the other worker.

More generally, Heuer et al. (1999) demonstrate that judgments of moral deserving mediate the relationship between respectful treatment and perceived fairness; people do not expect authorities to deliver respect unconditionally. And Skitka (2002, 2003; Skitka & Houston 2001, Skitka & Mullen 2002) argues that people are less attentive to concerns about process when certain outcomes involve moral mandates, e.g., that the innocent should be acquitted. Thus, due process considerations affected people's evaluations of a verdict in an ambiguous case, but when people received independent evidence that a defendant was innocent, a conviction was perceived to be unfair irrespective of the fairness of the prosecution and trial (Skitka & Houston 2001). In another study (Skitka 2002), deeply held moral beliefs were more influential than procedural fairness judgments in predicting acceptance of Supreme Court or legislative decisions that threatened those views. The boundary conditions on this moral mandate effect are still unclear; it is difficult to believe that these abstract values are more passionately held than litigant views about the right verdict in their own cases, and yet research reviewed above shows that both winners and losers at trial are quite responsive to process fairness considerations.

Are Procedural and Distributive Justice Substitutes?

Discussions of procedural justice tread a fine line between the questions "Does fair process matter?" and "Which matters more—process or outcomes?" The answer to the first question is decidedly yes; the second question may not be answerable in a meaningful, global way. Meta-analyses suggest that procedural and distributive justice judgments are moderately correlated [rho $= .64$ in Hauenstein et al.'s (2001) meta-analysis], and that each has independent effects on a variety of attitudinal and behavioral outcomes (Cohen-Charash & Spector 2001, 2002; Colquitt et al. 2001). For example, in separate studies of bank employees, engineers, and manufacturing employees, procedural justice has better predicted attitudes toward one's supervisors and organization, whereas distributive justice has better predicted pay satisfaction and job satisfaction (Folger & Konovsky 1989, McFarlin & Sweeney 1992, Sweeney & McFarlin 1993).

But direct horse race comparisons of predictor strength are problematic for a variety of reasons. The traditional variance-accounted-for index (squared correlation or standardized regression coefficient) is influenced by measurement error, by range restriction, and by the situational salience of each variable. Further complicating matters, some studies assess outcome favorability whereas others assess outcome fairness, and the former produce stronger fair process effects than the latter (Skitka et al. 2003). Moreover, the effects of monetary outcomes are not monotonic (Conlon et al. 1989).

Finally, and most importantly, procedural and distributive judgments have multiplicative, interactive effects on judgments of authorities and organizations. Across 45 different studies, Brockner & Wiesenfeld (1996) found that the typical pattern is that procedural justice has stronger effects when outcome ratings are low than when they are high, and outcome ratings have stronger effects when perceived procedural fairness is low than when it is high. (The former is the fair process effect; the latter has been called the fair outcome effect; Van den Bos & Lind 2002.)

In a fascinating program of organizational research that has received almost no notice in the law and social science literature, Allan Lind and Kees van den Bos (Lind 2001, Lind et al. 1993, Van den Bos & Lind 2002) have developed a theoretical model that integrates the relational model, research on expectancy and attributional effects, and the interactive impact of process and outcome considerations. At first glance, their fairness heuristic theory might appear to be a radical challenge to earlier thinking on procedural fairness because it has been used to demonstrate, in experimental settings, that under certain conditions it is possible to make fair process effects shrink. Under one reading, the fairness heuristic model is a cognitive account whereas the relational model is a motivational account. The new hypotheses in the fairness heuristic account are indeed cognitive. But I argue that the same core motivational logic drives both fairness heuristic theory and the earlier relational model. The new model is simply more explicit in treating one's relationship with authorities and the group as fundamental and procedural concerns as a means to that end.

Fairness heuristic theory starts with a proposition that has motivated many other psychological theories, the notion that people have a fundamental need to reduce uncertainty about the future. The "fundamental social dilemma" (Van den Bos & Lind 2002, p. 9) is that social life requires us to relinquish control over future outcomes to other people, leaving us vulnerable to their actions. The key innovation of the theory is the idea that information about process and information about outcomes serve to reduce uncertainty about others' motives, and hence the two can substitute for each other. Procedural fairness serves as a heuristic substitute when outcomes are ambiguous or unknown; similarly, outcome fairness can serve as a heuristic substitute when future procedures are not yet known. Firm knowledge of an authority's trustworthiness reduces the informational value of either source. Tyler & Huo (2002) invoke the label "fiduciary relationship" to make a similar point: "If we believe that a person is motivated by goodwill, we need not seek to anticipate his or her particular actions. Whatever that person does will be a good-faith effort to help us" (pp. 62–63).

Lind, Van den Bos, and their colleagues have been quite creative in creating new conditions for testing the model. They have shown that voice effects are weaker when an authority's trustworthiness is known to be positive or negative rather than unknown (Van den Bos et al. 1998); when uncertainty is not salient (Van den Bos 2001); when other actors' outcomes are known (Van den Bos et al. 1997a); when outcome information is provided before process information (Van den Bos et al. 1997b); and when the lack of voice is implicit rather than explicit (Van den Bos 1999). Note that procedural concerns are weaker but rarely eliminated in this research (see Tyler & Huo 2002). The upshot is not that procedures become unimportant, but rather that people sometimes glean the information they are seeking in other ways.

The fairness heuristic work has been used to interpret research in field settings (Lind et al. 2000, Lind et al. 1993), but to date most of the direct tests have occurred in the laboratory. At present we lack the kind of ecological data that would tell us where and when the special conditions created in the laboratory also occur in various applied settings (e.g., receiving outcome information before procedural information). The sheer bulk of field support for fair process effects suggests that these conditions are more likely to be the exception than the rule. So the theory is at present less useful for forecasting public responses than as a source of insights into the judgment processes underlying fairness judgments.

CULTURE, DIVERSITY, AND CONSCIOUSNESS

Procedural justice researchers began looking at the cross-national generality of their findings very early, perhaps owing to skepticism about whether favorable views of adversarial procedures reflected an endorsement of what was familiar to Americans. Although cultures do appear to differ in their support for adversarialism (e.g., Leung & Lind 1986), many studies have found that the underlying dynamics of fair process are similar. For example, Lind et al. (1997) found that relational variables played a similar role in mediating process effects among German, Hong Kong, and Japanese college students. Procedural justice variables were found to have a similar influence on employee attitudes in the United States and Bangladesh (Rahim et al. 2001), and in Germany, Hong Kong, and India (Pillai et al. 2001). Cohn et al. (2000) found that voice and impartiality factors in two survey vignettes had similar effects across seven countries.

The considerable convergence across samples has somewhat mitigated the methodological problems inherent in cross-cultural psychology. Cross-national psychological differences can be difficult to interpret because of considerable within-nation variability and the likely confounding influences of economics, education, socialization, language, and response biases. Morris & Leung (2000) argued that procedural justice researchers should directly assess important cultural differences at the individual level. For example, Brockner and colleagues (2000) conducted negotiation simulations in the People's Republic of China and in the United States. They found that perceived fair process in dealing with partners reduced the importance of outcome satisfaction on willingness to deal with the partner in the future and that this effect was more pronounced for Chinese than for U.S. participants. The cross-national difference was explained by the greater tendency of Chinese participants to describe their identity in terms of social interdependence rather than independence. Other studies have used Hofstede's (1980) "power distance" dimension, which taps the perceived acceptability of an arrogant or aloof stance among those high in social power or wealth. Voice effects are stronger among people with a lower tolerance for power distance, as is common in the United States and Germany relative to China or Mexico (Brockner et al. 2001, Tyler et al. 2000).

There is a much larger literature on group differences—by gender, ethnicity, race, and class—within the United States (see Tyler et al. 1997 for an extensive review). It is important here to distinguish three issues: (a) group differences in mean ratings of procedural justice and outcome satisfaction; (b) group differences in the meaning of procedural fairness, as determined by patterns of association with various antecedents and consequences; and (c) differences in the criteria people apply in within- versus between-group relationships.

Groups do differ in their judgments of the quality of the way they are treated by authorities, their satisfaction with the outcomes they receive, and the perceived legitimacy of government institutions (see Brooks & Jeon-Slaughter 2001, MacCoun 2001, Tyler & Huo 2002). For example, racial and ethnic groups report similar views of the courts, but African Americans consistently report more negative views of police conduct; they are about twice as likely to report low confidence in the police or the view that the police have low ethical standards (Bur. Justice Stat. 2003)

But most studies have found striking similarities across demographic groups in the antecedents and consequences of procedural fairness, suggesting a shared understanding of the concept (Tyler et al. 1997). For example, Lind et al. (1994) found a remarkably similar pattern of procedural rankings for European, Hispanic, and African American students in a study of different ways of resolving conflicts. Lind et al. (1990b) found that procedural fairness had similar effects on litigation ratings for white versus nonwhite, male versus female, and high- versus low-income litigants. Kulik et al. (1996; see also Sweeney & McFarlin 1997) found no significant differences in the way male and female tort litigants weighted various criteria in procedural justice ratings. Tyler & Huo (2002) compared a high-risk sample of

18- to 25-year-old minority males to other respondents in a general population survey. Both groups, to nearly an identical degree, emphasized procedural fairness (.84 versus .77) over outcome favorability (.11 versus .16) in their ratings of satisfaction with legal authorities (p. 158).

This apparently common understanding does not imply a common reliance on procedural fairness in judging authorities. A growing literature on the scope of justice shows that people do not always extend their standards for distributive and procedural justice to relationships outside their own groups (Messé et al. 1986, Opotow 1996). As the relational model and fairness heuristic theory would lead us to expect, the nature of the relationship with an authority figure moderates the relative weight citizens give to process versus outcomes. In a study of American workers and supervisors, and a second study of Japanese and Western English teachers in Japan, Tyler et al. (1998) found that a relational concern with fair treatment mattered more in within-group conflicts, whereas an instrumental concern with outcome favorability mattered more in across-group conflicts. Huo et al. (1996) surveyed union members of varying ethnicities about conflicts with their supervisors. They found that procedural fairness was generally associated with a willingness to accept supervisor decisions, except among those with a strong minority identification and a weak identification with American society—separatists. But such separatists are relatively rare. Analyzing data from a survey of Californians' encounters with legal authorities, Huo (2003) found that American and ethnic subgroup identities were positively rather than negatively associated. The key moderator of fair process concerns in this sample was identification with the superordinate group (America) rather than ethnic subgroup identity. Similarly, in an Australian survey, Wenzel (2004) found that perceived social norms were positively associated with tax compliance for most people, but that this link was significantly weaker among those who did not identify with the mainstream culture.

False Consciousness

Given the fragility and tension inherent in a multicultural society, evidence for a widely shared understanding of, and reliance upon, fair process concerns, even among those receiving undesired outcomes, would seem to be a cause for celebration. So it may seem churlish to state that many of us also find this somewhat troubling. Although it is beyond the scope of this review to argue the point, most readers will probably accept the assertion that the distribution of outcomes in our society is correlated with race, ethnicity, gender, and class in ways that strike many of us as patently unfair.

For many scholars, fair process effects are so robust that they raise the specter of "false consciousness"—the Marxist notion that political and market institutions keep the proletariat ignorant of capitalism's true nature (Cohen 1985, 1989; Fox 1993; Haney 1991; Jost 1995). This use of scare quotes is common when contemporary scholars use the term false consciousness, in part owing to embarrassment about mid-twentieth century Marxist social science, which most see as discredited and all see as unfashionable. But there is also discomfort with the implicit notion that we scholars can assert that ordinary people are mistaken in their understanding of their social world—a notion that seems politically elitist and epistemologically naive.

In the procedural justice domain, the concern is that authorities can use the appearance of fair procedure (dignity, respect, voice) as an inexpensive way to coopt citizens and distract them from outcomes that by normative criteria might be considered substantively unfair or biased. Cohen (1985) first raised a concern with the manipulative use of procedural justice in the context of participation procedures for corporate employees. Cohen argued that because employers and employees face a conflict of interests, limited participation may be used as a "strategic device to induce loyalty and commitment."

Surely the most evocative discussion of the manipulative use of fair treatment is Erving Goffman's (1952) classic essay "On Cooling the Mark Out." In the world of con artists, Goffman notes, to "cool the mark out" is to "define the situation for the mark in a way that makes it easy for him to accept the inevitable and quietly go home. The mark is given instruction in the philosophy of taking a loss." Goffman illustrates how a similar process occurs throughout social life such as, for example, at the complaint departments of retail stores. Goffman's discussion intriguingly anticipates the importance of status in the relational model of the fair process effect; e.g., he suggests that an effective cooling tactic is to offer the mark

> a status which differs from the one he has lost or failed to gain but which provides at least a something or a somebody for him to become. . .a lover may be asked to become a friend; a student of medicine may be asked to switch to the study of dentistry. . . . Sometimes the mark is allowed to retain his status but is required to fulfill it in a different environment: the honest policeman is transferred to a lonely beat; the too zealous priest is encouraged to enter a monastery; an unsatisfactory plant manager is shipped off to another branch. Sometimes the mark is "kicked upstairs" and given a courtesy status such as 'Vice President.' In the game for social roles, transfer up, down, or away may all be consolation prizes.

And of course, the potential for fair process cues to manipulate the citizenry has not escaped the attention of those in positions of authority. For example, in the course of a study of ADR in tort litigation, a collaborator of the author attended a judicial settlement conference in which the attorneys, with no clients present, hammered out a settlement they were comfortable with, but the plaintiff's attorney complained that his client might not accept it because she "wants her day in court." The judge put on his robe, called her into an empty courtroom, and sat her on the witness chair. After she told her story, she assented to the settlement. On another occasion, an insurance executive requested a meeting with the author and another justice researcher, asking how he might increase the formality of meetings between clients and insurance adjustors, in order to reduce the rate of contested claims. And examples are legion in world politics. *The New York Times* recently reported that the Zimbabwe dictator Robert Mugabe has recently allowed opposition candidates to operate with relatively little police interference; citing evidence for an elaborate plan to rig the upcoming election, the authors note that "many see Mr. Mugabe's loosening of the reins as a calculated gamble by someone supremely confident of victory" (Wines & LaFraniere 2005).

In his essay "Let Them Eat Due Process," Haney (1991) argued that the American preoccupation with due process—for example, the Supreme Court's due process framing of equal protection issues—diverts us from seriously confronting persistent and large social inequalities. Fox (1993) contends that the process emphasis of the American psychology and law community helps perpetuate this political dynamic rather than illuminate it. Fox (1993) decries a "procedural justice trap" by which "psychologists focused on procedural justice too easily dismiss substantive outcomes" and a "legitimacy trap" in which "psychologists accept the dominant assumption that legitimacy should be enhanced in order to gain greater compliance with the demands of legal authorities."

It is debatable whether these arguments are a fair critique of the psychology and law enterprise as a whole or of the procedural justice literature more specifically. The psychology and law community is largely preoccupied with efforts to challenge legal procedures that are biased or coercive—stacked police line-ups, interrogation methods that produce false confessions, the biasing effects of "death-qualified" voir dire on capital trial verdicts—not to mention the effects of race, gender, and social stigma on ostensibly evidence-based legal judgments. Moreover, procedural justice scholars have consistently and explicitly noted the risk of false consciousness in their writings (e.g., Lind & Tyler 1988, MacCoun et al. 1992, Tyler et al. 1997). Indeed, Tyler & McGraw (1986) published an entire article on the topic, arguing that "cultural socialization" induces citizens to "focus on opportunities to speak rather than on actual control over decisions."

Tyler and other procedural justice scholars have long noted the positive social benefits of fair process as a means of promoting social harmony and cooperation in the face of divergent interests and inevitable scarcity. But the procedural justice community has been reticent about exploring the darker side of the fair process phenomenon. For example, Tyler (1990, p. 148) argued that "the study of procedural justice is neutral about the quality of the existing legal system" and "whether those studied 'ought' to be more or less satisfied than they are with legal authorities." He more recently argued that his psychological model "does not address normative issues concerning whether people ought to defer to legal authorities and generally obey the law" (Tyler 2003, p. 285).

Actually, the gap between normative and empirical analysis is probably more apparent than real for this topic. Implicit in the notion of "false consciousness" is the possibility that there is "true consciousness." Without plunging into entangling debates about ontology on the one hand or welfare economics on the other, one can simply deploy strategies decision researchers routinely use to assess the accuracy of judgments and beliefs (see Hastie & Raskinski 1988). The false consciousness question implies a set of linkages—between procedural cues in the environment and citizen beliefs about process and outcomes; between actual outcomes and citizen beliefs; between procedural cues and the actual determination of outcomes; and so on. Without directly evaluating whether outcomes are just by criteria imposed by the researcher, one can empirically examine these linkages to identify the degree to which citizens have a distorted view of what is actually happening.

One strategy is to focus on the citizen, looking for a mismatch between what they want from a procedure and what it actually delivers. But defining "what they want" turns out to be surprisingly tricky.

For example, Tyler et al. (1999) report that people assess procedures differently before and after an outcome has been determined. Ex ante, their participants' procedural preferences reflected an instrumental concern with getting the best outcomes. But ex post, once an outcome had been determined, participants evaluated procedures based on the quality of the treatment they received. It is difficult to avoid the conclusion that the ex post view may reflect well-known processes of cognitive dissonance reduction. But there are also reasons to think that the predecision viewpoint was more valid. Miller (1999) has shown that American citizens overestimate the degree to which their own opinions and behavior are governed by self-interest. Similarly, Tyler and colleagues (1999) argue that participants' ex ante views reflected "the myth of self-interest," whereas their ex post views were grounded in their actual experience with a process. Which viewpoint should we take to represent citizen beliefs, the ex ante view or the ex post view? Psychological processes of distortion can occur both before and after a decision (Brownstein 2003).

Before we conclude that people are simply muddleheaded, it is worth noting that many psychologists view such mental adjustments as a sign of mental health. Thus, the famed Alcoholics Anonymous Serenity Prayer asks for "the serenity to accept the things I cannot change, the courage to change the things I can, and the wisdom to know the difference." The psychological coping literature distinguishes primary control (trying to change one's circumstances) from secondary control (trying to adjust to one's circumstances), each of which is necessary for successful psychological development (Skinner et al. 2003). Taylor & Brown (1988) review a large body of evidence that "overly positive self-evaluations, exaggerated perceptions of control or mastery, and unrealistic optimism are characteristic of normal human thought" (p. 193) and essential to healthy coping. Alloy & Abramson (1979) were the first to report that depressed people are actually more accurate than nondepressed people at perceiving response-outcome contingencies in the environment; they are "sadder but wiser."

Research on just-world theory (Hafer & Bègue 2005, Lerner 1980) and system justification theory (see Jost et al. 2004 for a review) shows how these mental adjustments can distort evaluations of objective distributions of outcomes in the environment. Just-world researchers have found that people will engage in victim-blaming to avoid the threatening conclusion that the world is arbitrary and unjust. In a related view, Jost and colleagues (2004) define "system justification" as the "process by which existing social arrangements are legitimized, even at the expense of personal and group interest" (p. 883) in the service of a psychological need to believe that the status quo is "legitimate and natural." Jost and colleagues cite experimental and field evidence for a variety of propositions consistent with the theory; for example: (*a*) people judge likely events as more desirable than unlikely events; (*b*) they deploy stereotypes in a manner that justifies the existing status ranking; (*c*) disadvantaged group members will misperceive or misrecall evidence in a manner that legitimizes their situation, and they will accept readily "placebic explanations" that justify their status (Kappen & Branscombe 2001); and (*d*) when lower status groups perceive the system as legitimate, they show outgroup favoritism rather than the ingroup favoritism typically observed in social psychology. The theory might also help to explain why the perception that courts are biased is more common among higher- rather than lower-income African Americans (Brooks & Jeon-Slaughter 2001). The role of system justification processes in procedural justice effects is still unclear, and there are reasons to believe the two approaches are dealing with two different set of phenomena. First, many of the most robust procedural fairness effects have involved civil disputes between pairs of ordinary citizens, where outcomes are equivocal with respect to their implications for the system. Second, the work by Huo and others suggests that ethnic minorities are not more likely to endorse procedural fairness, but—at least among separatists—less so.

Another strategy is to examine how citizens respond to procedures when their linkage to outcomes is made more explicit ex ante. Perhaps the most direct and powerful analysis of the issue is a remarkable experiment by Lind et al. (1990a; also see Avery & Quiñones 2002; McFarlin & Sweeney 1996). Correlational analyses by Earley & Lind (1987) suggested that the voice effect is not mediated by perceptions of perceived control, contrary to Thibaut & Walker's (1975) interpretation. To test this more directly, Lind and colleagues enrolled students in a work simulation task in which the experimenter determined the participants' workload. They were randomly assigned to one of three voice conditions. In a control condition, participants had no opportunity to offer the experimenter their opinion about what would be a reasonable workload goal. In a traditional voice condition ("predecision voice"), the experimenter described his tentative decision—a demanding work schedule—but encouraged the participants to express their views. After hearing their opinions, he announced as his final decision a work schedule more in line with student opinions. In a "postdecision voice" condition, the experimenter announced his decision, stated that it was final and not subject to change, but said that he was interested in their views and that he would welcome their comments. After hearing them out, he restated his initial decision, using what the authors call "a calm and reassuring tone." Lind and colleagues (1990) found that although predecision voice produced greater fairness ratings than postdecision voice, both conditions produced significant increases in perceived fairness and perceived control over the no-voice condition. The authors argued, "It is clear that, at least within the context and subject population we studied, fairness judgments are enhanced by the opportunity to voice opinions even when there is no chance of influencing the decision." Explicitly noting the risk of false consciousness, they suggest that a misattribution of control "could lead the individuals in question to believe that the decision-making procedure was fair even though, by objective criteria, it is patently unfair. . . . If the perception of fairness is enhanced even in the face of the relatively straightforward denial of control involved in our postdecision voice condition, voice-enhanced fairness is all the more likely to occur in situations where a decision maker actively hides the ineffectiveness of input-conditions that may well be more common in the real world than is postdecision voice."

Work on the psychology of the citizen sheds important light on the question of false consciousness, but perhaps greater progress can be made if there is a shift in focus from the citizen to the authority. How are procedures selected, how are they represented to citizens, and when are they deployed (see Edelman et al. 1993, 1999)? When authorities choose empty symbolic procedures, do they do so out of their own symbolic needs or for self-interested instrumental means? These are empirical questions that can be assessed via experimental simulations, observational field work, and statistical analysis.

The neglect of the dark side of procedural justice is unfortunate. As a psychological dynamic, procedural fairness is clearly a double-edged sword. Our poignant desire for voice and dignity makes it possible to promote cooperation and tolerance in a diverse society facing uncertainty, scarcity, and inevitable conflicts of interest. But these same needs leave us potentially vulnerable to manipulation and exploitation by those who control resources and the processes for distributing them. The scientific study of procedural justice provides a nonideological tool for studying the malevolent as well as the benevolent aspects of fair treatment.

DEDICATION

This essay is dedicated to the memory of Lawrence A. Messé, a warm, witty, and wise mentor and justice scholar.

**The *Annual Review of Law and Social Science* is online at
http://lawsocsci.annualreviews.org**

LITERATURE CITED

Alloy LB, Abramson LY. 1979. Judgment of contingency in depressed and nondepressed students: sadder but wiser? *J. Exp. Psychol. General.* 108:441–85

Anderson E. 1999. *Code of the Streets: Decency, Violence and the Moral Life of the Inner City.* New York: Norton

Anderson RA, Otto AL. 2003. Perceptions of fairness in the justice system: a cross-cultural comparison. *Soc. Behav. Personal.* 31:557–64

Associated Press. 2005. Court tells Los Angeles City Council to listen. *NY Times*, National Section, A15. Jan. 2

Avery DR, Quiñones MA. 2002. Disentangling the effects of voice: the incremental roles of opportunity, behavior, and instrumentality in predicting procedural fairness. *J. Appl. Psychol.* 87:81–86

Bandura A. 1986. *Social Foundations of Thought and Action: A Social Cognitive Theory.* Englewood Cliffs, NJ: Prentice-Hall

Baron RM, Kenny DA. 1986. The moderator-mediator variable distinction in social psychological research: conceptual, strategic, and statistical considerations. *J. Pers. Soc. Psychol.* 51:1173–82

Beckman HB, Markakis KM, Suchman AL, Frankel RM. 1994. The doctor-patient relationship and malpractice. Lessons from plaintiff depositions. *Arch. Intern. Med.* 154:1365–70

Bies RJ, Martin CL, Brockner J. 1993. Just laid off, but still a "good citizen?" Only if the process is fair. *Empl. Responsib. Rights J.* 6:227–38

Bies RJ, Tyler TR. 1993. The "litigation mentality" in organizations: a test of alternative psychological explanations. *Organ. Sci.* 4:352–66

Blader SL, Tyler TR. 2003. A four-component model of procedural justice: defining the meaning of a "fair" process. *Personal. Soc. Psychol. Bull.* 29:747–58

Bollen KA. 2002. Latent variables in psychology and the social sciences. *Annu. Rev. Psychol.* 53:605–34

Braithwaite J. 2002. *Restorative Justice and Responsive Regulation.* New York: Oxford Univ. Press

Brockner J, Ackerman G, Greenberg J, Gelfand MJ, Francesco AM, et al. 2001. Culture and procedural justice: the influence of power distance on reactions to voice. *J. Exp. Soc. Psychol.* 37:300–15

Brockner J, Chen Y, Mannix EA, Leung K, Skarlicki DP. 2000. Culture and procedural fairness: when the effects of what you do depend on how you do it. *Admin. Sci. Q.* 45:138–59

Brockner J, DeWitt RL, Grover S, Reed T. 1990. When it is especially important to explain why: factors affecting the relationship between managers' explanations of a layoff

and survivors' reactions to the layoff. *J. Exp. Soc. Psychol.* 26:389–407

Brockner J, Tyler TR, Cooper-Schneider R. 1992. The influence of prior commitment to an institution on reactions to perceived unfairness: the higher they are, the harder they fall. *Admin. Sci. Q.* 37:241–61

Brockner J, Wiesenfeld BM. 1996. An integrative framework for explaining reactions to decisions: interactive effects of outcomes and procedures. *Psychol. Bull.* 120:189–208

Brooks R, Jeon-Slaughter H. 2001. Race, income, and perceptions of the US court system. *Behav. Sci. Law* 19:249–64

Brownstein AL. 2003. Biased predecision processing. *Psychol. Bull.* 129(4):545–68

Bur. Justice Stat. 2003. *Sourcebook of criminal justice statistics online.* http://www.albany.edu/sourcebook/

Casey JT, Scholz JT. 1991. Beyond deterrence: behavioral decision theory and tax compliance. *Law Soc. Rev.* 25(4):821–43

Casper JD, Tyler R, Fisher B. 1988. Procedural justice in felony cases. *Law Soc. Rev.* 22:483–507

Cohen RL. 1985. Procedural justice and participation. *Hum. Relat.* 38:643–63

Cohen RL. 1989. Fabrications of justice. *Soc. Justice Res.* 3:31–46

Cohen-Charash Y, Spector PE. 2001. The role of justice in organizations: a meta-analysis. *Organ. Behav. Hum. Dec. Proc.* 86:278–321. Erratum. 2002. *Organ. Behav. Hum. Dec. Proc.* 89:1215

Cohn ES, White SO, Sanders J. 2000. Distributive and procedural justice in seven nations. *Law Hum. Behav.* 24:553–79

Collie T, Bradley G, Sparks BA. 2002. Fair process revisited: differential effects of interactional and procedural justice in the presence of social comparison information. *J. Exp. Soc. Psychol.* 38:545–55

Colquitt JA. 2001. On the dimensionality of organizational justice: a construct validation of a measure. *J. Appl. Psychol.* 86:386–400

Colquitt JA, Conlon DE, Wesson MJ, Porter CO, Ng KY. 2001. Justice at the millennium: a meta-analytic review of 25 years of organizational justice research. *J. Appl. Psychol.* 86:425–45

Conlon DE, Lind EA, Lissak RI. 1989. Nonlinear and nonmonotonic effects of outcome on procedural and distributive fairness judgments. *J. Appl. Soc. Psychol.* 19:1085–99

Cropanzano R, Goldman B, Folger R. 2003. Deontic justice: the role of moral principles in workplace fairness. *J. Organ. Behav.* 24:1019–24

Crosby F. 1976. A model of egoistical relative deprivation. *Psychol. Rev.* 83:85–113

De Cremer D. 2003. Why inconsistent leadership is regarded as procedurally unfair: the importance of social self-esteem concerns. *Eur. J. Soc. Psychol.* 33:535–50

De Cremer D, Alberts HJEM. 2004. When procedural fairness does not influence how positive I feel: the effects of voice and leader selection as a function of belongingness need. *Eur. J. Soc. Psychol.* 34:333–44

De Cremer D, van Knippenberg D. 2003. Cooperation with leaders in social dilemmas: on the effects of procedural fairness and outcome favorability in structural cooperation. *Organ. Behav. Hum. Dec. Proc.* 91:1–11

Deutsch M. 1975. Equity, equality, and need: What determines which value will be used as the basis of distributive justice? *J. Soc. Issues* 31:137–49

Earley PC, Lind EA. 1987. Procedural justice and participation in task selection: the role of control in mediating justice judgments. *J. Pers. Soc. Psychol.* 52:1148–60

Edelman LB, Erlanger HS, Lande J. 1993. Internal dispute resolution: the transformation of civil rights in the workplace. *Law Soc. Rev.* 27:497–534

Edelman LB, Uggen C, Erlanger HS. 1999. The endogeneity of legal regulation: grievance procedures as rational myth. *Am. J. Sociol.* 105:406–54

Farmer SJ, Beehr TA, Love KG. 2003. Becoming an undercover police officer: a note on fairness perceptions, behavior, and attitudes. *J. Organ. Behav.* 24:373–87

Fiske AP. 1992. The four elementary forms of sociality: framework for a unified theory of social relations. *Psychol. Rev.* 99:689–723

Folger R. 1984. Perceived injustice, referent cognitions, and the concept of comparison level. *Represent. Res. Soc. Psychol.* 14:88–108

Folger R, Cropanzano R, Timmerman TA, Howes JC. 1996. Elaborating procedural fairness: justice becomes both simpler and more complex. *Personal. Soc. Psychol. Bull.* 22:435–41

Folger R, Konovsky MA. 1989. Effects of procedural and distributive justice on reactions to pay raise decisions. *Acad. Manag. J.* 32:115–130

Folger R, Martin C. 1986. Relative deprivation and referent cognitions: distributive and procedural justice effects. *J. Exp. Soc. Psychol.* 22:531–46

Folger R, Rosenfield D, Grove J, Corkran L. 1979. Effects of "voice" and peer opinions on responses to inequity. *J. Pers. Soc. Psychol.* 37:2253–61

Folger R, Rosenfield DD, Robinson T. 1983. Relative deprivation and procedural justifications. *J. Pers. Soc. Psychol.* 45:268–73

Forster HP, Schwartz J, DeRenzo E. 2002. Reducing legal risk by practicing patient-centered medicine. *Arch. Intern. Med.* 162:1217–19

Fox DR. 1993. Psychological jurisprudence and radical social change. *Am. Psychol.* 48:234–41

French JR, Raven B. 1959. The bases of social power. In *Studies in Social Power*, ed. D Cartwright, pp. 150–67. Ann Arbor, MI: Inst. Soc. Res., Univ. Mich.

Galanter M. 1998. The faces of mistrust: The image of lawyers in public opinion, jokes, and political discourse. *Univ. Cincinnati Law Rev.* 66:805–45

Garonzik R, Brockner J, Siegel PA. 2000. Identifying international assignees at risk for premature departure: the interactive effect of outcome favorability and procedural fairness. *J. Appl. Psychol.* 85:13–20

Gibson JL. 1989. Understandings of justice: institutional legitimacy, procedural justice, and political tolerance. *Law Soc. Rev.* 23:469–96

Goffman E. 1952. On cooling the mark out: some aspects of adaptation to failure. *Psychiatry* 15:451–63

Gold LJ, Darley JM, Hilton JL, Zanna MP. 1984. Children's perceptions of procedural justice. *Child Develop.* 55:1752–59

Greenberg J. 2001. Studying organizational justice cross-culturally: fundamental challenges. *Intern. J. Confl. Manag.* 12:365–75

Hafer CL, Bègue L. 2005. Experimental research on just-world theory: problems, developments, and future challenges. *Psychol. Bull.* 131:128–67

Haney C. 1991. The Fourteenth Amendment and symbolic legality: let them eat due process. *Law Hum. Behav.* 15:183–204

Hans VP. 1993. Attitudes toward the civil jury: a crisis of confidence? In *Verdict: Assessing the Civil Jury System*, ed. RE Litan, pp. 248–81. Washington, DC: Brookings Inst.

Hastie R, Rasinski KA. 1988. The concept of accuracy in social judgment. In *The Social Psychology of Knowledge*, ed. D Bar-Tal, AW Kruglanski, pp. 193–208. Cambridge: Cambridge Univ. Press

Hauenstein NMA, McGonigle T, Flinder SW. 2001. A meta-analysis of the relationship between procedural justice and distributive justice: implications for justice research. *Empl. Responsib. Rights J.* 13:39–56

Hawkins SA, Hastie R. 1990. Hindsight: biased judgments of past events after the outcomes are known. *Psychol. Bull.* 107:311–27

Hegtvedt KA, Killian C. 1999. Fairness and emotions: reactions to the process and outcomes of negotiations. *Soc. Forces* 78:269–302

Heuer L, Blumenthal E, Douglas A, Weinblatt T. 1999. A deservingness approach to respect as a relationally based fairness judgment. *Personal. Soc. Psychol. Bull.* 25:1279–92

Heuer L, Penrod S. 1986. Procedural preference as a function of conflict intensity. *J. Pers. Soc. Psychol.* 51:700–10

Heuer L, Penrod S. 1994. Predicting the outcomes of disputes: consequences for disputant reactions to procedures and outcomes. *J. Appl. Soc. Psychol.* 24:260–83

Hickson GB, Clayton EW, Githens PB, Sloan FA. 1992. Factors that prompted families to file medical malpractice claims following perinatal injuries. *JAMA* 267:1359–63

Hofstede G. 1980. *Culture's Consequences: International Differences in Work-Related Values.* Newbury Park, CA: Sage

Huo YJ. 2003. Procedural justice and social regulation across group boundaries: Does subgroup identity undermine relationship-based governance? *Personal. Soc. Psychol. Bull.* 29:336–48

Huo YJ, Smith HJ, Tyler TR, Lind EA. 1996. Superordinate identification, subgroup identification, and justice concerns: Is separatism the problem; is assimilation the answer? *Psychol. Sci.* 7:40–45

Jost JT. 1995. Negative illusions: conceptual clarification and psychological evidence concerning false consciousness. *Polit. Psychol.* 16:397–424

Jost JT, Banaji MR, Nosek BA. 2004. A decade of system justification theory: accumulated evidence of conscious and unconscious bolstering of the status quo. *Polit. Psychol.* 25(6):881–920

Kappen DM, Branscombe NR. 2001. The effects of reasons given for ineligibility on perceived gender discrimination and feelings of injustice. *Br. J. Soc. Psychol.* 40(Pt. 2):295–313

Kelley HH, Thibaut J. 1978. *Interpersonal Relations: A Theory of Interdependence.* New York: Wiley

Kershaw TS, Alexander S. 2003. Procedural fairness, blame attributions, and presidential leadership. *Soc. Justice Res.* 16:79–93

Krehbiel PJ, Cropanzano R. 2000. Procedural justice, outcome favorability, and emotion. *Soc. Justice Res.* 13:339–60

Kulik CT, Clark SC. 1993. Frustration effects in procedural justice research: the case of drug-testing legislation. *Soc. Justice Res.* 6:287–99

Kulik CT, Lind EA, Ambrose ML, MacCoun RJ. 1996. Understanding gender differences in distributive and procedural justice. *Soc. Justice Res.* 9:351–69

Kwong JYY, Leung K. 2002. A moderator of the interaction effect of procedural justice and outcome favorability: importance of the relationship. *Organ. Behav. Hum. Dec. Proc.* 87:278–99

Lerner MJ. 1980. *The Belief in a Just World: A Fundamental Delusion.* New York: Plenum

Leventhal GS. 1980. What should be done with equity theory? New approaches to the study of fairness in social relationships. In *Social Exchange: Advances in Theory and Research*, ed. KJ Gergen, MS Greenberg, RH Willis, pp. 27–53. New York: Plenum

Levinson W, Roter DL, Mulooly JP, Dull VT, Frankel RM. 1997. Physician-patient communication: the relationship with malpractice claims among primary care physicians and surgeons. *JAMA* 277:553–59

Leung K, Lind EA. 1986. Procedural justice and culture: effects of culture, gender, and investigator status on procedural preferences. *J. Pers. Soc. Psychol.* 50:1134–40

Lind EA. 1990. *Arbitrating High-Stakes Cases: An Evaluation of Court-Annexed Arbitration in a US District Court.* Santa Monica: RAND

Lind EA. 2001. Fairness heuristic theory: justice judgments as pivotal cognitions in organizational relations. In *Advances in Organizational Behavior*, ed. J Greenberg, R Cropanzano, pp. 56–88. Stanford, CA: Stanford Univ. Press

Lind EA, Greenberg J, Scott KS, Welchans TD. 2000. The winding road from employee to complainant: situational and psychological determinants of wrongful termination claims. *Admin. Sci. Q.* 45:557–90

Lind EA, Huo YJ, Tyler TR. 1994. And justice for all: ethnicity, gender, and preferences for dispute resolution procedures. *Law Hum. Behav.* 18:269–90

Lind EA, Kanfer R, Earley PC. 1990a. Voice, control, and procedural justice: instrumental and noninstrumental concerns in fairness judgments. *J. Pers. Soc. Psychol.* 59:952–59

Lind EA, Kulik CT, Ambrose M, de Vera Park MV. 1993. Individual and corporate dispute resolution: using procedural fairness as a decision heuristic. *Admin. Sci. Q.* 38:224–51

Lind EA, Lissak RI. 1985. Apparent impropriety and procedural fairness judgments. *J. Exp. Soc. Psychol.* 21:19–29

Lind EA, MacCoun RJ, Ebener PA, Felstiner WLF, Hensler DR, et al. 1990b. In the eye of the beholder: tort litigants' evaluations of their experiences in the civil justice system. *Law Soc. Rev.* 24:953–96

Lind EA, Tyler TR. 1988. *The Social Psychology of Procedural Justice.* New York: Plenum

Lind EA, Tyler TR, Huo YJ. 1997. Procedural context and culture: variation in the antecedents of procedural justice judgments. *J. Pers. Soc. Psychol.* 73:767–80

Long JJ. 2003. Compliance in small claims court: exploring the factors associated with defendants' level of compliance with mediated and adjudicated outcomes. *Confl. Resolut. Q.* 21:139–53

MacCoun RJ. 1993. Drugs and the law: a psychological analysis of drug prohibition. *Psychol. Bull.* 113:497–512

MacCoun RJ. 2001. Public opinion about legal issues. In *International Encyclopedia of the Social and Behavioral Sciences*, ed. NJ Smelser, PB Baltes, pp. 8641–46. Amsterdam/New York: Elsevier

MacCoun RJ. 2005. Conflicts of interest in public policy research. In *Conflicts of Interest: Problems and Solutions from Law, Medicine and Organizational Settings*, ed. DA Moore, DM Cain, G Loewenstein, M Bazerman, pp. 233–62. London: Cambridge Univ. Press

MacCoun RJ, Lind EA, Hensler DR, Bryant DL, Ebener P. 1988. *Alternative Adjudication: An Evaluation of the New Jersey Automobile Arbitration Program.* Santa Monica, CA: RAND

MacCoun RJ, Lind EA, Tyler TR. 1992. Alternative dispute resolution in trial and appellate courts. In *The Handbook of Psychology and Law*, ed. DK Kagehiro, WS Laufer, pp. 95–118. New York: Springer Verlag

MacCoun RJ, Tyler TR. 1988. The basis of citizens' perceptions of the criminal jury: procedural fairness, accuracy and efficiency. *Law Hum. Behav.* 12:333–52

Makkai T, Braithwaite J. 1996. Procedural justice and regulatory compliance. *Law Hum. Behav.* 20:83–98

McFarlin DB, Sweeney PD. 1992. Distributive and procedural justice as predictors of satisfaction with personal and organizational outcomes. *Acad. Manag. J.* 35:626–37

McFarlin DB, Sweeney PD. 1996. Does having a say matter only if you get your way? Instrumental and value-expressive effects of employee voice. *Basic Appl. Soc. Psychol.* 18:289–303

Mellers BA, Baron J, eds. 1993. *Psychological Perspectives on Justice.* New York: Cambridge Univ. Press

Messé LA, Hymes RW, MacCoun RJ. 1986. Group categorization and distributive justice decisions. In *Justice in Social Relations*, ed. HW Bierhoff, RL Cohen, J Greenberg, pp. 227–48. New York: Plenum

Miller DT. 1999. The norm of self-interest. *Am. Psychol.* 54(12):1053–60

Miller DT. 2001. Disrespect and the experience of injustice. *Annu. Rev. Psychol.* 52:527–53

Mondak JJ. 1993. Institutional legitimacy and procedural justice: reexamining the question of causality. *Law Soc. Rev.* 27:599–608

Mook DG. 1983. In defense of external invalidity. *Am. Psychol.* 38:379–87

Morris MW, Leung K. 2000. Justice for all? Progress in research on cultural variation in the psychology of distributive and procedural justice. *Appl. Psychol.* 49:100–32

Morris MW, Leung K, Lyengar SS. 2004. Person perception in the heat of conflict: negative trait attributions affect procedural preferences and account for situational and cultural differences. *Asian J. Soc. Psychol.* 7:127–47

Murphy K. 2004. The role of trust in nurturing compliance: a study of accused tax avoiders. *Law Hum. Behav.* 28:187–209

New York Times. 2004. Making the rules to play by. April 19, p. A11

Opotow S. 1996. Affirmative action, fairness, and the scope of justice. *J. Soc. Issues* 52:19–24

Paternoster R, Bachman R, Brame R, Sherman LW. 1997. Do fair procedures matter? The effect of procedural justice on spouse assault. *Law Soc. Rev.* 31:163–204

Pillai R, Williams ES, Tan JJ. 2001. Are the scales tipped in favor of procedural or distributive justice? An investigation of the US, India, Germany, and Hong Kong (China). *Int. J. Confl. Manag.* 12:312–32

Poythress NG. 1994. Procedural preferences, perceptions of fairness, and compliance with outcomes: a study of alternatives to the standard adversary trial procedure. *Law Hum. Behav.* 18:361–76

Rahim MA, Magner NR, Antonioni D, Rahman S. 2001. Do justice relationships with organization-directed reactions differ across US and Bangladesh employees? *Int. J. Confl. Manag.* 12:333–49

Robbins TL, Summers TP, Miller JL, Hendrix WH. 2000. Using the group-value model to explain the role of noninstrumental justice in distinguishing the effects of distributive and procedural justice. *J. Occup. Organ. Psychol.* 73:511–18

Roberts K, Markel KS. 2001. Claiming in the name of fairness: organizational justice and the decision to file for workplace injury compensation. *J. Occup. Health Psychol.* 6:332–47

Rogosa D. 1980. A critique of cross-lagged correlation. *Psychol. Bull.* 88:245–58

Sheppard B, Vidmar N. 1980. Adversary pretrial procedures and testimonial evidence: Effects of lawyers' role and Machiavellianism. *J. Pers. Soc. Psychol.* 39:320–32

Sheppard BH. 1985. Justice is no simple matter: case for elaborating our model of procedural fairness. *J. Pers. Soc. Psychol.* 49:953–62

Shestowsky D. 2004. Procedural preferences in alternative dispute resolution: a closer, modern look at an old idea. *Psychol. Public Policy Law* 10:211–49

Skinner EA, Edge K, Altman J, Sherwood H. 2003. Searching for the structure of coping: a review and critique of category systems for classifying ways of coping. *Psychol. Bull.* 129:216–69

Skitka LJ. 2002. Do the means always justify the ends, or do the ends sometimes justify the means? A value model of justice reasoning. *Personal. Soc. Psychol. Bull.* 28:588–97

Skitka LJ. 2003. Of different minds: an accessible identity model of justice reasoning. *Personal. Soc. Psychol. Rev.* 7:286–97

Skitka LJ, Houston DA. 2001. When due process is of no consequence: moral mandates and presumed defendant guilt or innocence. *Soc. Justice Res.* 14:305–26

Skitka LJ, Mullen E. 2002. Understanding judgments of fairness in a real-world political context: a test of the value protection model of justice reasoning. *Personal. Soc. Psychol. Bull.* 28:1419–29

Skitka LJ, Winquist J, Hutchinson S. 2003. Are outcome fairness and outcome favorability distinguishable psychological constructs? A meta-analytic review. *Soc. Justice Res.* 16: 309–41

Skogan W, Frydl K, eds. 2003. *Fairness and Effectiveness in Policing: The Evidence.* Washington, DC: Natl. Acad. Press

Smith HJ, Tyler TR. 1996. Justice and power: When will justice concerns encourage the advantaged to support policies which redistribute economic resources and the disadvantaged to willingly obey the law? *Eur. J. Soc. Psychol.* 26:171–200

Smith HJ, Tyler TR, Huo YJ, Ortiz DJ, Lind EA. 1998. The self-relevant implications of the group-value model: group membership, self-worth, and treatment quality. *J. Exp. Soc. Psychol.* 34:470–93

Ståhl T, Van Prooijen J-W, Vermunt R. 2004. On the psychology of procedural justice: reactions to procedures of ingroup vs. outgroup authorities. *Eur. J. Soc. Psychol.* 34:173–89

Stalans L, Lind EA. 1997. The meaning of procedural fairness: a comparison of taxpayers' and representatives' views of their tax audits. *Soc. Justice Res.* 10:311–31

Strang H. 2004. *Repair or Revenge: Victims and Restorative Justice.* Oxford: Clarendon

Sweeney PD, McFarlin DB. 1993. Workers' evaluations of the "ends" and the "means": an examination of four models of distributive and procedural justice. *Organ. Behav. Hum. Dec. Proc.* 55:23–40

Sweeney PD, McFarlin DB. 1997. Process and outcome: gender differences in the assessment of justice. *J. Organ. Behav.* 18:83–98

Taylor SE, Brown JD. 1988. Illusion and wellbeing: a social psychological perspective on mental health. *Psychol. Bull.* 103:193–210

Thibaut J, Walker L. 1975. *Procedural Justice.* Hillsdale, NJ: Erlbaum

Thibaut J, Walker L. 1978. A theory of procedure. *Calif. Law Rev.* 26:1271–89

Tornblom KY, Vermunt R. 1999. An integrative perspective on social justice: distributive and procedural fairness evaluations of positive and negative outcome allocations. *Soc. Justice Res.* 12:39–64

Tyler TR. 1984. The role of perceived injustice in defendants' evaluations of their courtroom experience. *Law Soc. Rev.* 18:51–74

Tyler TR. 1988. What is procedural justice? Criteria used by citizens to assess the fairness of legal procedures. *Law Soc. Rev.* 22:103–35

Tyler TR. 1989. The psychology of procedural justice: a test of the group-value model. *J. Pers. Soc. Psychol.* 57:830–38

Tyler TR. 1990. *Why People Obey the Law.* New Haven, CT: Yale Univ. Press

Tyler TR. 1994. Psychological models of the justice motive: antecedents of distributive and procedural justice. *J. Pers. Soc. Psychol.* 67:850–63

Tyler TR. 2001. Public trust and confidence in legal authorities: What do majority and minority group members want from the law and legal institutions? *Behav. Sci. Law.* 19:215–35

Tyler TR. 2003. Procedural justice, legitimacy, and the effective rule of law. In *Crime and Justice: A Review of Research*, ed. M Tonry, 30:283–358. Chicago: Univ. Chicago Press

Tyler TR, Boeckmann RJ. 1997. Three strikes and you are out, but why? The psychology of public support for punishing rule breakers. *Law Soc. Rev.* 31:237–65

Tyler TR, Boeckmann RJ, Smith HJ, Huo YJ. 1997. *Social Justice in a Diverse Society.* Boulder, CO: Westview

Tyler TR, Degoey P. 1995. Collective restraint in social dilemmas: procedural justice and social identification effects on support for authorities. *J. Pers. Soc. Psychol.* 69:482–97

Tyler T, Degoey P, Smith H. 1996. Understanding why the justice of group procedures matters: a test of the psychological dynamics of the group-value model. *J. Pers. Soc. Psychol.* 70:913–30

Tyler TR, Folger R. 1980. Distributional and procedural aspects of satisfaction with citizen-police encounters. *Basic Appl. Soc. Psychol.* 1:281–92

Tyler TR, Huo YJ. 2002. *Trust in the Law: Encouraging Public Cooperation with the Police and Courts.* New York: Russell Sage Found.

Tyler TR, Huo YJ, Lind EA. 1999. The two psychologies of conflict resolution: differing antecedents of pre-experience choices and post-experience evaluations. *Group Process. Intergr. Relat.* 2:99–118

Tyler TR, Lind EA. 1990. Intrinsic versus community-based justice models: When does group membership matter? *J. Soc. Issues* 46:83–94

Tyler TR, Lind EA. 1992. A relational model of authority in groups. In *Advances in Experimental Social Psychology*, ed. MP Zanna, 25:115–91. San Diego, CA: Academic

Tyler TR, Lind EA, Huo YJ. 2000. Cultural values and authority relations: the psychology of conflict resolution across cultures. *Psychol. Public Policy Law* 6:1138–63

Tyler TR, Lind EA, Ohbuchi K, Sugawara I, Huo YJ. 1998. Conflict with outsiders: disputing within and across cultural boundaries. *Personal. Soc. Psychol. Bull.* 24:137–46

Tyler TR, McGraw KM. 1986. Ideology and the interpretation of personal experience: procedural justice and political quiescence. *J. Soc. Issues* 42:115–28

Tyler TR, Mitchell G. 1994. Legitimacy and the empowerment of discretionary legal authority: the United States Supreme Court and abortion rights. *Duke Law J.* 43:703–814

Tyler TR, Rasinski K. 1991. Procedural justice, institutional legitimacy and the acceptance of unpopular U.S. Supreme Court decisions: a reply to Gibson. *Law Soc. Rev.* 25:621–30

Van den Bos K. 1999. What are we talking about when we talk about no-voice procedures? On the psychology of the fair outcome effect. *J. Exp. Soc. Psychol.* 35:560–77

Van den Bos K. 2001. Uncertainty management: the influence of uncertainty salience on reactions to perceived procedural fairness. *J. Pers. Soc. Psychol.* 80:931–41

Van den Bos K, Lind EA. 2002. Uncertainty management by means of fairness judgments. *Adv. Exp. Soc. Psychol.* 34:1–60

Van den Bos K, Lind EA, Vermunt R, Wilke HAM. 1997a. How do I judge my outcome when I do not know the outcome of others? The psychology of the fair process effect. *J. Pers. Soc. Psychol.* 72:1034–46

Van den Bos K, van Prooijen J-W. 2001. Referent cognitions theory: the role of closeness of reference points in the psychology of voice. *J. Pers. Soc. Psychol.* 81:616–26

Van den Bos K, Vermunt R, Wilke HAM. 1997b. Procedural and distributive justice: what is fair depends more on what comes first than on what comes next. *J. Pers. Soc. Psychol.* 72:95–104

Van den Bos K, Wilke HAM, Lind EA, Vermunt R. 1998. Evaluating outcomes by means of the fair process effect: evidence for different processes in fairness and satisfaction judgments. *J. Pers. Soc. Psychol.* 74:1493–503

Van Prooijen J, Van den Bos K, Wilke HAM. 2002. Procedural justice and status: status salience as antecedent of procedural fairness effects. *J. Pers. Soc. Psychol.* 83:1353–61

Van Prooijen J, Van den Bos K, Wilke HAM. 2004. Group belongingness and procedural justice: social inclusion and exclusion by peers affects the psychology of voice. *J. Pers. Soc. Psychol.* 87:66–79

Vermunt R, Blaauw E, Lind EA. 1998. Fairness evaluations of encounters with police officers and correctional officers. *J. Appl. Soc. Psychol.* 28:1107–24

Vincent C, Young M, Phillips A. 1994. Why do people sue doctors? A study of patients and relatives taking legal action. *Lancet* 343:1609–13

Wagner K, Moriarty LJ. 2002. Perceived fairness of drug-testing policies: an application of Leventhal's principles of procedural justice. *Am. J. Crim. Justice* 26:219–33

Walster E, Walster G. 1975. Equity and social justice. *J. Soc. Issues* 31:21–43

Weber M. 1968. *Economy and Society: An Outline of Interpretive Sociology.* New York: Bedminster

Wendorf CA, Alexander S, Firestone IJ. 2002. Social justice and moral reasoning: an empirical integration of two paradigms in psychological research. *Soc. Justice Res.* 15:19–39

Wenzel M. 2002. The impact of outcome orientation and justice concerns on tax compliance: the role of taxpayers' identity. *J. Appl. Psychol.* 87:629–45

Wenzel M. 2004. Social identification as a determinant of concerns about individual-, group-, and inclusive-level justice. *Soc. Psychol. Q.* 67:70–87

Wilkinson RG. 1997. Health inequalities: relative or absolute material standards. *Br. Med. J.* 314:591–95

Wines M, LaFraniere S. 2005. For Zimbabwe, peaceful vote, but is it fair? *NY Times*, April 18, pp. A1, A6

Annu. Rev. Law Soc. Sci. 2005. 1:203–31
doi: 10.1146/annurev.lawsocsci.1.041604.115931
First published online as a Review in Advance on July 5, 2005

LAW, RACE, AND EDUCATION IN THE UNITED STATES

Samuel R. Lucas and Marcel Paret

*Department of Sociology, University of California, Berkeley, California 94720;
email: Lucas@demog.berkeley.edu; MParet@berkeley.edu*

Key Words   inequality, policy, ethnicity, discrimination

■ **Abstract**   After describing many of the features that structure educational opportunity, and how race interacts with these structures, we briefly relate a set of important orienting perspectives on the law-race relation. We divide issues of education into three categories: (*a*) inherently racialized aspects of law and education; (*b*) aspects of education that intersect race and the law; and (*c*) emerging issues in race, education, and the law. Treating desegregation, affirmative action, special education, gifted and talented education, tracking, high-stakes accountability, school finance, bilingual education, and legacy admissions, we identify key cases and controversies while critically evaluating relevant social science research. We close with a discussion of the law-race relation as revealed through its operation in the field of education.

INTRODUCTION

Education has been a site of racial contestation for decades, and the law has been a weapon in that social conflict throughout. From before the landmark *Brown v. Board of Education* (1954) case to the present, social science research has been party to the conflict. Hence, a burgeoning and diverse literature relevant to race, education, and the law has developed.

Before turning to that literature, however, we must make four observations. First, the very definition of race is contested in the contemporary period (Am. Anthropol. Assoc. 1998, Am. Sociol. Assoc. 2002, Harris & Sim 2002, Omi & Winant 1994, Omi 2001). Rather than engage that debate, we propose a working resolution based in the history that justifies the attention of the law to considerations of race. While not denying the potential importance of one's stated racial identity for one's own experience, and without affirming or denying the putative biological basis of race, we draw on the history of socially defined racial exclusion. In that history, racial classification turned not on what one felt but, instead, on what others allowed one to do. We believe that the exclusionary aspect of race may be as dominant now as it was in the past, and certainly remains important in the contemporary period. Thus, there is little need to address matters of personal identification or to resolve the biological facts of the phenomenon. Instead, one can attend to race with respect to its social role in determining how power will be wielded by significant social actors—teachers, principals, admissions committees, funding agencies, and more. It is that use of power that principally concerns the nexus of law, race, and education.

Second, the relationship of law, race, and education has developed over time. Undeniably, part of that development has entailed changes in the content of each aspect. Throughout, race has operated as a dimension along which power has been allocated to some and denied to others. We bracket changes in race, while acknowledging their importance (Anderson & Fienberg 2000, Omi 1997). Here, however, we focus on the changing internal aspects of law and education. Hence, although we attend to the present, we mention selected important historical developments in both.

Third, the law works differently for different stages of the educational process. Sometimes law applies in a straightforward fashion for all levels and types of education, whereas other times it applies narrowly.

Fourth, and most important, the role of law in race and education is not limited to the cases, rulings, and legislation that specifically mention or emphasize race. To limit attention to such matters is tempting, for there is certainly a great deal to cover within those confines, but to do so would be to deeply mischaracterize the relationship of race, education, and the law. Thus, a proper review of the phenomenon will not be so constrained.

Hence, it is important to attend to the history of race, education, and the law and to the different levels of education within which that relation is enacted, and to broaden our concern to areas in which legal principles are relevant if not explicitly invoked. Once one opens to considering the role of law in race and education as historically developing in a broadly construed field of power relations, it becomes necessary to outline at least briefly the broader structures that channel educational opportunity in the United States, at least contemporaneously. These structures often fall into place over time owing to processes that have a sometimes unrecognized racial dimension. Alternatively, these structures often sustain racial inequality through time, thus raising the possibility of legal attention now or in the future. Either way, their operation reflects acquiescence of, or active production by, the legal sphere, and thus requires attention in a thoroughgoing review.

Of course, there is insufficient space to outline every way in which the law might structure race and education, nor is there space to describe every complexity that attends those possibilities. Thus, this review treats selected major issues and closes by identifying an additional possibility not yet on the courts' docket. But, the effort begins by outlining education in the United States in general. It is to that task we now turn.

STRUCTURES OF OPPORTUNITY

Students are allocated to schools, and within schools to courses, classrooms, and teachers. Educational opportunity is structured by these allocations.

No one denies that schools differ in the resources at their disposal. For example, class size, computer availability, and less tangible resources such as disciplinary approaches and academic expectations all vary across schools and shape opportunities for learning (Mayer et al. 2000). Human capital, in the form of knowledgeable, experienced teachers, is also differentially distributed. Processes of teacher allocation often send more experienced teachers trained in their disciplines to wealthier schools and relegate students in poorer schools to studying with less experienced teachers untrained in the areas in which they teach (e.g., Mayer et al. 2000).

Resources are also allocated differentially inside schools. Clearly, students occupy different in-school structural locations. Some enter gifted and talented programs; others receive individualized education plans (IEPs), i.e., are placed in special education. Processes of general course assignment in a differentiated curriculum may eventuate in tracking—the systematic placement of students in courses of similar levels across subjects—even though formal tracking has declined since the mid-1960s (Carey et al. 1994, Moore & Davenport 1988, Oakes 1981). Evidence suggests that the assignment of students to courses occurs in concert with the assignment of the best teachers to the most advanced classes (e.g., Finley 1984), possibly exacerbating the impact of tracking.

Further, educational opportunities may vary among students within the same classroom, as teacher-student relationships and interaction are different for different students. These relationships influence teachers' perceptions of students' abilities, expectations for students' future performance, and behavior toward students (Ferguson 1998a). Thus, varying teacher perceptions, expectations, or treatment of students in the same classroom can have a profound impact on students' opportunities (e.g., Pallas et al. 1994).

Researchers have found that these factors matter. Family background matters for achievement (e.g., Coleman et al. 1966), but so do class size (Ehrenberg et al. 2001, Krueger & Whitmore 2002), computer use (Pres. Comm. Advis. Sci. Technol. Panel Educ. Technol. 1997), per-pupil expenditure (Krueger & Whitmore 2002), teachers' use of best practices (Elliott 1998), teacher academic skills and experience (Ferguson 1998b, Murnane & Phillips 1981), teacher perceptions and expectations (Ferguson 1998a), and student track location (Lucas & Gamoran 2002).

RACE AND STRUCTURES OF OPPORTUNITY

Race is associated with many outcomes of schooling, some of which are themselves inputs for later educational opportunity. Table 1 draws from several sources to document race-linked inequality in educational success. On the basis of the statistics

TABLE 1 Probability of having characteristics associated with educational success and opportunity

Characteristic	Student race/ethnicity					
	White	Black	Asian	Latino/a	Native American	Other
Early childhood[a]						
Mastering addition and subtraction by the spring of first grade	78.0	56.0	74.0	68.0	—	64.0
Being able to "read words in context" by the spring of first grade	50.0	33.0	57.0	40.0	—	35.0
High school[b]						
Achieving the NAEP highest math proficiency level, 17-year-olds, 1999	10.4	1.0	—	3.1	—	—
Taking a high-level combination of courses, 2000 high school graduates	31.5	28.9	37.8	28.4	16.2	—
High school or GED completion by 2000, NELS 1988 eighth grade cohort	94.0	91.0	99.0	87.0	—	—
High school dropout, 16- to 24-year-olds, 2001 (U.S. degrees only)	7.3	10.9	—	27.0	—	—
Postsecondary transition and completion[c]						
Postsecondary enrollment by 2000, if high school graduate, NELS 1988 eighth grade cohort	82.0	80.0	95.0	82.0	—	—
Postsecondary credential by 2000, if college entry, NELS 1988 eighth grade cohort	46.0	27.0	56.0	23.0	—	—
Bachelor's degree by 1992, 1980 high school sophomores	27.5	12.2	45.6	9.9	7.2	—
Additional[d]						
Special education placement for mental retardation, all grades, 1998	1.2	2.6	0.6	0.9	1.3	—
Placement in a gifted and talented program, all grades, 1998	7.5	3.0	10.0	3.6	4.9	—
Fear of being attacked or harmed at school in the last six months, 12- to 18-year-olds, 1999	3.9	9.0	—	8.1	—	4.2
Ever repeated a grade, all elementary and secondary students	9.0	18.0	7.0	13.0	18.0	—
Ever been suspended or expelled, all elementary and secondary students	15.0	35.0	13.0	20.0	38.0	—

[a]Early childhood sources: Rathbun et al. (2004: A-13, A-16).

[b]High school sources: Natl. Cent. Educ. Stat. (2003a, tables 107, 122, 140; 2003b, pp. 1–2).

[c]Postsecondary transition and completion sources: Natl. Cent. Educ. Stat. (2003a, table 309; 2003b, pp. 1–2).

[d]Additional sources: Donovan & Cross (2002, pp. 44, 51); Kaufman et al. (2001, p. 27); Natl. Cent. Educ. Stat. quick tables (http://www.nces.ed.gov/quicktables).

presented, it appears that across grades, intellectual domains, educational thresholds, and types of placement, white and Asian students do better and black and Latino/a students do worse. Evidence also indicates that educational opportunities are more restricted for minority students than for white students. For example, studies show that minority students tend to have less experienced teachers (Mayer et al. 2000), have larger class sizes (Boozer et al. 1992, Mayer et al. 2000), and use computers less often (Boozer et al. 1992).

These figures and others document race-linked differences in achievement and opportunity but do not explain the differences. Various theories exist (e.g., Fischer et al. 1996, Herrnstein & Murray 1994, Jencks & Phillips 1998). Socioeconomic differences alone do not explain racial inequality, as most race-linked differences decline but remain noteworthy after socioeconomic factors are controlled (e.g., Jencks & Phillips 1998). Hence, race appears to be a distinct phenomenon relevant for education.

ORIENTING PERSPECTIVES ON RACE AND THE LAW

Law is the midwife of race. In the 1600s, persons of every hue arrived on the eastern shores of the Atlantic, with indentured servants ready to work off their subjugation. But, as more and more colonists of a variety of social classes arrived from Europe, the prospect of social upheaval near shore led colonial elites to seek a safety valve. The frontier provided an option, but as Europeans advanced inland they encountered native peoples still living there. European settlers were not content to share the bounty. To justify their taking of the land and its abundant resources, Europeans sought to set themselves over and above the native peoples (Richter 2001). The developing concept of race became key to this undertaking, affording a way to preserve property as inviolate (thus maintaining status quo power relations among Europeans) while legitimating white ownership of what whites were taking from Native Americans. At the same time, indentured servitude of whites disappeared, while laws placed African Americans alone in perpetual slavery. Property as expectation, as dispositive possession, as first possession, indeed under various different conceptions, property rights came to depend on the race of the ostensible owner (Harris 1993). That dependence continued well beyond the colonial period.

For example, Harris (1993) analyzes cases in which plaintiffs have sought redress for being called nonwhite, noting that the courts have ruled that to allege that a white person is black is to cause injury [e.g., *Bowen v. Independent Publishing Co.* (1957)]. The courts have recognized no such proscription against calling a black person white. As Harris notes, the injury exists in part because of the expectations that those who are regarded as white may form, expectations of being able to conduct their affairs with the full weight of the United States government behind them and with the fullest possible autonomy consistent with a society of free persons. This expectation is a property right in whiteness and is endangered when one is accused of lacking whiteness. Indeed, material instances of racialized property rights are not confined to the distant past—Singer (1991) shows that the Supreme Court ruled in 1980 that there was no constitutional requirement that property seized from Native American tribes be justly compensated (Singer 1991, pp. 719–20).

Because of these patterns, some legal scholars conclude that whiteness is property. Although first possession may be said to define property, in actuality first *white* possession has defined the property-owner relation. Or, if property is an expectation of power over the possessed good, in actuality, only *whites'* expectations have been consistently enforceable. These scholars argue that without whiteness one's property claims are insecure.

Of course, centuries after the inception of the law-race relation, the reification of race complicates matters. The law may no longer be directly implicated in the maintenance of racial disadvantage. This possibility raises important questions. Is law in the more recent period a tool for racial justice? Or, instead, is the law-race relation epiphenomenal, spurious, driven by other more fundamental factors? And, if so, what other factors might be plausible candidates for such a powerful role?

Derrick Bell, upon noting the fluctuating extension and retrenchment of rights for African Americans, presents a thesis of interest convergence: the rights and well-being of African Americans will be advanced only when doing so matches the interests of the dominant, i.e., upper- and middle-class whites (Bell 1980, 2004). This thesis explains changes in the law by recourse to extralegal factors and motivations. This position sees the centuries as passing with little erosion in the fundamental role of law in protecting racially dominant groups. In this respect the perspective resonates with a separatist strain in African American activism, a strain identified with black nationalism, Marcus Garvey, and others.

In contrast, a commitment to pursue advancement and justice largely within the confines of the Constitution and U.S. institutions sees law as a potential weapon for disadvantaged groups seeking justice. Agnostic about the fundamental mover of the law, the law is still seen as a means for effecting real social change. The work of the NAACP, for example, reflects this strain of black activism.

These two visions have long been in tension in African American thought. These perspectives differently interpret the facts of race and the law. Education is one arena within which race and law come together. Consequently, awareness of these perspectives may aid our understanding, heightening our sensitivity to potential ambiguities as we consider the phenomenon of law, race, and education in the United States.

INHERENTLY RACIAL ASPECTS OF LAW AND EDUCATION

Race is relevant for education, and some educational issues are inherently racial. Racial desegregation is an issue only by virtue of the historic racial classification of students and concomitant denial of opportunities to nonwhites. Similarly, affirmative action with respect to race, which principally concerns postsecondary admissions, inherently entails the legal recognition of race in education.

Desegregation

The racial desegregation cases of the mid-twentieth century spawned major social change. They affected every level of formal education, and the early decisions reverberated through every sphere of social interaction in the United States. Separate but equal had been ruled constitutional in *Plessy v. Ferguson* (1896); *Brown v. Board of Education* (1954) was a landmark reversal of that position, a catalyst in the dismantling of the Jim Crow system.

In the wake of *Brown*, and as the desegregation effort unfolded, researchers attempted to ascertain the effects of desegregation on several outcomes, including achievement, attitudes, and cross-race interactions. In reviewing the desegregation effects literature, Wells (1995) notes that many of the early studies did not attend to the details of implementation. Focused on evaluating whether desegregation mattered, researchers designed studies as if specific details of desegregation policy, such as the voluntary or compulsory nature of the policy or the time between implementation and evaluation, were ignorable. According to Wells, this inattention to detail greatly reduced the value of those studies. Still, the best evidence suggests that desegregation raised the achievement of blacks while maintaining the achievement of whites (Wells & Crain 1994).

Research also indicates that blacks who attended desegregated schools obtained long-term gains in educational and occupational attainment (Wells 1995). At the same time, whites did not suffer short- or long-term losses owing to desegregation (Wells & Crain 1994). Further, effects extended beyond measured achievement, affecting cross-racial contact and student attitudes. However, these effects depended more on the racial composition of classes than the racial composition of schools (Wells 1995), and desegregated classrooms were not a given. Research shows that desegregated schools often gave way to in-school segregation, as schools used tracking in ways that led to racially identifiable classrooms (e.g., Metz 1978; Oakes 1985, 1995).

In-school resegregation was but one white response to school desegregation. As parents, teachers, principals, and district officials, many whites intensely resisted desegregation. Reporters chronicled the spread of segregation academies during the 1960s—the opening of private all-white schools in areas explicitly threatened with desegregation (Cleghorn 1970, *Time* 1969). Further, white urban out-migration—white flight—occurred after desegregation. Yet, research remains equivocal on whether school desegregation caused white flight (e.g., Smock & Wilson 1991).

One challenge with studying school desegregation effects on white flight is that several other factors may have pushed white migration, including cost advantages stemming from the building of the interstate highway system and from federal mortgage policies (e.g., Massey & Denton 1993). Of course, the racialized nature of these policies is well documented (e.g., Massey & Denton 1993, Bayor 1988). However, another difficulty with the statistical approaches to studying the causes of white flight is that the statistical models depend crucially on an important assumption. In the usual analysis, the researcher assumes that the objects of study (e.g., schools) are independent, such that what happens to one unit (e.g., a school) does not indicate and is not affected by what happens to others. This independence assumption can of course be relaxed in certain circumstances, but even so, the putative causal factor under investigation is assumed to affect objects under study more or less independently. This assumption of independence, unthinkingly applicable in most settings, appears untenable in the case of desegregation, an epochal intervention that touched "treated" and "untreated" institutions and their contexts in complex ways.

That the independence assumption does not apply to desegregation implies that the effort to discern a separable, statistically estimable effect on white enrollments of school desegregation is misplaced. At the time, school desegregation was not a precise, targeted intervention, no matter how much policy makers may have tried to design it to be just that. In the context of the 1950s, 1960s, and 1970s, if not later, school desegregation is more accurately conceived as part of a larger phenomenon of changing race relations, with changing or at least challenged power dynamics at its core. Arguably, residential dislocations (e.g., black urban in-migration; white urban out-migration), political party realignment, and more were consequences of this challenge.

Of course, this observation raises the question of what caused this challenge to power dynamics. Some scholars argue that changing geo-political realities led white elites to see a cost to continued de jure segregation (e.g., Bell 1980, Borstelmann 2001, Dudziak 2000). These researchers point to previous school desegregation cases that had failed to establish the unconstitutionality of separate schooling [e.g., *Roberts v. City of Boston* (1850)], as well as the State Department's amicus brief in *Brown*, which highlighted the international impact of continuing to segregate blacks. Alternatively, one might highlight as the cause of the challenge the migration patterns that brought blacks out of the South and into northern cities, thus increasing the national relevance of the issue.

Whatever the reason, many white nonelites continued to resist desegregation. By the late 1960s, judicial patience with resistance seemed at an end [e.g., *Green v. School Board of New Kent County* (1968)]. *Swann v. Charlotte-Mecklenburg Board of Education* (1971) intensified judicial action, with busing becoming a judicially approved tool for desegregating schools. As *Milliken v. Bradley* (1974) made compulsory busing across district boundaries for desegregation illegal, the ability of schools and families to avoid desegregation increased, greatly constraining the ability of urban districts to pursue desegregation. The difficulty posed by *Milliken* further motivated school finance litigation (see below). It also led some urban districts to seek ways to retain white students with the carrot of special programs (e.g., magnet schools) and choice rather than the perceived stick of racial desegregation.

But magnet school and other choice programs face some of the same challenges desegregation efforts encountered. Saporito & Lareau (1999) use statistical methods and in-depth interviewing to investigate parents' decision-making process when choosing between schools. They find that the major factor in white parents' selection of schools is the racial composition of the school. Indeed, Saporito & Lareau (1999) contend that white parents first eliminate from consideration schools identified as black, and then select from among the remaining schools, which are seen as white. Whites will choose white schools that are less safe, more poor, and lower achieving than some of the rejected black schools. Hence, Saporito & Lareau (1999) show that race is an important criterion for whites.

Predictably, therefore, on most measures, school desegregation appears to be stalled, or perhaps even to have regressed (e.g., Orfield et al. 1997). For example, in 1970 the typical black student attended a school that was 32% white. In 1993 the typical black student attended a school that was 33.9% white. In 1970 the typical Latino/a student attended a school that was 43.8% white; the comparable figure for 1994 was 30.6%. In the South, in 1964 the typical white student attended a school that was 2.3% black. By 1968, the figure was 23.4%, reaching a zenith of 43.5% in 1988. By 1994, however, the figure had fallen to 36.6%. Thus, some fear a trend toward resegregation (Orfield et al. 1997).

The possibility of resegregation is not the only concern; indeed, at times even success seems problem-laden. Noteworthy successes, such as Boston's voluntary program of city-suburb busing, in which urbanites may apply to attend suburban schools (Orfield et al. 1998), operate such that whites maintain control and bear few of the costs of desegregation. Also pointing to the ambivalence of success, evidence indicates that black teachers and administrators were sacrificed with the closure of formally dual systems of education (e.g., Ethridge 1979). If one wanted to maintain that role modeling is important to the achievement of disadvantaged students, then the demotion and firing of African American teachers and administrators is an unacknowledged step backward for the prospects of African American students.

Further, despite the plethora of studies, the most important research—studies of long-term effects, a decade in the making—did not inform the desegregation policy debate (Wells 1995). Still, it is unclear whether any research could have mattered; it may have been impossible in that context to placate the intransigence of white resistance. What followed *Brown* were programs that passed the costs of desegregation onto black and Latino/a children alone, processes that resegregated students inside schools, and movement of whites from the reach of desegregation— all of which appear consistent with Bell's interest-convergence thesis.

Affirmative Action

Affirmative action became official policy in 1969 with Office of Federal Contract Compliance (OFCC) Order Number 4 requiring federal contractors to take "affirmative action" to increase their employment of qualified, available blacks (Skrentny 2002). The policy quickly spread to education and to other groups (e.g., women, Asians). However, just as quickly the policy came under attack (e.g., Glazer 1975). In *Regents of the University of California v. Bakke* (1978) the

Supreme Court not only sharply circumscribed the means through which the policy could be implemented, but also severely limited the reasoning upon which schools could base adoption of affirmative action policy. No longer could schools address historic discrimination or respond to diffuse contemporary discrimination via affirmative action. After *Bakke*, a policy that elite institutions originally justified on the basis of a broad set of reasons could only be based on a desire for diversity.

Narrowing the justification of affirmative action increased interest in identifying the effects of affirmative action on diversity and the effects of diversity on outcomes, interests further spurred by the filing of *Grutter v. Bollinger* (2003) and *Gratz v. Bollinger* (2003), two cases that contested affirmative action in law school and undergraduate admissions at the University of Michigan, respectively. Yet, however interested scholars may be in discerning the effects of diversity and affirmative action, estimating such effects is difficult.

Perhaps given the difficulty of studying affirmative action effects, Hallinan (1998) proposes to infer the effects of diversity by reviewing evidence on the effects of desegregation. This is a mistake, because the context for studies of desegregation effects differs substantially from the context for inference concerning affirmative action. The key contextual difference concerns the voluntary or coercive nature of the policy and of student attendance.

Affirmative action is doubly voluntaristic. It concerns institutions' more or less voluntary policy to bring adults together, through what is also a largely voluntaristic process (college admissions and matriculation), to engage in learning across a wide set of domains. In contrast, desegregation is partially if not wholly coercive. Desegregation concerns oft-coerced institutions' efforts to educate children. In addition, some may be attending school under compulsion. Using the response of children in coercive institutions implementing a policy adults may not support to infer the effects of a voluntarily adopted intervention for voluntarily exposed adults seems unwise. Even though the estimated effect may be positive, differences in the allocation processes of the two interventions and their contexts render the estimates nontransferable. For example, affirmative action may have no effect; it could be that the factors that cause institutions to adopt affirmative action also cause other outcomes. If so, failing to account for the voluntary adoption of affirmative action will lead to analyses that incorrectly attribute effects to affirmative action.

Indeed, because of the voluntaristic nature of college and postcollege admissions, drawing inferences about the effect of diversity and/or affirmative action is exceedingly difficult in any case. The ideal study would consider a broad range of outcomes for both the targets of affirmative action and others. Outcomes would eschew self-reports of "comfort with those of other races," for example, in favor of psychometrically validated attitude scales, behavioral indicators, and economic and occupational outcomes. At the same time, the ideal study would control for nonrandom sorting into institutions on observable and unobservable factors, and how those factors themselves might affect outcomes. Successful accomplishment of this effort would also take seriously critics' claim that affirmative action leads to mismatch between student capabilities and institutional level—the fit hypothesis

(Thernstrom & Thernstrom 1997). Because it is this sorting that complicates the comparisons needed to discern a causal effect (Holland 1986), regardless of one's assessment of the fit hypothesis, accounting for the process that allocates students to institutions is essential for an effective study of the causal effect of affirmative action. Of course, no such ideal study exists.

However, affirmative action is not unique in this regard; rarely are policies evaluated on the basis of ideal designs in part because such designs are often extremely complex, incredibly expensive, and sometimes impossible to implement. Yet, public policy must be made, and suggestive research can usefully inform policy decisions.

Absent the ideal study of affirmative action effects, some suggestive research does exist. Lempert et al. (2000a) analyze the law school and post–law school records of minorities and nonminorities, concluding that minority University of Michigan law school graduates are exceedingly successful. Indeed, minority graduates equal the incomes and job satisfaction of whites and exceed the public service of whites. The study usefully controls for admissions information, namely Law School Admissions Test (LSAT) scores; they find that LSAT scores predict grades in law school but do not predict success after law school.

One weakness of Lempert et al. (2000a), however, plagues any study of one institution. Affirmative action is a policy that can alter the composition of practicing and nonpracticing institutions. If composition matters—and research such as that of Kanter (1977) suggests it does—then the effect of affirmative action cannot be discerned by assessing the success of the graduates from any one institution (e.g., Nelson & Payne 2000, Sander 2000). If composition in one institution is adjusted on the basis of affirmative action, it may force negative adjustments in other institutions. For this reason, therefore, single-site studies are less informative than one might presume.

Bowen & Bok (1998) address this problem by studying 28 selective institutions. The analysis is based on college application, college transcript, and follow-up survey data for black and white students enrolling at 28 liberal arts and research universities in 1976 and 1989, and data for all 1989 applicants at 5 of the 28 institutions. They conclude that owing to pre-college racial achievement disparities, race-neutral admissions policies would substantially reduce black enrollment, particularly at the most selective institutions. They also note that racial preferences in admissions have little impact on white students, as the chance of a white applicant being admitted would increase by less than 2% if all the affirmative action positions were allotted to white applicants.

Bowen & Bok (1998) find little evidence supporting the fit hypothesis. However, their analysis of the fit hypothesis is insufficient. Essentially, they find that the more selective the institution, the better students do regardless of race. But the fit hypothesis does not imply equal black success regardless of college selectivity. Instead, the hypothesis maintains that if the graduation rates for blacks are 82%, 81%, and 75% for colleges of high, medium, and low selectivity, respectively, under affirmative action, then absent affirmative action the graduation rates might be, say,

85%, 82%, and 81% across the different selectivity categories. Thus, even though fewer blacks would attend the most selective colleges, more blacks would graduate overall because of better fit. This claim is unchanged even if there are extensive controls because the fit hypothesis is about unobservable variables. One cannot address this hypothesis merely by comparing the graduation rates of blacks at differently selective institutions. Instead, one must employ an experimental design with random assignment to colleges, which will break the relationship between unobserved factors' effects on admission and success. As this design is unethical, one can employ a statistical model, such as the endogenous switching regression model (e.g., Gamoran & Mare 1989, Mare & Winship 1988) that simultaneously accounts for nonrandom assignment to sectors and success within the sector. Only such analyses can directly address the fit hypothesis. Hence, at this point the fit hypothesis cannot be rejected.

Keith et al. (1985) use the complete set of institutions in the population, studying the 1975 cohort of medical school graduates. They find that minority physicians had a higher proportion of Medicaid patients and were more likely to practice in locations federally defined as suffering a shortage of health care providers. Yet, minorities were less likely to have become board certified nine years later, a disparity only partly explained by undergraduate record. Keith et al. (1985) speculate that minority physicians may treat a population less aware of the meaning of board certification, lowering the incentive for physicians to seek certification.

The Keith et al. design allows inference to the full range of institutions. Yet, a disadvantage of the Keith et al. and Lempert et al. studies is that they presume that all black and Latino/a candidates enter institutions only through affirmative action. This assumption implies that blacks and Latino/as could never enter elite institutions or professions absent affirmative action, and also implies that all others were admitted meritocratically. Thus, the comparison is inappropriate; the research compares the performance of blacks, Latino/as, and whites and presumes to be comparing the performance of affirmative action and non–affirmative action admittees. Instead, one should cross-classify admittees by race and reason for admission. Candidates admitted on the basis of grades and test scores might form one stratum. Other strata would include those admitted for affirmative action, legacy status, state residence, and such. Strata could even be formed to reflect mixed-motive admittees. One could then cross-classify the admission strata by race/ethnicity. Ideally, those in all allegedly nonmeritocratic admissions categories would be compared to those admitted for allegedly meritocratic reasons.

Although Lempert et al. (2002b) contend that all African Americans, regardless of reason for admission, gain with increasing diversity, and thus that across-race comparisons are appropriate, they attempt to address the issue by statistically allocating students to reason-for-admission strata on the basis of observable characteristics. Findings remain unchanged. Still, the reanalysis remains contestable because the allocation occurred on the basis of matriculants, not applicants, and it is unclear whether matriculants alone provide enough information to deduce accurately the admission stratum of a candidate.

In addition to its implication for appropriate comparisons in research, the assumption that all minorities are affirmative action admittees, an assumption embedded in the research, is consistent with the claim that affirmative action stigmatizes all students of the targeted group (e.g., Herrnstein & Murray 1994). However, stigmatization of students of color has many plausible causes (Loury 2002). Thus, there is no solid empirical research on this potential effect of affirmative action; it is too early to conclude that affirmative action per se stigmatizes minority candidates.

Equally important, no study effectively assesses the impact of affirmative action on nonminorities. Some research has attempted to assess the impact of diversity on outcomes for nonminority students (e.g., Gurin et al. 2002, Hu & Kuh 2003, Pascarella et al. 2001, Whitla et al. 2003). But these studies do not account for the voluntary element of enrollment in college and college classes and often use self-reports of valuing diversity experiences as an outcome. Hence, these studies do not address the challenges that bedevil causal inference in this area.

Several responses have followed as affirmative action has come under attack [e.g., *Hopwood v. State of Texas* (1994)]. Some states have adopted so-called 10% plans for college admission, where the top 10% of students in each high school are eligible to attend the state university. Research suggests that these plans have complex results that may not sustain the levels of diversity previously observed (e.g., Tienda et al. 2003). Also, such plans cannot be used for postcollege admissions. Some commentators have called for the abandonment of race-based affirmative action and the adoption of class-based affirmative action (e.g., Kahlenberg 1996). However, as Kane (1998) demonstrates, although underrepresented minorities are more likely to be poor, because they are also numerical minorities, the numbers of minorities on campus cannot be sustained through class-based affirmative action.

The sole remaining legal justification for affirmative action is diversity. Ironically, evidence suggests that the diversity aim can be met, at least partially, without positively affecting native-born minorities. Hoxby (1998) found that blacks and Latino/as were crowded out of very selective institutions, the very institutions most likely to practice affirmative action, by more socioeconomically advantaged international students of the same demographic group. At the same time, socioeconomically disadvantaged, native-born African American and Latino/a students in less selective institutions encountered foreign nationals of similar circumstances competing for the same scarce financial aid dollars. Hence, the diversity rationale does not sufficiently target admission opportunities for an institution to address collaterally any of the other, now illegal, aims affirmative action may formerly have accomplished.

Institutions must be seeking diversity for pedagogical reasons in order to justify affirmative action. Certainly, in this socio-legal environment, research into the effects of affirmative action, especially research that addresses the challenges already described, could be useful for public policy and for social scientific understanding. However, note that another interpretation of the courts' reasoning on affirmative action is that colleges' and universities' efforts to include blacks, Latino/as, and Native Americans must be justified on the basis of what it means for the educational experiences of whites. A better exhibit in the case for the interest-convergence thesis is difficult to imagine.

LAW, EDUCATION, AND THE INTERSECTION OF RACE

Many other education issues besides affirmative action and desegregation have racial dimensions. Sometimes the racial dimensions become implicated in legal processes. We provide a few examples here.

Special Education and Gifted and Talented Education

Special education is a nonracialized policy with clear racial relevance. In the past handicapped students were often prevented from attending school. The Education of All Handicapped Children Act of 1975 essentially recognized a right to public education for all students regardless of handicapped status. Re-authorizations [e.g., Individuals with Disabilities Education Act (IDEA)], legal rulings [e.g., *Larry P. v. Riles* (1972)], and institutional developments have affirmed this principle, as well as others: Students in need of special education should be allocated to the least restrictive environment; assignment to special education must provide due process protections; and parents must be formally involved in the process (Reschly 2000).

Processes that culminate in special education assignment have been foci of legal and scholarly attention. The special education assignment process for judgmental disabilities (as opposed to medical disabilities, such as blindness or deafness) usually begins by a teacher referring a child for evaluation. Evidence suggests that teachers are more likely to refer students with behavioral difficulties that disrupt other students (e.g., Shaywitz et al. 1990). Some evidence also indicates that white teachers are biased when making judgments about minority students (e.g., Downey & Pribesh 2004, Zucker & Prieto 1977), although other evidence suggests the absence of teacher bias against minority students (e.g., Tobias et al. 1983).

However, even in the absence of bias, the process through which students are assigned to special education does not involve a general assessment of all students. Consequently, the true incidence of need for special education is unknown. This makes it impossible to assess whether the figures on racial disparity in special education reflect overassignment, underutilization, or some complex combination of both (e.g., Donovan & Cross 2002). Indeed, it is impossible to determine whether groups with the highest proportion of utilization are still underutilizing special education.

The problems increase as one moves further into the special education evaluation process. The disability categories and their use vary dramatically across states. A child diagnosed as mentally retarded in one state might be diagnosed as learning disabled in the neighboring state, even though nothing in the student's presentation may have changed (Donovan & Cross 2002).

These variations occur in part because there are no solid, clinically defined consensus markers that necessitate special education placement. Certainly, the use of intelligence tests in the evaluation process led to litigation charging that minority students were being incorrectly assigned to special education on the basis of biased tests [*Larry P. v. Riles* (1972)]. Still, states use different IQ tests with different properties, different IQ test cut-offs for placement, and different placement categories—all culminating in a process that appears arbitrary, despite the requirement for parental consent to special education placement. Courts have rejected arbitrary assignment processes in other contexts [e.g., in employment in *Richardson v. Lamar County Board of Education* (1989)]. It may be that students' disparate presentation, coupled with the lack of a practical consensus around clinically validated diagnostic criteria, has left in place an arbitrary assignment process. In that context, eliminating standardized testing would increase the power of unstandardized judgments, leaving even more room for potential (racial) bias.

Finally, special education is a treatment, but research on treatment effectiveness is limited, although increasing. Part of the challenge with assessing effectiveness stems from the disparate categorical systems and assignment criteria; part of the challenge flows from disagreement as to the goals of special education. Still, a National Research Council report was able to identify a set of promising approaches for special education instruction (Donovan & Cross 2002). However, problems remain in assuring that effective approaches are widely adopted, no easy task given the widely varying state systems.

Thus, although IDEA is federal law, and a federal monitoring effort is ongoing, the ability to discern national patterns or local biases is seriously compromised by the power of teacher judgment, district variability, and state idiosyncrasy.

African American, Latino/a, and Native American students have lower enrollment in gifted and talented education (GATE) than do whites and Asians (see Table 1). GATE is even more unsystematized than special education. No federal law governs the existence of the program. Thus, while students in need of special education are entitled, there is no federally guaranteed entitlement to GATE programs (Heim 1998). Evidence suggests, however, that there may be large underassignment of minorities to GATE. Woods & Achey (1990) found that with more intensive evaluation, but without altering admission criteria, they increased the number of minority student admits to a grade 2 through 5 GATE program by 181%. Minority proportion in GATE doubled, from approximately 13% to over 27%.

Tracking

Special education and GATE remove students from the general school population. Curriculum differentiation—the division of a school subject into different courses—allows the allocation of general population students to targeted instruction of differing rigor. Formerly, curriculum differentiation occurred in concert with formal tracking, in which students were assigned to one program (e.g., general, vocational, college preparatory) that determined their academic course taking. In *Hobson v. Hansen* (1967), the Court ruled that the tracking system of Washington, DC, was unconstitutional because it denied African American students equal opportunity. By the mid- to late 1970s, formal tracking had declined precipitously (Moore & Davenport 1988, Oakes 1981). By 1990, less than 15% of schools engaged in formal tracking (Carey et al. 1994).

However, even in the absence of overarching programs, students are assigned to similar levels of courses across disparate subjects more than their profile of achievement would predict (Lucas 1999). This phenomenon, termed de facto tracking (Lucas 1999), renders discourse on tracking relevant even with the decline of formal institutional mechanisms.

Analysts have studied the assignment of students to tracks. The research on racial disparity remains equivocal. Local studies produce a wide array of findings. For example, Mickelson (2001) finds black disadvantage in Charlotte-Mecklenburg, North Carolina; in contrast, Garet & DeLany (1988) find black advantage in four districts in California. At the very least, therefore, tracking may be used in some locales to segregate students by race intentionally or in ways that have that effect. Oakes's (1995) research on the San Jose, California, and Rockford, Illinois, school systems documented the inconsistent application of opaque course assignment criteria and the assignment of students to tracks in ways that led courses to include broad ranges of prior achievement. Because narrowing the achievement range in classes is a key technical rationale for tracking, the broad range of achievement in the classes suggests that the technical basis was somehow undone. Finally, Oakes (1995) observes that blacks and Latino/as were concentrated in lower level courses.

Statistical analysis of nationally representative data that controls for nonrandom assignment to tracks indicates that tracking exacerbates black and Latino/a achievement disadvantage (Lucas & Gamoran 2002). The most recent cohort shows no net black-white or Latino/a-white difference in college preparatory course taking. However, all three groups lag behind Asians in college preparatory placement, even after prior achievement is controlled. Thus, race appears to matter in college preparatory opportunities.

Of course, the role of race/ethnicity is only incompletely reflected in analyses of individual students' prospects for success. Racial/ethnic dynamics also partially determine the very structures students navigate. Tracking is a pedagogical structure that need not be linked to race. However, evidence indicates that tracking is more pronounced when a school has greater racial/ethnic diversity (e.g., Braddock 1990); once racial/ethnic diversity and class diversity of the school are simultaneously considered, both matter, even after the role of the distribution of students' prior achievement is controlled (Lucas & Berends 2002). This pattern of results suggests that tracking is not only a technical pedagogic device, as Hallinan (1994) maintains, but also a mechanism of exclusion and segregation, as Oakes (1994) contends. Ignoring tracking's racial connection is to fundamentally misunderstand the schools and how their operation may maintain power relations.

High-Stakes Accountability:
The Case of "No Child Left Behind"

The No Child Left Behind Act (NCLB), signed into law in 2002, requires schools to evaluate student achievement overall, as well as achievement of economically disadvantaged students, students in special education, limited English proficiency students, and students in each major racial/ethnic group at the school. At least 95% of students in each category must take part in the testing or the school cannot show adequate yearly progress (AYP) for the subgroup. Schools must show AYP for all subgroups and for the school as a whole to avoid sanctions. The sanctions for Title I schools are harshest; should a Title I school consistently fail to show AYP, the school may be forced to pay for students wishing to transfer to other schools in the district and eventually may be forced to replace teachers and/or administrators.

Because it requires improvement for students of all races and links failure to demonstrate across-the-board improvement to negative consequences, NCLB is a racialized law (Edley 2002, Losen 2004). Interestingly, in contradiction to this racialized approach to educational legislation, the Bush administration that signed NCLB into law also presented an amicus brief in *Grutter v. Bollinger* (2003) arguing against recognition of race in postsecondary admissions (United States 2003).

NCLB has several potential consequences. First, it may restructure incentives. Schools with a modest number of minority students will have an increased incentive to spur these students' achievement growth.

Second, NCLB may also potentially rearrange attitudes toward existing means of student evaluation. For example, in the area of special education, in the past educators have argued that IQ tests are appropriate for evaluating students [e.g., *Larry P. v. Riles* (1972)]. NCLB focuses on improvement in achievement as indicated by achievement tests of state design or selection. Psychometricians, however, contend that the difference between intelligence tests and achievement tests is tenuous and that intelligence can scarcely be increased (e.g., Carroll 1997, Herrnstein & Murray 1994). Thus, if it proves difficult to demonstrate improvement for (minority) students using standardized achievement tests, the advent of NCLB's negative sanctions may lead school administrators faced with reassignment or termination to argue that achievement tests and intelligence tests are the same, and therefore the achievement tests are unable to demonstrate student improvement, perhaps especially for black and Latino/a students.

Third, NCLB may distort instruction. Because NCLB is relatively new, the full process remains unobserved. Yet Texas, a state that enacted NCLB-like school accountability legislation early, may suggest how the intervention works when implemented. For example, one educator response to the Texas Assessment of Academic Skills (TAAS) goes beyond teaching to the test. In classic teaching to the test, the content of the test drives the curriculum. If the test is designed to reflect broad curriculum goals, aligning the curriculum to the test could be a positive development. McNeil (2000) documents that in at least some locales, however, the response to TAAS has been to teach to the test design. Students are instructed daily in test-taking strategies. Memorable cheers, such as "Three in a row? No, No, No!" remind students who were instructed that

> if you see you have answered "b" three times in a row, you know ("no, no, no") that at least one of those answers is likely to be wrong, because the maker of a test would not be likely to construct three questions in a row with the same answer-indicator (McNeil 2000, p. 235).

McNeil shows that these kinds of instructional responses followed introduction of TAAS, a high-stakes accountability system.

One problem with test-focused accountability systems is that students may not be motivated to take the test or to excel at the test. Texas responded by requiring students to pass the TAAS in order to graduate. Litigation followed. In *GI Forum et al. v. Texas Education Agency et al.* (2000) plaintiffs argued that the high-stakes TAAS had a disparate impact on Latino/a and African American students and violated due process protections by denying minority students and non-English speakers equal learning opportunities (Saucedo 2000). However, the court ruled for the defendants, concluding that the plaintiffs had shown neither intentional discrimination nor the absence of offsetting positive effects. Saucedo (2000) notes that defendants both rebutted plaintiffs' disparate impact claim that alternatives for accomplishing state aims existed, and successfully pointed to alternative explanations for racial disparity in TAAS results. In response, Saucedo (2000) calls for future plaintiffs to compare states with and without exit exams, and to conduct analyses to document the net association with outcomes and race. Interestingly, the case was brought on behalf of students at risk of being denied high school diplomas. As discussed earlier, future cases may be brought by school personnel at risk of being terminated. It is unclear whether due process protections will make more of a difference in an employment context, and if they do, what that will mean for students.

Finally, NCLB recalls the distinction between equality of opportunity and equality of result (Coleman 1968). NCLB is an equality of result law, where the result is achievement growth. The accountability logic in NCLB makes merely providing opportunity insufficient, constituting an important policy change. Although the results are at present unclear, NCLB may help reduce racial inequality of measured achievement, should it succeed. Of course, the ultimate result depends on whether instruction inside schools does not become so oriented to test design that education suffers. But NCLB suggests that law can be a tool for preventing racial/ethnic disparities from increasing, and therefore supports a more optimistic read of the law-race relation.

School Finance

NCLB redirects attention from resources to outcomes. But resources are needed for outcomes to be positive. Indeed, although *Brown v. Board of Education* (1954) is remembered for its role in eliminating de jure segregation, the plaintiffs' primary education goal was achieving equal educational opportunities and resources for racial minorities. Against a backdrop of expanding public education systems during the first half of the twentieth century, blacks' participation remained limited. Not only were blacks less likely to be enrolled in school than whites (Jaynes & Williams 1989, p. 333), but also the schools that black students did attend were underfunded and low on resources (e.g., Moses 1941). Thus, securing equal educational opportunities in the form of equal institutional resources was a major goal of *Brown* and the larger Civil Rights movement (Valverde 2004).

School equity remains a key issue, one in which the courts have continued to play a primary role. Equal opportunity is difficult to define, with conceptions of school equity shifting over time (Berne & Stiefel 1999). For example, school equity might focus on inputs (e.g., expenditures), processes (e.g., classroom instruction and tracking), or outputs (e.g., academic achievement), and it might use states, districts, schools, or groups of students as the unit of analysis. In one line of argument and research, the emphasis has shifted from inputs to outputs, and from equalizing resources to achieving adequacy, i.e., resources sufficient for a school to meet absolute output standards. A more recent discussion of improved school finance attempts to redirect the focus to how funds are used (e.g., to implement effective practices within schools and classrooms), as opposed to just equalizing their distribution (Grubb et al. 2004).

The courts have been a key arena for challenging school finance policy and ensuring school equity (Berne & Stiefel 1999, Minorini & Sugarman 1999). In *San Antonio Independent School District v. Rodriguez* (1973), the Supreme Court ruling, that despite apparent funding inequalities the Texas school finance system was constitutional, led to the federal retreat from a possible role in school equity conflicts. Since that time, struggles over school equity have been confined to the local and state levels, where litigants have been able to use state constitutions that assign states responsibility for providing education to argue that the state must provide equal access to education.

Court battles in over 40 states have worked to reshape state educational policy substantially (Minorini & Sugarman 1999, Evans et al. 1999). This reform effort is prominently displayed in California, home to the first successful and perhaps most influential state school finance equity lawsuit (Minorini & Sugarman 1999). In *Serrano v. Priest* (1971, also known as *Serrano I*), the court ruled that a student's educational opportunity must not be associated with the wealth of her school district. This was an important decision, given the heavy role of local property taxes in determining educational funding levels and the large racial disparities in wealth (Oliver & Shapiro 1995). Thus, through *Serrano I* and three followup cases, the state court endeavored to equalize per-pupil spending in California. This effort, though, was countered by Proposition 13, an initiative approved by voters in 1978, which limited property taxes and required a two-thirds legislative majority to increase state taxes. As a result, California experienced an overall decrease in statewide education spending and an increase in state categorical grants (e.g., for special education), both of which undermined efforts to equalize general-purpose spending (Grubb et al. 2004, Minorini & Sugarman 1999).

Further, and in line with the recent focus on adequacy rather than equity, scholars have pointed to persisting inequalities in resources between California schools (Grubb et al. 2004). Ensuring equal school resources—such as textbooks, certified teachers, and physical facilities—remains an elusive goal, as evidenced by the results of discovery in *Williams v. State of California.*

It remains unclear whether, in this arena, we are observing the impact of race-linked interest divergence, the difficulty of arranging complex organizations to match a fundamental American commitment to individual rights, or something else.

Bilingual Education

Technically, bilingual education—the use of non-English languages in classroom instruction—is not a racial issue. Whites speak a plethora of languages, and many minorities speak English. Yet, bilingual education is a racialized arena of education and the law because of the combination of immigration patterns, legal requirements of schools, and racial residential segregation.

Legislation and court rulings have played a key role in structuring educational opportunity for English language learners (ELL)—students from non-English backgrounds with low proficiency in the English language. Passed in 1964, Title VI of the Civil Rights Act forbade discrimination on the basis of race, color, or national origin in federal programs and public education. In 1968, Congress passed the Bilingual Education Act (BEA), which committed federal funds to develop programs for students with limited English language skills. The Supreme Court affirmed this commitment to ELL students, ruling in *Lau v. Nichols* (1974) that San Francisco schools were in violation of the Civil Rights Act by not offering special instruction to all Chinese students.

The BEA, Title VII of the Elementary and Secondary Education Act (ESEA), was expanded throughout the 1970s and 1980s and remained in place until 2002, when it was transformed into the English Language Acquisition Act, Title III of NCLB. While recognizing the need for special services to meet the needs of language-minority students, the BEA did not specifically stipulate whether the funds should be used for bilingual (i.e., native-language instruction) programs or more English-based programs. Some scholars, however, have criticized the legislation for emphasizing English language skills over developing bilingualism and biculturalism among students (e.g., Lyons 1990).

Programs for ELL students have proliferated since the mid-1960s. A wide variety of programs are offered, and evaluations of program effectiveness are often hindered by diversity within broad program types. Most ELL students, however, are in one of two programs: transitional bilingual education (TBE) programs that use some native-language instruction in academic areas but focus on moving students to English-only instruction; and English-as-a-second-language (ESL) programs that focus exclusively on learning English language skills (i.e., with minimal academic content) (August & Hakuta 1997). Programs intended to foster native-language proficiency among ELL students (maintenance bilingual education) or shared language development between ELL and native-English speakers are rare.

Some large-scale national program evaluations have been conducted, although flawed research designs, weak operationalization of key concepts, and sample attrition weaken the validity of the findings (Burkheimer et al. 1989, Dannoff 1978, Ramirez et al. 1991). Nonetheless, a National Research Council review of the statistical methods in two of these studies found noteworthy evidence of positive effects of Spanish language instruction during kindergarten and first grade on English reading achievement (Meyer & Fienberg 1992). And meta-analyses of large numbers of smaller program evaluations have found positive effects of bilingual education in multiple academic areas (Greene 1998, Willig 1985). Evidence suggests that native-language instruction tends to have modest positive effects on the achievement of language-minority students.

Interpreting the Civil Rights Act as requiring non-English instruction is a noteworthy advance for egalitarian principles..However, the implication of this interpretation on the ground may ultimately exacerbate racial inequality. Owing to de facto racially/ethnically segregated schooling, costs of bilingual education do not fall equally on all schools. Instead, the mandate has increased costs in schools with a large amount of language diversity, schools and districts that are often already underresourced. As Betts (1998) and Van Hook (2002) document, without legal requirements of adequate funding for all schools, the bilingual mandate of providing opportunity to non-English speakers has concentrated the costs of the policy on the often poor children of native-born citizens of Latino/a and African American heritage. This has lowered the educational attainment of native-born minority students (Betts 1998).

EMERGENT ISSUES IN RACE, EDUCATION, AND LAW: THE ILLUSTRATIVE CASE OF LEGACY ADMISSIONS

Bell (2004) argues that minority interests are given priority only when those interests converge with the interests of dominant segments of dominant racial groups. If the thesis is accurate, one should recognize a theoretically appropriate ranking of priorities in areas that have yet to emerge as arenas of racial contestation. Identifying such areas is difficult, of course, but a provisional candidate in education concerns legacy admissions for elite institutions.

Affirmative action is often described as violating the principle of merit (e.g., Herrnstein & Murray 1994). Legacy admissions—the practice of advantaging children of alumni in the admissions process—would seem to be a pathway through which some attain elite college admission without necessarily demonstrating merit. Evidence indicates that African Americans, formerly barred from attending some state institutions, as well as Latino/as are disadvantaged by the legacy policy because they just cannot have comparable numbers of college matriculants in the previous generation because their parents and grandparents were denied opportunities to become qualified and were often barred from attending when qualified (Howell & Turner 2004). At selective institutions, the gross legacy advantage is significant, as admissions rates of legacies are twice the rate of all applicants (Bowen & Bok 1998, Lamb 1993). Controlling for other aspects of candidates' records, research indicates that the legacy advantage remains substantial, exceeding the advantage of minority status in 1999 (Shulman & Bowen 2000).

The opening of elite institutions' doors has allowed formerly excluded groups to catch up. Research projections suggest, however, that it will take some 20 years for black applicants to the University of Virginia, the flagship institution of that state, to near their population proportion (Howell & Turner 2004). In short, approximately 20 cohorts of African American students will need to pass through the educational system before the legacy advantage becomes equally available.

To this point, one might surmise that this is simply a story of the slow but inexorable dissolution of racial exclusion. However, Howell & Turner (2004) observe that the numbers of potential legacies will soon grow to a point at which maintaining current patterns of admissions rates will require vastly increasing the size of the institution. Hence, just as African American and Latino/a candidates approach the chance of benefiting as much as whites from legacy policy, demographic facts will place the policy under threat. Thus, legacy admission policy presents a fortunate opportunity to assess the fundamental law-race relation. If legacy policy falls to a concerted commitment to racially neutral indices of merit, or is sustained without modification through and after the period of racial equality in legacy opportunities, then that would be inconsistent with Bell's thesis. However, if the policy hangs on until racial parity in legacy status is approached, yet then suddenly becomes practically irrelevant, is formally withdrawn, or is displaced by some other race-linked characteristic, that would be more consistent with the interest-convergence thesis. Students of race, law, and education may find it useful to watch the debate on and prospects of legacy admissions in the coming quarter century, to aid their efforts to adjudicate between disparate theses of the law-race relation in the United States.

DISCUSSION

A great deal of social science research has been conducted in the area of race and education. That research has rarely if ever been determinative of legal or policy outcomes. Yet, social science research is common in court and other venues in which the law is interpreted and developed. Even when not determinative, research can be influential and useful, revealing whether and how race matters in education and sensitizing policymakers and citizens to the complexities involved.

Education is one, albeit important, area of social life and policy. Yet, the relationship between law and race transcends the field of education. Education, furnishing examples of the law-race relation, is a particularly advantageous forum for studying this relation because education often involves relatively nonthreatening beings in need of societal support in a myriad of ways, i.e., children. How the law acts around race in the field of education, a field in which the weakest members of society are encountered, can be very revealing of the basic law-race relation.

The law-race relation in education is not straightforward, varying across domains. Its character differs across the areas of desegregation, affirmative action, special education, tracking, high-stakes accountability, bilingual education, legacy admissions, and other issues, such as grade retention and school discipline. Thus, the law-race relation is manifest in the development of education in the United States, and superficial aspects of the relation change over time.

At a more fundamental level, though, the relation remains unclear. Consistent with Bell's interest-convergence thesis, law often has seemed most powerfully on the side of minority students when its operation served the interests of children of both minority and dominant groups. However, at other times law has seemed to support ostensible minority interests (e.g., affirmative action). These countercurrents make it impossible to simply characterize the fundamental law-race relation as it pertains to education.

In light of the equivocal evidence, one might reason that the inequalities are so stark (see Table 1) that only sustained neglect or outright antagonism can explain the patterns. Thus, one may conclude that racial groups have inherently antagonistic interests and that the law cannot be egalitarian. In this view, the interest-convergence thesis indicates that the law is ultimately concerned with protecting the interests of dominant whites and will never recognize and promote minority interests. One response, therefore, is to reject formulations requiring compromise with interests that are fundamentally antagonistic, for such compromise will never lead to fundamental change. Instead, a direct confrontation of dominant white interests, no matter how long it takes, holds the most promise of restructuring American institutions for racial justice.

An alternative vision takes the equivocal results to heart, and observes that for minority interests to motivate effective action they must first find articulation. Any possible harmony of minority and majority interests can only be recognized if minorities, regardless of their possible disenfranchisement, act as if existing institutional structures can and will be responsive in service to minority interests. In this view, one should not be surprised that action is most likely when cohesion between the interests of racial minorities and dominant racial groups is discovered or developed; that is the political norm. Further, even though races as such may have antagonistic interests owing to the historic construction of race through property relations, the interests that precede that historical development are not antagonistic. Thus, shared interests can often be discovered or developed, depending on how the case is made.

For both responses, the interest-convergence thesis, even if ultimately shown to be true, need not imply a thoroughgoing pessimism. Instead, accepting the veracity of the thesis, if true it be, can provide one step toward responding effectively to the conditions the truth of the position ostensibly lays bare. Both responses agree— regardless of the conditions of any given moment, the fundamental relation of law, race, and education is not so determined that it cannot be fashioned anew.

ACKNOWLEDGMENT

We thank Carol Greenberg and Goodwin Liu for comments on an earlier draft and Jeanne Powers and Leticia Saucedo for helpful suggestions of additional literature.

The *Annual Review of Law and Social Science* **is online at**
http://lawsocsci.annualreviews.org

LITERATURE CITED

Am. Anthropol. Assoc. 1998. *American Anthropological Association statement on 'race.'* http://www.aaanet.org/stmts/racepp.htm

Am. Sociol. Assoc. 2002. *Statement of the American Sociological Association on the importance of collecting data and doing social scientific research on race.* http://www.asanet.org/governance/racestmt.html

Anderson M, Fienberg S. 2000. Race and ethnicity and the controversy over the U.S. Census. *Curr. Sociol.* 48:87–110

August D, Hakuta K. 1997. *Improving Schooling for Language-Minority Children: A Research Agenda.* Washington, DC: Natl. Acad. Press

Bayor BH. 1988. Roads to racial segregation: Atlanta in the twentieth century. *J. Urban Hist.* 15:3–21

Bell D. 1980. *Brown v. Board of Education* and the interest-convergence dilemma. *Harvard Law Rev.* 93:518–33

Bell D. 2004. *Silent Covenants:* Brown v. Board of Education *and the Unfulfilled Hopes for Racial Reform.* New York: Oxford Univ. Press

Berne R, Stiefel L. 1999. Concepts of school finance equity: 1970 to the present. See Ladd et al. 1999, pp. 7–33

Betts JR. 1998. Educational crowding out: Do immigrants affect the educational attainment of American minorities? In *Help or Hindrance: The Economic Implications of Immigration for African-Americans*, ed. DS Hammermesh, FD Bean, pp. 253–81. New York: Russell Sage Found.

Boozer MA, Krueger AB, Wolkon S. 1992. *Race and school quality since* Brown vs. Board of Education. NBER Work. Pap. No. 4109. Natl. Bur. Econ. Res.

Borstelmann T. 2001. *The Cold War and the Color Line: American Race Relations in the Global Arena.* Cambridge, MA: Harvard Univ. Press

Bowen v. Independent Publishing Co., 96 SE 2d 564, 565 (S.C. 1957)

Bowen WG, Bok D. 1998. *The Shape of the River: Long-Term Consequences of Considering Race in College and University Admissions.* Princeton, NJ: Princeton Univ. Press

Braddock JH II. 1990. Tracking the middle grades: national patterns of grouping for instruction. *Phi Delta Kappan* 71:445–49

Brown v. Board of Education, 347 U.S. 483 (1954)

Burkheimer GJ Jr, Conger AJ, Dunteman GH, Elliott BG, Mowbray KA. 1989. Effectiveness of services for language-minority limited-English-proficient students. *Tech. Rep.* 2 Vols. Research Triangle Park, NC: Research Triangle Inst.

Carey N, Farris E, Carpenter J. 1994. *Curricular Differentiation in Public High Schools: Fast Response Survey System E.D. Tabs.* Rockville, MD: Westat

Carroll JB. 1997. Psychometrics, intelligence, and public perception. *Intelligence* 24:25–52

Cleghorn R. 1970. Segregation academies: the Old South tries again. *Saturday Rev.*, May 16

Coleman JS. 1968. The concept of equality of educational opportunity. *Harvard Educ. Rev.* 38:7–22

Coleman JS, Campbell EQ, Hobson CJ, McPartland J, Mood AM, et al. 1966. *Equality of Educational Opportunity.* Washington, DC: US Dep. Health Educ. Welf.

Dannoff MN. 1978. Evaluation of the impact of ESEA Title VII Spanish-English bilingual education programs. *Tech. Rep.* Washington, DC: Am. Inst. Res.

Donovan MS, Cross CT. 2002. *Minority Students in Special and Gifted Education*. Washington, DC: Natl. Acad. Press

Downey DB, Pribesh S. 2004. When race matters: teachers' evaluations of students' classroom behavior. *Sociol. Educ.* 77:267–82

Dudziak ML. 2000. *Cold War Civil Rights: Race and the Image of American Democracy*. Princeton, NJ: Princeton Univ. Press

Edley C Jr. 2002. Testimony of Professor Christopher Edley, Jr., Committee on Education and the Workforce "Implementation of the No Child Left Behind Act," July 24, 107th Congr., 2nd sess. http://edworkforce.house.gov/hearings/107th/fc/hr1implement72402/edley.htm

Ehrenberg RG, Brewer D, Gamoran A, Willms JD. 2001. Does class size matter? *Sci. Am.* 285(5):79–85

Elliott M. 1998. School finance and opportunities to learn: Does money well spent enhance students' achievement? *Sociol. Educ.* 71:223–45

Erickson RJ, Simon R. 1998. *The Use of Social Science Data in Supreme Court Decisions*. Chicago: Univ. Illinois Press

Ethridge SB. 1979. Impact of the 1954 *Brown v. Topeka Board of Education* decision on black educators. *Negro Educ. Rev.* 30:217–32

Evans WN, Murray SE, Schwab RM. 1999. The impact of court-mandated school finance reform. See Ladd et al. 1999, pp. 72–98

Ferguson RF. 1998b. Can schools narrow the black-white test score gap? See Jencks & Phillips 1998, pp. 318–74

Ferguson RF. 1998a. Teachers' perceptions and expectations and the black-white test score gap. See Jencks & Phillips 1998, pp. 273–317

Finley MK. 1984. Teachers and tracking in a comprehensive high school. *Sociol. Educ.* 57:233–43

Fischer CS, Hout M, Jankowski MS, Lucas SR, Swidler A, Voss K. 1996. *Inequality by Design: Cracking the Bell Curve Myth*. Princeton, NJ: Princeton Univ. Press

Gamoran A, Mare RD. 1989. Secondary school tracking and educational inequality: compensation, reinforcement, or neutrality? *Am. J. Sociol.* 94:1146–83

Garet MS, DeLany B. 1988. Students, courses, and stratification. *Sociol. Educ.* 61:61–77

GI Forum et al. v. Texas Education Agency et al., 87 F. Supp. 2d 667 (W.D. Tex. 2000)

Glazer N. 1975. *Affirmative Discrimination: Ethnic Inequality and Public Policy*. Cambridge, MA: Harvard Univ. Press

Gratz v. Bollinger, 539 U.S. 244 (2003)

Greene J. 1998. A meta-analysis of the effectiveness of bilingual education. *Res. Rep.*, sponsored by Tomas Rivera Policy Inst., Public Policy Clinic, Dep. Gov., Univ. Texas, Austin, Program Educ. Policy Gov., Harvard Univ.

Grubb N, Goe L, Huerta LA. 2004. The unending search for equity: California policy, the "improved" school finance, and the *Williams* case. *Teach. Coll. Rec.* 106:2081–101

Grutter v. Bollinger, 539 U.S. 306 (2003)

Gurin P, Dey EL, Hurtado S, Gurin G. 2002. Diversity and higher education: theory and impact on educational outcomes. *Harvard Educ. Rev.* 72:330–66

Hallinan MT. 1994. Tracking: from theory to practice. *Sociol. Educ.* 67:79–84

Hallinan MT. 1998. Diversity effects on student outcomes: social science evidence. *Ohio State Law J.* 59:733–54

Harris CI. 1993. Whiteness as property. *Harvard Law Rev.* 106:1707–91

Harris DR, Sim JJ. 2002. Who is multi-racial? Assessing the complexity of lived race. *Am. Sociol. Rev.* 67:614–27

Heim AS. 1998. Gifted students and the right to an ability-appropriate education. *J. Law Educ.* 27:131–38

Herrnstein RJ, Murray C. 1994. *The Bell Curve: Intelligence and Class Structure in American Life*. New York: Free Press

Hobson v. Hansen, 265 F. Supp. 902, DDC (1967)

Holland PW. 1986. Statistics and causal

inference (with comments). *J. Am. Stat. Assoc.* 396:940–70

Hopwood v. State of Texas, 861 F. Supp. 551 (W.D. Tex. 1994)

Howell C, Turner SE. 2004. Legacies in black and white: the racial composition of the legacy pool. *Res. High. Educ.* 45:325–51

Hoxby CM. 1998. Do immigrants crowd disadvantaged natives out of higher education? In *Help or Hindrance: The Economic Implications of Immigration for African-Americans*, ed. DS Hammermesh, FD Bean, pp. 282–312. New York: Russell Sage Found.

Hu S, Kuh GD. 2003. Diversity experiences and college student learning and personal development. *J. Coll. Stud. Dev.* 44:320–34

Jaynes GD, Williams RM Jr. 1989. *A Common Destiny: Blacks and American Society*. Washington, DC: Natl. Acad. Press

Jencks C, Phillips M, eds. 1998. *The Black-White Test Score Gap*. Washington, DC: Brookings Inst. Press

Kahlenberg RD. 1996. *The Remedy: Class, Race, and Affirmative Action*. New York: Basic Books

Kane TJ. 1998. Racial and ethnic preferences in college admissions. See Jencks & Phillips 1998, pp. 431–56

Kanter RM. 1977. *Men and Women of the Corporation*. New York: Basic Books

Kaufman P, Chen X, Choy SP, Peter K, Ruddy SA, et al. 2001. *Indicators of School Crime and Safety: 2001*. Washington, DC: Natl. Cent. Educ. Stat.

Keith SN, Bell RM, Swanson AG, Williams AP. 1985. Effects of affirmative action in medical schools: a study of the class of 1975. *New Engl. J. Med.* 313:1519–25

Krueger AB, Whitmore DM. 2001. The effect of attending a small class in the early grades on college-test taking and middle school tests results: evidence from Project STAR. *Econ. J.* 111:1–28

Krueger AB, Whitmore DM. 2002. Would smaller classes help close the black-white achievement gap? In *Bridging the Achievement Gap*, ed. JE Chubb, T Loveless, pp. 11–46. Washington, DC: Brookings Inst.

Ladd HF, Chalk R, Hansen JS, eds. 1999. *Equity and Adequacy in Education Finance*. Washington, DC: Natl. Acad. Press

Lamb JD. 1993. The real affirmative action babies: legacy preferences at Harvard and Yale. *Columbia J. Law Soc. Probl.* 26:491–521

Larry P. v. Riles, 343 F. Supp. 1306, ND Cal. (1972)

Lau v. Nichols, 414 U.S. 563 (1974)

Lempert RO, Chambers DL, Abrams TK. 2000a. Michigan's minority graduates in practice: the river runs through law schools. *Law Soc. Inq.* 25:395–505

Lempert RO, Chambers DL, Abrams TK. 2000b. Michigan's minority graduates in practice: answers to methodological queries. *Law Soc. Inq.* 25:585–97

Losen DJ. 2004. Challenging racial disparities: the promise and pitfalls of the No Child Left Behind Act's race-conscious accountability. *Howard Law J.* 47:243–98

Loury G. 2002. *The Anatomy of Racial Inequality*. Cambridge, MA: Harvard Univ. Press

Lucas SR. 1999. *Tracking Inequality: Stratification and Mobility in American High Schools*. New York: Teach. Coll. Press

Lucas SR, Berends M. 2002. Sociodemographic composition, correlated achievement, and de facto tracking. *Sociol. Educ.* 75:328–48

Lucas SR, Gamoran A. 2002. Tracking and the achievement gap. In *Bridging the Achievement Gap*, ed. JE Chubb, T Loveless, pp. 171–98. Washington, DC: Brookings Inst.

Lyons JJ. 1990. The past and future directions of federal bilingual-education policy. *Ann. Am. Acad. Polit. Soc. Sci.* 508:66–80

Mare RD, Winship C. 1988. Endogenous switching regression models for the causes and effects of discrete variables. In *Common Problems in Quantitative Social Research*, ed. JS Long, pp. 132–60. Beverly Hills, CA: Sage

Massey D, Denton NA. 1993. *American Apartheid: Segregation and the Making of the Underclass*. Cambridge, MA: Harvard Univ. Press

Mayer DP, Mullens JE, Moore MT. 2000. *Monitoring School Quality: An Indicators Report*. Washington, DC: Natl. Cent. Educ. Stat.

McNeil LM. 2000. *Contradictions of Reform: The Educational Costs of Standardized Testing*. New York: Routledge

Metz MH. 1978. *Classrooms and Corridors: The Crisis of Authority in Desegregated Secondary Schools*. Berkeley: Univ. Calif. Press

Meyer MM, Fienberg SE. 1992. *Assessing Evaluation Strategies: The Case of Bilingual Education Strategies*. Washington, DC: Natl. Acad. Press

Mickelson RA. 2001. Subverting Swann: first- and second-generation segregation in Charlotte-Mecklenburg schools. *Am. Educ. Res. J.* 38:215–52

Milliken v. Bradley, 418 U.S. 717 (1974)

Minorini PA, Sugarman SD. 1999. School finance litigation in the name of educational equity: its evolution, impact, and future. See Ladd et al. 1999, pp. 34–71

Moore DR, Davenport S. 1988. *The New Improved Sorting Machine*. Madison: Univ. Wis., Sch. Educ., Natl. Cent. Eff. Second. Sch. ERIC Doc. Reprod. Serv. No. ED 316942

Moses ER. 1941. Indices of inequalities in a dual system of education. *J. Negro Educ.* 10:239–44

Murnane RJ, Phillips BR. 1981. Learning by doing, vintage, and selection: three pieces of the puzzle relating teaching experience and teaching performance. *Econ. Educ. Rev.* 1:453–65

Natl. Cent. Educ. Stat. 2002. *Early Childhood Longitudinal Study—Kindergarten Cohort Longitudinal Kindergarten–First Grade Public-Use Child File*. Washington, DC: Natl. Cent. Educ. Stat.

Natl. Cent. Educ. Stat. 2003a. *Digest of Education Statistics*. Washington, DC: Natl. Cent. Educ. Stat.

Natl. Cent. Educ. Stat. 2003b. *Issue Brief: Racial/Ethnic Differences in the Path to a Postsecondary Credential*. Washington, DC: Natl. Cent. Educ. Stat.

Nelson RL, Payne MR. 2000. Minority graduates from Michigan Law School: differently successful. *Law Soc. Inq.* 25:521–26

Oakes J. 1981. Tracking policies and practices: school by school summaries: a study of schooling in the United States. *Tech. Rep. Ser. No. 25*, Los Angeles, Univ. Calif. Graduate Sch. Educ. ERIC Doc. Reprod. Serv. No. ED 214893

Oakes J. 1985. *Keeping Track: How Schools Structure Inequality*. New Haven, CT: Yale Univ. Press

Oakes J. 1994. More than misapplied technology: a normative and political response to Hallinan on tracking. *Sociol. Educ.* 67:84–89

Oakes J. 1995. Two cities' tracking and within-school segregation. *Teach. Coll. Rec.* 96:681–90

Oliver ML, Shapiro TM. 1995. *Black Wealth/White Wealth: A New Perspective on Racial Inequality*. New York: Routledge

Omi M. 1997. Racial identity and the state. *Law Inequal.* 15:7–23

Omi M. 2001. The changing meaning of race. In *America Becoming: Racial Trends and Their Consequences*, ed. NJ Smelser, WJ Wilson, F Mitchell, pp. 243–63. Washington, DC: Natl. Acad. Press

Omi M, Winant H. 1994. *Racial Formation in the United States: From the 1960s to the 1990s*. New York: Routledge. 2nd ed.

Orfield G, Bachmeier MD, James DR, Eitle T. 1997. Deepening segregation in American public schools: a special report from the Harvard project on school desegregation. *Equity Excell. Educ.* 30(2):5–24

Orfield G, Arenson J, Jackson T, Bohrer C, Gavin D, Kalejs E, et al. 1998. Summary of "City-Suburban Desegregation: Parent and Student Perspectives in Metropolitan Boston," a report by the Harvard Civil Rights Project. *Equity Excell. Educ.* 31(3):6–12

Pallas AM, Entwisle DR, Alexander KL, Stluka MF. 1994. Ability-group effects: instructional, social, or institutional? *Sociol. Educ.* 67:27–46

Pascarella ET, Palmer B, Moye M, Pierson CT. 2001. Do diversity experiences influence the development of critical thinking? *J. Coll. Stud. Dev.* 42:257–71

Phillips M, Brooks-Gunn J, Duncan GJ, Klebanov P, Crane J. 1998. Family background, parenting practices, and the black-white test score gap. See Jencks & Phillips 1998, pp. 103–45

Plessy v. Ferguson, 163 U.S. 537 (1896)

Pres. Comm. Advis. Sci. Technol. Panel Educ. Technol. 1997. *Report to the President on the Use of Technology to Strengthen K-12 Education in the United States.* Washington, DC: Exec. Off. Pres., Pres. Counc. Advis. Sci. Technol. http://www.ostp.gov/PCAST/k-12ed.html

Ramirez DJ, Yuen SD, Ramey DR, Pasta DJ. 1991. Final report: national longitudinal study of structured-English immersion strategy, early-exit and late-exit transitional bilingual education programs for language-minority children. Vols. I, II. *Tech. Rep.* Aguirre Int., San Mateo, CA

Rathbun A, West J, Germino-Hausken E. 2004. *From Kindergarten Through Third Grade: Children's Beginning School Experiences.* Washington, DC: Natl. Cent. Educ. Stat.

Regents of the University of California v. Bakke, 438 U.S. 265 (1978)

Reschly DJ. 2000. Assessment and eligibility determination in the Individuals with Disabilities Act of 1997. In *IDEA Amendments of 1997: Practice Guidelines for School-Based Teams*, ed. CF Telzrow, M Tankersley, pp. 65–104. Bethesda, MD: Natl. Assoc. Sch. Psychol.

Richardson v. Lamar County Board of Education, 729 F. Supp. 806 (M.D. Ala. 1989)

Richter DK. 2001. *Facing East from Indian Country: A Native History of Early America.* Cambridge, MA: Harvard Univ. Press

Roberts v. City of Boston, 59 Mass. (5 Cush.) 198 (1850)

San Antonio Independent School Dist. v. Rodriguez, 411 U.S. 1 (1973)

Sander R. 2000. The tributaries to the river. *Law Soc. Inq.* 25:557–64

Saporito S, Lareau A. 1999. School selection as a process: the multiple dimensions of race in framing educational choice. *Soc. Probl.* 46:418–39

Saucedo LM. 2000. The legal issues surrounding the TAAS case. *Hisp. J. Behav. Sci.* 22:411–22

Serrano v. Priest, 5 Cal. 3d 584 (1971)

Shaywitz SE, Shaywitz BA, Fletcher JM, Escobar MD. 1990. Prevalence of reading disability in boys and girls: results of the Connecticut Longitudinal Study. *JAMA* 264:998–1002

Shulman JL, Bowen WG. 2000. *The Game of Life: College Sports and Educational Values.* Princeton, NJ: Princeton Univ. Press

Singer JW. 1991. Re-reading property. *New Engl. Law Rev.* 26:711–29

Skrentny JD. 2002. *The Minority Rights Revolution.* Cambridge, MA: Belknap Press of Harvard Univ. Press

Smock PJ, Wilson FD. 1991. Desegregation and the stability of white enrollments: a school-level analysis, 1968–84. *Sociol. Educ.* 64:278–92

Swann v. Charlotte-Mecklenburg Board of Education, 402 U.S. 1, 32 (1971)

Thernstrom S, Thernstrom A. 1997. *America in Black and White: One Nation, Indivisible.* New York: Simon & Schuster

Tienda M, Cortes K, Niu S. 2003. *College attendance and the Texas top 10 percent law: permanent contagion or transitory promise?* Presented at Conf. Expand. Oppor. High. Educ., Sacramento, CA, October 23–25. http://www.texastop10.princeton.edu/publications/tienda101803.pdf

Time. 1969. Last refuge. *Time*, Nov. 14

Tobias S, Zibrin M, Menell C. 1983. Special education referrals: failure to replicate student-teacher ethnicity interaction. *J. Educ. Psychol.* 75:705–7

United States. 2003. Brief of the United States as Amicus Curiae supporting petitioner, *Grutter v. Bollinger*, 539 U.S. 306 (2003). http://www.umich.edu/~urel/admissions/legal/gru_amicus-ussc/us-gru.pdf

Valverde LA. 2004. Equal educational

opportunity since *Brown*: four major developments. *Educ. Urban Soc.* 36:368–78

Van Hook J. 2002. Immigration and African-American educational opportunity: the transformation of minority schools. *Sociol. Educ.* 75:169–89

Wells AS. 1995. Reexamining social science research on school desegregation: long- versus short-term effects. *Teach. Coll. Rec.* 96:691–706

Wells AS, Crain RL. 1994. Perpetuation theory and the long-term effects of school desegregation. *Rev. Educ. Res.* 60:531–55

Whitla DK, Orfield G, Silen W, Teperow C, Howard C, Reede J. 2003. Educational benefits of diversity in medical school: a survey of students. *Acad. Med.* 78:460–66

Williams ML. 1996. Racial diversity without racial preferences. *Chron. High. Educ.* Nov.15, p. A64

Williams v. State of California, Super. Ct. San Francisco, No. CGC-00-312236 (settled 2004)

Willig AC. 1985. A meta-analysis of selected studies on the effectiveness of bilingual education. *Rev. Educ. Res.* 55:269–317

Woods SB, Achey VH. 1990. Successful identification of gifted racial/ethnic students without changing classification requirements. *Roeper Rev.* 13(1):21–26

Zucker SH, Prieto AG. 1977. Ethnicity and teacher bias in educational decisions. *Instr. Psychol.* 4:2–5

Annu. Rev. Law Soc. Sci. 2005. 1:233–54
doi: 10.1146/annurev.lawsocsci.1.041604.115843
Copyright © 2005 by Annual Reviews. All rights reserved
First published online as a Review in Advance on July 8, 2005

LAW FACTS

Arthur L. Stinchcombe

Department of Sociology, Northwestern University, Evanston, Illinois 60208;
email: a-stinch@northwestern.edu

Key Words evidence, procedure, socio-legal scholarship, law in action versus law
on the books

■ **Abstract** This review article is not dedicated to a subject matter of research.
Instead it outlines various kinds of facts commonly used to analyze the relations of law
and society. To illustrate, it gives examples of eight distinct kinds of facts on how action
departs from relevant laws on the books: actions in crusades; actions following deep
norms when coordination norms are in conflict with them; police culture undermining
legal citizen protection; corruption; legal pluralism as in colonies; crucial missing
facts on behavior deliberately left out of the law of contract and similar laws to create
flexibility; and disagreements between public opinion and the law. Each of these and
more are then analyzed in terms of what is distinctive about them and of the kind of
law and society theories they bear on.

CRUCIAL FACTS ABOUT LAW AND SOCIETY: INTRODUCTION

This essay is a review of a single aspect of the law and society tradition, so it is
not a review of a body of literature in the usual *Annual Review* sense. I analyze
how different branches of the law and society literature identify facts crucial to
their research. I argue that very little depends on the epistemological status of the
facts, although no one prefers false to true except for sound reasons [for example,
the reasons that led the U.S. Supreme Court to classify Long Island as a peninsula
in *U.S. v. Maine* (1986)]. Instead, the way facts are identified depends on the
theoretical interests of the subcommunity of scholars, or of practitioners who have
to use facts to support theories on which they hope to base their practice.

Sometimes there is a fairly close relationship between the centrality of a particular kind of fact and a discipline. For example, I argue that what Karl Llewellyn
(1960) calls a "singing reason" in his book on common law cases in appeals courts
is a "fact" about a reason; such a fact neatly explains many precedents (which
makes it sing) and afterwards causes the fact's own precedent to rule. The people
who regard it as their job to find or propose such facts are almost all either professors of law or appeals court judges, I think (although I will use an example written
by an economist, John R. Commons).

1550-3585/05/1209-0233$20.00

Most social scientists and historians of law hardly recognize an entity like "singingness" as a fact at all and think they have epistemological reasons for that distinction. But if they were as interested as Llewellyn was in which precedents become canonical and what distinguishes reasons that sing, they could find good, positivist ways to approach singingness. Psychophysics is not baffled by making positivist efforts to measure perception of weights; a psychophysics of the singingness of reasons should be only a trifle more difficult. Instead, the explanation of why these facts are central to law reviews and appellate opinions, and why great law professors and great judges are recognized by singing reasons, is the special theoretical nature of predicting future decisions from precedents. As it happens, most scholars interested in this question are in law schools or on appellate benches.

I focus, however, on the theoretical reasons that facts are interesting and fundamental, rather than the organization of disciplines. When I think there is a moderate correlation between a kind of fact and a discipline, I will mention it. But I will not be surprised to find, in the midst of the law professors and appellate judges, the odd economist who tells the typical tale that makes a singing reason a fact about a precedent, and makes it sing more by writing a fugue on it. The following is a brief outline of the sorts of facts I analyze here and how they differ from one another, before going into detail about each kind.

I start with singing reasons as facts, partly because the legitimacy of lawyers as scholars of law and society is a contentious issue on which I take a generous position; the point is that elegant argument is a social force in law, and facts about elegance are therefore crucial. Singing reasons are elegant reasons.

Then I deal with who-wins facts (or inequality facts), law-on-the-books versus law-in-life facts of eight different kinds, *longue durée* facts, proliferation facts, law facts about representation and jurisdictions, situational or ethnographic facts that shape decisions, and finally bargaining and discussion about what legislation and interpretation will be. I leave facts about lawyers' training, work, and careers out because I know very little about them.

I analyze these kinds of facts according to the theoretical reasons for using such facts. For example, perhaps the central kind of fact for most sociologists of law is who wins in court or in the creation of legislation, the social stratification aspect of the law. Sometimes such facts are general across many parts of legal behavior, such as the fact that repeat players (e.g., insurance companies) are likely to win. Some are quite specific to a particular kind of legal case, such as the fact that in rape cases it is very hard for a victim of either sex to establish lack of consent, which produces a stratification that generally favors men rather than women. Some are features of the boundaries of the legal order, as when in times of revolution or conquest it is quite hard for any legal dispute to be resolved by court decisions. When no one has a legal arena to win in, it is a legal fact that no one wins by legal processes.

But sociologists have no monopoly on this kind of fact because political scientists often study the inequalities of law caused by variations in how the boundaries of electoral district and issue jurisdictions of courts create different inequalities in different countries (e.g., Stepan 2004). Historians and historical anthropologists have studied the interplay between forms of legal systems and amount and kind of inequality in economic production [e.g., Merry 2000, Lattimore 1967 (1940), Sahlins 1958]. Law and economics addresses monopolistic inequalities of some kinds of legal regulation, especially, for example, those that create more civil service jobs. They also study why the negative externalities of economic development ought not give rise to tort claims (Posner 1972), arguing that this stratification by economic function serves the collective good, if not the good of the fifth driver who did not stop at the same obscure crossing. So facts about who wins, and so the stratification effects of law (and stratification's effects on law), have various epistemological forms and various disciplinary requirements of solidity of a fact. But they have in common the purpose of explaining inequalities.

The relationship between law on the books and law in social life has many subtypes. The brief reason that there are many kinds of such facts is that social life is very various and so creates many kinds of pressures for departures from formal law. The reasons that secret police interrogation behavior departs from what the law of evidence specifies are quite different from the reasons that American juries have to be instructed in the law and on the specific legal issue at stake by a judge, because their everyday sense of justice may not conform with the law. Both of these reasons differ from the reasons that businessmen in dispute with each other do not start by quoting the contract but by interpersonally complaining and bargaining in order not to destroy a valuable relationship. My list of eight kinds of law-on-the-books versus law-in-life facts is a primitive form of theorizing. But because every form of social life has its own consequences, a list of the kinds of facts in the broad category of departures of life from law is all I can manage here.

A *longue durée* fact is a trend (here in legal culture and behavior) that changes continuously and slowly for very long periods of time. For example, the number of phenomena in a given area of social life regulated by law tends to increase with time. The proportion of all commerce that involves contracts that cross national boundaries has increased steadily for several centuries, while the number of cows in the neighbor's corn in trespass law has decreased. Obviously, historians are in general more competent at finding such facts, but a wide variety of disciplines use them in some part of their reasoning.

A proliferation fact is usually a *longue durée* fact, increasing steadily and slowly, but it has special features because it branches from previous law and regulation. And sometimes the rate of proliferation is astounding: *longue*, for the proliferation of human subjects' regulation in university research or for the complexity of a medical insurance contract for a care provider's services, is a month or two.

The development of jurisdictions, such as legislative, judicial, and administrative autonomy given to the states by the Tenth Amendment of the U.S. Constitution, or the one main limitation of the Commerce Clause by that amendment, are historical creations, and their interpretations have proliferated (e.g., see Levi 1949). But the inequality that this produces—for example, that Rhode Island and Alaska have equal representation in the Senate as California and New York, or that most big corporations have access to federal U.S. courts for actions in California even if they are located in Delaware—generates proliferation of jurisdictional law. Delaware therefore makes corporate law for all of America (and so to some degree for all the world), a deep fact of the political organization of legal matters (Romano 1997). Jurisdictional law therefore is a special kind of creator of legal inequality of legislative and court representation, and the social and political shaping of such law consequently creates law facts of great significance. But the proliferation fact illustrated by Levi is not the same as the inequality fact analyzed by Romano.

Situational facts derive from the elementary consideration that, as every social action has to be done by people, so every legal action has to be done in a particular time and place with its defined composition, purpose (or lack thereof), normative structure, and information availability. Those situational variables often determine which laws apply, which influences are brought to bear on legal decisions, which incentives of the various people shape the social interaction, what language is to be spoken, and what norms of turn-taking apply. Such matters are often of the greatest legal importance. The main way to find out about such situational matters is ethnography, watching what happens in situations and interviewing people about what has been going on, so anthropologists and their imitators in sociology are dominant generators of such facts. But some kinds of situations produce documents that record what went on (for example, records for legislative debates are common in democracies), or at least what the outcome was (e.g., when a negotiation produces a contract or a jury produces a verdict). And, of course, experimental social psychologists can produce simulated legal situations (e.g., jury deliberations) to study the processes that presumably go on in their real analogues.

Discourse is one of the central things shaped by the nature of the situation. Because the law is a system of meanings, and meanings are the central thing shaped by discourse, a big subtype of situational variation is what sort of discourse goes on in it. Discourse and the meanings it carries are so important, and so extended by writing to many other situations, that they deserve separate treatment. Especially crucial to legislation and to the formation of contracts in the civil law are the interrelations between discourse that can be described by the term bargaining and the kind that can be described as discussion. A crucial fact about many contracts that last a long time, for example, is that, during the existence of the contract, a good deal of discussion happens about what is wise between the parties and what we should do to deal with a new situation (Macaulay 1966, 1996). But the terms of many other contracts are hardly ever discussed either before or after the commitment is made—these are often called contracts of adhesion.

Similarly, constitutional conventions differ from ordinary legislative meetings by a high ratio of discussions of general values and a lower ratio of discussion about who gets what out of various flows of money or material goods (Elster 1994). Thus, a crucial kind of legal fact is the nature of the discourse, especially the amount of bargaining versus general discussion of the wisdom of laws and remedies, behind a given legal outcome: a constitution, a performance under a contract, or the content of a contract or of a piece of legislation.

This is, for example, a central topic in modern political and legal philosophy (Habermas 1984, 1989). But like most philosophical topics, the rest of the disciplines will not leave the questions (and therefore the facts relevant to them) to the philosophers (e.g., on Habermas's main topic, see Speier 1950/1952—Speier was a historical sociologist). The rest of this essay tries to identify the distinctive place of these varieties of law facts in the theory of the relationship between law and society.

SINGING REASONS AS FACTS OF LAW

Many of the arguments about the law in appellate opinions and law journal articles seem factual to lawyers because they are organized around what Karl Llewellyn called singing reasons (Llewellyn 1960, *passim*). For example, the American law about restraint of trade needs to distinguish between a cartel that is an illegal price-fixing scheme and a corporation that is permitted, say, to keep the Mercury models of cars from competing with Ford models. Many of the distinctions such law makes can be summed up in the concept that Ford Motor Company carries on a business and is a going concern, whereas a cartel consists of an arrangement among a number of separate going concerns [the concept of the law of going concerns and going concern value is developed in Commons (1924/1974), especially chapter 5].

Showing that a great many precedents can be summed up in a singing reason that draws a well-defined line between managing a business and a conspiracy in restraint of trade by developing a legal concept of going concern is a fact of law. That a business must have a price policy for its lines of products, whereas two or more separate businesses should not have a price policy in restraint of trade, sums up an intuition behind many precedents. Some of the indicators of this concept are the following: A going concern has a common fund of resources that is replenished by revenues from its various products of services; it produces a common profit that is possessed by a management that authorizes a variety of unified policies to manage that fund; it buys and sells parts of its fund of resources and of the additions of its own products and puts the receipts into the fund; and it is owned in such a way that owners can reconstruct the management of the entity governing the fund. Precedents that use one or another of these indicators to show the carrying on of a business are thus unified into a central intuition of what the law really is about, what the fact was that was being established in all of the indicators in the precedent.

Thus, a singing reason using this concept of a going concern makes it natural that the Mercury division cannot develop a car to compete with Ford models because that would be bad management for the profitability of the business being carried on by the Ford Motor Company; its internal restraint of trade is what Commons [1974 (1924)] calls a "working rule" of the going concern.

The working rule of the going concern is a fact of law because it predicts the things future courts will use as criteria in a judgment in such cases. It gathers previous precedents into a convenient package that courts can then use to distinguish carrying on a business from restraint of trade, although both in fact restrain competition. It is useful in turn in establishing that a judgment that an anticompetitive act like restraining Mercury is part of carrying on a business when done by Ford but is a conspiracy in restraint of trade if agreed to between the Chevrolet Division of General Motors and the Mercury Division of Ford. The concept then appears in legal activity mainly in determining what are called legal facts about the world. But the concept and the reason it is embedded in is also a fact about the law because it is "what we meant all along." What we meant all along was manifested in the various reasons for using, say, separate profits, or the lack of a common management, or the lack of a common fund of resources owned by a legal personality, as evidence that a common pricing policy was a restraint of trade.

Part of the facticity is derived from the opinion's or law review article's narrative of a series of precedents being a "straining for" clarity in the legal definition of a set of situations to which the law is relevant. Thus, Commons [1974 (1924)], though an economist by trade, was writing a historical narrative of how the forms of ownership and contract of the capitalism of his time came into existence. That narrative came from a set of cases, for instance a case that established that the name of a business could be sold with the business and that sale protected against the former owner starting a business in the same trade with his name. This case is of course defining the name and the goodwill of a going concern as part of the fund of resources of the business, and so to be sold with the business. When such a precedent gets incorporated into a narrative of a struggle to distinguish business units as property (separate from particular assets), it is a heroic effort by a judge or an economist.

But *if* it is not a singing reason that does all that work, then a precedent does not become a crucial fact. For example, it is a singing reason of ancient vintage that a contract becomes final when an offer (defined in an appropriate legal way for the line of business) is accepted (appropriately). When it comes to be defined in a precedent that an offer becomes a contract when the acceptance is mailed (rather than when the offeror received the acceptance), and the date of the postmark is taken as the acceptable evidence of when it was mailed, the precedent all seems arbitrary. It allows the acceptor, but not the offeror, to rely on the contract during the time between mailing and delivery. But a failure of the postal service to postmark the acceptance would not naturally be interpreted by any such singing reason because this precedent's reason does not in fact sing. Thus, the precedent is not a fact about the law likely to be in a law review article, unless it is an article (Friedman 1966) on "legalism," on law that is not really law in the deep sense.

Perhaps the clearest example of the power of singing reasons in the law and society literature is the law and economics movement. The elegance, power, and economy of modern neoclassical economics is as seductive as Euclid. Edna St. Vincent Millay formulates the value of singing reasons as: "Euclid alone/Has looked on Beauty bare." I am reminded, however, of Erving Goffman's comment on Talcott Parsons's general theory, so much inspired by his (faulty) appreciation of the economic theory of his day: "I wish social theory were as easy as Talcott thinks it is." Specifying all the trade-offs in the utility function being maximized by the law is not as easy as Judge Posner thinks. It is lovely stuff, all the same.

LAW FACTS ON INFORMAL DEPARTURES
FROM LAW ON THE BOOKS

Because pressures for informal departures from the law come from society, and because society itself varies from one segment to another, one time to another, one society to another, one situation to another, facts about informal departures from the law are as various as the whole of the social sciences. In this section, I give a disorganized list with brief explications of why departures are distinct. I do not, however, treat facts about when people want to stick strictly to the written law (see Bernstein 1996).

1. Crusades, true believers, and the military exception: When intense social interaction takes place in a group defined by its value differences from some enemy, and intensity of opposition is magnified by the isolation of the conflict from outside influences, and especially from defenders or tolerators of the enemy, then law, punishment, restriction of exchange, and negotiation come to be seen as weapons in the conflict. The Crusades against Muslim dominance of the Holy Land combined such value differences on religion with the "military exception" to ordinary civilized law. Riot control law, occupied territories law, and police chase laws are similar except that they do not usually dominate the whole environment. They instead create pockets of special laws not effectively reviewable by the courts and often not responsive to legislation. When civilian presidents, or kings and queens, want exceptions from ordinary law, they start calling themselves the commander in chief. What we used to call totalitarianism is chiefly built out of careful exemption of parts of the ideological police from public legal or legislative review and so is similar to the military exception. These exceptions from review are often explicit, as in the *Geheime* (secret) in the Gestapo's name, but are often cloaked by words like "classified information" or "operational" or even just "special." Such informal departures from law on the books are often carried out by authorized officials of the state, state terrorism. The disassembly of such structures is an especially difficult part of the transition from totalitarian to other kinds of political rule (Stinchcombe 1995).

2. Deep norms versus coordination norms: Closely related to the crusade type of departure from law on the books is the professional type. It is similarly driven by values, but values that legalized institutions are themselves supposed to serve. For example, in the United States, there is a law that emergency rooms cannot turn away people in danger of dying because they cannot pay. But this law does not arrange for anyone else to pay. It calls on the deep medical professional values embedded in the Hippocratic Oath and also embedded

in the social structure of hospitals. The formal structure also specifies that medical bills be paid, but it does not specify who else but the poverty-stricken victim of an accident is supposed to pay. Emergency rooms in the United States obey Hippocrates rather than the civil law that says that they are entitled to be paid, a losing proposition for hospitals. Many hospitals close because they cannot find anyone else to overcharge so they can pay for patients who cannot, who fill their emergency room. Without embedding the obligatory treatment regulation in the deep norm that physicians should save lives if they can, strikes by emergency room personnel might force the conflict of laws to be resolved. Hopefully someone would then agree to pay. As it is, the business managers of the hospital have to enforce what amounts to a lockout, often by going bankrupt or abolishing the hospital. Professional values trump ordinary civil law but not bankruptcy law.

3. Police culture: A particularly intransigent problem of professionally embedded law is police subculture. The police are supposed to solve crimes and arrange for criminals to be punished by bringing a case in court. The political and legal guidance of the professional objectives of police partly determines how variations in this culture of professional duty are shaped. But in a large fraction of jurisdictions (especially in the United States), the prosecutor's office most directly shapes police criteria of success. As a result, at the base of police culture is a culture of effectiveness rather than a culture of legality. Departures from the law on the books in interrogation procedures and arrests are law facts central to the illegality of professional but informal police behavior. The widespread presence of plea bargaining in American criminal justice is forced on the prosecutor-police system in part by overloaded judges. The formally illegal bargaining that often takes place, and the heavier sentences for those who plead not guilty that provide the informal incentive system, are the judges' contribution to prosecutorial-police undermining of the criminal law system. As noted above, this police departure from law is more common in "secret" police.

4. Corruption: We can identify two main types of corrupt informal structures that cause departures of informal behavior from the law. I call these two types commercial and political. When laws try to repress or tax heavily commerce in goods that customers will pay a lot for (the main cases are recreational addictive drugs, prostitution, gambling, and zoning decisions), behavior that departs from the law is very profitable. A good deal of money can flow to public officials or legislators who create a reliable subsystem for the sale of permissions (by legitimate legislation or illegitimate exemption) to carry on the trade. This flow of money tends to create informal commercial networks and subcultures to produce that reliable flow of permissiveness. Political corruption, in contrast, tends to happen when formal government implicitly reserves political privileges, theoretically available to all, for the richer and more educated. Typical examples include administering civil service tests

that exclude poorly educated people from jobs they could perfectly well do, or the provision of information and discussion only in the native language in a city with many immigrants, or locating schools only in cities a long way from rural children. Thus privileging the rich and well-educated tends to produce "machine" politicians who can help the poor, immigrants, and rural people. As a machine politician told Lincoln Steffens (Merton 1968/1948, p. 149), "I think there's got to be in every ward somebody that any bloke can come to—no matter what he's done—and get help. Help, you understand; none of your law and justice, but help."

5. Symbolic law: Sometimes laws are passed for rhetorical reasons rather than as matters of enforceable policy. When no monies are voted for enforcement of fair employment laws, employers learn that the law was intended as a moral symbol of equality, not as a law that would actually change anything. Sometimes this symbolism takes the subform of an assertion of authority that may someday be filled in, as when the tsars of Russia proclaimed autocracy (*samoderzhavie*) as the central ideology but had fewer civil servants per thousand inhabitants than Western powers and not enough money to feed the army. The army, the core enforcer, therefore had to earn its keep by working in the fields and could not find time to drill or to practice the use of weapons. Autocracy then was symbolic, although pretty destructive for a symbol. Another type of symbolic law involves making crimes of behavior such as prostitution or selling bets on the numbers, even though legislators know the victims will not provide evidence. They are often called consensual crimes. The laws that make them crimes are also symbolic law. In all forms of law effective only as symbols, the law fact of informal departure from the law on the books is designed into the law itself.

6. Legal pluralism: In similar fashion, sometimes a law is intended to apply to only one part of the population, while a different, and sometimes contradictory, law is intended for another part of the population. Such legal systems are also designed to create departures from the laws on at least one of the books. Such informal acting according to different laws always requires in its turn a third separate law for transactions or crimes across the boundaries (Benton 2002). Most facts of this kind are about colonial situations or occupation governments, but they are also sometimes created by extraterritoriality negotiated to get foreigners to enter special "free ports" or "industrial zones" (e.g., Herlihy 1986, pp. 23–34). And almost all come about through some combination of war and diplomacy, so the facts are disproportionately found by historians.

7. Missing law facts—the performances parts of contracts: Securities markets are about the only place where we have extensive data of the contents of contracts, the performances that we learn about in elementary courses on the law of contracts. It is very difficult for social scientists to get a sample of contracts to look at. Occasionally we are lucky and, for example, the

contents of a contract of Frank Lloyd Wright become known because it was so often a matter of contention and Wright was a great architect, worthy of documenting (Macauley 1996). Quite often, specialized arbitration tribunals show that dispute resolution requires some detailed knowledge of the meaning of descriptions of performances in a particular trade. But this means then that the informal understandings are built into the legal obligations created by the contract (Stinchcombe 2001, pp. 55–75). When this reaches the level of specialized bodies of law, as in marine insurance, and a specialized, independent profession of classification societies provides standards of seaworthiness that are the basis of the insurance ratings, then there can be independent sources on the contents of the contracts, published by classification societies. Requests for proposals in public tenders may be valuable sources, but usually considerable secrecy surrounds the actual proposals.

Other examples include the contracts in status law (e.g., marriage contracts and labor contracts) in which it is of the essence that the performances change with the situation. The statuses of the people to the contract and the broad responsibilities of those statuses are described vaguely in the agreement. An oath of fealty in feudal law, the trusteeship of an estate or a mutual fund, or "to have and to hold, 'til death do us part" give the tone of the performance description of such agreements. In some sense, then, we have grossly deficient facts on the substance of the performances in contracts or the actual patterns of behavior in fiduciary relationship agreements. Obviously, there are various subcultures in which people understand each other about the performances implied in contracts, or else the law of such contracts would be useless.

To exaggerate a bit, we know everything about legal contracts except what they are for. Perhaps the central illusion of the law and economics movement is that all the description of performances in the contracts can be summed up in the risks in the money flows. These risks are crucial to motivation of contracts and fiduciary agreements, but they do not get buildings built nor children cared for. Because the law of contracts or of marriages is supposed to enclose the contents, it is not really a departure from the law on the books. But Thorstein Veblen somewhere complains that one cannot tell whether contractual behavior is sharp salesmanship or fraud until a court decides; Veblen points to a gap in our scholarship.

8. Public opinion and legal arrangements: A broad fact about the informal setting of the law is that an interviewer or an ethnographer cannot get ordinary people, individually or in groups, to reproduce the law on the books as their sense of justice. Some parts of procedural law, such as the right for one's side of a dispute to be heard by an impartial tribunal, are widely supported in public opinion. But it is very hard, for example, to convince people who believe that racial equality is a good thing to approve of any system to pay for the enforcement of this ideal, or to approve punishing people who discriminate, or to think that courts should decide whether to

integrate schools. It is an obvious fact that judges instruct juries on the law and on the legal definition of the factual issue. It is not obvious, however, whether the juries learn that lesson well. Those of us whose profession includes reading essays of students, to whom we have taught easier things than the law of evidence, are inclined to be suspicious. Thus, there are facts that show that most uninstructed individual and small group public opinion is naive about the law, and is especially naive about what it takes to enforce legally embedded values. Facts about how the cognitions of law and the administration of law are different in the legal and governmental elite than in the general public have been central since the early discussions of the relation between law and custom. Stratification by naiveté about the law is therefore a central source of facts about departures of social life from the law on the books.

THE FACT OF WHO WINS

Much of the social science literature on law takes as the fundamental fact who wins. This fact becomes especially fundamental when one can show that social inequalities determine who wins rather than the facts of the case, as a fair trial would have found them to be. Thus, Donald Black (1976) wants to construct a pure sociology of law with only facts about inequalities in who wins, and facts about who wins should be sufficiently represented by vertical distance. The fundamental fact is unfairness [although the fact that unfairness is unfair is not itself a scientific fact to Black (1976)]. Thus, it would not be a fundamental fact about who wins if, say, more people in Corsica (Gould 2003), the United States, Colombia, and Mexico are convicted of murder because there are more murders there than in England or Norway or non-Corsican France. That is a fact of criminology, not a fact about the law. Similarly, it is not as interesting a fact as it should be that white-collar theft by fraud and embezzlement totals more money than that stolen by the poor because the rich can steal more money at a time. That, again, is criminology. The who-wins fact is that white-collar thieves more often get light sentences or get off altogether.

There are three main subforms of the who-wins facts, which I call discrimination facts, better lawyers facts, and repeat players facts. [A special form of surprise facts is about not much caring who wins, as when Palestinians bring cases against the Israeli army, knowing they will lose, because they want to hear the justice of their case proclaimed (Shamir 1991). I do not deal with this last form.]

Discrimination facts come in two main forms: unfair laws and unfair enforcement. Thus, the famous fact noted by Hannah Arendt that the evil of Nazi genocide was banal, that Eichmann was just doing his job, is an argument that it was the law that was evil, not Eichmann (or at least his personal evil was not the essence of Nazi unfairness to Jews). Similarly, the status laws of *Ständestaat* regimes, that only noblemen could be military officers, or that Jews had to live in the conquered provinces within the Pale in Tsarist Russia, are fascinating facts because the law itself is discriminatory rather than the courts' application of it to specific cases. These are often favorite facts of historians; the slavery part of the American Civil War and Jewish-Ukrainian relations are central topics of historians of the United States and of the Ukrainian part of Russia or Poland because the system was unfair on its face.

But the sociologists' favorite kind of facts are that the courts (or police, or prosecuting attorneys, or sentencing judges, or prison authorities) are unfair in the application of fair laws. Sociologists want to know that a law pretending to be fair (such as the much higher penalties against crack cocaine than the same dose in powder) is unfair (because crack is mainly used by blacks and powder by whites). But it is perhaps even more interesting to sociologists that the law is itself administered so that blacks are convicted more often and get longer sentences even when using the other race's drug.

The fundamental facts for white-collar crime are much more often of the better lawyers variety. One main form of this kind of fact relies on deep pockets combined with good lawyers to make the civil law process much more expensive, so a poorer disputant has to settle or withdraw. It is the unfairness of a poker game in which one of the players raises so much that the other players cannot call him. But better lawyers can also write better writs of error to appeal decisions, so getting multiple chances to win. They can have all the evidence for a criminal charge of their opponent on their computer for their own simultaneous civil trial, by an agreement of the prosecutor with no computer resources. Then they agree to wipe the evidence out if the counterparty settles the civil claim, thus concealing the crime. Such a fact does not get its fire from evil people who discriminate, or evil laws, but from evil consequences of routine legal processes. It is fascinating the way Franz Kafka is fascinating, not the way a Gestapo officer's evil in a holocaust movie is fascinating.

Repeat player facts are very often about the multiple ways that organizations do much better than mere folks do in the legal system, starting with the shape of the law or of contracts and ending with the suit being dropped, or never started. Hospitals and physicians know a lot about avoiding malpractice suits—for example, about how a consent form has legal consequences in cases of alleged malpractice, consequences that are not explained when the patient signs it (Heimer et al. 2005). One's automobile insurance company sends amendments to one's contract when it sends the bill, without consultation or negotiation about the new contract. The police are often thought by juries to be better witnesses than the accused, even when their testimony is not accurate. The insurance company has a continuing relation with repeat lawyers, whereas the insured gets a lawyer who works for a proportion of the settlement or verdict. That lawyer has both practical powers and motives to settle, whether the client wants to go to court or not. The accused in a criminal trial mostly uses a part-time or inexperienced public defender, and police volunteer no exculpatory evidence, having continuing friendly relations with the prosecutor.

Such repeat player facts are not as dramatically evil as genocide or discrimination. Rich white male passengers get the same (now secret rather than printed on the back of the ticket) denials of liability as the black single mother. Inequality is less personal, more routine, and, in some fundamental sense, egalitarian. We never thought we might be equal to the insurance company or the hospital, so we are not humiliated or irritated when everything is arranged for them, not for us.

LONGUE DURÉE FACTS

When in several places Max Weber writes about the rationalization of law (and of many other things), he treats it as one fact that is a summary of a great many facts, cumulated in a single direction over a very long time. A posing of this particular kind of cumulation is more clearly laid out in Yaney (1973, pp. 3–9) for a single entity over two centuries. Such reasoning has come to be known under the label used by the French *Annales* school of historians, *longue durée*, used here as an adjective. An ideal-typical fact of this sort is Le Roy Ladurie's (1966, pp. 53–57) analysis of cereal grains slowly evolving from their ancestral adaptation to Middle Eastern climates to colder and colder climates through trial plantings and sowings, edging northward in France, eventually making the northern Seine-Loire plains a dominant grain area. Most *longue durée* facts in the law and society literature do not have this elegant concreteness, with the long history of the latitudes built into the *longue durée* evolution of seed grains. But hardly anyone would doubt that the rationalization of law to a form that takes three years of law school, and some apprenticeship as an associate, to practice well is a long-term development. They may disagree with Weber that the main direction of change is getting more rational.

Another principal theoretical problem whose investigation generates *longue durée* facts is the incorporation of distinct legal systems and customary law into a ruling legal system—the problem of the decline of pluralism in law. The core mechanisms here are generally two: disputes over the jurisdiction of customary or native law, gradually overturning exemptions of natives from colonial law, and superior economic and political power and effective legitimacy of the law of the conqueror. Examples are the comparative study by Benton (2003), the study by Merry (2000) on Hawaii, and the study by Charrad (2001) on North Africa. A more ancient such pattern, reversed, is the nomadic conquerors of China and of some oasis cultures being successively incorporated into Chinese or oasis cultures, having their plural customs and laws erased by the legal culture of the conquered [Lattimore 1967 (1940)]. The law of the conqueror became the law of the conquered in the *longue durée*, except when the conquerors were poorer.

PROLIFERATION FACTS IN LAW AND REGULATION

Some parts of law and regulation start small, then branch into many varieties. At first those who tested dangerous drugs had to inform subjects of the risks involved. But dangers to people being investigated are generative. Bureaucratic systems, Douglas (1985) suggests, invent dangers, then new dangers, coming from those low in the system or outside it. They then invent laws and regulations, and then again still more laws and regulations, to control these dangers. Similarly, when asking questions of people who were free not to answer started to be thought dangerous to them, rules were invented for reviewing survey interviews for dangers, and now world-class physicians being interviewed by graduate students have to sign consent forms saying that they have been informed of the dangers to them of the interview. Everyone is vulnerable now.

Similarly, when deaths from some food supplements were reported in the news, regulators then expanded drug regulation to cover the dangers. Then people noticed that hamburgers and fries have long-run dangers, so class-action torts have tried to expand the legal regulation of diets more generally. Adversary systems as well as bureaucratic systems are motivated to find new dangers, and adversaries sue about them (Kagan 2001).

Dangers are then sources of proliferation facts of the law. But intellectual property also proliferates, so that CDs from the United States cost a great deal more in other countries than in the United States because intellectual property treaties create more monopolistic markets elsewhere than in their land of origin. Antitrust or procompetition legislation of other countries can be treated as invasions of intellectual property (Braithwaite & Drahos 2000, pp. 360–98; also pp. 56–66, 79–85, 404, 564–571). The proliferation of court cases in poorer or smaller countries challenging an advanced country's intellectual property monopoly follows from the proliferation of things that can be patented or copyrighted and the lengthening duration of the copyright or patent. Both these proliferations therefore cause case law to proliferate. Then we need more law school professors specializing in intellectual property.

Similarly, jurisdictional law proliferates as the complexity of central legislation and also of provincial or local legislation increases, so there are more legally defined situations in which jurisdiction has to be allocated. The No Child Left Behind Act effectively establishes jurisdiction over how local taxes are spent if student test scores do not improve faster (test scores have improved by about a standard deviation since World War II in the United States, using the same tests that were used for recruits to the World War II military on present-day populations). The main apparent cause of test score improvements is increased average time in school of all population groups. Increased time within school each year, or increased number of years in school overall, are of course very expensive and are explicitly excluded in the legislation. Thus, the main technology known to be successful in raising test scores, time in school, is excluded. But the ineffectiveness of alternative technologies then produces a proliferation of excuses in the act's implementation. This raises conflicts between jurisdictions of school boards and the national government. Jurisdictional law is in some sense the purest law, having to do only with arrangements internal to the legal system. For that reason, when Levi (1949) wrote a book on legal reasoning, he chose especially the part of commercial law having to do with the Commerce Clause, and the part of family law having to do with federal jurisdiction over the interstate movement of prostitutes (the white slave trade, as it was called then). Making immorality an interstate transaction thus caused jurisdictional law to proliferate.

Proliferation is a general process, so contracts and standard operating procedures usually get longer. The ratios of phone numbers for administrative and regulatory university officials to phone numbers for faculty increase over time; pounds of paper to respond to per week increase; memos one answered last week, whose answers were not read, cause the proliferation of requests to repeat oneself. A central trouble of tsarist autocracy was that the tsar could not read the memos from his provincial governors (Robbins 1987); this, of course, caused the proliferation of central government departments, of inquiries into imperfect reports, of summonses to Moscow, and thus the lengthening and increased frequency of memos for the autocrat.

Changes in the overall structure of law and regulation then are shaped by differential proliferation rates in different subparts of the law (March et al. 2000). Thus, one can study which aspects of the university are being more intensely regulated by studying which subparts of the administration have most increased their number of telephones, which parts of the faculty handbook have gained the most pages, which new reports are required from lower units, and about which topics new rules have been written.

LAW FACTS ON JURISDICTION AND REPRESENTATION

Both legislative and court jurisdictions are formally divided between central and provincial governments in federal systems, and informally so divided elsewhere. Federal systems, formal and informal, vary widely in their representation systems, who elects the legislators, and who can appeal to which courts on what issues.

For example, in the territorial upper houses in Belgium and India, provinces have nearly population-proportional representation, whereas in the United States, Brazil, and Russia representation is very unequal, and representatives of very small provinces essentially have veto power over national policy (Stepan 2004). In the United States, national corporations and wholesale commercial businesses have more access to federal courts, while small retail, construction, and real estate enterprises have very little, because of the Commerce Clause and the treaties jurisdiction of the central government.

In essentially all formally federal countries, and within many of their provincial subunits, special jurisdictions are created for special purposes. Ports, airports, railroads, capital cities, tribal reserves, natural resources, military installations, and prisons are almost always special jurisdictions and have special appeals procedures. Many other kinds of regimes also create special jurisdictions, often with separate policy making and dispute resolution systems. Special jurisdictions mean necessarily privileged special interests or the specially disprivileged. People who live near oil wells are routinely excluded and powerless, in both legislation and litigation; corporations that exploit oil wells are the reverse. When regions present a special combination of problems and opportunities, special departments are created to deal with them; we are not surprised when the conquest of Siberia, not at all like the rest of Russia, called for a Siberian *Prikaz* (department or ministry) in the central government, reporting to the tsar. Although this sounds like technical law, the sort of thing only lawyers pay attention to, political and legal powers are differently distributed in different societies, and differently distributed to different social locations within societies. Tribal chieftains and exploiters of oil wells are frequently on airplanes flying into the capital city; tribal farmers or ranchers near an oil well are frequently absent from the same airplanes. The frequent precariousness of democracy and federalism in oil-exporting countries, and the special eagerness for intensely partisan redistricting in Texas, may reflect the special politics of natural resources' special jurisdictions.

The social determinants of such inequalities of legislation and litigation are, in the first place, deeply historical, and in the second place, deeply political. They seem to be more historical and political when they are implicated in ethnic conflicts. The radical egalitarianism of Belgium and India in the upper house representation system may reflect ethnic conflict so deep and various that only universalism and equity are viable alternatives for jurisdictional law. Wherever one finds many territorially segregated ethnicities or economic interests, jurisdictional inequalities are likely to dominate politics, schooling, the law of property in land and the resources under it, and who is licensed to carry a gun. In such polities, the losing party is less likely to think it might win next time. Law facts on variations in jurisdictional structure and the resulting inequalities of representation and legal access are well known, but they have a very small part in our theory of law and society. And that is a bad thing.

LAW IS SITUATIONAL: ETHNOGRAPHIC FACTS ABOUT LAW

Sodomy statutes are rarely enforced against married couples, and marital rape cases are rarely punished with criminal penalties because evidence that could be used in court does not leave the domestic situation. But murder offenses are also largely committed in domestic situations and are cleared by arrest far more often than burglary or robbery offenses because murder offenders were known by the police and other witnesses to be on the scene. Domestic situations compared with public situations have opposite effects, concealing some crimes and displaying others (Stinchcombe 1963). Broadly speaking, many domestic offenses are more likely to be treated with therapeutic remedies than criminal or damages remedies because of the close relations between domestic situations and intimacy. The intimacy of domestic life is often protected in law, and the information barriers around domestic life often have legal standing. For example, spouses in the United States routinely cannot (or at least cannot be forced to) testify against each other. The value of privacy is often about situational boundaries of valued intimacy.

Ethnographers have much the same troubles observing domestic legal facts as do police officers. Both rarely find burglaries invading domestic space through patrolling the streets; both meet the burglars (or murderers) mainly in court. Thus, scholarly situational facts and variations between domestic and public situations turn out to be mostly facts about courtrooms or other dispute resolution situations, after the dispute comes to light. The walls, doors, and locks define information flows legally and so shape what information gets past the door into the light. The law is more public in ethnography, as well as in police experience, than in life. All sorts of potentially interesting facts are unobservable. As a result, incidence of domestic crimes is estimated by victim interviews rather than by arrest records, so situational variations among crimes directly shape our epistemology. It also shapes the blank places in our theories—we know little about the history of the interaction situation behind most types of domestic crimes, and what we do know is what appears in court. We know police never see most burglaries but only the effects of burglary, which are very visible. People often report burglary for insurance purposes; the burglars themselves are carefully invisible.

Very often in the ethnography of law, the crucial facts have to do with the character of gatherings within situations. For example, divorces in western states of the United States in the 1800s were fairly often obtained through acts of a legislature rather than of a court, especially when the woman being divorced was in the East and the new wife was a local woman. Usually no representative was present except the person representing the husband, a situational fact about the character of the hearing. In the legislative divorces, that representative hardly ever bothered to notify the now-former wife. Legislative decision on particular cases was also characteristic of immigration in the mid-1900s in the United States. But immigration officials were not called to testify that this exception to the law would benefit the public; usually getting a few such cases through was a privilege of the legislator. Having such cases decided in a legislature is quite different from proceeding with a hearing in which the representatives of one side of the dispute must answer the opposite side, as was usually true in courts and administrative hearings.

American adversarial hearings arrange the authority of the attorneys of the parties and the judge differently than judge-led hearings, and this shapes the kinds of evidence and discovery procedures that supply flows of evidence to the situation (Kagan 2001). Police working for the investigating judge may seek and provide the court with evidence of innocence more reliably than those who work for the prosecuting attorney. That is, the characteristics of role definition in the chamber of judgment shapes who gets represented how, as well as who controls what evidence on the facts. Who is represented and who controls evidence in turn shape a series of situations, especially interrogations, conducted by the police.

But much of the literature interested in situational facts is interested also in how the law gets into the situation. For example, local community participation in judgment changes the presentation of evidence, the presentation of the law, and the presentation of custom. The trade-offs between law, punishment, therapy, custom, and remedies are generally thought to be shaped by local participation, and that is often thought to be a good thing. But this in turn means that a disproportionate share of ethnographic facts are about situations of alternative dispute resolution (e.g., Strang 2002, Strang & Braithwaite 2001). Very often facts about such alleged effects of situational arrangements are central to proposals to reform legal processes, or of court hearings oriented to continuing reformation of, say, drug addicts, habitual petty criminals, prostitutes, or errant youth. Often the central factual allegations about such changes in the situation or in the structure of the gathering subtend a dimension from formal to informal, with informal settings reducing recidivism or the level of conflict.

The central arguments in support of informal situations are that more values may be introduced than those embedded in the contract or indictment, more evidence than strictly pertinent (e.g., about character or social support or past efforts at reform or previous convictions) and more alternative remedies. It is often a special kind of situational fact that political loyalties and values may be taken into account, as in many communist judgment processes. More generally, the *khadi* justice that Weber implicitly attributed to the Muslim religious training of the judge is more often nowadays seen as the outcome of the judge manipulating the situation to "shame and restore," rather than punish. Of course, in other times and places, going over to (or safeguarding) a justice of the peace system is thought to have had the same virtues and faults as alternative dispute resolution or *khadi* religious training. Naturally, if informality bleeds other values into dispute resolution, whether this is a good thing depends on which values are introduced. When and where such dispute resolution situations produce records, historians, as well as ethnographers and reformers, create facts by comparing them. Justices of the peace, the posse for arrests, and the lynch mob have often been studied with historical facts.

The notion that juries decide facts seems to be descended from the idea that one's neighbors in traditional societies generally already knew the relevant facts. A gathering of neighbors to come to a consensus on a land tenure matter was an administrative convenience for investigation, as well as judgment. And the notion that the jury will find out the law from the judge (as influenced by the adversary attorneys), rather than the jury determining that as well, is a *longue durée* fact about how court situations have been transformed. Often increased differentiation of roles in legal situations is a *longue durée* fact. Now juries in Anglo-American law are specifically distinguished from witnesses, and a witness is excluded from being a juror.

Very often facts about situations become significant when they come in a series, as when couple counseling comes before a divorce case, arrest comes before indictment, which comes before trial or pleading, which comes before sentencing. In such cases, what the situational variation is supposed to achieve is often specified in the law, so that the counselor cannot grant a divorce (e.g., because of the informal fact that that man is impossible to deal with), nor can the police officer participate in the sentencing. Severe punishment for disrespect of police officers sometimes characterizes police arrest behavior (Black 1971)—in some societies disrespect may be, in effect, a capital offense (see Gould 2003). It is crucial here that arrest takes place outside the situation of a courtroom.

Correspondingly, the norms and social structure internal to the situations that form the series are shaped to take into account the special virtues or special liabilities of such norms. Police officers are not less concerned with law and order than judges, but because they are not in a situation to hear two carefully prepared contending arguments and submissions of evidence, they have different norms, different legal powers, a different pace and urgency of work, and different superiors to answer to.

BARGAINING AND DISCUSSION OF LEGISLATION AND CONTRACTS AS LAW FACTS

Jon Elster (1994) compares the U.S. Constitutional Convention with the Constituent Assembly that was part of the French Revolution and distinguishes two contrasting forms of discourse: general argument and bargaining. Bargaining was much more salient among the American states becoming united rather than confederated [for the development of the form of discourse appropriate for democracy in France, see also Markoff's (1996) marvelous study of the discussion between the legislature and rural France (pp. 427–515); Speier (1950/1952); Habermas (1984, 1989); and further in the United States, Polsby (1968)]. The two types of discourse, bargaining and discussion, are organized differently, with different effects. Thus, broadly speaking, public opinion is mostly discussion of what is valuable and wise, whereas legislative discussion and talk in constitutional conventions is a mixture of speechmaking that gives an analysis of implementation and the formulation of laws and bargaining about who benefits and who has what powers during that implementation. In the infamous motto of the American trade union leader, Jimmy Hoffa, "There are two kinds of political action. You can make speeches, or you can give money. We [Teamsters] give money." A more common form of bargaining in legislation is trading votes, but in contracts trading money is more common.

Newspapers and salons are the prototype of public opinion. Speier's (1950/1952, pp. 328–29) note on the centrality of publishing the budget is indicative of the interdependence of bargaining and discussion, even under an absolutist king of France. One cannot discuss a bargain without knowing who gets what; the budget is central data on that. Thus, a crucial fact about the tsarist late-nineteenth-century reforms that created quasi-democratic institutions at local levels is that almost all implementation was still in the hands of a local council consisting of civil servants appointed by the center, and the center was in its turn governed by a council, consisting again entirely of civil servants or representatives of the nobility. Speechmaking was sharply distinguished from (budgeted) implementation, and local implementation was much more centralized than local speechmaking in the *zemstvo* (Robbins 1987, pp. 20–42, 91–123). Autocratic democratization was intimately dependent on the relationships between bargaining and discussion, which made implementation not very democratic.

Bargaining about legislation involves the exploration, often off the floor, of what each participant wants, what each controls that he or she will trade for it, what the relative priorities are of each participant for the various components of the legislation, and what things that are being traded can be discussed publicly. Discussion can roughly be divided into two main parts, the first related to the general values being expressed in the legislation and the second related to the implementation strategy that can bring those values to realization. If contracts are thought of as legislation for the parties to the contract, then the same contrast can be found (to be sure with fewer general values and more implementation) within talk in negotiation; one can discuss what is wise, then bargain about who gets what benefits and who bears what costs.

CONCLUSION

In some sense a conclusion to a list of kinds of facts of this sort is as inappropriate as a conclusion to a dictionary. I do, however, want to comment briefly on what I have learned by focusing on the variety of facts in the study of law and society, rather than the variety of ideas. First, the discussion above seems to me to testify to the inherently interdisciplinary character of the study of law and society. Each kind of fact is the property of many disciplines, and of many theories. Second, the discussion seems to me to show, better than a discussion of theories or approaches, how many different ideas are interesting to the field. Looking at ideas from the point of view of the facts to which they are relevant, rather than from the point of view of how they differ from other ideas, is inherently eclectic. For example, in the discussion of jurisdictional facts above, the only advice on theory is to wish there were at least one theory of the social determinants and consequences of jurisdictional law. By concentrating on the facts, one does not have to put down a hypothesis to reject (which we do not really have for jurisdictional law), for there are many wonderful ones, suggested by the facts, to accept tentatively. Third, I became convinced again that a library is a wonderful research tool.

ACKNOWLEDGMENTS

My title of emeritus means that I am off the merit system, and so not to blame for any deficiencies of this paper. Kim Lane Scheppele is the ultimate cause of my writing this paper. She has, however, pointed out that a list is inherently disorganized, and she wished for a better theoretical structure. My failure in that regard is my own; that due to the inherent nature of the task is hers.

The *Annual Review of Law and Social Science* is online at
http://lawsocsci.annualreviews.org

LITERATURE CITED

Benton LA. 2002. *Law and Colonial Cultures: Legal Regimes in World History: 1400–1900.* Cambridge, UK: Cambridge Univ. Press

Bernstein LE. 1996. Symposium: law, economics, and norms: merchant law in a merchant court: rethinking the code's search for immanent business norms. *Univ. Penn. Law Rev.* 144:1765–831

Black DJ. 1971. The social organization of arrest. *Stanford Law Rev.* 32 (1):1087–111

Black DJ. 1976. *Behavior of Law.* New York: Academic

Braithwaite J, Drahos P. 2000. *Global Business Regulation.* Cambridge, UK: Cambridge Univ. Press. 704 pp.

Charrad MM. 2001. *Women's Rights: The Making of Postcolonial Tunisia, Algeria, and Morocco.* Berkeley: Univ. Calif. Press. 341 pp.

Commons JR. 1974 (1924). *Legal Foundations of Capitalism.* Clifton, NJ: Augustus M. Kelly. 394 pp.

Douglas M. 1985. *Risk Acceptability According to the Social Sciences.* New York: Russell Sage Found. 115 pp.

Elster J. 1994. Argumenter et negocier dans deux assemblées constituants. *Revue francaise de science politique* 44(2):187–256

Friedman LM. 1966. O. legalistic reasoning: a footnote to Weber. *Wis. Law Rev.* 148:171

Gould RV. 2003. *Collision of Wills: How Ambiguity About Social Rank Breeds Conflict.* Chicago: Univ. Chicago Press. 203 pp.

Habermas J. 1984. *The Theory of Communicative Action.* Vol. 1. *Reason and the Rationalization of Society.* Trans. T McCarthy. Boston: Beacon

Habermas J. 1989. *The Theory of Communicative Action.* Vol. 2. *Lifeword and System: A Critique of Functionalist Reason.* Trans. T McCarthy. Boston: Beacon

Heimer CA, Petty JC, Culyba RJ. 2005. Risk and rules: the legalization of medicine. In *Organizational Encounters with Risk*, ed. B Hutter, M Power. Cambridge, UK: Cambridge Univ. Press. In press

Herlihy P. 1986. *Odessa: A History, 1794–1914.* Cambridge, MA: Harvard Univ. Press, Harvard Ukrainian Res. Inst. 411 pp.

Kagan RA. 2001. *Adversarial Legalism: The American Way of Law.* Cambridge, MA: Harvard Univ. Press

Lattimore O. 1967 (1940). *Inner Asian Frontiers of China.* Boston: Beacon. 585 pp. 2nd ed.

Le Roy Ladurie E. 1966. *Les paysans de Languedoc.* Paris: Mouton. 1034 pp.

Levi EH. 1949. *An Introduction to Legal Reasoning.* Chicago: Univ. Chicago Press. 104 pp.

Llewellyn KN. 1960. *The Common Law Tradition: Deciding Appeals.* Boston: Little Brown. 565 pp.

Macaulay S. 1966. *Law and the Balance of Power: The Automobile Manufacturers and Their Dealers.* New York: Russell Sage Found. 224 pp.

Macaulay S. 1996. Organic transactions: Frank Lloyd Wright and the Johnson Building. *Wis. Law Rev.* 27:75–121

March JG, Schulz M, Zhou X. 2000. *The Dynamics of Rules: Change in Written Organizational Codes.* Stanford, CA: Stanford Univ. Press. 228 pp.

Markoff J. 1996. *The Abolition of Feudalism: Peasants, Lords, and Legislators in the French Revolution.* University Park: Penn. State Univ. Press. 689 pp.

Merry SE. 2000. *Colonizing Hawaii: The Cultural Power of Law.* Princeton, NJ: Princeton Univ. Press. 371 pp.

Merton RK. 1968/1948. Manifest and latent functions. In *Social Theory and Social Structure*, ed. RK Merton, pp. 73–138. New York: Free Press. 702 pp. 1968 enlarged ed.

Polsby NW. 1968. The institutionalization of the House of Representatives. *Am. Polit. Sci. Rev.* 62:144–68

Posner RA. 1972. *Economic Analysis of Law.* Boston: Little Brown. 747 pp.

Robbins RG. 1987. *The Tsar's Viceroys: Russian Provincial Governors in the Last Years of the Empire.* Ithaca, NY: Cornell Univ. Press. 272 pp.

Romano R. 1997. State competition for corporate charters. In *The New Federalism: Can the States Be Trusted?*, ed. JA Ferejohn, BR Weingast, pp. 129–54. Stanford, CA: Hoover Inst. Press, Stanford Univ. 170 pp.

Sahlins MD. 1958. *Social Stratification in Polynesia.* Seattle: Univ. Wash. Press. 306 pp.

Shamir R. 1991. Litigation as consummatory action: the instrumental paradigm reconsidered. *Stud. Law Polit. Soc.* 11:41–67

Speier H. 1950/1952. The historical development of public opinion. In *Social Order and the Risks of War*, ed. H Speier, pp. 323–28. New York: Stewart. 497 pp.

Stepan A. 2004. Toward a new comparative politics of federalism, multinationalism, and democracy: beyond Rikerian federalism. In *Federalism and Democracy in Latin America*, ed. EL Gibson, pp. 29–84. Baltimore, MD: Johns Hopkins Univ. Press. 377 pp.

Stinchcombe AL. 1963. Institutions of privacy in the determination of police administrative practice. *Am. J. Sociol.* 69(2):150–60

Stinchcombe AL. 1995. Lustration as a problem of the social basis of constitutionalism. *Law Soc. Inq.* 20(1):245–73

Stinchcombe AL. 2001. *When Formality Works: Authority and Abstraction in Law and Organizations.* Chicago: Univ. Chicago Press. 208 pp.

Strang H. 2002. *Repair or Revenge: Victims and Restorative Justice.* Oxford: Clarendon. 298 pp.

Strang H, Braithwaite J, ed. 2001. *Restorative Justice and Civil Society.* Cambridge, UK: Cambridge Univ. Press. 250 pp.

U.S. v. Maine, 475 U.S. 89 (1986)

Yaney GL. 1973. *The Systematization of Russian Government: Social Evolution in the Domestic Administration of Imperial Russia, 1711–1905.* Urbana: Univ. Ill. Press

Annu. Rev. Law Soc. Sci. 2005. 1:255–84
doi: 10.1146/annurev.lawsocsci.1.041604.120002
Copyright © 2005 by Annual Reviews. All rights reserved
First published online as a Review in Advance on July 19, 2005

REAL JURIES

Shari Seidman Diamond[1] and Mary R. Rose[2]

[1]Northwestern University Law School and American Bar Foundation, Chicago, Illinois
60611; [2]Department of Sociology, University of Texas, Austin, Texas 78712-1088;
email: s-diamond@law.northwestern.edu, mrose@mail.la.utexas.edu

Key Words   decision making, law, damages, death penalty

■ **Abstract**   The elaborate efforts of the legal system to control and channel jury
behavior reveal a mistrust of an institution that also attracts extravagant praise. We look
at the jury by examining research on real juries drawn from archival studies and post-
trial surveys and interviews, as well as from the deliberations of real juries. We show
how the methods used by courts to gather and select jurors affect the representativeness
and legitimacy of the jury. We also examine the evidence underlying skepticism about
jury verdicts and decision making, focusing on cases that pose special challenges to
jurors, particularly those involving complex evidence, legal complexity, and the death
penalty. We then consider how optimal jury trials can be achieved.

> Even twelve experienced judges, deliberating together, would probably not func-
> tion well under the conditions we impose on the twelve inexperienced laymen
> [Judge Jerome Frank, *Courts on Trial* (1949), p. 120].

> Juror #4 (discussing the testimony of an expert physician in a medical malpractice
> case): What I would like to have is 40 [specialists] and show them the [test results]
> and okay, get a survey and is this significant or is this not significant and would
> they have [done what the defendant did]? [Deliberating juror from the Arizona
> Filming Project (Diamond et al. 2003)]

INTRODUCTION

The jury, with its constitutional pedigree, is a fixture in the American legal system
and a symbol of American democracy that has impressed outside observers since
Tocqueville. The subject of both extravagant praise and vitriolic criticism, juries
decide not only cases involving multimillion dollar claims and severe permanent
injury, but also whether a defendant will spend years in prison or be sentenced to
death. Yet public debate about the trust we place in the jury raises questions not
only about the nature of jury verdicts but also about their legitimacy in light of
jury composition. Implicated here are the strains that arise when the legal system
subjects conscripted citizens to extensive scrutiny and vetting before permitting
them to serve as jurors. Once the trial begins, ambivalence about entrusting the
resolution of serious disputes to laypersons who lack specialized technical or legal

expertise has led to elaborate efforts to control and channel jury behavior. The result is a generally polite but palpable tug of war with the jury.

To assess the product of this sensitive balancing act, we examine the research on real juries, point to some shortcomings, and discuss prospects for improvement. We focus on those areas in which issues of trust frequently arise: the selection of the citizens who serve as jurors; the verdicts of juries, particularly civil juries; comparisons between jury decisions and those of judges; and cases that pose special challenges to jurors because of evidentiary or legal complexity or the high-stakes instance of death penalty decisions. Real juries provide the most appropriate source in considering these issues because the ubiquitous research on jury simulations cannot fully enact important variables or environmental features (e.g., methods of jury selection or lengthy cases). Moreover, lurking in the background of all jury simulation research is the question of how well the findings, even those obtained from the more elaborate efforts using jury pool members, videotaped trials, and courtroom settings, mirror the behavior of real juries. Thus, although our primary focus is on research on real juries, we occasionally compare the results from studies of simulated and real juries.

JURY COMPOSITION AND THE SIGNIFICANCE OF WHO SERVES

The composition of juries conveys a powerful political message about legitimacy. People regard trials as less trustworthy and fair—especially trials resulting in unpopular verdicts—when verdicts come from more homogenous juries (see Ellis & Diamond 2003). A belief that the racial composition of the jury determines outcomes has even affected support for the jury in nefarious ways. For example, in 1957 U.S. senators from the South responded to President Eisenhower's proposed civil rights legislation by including a provision requiring juries to decide whether an individual's voting rights had been violated (Caro 2002). At that time, minorities were rarely selected as jurors, and the segregationists of 1957 believed that all-white juries in their states would not follow the law by punishing those who violated the voting rights of African Americans.

The literature examining both experimental simulations and real jury data on the relationship between race and jury decision making reveals a more complicated picture (see, e.g., Conley et al. 2000, Garvey et al. 2004, Pfeifer & Ogloff 1991, Sommers & Ellsworth 2003). Although jury representativeness has increased in the past few decades, conviction rates in criminal cases have remained remarkably stable (Vidmar et al. 1997). The impact of demographic characteristics, including race, on jury decision making is often dramatically overestimated, especially given the far stronger effect that the weight of the evidence has in determining verdict outcomes. For example, Garvey et al. (2004) analyzed the reported first votes and jury verdicts of 3000 jurors in four major metropolitan areas. Strength of the evidence was a consistent and strong predictor of jurors' first votes. Race had some predictive value, but only in some jurisdictions for some offenses for some defendants. Thus, African American jurors in the District of Columbia sitting in drug cases were more likely to favor an acquittal of an African American defendant on their first votes than were white jurors in those cases. Even in those cases, however, race had no detectable influence on jury verdicts. In contrast, there are at least some types of cases in which racial composition of the jury as a whole correlates with outcomes (e.g., Baldus et al. 2001). The effects on perceived fairness suggest that attention to representativeness would be warranted, even if it did not influence outcomes.

Two distinct phases in jury selection contribute to ensuring or undermining the representativeness of the jury: (*a*) summoning and qualifying jurors (pre-courthouse) and (*b*) selecting a jury after questioning at the courthouse (voir dire). As we note below, the meaning of a fair jury and challenges to achieving it are distinct at each stage.

From the Community to the Courthouse

Jury composition has changed substantially over the past 40 years. At the federal court level, Congress worked to improve the representativeness of juries through the 1968 Jury Selection and Service Act, which required—following the landmark 1965 Voting Rights Act—use of voter registration rolls as juror source lists, as well as a plan for summonses to be sent randomly. This legislation overturned prior regimes in which local officials selected citizens for jury service based on their community ties and status (Van Dyke 1977, p. 86). The 1970 Uniform Jury Selection and Service Act, which provides a model statute for states to adopt, also endorses random selection, as well as supplementation of voter rolls with other lists (Van Dyke 1977, p. 99). According to a Bureau of Justice Report (Rottman et al. 2000), only a handful of states now mandate voter registration as their exclusive source list. Most states now use the voter rolls and supplement them with other source lists (e.g., drivers license and tax lists). A majority of the states have eliminated all occupational exemptions, broadening the range of citizens potentially available to serve as jurors (Rottman et al. 2000).

Despite these improvements, the persistent reality is that the prospective jurors assembled in courthouses and the empanelled juries that decide cases are systematically different from the communities from which they were drawn (Curriden 2001, Fukurai et al. 1993, Johnson & Haney 1994, Levin 2005, Walters et al. 2005). They are typically more likely to be white, better educated, wealthier, and older. A critical empirical question is what processes lead to this result.

Research has pointed to several institutional practices that can limit representation. Fukurai and colleagues (1993) note that less frequent updating of address lists will underrepresent the poor and the young, both of whom move frequently and are less likely to own their homes. In addition, biases in source lists affect who will be called. For example, according to the Current Population Survey, eligible (i.e., citizens over age 18) Hispanics/Latinos and Asian Americans are far less likely to register to vote than are African Americans and non-Hispanic whites (Lopez 2003). More than one study has shown that eligible Hispanics are underrepresented in large counties (Fukurai et al. 1993, Walters et al. 2005), even in counties where African American representation is comparable to the adult population (Hays & Cambron 1999).[1] Some courts have begun to use the Internet to qualify and schedule jury service (Marder 2001). This innovation can be remarkably efficient and convenient for users, but it may inadvertently undermine representativeness by reducing non-response rates only among wealthier and better educated prospective jurors who have regular access to and proficiency with the Internet.

Finally, resource constraints pose a profound barrier to representation. The paltry compensation provided to jurors contributes to the underrepresentation of low-income people of any racial/ethnic group. In Dallas County, Texas, for example, which currently compensates jurors at a rate of $6–$10 a day (Curriden 2001), just 13% of the jury pool earned less than $35,000 a year, whereas more than 39% of the county's citizens fell into this group (M. Curriden, personal communication). (Beginning in 2006, jurors in Texas will receive up to $40 a day.) Low rates of compensation affect citizen participation through two routes. First, the prospect of low compensation or the hardship of time away from work deters citizens from responding to a jury summons (Boatright 1999). In addition, financial hardship may lead the court to excuse jurors who simply cannot afford the "luxury" of jury service (Fukurai & Butler 1991).

Although the jury receives strong support from the citizenry in the abstract (Harris Interactive 2004, MacCoun & Tyler 1988), citizens are often reluctant to respond to a summons because of unrealistic expectations about what their service will likely entail. News accounts of high-profile cases lasting many months present a stark contrast with the reality that the average juror is likely to serve only a day or two given the growing number of "one day or one trial" systems and the fact that the typical trial lasts a few days (Boatright 1999). Some prospective jurors express a lack of confidence in their ability to serve (Boatright 1999), even though such concerns are likely unwarranted, especially because no juror decides a case alone. Although no study shows that additional educational campaigns would alter misperceptions, actual service does appear to promote largely positive perceptions of the jury system, and a majority of those who have served report that they were well treated (Consolini 1992, Diamond 1993b, Rose 2005).

---

[1] Apart from voter registration rates, the requirement that jurors be fluent in English can affect the participation rates of groups like Hispanic/Latinos and Asian Americans (Fukurai et al. 1993, p. 54). The remedy for this issue, however, is not fully clear, given the cost of providing translators to citizens who are not fluent in English—an accommodation generally available only to those with a language disability like deafness (see Kisor 2001). A 2000 state supreme court ruling in New Mexico (*State ex rel. Martinez v. Third Judicial District Court*) required the state to supply translators for non-English speaking jurors who require their services; other states, even those with substantial non-English-speaking populations, have not yet followed.

Researchers have studied some methods that courts might use to meet the challenge of ensuring a representative jury pool (Ellis & Diamond 2003, Fukurai et al. 1991, Munsterman & Hall 2003). Selection practices may not be based on race [e.g., by explicitly oversampling minority residents (*U.S. v. Ovalle* 1998)], but other approaches are available that may increase representativeness more generally. For example, courts could sample from census tracts or zip codes on the basis of the historical yield of eligible jurors from those locations, adjusting the proportion of summonses simply on the basis of previous yield rates, and further adjusting the proportions over time to reflect changes. Such proposals assume that prospective jurors within sampling units are homogeneous on factors that influence response rates. If true, this stratified, random-sampling approach would automatically correct for differential representativeness by race, income level, or any other characteristic that is correlated with the factors that lead to a reduced rate of yield from jury summonses, such as high mobility or hardship.

Jury Selection in the Courtroom

VOIR DIRE AND THE JUDGE   Once a sample of citizens appears in the courthouse, selection issues change, and a different struggle emerges in identifying the jurors who will decide a particular case. Questions about a fair cross-section of prospective jurors give way to questions about a given juror's ability and willingness to be fair, that is, to decide the case on the basis of the evidence and the law. An unbiased jury excludes those with explicit conflicts of interest with the case (e.g., blood relatives of one of the parties, their representatives, or a witness); those with specific prejudices (e.g., jurors who have made up their minds that the defendant is guilty or innocent; Vidmar 1997); and those with generic prejudice (e.g., jurors who assume that anyone charged with a particular type of offense, such as child molestation, must be guilty; Vidmar 1997).

The tug of war in the courtroom occurs because judges, in particular, must manage multiple issues and interests while assessing the level of juror bias. First, jurors value protection of their privacy (Rose 2005), even while voir dire is presumptively open to the public, and decision makers, especially attorneys, seek to learn as much as possible about life experiences and attitudes that might affect how jurors see the case. Such experiences could include issues that are difficult to discuss in open court, for example previous criminal history or other legal dealings. One study found that as many as 25% of jurors selected for criminal cases had not volunteered information during voir dire about their own or relatives' prior criminal victimizations (Seltzer et al. 1991). Some courts offer prospective jurors the opportunity to discuss sensitive areas at the bench or in chambers or to respond to voir dire questions on a preliminary questionnaire that is made available to the parties. The use of juror questionnaires may facilitate more efficient collection of individualized information from prospective jurors, but no research to this point has tested the effects of juror questionnaires on juror disclosure or on the exercise of challenges.

Second, both judges and jurors have interests in keeping the time spent on voir dire to the minimum necessary to make intelligent and accurate decisions about juror impartiality. This may explain why, despite risks of privacy threats, social influence, and jurors' self-presentation concerns, most judges initially—and often exclusively— question jurors as a group and ask people to volunteer publicly when a question is applicable to them (Bermant 1977, Hannaford-Agor & Waters 2004). Although potentially less time consuming, this procedure is comparatively less effective at gathering information about bias. After observing a number of people remain silent during questioning, one trial judge instituted a practice of privately, explicitly asking jurors who remained silent whether they had any information to add (Mize 1999). Of those who had been silent, 20% responded to the judge's individual follow-up questions with case-relevant information, some revealing severe difficulties or conflicts (e.g., a juror who was unable to understand the proceedings or, in one case, was the fiancé of the defendant). Nietzel & Dillehay (1982; see also Nietzel et al. 1987) found higher rates of sustained "challenges for cause"[2] when judges in capital cases allowed for individual, sequestered questioning rather than group questioning.

Finally, while encouraging jurors to be honest about their reservations or concerns about their fairness, judges also take steps to prevent jurors from too easily talking their way out of service by emphasizing (rather than minimizing or hiding) potential conflicts or superficially held opinions. Observations of actual jury selections indicate that judges spend significant time impressing upon jurors the court's need for their services (Balch et al. 1976, Johnson & Haney 1994, Rose 2005) and that judges attempt to rehabilitate those jurors who express reluctance about their abilities to serve, for example, by reducing the issue to whether the juror can or cannot follow the law (Diamond et al. 1997). This practice of emphasizing jurors' sense of duty and of extracting promises from jurors to set aside strong feelings or early intuitions about the case has implications for representativeness. Although such juror promises may not be reliable indicators of fairness, if a system of excuses for cause relied on category-based presumptions about bias—e.g., that a juror who was once a victim of a crime cannot be fair in a criminal case—there would be other negative consequences for the composition of the remaining jury pool. For example, in 2003 African Americans were 30% more likely than whites to have been a victim of a violent crime (Bur. Justice Stat. 2005).

To date, no comprehensive study has mapped out precisely how the management of these multiple interests and issues affect the representation of different groups of prospective jurors. Nor is there evidence that members of various demographic groups react differently to the structure of voir dire questioning (e.g., to private versus public questioning). Research has tended to focus almost exclusively on attorneys' evaluations of jurors' attitudes and subsequent use of peremptory challenges

---

[2]A challenge for cause is attempted when a prospective juror, through word or life circumstance, indicates an inability to be fair; a challenge is sustained if the judge agrees that the juror cannot be fair and excuses the juror from serving on that trial.

to excuse a subset of prospective jurors, and, indeed, this adversarial input into juries reflects serious tensions in the management of jury selection.

THE ROLE OF ADVERSARIES AND THE PEREMPTORY CHALLENGE   In exercising peremptory challenges, the parties can excuse a limited number of prospective jurors from serving on a particular case. The peremptory challenge, unlike the challenge for cause, traditionally required no explanation, but that changed in *Batson v. Kentucky* (1986). The U.S. Supreme Court held that it is unconstitutional to excuse potential jurors on the basis of their race. Despite this and other rulings,[3] African Americans are disproportionately likely to be dismissed by the prosecution, whereas whites are disproportionately likely to be struck by the defense (Baldus et al. 2001, Rose 1999). Although in the aggregate African Americans and whites may serve on juries at rates roughly comparable to their representation in the jury pool (Rose 1999), such representativeness may break down when the jury pool includes a small proportion of minorities or when subgroup representation is examined. Baldus and colleagues (2001) analyzed a large data set (over 317 capital cases) from Philadelphia and controlled for multiple variables (e.g., occupational category, answers to categories of voir dire questions). Although both sides' peremptories were patterned on race, prosecution challenges tended to eliminate the small group of young, African American men, particularly in trials involving an African American defendant and a white victim.

A number of commentators have called for eliminating peremptory challenges in order to improve jury representativeness (Amar 1995; *Batson v. Kentucky* 1986, Marshall, J., concurring; Hoffman 1997). Others have suggested that representativeness can be increased without a sacrifice in impartiality by reducing the number of peremptory challenges (Baldus et al. 2001, Finkelstein & Levin 1997, Hannaford-Agor & Waters 2004). Although the correct number is unclear and probably varies with the nature of the case, given the complicated mix of competing goals (e.g., privacy protection versus thoroughness, efficiency versus encouraging honest answers), some level of adversarial input in choosing jurors may act as a

---

[3]Attorneys must explain their challenges if the opposing party establishes a prima facie case that a challenge was based on race (*Batson v. Kentucky* 1986; *Georgia v. McCollum* 1992; *Powers v. Ohio* 1991) or gender (*J.E.B v Alabama, ex rel T.B.* 1994)—an allegation of a so-called *Batson* violation. To defend against the allegation, the attorney must provide the judge with a race-neutral explanation for the peremptory strike being challenged. The objecting party must prove that even trivial-sounding reasons are pretexts for intentional discrimination, a substantial hurdle, particularly because U.S. Supreme Court rulings in this area give a great deal of deference to trial judges' impressions of the attorneys' explanations for their peremptory strikes (*Purkett v. Elem* 1995). Melilli (1996) catalogued explanations offered in published opinions dealing with *Batson* violations. When challenges were disputed, attorneys failed to convince the judge that their motivations were race neutral only about 18% of the time, most often because the lawyer expressed concerns about a juror of one race but had not challenged a similarly situated juror of another race (Melilli 1996, p. 479).

safety valve for ensuring that people suspected of minimizing or failing to admit bias can be eliminated (Hannaford-Agor & Waters 2004, Rose 2003). Rose (2003) found that excused jurors who attributed their peremptory dismissal to prior experiences with the courts or to how they responded to voir dire questions (e.g., by hesitating in their response to an inquiry) had significantly greater concerns about their abilities to be fair than jurors who suspected they were removed for more tangential reasons. Thus, although attorneys are limited in their ability to predict juror verdict preferences (e.g., Zeisel & Diamond 1978), peremptory challenges do appear to eliminate some potentially unsuitable jurors who would not be subject to a challenge for cause. In sum, the central meaning of a fair jury at the voir dire stage is a group whose members are not biased against one party or another. This requires a vetting of their attitudes that can be made difficult by concerns about privacy and efficiency as well as about the need to ensure that people are not either shirking their responsibility to serve or failing to admit to or even recognize socially undesirable biases that would prevent them from being fair. The representativeness of jury panels can be diminished at this stage through attorneys' strategic uses of their peremptory challenges; however, peremptories are used as part of the complicated system for managing the various tensions and interests in selecting a fair jury. Thus, it is not clear that eliminating attorney input into selection would, in practice, result in more impartial juries or in panels that the public finds more legitimate or trustworthy.

JURY VERDICTS

The most basic source of public mistrust of the jury is with the results of its cases. This has been especially true of the civil jury, although acquittals or convictions in some high-profile cases produce suspicions aimed also at the criminal jury. In this section, we review studies of jury verdicts and consider how these results look in light of available external standards, especially how judges might rule.

Public Perception and Civil Jury Data

Critics often charge, and a majority of the public believes, that jurors are biased in favor of plaintiffs, awarding damages for frivolous claims and giving excessive and erratic awards (for reviews, see Kritzer 2001, Saks 1998). These suspicions, focused primarily on the tort system, have fueled an active reform agenda (e.g., legislative caps on jury awards for pain and suffering). Yet empirical studies of the tort system offer little support for this picture of extravagant and unwarranted juror generosity. According to data from the nation's 75 largest counties, plaintiffs prevail on liability on average about half the time (Cohen & Smith 2004), a success rate that is itself inflated because liability is either uncontested or only partially contested in some percentage of the cases counted as plaintiff wins (Diamond et al. 2003). Of course, it is not clear what the win rate ought to be, but plaintiffs clearly cannot anticipate that jurors will automatically be receptive to their claims. This conclusion holds even when cases involve corporate defendants (Hans 2000). The deliberations of real jurors (Diamond et al. 2003) show substantial juror skepticism about plaintiff claims and a reluctance to make unwarranted damage awards.

A recent study of malpractice claims, based on evidence from the Texas Department of Insurance, directly contradicts contentions that the sharp increases in insurance rates for medical malpractice in the past decade are the result of jury behavior or a tort crisis (Black et al. 2005). The study revealed no increase in the number of claims, no increase in the median or mean pay outs, and no change in the percentage of claims with payments of more than $1 million. Seabury and colleagues (2004) analyzed 40 years of jury awards and found evidence that increases in nonautomobile tort awards (e.g., medical malpractice, products liability) stem from increases in claimed costs of injuries rather than from changes in jury behavior.

The clearest indication that jury verdicts do not reflect popular perceptions comes from the few studies in which external measures of strength of evidence exist. These studies find that jury verdicts on liability are consistent with other assessments of the evidence. Taragin and colleagues (1992) examined independent physician assessments, routinely sought by malpractice insurers, of the defensibility of a given physician's care. This rating strongly predicted a plaintiff win: 42% of cases deemed indefensible resulted in payment, whereas only 21% of those labeled defensible did so. These authors note potential error in this latter rating and suggest that payments in truly defensible cases are even less frequent. In other research that considered both settlements and jury trials, injuries that independent physicians rated as avoidable were more likely to result in payment to a plaintiff (Sloan & Hsieh 1990; see also Sloan et al. 1993). Finally, Hannaford et al. (2000) asked judges who heard the exact same case that the jury heard to rate the strength of evidence; strength of evidence was the strongest predictor of a plaintiff's verdict on liability.

One area needing further research concerns the amount of variability in jury awards when two cases involve the same injury or cause of action. Simulation research suggests that even when case characteristics are held constant, jury liability verdicts and damage awards vary, sometimes in legally inappropriate ways (e.g., Saks et al. 1997). Experimenters can manipulate the amount of loss sustained in simulations, but the available measures of severity of injury in real jury data are generally limited and represent crude proxies for the real variables of interest. For example, many studies of damage awards have used a nine-point scale to assess the severity of injury, consistently showing a significant positive correlation between the scale value and damage awards (Daniels & Martin 1995). Such archival studies of damages find substantial variance unaccounted for by the severity scale, however, particularly with respect to the so-called pain and suffering component (e.g., Bovjberg et al. 1989, Vidmar et al. 1998). It is unclear how much of this unexplained variance is due to the myriad of relevant differences across plaintiffs that are not captured by this single measure. Even precisely the same injury can have vastly different implications for the compensation of different plaintiffs that a jury might reasonably consider. A classic example is the difference between the loss of a finger for a professional violinist versus a professor or a factory worker. There is also substantial variability in punitive damage awards, which we discuss next.

The Special Case of Punitive Damages

In a small percentage of civil cases, the jury is permitted to award punitive damages to punish the defendant in a civil case and to deter both the wrongdoer and others. The jury does so only upon finding that the behavior in question was particularly egregious (e.g., involved wanton, willful, malicious, or reckless conduct that showed an indifference to the rights of others). Jurors are typically given no further guidance in setting punitive damage amounts. Such awards are rare (occurring in 6% of tort and contract cases in which a plaintiff won damages; Cohen & Smith 2004) but have attracted enormous attention from scholars, the press, and the courts (for reviews, see Greene & Bornstein 2003, Sunstein et al. 2002) owing to a small number of unusually high awards.

Studies of real jury verdicts on punitive damages again show a disconnect between the typical assumption about jury behavior and actual results. Although juries make some multimillion dollar "mega awards" (Hersch & Viscusi 2004), the median punitive damage award in 2001 was $50,000 (Cohen & Smith 2004). Punitive damage awards are more likely to be awarded in some types of cases—such as intentional misconduct cases—than they are in the types of cases that capture press attention, such as medical malpractice or products liability cases. Attempts to compare the punitive damage awards of judges and juries have yielded mixed results (Eisenberg et al. 2001–2002, Hersch & Viscusi 2004), but as Eisenberg and his colleagues acknowledge, and we discuss in more detail below, there is no evidence that judges and juries see the same stream of cases. As a result, the comparisons of judge and jury punitive damage verdicts are difficult to interpret.

Finally, as with compensatory awards, punitive damage amounts can be highly variable. Again, equating two cases, in this instance on the severity of conduct, is no simple matter. Research typically uses the compensatory amount as a gauge of the conduct's harmfulness. Eisenberg and colleagues (1997, 2001–2002) find that approximately half of these awards can be explained by just a few variables, including the compensatory amount. Others (e.g., Karpoff & Lott 1999) find similar results, but note that this level of predictability occurs only when the cases examined are those that resulted in punitive damage assessments. The level of explained variance drops to approximately 2% when one attempts to predict both whether punitive damages will be assessed and what the amount will be. The principle of optimal deterrence requires accurate predictions of whether damages are likely to be awarded and the size of the likely damages for behavior that can be a cost of doing business. In this way, businesses can predict the risks associated with, for example, developing a new product. However, punitive damages also aim at punishing conduct that is highly egregious and not part of acceptable business practice (e.g., dumping toxic waste into a garbage can that neighborhood children could access; Vidmar & Rose 2001; see also Rustad & Koenig 1995). The Supreme Court has recognized both retribution and deterrence as goals for punitive damages in its recent rulings (e.g., *Cooper Industries v. Leatherman Tool Group* 2001), while making clear that the amount of punitive damages should bear some relationship to compensatory awards. In light of the low frequency of punitive damages and the strong relationship between compensatory damages and the level of punitive damages, the availability of reductions in unusually large punitive damages on appeal may offer a reasonable way of containing punitive awards that exceed either their deterrent or their retributive value.

How Do Judge and Jury Decisions Differ?

Another approach to assessing whether jury verdicts merit concern or trust is to compare them with the verdict that the judge, the other primary trier of fact, would reach. In jury-eligible civil cases, both parties must waive the right to a jury trial. In criminal cases, the prosecutor in many states can insist on a jury despite the defendant's waiver, although in practice prosecutors rarely do. In criminal cases, therefore, it is generally the defendant's decision as to whether a jury or a judge will decide the case. Thus, party preferences in both civil and criminal cases eligible for jury trial determine who the decision maker will be.[4] This nonrandom allocation of cases between judge and jury poses a large obstacle for researchers interested in comparing the decisions of judges and juries. Modeling that selection process is a complex matter. If, for example, juries were generally more pro-plaintiff than judges, bench trials in civil cases would disappear because the plaintiff would always insist on a jury. In fact, a recent study of trials in 75 of the nation's largest counties showed that bench trials accounted for nearly one in four trials (Cohen & Smith 2004). In addition, because so few civil cases result in trials rather than in settlement or other dispositions, a second layer of selection may affect which jury versus bench cases actually go to trial. A strong version of Priest & Klein's (1984) selection theory assumes that the cases going to trial should be those in which the parties substantially differ in their perceptions of what will happen at trial, taking into consideration who the trier of fact will be. By that account, overall win rates before judges and juries should not differ. Yet, Clermont & Eisenberg (1992) found that differential win rates in federal trials varied across categories of cases, with plaintiffs winning significantly more often before judges in three major tort categories and winning significantly more often before juries in two others. That finding leaves three possibilities: (*a*) that the cases differed, despite selection theory's assumption that they should be equivalently strong, in large part because one or both litigants miscalculated their probability of prevailing; (*b*) that the judges and juries differed in their response to equivalent sets of cases; or (*c*) some combination of the two.

---

[4]Because parties generally must wait longer for a jury trial, they may agree to a bench trial if both are anxious to proceed to trial, even if one or both might prefer a jury if delay was not an issue.

In an effort to avoid the potential case allocation selection effects, researchers comparing the outcomes of judge and jury trials have attempted to control for the influence of other variables. For example, Clermont & Eisenberg (1992) showed that the patterns they observed persisted when they controlled for locale. Nonetheless, as Clermont and Eisenberg acknowledge, a host of other differences between judge and jury trials may account for any differences (or similarities) they observed (see also Eisenberg et al. 2001–2002). The problem persists within categories of cases. Moore (2000) examined patent cases decided by juries and judges. Her data reveal that 58% of the decisions on the issue of willful infringement were jury rather than judge decisions, whereas 39% of the decisions on enforceability were decided by juries rather than judges (Moore 2000, values computed from table 4), indicating a systematic difference in the allocation of cases to jury and judge trials and undermining the interpretability of differences (or similarities) in liability verdicts and awards. Moreover, Moore (2002) finds that the judge and jury verdicts in patent cases are equally likely to be reversed on appeal, even when the appealed issues are broken down by subject matter, a pattern inconsistent with the claim that a jury is less competent than a judge to decide a complex patent case. Nonetheless, even this result is ambiguous. Although a judicial opinion by the trial judge in a bench trial may reveal judicial error, no comparable record is available from a jury trial, so equal reversal rates may not reflect similar qualities of the decisions reviewed on appeal.

A few researchers have compared judge and jury verdicts in criminal trials. Levine (1983) compared conviction rates in jury and bench trials in the 1970s, reporting higher conviction rates in jury trials in seven of nine jurisdictions and attributing the difference to "a conservative reaction of a people racked by excessive crime" (p. 86). Yet the strategic choice involved when a criminal defendant waives a jury is even more likely to affect the outcome in a criminal case than in a civil case where both parties must waive the jury. If, for example, the defendant waives a jury only when the applicable law favors an acquittal on the assumption that the judge will be more likely to recognize that strong legal advantage, then cases decided by judges will be more likely to result in acquittals because of the cases they receive owing to this selection process.

To address the selection problems that arise in comparing judge and jury verdicts, Kalven & Zeisel (1966) developed an ingenious approach that other researchers have emulated. In their classic study of jury trials, Kalven and Zeisel asked trial judges to fill out questionnaires in over 3500 criminal and 4000 civil jury trials, indicating the characteristics of the case, the jury's verdict, and how the judge would have decided the same case in a bench trial. Because the judges were indicating their preferred verdicts on precisely the same trials that the juries decided, there could be no question about whether the cases were comparable (although the method says nothing about how juries would decide the cases that result in bench trials). The judge and jury agreed in 78% of the cases on whether or not to convict. When they disagreed in the criminal cases, the judge would have convicted when the jury acquitted in 19% of the cases and the jury convicted when the judge would have acquitted in 3% of the cases, a net leniency rate of 16%. Disagreement rates were higher in cases that the judge characterized as close, but did not increase when the judge characterized the evidence as difficult rather than easy to understand.

The agreement on liability in civil cases was also 78%, but disagreement was almost equally divided: in 12% of the cases the jury found for the plaintiff while the judge favored the defense, and in 10% of the cases the jury found for the defense while the judge would have made an award. Jury awards were about 20% higher than those the judge would have given. Unfortunately, Kalven and Zeisel concentrated almost exclusively on the criminal jury data in their volume *The American Jury*, so little more is known from their classic study about the results for the real civil juries. Moreover, the data were collected in the 1950s, and jury trials have undergone substantial changes in the past 50 years. Both the jury and the judiciary have become more representative of the community, although the jury has undergone greater change. For example, it was not until 1975 that the U.S. Supreme Court ruled in *Taylor v. Louisiana* (1975) that the Sixth Amendment forbade the exemption of women from jury duty. The law, too, has changed significantly in a number of areas. Plaintiffs in tort cases, for example, were traditionally barred from recovery by any contributory fault for their injury. Today, most jurisdictions apply a comparative fault standard. The plaintiff who bears some responsibility for her injury can receive partial recovery, generally reduced in proportion to the plaintiff's fault, from a defendant who is also at fault.

Several smaller, more recent studies using the Kalven-Zeisel method have shown remarkably similar patterns in criminal cases. Heuer & Penrod (1994) found a 74% agreement and a net leniency of 20%. In a study designed to investigate hung jury rates in four jurisdictions, with two jurisdictions selected for their higher-than-average hung jury rates, Eisenberg and colleagues (2005) found 75% agreement, with a net leniency of 13%. The agreement rates varied by jurisdiction (between 64% and 89%), with three of the four jurisdictions showing the same pattern of greater leniency by juries that Kalven and Zeisel found.

More recent studies in civil cases have shown a pattern of results less consistent with that observed by Kalven and Zeisel. Heuer & Penrod (1994) found an agreement rate on liability of 63%, with the jury finding for the plaintiff in 18% and for the defendant in 19% of disagreement cases. Diamond et al. (2003) found an agreement rate of 77%. Hans (1998) obtained judicial ratings on the strength of the evidence favoring the plaintiff or defendant on a 7-point scale. When the judge rated the case as favoring one side or the other (1–3 or 5–7), the jury's verdict agreed with that position 74% of the time, but in the disagreement cases, the jury favored the plaintiff 19% of the time and the defendant 7% of the time.

Most of these smaller, more recent studies were carried out in one or just a few jurisdictions. The Eisenberg et al. (2005) analysis included 318 trials across 4 jurisdictions, and the remaining studies each described results based on 125 or fewer cases from a single jurisdiction. To evaluate adequately whether and how jury verdicts have changed over time and how similar patterns are across jurisdictions calls for a large-scale, national replication of the Kalven-Zeisel study. Moreover, the Kalven-Zeisel research had some weaknesses that a modern replication could remedy. In explaining the disagreements between judge and jury, Kalven and Zeisel focused on the disagreement cases, had to rely exclusively on the judge for information about the case, and generally tested for relationships using univariate analyses. In contrast, the National Center for State Court's hung jury study analyzed by Eisenberg et al. (2005), albeit involving a substantially smaller sample, incorporated juror surveys and information on jury composition. Using multivariate analyses, Eisenberg et al. obtained results that support the overall Kalven-Zeisel findings of a higher threshold for conviction by juries. The pattern of disagreement associated with juror characteristics introduced some additional complexities. Juries with more well-educated members were more likely to acquit when the judge would have convicted than were juries with less well-educated members. Neither race nor gender was consistently related to judge-jury disagreement across sites (Eisenberg et al. 2005, Garvey et al. 2004).

No comparable study of civil cases exists. Indeed, in their original volume, Kalven & Zeisel (1966) provided only the barest description of the overall agreement-disagreement rates from the civil jury data. In view of the insights that such a study of the civil jury could provide, the case for a modern Kalven-Zeisel replication is even stronger for the civil jury than for the criminal jury. At this point, the available judge-jury comparison data do not support fears that juries tend to reach unjustified decisions or that they are substantially at odds with the views that judges would take. A closer look at the process of jury decision making is generally consistent with that pattern, but it also identifies some areas that provide particular challenges for the jury.

JURY DECISION MAKING

Jurors are charged with two tasks in arriving at their verdicts: to find the facts and to apply the law from the judge's instructions to those facts. Questions about the jury arise from both sources. Here, we consider the evidence on jury reactions to the evidence and the law, as well as juror response to the difficult task of deciding on death in capital cases.

Deciding Ordinary Cases

In an ordinary criminal or civil trial, the trier of fact must work out differences that the opposing sides were unable to resolve by themselves or with the assistance of their attorneys. The jury or judge must not only evaluate and compare the credibility of conflicting accounts of past events and mental states, but may also have to determine whether injuries or other damages occurred and what caused those injuries. In the typical tort case, the jury must decide whether the defendant's behavior was negligent by determining not only what the defendant actually did, but also what it would have been reasonable to do in the circumstances.

Faced with these tasks, the jurors sensibly engage in an active evaluation of the competing claims to arrive at a plausible interpretation of the evidence presented at trial. Although jurors often differ in the narratives they consider most plausible as they reconstruct prior events from these conflicting sources, the jurors' recall and comprehension of the evidence in the ordinary trial are generally high. This pattern is revealed both on post-deliberation tests of comprehension in simulation research (e.g., Diamond & Casper 1992, Hastie et al. 1983) and in the discussions of the Arizona civil juries (Diamond et al. 2003). Jurors regularly scrutinize the claims of plaintiffs with a skeptical eye and apply common sense norms of behavior to judge whether a party's behavior was negligent and to sort out the competing and inconsistent claims. Jurors evaluate not only the credentials and experience of the experts, but also the content of their testimony. And, in general, jurors rely on as well as test each other's impressions, correcting errors in recall and inference.

Consistent with the widely accepted story model (Pennington & Hastie 1991) developed to explain individual juror judgments in criminal cases, jurors attempt to reconstruct a plausible account of what led to the plaintiff's suit. The jury's account, however, includes more than the story model would suggest. For example, jurors try to understand not only what led to the injury that eventuated in the plaintiff's complaint, but also why the case did not settle (e.g., was the plaintiff too greedy?). In the process, they draw on their own experiences with issues like insurance and prior accidents and injuries (Diamond & Vidmar 2001). In addition, their search for explanations builds on basic normative value judgments in assessing when behavior is reasonable. For example, when should a plaintiff be entitled to recover for injuries that occurred when he or she slipped and fell on a crack? How big must the crack be to constitute negligence on the part of the owner of the property? Jurors use these value judgments in integrating evidence and applying it to reach a verdict.

No evidence from close studies of jury decision making inside or outside the laboratory indicates that juries are extravagant dupes of frivolous claims in ordinary cases, although some of the rhetoric of tort reform suggests that they are (Diamond 2003). More serious concerns about the trustworthiness of the jury focus not on ordinary cases but on cases that involve unusually complex testimony.

Complex Evidence

Modern litigation includes a growing number of trials with complex scientific or technical evidence from expert witnesses on topics unfamiliar to most jurors (and judges). Jurors (and judges) are asked to evaluate and compare the testimony of credentialed professionals addressing arcane issues, sometimes the object of vigorous dispute among respected experts on opposing sides. Although questions about how the jury handles complexity are raised most often about the civil jury, DNA evidence and white collar crimes involving complex financial transactions mean that complexity is not exclusively the preserve of civil litigation.

Most jury cases, both criminal and civil, last only a few days, but a small percentage extend for weeks or even months and may involve numerous witnesses, including multiple experts. The many hours and days of testimony place unusual demands on the attention and memory of the decision maker in a lengthy trial. The 13 cases that Lempert (1993) analyzed in evaluating jury performance in complex cases had a median length of two months. Not surprisingly, when researchers asked jurors, attorneys, and judges to rate the complexity of the criminal trial in which they had participated, duration was a consistent and strong predictor of trial complexity for all three groups (Heise 2004). But trials can also be complex, holding length constant, with increases in the technical challenge of the evidence, including expert testimony and the difficulty of the legal standards that the jury is called upon to apply.

Complex expert testimony tests both judges and juries (*Daubert v. Merrell-Dow Pharm., Inc.* 1995). Faced with expert testimony, jurors could avoid the challenge by ignoring the expert testimony or by deferring to an expert based strictly on the expert's credentials and not on an evaluation of the content of the testimony. Yet evidence obtained from observing the behavior of jurors during trials and deliberations, as well as from post-trial interviews with real jurors, indicates that jurors spend considerable time discussing the content of expert testimony (Vidmar & Diamond 2001). This effort is consistent with central processing (Eagly & Chaiken 1993), which occurs when an individual attends to the quality of an argument, rather than relying on peripheral processing, a mental shortcut to an evaluation. Jurors would be engaged in peripheral processing if they merely compared the credentials of two opposing experts and accepted the opinions of the more prestigious source.

Jury instructions explicitly tell jurors to evaluate the expert's testimony "considering the witness's qualifications and experience" along with the reasons given for the opinions and all the other evidence in the case. As instructed, jurors do consider the expert's education and experience, but they also focus on the content of the testimony (Vidmar & Diamond 2001).

Moreover, jurors recognize that the experts are appointed by the parties, which encourages jurors to be skeptical about what they hear (Shuman et al. 1996). The adversary setting, however, does not disclose to the jurors how distorted the balance in testimony may actually be. If each side has an expert, the jurors may not be told that one side's expert is among thousands holding the same view, whereas the other side's expert is the only person willing to testify to the opposing position (Gross 1991). Thus, the challenge of evaluating the testimony of equally credentialed and articulate experts is substantial. Jurors' frustrations can be palpable, as indicated in the excerpt at the beginning of this review from the juror who questioned the representativeness of the expert opinion she was receiving from the witness stand.

Other juror behaviors also reveal central processing of expert testimony. When jurors are permitted to submit questions during trial, a disproportionate number of their questions are for the expert witnesses (Diamond et al. 2004, Mott 2003). The juror questions for the experts focus primarily on efforts to clarify their testimony or to understand the bases for their opinions. In general, increases in case complexity are associated with increases in juror scrutiny of the evidence. For example, in the Arizona Filming Project, the longer the trial, the longer jurors discussed the evidence before taking an initial vote ($r = .54$) (Diamond et al. 2003). Jurors in Arizona are permitted to take notes, and the jurors referred to their notes more frequently during deliberations when the trial was complex, even after controlling for the length of the deliberation.

Studies comparing judge and jury verdicts in the same cases have found no evidence that disagreement rates rise with the complexity of the evidence (Eisenberg et al. 2005, Heuer & Penrod 1994, Kalven & Zeisel 1966). Both juries and judges may perform less than optimally when faced with complex evidence. In particular, there is evidence that judges as well as laypersons have difficulty with probabilistic and quantitative testimony (e.g., Wells 1992). Although the modern jury may include one or more members with some quantitative background who can assist with the technical evidence, and several studies show that juries do make such use of their most competent members, the trial court judge without quantitative training must turn elsewhere for help. A general challenge remains for litigants and the legal system: to educate the trier of fact.

Several researchers who have interviewed jurors following complex cases have found substantial levels of comprehension on the main issues of the case, including the expert testimony (Am. Bar Assoc. 1989, Vidmar 1995). Others have found significant sources of misunderstanding about complex expert testimony (Sanders 1998, Selvin & Picus 1987; in both instances there was a failure to understand epidemiological evidence). In a detailed review of 13 complex cases, Lempert (1993, p. 234) concluded that juries were not "befuddled by complexity" and that they usually reached defensible decisions. He noted that mistakes were often attributable to deficiencies in the presentation of the evidence or jury instructions, raising issues that are not unique to complex cases.

Understanding and Applying the Law

The jury's role in interpreting the law has changed substantially over time, triggering an uneasy struggle over the position and impact of the law in jury trials. Early juries were regarded as equal to the judge in their ability to interpret the common law (Perlman 1986). The rationale was that juries shared the values and knew the rules of ordinary transactions on which the common law was built. The ability of the jury to intuit legal norms and contingencies declined with the increased complexity of the modern legal environment. The development of the adversary system, a professional judiciary, and the rules of evidence led to efforts to impose legal constraints on the jury. Judges now charge the jurors that they must apply the law as the judge describes it to the facts as the jury finds them (*Sparf & Hansen v. United States* 1895). Yet the vehicle for informing the jury about the law has changed very little over time. Although literacy has grown and jurors generally must be able to read and write English, the oral tradition for conveying legal instructions persists, and jurors in many courts do not receive a written copy of the jury instructions to refer to either while the judge reads the instructions to the jury or during jury deliberations (Rottman et al. 2000).

The jury's decision can accurately reflect the relevant legal framework either if the jury correctly anticipates and accepts the applicable law or if the jury is informed by and follows the judge's instructions. Yet legal standards are not always obvious, and jurors do not always succeed in applying the legal instructions they are given, not because they actively resist but because the legal education provided at trial is remarkably awkward, frequently incomplete, and in some respects almost obstinately opaque.

Many legal concepts are abstract and difficult, presenting a serious challenge to clear communication. Standardized "pattern jury instructions" approved by committees of judges and attorneys in most jurisdictions are designed to avoid legal error, with little effort invested in ensuring clear communication. Not surprisingly, studies testing the ability of laypersons to understand legal concepts as presented in jury instructions have repeatedly revealed poor performance (for a review, see Lieberman & Sales 1997).

Researchers conducting most of the research on comprehension of jury instructions have relied on simulations, leading critics to raise the possibility that jurors instructed in the context of a real trial may be more motivated to grasp legal concepts and may be aided by the trial context in understanding their meaning (*Free v. Peters* 1993). Moreover, most of the simulations have tested individuals who did not deliberate and thus did not have the benefit of any information they might have gleaned from group discussion. The few researchers who have addressed these concerns by administering post-trial questionnaires to real jurors (Kramer & Koenig 1990, Reifman et al. 1992, Saxton 1998) have replicated the findings of simulations demonstrating weaknesses in juror understanding of legal instructions. By comparing the accuracy of responses from jurors who served on certain types of trials with those of jurors who sat on different types of trials, Reifman and colleagues (1992) tested not only how accurate jurors exposed to those particular instructions in cases were, but also whether they were more accurate than those who had not been exposed to those particular instructions. They found that instructions improved understanding of procedural issues but produced no improvements in substantive legal understanding. The jurors were tested at the end of their two-month service, suggesting that the poor showing might be due to faulty recall as opposed to miscomprehension, but a similar effort that focused on potentially difficult legal concepts tested jurors immediately after they completed a criminal trial, and it also showed substantial misunderstanding (Kramer & Koenig 1990). Although instructed jurors performed better than uninstructed jurors, even instructed jurors displayed areas of substantial miscomprehension. Moreover, the difficulty in understanding jury instructions could not be attributed to low educational levels: More educated as well as less educated jurors showed comprehension problems for some concepts. Saxton (1998) examined post-trial juror comprehension on a range of legal issues in both criminal and civil cases. Although instructed jurors showed better comprehension overall, jurors still revealed some substantial holes in their understanding.

In all these questionnaire studies, some of the questions used to gauge juror comprehension were themselves difficult to understand. For example, one question asked whether it is true or false that "a reasonable doubt must be based only on the evidence that was presented in the courtroom, not on any conclusion that you draw from the evidence." This statement is false, because the juror can draw inferences from the evidence on reasonable doubt or any other matter, but a doubt based on the evidence is a conclusion drawn from the evidence. Nonetheless, many of the test questions were drawn directly from the language in the jury instructions themselves, so a failure to understand the questions likely tracked a failure to understand the instructions as well.

The persistent evidence that jury instructions frequently miscommunicate reveals several explanations for this unnecessary struggle between jurors and the law. An obvious first obstacle to jury comprehension is that unfamiliar terms and unnecessarily convoluted sentences are common in jury instructions. Researchers have shown that rewriting instructions in "plain English" can dramatically improve juror comprehension (e.g., Elwork et al. 1982, Wiener et al. 2004). Some states have made an effort to rewrite pattern instructions, and recently California included linguist Peter Tiersma on the pattern instruction committee to assist in clarifying the language used in the instructions (Judic. Counc. Calif. Advis. Comm. 2004). To provide optimum instructions on the law, the attempt to clarify the language of legal instructions needs to be accompanied by a regular testing program that evaluates whether changes in the instructions will successfully improve laypersons' understanding of the law. When Diamond & Levi (1996) rewrote jury instructions in death penalty cases, their experiment showed that the rewritten instructions improved comprehension by laypersons, but some changes in the language were more influential than others. Other studies have revealed that recommended changes in the language of instructions may either produce only minimal improvements in comprehension (Severance & Loftus 1982) or may actually introduce new sources of error (Charrow & Charrow 1979).

Writing comprehensible jury instructions is not merely a matter of using simpler language and improving grammatical structure and organization. Instructions often contain words that appear familiar but have specific technical meanings that may be quite different from their most common definition. For example, an aggravating circumstance is a reason to impose the death penalty, whereas in common use it means merely an annoyance or irritation (Diamond 1993a, Haney & Lynch 1997).

Another obstacle to communication is the failure to acknowledge jurors' beliefs and expectations. Courts generally avoid any reference to a topic that jurors should not be discussing during deliberations, on the assumption that jurors will not discuss an issue if the court does not mention it. As a result, jurors regularly discuss topics, such as the plaintiff's and defendant's insurance and attorney's fees (Diamond & Vidmar 2001) without court guidance, making assumptions that may or may not be either factually accurate or legally correct. Blindfolding the jury to a legally irrelevant question, that is, simply avoiding any mention of it, can be an effective method of jury control. It can function effectively, however, only when the question is unlikely to occur to the jurors (e.g., whether the defendant subsequently repaired the steps after the plaintiff tripped and fell) or, if it does occur to the jury, when the jurors are not likely to assume that they can figure out the answer if the trial does not supply one (e.g., the contents of settlement negotiations) (Diamond & Vidmar 2001).

In principle, jurors can clarify their legal misunderstandings by interrupting their deliberations and submitting a written question to the judge. Jury surveys indicate, however, that jurors may be inappropriately sanguine about their ability to make sense of jury instructions (Diamond 1993b, Reifman et al. 1992, Saxton 1998). As a result, the legal system cannot depend on the jurors to submit questions when the instructions are not illuminating. Moreover, the procedures used to submit questions during deliberations may discourage jurors from using the opportunity to clarify ambiguities in the law. Jurors submitting a question during deliberations must summon the bailiff who then informs the judge. Once the jury begins deliberations, the parties and the judge turn to other matters and convene again only if the jury has a question or announces its verdict. If the jury submits a question, the judge in turn must consult with the parties and determine whether or how to answer the question, either in a note sent back with the bailiff or by bringing the jury back to the courtroom. Either way, the jurors swiftly learn that it can take a long time to get an answer if they have a question. When the jury does submit a question during deliberations, judges are often hesitant to supply a direct response that goes beyond the language of the original legally approved instructions. Instead the judge may direct the jury to a particular section of the jury instructions (*Weeks v. Angelone* 2000; Diamond & Vidmar 2001, p. 1901) or simply tell the jury to consult the instructions (Severance & Loftus 1982) or to rely on the jury members' collective memory. These limited responses miss an opportunity to prevent an error by a conscientious jury attempting to follow the judge's instructions (Diamond & Vidmar 2001, p. 1902).

Thus far we have assumed that legal instructions fail primarily when they do not effectively convey the relevant legal standard. A more insidious miscommunication can arise if the jurors do not trust what they are being told. The task in determining the sentence in a capital case appears straightforward, even if difficult: to determine whether the defendant deserves death. Yet phrasing the question in those terms, as legal instructions generally do, ignores the real decision that the jurors must make, namely, which of two penalties is more appropriate for the defendant. Until *Simmons v. South Carolina* (1994), jurors were never informed what sentence the defendant would receive if not sentenced to death, even when they specifically asked. Since *Simmons*, if the prosecutor chooses to present arguments about the defendant's future dangerousness, and if life in prison without the possibility of parole is the only alternative sentence, jurors must be told that the defendant will receive such a sentence if he or she is not sentenced to death. Yet some jurors interviewed in the Capital Jury Project expressed the view that a defendant not sentenced to death would in fact ultimately be released, even when they were told there would be no parole from a life sentence (Bowers & Steiner 1999). Thus, owing to a mistrust of the system, a juror who would prefer a sentence of life without the possibility of parole might vote for a death sentence as the only way to ensure that the defendant will never be released. If this concern about future dangerousness remains unaddressed, the jurors are effectively reaching life and death decisions uninformed about the nature of the choice they are being asked to make.

The failures in jury instructions do not leave the jury without resources. Unschooled in the relevant law, the jury applies a rough and ready sense of justice that may not deviate substantially from the decision that it would reach if it were guided by clear communication of the relevant legal standards. But in light of the evidence that important deviations do occur between the jury's common sense legal standards and understandings and the legal guidance that the jury purportedly receives, better communication with the jury about the law represents a crucial and underappreciated way to optimize jury performance.

Juries in Death Penalty Cases

In ordinary felony cases in most jurisdictions (King & Noble 2004), jurors decide only whether or not the defendant is guilty of one or more charges. The dramatic exception to this pattern occurs in capital cases. Death penalty sentences are now the exclusive preserve of the jury, both in the federal system and in the 38 states that permit capital punishment.[5] Perhaps no jury issue demands more from the citizens who serve as jurors. In addition to the stress associated with the death penalty decision itself and the frequently disturbing circumstances of the alleged offense, capital sentencing calls upon jurors not simply to reconstruct what happened, but also to evaluate the severity of the defendant's behavior in light of circumstances and match it with a penalty that will either spare the defendant or take his or her life. Capital sentencing has stimulated significant scholarship and criticism of the jury, encompassing critiques concerning the composition of the death-qualified jury, racial bias in the imposition of the death penalty, death-prone tendencies of jurors stimulated by unrealistic estimates of dangerousness and expectations of early release, and lack of comprehension of legal instructions. The U.S. Supreme Court responded to earlier social science scholarship on death-qualification by rejecting evidence from jury simulations (*Lockhart v. McCree* 1986) and dismissing findings pointing to racial bias based on archival research (*McCleskey v. Kemp* 1987).

The Supreme Court's negative reactions to other methods of research in part stimulated the Capital Jury Project, a national research program in which

---

[5]In *Ring v. Arizona* (2002), the U.S. Supreme Court ruled that juries, rather than judges, must decide the aggravating and mitigating facts that go into determining whether a defendant should be put to death, declaring unconstitutional the systems then in place in five states that left death penalty determinations to judges. Although the courts have yet to speak on the constitutionality of systems in four other states in which advisory juries recommend life or death, but a judge makes the final determination, many observers believe that *Ring* effectively overturned those systems as well.

interviewers conducted 3- to 4-hour post-trial interviews with jurors who had served in 20 to 30 capital cases in each of 14 states (Bowers 1995, Bowers & Foglia 2003). The 354 capital cases were chosen to provide equal numbers of life and death verdicts. By interviewing several jurors from each case, the researchers were able to check for the reliability of jurors' retrospective reports about deliberations. Some of their results, however, focus on individual juror's self-reports on their own earlier perceptions and reactions, precisely those most susceptible to distortions of memory and reporting and less subject to cross-checking. For example, the researchers questioned jurors on what they thought the punishment should be after deciding on the defendant's guilt but before hearing any evidence from the sentencing stage of the trial. Half (50.8%) reported being undecided at that point, the legally appropriate position, but the remaining jurors recalled having a view, with 30.3% favoring death and 18.9% opposing death. A majority of those who said they initially favored death (59.5%) also said that they never changed from that early position. If those recollections are correct, they signal a premature inclination toward death and a lack of openness to mitigation evidence. There is another way to view these data, however. Deciding to sentence someone to death is by all accounts perceived by jurors as a heavy burden, and the only way to lighten that burden is to be convinced that it was the only option, the right thing to do. Cognitively rewriting the unavoidability of the decision (there never was any other choice) would be an understandable post-verdict mechanism distorting recall of a juror's earlier position. The Capital Jury Project, of course, had no choice in how it conducted the research: It could not interview jurors on their positions during the trial or sentencing proceedings, so it could only obtain retrospective reports from jurors about their earlier positions. Nonetheless, the post-trial data by themselves are weak for inferring premature decision making. Similar problems occur in all post-trial interview studies of jurors, but they are particularly problematic when the juror is asked to recall a belief at an earlier time, rather than a specific action taken (e.g., the vote a juror cast on a first ballot; Garvey et al. 2004).

Other data persuasively point to premature decision making by some jurors in capital cases. Death penalty jurisprudence requires that jurors be willing and able to follow the judge's instructions to consider both aggravating and mitigating evidence in deciding whether to sentence a defendant to death. The judge must excuse prospective jurors for cause if the jurors indicate during jury selection that they would automatically impose a death sentence if the defendant is convicted or if they say they would never be willing to impose a death sentence.[6] Yet nearly 3 in 10 jurors from the Capital Jury Project, despite surviving jury selection, reported in their post-trial interviews that they viewed death as the only acceptable punishment for five of six different kinds of murder (Bowers & Foglia 2003, p. 62). Seventeen percent of the jurors reported that only death was acceptable as a punishment for

---

[6]Actually, the requirement is more stringent: A juror must be excluded if his or her feelings about the death penalty would prevent or "substantially impair" the juror's performance of his or her duties in accordance with the judge's instructions on the law (*Wainright v. Witt* 1985).

all six kinds of murder, including a killing in the course of another crime (felony murder). Unless service as a juror on a capital trial caused these jurors to become unwilling to consider mitigating factors, these "automatic death penalty" jurors should have been disqualified from serving in a capital cases.

The Capital Jury Project also provides a chilling picture of the relationship between the racial composition of the jury, as described by the converging reports on racial and gender composition from multiple jury members, and the verdicts for black defendants on trial for killing white victims (Bowers et al. 2001, pp. 190–91). When there was at least one black male on the jury, 40% of those defendants in the sample were sentenced to death. The figure jumped to 72% when not a single black male was a juror (figures computed from Bowers et al. 2001, table 1). Although, as Bowers and his colleagues acknowledge, the cases may have differed on other dimensions, this startling contrast raises a serious and plausible suggestion that the presence of a black male juror carried some significance in these interracial capital cases either in opposing death or in changing the reaction of the other jurors to this interracial offense. That suspicion is reinforced by the absence of any relationship between the number of black male jurors and death sentences for white-on-white offenses and a somewhat inconsistent pattern for black-on-black offenses. This pattern has an eerie resonance with the early finding by Baldus and colleagues (1990) that black defendants in Georgia who were convicted of killing white victims were more likely to receive the death penalty than were black defendants convicted of killing black victims, and it takes on particular significance in view of the more recent evidence that *Batson v. Kentucky* (1986) has failed to prevent disproportionate exclusion of black jurors from capital juries (Baldus et al. 2001).

THE OPTIMAL JURY TRIAL

Research on jury decision making generally reveals that a jury is a motivated problem solver that uses reasonable strategies to understand and evaluate incomplete and conflicting evidence. Nonetheless, standard trial procedures designed to control and channel jury decision making unnecessarily undermine the jury's efforts to deal with complex evidence and law. Some courts have recently implemented a variety of innovations that attempt to overcome some of these constraints and to assist jurors in understanding what they are hearing in court and to arrive at verdicts that reflect the evidence and the jury instructions. These innovations include permitting jurors to take notes, allowing them to submit questions for witnesses during the trial, and instructing them that they can discuss the evidence among themselves during breaks in the trial as long as they reserve judgment until they have heard all the evidence. Research evaluating these innovations suggests that their effects are modest but that they do, in some cases, facilitate comprehension, particularly in complex trials (Diamond et al. 2003, Heuer & Penrod 1988). A few courts have also attempted to improve jury instructions, providing preliminary instructions at the beginning of the trial, rewriting instructions in plain English, and providing written copies of the instructions for jurors to consult during deliberations (Heuer & Penrod 1989). Some simulation research suggests directions for further improvements in jury trial procedures. For example, FosterLee and colleagues (2000) found that jurors who received written reports summarizing an expert's testimony before the expert testified showed enhanced understanding of the testimony. Similarly, to combat spillover effects between judgments about liability and damages, Sanders (1998) suggests greater use of bifurcated trials. The effects of other proposed innovations, such as back-to-back experts (to facilitate direct comparison of opposing testimony), periodic summaries by the attorneys, and the delivery of jury instructions before rather than after closing arguments, have not yet been assessed, but each proposal offers the promise of better communication with the modern jury. An even more radical change in procedure would invite jurors to ask questions about the law before beginning deliberations, providing an opportunity to check more directly for, and to address, both misunderstandings and areas of skepticism (e.g., how long a life sentence actually is). Informed by substantial research revealing jurors as active decision makers, these innovations reject the passive "potted plant" image of the traditional jury (Damaska 1997) and attempt to treat the courtroom as an educational setting in which informed decision makers are assisted rather than controlled (Dann 1993). Yet the rules of evidence impose some barriers that currently may stand in the way of such efforts and prevent juries from achieving optimal performance. For example, if concerns about horizontal inequity (similar cases resulting in differing awards) are warranted, they could be addressed with assistance from a procedure that permitted attorneys to share with the jury a set of awards previously given in comparable cases (the judge would act as gatekeeper to ensure that the cases selected were not aberrant). Judges have turned to such sources in assessing whether an award was excessive or inadequate (Diamond et al. 1998, p. 321), but in a jury trial, other jury awards would be excluded from the jury's consideration as irrelevant or prejudicial.

CONCLUSION

The picture of real juries that emerges from this review provides little evidence that the jury fails to live up to the trust placed in it. Juries make mistakes and they display evidence of bias, but there is no convincing evidence that another decision maker would do better. Nonetheless, those interested in optimizing modern jury trials would do well to reconsider Judge Jerome Frank's lament (1949, p. 120) that "even twelve experienced judges, deliberating together, would probably not function well under the conditions we impose on the twelve inexperienced laymen." That juries perform as well as they do does not mean that they could not do better with some appropriate assistance.

ACKNOWLEDGMENTS

The authors thank Richard Lempert, Paula Hannaford-Agor, Tom Munsterman, Beth Murphy, and Max Schanzenbach for their comments and suggestions on a draft of this article.

The *Annual Review of Law and Social Science* is online at
http://lawsocsci.annualreviews.org

LITERATURE CITED

Amar AR. 1995. Reinventing juries: ten suggested reforms. *Univ. Calif. Davis Law Rev.* 28:1169–94

Am. Bar Assoc. 1989. Jury comprehension in complex cases. *Rep. Spec. Comm. ABA Sect. Litig.*, Am. Bar Assoc., Chicago

Balch RW, Griffiths CT, Hall EL, Winfree LT. 1976. The socialization of jurors: the voir dire as a rite of passage. *J. Crim. Justice* 4:271–83

Baldus DC, Woodworth G, Pulaski CA Jr. 1990. *Equal Justice and the Death Penalty: A Legal and Empirical Analysis.* Boston: Northeast. Univ. Press

Baldus DC, Woodworth G, Zuckerman D, Weiner NA, Broffit B. 2001. The use of peremptory challenges in capital murder trials: a legal and empirical analysis. *Univ. Penn. J. Const. Law* 3:3–169

Batson v. Kentucky, 476 U.S. 79 (1986)

Bermant G. 1977. *Conduct of the Voir Dire Examination: Practices and Opinions of Federal District Judges.* Washington, DC: Fed. Judic. Cent. 32 pp.

Black B, Silver C, Hyman D, Sage W. 2005. *Stability, not crisis: medical malpractice claim outcomes in Texas, 1988–2002.* Work. Pap. No. 30, Dep. Law Econ., Univ. Tex.

Boatright RG. 1999. Why citizens don't respond to jury summonses and what courts can do about it. *Judicature* 80:156–64

Bovjberg RR, Sloan FA, Blumstein JF. 1989. Valuing life and limb in tort: scheduling "pain and suffering." *Northwest. Law Rev.* 83:908–76

Bowers WJ. 1995. The Capital Jury Project: rationale, design, and a preview of early findings. *Indiana Law J.* 70:1043–102

Bowers WJ, Foglia WD. 2003. Still singularly agonizing: law's failure to purge arbitrariness from capital sentencing. *Crim. Law Bull.* 51:51–86

Bowers WJ, Steiner BD. 1999. Death by default: an empirical demonstration of false and forced choices in capital sentencing. *Tex. Law Rev.* 77:605–717

Bowers WJ, Steiner BD, Sandys M. 2001. Death sentencing in black and white: an empirical analysis of the role of jurors' race and jury racial composition. *Univ. Penn. J. Const. Law* 3:171–274

Bur. Justice Stat. 2005. *Victim characteristics.* http://www.ojp.usdoj.gov/bjs/cvict_v.htm#race. Accessed March 11

Caro R. 2002. *Master of the Senate: The Years of Lyndon Johnson.* New York: Knopf. 1200 pp.

Charrow RP, Charrow VR. 1979. Making legal language understandable: a psycholinguistic study of jury instructions. *Columbia Law Rev.* 79:1306–74

Clermont KM, Eisenberg T. 1992. Trial by jury or judge: transcending empiricism. *Cornell Law Rev.* 77:1124–77

Cohen TH, Smith SK. 2004. Civil trial cases and verdicts in large counties, 2001. *Bur. Justice Stat. Bull.* NCJ-202803, US Dep. Justice, Washington, DC. http://www.ojp.usdoj.gov/bjs/abstract/ctcvlc01.htm

Conley JM, Turnier WJ, Rose MR. 2000. The racial ecology of the courtroom: an experimental study of juror response to the race of criminal defendants. *Wis. Law Rev.* 2000:1185–220

Consolini P. 1992. *Learning by doing justice: jury service and political attitudes.* PhD thesis. Univ. Calif. Berkeley

Cooper Industries, Inc. v. Leatherman Tool Group, Inc., 532 U.S. 424 (2001)

Counc. Court Excell. 1998. *Juries for the Year 2000 and Beyond: Proposals to Improve the Jury Systems in Washington DC.* Washington, DC: Dist. Columbia Jury Proj.

Curriden M. 2001. The American jury: a study

in self-governing and dispute resolution. *South. Meth. Law Rev.* 54:1691–94

Damaska MR. 1997. *Evidence Law Adrift.* New Haven, CT: Yale Univ. Press. 160 pp.

Daniels S, Martin J. 1995. *Civil Juries and the Politics of Reform.* Evanston, IL: Northwest. Univ. Press

Dann BM. 1993. "Learning lessons" and "speaking rights": creating educated and democratic juries. *Indiana Law J.* 68:1229–79

Daubert v. Merrell Dow Pharmaceuticals, Inc., 509 U.S. 579 (1993)

Daubert v. Merrell Dow Pharmaceuticals, Inc. 43 F.3d 1311 (9th Cir. 1995)

Devine DJ, Clayton LD, Dunford BB, Seying R, Pryce J. 2001. Jury decision making: 45 years of empirical research on deliberating groups. *Psychol. Public Policy Law* 7:622–727

Diamond SS. 1993a. Instructing on death: psychologists, juries, and judges. *Am. Psychol.* 48:423–34

Diamond SS. 1993b. What juries think: expectations and reactions of citizens who serve as jurors. In *Verdict: Assessing the Civil Jury,* ed. R Litan, pp. 282–305. Washington, DC: Brookings Inst.

Diamond SS. 2003. Truth, justice, and the jury. *Harvard J. Law Public Policy* 26:143–55

Diamond SS, Casper JD. 1992. Blindfolding the jury to verdict consequences: damages, experts, and the civil jury. *Law Soc. Rev.* 26: 513–63

Diamond SS, Ellis L, Schmidt E. 1997. Realistic responses to the limitations of *Batson v. Kentucky. Cornell J. Law Public Policy* 7: 77–95

Diamond SS, Levi JN. 1996. Improving decisions on death by revising and testing jury instructions. *Judicature* 79:224–32

Diamond SS, Rose MR, Murphy B. 2004. Jurors' unanswered questions. *Court Rev.* 41: 20–29

Diamond SS, Saks MJ, Landsman S. 1998. Juror judgments about liability and damages: sources of variability and ways to increase consistency. *DePaul Law Rev.* 45:301–25

Diamond SS, Vidmar N. 2001. Jury room ruminations on forbidden topics. *Va. Law Rev.* 87:1857–915

Diamond SS, Vidmar N, Rose MR, Ellis L, Murphy B. 2003. Juror discussions during civil trials: studying an Arizona innovation. *Ariz. Law Rev.* 45:1–81

Eagly A, Chaiken S. 1993. *The Psychology of Attitudes.* New York: Harcourt Brace

Eisenberg T, Goerdt J, Ostrom B, Rottman B, Wells M. 1997. The predictability of punitive damages. *J. Leg. Stud.* 26:623–77

Eisenberg T, Hannaford-Agor P, Hans VP, Waters NL, Munsterman GT, et al. 2005. Judge-jury agreement in criminal cases: a partial replication of Kalven & Zeisel's *The American Jury. J. Empir. Leg. Stud.* 2:171–207

Eisenberg T, LaFountain N, Ostrom B, Rottman D, Wells MT. 2001–2002. Juries, judges, and punitive damages: an empirical study. *Cornell Law Rev.* 87:743–82

Ellis L, Diamond SS. 2003. Race, diversity, and jury composition. *Chicago-Kent Law Rev.* 78:1033–58

Elwork A, Sales BD, Alfini JJ. 1982. *Making Jury Instructions.* Charlottesville, VA: Michie

Finkelstein MO, Levin B. 1997. Clear choices and guesswork in peremptory challenges in federal criminal trials. *J. R. Stat. Soc.* 160: 275–88

ForsterLee L, Horowitz I, Athaide-Victor E. 2000. The bottom line: the effect of written expert witness statements on juror verdicts and information processing. *Law Hum. Behav.* 24:259–70

Frank J. 1949. *Courts on Trial.* Princeton, NJ: Princeton Univ. Press. 441pp.

Free v. Peters, 12 F.3d 700 (1993)

Fukurai H, Butler EW. 1991. Organization, labor force, and jury representation: economic excuses and jury participation. *Jurimetr. J.* 32:49–69

Fukurai H, Butler EW, Krooth R. 1991. A cross-sectional jury representation or systematic jury representation: simple random and cluster-sampling strategies in jury selection. *J. Crim. Justice* 19:31–48

Fukurai H, Butler EW, Krooth R. 1993. *Race and the Jury: Racial Disenfranchisement and the Search for Justice.* New York: Plenum

Galanter M. 2004. The vanishing trial: an examination of trials and related matters in federal and state courts. *J. Empir. Leg. Stud.* 26:459–570

Garvey SP, Hannaford-Agor P, Hans VP, Mott NL, Munsterman GT, Wells MT. 2004. Juror first votes in criminal trials. *J. Empir. Leg. Stud.* 1:371–98

Gastil J, Deess EP, Weiser P. 2002. Civic awakening in the jury room: a test of the connection between jury deliberation and political participation. *J. Polit.* 64:585–95

Georgia v. McCollum, 505 U.S. 42 (1992)

Greene E, Bornstein B. 2003. *Determining Damages: The Psychology of Jury Awards.* Washington, DC: Am. Psychol. Assoc.

Gross SR. 1991. Expert evidence. *Wis. Law Rev.* 1991:1113–232

Haney C, Lynch M. 1997. Clarifying life and death matters: an analysis of instructional comprehension and penalty phase closing arguments. *Law Hum. Behav.* 21:575–95

Hannaford-Agor P, Hans VP, Mott NL, Munsterman GT. 2002. *Are Hung Juries a Problem?* Williamsburg, VA: Natl. Cent. State Courts, Natl. Inst. Justice

Hannaford-Agor PL, Waters NL. 2004. *Examining Voir Dire in California.* San Francisco: Calif. Admin. Off. Courts

Hannaford PL, Hans VP, Munsterman GT. 2000. Permitting jury discussion during trial: impact of the Arizona reform. *Law Hum. Behav.* 24:359–82

Hans VP. 1998. The illusions and realities of jurors' treatment of corporate defendants. *DePaul Law Rev.* 48:327–53

Hans VP. 2000. *Business on Trial: The Civil Jury and Corporate Responsibility.* New Haven, CT: Yale Univ. Press

Harris Interactive 2004. *Jury service: Is fulfilling your civil duty a trial?* http://www.abbanews.org/releases/juryreport.pdf. Accessed June 13, 2005

Hastie R, Penrod S, Pennington N. 1983. *Inside the Jury.* Cambridge, MA: Harvard Univ. Press. 277 pp.

Hays JR, Cambron S. 1999. Courtroom observation of ethnic representation among jurors in Harris County, Texas. *Psychol. Rep.* 85:1218–20

Heise M. 2004. Criminal case complexity: an empirical perspective. *J. Empir. Leg. Stud.* 1:331–69

Hersch J, Viscusi WK. 2004. Punitive damages: how judges and juries perform. *J. Leg. Stud.* 33:1–36

Heuer L, Penrod S. 1988. Increasing jurors' participation in trials: a field experiment with jury notetaking and question asking. *Law Hum. Behav.* 12:231–61

Heuer L, Penrod S. 1989. Instructing jurors: a field experiment with written and preliminary instructions. *Law Hum. Behav.* 13:409–30

Heuer L, Penrod S. 1994. Trial complexity: a field investigation of its meaning and effects. *Law Hum. Behav.* 18:29–51

Hoffman MB. 1997. Peremptory challenges should be abolished: a trial judge's perspective. *Univ. Chicago Law Rev.* 64:809–71

J.E.B. v. Alabama, ex rel. T.B., 511 U.S. 127 (1994)

Johnson C, Haney C. 1994. Felony voir dire: an exploratory study of its content and effect. *Law Hum. Behav.* 18:487–506

Judic. Counc. Calif. Advis. Comm. 2004. *Calif. Civil Jury Instructions.* Newark, NJ: Lexis-Nexis/Matthew Bender

Kalven H Jr, Zeisel H. 1966. *The American Jury.* Chicago: Univ. Chicago Press. 559 pp.

Karpoff JM, Lott JR. 1999. On the determinants and importance of punitive damage awards. *J. Law Econ.* 42:527–73

King NJ, Noble RL 2004. Felony jury sentencing in practice: a three-state study. *Vanderbilt Law Rev.* 57:885–962

Kisor CA. 2001. Using interpreters to assist jurors: a plea for consistency. *Chicano-Latino Law Rev.* 22:37–54

Kramer GP, Koenig DM. 1990. Do jurors understand criminal jury instructions? Analyzing the results of the Michigan Juror

Comprehension Project. *Univ. Mich. J. Law Ref.* 23:401–37

Kritzer HM. 2001. Public perceptions of civil jury verdicts. *Judicature* 85:78–82

Lempert RO. 1993. Civil juries and complex cases: taking stock after twelve years. In *Verdict: Assessing the Civil Jury System*, ed. R Litan, pp. 181–247. Washington, DC: Brookings Inst.

Levin H. 2005. Are jurors undereducated? An empirical study with surprising results. *Univ. Conn. Law Rev.* In press

Levine JP. 1983. Jury toughness: the impact of conservatism on criminal verdicts. *Crime Delinq.* 29:71–87

Lieberman JD, Sales BD. 1997. What social science teaches us about the jury instruction process. *Psychol. Public Policy Law* 3:589–644

Lockhart v. McCree, 476 U.S. 162 (1986)

Lopez MH. 2003. Electoral engagement among Latinos. *Latino Research @ ND* 1:1–8. http://www.nd.edu/~latino/research/pubs/LRNDv1n2.pdf

MacCoun RJ, Tyler TR. 1988. The basis of citizens' perceptions of the criminal jury: procedural fairness, accuracy, and efficiency. *Law Hum. Behav.* 12:333–52

Marder NS. 2001. Juries and technology: equipping jurors for the twenty-first century. *Brooklyn Law Rev.* 66:1257–99

McCleskey v. Kemp, 481 U.S. 279 (1987)

Melilli KJ. 1996. *Batson* in practice: what we have learned about *Batson* and peremptory challenges. *Notre Dame Law Rev.* 71:447–503

Merritt DJ, Barry K. 1999. Is the tort system in crisis? New empirical evidence. *Ohio Law J.* 60:315–98

Mize G. 1999. On better jury selection: spotting UFO jurors before they enter the jury room. *Court Rev.* 36:10–15

Moore KA. 2000. Judges, juries, and patent cases—an empirical peek inside the black box. *Mich. Law Rev.* 99:365–406

Moore KA. 2002. Juries, patent cases, and a lack of transparency. *Houston Law Rev.* 39:779–802

Mott NL. 2003. The current debate on juror questions: to ask or not to ask, that is the question. *Chicago-Kent Law Rev.* 78:1099–125

Munsterman GT, Hall DJ. 2003. *Jury Management Study: Kent County, Michigan*. Williamsburg, VA: Natl. Cent. State Courts

Nietzel MT, Dillehay RC. 1982. The effects of variations in voir dire procedures in capital murder trials. *Law Hum. Behav.* 36:1–13

Nietzel MT, Dillehay RC, Himelain M. 1987. Effects of voir dire variations in capital trials: a replication and extension. *Behav. Sci. Law* 5:467–78

Pennington N, Hastie R. 1991. A cognitive theory of juror decision making: the story model. *Cardozo Law Rev.* 13:519–57

Perlman H. 1986. Pattern jury instructions: the application of social science research. *Neb. Law Rev.* 65:520–57

Pfeifer JE, Ogloff JR. 1991. Ambiguity and guilt determinations: a modern racism perspective. *J. Appl. Soc. Psychol.* 21:1713–25

Powers v. Ohio, 499 U.S. 400 (1991)

Priest GL, Klein B. 1984. The selection of disputes for litigation. *J. Leg. Stud.* 13:1–55

Purkett v. Elem, 514 U.S. 765 (1995)

Reifman A, Gusick SM, Ellsworth PC. 1992. Real jurors' understanding of law in real cases. *Law Hum. Behav.* 16:539–54

Ring v. Arizona, 536 U.S. 584 (2002)

Rose MR. 1999. The peremptory challenge accused of race or gender discrimination? Some data from one county. *Law Hum. Behav.* 23:695–702

Rose MR. 2003. A voir dire of voir dire: listening to jurors' views regarding the peremptory challenge. *Chicago-Kent Law Rev.* 78:1061–98

Rose MR. 2005. A dutiful voice: justice in the distribution of jury service. *Law Soc. Rev.* 39:601–34

Rottman DB, Flango CR, Cantrell MT, Hansen R, LaFountain N. 2000. State Court Organization 1998. *Bur. Justice Stat. Rep. NCJ-178932*, US Dep. Justice, Williamsburg, VA. http://www.ojp.usdoj.gov/bjs/pub/pdf/sco98.pdf

Rustad M, Koenig T. 1995. Reconceptualizing punitive damages in medical malpractice: targeting amoral corporations, not "moral monsters." *Rutgers Law Rev.* 47:975–1008

Saks MJ. 1976. The limits of scientific jury selection: ethical and empirical. *Jurimetr. J.* 17:3–22

Saks MJ. 1998. Public opinion about the civil jury: can reality be found in the illusions. *DePaul Law Rev.* 48:221–45

Saks MJ, Hollinger LA, Wissler RL, Evans DL, Hart AJ. 1997. Reducing variability in juror awards. *Law Hum. Behav.* 21:243–56

Sanders J. 1998. *Bendectin on Trial: A Study of Mass Tort Litigation.* Ann Arbor: Univ. Mich. Press. 296 pp.

Saxton B. 1998. How well do jurors understand jury instructions? A field test using real juries and real trials in Wyoming. *Law Water Law Rev.* 33:59–189

Seabury SA, Pace NM, Reville RT. 2004. Forty years of civil jury verdicts. *J. Empir. Leg. Stud.* 1:1–25

Seltzer R, Venuti MA, Lopes GM. 1991. Juror honesty during the voir dire. *J. Crim. Justice* 19:451–62

Selvin M, Picus L. 1987. *The debate over jury performance: observations from a recent asbestos case.* RAND Doc. R-3479-ICJ. RAND, Santa Monica, CA. 110 pp.

Severance LJ, Loftus EF. 1982. Improving the ability of jurors to comprehend and apply criminal jury instructions. *Law Soc. Rev.* 17: 198–233

Shuman DW, Champagne A, Whitaker E. 1996. Assessing the believability of expert witnesses: science in the jury box. *Jurimetr. J.* 37:23–33

Simmons v. South Carolina, 512 U.S. 154 (1994)

Sloan FA, Githens PB, Clayton EW, Hickson GB, Gentile DA, Partlett DF. 1993. *Suing for Medical Malpractice.* Chicago: Univ. Chicago Press. 276 pp.

Sloan FA, Hsieh CR. 1990. Variability in medical malpractice payments: Is the compensation fair? *Law Soc. Rev.* 24:997–1039

Sommers SR, Ellsworth PC. 2003. How much do we really know about race and juries? A review of social science theory and research. *Chicago-Kent Law Rev.* 78:997–1031

Sparf & Hansen v. U.S., 156 U.S. 51 (1895)

State ex rel. Martinez v. Third Judicial Dist. Court, Vol. 39, No. 7, SBB 12 (N.M. 2000)

Sunstein CR, Hastie R, Payne JW, Schkade DA, Viscusi WK. 2002. *Punitive Damages: How Juries Decide.* Chicago: Univ. Chicago Press

Taragin MA, Willet LR, Wilczek AP, Trout R, Carson JL. 1992. The influence of standard of care and severity of injury on the resolution of medical malpractice claims. *Ann. Intern. Med.* 117:780–84

Taylor v. Louisiana, 419 U.S. 522 (1975)

U.S. v. Ovalle, 136 F.3d 1092 (1998)

Van Dyke JM. 1977. *Jury Selection Procedures: Our Uncertain Commitment to Representative Juries.* Cambridge, MA: Ballinger

Vidmar N. 1995. *Medical Malpractice and the American Jury: Confronting the Myths About Jury Incompetence, Deep Pockets, and Outrageous Damage Awards.* Ann Arbor: Univ. Mich. Press. 336 pp.

Vidmar N. 1997. Generic prejudice and the presumption of guilt in sex abuse trials. *Law Hum. Behav.* 21:5–25

Vidmar N, Beale SS, Rose MR, Donnelly LF. 1997. Should we be rushing to reform the criminal jury? Consider conviction rate data. *Judicature* 80: 286–90

Vidmar N, Diamond SS. 2001. Juries and expert evidence. *Brooklyn Law Rev.* 66:1121–80

Vidmar N, Gross F, Rose MR. 1998. Jury awards for medical malpractice and post-verdict adjustment of those awards. *DePaul Law Rev.* 48:265–99

Vidmar N, Rose MR. 2001. Punitive damages by juries in Florida: *in terrorem* and in reality. *Harvard J. Legisl.* 38:487–513

Wainright v. Witt, 469 U.S. 412 (1985)

Walters R, Marin M, Curriden M. 2005. Are we getting a jury of our peers? *Tex. Bar J.* 68:144–46

Weeks v. Angelone, 528 U.S. 225 (2000)

Wells GL. 1992. Naked statistical evidence of liability: Is subjective probability enough? *J. Pers. Soc. Psychol.* 62:739–52

Wiener RL. 2004. Guided jury discretion in capital murder cases: the role of declarative and procedural knowledge. *Psychol. Public Policy Law* 10:516–76

Zeisel H, Diamond SS. 1978. The effect of peremptory challenges on jury and verdict: an experiment in a Federal District Court. *Stanford Law Rev.* 30:491–531

Annu. Rev. Law Soc. Sci. 2005. 1:285–306
doi: 10.1146/annurev.lawsocsci.1.041604.115915
First published online as a Review in Advance on July 25, 2005

FEMINISM, FAIRNESS, AND WELFARE:
An Invitation to Feminist Law and Economics

Gillian K. Hadfield

*University of Southern California Law School, Los Angeles, California 90089;
email: ghadfield@law.usc.edu*

Key Words   welfare economics, care, justice, efficiency, normative, ethics

■ **Abstract**   In recent years there has been a renewed effort to ground conventional law and economics methodology, with its exclusive focus on efficiency and income redistribution through the tax system, in modern welfare economics (Kaplow & Shavell 1994, 2001). This effort raises a challenge to the possibility of a feminist law and economics: Is it possible to be a good (welfare) economist and still maintain the ethical and political commitments necessary to address feminist concerns with, for example, rights, inequality, and caring labor? In this review, I argue that modern welfare economics, rather than supporting the ethical minimalism of conventional methodology advocated by Kaplow and Shavell, ratifies the need for an ethically and politically informed economic analysis. Feminists can, and should, use the tools of both positive and normative economics to analyze feminist issues in law.

INTRODUCTION

Law and economics scholarship has conventionally adopted a methodological strategy of focusing exclusively on the efficiency implications of legal rules. As Sanchirico (2000, 2001) has observed, for a long time this method was taken for granted, but in recent years there has been a resurgence of efforts to ground this methodology more formally in welfare economics. These efforts are largely attributable to Louis Kaplow and Steven Shavell who, in a series of papers and later a book, have defended two basic methodological claims for law and economics. The first is the familiar claim that efficiency and equity (distribution) considerations should be isolated, meaning that legal rules should be chosen exclusively on the basis of efficiency and that distributive goals should be addressed through the tax system (Shavell 1981, Kaplow & Shavell 1994). The second is a more dramatic claim that "fairness" considerations should play no independent role in the choice of legal rules (or any other policies, including tax policies); by "fairness" Kaplow and Shavell mean any considerations that are not based on welfare effects. Put together, the Kaplow and Shavell work amounts to the following three-step defense of standard law and economics methodology: (*a*) Welfare is the only relevant criterion for the evaluation of legal rules, (*b*) welfare consists of efficiency and distribution, and (*c*) efficiency is the only proper criterion for the evaluation of legal rules because distributive goals are more efficiently pursued through the tax system than through the legal system.

This conventional methodology poses a problem for feminists in law who want to use economics as a tool for analyzing legal rules and policies. Efficiency is too narrow a normative criterion and income redistribution too limited [and, perhaps, politically dangerous (McCluskey 2003)] a response to the problem of inequality and other feminist ethical commitments. This may explain why feminist law and economics is still largely an aspirational field of study, rather than a body of work that an *Annual Review* can survey and critique. Although there are some efforts to analyze, for example, tax and welfare policies (Alstott 1996, McCaffery 1997, Staudt 1996, McCluskey 2003), family law (Carbone 1990, Carbone & Brinig 1991, Brinig & Crafton 1994, Singer 1994, Estin 1995, Brinig 2000), employment law (Hadfield 1993, 1995a), contract law (Trebilcock 1993; Hadfield 1995b, 1998a; Brinig 1995), and corporate law (Sarra 2002) from a feminist economics perspective, by and large there has been little development in this field since Hadfield (1998b) attempted to define its scope. [For a recent book-length treatment of the issues at the intersection of feminism and economics, both critical and hopeful, see Fineman & Dougherty (2005).] Feminist analysis in law has, in general, not flourished in the last decade. Rosenbury (2003) found, for example, that the number of articles on women or gender published in leading law reviews fell by approximately one half over the last decade, and most of the work was done by established (tenured) scholars and not those newly entering legal academics.

And yet, in theory, economics possesses many attractive features for feminists: It provides careful tools for systematically analyzing the effects of legal rules and evaluating the impact of those effects on those we care about. It draws attention to the need for explicit assumptions about how people behave, what resources they have available, what constraints they face, what information they have. It emphasizes the dynamic interaction, both strategic and nonstrategic, between people and institutions. It is organized around the concept of equilibrium, drawing focus to the forces that stabilize the outcomes we want and that possibly resist change to the outcomes we do not want. And, we hope, it gives us a basis for careful assessments about which rules and policies will improve well-being. But if adopting law and economics methodology means restricting one's work to efficiency analysis and income redistribution, then the value of economics is substantially limited. I have argued elsewhere (Hadfield 1998b) that feminists can continue to use the positive (descriptive and predictive) tools of economics while conducting normative analysis informed by nonefficiency criteria. This response to the expanding claims for law and economics methodology, articulated most forcefully by Kaplow and Shavell, however, is inadequate, for they claim that welfare economics requires the law and economics analyst to eschew fairness claims and that the only proper economic criterion for assessing legal rules is efficiency. These are challenges to the possibility of a coherent feminist law and economics, and I take up those challenges here. I argue that neither of the claims Kaplow and Shavell put forward about coherent law and economics methodology excludes the type of welfare economics that feminists should embrace: a welfare economics that is politically and ethically engaged and that is capable of addressing feminist commitments. Indeed, I argue, the only coherent welfare economics available is one that integrates the type of normative commitments that a field of study such as feminist law and economics requires.

FAIRNESS, WELFARE, AND THE GOAL OF ETHICAL MINIMALISM

Among the social sciences used in legal analysis, economics is clearly the most influential. Whereas other social science methods have substantial sway in particular areas—psychology where law makes judgments about competence or analyzes decision making, for example; history where the genesis of legal doctrines or practices is relevant; political science when the workings of political institutions are under scrutiny—economics managed in the 1970s to break free from disciplinary boundaries that limited the use of economics to areas where the law was regulating market conduct, notably antitrust law. Economists and economically minded legal scholars began to draw on economic models of behavior and social choice to analyze essentially all of law: torts, property, family law, corporate law, environmental law, poverty law, constitutional law, and so on.

Economics gained this ascendancy in legal scholarship, I believe, because of two seemingly opposed attributes of economic methodology. First, unlike many social sciences, economics makes both positive and normative claims, whereas much of social science is exclusively positive. Thus, economics helps lawyers, jurists, and legal scholars to predict not only what will happen if a particular rule is adopted or how to decide whether particular factual predicates of a rule are met; it also provides guidance about which rules to adopt. Economics thus speaks to the essential normativity of law and legal decision making. Paradoxically, however, it is a second claim, to ethical minimalism, that makes economics especially attractive and also explains why economics in its normative dimension is also more influential than many overtly normative legal theories, such as critical legal studies, critical race theory, libertarianism, or, indeed, feminist legal theory. The normativity of conventional law and economics is based on the concept of efficiency and the purportedly noncontroversial claim that a legal rule or policy that makes everyone better off and no one worse off (the Pareto criterion) or, slightly more controversial, that generates sufficient benefits for winners to potentially compensate losers (the Kaldor-Hicks criterion) should be adopted. Economics, therefore, offers legal decision makers relief from otherwise seemingly intractable ethical and political debates about fairness or justice.

Economics manages this apparently paradoxical state—normative power with minimal normative content—through various separability claims. Kaplow

& Shavell (1994) have emphasized one particularly powerful separability claim, namely that whatever our distributional goals or equity concerns, we will do better as a society (in the uncontroversial Pareto sense) if we look only to the efficiency criterion in selecting legal rules, leaving distributional considerations to the tax and welfare system. This is a variant on the more fundamental claim of the second welfare theorem, and in the next section I discuss that claim from a feminist perspective.

Kaplow & Shavell's (2001) work on "fairness versus welfare" delves into the justification for using welfare economics to evaluate legal rules in the first place. As good economists, they purport to be making a minimally normative claim: Legal rules and policies should be assessed in terms of their impact on the well-being of individuals; any slavish application of fairness principles (defined to be principles that look to factors other than the well-being of individuals) will, logically, lead in some circumstances to social choices that make everyone worse off. That, say Kaplow and Shavell, would violate the minimalist Pareto criterion, and we should all agree that such results should be rejected.

Feminists may have a harder time criticizing Kaplow and Shavell's fairness versus welfare claim than their separability claim. After all, most feminists ground their normative commitments in concerns about well-being, particularly women's well-being; few feminists are interested in pursuing abstract justice principles for the sake of principle. These are the lessons, for example, of Gilligan (1982), Noddings (1984), and Tronto (1993) on the feminist ethic of care, an ethic of particularistic attention to the needs of others in concrete circumstances. These commitments would seem to make feminists largely agreeable to the idea that legal rules should be evaluated exclusively in terms of well-being.

Kaplow and Shavell's approach, however, is not one that feminists working in law and economics should accept as a methodological framework. Many of the attributes of fairness and justice that feminists are particularly concerned with generally cannot be represented in the sorts of social welfare functions that Kaplow and Shavell have in mind. Hidden in their apparently capacious appeal to well-being as opposed to abstract principle are many much more restrictive, strongly normative conditions. The welfare economics Kaplow and Shavell are advocating is the narrowest form of welfare economics and precisely the one that seems to lead inexorably to the crabbed focus on efficiency, reducing fairness or justice concerns to problems of income distribution. And indeed this is their overall project: to justify conventional law and economics methodology. Feminists, who should welcome welfare economics on the whole as a systematic method of paying attention to the particular needs and well-being of individuals, should look to modern welfare economics for how it struggles to integrate into social welfare functions considerations such as concern with rights, interpersonal comparisons of well-being, objective criteria of well-being, the unique attributes of goods such as care that create the capacity for well-being or primary goods such as dignity, the inadequacy or unacceptability of some preferences, and the importance of processes and not merely outcomes. That is, feminists should with confidence reject the ethical minimalism of conventional law and economics' exclusive focus on efficiency, taking up the more overt engagement with fairness and justice concerns that, in fact, animate modern welfare economics. I take up this argument in the section below on Fairness and Social Welfare Functions.

SEPARABILITY AND THE SECOND WELFARE THEOREM

Welfare economics is powerful because of its methodological implications. The first theorem of welfare economics says that perfect markets—ones with full information, complete divisibility and tradeability of goods, no externalities, no increasing returns to scale in production, and well-behaved preferences[1]—will result in an allocation of goods (resources) that is Pareto efficient, meaning no member of society could be made better off under an alternative distribution without making some other member of society worse off. This result grounds the focus by neoclassical economists (including those working in law and economics) on creating market mechanisms and identifying market failures and missing markets.

The first welfare theorem can support final allocations of goods and resources, however, that violate our considered judgments about what is fair or just. An allocation that is Pareto efficient may allocate all goods to one person or one class of people; this is because the test for Pareto efficiency has to consider whether any member of society would prefer the initial allocation of goods to the one that would result from market trades. Thus, those that are well-off in the initial allocation must be at least as well-off in the final allocation.

The second welfare theorem allows those using welfare economics to implement (particular) views about fairness and justice. The second theorem says that any feasible Pareto-optimal final allocation (for example, one with an equal distribution of goods or income) can be reached through (perfect) markets through a manipulation of the initial allocation of goods or income. The methodological implication is what I have referred to as the separability claim: If markets are perfect, then they can be relied upon to achieve efficiency in production and allocation, whereas distributive concerns stemming from considerations of fairness or justice can be addressed through changes in the initial distribution of goods.

These two theorems account for the tremendous power of economic analysis and its persuasive attractiveness to applied policy making: They give a carefully reasoned justification for a focus on efficiency (the creation and correction of markets) in legal and policy design that does not require the abandonment of (or agreement on) the fair or just allocation of goods or resources.

The requirements of the first and second welfare theorems are very strong. Few if any markets are perfect. Moreover, the types of reallocations required by the

---

[1]Preferences are said to be well behaved when they are monotonic and convex: Utility increases with any increase in the quantity of a good consumed (nonsatiation) at a diminishing marginal rate.

second welfare theorem—initial lump sum reallocation as opposed to distortionary taxes on income—are practically impossible. Yet the generality and elegance of these theorems are such that in making practical judgments about how to proceed with policymaking, the norms of economists tend to reflect a determination that the imperfections in markets and taxation methods are generally not sufficient reason to abandon the power of the separability claim.

Shavell (1981) and Kaplow & Shavell (1994) demonstrate the implications of such practical judgments for law and economics methodology. They specifically address the problem of distortionary taxes and conclude that the essential separability result continues to justify an exclusive focus in the design of legal rules on efficiency. Their reasoning is that any labor supply distortions created by the tax system will be replicated in the legal system if legal rules are used not only to achieve efficiency but also to redistribute income. Thus, legal rules chosen to achieve both efficiency and equity goals will contain a "double distortion" relative to a regime in which legal rules are chosen exclusively on the basis of efficiency and taxes are used for redistribution.

Sanchirico (2001) has highlighted at least one problem with this conclusion based on the "theory of the second-best" (Lipsey & Lancaster 1956). That theory tells us that, as a mathematical matter, adding up distortions is invalid: If one market fails to meet the assumptions of the first welfare theorem (is "distorted"), then we cannot conclude that eliminating a distortion in another market will increase efficiency. Kaplow and Shavell's separability claim, however, has to be seen as an exercise not just in mathematical reasoning but also in practical methodological judgment. It reflects a common judgment made by economists in practice to ignore the implications of the theory of the second-best: Partial equilibrium efficiency analysis is standard fare in the economics literature. Although Kaplow and Shavell have not responded directly to Sanchirico's "second-best" critique (they have responded to other criticisms he offers[2]), their implicit judgment appears to be that it is more likely than not that in practice the efficiency distortions that will be introduced if legal rules are used to redistribute income will not offset the labor market distortions that such rules will create. Because the labor market distortion (Kaplow and Shavell claim) will be the same whether redistribution is accomplished through a legal rule or a tax, the efficiency distortion will indeed be additive. [The claim that people will respond equivalently to redistribution through the tax system and the legal system has been criticized by Jolls (1998), Sanchirico (2000, 2001), and Avraham et al. (2004).]

Whatever the merits of the "second-best" judgments Kaplow and Shavell have employed, however, for feminists, there are deeper concerns about the exercise of practical judgment that underlies the application of the separability claim in law

---

[2]Sanchirico (2001) argues that Kaplow and Shavell have not adequately responded to what he calls the "efficiency as non-sequitur" critique. This critique emphasizes that not all redistributive legal rules are conditioned on income, and hence redistribution through legal rules cannot be replicated by an equivalent tax.

and economics. Even in a world in which perfect nondistorting income or resource redistributions are available, or a world in which Kaplow and Shavell are correct about the relative distortions afforded by redistribution through the tax and legal systems, the separability claim should be rejected in many cases by feminists.

Recall that the second welfare theorem assumes a world in which all goods (sources of utility or well-being) are tradeable and divisible and there are no externalities that cannot be made tradeable. These are assumptions that fail for values that feminists specifically emphasize. I explore the failure of these assumptions with respect to two subjects of concern to feminists: rights (such as rights with respect to autonomy and with respect to freedom from discriminatory or harassing treatment) and caring labor.

Rights

Rights—such as the right to make one's own choices (about abortion, for example, but also about whether to enter into a contract or to work for a given employer) or to be free of discrimination or harassment in the workplace—can be analyzed instrumentally in terms of how they promote women's ability to generate income and opportunities to secure their well-being. Rights, however, are also important sources of well-being in and of themselves. This is an important point because whereas the things that rights may afford women—a discrimination-free workplace, employment, contracts, the deferral of childbearing—may be tradeable goods that can be obtained through markets, rights themselves are not tradeable goods.

Consider for example a right to be free of discrimination in the form of harassment in the workplace. A harassment-free workplace is a potentially tradeable good. Employers can compete for employees by offering such a workplace, and they can compete in the goods and services market through their choice of workplace environment and hence the cost to them of obtaining labor. [Becker (1971) employs a standard model of labor markets to argue that discrimination—understood as employer animus-based preferences for discrimination—will be competed away as a result of its inefficient use of resources.] To the extent that our social welfare function seeks to allocate the benefits of a harassment-free workplace to employees generally or to women in particular, income transfers could conceivably enable such employees to demand such a workplace, that is, to avoid harassing workplaces (or to obtain other goods that give them an equivalent level of utility). Similarly, to the extent that workplace harassment lowers women's wages and employment opportunities (by increasing the cost to them of different occupations, for example, or decreasing either their incentives to invest in human capital or their capacity to signal their abilities), the market allocation of income that results in a world of harassment can be corrected through redistribution. In these ways, harassment reduces women's well-being because it denies women the things that produce well-being such as wages or workplace opportunities or pleasant working environments. Harassment itself can be a "bad" that women would like to have less of in a final allocation; they can purchase that allocation if they have sufficient wealth (perhaps as a result of subsidies in the tax system) to avoid harassing workplaces.

A right to be free of harassment can be a source of value to women because it alters their opportunities to purchase the goods that a harassment-free workplace generates and it changes the price of these goods. This is the classic Coasian understanding of legal rights: Rights play an instrumental role in achieving the efficient allocation of goods or resources. Seen in this framework, the separability thesis seems natural: focus on the efficient allocation of the underlying goods or resources (with a market-determined price for harassing environments, for example); if the resulting distribution of goods or resources differs from what we judge to be just or fair (if harassment-free environments are too expensive and hence too many women cannot afford them), then redistribute income (possibly through the allocation of a right that allows a woman to demand compensation for harassment) to achieve the preferred outcome.

A right, however, may also be a source of value in and of itself. It may not be perceived merely as an instrument to obtain other goods. A right to be free of workplace harassment may be valued differently than a harassment-free workplace. The right expresses a social, political, and moral status. It is a manifestation of dignified and equal relations. The adjudication of a right to be free of harassment entails a public avowal of how a person must be treated by employers, by men, by those with power. The holding of a right entitles a person to trigger the state's exercise of public power: to obtain an accounting of wrongdoing and to declare, at least, when a wrongdoing has occurred.

Rights are not divisible goods capable of being produced and traded in markets. An individual can buy more or less harassment in the workplace, she can conceivably purchase more or less of a contract right to be free of harassment, but she cannot buy more or less of a public right to be free of harassment. There is no way to adjust our distribution of income so as to enable her to purchase this public right. We may be able to increase her income and thereby increase her capacity to influence collective choice processes (such as majority voting) that produce the right, but that is a different story.

The methodological point for feminist law and economics is clear: It is insufficient to focus exclusively on the efficiency characteristics of discrimination laws, not because the efficiency, or even economic well-being, criterion is inapposite in this area but because the economic theory that justifies the focus on efficiency fails on its own terms. This is not to say that feminists should not be concerned about the efficiency losses—understood as distortions in the allocation of resources and efforts—that may arise in the labor market as a consequence of discrimination laws that interfere with employer discretion. [For examples of this type of analysis, see Posner (1989) and Donohue (1986, 1989).] Being a feminist economist must mean, at a minimum, an appreciation of the fact that laws that on their face are intended to improve the lot of women may in fact make them worse off, as could happen if discrimination laws left women increasingly unemployed. Rather, the point is that feminists venturing into the law and economics analysis of discrimination laws, arguing as economists, are entitled to reject an exclusive focus on efficiency precisely because an important source of value (the value of rights qua rights) is not subject to the claims of the separability thesis: We cannot correct any market distortion in the final production and allocation of this right through redistribution policies. Money cannot buy everything. Even if it can buy what rights can buy, it cannot buy the rights themselves.

Caring Labor

Feminist economics has, to the dismay of its small but dedicated band of practitioners, not made large strides over the past decade in putting issues on the agenda of mainstream economics (Ferber & Nelson 2003). But one area in which feminist economics has registered some success, and which Power (2004) identifies as a first principle for feminist economic method, is the analysis of care and caring labor. England & Folbre (2003) and Folbre (2003), for example, relate the analysis of caring labor—labor that is directed to producing capabilities in others, is (sometimes) supplied through intrinsic motivation and possesses unique attributes when supplied by individuals with nonmonetary motivations (such as parents), and is often supplied to beneficiaries who are not capable of judging quality or contracting for services (children, for example)—to the analysis of new institutional economics in general and incomplete contracting in particular. Taylor (1998) presents an economic model of caring that relates optimal care decisions to the costs of identifying those in need in small (family) versus large (organizational) populations and the relative cost of time for men and women.

The assumptions of the second welfare theorem fail profoundly with respect to the production, organization, and quality of caring labor. Caring labor has significant public good attributes, particularly if we emphasize the relationship between quality care of children and the production of social capital in the form of norms of honesty, trust, civic engagement, reciprocity, respect for law, and so on. There are also positive externalities associated with the production of capabilities that underlie the development of human capital, externalities that redound to the benefit not only of the person cared for but also to the benefit of society at large in the form of an educated workforce and polity, the resources for innovation, and so on.

The complex nature of caring labor means that conventional methods of addressing public goods and externalities problems are inadequate. To induce caring labor, we must generate an effective demand for caring labor. The demand could arise in the beneficiaries of care, in the providers of care, or in the public generally. Many of the direct beneficiaries of care, however, are unable to assess the value of care or transact for the provision of care (because they are children or because they are unwell, for example). Transferring resources to these beneficiaries, or their agents, is likely to increase the supply and quality of care provided in the market, but failures in the demand exercised by those in need of care mean that the result will not be optimal.

Alternatively, we could assume that those who supply caring labor through intrinsic motivation (such as parents or other family members) fully internalize the benefits to those for whom they care, in which case the supply of caring labor is a function of what is conventionally described as the labor/leisure choice. In this framework, the second welfare theorem would seem to be relevant: One may achieve the desired final allocation by redistributing income and thereby adjusting the price of leisure, leading to a final efficient determination of how much time is spent on care. This is one way in which feminists have framed the problems that women, in particular, face in spending as much time as they would like with their children and other family members.

There are (at least) two problems with this approach, even within conventional neoclassical frameworks. First, it is probably empirically inaccurate to assume that caregivers (mothers and fathers, for example) fully internalize the benefits of their caring labor as experienced by those for whom they care. It is not (just) that people are not perfectly altruistic and thus may fail to choose optimal levels of care for others, spending too much of their income and time on themselves and not enough on their dependants. It is, as Folbre (1994) has emphasized, that caregivers (particularly, in practice, women) incur various costs in providing care. They face trade-offs. When women care for others, they reduce their investments in human capital; they make themselves dependent on relationships that may circumscribe their autonomy, their mobility, their opportunities, or their well-being and that may end, such as in divorce, injury, or death.

Second, even if women receive substantial income transfers to compensate them for the costs of providing care to others, this compensation will not lead to an efficient allocation of women's time between paid labor and caring labor through market transactions. The structures of the workplace restrict the labor/leisure bundles that are available because, for example, production is often characterized by network externalities. Consider the scheduling of the work day. There are network externalities associated with common or at least overlapping work hours created by the need for collaboration, coordination, and communication with coworkers. The determination of work hours is thus potentially subject to conflicts of interest among workers and so must be determined through some collective mechanism—hierarchical authority (delegation to a manager) in the ordinary firm, or deliberation and possibly voting in a collaborative workplace. In such settings, the market does not produce efficient results. And, again, no amount of monetary redistribution can produce the allocation we may prefer as a society.

Can we solve the problems by conceptualizing caring labor as a public good, demanded by the state rather than individuals and produced by or purchased in the market by the state? Clearly we can generate substantial quantities of caring labor through this mechanism; this is what publicly funded childcare, education, hospitals, institutions, etc., provide. The fact that care provided by non-market providers—those who are intrinsically motivated to care, with whom the beneficiary has a long-term relationship—is fundamentally different from the care provided by market providers (England & Folbre 2003), however, means that the state cannot achieve the optimal outcome through public production or purchase.

The lesson for feminists in law and economics is that the separability result has to be squarely rejected when particular legal rules under study have an impact on the provision of caring labor in the economy. The sweep of this implication is broad. All of modern corporate law and economics, for example, focuses on the efficiency of corporate governance, understood as maximization of returns to shareholders. Corporate governance, however, has implications for the organization of the workplace, which has implications—profound implications—for the provision of caring labor. The unique attributes of caring labor, however, as we have just seen, imply that we cannot simply maximize the wealth of shareholders—the profits of firms—and then redistribute income to achieve the socially preferred level of caring labor. Similarly, workplace regulations—hours legislation, parental leave policies, minimum wages, and so on—have to be evaluated not merely in light of efficiency concerns but also in light of ultimate social preferences for the production and quality of caring labor. Indeed, rejecting the separability thesis in this area would help feminist law and economics scholars to emphasize the social value of caring labor, indeed, the efficiency of caring labor, in light of its role in producing valuable social and human capital. The separability thesis suggests that the only interest we have in manipulating a market allocation through redistribution is in adjusting the relative wealth and consumption of individuals. A more careful economic analysis of caring labor sees not merely what is fair or just about maternity leave policies or workplace regulation but also what is, fundamentally, socially valuable.

Separability and Practical Judgment

The adoption of the separability claim in law and economics is ultimately a matter of practical judgment: When is it reasonable in practice, in light of real-world failures of the assumptions of perfect markets, to continue to rely on the second welfare theorem to justify a focus on the efficiency of legal rules? There are undoubtedly many settings in which this is an appropriate methodological move. Feminists in law and economics should be attentive to the normative quality of those practical judgments and the way, in fact, they reflect substantive views about what is valuable, what is important, and why. In making those judgments, the normative minimalism of the separability claim may be abandoned. This is what happens when law and economics scholars adopt the separability claim in the analysis of discrimination law or corporate governance: In treating normative concerns about equality or care as equity or distributional concerns—to be efficiently addressed through income transfers rather than through legal rule design—they implicitly assume that rights have only instrumental value or that the supply of caring labor is a leisure/labor choice that caregivers (such as parents) make. It is appropriate at that point for feminists to make these implicit normative claims apparent and to insist that law and economics analysis adopting these claims defend not only their economic reasoning but also their normative judgments.

FAIRNESS AND SOCIAL WELFARE FUNCTIONS

Feminists in law and economics who reject the use of separability in the analysis of legal rules and policies—who insist that equity considerations cannot be cabined off to allow an exclusive focus on efficiency—may nonetheless continue to work squarely within the neoclassical framework. Rejecting separability within that framework means working directly with a social welfare function to determine the desirability of a legal rule. Methodologically, the question for feminists is then whether working within that framework in law and economics is inconsistent with feminists' particular normative commitments, such as to the importance of rights and the impact of corporate governance and workplace regulation on the organization, quantity, and quality of caring labor. As framed by Kaplow & Shavell (2001), do feminists have to give up fairness in order to work with the concept of welfare?

Kaplow and Shavell make the basic claim that the only defensible normative criteria are those that evaluate legal rules and policies in terms of their impact on the welfare of individuals. They distinguish these welfare criteria from fairness criteria by adopting an idiosyncratic (Waldron 2003) definition of fairness: They use the term fairness exclusively to mean normative considerations that do not ultimately rest on the impact of a rule or policy on individuals' welfare. So, for example, they rule out decision criteria such as that "surrogacy contracts should be enforced because they promote women's autonomy," or that "surrogacy contracts should not be enforced because they degrade women," or that "women have a right to choose how they use their bodies, and this encompasses the right to decide to be a surrogate." They advocate instead that all of our discussions should be of the form, "Are the people we include in our social welfare function (surrogates, childless couples, unborn children, existing children, etc.) made better or worse off by a policy of enforcing surrogacy contracts?" Having defined fairness to be principles that ignore the welfare implications of a rule or policy, the basis for their claim is then a simple application of the economist's conventional, minimalist, Pareto criterion: Rules and policies should be rejected if they make someone worse off and no one better off. If there are circumstances in which enforcing surrogacy contracts to promote women's autonomy makes everyone worse off or makes someone worse off and no one better off, then, Kaplow and Shavell ask, what is the point in doing that? What sense can it make to say that autonomy for women is a good thing if it does not make at least someone better off? And if the application of this principle always makes a least someone better off (such as the woman exercising her autonomy), then we are doing welfare analysis.

The claim is, frankly, a fairly powerful one, for the same reasons that conventional neoclassical economics has been so powerful as a normative social science: It has minimal normative content. Although many in law and economics have criticized the opposition of welfare and fairness in Kaplow and Shavell's work (Chang 2000, Dorff 2002, Craswell 2003, Farber 2003, Kornhauser 2003, McDonnell 2003), it is hard to argue with the minimalist claim that ultimately all laws and policies should be evaluated on the basis of whether they improve the well-being of actual people. Feminists, in particular, will not find anything objectionable in the idea that social choice should be governed by concrete attention to people's well-being in fact. Commitment to a principle that, systematically at least, made everyone worse off in any way we considered relevant would seem to reflect a foolish, abstract adherence to principle. And yet there is something quite jarring about the Kaplow and Shavell claim, something that seems to be much more dramatic as a normative claim, even for feminists who seek to do law and economics.

The objectionable part of Kaplow and Shavell's claim, from a feminist perspective, is the narrow form of welfare economics that they advocate, one that leads naturally to the narrow focus on efficiency in legal rules and that limits fairness concerns to income distribution. They are, indeed, engaged in the project of justifying conventional law and economics methodology. But feminists in law and economics should pay careful attention to the fact that their argument seems to suggest that by conceding the congenial claim that well-being should be the criterion of social choice we must also logically accept that nothing matters except efficiency in legal rules and income redistribution. In fact, this does not follow. Feminists can agree that welfare is the appropriate criterion, and even that welfare economics is a valuable methodological framework, without ending up at conventional law and economics and the narrow focus on efficiency and income distribution.

Kaplow and Shavell are advocating not merely that legal rules should be evaluated exclusively in terms of individual well-being; they are advocating that well-being, for the purposes of guiding social choice, be evaluated exclusively in radically subjective terms[3] and that only subjective utility information be used to construct a social welfare function.[4] But it is well known in modern welfare economics that such a social welfare function is a highly problematic, perhaps incoherent, concept. Feminists can, and should, join mainstream welfare economists in rejecting the restriction to subjective utility information in constructing social welfare functions.

Impossibility and Interpersonal Comparisons of Utility

The roots of modern welfare economics rest in a set of results deeply pessimistic about the possibility of systematic social choice. Traditional welfare economics dates back to Bentham (1996 [1789]) and the proposal that social choice be governed by a strictly utilitarian calculus, maximizing the total subjectively evaluated utility of a community, without regard to the distribution of utility within the community. This approach to social choice dominated economics until the 1930s

---

[3] "The only limit on what is included in well-being is to be found in the minds of individuals themselves, not in the minds of analysts" (Kaplow & Shavell 2001, p. 980).

[4] "Social welfare is postulated to be an increasing function of individuals' well-being and to depend on no other factors" (Kaplow & Shavell 2001, p. 985).

when, as described by Amartya Sen, who received the Nobel Prize for his work in welfare economics in 1998, "utilitarian welfare economics came under severe fire . . . .[E]conomists came to be persuaded by arguments presented by Lionel Robbins and others (deeply influenced by 'logical positivist' philosophy) that interpersonal comparisons of utility had no scientific basis" (Sen 1999, p. 352). Interpersonal comparisons of utility are necessary to construct a utilitarian social welfare function because all utility has to be reduced to a common metric. This is the basis for the minimalist move in neoclassical economics, the retreat to the Pareto criterion and to the first and second welfare theorems. Under this approach, the problem of interpersonal comparisons of utility and the construction of a social welfare function in fact are put aside in favor of the demonstration that, assuming that the construction of such a social welfare function might be possible, perfect markets will achieve Pareto optimal outcomes, and redistribution of endowments can select any outcome that maximizes social welfare.

Then, in 1951, Kenneth Arrow proved a rather distressing result with wide-reaching consequences: In the absence of interpersonal comparisons of utility, no social welfare function that is based exclusively on individual subjective preferences—which takes into account no other information to select optimal social outcomes—exists (Arrow 1951). Formally, Arrow showed that a social ordering over possible allocations that satisfies minimal conditions—it does not track the preferences of any single member of the society (nondictatorship), it chooses between alternative allocations exclusively on the basis of the preferences of individuals between those allocations (independence of irrelevant alternatives), and it places no restrictions on the preferences individuals might hold (unrestricted domain)—fails to establish a complete, transitive ordering over outcomes, the definition of rational choice.

Kaplow and Shavell avoid the impossibility result (although they do not discuss it) by assuming that interpersonal comparisons of utility are possible and, indeed, are possible to the extent that the social welfare function can be based not only on total welfare but also on the distribution of welfare among individuals. But they do not explain how such interpersonal comparisons are to be made and thus do not explain how they resolve the very problem that led welfare economists in the 1930s to abandon the concept of an aggregate social welfare function based exclusively on subjective utilities, the problem that led to the minimalist Pareto criterion and ultimately to the impossibility result. Indeed, Kaplow and Shavell do not explain how the analyst who is encouraged to endorse welfare economics as the framework for all legal rule and policy evaluation (and recall, their claim is the strong one that any other framework fails to be logically consistent and conflicts with the Pareto criterion) is to engage in interpersonal comparisons without taking into account information other than individual subjective utility assessments.

In fact, the lesson of modern welfare economics is that it is not possible to construct a social welfare function without taking into account information other than individual subjective utility. That is, the welfare economics Kaplow and Shavell are advocating does not exist, and one can follow their recommendation to eschew any efforts to judge what is good or bad for individuals, what is fair or just in aggregating individual well-being to arrive at social choices, only by ignoring the demonstrated inconsistencies in such an approach. Arrow (1977) shows this clearly. In this work, and in response largely to the efforts of other welfare economists such as Hammond (1976) to reconcile welfare economics with Rawls (1971), Arrow takes on the challenge to construct a social welfare function that includes interpersonal comparisons of utility, seeking the most minimal version of such comparisons that overcomes the problem of impossibility. The metric he arrives at (a utility function defined over goods—such as wine—and the attributes that lead to the derivation of utility from the consumption of goods—such as the capacity to enjoy wine) accomplishes what a method of interpersonal comparisons requires, namely the reduction of all utility to a single comparable metric. But it does so at a price that Arrow himself finds troubling:

> [R]educing an individual to a specified list of qualities is denying his individuality in a deep sense. In a way that I cannot articulate well and am none too sure about defending, the autonomy of individuals, an element of mutual incommensurability among people, seems denied by the possibility of interpersonal comparisons. No doubt it is some such feeling as this that has made me so reluctant to shift from pure ordinalism, despite my desire to seek a basis for a theory of justice (Arrow 1977, p. 225).

Kaplow and Shavell also reject this solution when they insist that the only criterion of well-being has to be the individual's subjective assessment of well-being and not that of the analyst's: As Arrow's own view of his solution makes clear, reducing individual well-being to a single metric requires that individuals all be in some fundamental sense the same, and the designation of any such metric would require an outside analyst to determine what it is that produces utility, in the same way, for anyone.

As Sen (1985) has explained, the fundamental source of the impossibility result is the neutrality that is implied by the type of social welfare function Kaplow and Shavell have in mind. If the only measure of utility we admit is the individual's subjective valuation, and if the only aggregation we allow is that which takes into account only these subjective preferences, then it follows that our social choices must be indifferent to the sources of individual utility, to the particular goods that individuals obtain in alternative allocations. Social choices cannot weight preferences according to any information about the particular things individuals value; in this framework, social choice is committed to neutrality as between promoting one person's utility by, for example, affording them opportunities to degrade others and promoting another person's utility by affording them greater dignity or autonomy. This is the sense in which the type of social welfare function Kaplow and Shavell have in mind rules out a wide array of ethical frameworks and judgments, and in particular rules out the kinds of normative commitments that feminists hold.

In this framework, social choices also cannot be determined by the nature of particular states of the world, by comparing the content of particular allocations.

The Rawlsian approach to justice, for example, is incompatible with the Kaplow and Shavell version of welfare economics. Rawls's conception of justice requires attention not merely to the utility of individuals but also to their access to what he calls primary goods: basic rights and liberties (such as freedom of thought), freedom of movement, and free choice of occupation, the social bases of self-respect, powers and prerogatives of positions of authority, and income and wealth (Rawls 2001, p. 58). Primary goods are the things individuals need to realize well-being as "free and equal persons living a complete life" (Rawls 2001, p. 58). Rawls's theory of justice addresses the just distribution of primary goods: The first principle of justice requires that "each person has the same indefeasible claim to a fully adequate scheme of equal basic liberties" (Rawls 2001, p. 42), and the second principle requires that any social and economic inequalities must be attached to positions available to all under conditions of fair equality of opportunity and be to the greatest benefit of the least advantaged. Rawls's approach is affirmatively about promoting individual well-being; it is a considered assessment of what produces well-being.

As Kaplow and Shavell acknowledge (Kaplow & Shavell 2001, fn. 54), Rawlsian justice is incompatible with the welfare economics they advocate because it takes into account more than subjective utility assessments; it also takes into account the particular attributes of underlying goods and objective indicia of well-being such as the capacity to exercise choice and to access sources of power and income. But, as we have seen, any coherent social welfare function must take into account information beyond the subjective utility assessments of individuals. Otherwise we are back at Arrow's impossibility result. The dilemma for Kaplow and Shavell is then essentially this: They insist that individuals can be the only judge of what they individually value in any aggregation of preferences into a social welfare function, and yet any coherent social welfare function must take into account information other than these subjective preferences.

Thus, Kaplow and Shavell's claim is not really that the only coherent approach to legal analysis is to use welfare economics because their specific approach to welfare economics does not allow for the construction of a social welfare function. Their claim reduces to a much more idiosyncratic and contestable one, namely that legal rules and policies should be chosen in light of what promotes each individual's own conception of their utility, rather than some analyst's conception of their well-being. They reject fairness principles because they are not, by definition, equivalent to individual subjective preference rankings. They insist that the only valid social choices are those that choose in the way individuals would choose. But this does not resolve the fundamental problem of social choice: How do we choose when our choices affect not just one but many? How do we resolve conflicts, such as the conflict between someone who derives pleasure from domination and the one who suffers under that domination? How do we allocate common resources? How do we organize activities that produce goods, and how do we distribute the fruits of those efforts? How do we respond to poverty and oppression?

Kaplow and Shavell's framework responds in a narrow way, the only way that is consistent with their fundamental commitment to individual subjective utility. They respond, as they set out to do, with conventional law and economics: efficiency and income redistribution. Efficiency is acceptable because it does not require interpersonal comparisons of utility and is not social choice; rather, it takes as a given an existing distribution of endowments and capabilities and institutions and preferences and simply asks, could we make everyone better off by changing our rules? All the questions of social choice, where conflicts and trade-offs between individuals are at stake, are relegated to a single acceptable instrument: income redistribution. Income redistribution is acceptable to their framework because it allows for interpersonal comparisons in a common metric, the only good that Kaplow and Shavell will allow the analyst to assume is universally valued by individuals: money. They refer to this sometimes as the distribution of well-being, but given their refusal to allow information about the allocation of specific goods into the equation (hence ruling out redistribution of goods, rather than income), they are in fact only referring to income, the fungible resource that individuals can then use to choose which among the goods available to them they should purchase.

Feminists can confidently reject this effort to collapse all of our fairness, justice, and equity concerns to income distribution. And they can do so on the very grounds that Kaplow and Shavell want to use to justify their narrow framework. As feminists emphasize, there are values that human beings receive from nontradeable goods such as the right to be free of harassment, the entitlement to dignity and equality in social processes, or the care that is embedded in particular non-market relationships such as the family. As I have already argued with respect to the rejection of the separability claim, these are goods that cannot be secured through income redistribution and markets. If we are committed in fact to the capaciousness of respecting the diversity of values individuals hold, then clearly we cannot rule out, as Kaplow and Shavell implicitly do, these nonmarket goods. The import of feminism here is to emphasize the importance of these goods, to say that these are not marginal considerations or empirically unlikely preferences that can be brushed aside in the practical judgments about methodology that law and economics analysts, like all analysts, must make. Kaplow and Shavell cannot reconcile any a priori limitation on the importance of nonmarket goods with their premise that "the notion of well-being used in welfare economics is comprehensive in nature. . .incorporat[ing] everything that an individual might value" (Kaplow & Shavell 2001, p. 979).

Nor can Kaplow and Shavell reconcile with their commitment to a comprehensive welfare economics their view that well-being is not merely subjective but is idiosyncratic and inscrutable as to each individual, accessible only through empirical methods and not through philosophical or other theoretical inquiry into the nature of human well-being. Feminist claims, like most ethical claims, about what is fair are, in fact, claims about what produces well-being for any human being. The claim that autonomy is a good thing, for example, appeals to a universal human nature that values the capacity for self-direction in life. Those who do not value this, we often judge, are operating under a false understanding of what promotes their own, subjective sense of well-being. It is a contestable claim, to be sure. But

Kaplow and Shavell provide no reason to rule out, a priori, the possibility that claims about universal sources of well-being are correct.

Indeed, Kaplow and Shavell's own defense of conventional law and economics methodology requires that a set of claims about the universal value of some goods be true. Although they do not articulate a theory of income distribution, any articulation of their position would require recognition of a fundamental point made by Rawls and Sen, namely, that in order for income to produce utility, individuals must have liberty. Specifically, Kaplow and Shavell's emphasis on income distribution as an instrument for adjusting the distribution of well-being assumes that every person has the liberty to participate in exchange. The relationship between income distribution and well-being also rests on the implicit assumption that all people possess the human and social capital necessary to evaluate trades and carry them through. In an extended economy with noninstantaneous exchange, this implies the capacity to contract and to access formal and informal mechanisms for enforcing trades. It is thus straightforward to derive fairness principles strictly from universal claims about the subjective well-being of individuals: All are entitled to equal access to markets and to trade on the same terms.

In a similar vein, feminists' principled claims such as "women should have a right to be free of harassment" can clearly play a role in defining what it means to be better off or worse off, and in any given policy or legal rule choice, the claim that the choice should be governed by the principle can clearly be a claim that, in this setting, our social welfare function is characterized by a reduced form rule: Harassment is wrong, reducing the well-being of all under all states of the world. There is no reason why a social welfare function cannot take the form, "We are all better off in a world free of gender inequality." A social welfare function taking this form simply adopts a view of preferences that reflects the position taken by many welfare economists when struggling with what to do with malevolent preferences, such as a preference for the domination of others; these are not "well-informed" preferences; these are preferences that it would be "welfare-maximizing to change;" or these are "unethical" preferences [for discussions about the nature of preferences, see Brock (1973), Nunan (1981), Hammond (1989)]. And if the social welfare function takes that form, then it is perfectly appropriate—indeed, mathematically elegant, to adopt a core value of neoclassical economics—to evaluate choices not by reference to a full-blown social welfare function but rather by reference to this derived principle. Indeed, this is precisely the strategy of traditional welfare economics and the first welfare theorem: We can proceed without specifying the social welfare function because by this proof we show that maximization of the value of any social welfare function can be obtained merely by following the principle of promoting free and voluntary exchange in markets.

In practice, economists routinely appeal to reduced-form principles of this type, despite the lessons of the second-best theorem that tell them that maximization requires specification of a social welfare function. They routinely judge that those lessons can be ignored and simpler principles used to determine what is social welfare maximizing: reduce transaction costs, create tradeable goods (such as pollution rights), enforce agreements on the terms set by the parties, protect property rights in ideas and inventions, eliminate obstacles to the entry of competitors into a market, etc. This is the stuff of law and economics: the application of reduced-form principles. There is simply no basis for the judgment, no basis that feminist law and economics scholars should accept, for not similarly expecting that the difficult problem of deciding what it means to say people are better or worse off, even within the framework of welfare economics, will also have simple implications for particular legal and policy choices: promote women's autonomy, support investments in caring labor, eliminate gender discrimination in the workplace. A good economist will of course think through whether or not the application of such a principle in a given case will, in fact, lead to worse outcomes; whether poverty, for example, will result from a particular application of a principle that "women's autonomy should be promoted." Indeed, this is precisely the dilemma many feminists struggle with when it comes to determining what the right result might be, for example, in extending the principle of freedom of contract to surrogacy (Hadfield 1995b, 1998a).

But a dilemma feminists do not have to struggle with is the choice between fairness and welfare: Modern welfare economics recognizes that any social choice must be informed by more than purely subjective utility information; it must take into account the underlying qualities of what creates human well-being. As Sen has framed this with respect to feminist concerns in particular:

> There have been many recent investigations of gender inequality and women's deprivation in terms of undernutrition, clinically diagnosed morbidity, observed illiteracy, and even unexpectedly high mortality.... Such interpersonal comparisons can easily be a significant basis of studies of poverty and of inequality between the sexes. They can be accommodated within a broad framework of welfare economics and social choice (enhanced by the removal of informational constraints that would rule out the use of these types of data) (Sen 1999, p. 363).

CONCLUSION

The vast majority of legal debates are among people who take seriously the importance of well-being and who share diverse and rich views about what promotes well-being, in the long- and short-run. It is misguided, and misrepresents modern welfare economics, to suggest that there is a conflict between a commitment to fairness and to well-being, or that a law and economics methodology must be limited to a focus on efficiency and income redistribution. Clearly, conceptions of well-being that encompass claims about the distribution of specific rights and specific goods fall within the domain of economic analysis. The great virtue of doing law and economics is that it emphasizes the need to articulate the effects of legal rules, in the long- and short-run, and to be systematic about exploring the more subtle consequences of legal rules and policies. Economics can help us identify cases when, indeed, we can safely focus on efficiency and material consequences or employ the separability thesis to parcel out our various goals to different legal instruments. Feminists analyzing the desirability of different legal rules should be looking to economic analysis for careful modeling, explicit attention to assumptions, and carefully specified behavioral models. They should be using economic tools to focus on the implications of strategic behavior, information dynamics, and equilibrium forces. They should be doing careful empirical work to describe the phenomena they study and to test the hypotheses they formulate. And they should embrace welfare economics and its explicit attention to the components of a social welfare function. But they should reject the claim that doing welfare economics means doing conventional law and economics, focusing on efficiency and limiting fairness concerns to income distribution, and they should reject the separability thesis when the conditions that make that thesis relevant do not hold, as they do not for many issues of importance in feminist analysis.

Sandra Harding wrote in 1995 that feminist economists should be seeking not to undermine objectivity in economics but rather to promote a stronger form of objectivity (Harding 1995). Doing feminist law and economics should similarly be an exercise not in cutting back on the grounding of our methodology in welfare economics, but rather in embracing the overtly normative nature of that exercise, one that requires, not relinquishes, ethics and politics. As Sen (1999) has observed, as modern welfare economics has evolved, it has drawn closer to moral philosophy, to the effort to say substantively what it means for individuals to enjoy well-being. This is a project feminists in law and economics should also take up as their own.

ACKNOWLEDGMENTS

My thanks to Chris Sanchirico and Andrei Marmor for helpful comments.

The *Annual Review of Law and Social Science* is online at http://lawsocsci.annualreviews.org

LITERATURE CITED

Alstott AL. 1996. Tax policy and feminism: competing goals and institutional choices. *Columbia Law Rev.* 96:2001–81

Arrow KJ. 1951. *Social Choice and Individual Values.* New York: Wiley

Arrow KJ. 1977. Extended sympathy and the possibility of social choice. *Am. Econ. Rev.* 67:219–25

Avraham R, Fortus D, Logue K. 2004. Revisiting the roles of legal rules and tax rules in income redistribution: a response to Kaplow and Shavell. *Iowa Law Rev.* 89:1124–58

Becker G. 1971. *The Economics of Discrimination.* Chicago: Univ. Chicago Press

Bentham J. 1996 (1789). *Introduction to the Principles of Morals and Legislation.* New York: Oxford Univ. Press

Brinig MF. 1995. A maternalistic approach to surrogacy. *Va. Law Rev.* 81:2377–99

Brinig MF. 2000. *From Contract to Covenant: Beyond the Law and Economics of the Family*. Cambridge, MA: Harvard Univ. Press

Brinig MF, Crafton SM. 1994. Marriage and opportunism. *J. Leg. Stud.* 23:869–94

Brock DW. 1973. Recent work in utilitarianism. *Am. Philos. Q.* 10:241–76

Carbone J. 1990. Economics, feminism and the reinvention of alimony: a reply to Ira Ellman. *Vanderbilt Law Rev.* 43:1463–501

Carbone J, Brinig MF. 1991. Rethinking marriage: feminist ideology, economic change, and divorce reform. *Tulane Law Rev.* 65:953–1010

Chang HF. 2000. A liberal theory of social welfare: fairness, utility and the Pareto principle. *Yale Law J.* 110:173–235

Craswell R. 2003. Kaplow and Shavell on the substance of fairness. *J. Leg. Stud.* 32:245–75

Donohue JJ. 1986. Is Title VII efficient? *Univ. Penn. Law Rev.* 134:1411–31

Donohue JJ. 1989. Prohibiting sex discrimination in the workplace: an economic perspective. *Univ. Chicago Law Rev.* 56:1337–68

Dorff MB. 2002. Why welfare depends on fairness: a reply to Kaplow and Shavell. *South. Calif. Law Rev.* 75:847–98

England P, Folbre N. 2003. Contracting for care. See Ferber & Nelson 2003, pp. 61–79

Estin AL. 1995. Economics and the problem of divorce. *Univ. Chicago Law School Roundtable* 2:517–97

Farber DA. 2003. What (if anything) can economics say about equity? *Mich. Law Rev.* 101:1791–823

Ferber MA, Nelson JA. 2003. *Feminist Economics Today: Beyond Economic Man*. Chicago: Univ. Chicago Press

Fineman MA, Dougherty T. 2005. *Feminism Confronts Homo Economicus: Gender, Law and Society*. Ithaca, NY: Cornell Univ. Press

Folbre N. 1994. *Who Pays for the Kids? Gender and the Structures of Constraint*. New York: Routledge

Folbre N. 2003. "Holding hands at midnight": the paradox of caring labor. In *Toward a Feminist Philosophy of Economics*, ed. DK Barker, E Kuiper, pp. 213–30. New York: Routledge

Gilligan C. 1982. *In a Different Voice: Psychological Theory and Women's Development*. Cambridge, MA: Harvard Univ. Press

Hadfield GK. 1993. Households at work: beyond labor market policies to remedy the gender gap. *Georgetown Law J.* 82:89–107

Hadfield GK. 1995a. Rational women: a test for sex-based harassment. *Calif. Law Rev.* 83:1151–89

Hadfield GK. 1995b. The dilemma of choice: a feminist perspective on *The Limits of Freedom of Contract*. *Osgoode Hall Law J.* 33:337–51

Hadfield GK. 1998a. An expressive theory of contract: from feminist dilemmas to a reconceptualization of rational choice in contract law. *Univ. Penn. Law Rev.* 146:1235–85

Hadfield GK. 1998b. Law-and-economics from a feminist perspective. In *The New Palgrave Dictionary of Economics and the Law*, ed. P Newman, 2:455–59. New York: Palgrave Macmillan

Hammond PJ. 1976. Equity, Arrow's conditions, and Rawls' difference principle. *Econometrica* 44:793–804

Hammond PJ. 1989. *Interpersonal comparisons of utility: why and how they are and should be made*. Work. Pap., Dep. Econ., Stanford Univ. http://www.stanford.edu/~hammond/icuSurvey.pdf

Harding S. 1995. Can feminist thought make economics more objective? *Fem. Econ.* 1:7–32

Jolls C. 1998. Behavioral economics analysis of redistributive legal rules. *Vanderbilt Law Rev.* 51:1653–77

Kaplow L, Shavell S. 1994. Why the legal system is less efficient than the income tax in redistributing income. *J. Leg. Stud.* 23:667–81

Kaplow L, Shavell S. 2001. Fairness versus welfare. *Harvard Law Rev.* 114:961–1388

Kornhauser LA. 2003. Preferences, well-being, and morality in social decisions. *J. Leg. Stud.* 32:303–29

Lipsey RG, Lancaster K. 1956. The general theory of the second best. *Rev. Econ. Stud.* 11:11–12

McCaffery EJ. 1997. *Taxing Women.* Chicago: Univ. Chicago Press

McCluskey MT. 2003. Efficiency and social citizenship: challenging the neoliberal attack on the welfare state. *Indiana Law J.* 78:783–876

McDonnell B. 2003. The economists' new arguments. *Minn. Law Rev.* 88:86–118

Noddings N. 1984. *Caring: A Feminine Approach to Ethics and Moral Education.* Berkeley: Univ. Calif. Press

Nunan R. 1981. Harsanyi vs. Sen: Does social welfare weigh subjective preferences? *J. Philos.* 78:586–600

Posner RA. 1989. An economic analysis of sex discrimination laws. *Univ. Chicago Law Rev.* 56:1311–35

Power M. 2004. Social provisioning as a starting point for feminist economics. *Fem. Econ.* 10:3–19

Rawls J. 1971. *A Theory of Justice.* Cambridge, MA: Harvard Univ. Press

Rawls J. 2001. *Justice as Fairness: A Restatement.* Cambridge, MA: Harvard Univ. Press

Rosenbury L. 2003. *Feminist legal scholarship: chartings topics and authors, 1978–2002.* Work. Pap. 03–11–01. Wash. Univ. St. Louis, Law School

Sanchirico CW. 2000. Exchange: should legal rules be used to redistribute wealth? Taxes versus legal rules as instruments for equity: a more equitable view. *J. Leg. Stud.* 29:797–820

Sanchirico CW. 2001. Deconstructing the new efficiency rationale. *Cornell Law Rev.* 86:1003–89

Sarra J. 2002. The gendered implications of corporate governance change. *Seattle J. Soc. Just.* 1:457–97

Sen A. 1985. *Social Choice and Justice*: a review article. *J. Econ. Lit.* 23:1764–76

Sen A. 1999. The possibility of social choice. *Am. Econ. Rev.* 89:349–78

Shavell S. 1981. A note on efficiency vs. distributional equity in legal rulemaking: should distributional equity matter given optimal income taxation? *Am. Econ. Rev.* 71:414–18

Singer JB. 1994. Alimony and efficiency: the gendered costs and benefits of the economic justification for alimony. *Georgetown Law J.* 82:2423–60

Staudt NC. 1996. Taxing housework. *Georgetown Law J.* 84:1571–647

Taylor R. 1998. The ethic of care versus the ethic of justice: an economic analysis. *J. Socio-Econ.* 27:479–93

Trebilcock MJ. 1993. *The Limits of Freedom of Contract.* Cambridge, MA: Harvard Univ. Press

Tronto JC. 1993. *Moral Boundaries: A Political Argument for an Ethic of Care.* New York: Routledge

Waldron J. 2003. Locating distribution. *J. Leg. Stud.* 32:277–301

Annu. Rev. Law Soc. Sci. 2005. 1:307–22
doi: 10.1146/annurev.lawsocsci.1.041604.115840
Copyright © 2005 by Annual Reviews. All rights reserved
First published online as a Review in Advance on August 9, 2005

CRIMINAL DISENFRANCHISEMENT

Christopher Uggen,[1] Angela Behrens,[1] and Jeff Manza[2]

[1]Department of Sociology, University of Minnesota, Minneapolis, Minnesota 55455;
[2]Department of Sociology, Northwestern University, Evanston, Illinois 60208-1330;
email: uggen@atlas.socsci.umn.edu, behr0055@umn.edu, manza@northwestern.edu

Key Words voting, felony, suffrage, punishment

■ **Abstract** Felon disenfranchisement has recently emerged as an issue of intense public concern and scholarly interest. This review highlights the broad range of socio-legal issues implicated by the practice of denying convicted felons the right to vote by considering the history, impact, and contemporary legal and scholarly debates surrounding the practice. Although race-neutral on their face, many U.S. laws stem from a history of racial discrimination and serve as an example of advantaged groups using the law as a mechanism to control disadvantaged groups. The practice of disenfranchising criminals has survived numerous legal challenges, raising questions about the fundamental nature of the right to vote in the United States and the representativeness of a democracy that systematically excludes a large group of citizens.

INTRODUCTION

Felon disenfranchisement, the practice of removing the right to vote upon conviction for a felony-level offense, highlights a broad set of issues in socio-legal studies. The case of felon voting restrictions in the United States shows how one set of legal practices cuts across a wide range of topics. For example, felon disenfranchisement laws have played a role in the country's racialized history and in recent elections. Moreover, U.S. practices are distinct internationally for their severity. Disenfranchising criminal offenders is also linked to mass incarceration, and the practice exemplifies a larger set of collateral consequences that follow a conviction. Finally, these laws raise questions about the status of voting as a right of all adult citizens. Our review of recent developments in the law and social science literature on felon disenfranchisement emphasizes both legal and political implications of the practice.

In the United States, 48 states currently limit voting rights on the basis of a felony conviction, but states exhibit large variation concerning the length of their bar on voting. State laws range from indefinite disenfranchisement that extends beyond completion of any criminal sentence to no disenfranchisement whatsoever. Only Maine and Vermont currently allow all people convicted of felonies to vote, including those serving time in prison. At the other extreme, 13 states disenfranchise some or all ex-felons (people who have completed a sentence for a felony

1550-3585/05/1209-0307$20.00   **307**

conviction). The constitutionality and validity of these laws have been questioned repeatedly, primarily as an infringement upon the fundamental right to vote and as a mechanism that dilutes or denies the right to vote on the basis of race. While many other democratic countries have some form of disenfranchisement related to criminal convictions, the severity of American disenfranchisement laws stands as an anomaly against the international norm, both substantively and procedurally (Demleitner 2000, Rottinghaus 2003).

At present, felon disenfranchisement laws account for over 5 million people in the United States who cannot vote (Manza & Uggen 2005). This is the largest group of disenfranchised adult American citizens (Keyssar 2000). Of the estimated 5.3 million disenfranchised felons in 2004, only 26%, or 1.4 million, were actually in prison or in jail. The rest were either living in their communities as felony probationers (1.3 million or 25% of the total), parolees (477,000 or 9%), or as *former* felons who reside in states in which they are ineligible to vote (2 million, or 39%).

Together, these disenfranchised citizens represent more than 2% of the voting-age population and hold the power to affect election outcomes in close races (Uggen & Manza 2002). Historically, states have not always disenfranchised for a felony conviction with such zeal, as the key developments in these laws occurred during the late nineteenth century.

THE INSTITUTIONALIZATION OF FELON DISENFRANCHISEMENT IN THE UNITED STATES

American felon disenfranchisement laws date to colonial times and have roots in European laws (Ewald 2002a, Itzkowitz & Oldak 1973). Colonial disenfranchisement laws in the United States were limited in scope as to both the length of disenfranchisement and the range of offenses precipitating the loss of voting rights (Ewald 2002a). Rather than serving as a consequence to the equivalent of a modern-day felony, voting rights were generally restricted for "moral" violations, such as drunkenness. Offenses such as electoral bribery resulted in the permanent loss of voting rights in some states, whereas the loss was temporary for other acts (Ewald 2002a).

Throughout the nineteenth and early twentieth centuries, more states began to tie voting rights to criminal convictions (Behrens et al. 2003). These provisions, however, still limited the loss of voting rights, either by applying to few crimes or by only empowering the state legislature to pass a disenfranchisement law. It was not until the end of the nineteenth century that it became common practice for states to disenfranchise based solely on a felony conviction. The Reconstruction period was one of particular change. Between 1865 and 1900, 19 states adopted or amended laws restricting the voting rights of criminal offenders (Manza & Uggen 2005). Many states added provisions to new or revised state constitutions, while legislatures in other states passed new laws. Compared to the disenfranchisement laws of the colonial period, these new laws were wide reaching, encompassing all felonies without attention to the underlying crime and disenfranchising indefinitely (Behrens et al. 2003).

Because most states already had the most restrictive form of disenfranchisement in place by the early twentieth century, the development of felon disenfranchisement in this century was primarily an issue of numbers rather than legal changes. In fact, the tide had begun to turn by the Civil Rights era. Over the past 40 years, restrictions on the voting rights of felons have diminished significantly. A wave of liberalizing changes began in the early 1960s and stretched through the mid-1970s. In this period, 17 states eliminated their ex-felon disenfranchisement laws, restoring voting rights automatically upon completion of one's sentence (Behrens et al. 2003). Nevertheless, the development of the criminal justice system (Friedman 1993), the expansion of offenses deemed felonies (e.g., Itzkowitz & Oldak 1973), and the historically unprecedented escalation of criminal punishment in the United States in the past 30 years (e.g., Pettit & Western 2004) all contributed to increases in the size of the disenfranchised population even as the laws became less restrictive.

WHY CONNECT VOTING TO CRIMINAL PUNISHMENT?

Explanations for stripping voting rights on the basis of a felony conviction vary, and many scholars question the legality of this long-standing practice. The loss of voting rights is not the only collateral consequence imposed for a criminal conviction (Mauer & Chesney-Lind 2002), and some supporters of felon disenfranchisement use this point to justify coupling punishment and voting rights; disenfranchisement, they argue, is no different than restricting the right to own a firearm or to work in certain occupations (Clegg 2004a,b; Ponte 2003; Sloan 2000). These arguments generally follow a social contract approach: A criminal act is a breach of the social contract, and a person should consequently lose the right to participate in electing the officials who make the law. Excluding those who have shown themselves to be untrustworthy thus protects the integrity of the ballot box (Clegg 2001). This rationale resembles that found in ancient Greece and Rome and later in medieval Europe in which "civil death" penalties accompanied criminal punishment (Ewald 2002a, Pettus 2005). Viewed in this light, the criminal code is a narrowly crafted expression of societal consensus against crime, whereby violation of that code justifies the loss of certain civil rights.

Alternatively, many scholars have viewed the connection between voting and crime as a product of group conflict rather than societal consensus. From this perspective, the history of felon disenfranchisement in the United States exemplifies a trend in which advantaged groups with powerful interests use law as a tool to maintain their dominant position. This has been argued particularly with respect to racial inequality, as evidenced by the disproportionate share of disenfranchised African American voters (Hench 1998, Shapiro 1993).

Opponents of disenfranchisement also argue that it is an unconstitutional practice that infringes upon the fundamental right to vote. Categorically denying the right to vote to former as well as current offenders is certainly out of step with the international consensus, and further, it may impede ex-felons' reintegration into society (Demleitner 2000, Fletcher 1999, Itzkowitz & Oldak 1973, Uggen et al. 2004, Uggen & Manza 2004b).

The Penological Rationale for Disenfranchisement

Because it operates as a sanction tied to a criminal offense, felon disenfranchisement should serve some purpose related to punishment. Disenfranchisement appears to have been initially premised upon both retributive and deterrence theories. In earlier periods, small communities could impose disenfranchisement as a public sanction whereby all would see the stigma and exclusion resulting from unlawful behavior (Itzkowitz & Oldak 1973).

A recent *amici curiae* brief signed by 20 criminologists in a challenge to New Jersey's disenfranchisement law, however, rejects the idea that disenfranchisement serves any of the legitimate purposes of punishment (Brief for *Amici Curiae* 2004; see also von Hirsch & Wasik 1997). We consider felon disenfranchisement in light of four of the primary justifications of punishment: (*a*) to exact retribution or vengeance for the victims; (*b*) to deter offenders and others from committing crimes; (*c*) to incapacitate or prevent them from committing further crimes; and (*d*) to rehabilitate or reform offenders.

RETRIBUTION   Retribution is based on the principle that those who have committed crimes should suffer for the harm they caused others. Proponents of retribution argue that punishment should fit the crime already committed rather than future crimes that the person or others might commit (von Hirsch 1976). Retribution thus demands sanctions proportionate to the seriousness of the offense and to the degree of the offender's culpability. More blameworthy offenders who cause greater harm should thus face greater punishment. Felon disenfranchisement is retributive because the denial of voting rights exacts some degree of vengeance from felons. The blanket disenfranchisement of all people convicted of felonies, however, calls into question the proportionality of the punishment. Moreover, losing the right to vote is a collateral sanction: It is imposed in addition to the criminal sentence. Particularly in states with lifetime disenfranchisement, this punishment extends far beyond the sentence for past criminal conduct. In most cases, disenfranchisement thus does not appear to fit the crime committed.

DETERRENCE   Whereas retribution redresses crime already committed, deterrence focuses on preventing future crime by either the offender or others. Specific deterrence seeks to deter the individual offender from committing another crime. General deterrence, on the other hand, seeks to dissuade the general public from engaging in crime. Felon disenfranchisement could hypothetically serve either deterrent purpose, especially because some people attach great significance to the right to vote (Uggen & Manza 2004a). For a deterrent to be effective, however, the consequences must be known to would-be offenders when they are contemplating committing a crime. In the case of felon disenfranchisement, this seems improbable for several reasons. First, most people are uncertain about when and where voting restrictions are imposed (Manza & Uggen 2005). Second, the marginal deterrent value of disenfranchisement over and above that of more immediate and severe penalties may be insufficient to significantly alter the criminal calculus. Even if people know they will forfeit voting rights if apprehended and convicted, this loss likely pales in comparison to the wholesale deprivations that accompany incarceration (see, e.g., Sykes 1958).

INCAPACITATION   Incapacitation involves reducing or eliminating the opportunity to commit subsequent offenses by restraining or isolating offenders (Cohen 1987). Today, this typically involves institutional confinement, although in the past bodily mutilation and death were also widely used. It is difficult to justify felon disenfranchisement with the argument that it incapacitates ex-felons from committing general crimes or election crimes specifically. First, disenfranchisement affects only a narrow range of activities. Thus, removing the right to vote cannot prevent people from committing other crimes unrelated to voting. Second, even for the few convicted of political crimes such as electoral fraud, the ability of felon disenfranchisement to prevent repeat offending is questionable. People convicted of making illegal campaign contributions, for example, would not be restrained from doing it again by restricting their right to vote on election day. In short, although disenfranchisement prevents individuals from voting, it cannot incapacitate them from committing crime. It prevents political participation, but not criminal activity.

REHABILITATION   The final major goal of punishment is to rehabilitate offenders so that they will not commit crimes in the future. During the "get tough" period in penology that began in the mid-1970s, critics successfully challenged the legitimacy and effectiveness of rehabilitation as a correctional philosophy (see, e.g., Martinson 1974). More recently, however, criminologists have reaffirmed rehabilitation, challenging the "nothing works" dictum and developing new evidence that certain treatments, such as cognitive-behavioral therapy, reduce recidivism (Cullen 2005, Lin 2000). Disenfranchisement might be rehabilitative if reenfranchisement served as a reward for good behavior. Yet restoration of voting rights is rarely conditioned on good behavior. Instead, it is triggered automatically when a sentence is completed or a waiting period has passed. The reward logic is perhaps most plausible in states disenfranchising offenders indefinitely (such as Florida), but in many such states restoration procedures are so cumbersome as to diminish any possible rehabilitative goal.

More generally, there are several reasons to conclude that restricting voting rights hinders rehabilitative efforts to bring about positive changes in offenders and their behavior. Indeed, it is likely that invisible punishments such as disenfranchisement act as barriers to successful rehabilitation (Travis 2002). It is much more plausible to think that participation in elections as stakeholders might reduce recidivism. As a fundamental act of citizenship, voting may foster respect for laws, criminal and otherwise, and the institutions that make and enforce them. One Minnesota study considered the relationship between voting in 1996 and subsequent criminal history. Among people with an arrest history, about 27% of nonvoters were rearrested, relative to 12% of voters in the sample. These results suggest that there is at least a correlation between voting in 1996 and recidivism in 1997–2000 among people who have had some official contact with the criminal justice system (Uggen & Manza 2004a).

In short, disenfranchisement is only loosely related to the justifications of punishment typically associated with criminal sanctions. Although critics find little justification for felon disenfranchisement, however, proponents offer numerous defenses of the practice.

Other Justifications for Disenfranchisement

One set of arguments in support of felon disenfranchisement relates to maintaining what is sometimes referred to as "the purity of the ballot box" (*Washington v. State* 1884). In the philosophical arguments associated with the republican tradition, for example, the political community remains viable only insofar as it consists of citizens who respect the rules of democratic procedure and can be expected to live within the norms those rules generate. In contemporary variants of these arguments, the presence of criminals within the polity potentially erodes confidence in elections by contaminating clean votes with "dirty" ones. Kentucky Senator Mitch McConnell invoked this idea during a 2002 debate in the U.S. Senate over disenfranchisement: "States have a significant interest in reserving the vote for those who have abided by the social contract that forms the foundation of representative democracy.... [T]hose who break our laws should not dilute the votes of law-abiding citizens" (*Congressional Record* 2002, p. S802).

A second set of arguments concerns the impact of allowing people convicted of felonies to vote. Having exhibited a propensity to violate the social contract on at least one previous occasion, these arguments suggest, felons cannot be trusted to exercise the franchise responsibly. In the Senate debate over proposed legislation to reenfranchise people who had completed their sentences, Senator McConnell argued that, among other things, removing disenfranchisement could lead to "'jailhouse blocs' banding together to oust sheriffs and government officials who are tough on crime" (*Congressional Record* 2002, p. S802).

A related justification concerns fraud, which might be expected among those convicted of political crimes (e.g., vote fraud, campaign finance fraud). These offenders represent a very small proportion of all convicted felons, however, and it is hard to find systematic evidence that serial political offenders constitute a significant actual or potential threat. For the great bulk of criminal offenders who have not been convicted of political offenses, the claim that they could or would "band together" to use the ballot improperly to scale back criminal laws, elect weak-on-crime sheriffs, or generally skew electoral results is, to put it charitably, an unproved hypothesis. There are two possible interpretations of these claims: (*a*) Nonpolitical offenders are more likely to commit vote fraud than nonoffenders, or (*b*) offenders would band together to vote a certain way that would produce an improper outcome of some kind. To our knowledge, no empirical evidence supports either interpretation. Moreover, such arguments are problematic in a democratic polity, where the right to vote is not premised on how one plans to vote.

Defenses of disenfranchisement laws based on states' rights arguments are probably the most widely deployed approaches. The argument is straightforward: The Constitution vests the states with the right to decide who can vote, and but for the explicit exceptions spelled out in various constitutional amendments, states are free to decide which criteria they want to use. Supporters of these arguments are on firm legal ground based on judicial decisions to date. As discussed below, the Supreme Court has held that states can restrict the right to vote on the basis of a felony conviction. Supporters have pointed to the diversity of state felon disenfranchisement laws to assert that in practice each state adopts laws consistent with the political ideology of its citizens. For example, Alabama Senator Jeff Sessions asserted in a U.S. Senate debate, "I think this Congress, with this little debate we are having on this bill, ought not to step in and, with a big sledge hammer, smash something we have had from the beginning of this country's foundation—a set of election law in every State in America. . . . To just up and do that is disrespectful to them" (*Congressional Record* 2002, p. S803). Critics challenge this view by noting that states' rights arguments have historically been invoked to justify continuing racially discriminatory practices. In fact, many commentators have suggested that the origins and persistence of felon disenfranchisement in the United States are tied to their racial origins and contemporary racial impact (Harvey 1994, Hench 1998).

Race and Disenfranchisement

Felon disenfranchisement laws are race-neutral on their face; anyone convicted of a felony faces disenfranchisement. Although this fact is key for some scholars (e.g., Clegg 2001, 2004a) and central for many courts [e.g., *Wesley v. Collins* (1986); *Johnson v. Bush* (2004); *Farrakhan v. Locke* (1997)], the historical and social circumstances surrounding felon disenfranchisement indicate that the practice is closely linked to race (Behrens et al. 2003, Harvey 1994, Hench 1998). That felon disenfranchisement laws began to flourish in the late nineteenth century is unsurprising to many given the disparate impact of the laws on racial minorities, particularly African Americans. In the 2004 presidential election, for example, over 8% of the African American voting-age population was disenfranchised because of a past felony conviction (compared to less than 2% of the non–African American voting-age population) (Manza & Uggen 2005).

Until the adoption of the Fourteenth and Fifteenth Amendments, states were generally free to impose conditions on the right to vote or even to wholly exclude particular groups from voting (Keyssar 2000). In 1868, the Fourteenth Amendment extended citizenship to all persons born in the United States, regardless of race, thus nullifying the Supreme Court's infamous holding a decade earlier in *Dred Scott* (*Scott v. Sandford* 1856). The Fifteenth Amendment, added two years later in 1870, eliminated states' right to disenfranchise on the basis of race. Thus, during this period, states potentially lost significant power with respect to controlling access to the ballot.

In 1850, 11 of the 32 existing states disenfranchised for a felony conviction. In contrast, by the time of the Fifteenth Amendment in 1870, 28 of the then 38 states had done so (Behrens et al. 2003). States' attempts to undermine the Fourteenth and Fifteenth Amendments by effectively preventing African Americans from voting have been well documented (e.g., Kousser 1974; Perman 2001; US Comm. Civil Rights 1975, 1981; Vallely 2004). Felon disenfranchisement can therefore be viewed as yet another attempt to limit the pool of eligible voters to advantaged groups (e.g., Chin 2002a, Fletcher 1999, Harvey 1994, Hench 1998, Shapiro 1993). In keeping with this view, a study of historical changes to state felon disenfranchisement laws between 1850 and 2002 found that the percentage of nonwhite persons incarcerated in a state's prison system was a strong and consistent predictor of passage of a more restrictive disenfranchisement law (Behrens et al. 2003).

LEGAL CHALLENGES TO FELON DISENFRANCHISEMENT LAWS

Felon disenfranchisement in the United States thus developed in a way that saw powerful groups taking a narrowly defined practice in ancient Europe and colonial America and broadening it to suppress perceived threats to power as historically disadvantaged groups gained legal rights. Following the Civil War, the Fourteenth Amendment forced states to choose between extending suffrage to all males or losing some congressional representation. In creating this choice, Section Two of the amendment made an exception for states that disenfranchised males "for participation in rebellion, or other crime." It is this phrase that the Supreme Court relied upon to uphold the practice of excluding persons with felony convictions from voting.

In *Richardson v. Ramirez* (1974), the principal Supreme Court case addressing felon disenfranchisement, the Court held that Section Two of the amendment amounted to an "affirmative sanction" of felon disenfranchisement. Despite upholding the practice, the Supreme Court carved out an exception a decade later in *Hunter v. Underwood* (1985). In *Hunter*, the Court invalidated Alabama's disenfranchisement law because of the clear record evidencing a racially discriminatory intent when an all-white constitutional convention passed a restriction in 1901 (State of Alabama 1901).

In the 1960s, the Warren Court repeatedly expounded the fundamental nature of the right to vote and invalidated numerous restrictions on that right [e.g., *Kramer v. Union Free School District* (1969), *Reynolds v. Sims* (1964), *South Carolina v. Katzenbach* (1966)]. Despite this strong precedent, felon disenfranchisement has eluded the same fate as other restrictions on the right to vote. The legality of the entire practice rests primarily on the *Ramirez* decision. The decision has been the subject of much criticism, and the jurisprudence and scholarship that have developed in the area continue to raise a key question: How do these laws persist when they limit a fundamental right, they are the product of a racially discriminatory history, and they are markedly out of step with international practices and American public opinion?

Challenging Disenfranchisement Under the Equal Protection Clause

Challenges to felon disenfranchisement laws since *Ramirez* have been mostly unsuccessful, as courts have found the topic to be a settled issue. In cases using the equal protection clause and the status of voting as a fundamental right to challenge the overall validity of disenfranchising, courts generally cite *Ramirez* and *Hunter* with little additional analysis [e.g., *Cotton v. Fordice* (1998), *Owen v. Barnes* (1983), *Woodruff v. Wyoming* (2002)].

Other challenges have attempted to use *Hunter* and allege a discriminatory intent on the part of the state actors who enacted a felon disenfranchisement law. These challenges, however, have not been successful since *Hunter* because discriminatory intent is difficult to prove and few cases provide a record as clear as that of the Alabama law adopted in 1901 (e.g., *Wesley v. Collins* 1986). Further, despite acknowledging the existence of a discriminatory intent at the time a felon disenfranchisement law was originally passed, a few courts have held that the taint of such an intent was removed because later legislatures had retained the law (e.g., *Cotton v. Fordice* 1998; cf. Chin 2002b).

Challenging Disenfranchisement Under the Voting Rights Act

Race-based challenges to felon disenfranchisement laws have produced more variation in judicial analysis but have also yielded few changes to the laws thus far. These challenges are generally based on the Fifteenth Amendment or Section Two of the Voting Rights Act (VRA) of 1965 and assert that disenfranchisement laws serve either to dilute or to deny the right to vote on the basis of race. Congress passed the VRA with the intent to enforce the Fifteenth Amendment and "banish the blight of racial discrimination in voting" (*South Carolina v. Katzenbach* 1966). The VRA, as amended in 1982, requires courts to analyze all voting-related claims of racial discrimination using a results-based test that considers the "totality of the circumstances." The original VRA required evidence of a discriminatory intent (*City of Mobile v. Bolden* 1965), but the ineffectiveness of this standard (e.g., US Comm. Civil Rights 1975, 1981) prompted the 1982 amendment.

Given the history of felon disenfranchisement, the VRA test would at first appear to provide a good fit for felon disenfranchisement laws. Using it, however, has thus far proved to be an uphill battle. Courts have either held that Congress did not intend for the VRA to apply to felon disenfranchisement and it therefore cannot be used to challenge the laws (e.g., *Muntaquim v. Coombe* 2004) or they have been unsympathetic to arguments considering historical racial discrimination and continuing discrimination in state criminal justice systems (e.g., *Wesley v. Collins* 1986).

A 2003 decision by the Ninth Circuit recognized the importance of considering historical and social circumstances when evaluating felon disenfranchisement. In *Farrakhan v. Washington* (2003), the plaintiffs asserted that the combination of disenfranchisement and racial disparities in Washington's criminal justice system served to deny the right to vote on the basis of race. The district court refused to consider the disparities as part of the totality of the circumstances. Instead, the court looked only at the text of the state's law, which prohibits people who have completed their sentences from voting. This, the Ninth Circuit held, was an error (*Farrakhan v. Washington* 2003). The court noted that a VRA analysis must consider "how a challenged voting practice *interacts with* external factors such as 'social and historical conditions' to result in denial of the right to vote on account of race or color" [*Farrakhan v. Washington* (2003) at 1011–12, quoting *Thornburg v. Gingles* (1986)]. The legal consequences of this type of analysis remain to be seen. Although a panel of the Eleventh Circuit agreed with the Ninth Circuit in a challenge to Florida's disenfranchisement law, that decision was vacated, and, en banc, the court ultimately upheld Florida's disenfranchisement of people who have completed their sentences (*Johnson v. Governor* 2005).

Felon disenfranchisement has also been challenged under a host of other constitutional provisions. For the most part, however, these claims have been unsuccessful. The practice has been challenged under the First Amendment as an infringement upon the right of political speech (e.g., *Johnson v. Bush* 2004; Winkler 1993), under the Eighth Amendment as cruel and unusual punishment [e.g., *Woodruff v. Wyoming* (2002) at 201; *Farrakhan v. Locke* (1997) at 1307; *McLaughlin v. City of Canton* (1995); Karlan (2004); Thompson (2002)], and under the Twenty-Fourth Amendment as a poll tax [for states charging an application fee to apply for restoration of voting rights; *Johnson v. Bush* (2004) at 1292; Mondesire (2001)].

Critiquing Judicial Review of Felon Disenfranchisement

Courts' approaches to analyzing felon disenfranchisement laws elicit two main critiques: First, the Supreme Court's reliance on Section Two of the Fourteenth Amendment in *Richardson v. Ramirez* (1974) was wrong, and its interpretation of the provision is problematic; and second, with regard to race-based claims, courts are incorrect to insist that the laws bear no relation to race. This latter critique exemplifies differences between legal and sociological understandings of causality. Whereas the legal field often disengages law from historical and social circumstance, sociologists draw upon probabilistic notions of causation and look to patterns of statistical associations in populations.

Because of the basis on which the *Ramirez* Court upheld the constitutionality of felon disenfranchisement, the validity of the practice (from a legal perspective) hinges on the meaning of Section Two of the Fourteenth Amendment. Voting is considered a fundamental right, and laws that limit the right to vote are generally subjected to a strict scrutiny standard of review, which requires a compelling state interest and narrowly tailored means to attain that interest (e.g., *Reynolds v. Sims* 1964). Thus, without Section Two, laws limiting the right to vote on the basis of a felony conviction would be subjected to the same analytical scrutiny as other voting rights cases.

The *Ramirez* Court's reliance on Section Two has been heavily criticized, with most following Justice Thurgood Marshall's dissent, which accused the Court of an "unsound historical analysis" [*Richardson v. Ramirez* (1974) at 56, J. Marshall, dissenting; Fletcher (1999), Tribe (1988)]. The Court used a narrow textualist approach in reaching its conclusion that the reference to "other crime" encompassed felonies. The Court commented that "how it became part of the Amendment is less important than what it says and what it means" [*Richardson v. Ramirez* (1974) at 26]. The Court therefore took the phrase "or other crime" on its face to support felon disenfranchisement laws and to remove them from a traditional voting rights analysis. The Court also pointed to extant state felon disenfranchisement laws at the time the Fourteenth Amendment was passed; if states were admitted to the Union with these laws intact, the Court reasoned, then the laws must not have been contrary to the meaning of the Fourteenth Amendment [*Richardson v. Ramirez* (1974) at 48–49].

A common critique of the Court's position is that Section Two of the Fourteenth Amendment itself no longer carries any force. Its purpose was to enfranchise African Americans, a feat accomplished with the addition of the Fifteenth Amendment just two years after the Fourteenth Amendment took effect (e.g., Chin 2004, Flack 1908). As one scholar has stated, the goal of Section Two was to create a dilemma for southern states, forcing them either to "give blacks the vote (an unthinkable choice) or lose representation in Congress (an unacceptable choice)" (Bond 1997, p. 123). The history concerning the addition of "or other crime" to Section Two is not well documented, but given the Civil War context, the most likely targets of the phrase were former Confederate soldiers (Itzkowitz & Oldak 1973).

In short, Section Two had a limited historical purpose that was accomplished by the adoption of the Fifteenth Amendment, an amendment that some argue repealed Section Two (Chin 2004, Flack 1908). Moreover, even during those two intervening years, Section Two's threat of reduced representation was rarely enforced: "[D]espite its sweeping language, Section 2 turned out to be toothless because neither Congress nor the courts ever showed themselves willing to pull the trigger, despite roughly a century of black disenfranchisement in the South" (Karlan 2001, p. 596, footnote 26).

Courts' dismissals of a connection between race and felon disenfranchisement have similarly garnered criticism. These criticisms charge that it is not difficult to link the two issues and that legal protections should bar this form of disenfranchisement. From this perspective, the passage of the VRA and its 1982 amendments demonstrate that the Fourteenth and Fifteenth Amendments alone were not enough to eliminate discrimination in the voting context. States used a range of other tactics that operated to maintain a selective electorate, despite seeming racial neutrality (e.g., poll taxes and literacy tests). Felon disenfranchisement laws developed at the same time as many of these practices, and critics argue that the laws similarly do not operate in a race-neutral way (e.g., Behrens 2004, Harvey 1994, Hench 1998). Racial disparities exist at nearly every stage of the criminal justice system, ranging from stereotypes about who commits crime, to arrest rates, and, most notably, to incarceration rates (e.g., Mauer 1999, Pettit & Western 2004). Thus, when disenfranchisement results from a felony conviction, its primary effect is to disproportionately deny or dilute the voting power of minority groups.

THE IMPACT OF FELON DISENFRANCHISEMENT

The effects of felon disenfranchisement are far reaching, and the practice has an impact on a wide range of social institutions beyond law. Changes within the criminal justice system, such as the trend toward greater incarceration and get tough approaches to crime, have resulted in the exclusion of an increasingly large segment of the population from the electorate. This exclusion, in turn, results in even further marginalization of those groups whose voting strength is diluted by the practice.

The size of the disenfranchised population has grown to a point such that it now holds the power to change the outcomes of closely contested elections. One study indicates that but for felon disenfranchisement laws, seven races for seats in the United States Senate would have turned out differently, which would have also changed the overall partisan composition of Congress during the 1990s (Uggen & Manza 2002). Similarly, the 2000 presidential election was decided by 537 votes in the state of Florida (Federal Election Commission 2001). If the state had permitted to vote only those persons who had completed their sentences and were no longer under any correctional supervision, Al Gore would likely have defeated George W. Bush by a margin of at least 30,000 votes (Uggen & Manza 2002), thus changing the overall outcome of the election.

The existence of felon disenfranchisement laws affects elections in other ways as well. Press reports suggest that many election officials are unaware of their state's laws and mistakenly believe that a felony conviction in any state permanently removes the right to vote (e.g., Hoffman 2003). Similarly, many people with felony convictions mistakenly believe they can never vote again (e.g., Frosch 2004, Manza & Uggen 2005, McCain 2004, Witkowsky 2004). These problems point to an additional aspect of disenfranchisement: The size of the disenfranchised population that is practically (as opposed to legally) disenfranchised may be much larger when accounting for misinformation and other practical concerns, such as people in jail (either awaiting trial or serving a misdemeanor sentence) who do not have ready access to a polling place or absentee ballots (Kalogeras 2003). Finally, removing approximately 5 million mostly low-income citizens from the electorate is likely to have shifted the positions of the major parties on many issues. For example, it is easier to disregard the concerns of low-income voters on economic issues when millions of such voters are legally disenfranchised.

INTERNATIONAL PRACTICES AND PUBLIC SUPPORT FOR FELON DISENFRANCHISEMENT

The United States is not alone in disenfranchising people as a consequence for a felony conviction. American practices of disenfranchisement, however, are distinct for their scope and severity. Many nations specifically provide for the right of incarcerated persons to vote, but others restrict the voting rights of prisoners only under specific circumstances, such as conviction for election tampering or treason (Demleitner 2000, Ewald 2002b, Manfredi 1998, Rottinghaus 2003). Of the few countries that disenfranchise nonincarcerated persons, most automatically restore voting rights after a waiting period that commences upon release from prison (Rottinghaus 2003). With the exception of Belgium, the United States stands alone in disenfranchising large numbers of nonincarcerated persons for lengthy or indefinite periods (Rottinghaus 2003).

Within the United States, most forms of felon disenfranchisement do not enjoy widespread support. One survey found that 80% of people polled oppose disenfranchising people who have completed their sentences (Manza et al. 2004). Experimental manipulations varying the type of conviction have shown that support diminishes depending on the seriousness of the crime the person committed, but nevertheless a majority support reenfranchisement upon release, even for serious crimes. Similarly, a clear majority support voting rights for probationers and parolees. Approval diminishes, however, with respect to prisoners; less than one third responded that prisoners should be able to vote (Manza et al. 2004, Pinaire et al. 2003).

CONCLUSION

Felon disenfranchisement laws have a long history and a continuing impact on electoral politics. In the United States these laws emerged from conflicts based on race and power as they presented an indirect but effective way to quell the threat of an expanded electorate. For many years, the practice went unquestioned, but a rising movement and burgeoning scholarly literature have critically examined this important exception to the taken-for-granted right to vote in the United States. Although social movements and legal reforms during the Civil Rights era led many states to amend their laws to a less restrictive regime, no state has ever wholly abolished a felon disenfranchisement law. Moreover, the widespread nature of the practice continues to exert dramatic and wide-ranging effects that change the tenor of the political climate in the United States.

The *Annual Review of Law and Social Science* is online at
http://lawsocsci.annualreviews.org

LITERATURE CITED

Behrens A. 2004. Voting—not quite a fundamental right? A look at legal and legislative challenges to felon disfranchisement laws. *Minn. Law Rev.* 89:231–75

Behrens A, Uggen C, Manza J. 2003. Ballot manipulation and the "menace of Negro domination": racial threat and felon disenfranchisement laws in the United States, 1850–2002. *Am. J. Sociol.* 109:559–605

Bond JE. 1997. *No Easy Walk to Freedom: Reconstruction and the Ratification of the Fourteenth Amendment.* Westport, CT: Praeger. 312 pp.

Brief for *Amici Curiae* at 9–33, *NAACP v. Harvey*, No. A-6881–03T5, N.J. Super. Ct. App. Div., filed Dec. 15, 2004

Chin GJ. 2002a. Race, the war on drugs, and the collateral consequences of criminal conviction. *J. Gender Race Justice* 6:253–75

Chin GJ. 2002b. Rehabilitating unconstitutional statutes: an analysis of *Cotton v. Fordice*, 157 F.3d 388 (5th Cir. 1998). *Univ. Cinn. Law Rev.* 71:421–55

Chin GJ. 2004. Reconstruction, felon disenfranchisement, and the right to vote: Did the Fifteenth Amendment repeal Section Two of the Fourteenth? *Georgetown Law J.* 92:259–316

City of Mobile v. Bolden, 446 U.S. 55 (1965)

Clegg R. 2001. Who should vote? *Tex Rev. Law Polit.* 6:159–78

Clegg R. 2004a. Perps and politics: why felons can't vote. *Natl. Rev. Online*, Oct. 18. http://www.nationalreview.com/clegg/clegg 200410180844.asp

Clegg R. 2004b. Should ex-felons be allowed to vote? *Leg. Aff.* http://www.legalaffairs.org/ webexclusive/debateclub_disenfranchisemen t1104.html

Cohen J. 1987. The incapacitation effect of imprisonment: a critical review of the literature. In *Deterrence and Incapacitation: Estimating the Effects of Criminal Sanctions on Crime Rates: Report of the National Research Council Panel on Research on Deterrent and Incapacitative Effects*, ed. A Blumstein, J Cohen, D Nagin, pp. 187–243. Washington, DC: Natl. Acad. Sci.

Congressional Record. 2002. 107th Congr., 2nd sess., Vol. 148. Debate on Equal Protection of Voting Rights Act of 2001, Feb. 14, pp. S797–809

Cotton v. Fordice, 157 F.3d 388 (5th Cir. 1998)

Cullen FT. 2005. The twelve people who saved rehabilitation: how the science of criminology made a difference. *Criminology* 43:1–42

Demleitner NV. 2000. Continuing payment on one's debt to society: the German model of felon disenfranchisement as an alternative. *Minn. Law Rev.* 84:753–804

Ewald AC. 2002a. "Civil death": the ideological paradox of criminal disenfranchisement law in the United States. *Wis. Law Rev.* 2002:1045–137

Ewald AC. 2002b. *Of constitutions, politics, and punishment: criminal disenfranchisement law in comparative context.* Presented at Annu. Meet. Am. Polit. Sci. Assoc., Boston, Aug 29–Sept. 1

Farrakhan v. Locke, 987 F. Supp. 1304 (E.D. Wash. 1997)

Farrakhan v. Washington, 338 F.3d 1009 (9th Cir. 2003), *cert. denied sub nom. Locke v. Farrakhan*, 125 S.Ct. 477 (U.S. Nov. 8, 2004) (No. 03–1597)

Federal Election Commission. 2001. *Federal Elections 2000: Election Results for the U.S. President, the U.S. Senate and the U.S. House of Representatives.* Washington, DC: FEC

Flack HE. 1908. *The Adoption of the Fourteenth Amendment.* Baltimore: Johns Hopkins Press. 285 pp.

Fletcher GP. 1999. Disenfranchisement as punishment: reflections on racial uses of infamia. *UCLA Law Rev.* 46:1895–907

Friedman LM. 1993. *Crime and Punishment in American History.* New York: Perseus. 577 pp.

Frosch D. 2004. The ex factor: prison-reform groups work to educate former felons on their voting rights. *In These Times* 28(20):6

Harvey AE. 1994. Ex-felon disenfranchisement and its influence on the black vote: the need for a second look. *Univ. Penn. Law Rev.* 142:1145–89

Hench VE. 1998. The death of voting rights: the legal disenfranchisement of minority voters. *Case Western Reserve Law Rev.* 48:727–89

Hoffman W. 2003. Some counties may not let felons vote. *Idaho Statesman.* Aug. 25

Hunter v. Underwood, 471 U.S. 222 (1985)

Issacharoff S, Karlan PS, Pildes RH. 1998. *The Law of Democracy.* New York: Foundation. 788 pp.

Itzkowitz H, Oldak L. 1973. Restoring the ex-offender's right to vote: background and developments. *Am. Crim. Law Rev.* 11:721–70

Johnson v. Bush, 214 F.Supp.2d 1333 (S.D. Fla. 2002), *rev'd* 353 F.3d 1287 (11th Cir. 2003), *vacated by* 377 F.3d 1363 (11th Cir. 2004)

Johnson v. Governor, 405 F.3d 1214 (11th Cir. 2005), *petition for cert. filed* (U.S. Aug. 10, 2005) (No. 00-3542)

Kalogeras S. 2003. *Jail-Based Voter Registration Campaigns.* Washington, DC: Sentencing Proj. 7 pp.

Karlan PS. 2001. Unduly partial: the Supreme Court and the Fourteenth Amendment in *Bush v. Gore. Fla. State Univ. Law Rev.* 29:587–602

Karlan PS. 2004. Convictions and doubts: retribution, representation, and the debate over felon disenfranchisement. *Stanford Law Rev.* 56:1147–70

Keyssar A. 2000. *The Right to Vote: The Contested History of Democracy in the United States.* New York: Basic Books. 496 pp.

Kousser JM. 1974. *The Shaping of Southern Politics: Suffrage Restriction and the Establishment of the One-Party South, 1880–1910.* New Haven, CT: Yale Univ. Press. 319 pp.

Kramer v. Union Free School District, 395 U.S. 621 (1969)

Lin AC. 2000. *Reform in the Making: The Implementation of Social Policy in Prison.* Princeton, NJ: Princeton Univ. Press

Manfredi C. 1998. Judicial review and criminal disenfranchisement in the United States and Canada. *Rev. Polit.* 60:277–305

Manza J, Brooks C, Uggen C. 2004. Public attitudes toward felon disenfranchisement in the United States. *Public Opin. Q.* 68:275–86

Manza J, Uggen C. 2004. Punishment and democracy: the voting rights of nonincarcerated criminal offenders in the United States. *Perspect. Polit.* 2:491–505

Manza J, Uggen C. 2005. *Locked Out: Felon Disenfranchisement and American Democracy.* New York: Oxford Univ. Press. In press

Martinson R. 1974. What works? Questions and answers about prison reform. *Public Int.* 35:22–54

Mauer M. 1999. *Race to Incarcerate.* New York: New Press. 224 pp.

Mauer M. 2004. Should ex-felons be allowed to vote? *Leg. Aff.* http://www.legalaffairs.org/webexclusive/debateclub_disenfranchisement1104.html

Mauer M, Chesney-Lind M. 2002. *Invisible Punishment: The Collateral Consequences of Mass Imprisonment.* New York: New Press. 288 pp.

McCain M. 2004. Getting out the vote to ex-cons; initiative aims to fix misconception that rights never restored. St. Paul, MN, *Pioneer Press*, Aug. 9, p. A1

McLaughlin v. City of Canton, 947 F.Supp. 954 (S.D. Miss. 1995)

Mondesire JW. 2001. Felon disenfranchisement: the modern day poll tax. *Temple Polit. Civil Rights Law Rev.* 10:435–41

Muntaquim v. Coombe, 366 F.3d 102 (2d Cir. 2004), *cert. denied* 125 U.S. 480 (U.S. Nov. 8, 2004) (No. 04–175), reh'g granted, 396 F.3d 95 (2d Cir. 2004)

Owen v. Barnes, 711 F.2d 25, 27 (3d Cir. 1983)

Perman MC. 2001. *The Struggle for Mastery: Disenfranchisement in the South, 1888–1908.* Chapel Hill: Univ. N. C. Press

Pettit B, Western B. 2004. Mass imprisonment and the life course: race and class inequality in U.S. incarceration. *Am. Sociol. Rev.* 69:151–69

Pettus KI. 2005. *Felony Disenfranchisement in America: Historical Origins, Institutional Racism, and Modern Consequences.* New York: LFB Scholarly

Pinaire B, Heumann M, Bilotta L. 2003. Barred from the vote: public attitudes toward the disenfranchisement of felons. *Fordham Urban Law J.* 30:1519–50

Ponte L. 2003. Jesse Jackson: a real con man. *FrontPage Magazine.com*, July 18. http://frontpagemag.com/Articles/ReadArticle.asp?ID = 8979

Reynolds v. Sims, 377 U.S. 533 (1964)

Richardson v. Ramirez, 418 U.S. 24 (1974)

Rottinghaus B. 2003. *Incarceration and Enfranchisement: International Practices, Impact and Recommendations for Reform.* Washington, DC: Int. Found. Elect. Syst. 46 pp.

Scott v. Sandford, 60 U.S. 393 (1856)

Shapiro AL. 1993. Challenging criminal disenfranchisement under the Voting Rights Act. *Yale Law J.* 103:537–66

Sloan J. 2000. Debate continues over felons' voting. Tampa, Fla. *Tampa Tribune*, Dec. 17, p. 14

South Carolina v. Katzenbach, 383 U.S. 301, 308 (1966)

State of Alabama. 1901. *Journal of the Proceedings of the Constitutional Convention of the State of Alabama.* Montgomery, AL: Brown. 1888 pp.

Sykes GM. 1958. *The Society of Captives: A Study of a Maximum Security Prison.* Princeton, NJ: Princeton Univ. Press

Thornburg v. Gingles, 478 U.S. 30, 47 (1986)

Thompson ME. 2002. Don't do the crime if you ever intend to vote again: challenging the disenfranchisement of ex-felons as cruel and unusual punishment. *Seton Hall Law Rev.* 33:167–205

Travis J. 2002. Invisible punishment: an instrument of social exclusion. In *Invisible Punishment: The Collateral Consequences of Mass Imprisonment*, ed. M Mauer, M Chesney-Lind, pp. 15–36. New York: New Press

Tribe LH. 1988. *American Constitutional Law.* New York: Foundation. 1778 pp.

Uggen C, Manza J. 2002. Democratic contraction? The political consequences of felon disenfranchisement in the United States. *Am. Sociol. Rev.* 67:777–803

Uggen C, Manza J. 2004a. Lost voices: the civic and political views of disfranchised felons. In *Imprisoning America: The Social Effects of Mass Incarceration*, ed. M Pattillo, D Weiman, B Western, pp. 165–204. New York: Russell Sage Found.

Uggen C, Manza J. 2004b. Voting and subsequent crime and arrest: evidence from a community sample. *Columbia Human Rights Law Rev.* 36:193–215

Uggen C, Manza J, Behrens A. 2004. Less than the average citizen: stigma, role transition, and the civic reintegration of convicted felons. In *After Crime and Punishment: Pathways to Offender Reintegration*, ed. S Maruna, R Immarigeon, pp. 261–93. Devon, UK: Willan. 288 pp.

US Comm. Civil Rights. 1975. *The Voting Rights Act: Ten Years Later.* Washington, DC: US GPO. 483 pp.

US Comm. Civil Rights. 1981. *The Voting Rights Act: Unfulfilled Goals.* Washington, DC: US GPO. 265 pp.

Vallely RM. 2004. *The Two Reconstructions.* Chicago: Univ. Chicago Press. 330 pp.

von Hirsch A. 1976. *Doing Justice: The Choice of Punishments.* New York: Hill & Wang

von Hirsch A, Wasik M. 1997. Civil disqualifications attending conviction: a suggested conceptual framework. *Cambridge Law J.* 56:599–624

Washington v. State, 75 Ala. 582, 585 (1884)

Wesley v. Collins, 605 F.Supp.2d 802 (M.D. Tenn. 1985), *aff'd* 791 F.2d 1255 (6th Cir. 1986)

Winkler A. 1993. Expressive voting. *N. Y. Univ. Law Rev.* 68:330–88

Witkowsky K. 2004. Registering ex-cons to vote in Montana. *Day to Day*, National Public Radio, Oct. 5

Woodruff v. Wyoming, 49 Fed. Appx. 199 (10th Cir. 2002)

Annu. Rev. Law Soc. Sci. 2005. 1:323–68
doi: 10.1146/annurev.lawsocsci.1.041604.115938
Copyright © 2005 by Annual Reviews. All rights reserved
First published online as a Review in Advance on August 19, 2005

AFTER LEGAL CONSCIOUSNESS

Susan S. Silbey

*Department of Anthropology, Massachusetts Institute of Technology, Cambridge,
Massachusetts 02139; email: ssilbey@mit.edu*

Key Words   ideology, hegemony, everyday life

■ **Abstract**   Legal consciousness as a theoretical concept and topic of empirical research developed to address issues of legal hegemony, particularly how the law sustains
its institutional power despite a persistent gap between the law on the books and the
law in action. Why do people acquiesce to a legal system that, despite its promises
of equal treatment, systematically reproduces inequality? Recent studies have both
broadened and narrowed the concept's reach, while sacrificing much of the concept's
critical edge and theoretical utility. Rather than explaining how the different experiences of law become synthesized into a set of circulating schemas and habits, the
literature tracks what particular individuals think and do. Because the relationships
among consciousness and processes of ideology and hegemony often go unexplained,
legal consciousness as an analytic concept is domesticated within what appear to be
policy projects: making specific laws work better for particular groups or interests.

INTRODUCTION

Legal consciousness is an important, conceptually tortured, and ultimately, I have
come to think, compromised concept in law and society scholarship. A product of
critical shifts in the theoretical arsenal of socio-legal research,[1] this concept's development and deployment may have betrayed the insight it was meant to achieve.
Before it is tossed into the storage closet of academic fashion, however, I provide
a history of its emergence, a review of its uses and major findings in the literature,
and an explanation for why it might be time to move on.

Legal consciousness as a theoretical concept and topic of empirical research
developed within law and society in the 1980s and 1990s to address issues of
legal hegemony, particularly how the law sustains its institutional power despite a
persistent gap between the law on the books and the law in action. Why do people
acquiesce to a legal system that, despite its promises of equal treatment, systematically reproduces inequality? It became associated with studies of legal culture
more generally, and since the late 1990s, empirical study of legal consciousness

---

[1]I use the terms law and society and socio-legal research interchangeably. Although the
latter term was originally used more in Europe, it has become conventional in the United
States as well.

has become a growth industry. Recent studies of legal consciousness have both broadened and narrowed the concept's reach, while sacrificing much of the concept's critical edge and theoretical utility. Rather than explaining how the different experiences of law become synthesized into a set of circulating, often taken-for-granted understandings and habits, much of the literature tracks what particular individuals think and do. Because the relationships among consciousness and processes of ideology and hegemony often go unexplained, legal consciousness as an analytic concept is domesticated within what appear to be policy projects: making specific laws work better for particular groups or interests. In this review, I offer an invitation to recapture the theoretical promise for studies of legal consciousness.

WHY LEGAL CONSCIOUSNESS? LEGACIES FROM LAW AND SOCIETY RESEARCH

The story of law and society, with different foci, has been told several times (Lipson & Wheeler 1986, Silbey & Sarat 1987, Sarat & Silbey 1988, Dezalay et al. 1989, Levine 1990, Sarat & Kearns 1993, Sarat et al. 1998, Garth & Sterling 1998, Tomlins 2000, Erlanger 2005). Here, I show that the concept of legal consciousness was implicated in the earliest law and society research. Seeing itself as a critical enterprise, removed from mainstream legal discourse as well as from the authority of the legal profession, law and society scholarship has been traditionally less concerned with what the law *is* than with what the law *does*. Taking up the agenda posed by Roscoe Pound (1910) and the American legal realists in the beginning of the twentieth century (Kalman 1986, Schlegel 1995), law and society scholars at mid-century explored empirically the processes and consequences of implementing and administering the law. They found, repeatedly, the ineffectiveness of law: a persistent, troublesome gap between the law on the books and the law in action (Pound 1910, Sarat 1985). In accounting for this gap, socio-legal research depicted how power is instantiated in all sorts of legal relations and demonstrated not only that social organization matters but also how it matters. In almost every piece of empirical research on law, the insight was confirmed. In historical studies of litigation, in studies of policing, in studies of the legal profession, in histories of how particular legal doctrines and offices developed, in studies of court cultures and judicial biographies, in studies of the regulation of business, and in the extensive literature on crime control, research showed that organization, social networks, and local cultures shaped the uses and consequences of law. Moreover, by the 1970s and 1980s, it was becoming increasingly clear that viewing law primarily as a tool of public policy designed to achieve pre-established purposes, whether an effective or failed tool, obscured the aggregate and cumulative contributions law made to sustaining a common culture, historical institutions, and particular structures of power and inequality.

The developing corpus of law and society research demonstrated that, despite aspirations to due process and equality before the law, the "haves" regularly and systematically "come out ahead" (Galanter 1974; see Kritzer & Silbey 2003). In what became a canonical statement synthesizing law and society research to that time, Galanter argued that the basic form of legal development through case-by-case adjudication privileged repeat players who, anticipating recurring legal engagements, have lower stakes in the outcome of any particular case. Repeat players have resources to pursue long-term strategies and plan for legal problems by arranging transactions and compiling a record to justify their actions. Thus, repeat players can orchestrate litigation to produce rule changes in their favor. Galanter did not argue that members of the dominant class, or organizations with great wealth, always win in litigation. Rather, he focused on the consequences of systemic organizational processes that create structural advantage for repeat players.

In modern, pluralistic democracies, due process, treating like cases the same, and equality before the law—the foundations of legal liberalism—name the most widely shared and philosophically sustained conceptions of justice (Rawls 1971, 2001). Thus, in documenting a gap between the law on the books and the law in action, and in specifying how social organization and legal procedures reproduced structured inequalities rather than equal treatment, law and society research produced a significant critique of the justice possible through law. By relying on ordinary social logics, local cultural categories and norms, the research had shown that legal action both reflected and reproduced other features and institutions of social life where power and prejudice were unconfined by the techniques of legal procedure. Although the uses of law were shown to be diverse and situationally structured, the seemingly individualized, disparate decisions of legal actors cumulated to reflect the wider array of social forces more than the facts of specific incidents. In its cumulative message, the research challenged the aspirations of those who saw in the law the possibilities of a rationally grounded morality (Fuller 1964), a mechanism for confining arbitrary power (Selznick 1961, 1969), or progressive scholars' pragmatic policy agendas.

The general thrust of the empirical research confirmed Weber's hypothesized iron cage of bureaucratic, legal, and technological rationalization. Rather than a machine-like system of constrained action coordinated to achieve officially established goals, it described "an acephalous system in which all are obedient subordinates tending to their particular tasks, and no one is responsible for the overall outcome" (Pitkin 1993, p. xiv). Although it is possible to have action without systematic goals, without any one in charge, having no coordinated purpose may not avoid systematic outcomes. "The rule of Nobody is not no-rule," Arendt wrote, "and where all are equally powerless we have a tyranny without a tyrant" (1972, p. 178). The progressive triumphalism that had animated the law and society movement's birth, the confidence that progressive social change could be achieved through law, was slowly giving way to a growing pessimism about what was beginning to seem like an inherent structural connection between the legal form and the forms of inequality and domination characteristic of industrial capitalism (Kalman 1996).

At the same time that social scientists were documenting the power of bureaucratic-legal authority—how republics were being turned into bureaucracies, as Arendt wrote—European observers and writers were making comparisons between the systems of Eastern Europe under Soviet supervision and post-industrial consumer capitalism in the West. Vaclav Havel, for example, described the Czechoslovakian situation as "post-totalitarian" because it relied for its power, for the most part, not on terror but on a routinized administrative bureaucracy and on the habitual, cynical apathy of the population to acquiesce to their own subordination and domination. He worried aloud that the experience of these post-totalitarian systems might be "a kind of warning to the West, revealing its own latent tendencies" toward concentrated, unrestrained power (Havel 1985, pp. 38–39). In both Arendt's and Havel's analyses, they discerned something worse than the common tyranny of a monarch or small manipulative elite. They came to believe that we, the people, were collectively imprisoning rather than freeing ourselves (Pitkin 1993, p. xv).

To know what law does and how it works, we needed to know how "we the people" might be contributing to the law's systemic effects, as well as to its ineffectiveness. If law failed to meet its public aspirations, how did it retain support among the people and how did it continue to achieve the sense of consistency, accessibility, fairness, and thus legitimacy? How could we explain what looked like unrelenting faith in and support for legal institutions in the face of what appeared to be consistent distinctions between ideal and reality, law on the books and law in action, abstract formal equality and substantive, concrete material inequality? We needed to find out more about the consistency or, conversely, the fissures in what looked like consistent allegiance to the rule of law. To answer these questions, we needed to know not only how and by whom the law is used, but also when and by whom it is not used. Thus, we needed to learn what using or not using the law signified to the populace. We had already learned that "neither the purposes nor the uses of any specific law are fully inscribed upon it.... [T]he meaning of any specific law, and of law as a social institution, [could] be understood only by examining the ways it is actually used" (Silbey & Bittner 1982, p. 399). Not only would we have to seek out the range of variation in uses and interpretations of law, but we might also have to assess, and perhaps redefine, what we mean by using the law. Thus, in the 1980s, "the ways law is experienced and understood by ordinary citizens" (Merry 1985), i.e., legal consciousness, became a central focus for some law and society scholars.

This reorientation had three components. First, it abandoned a "law-first" paradigm of research (Sarat & Kearns 1993). Rather than begin with legal rules and materials to trace how policies or purposes are achieved or not, scholars turned to ordinary daily life to find, if there were, the traces of law within. They were as interested in the absences and silences where law could have been and was not as much as they were interested in the explicit signs of positive law. Law and society had already moved beyond what Lawrence Friedman (1975, p. 29) identified as lawyer's law ("ideas, problems or situations of interest to legal practitioners and theorists") to legal acts ("rules and regulations of the modern state, the processes of administrative governance, police behavior") and legal behavior (the unofficial as well as official work of legal professionals). Researchers now attended to the unofficial, non-professional actors—citizens, legal laymen—as they took account of, anticipated, imagined, or failed to imagine legal acts and ideas. It shifted empirical focus from a preoccupation with both legal actors and legal materials to what had in European social theory been designated as the life-world, the everyday life of ordinary people (Lefebvre 1968, 1991 [1958]; Schutz & Luchman 1989 [1973]; Ginzburg 1976; for a recent critique of the uncritical valorization of the everyday in socio-legal studies, see Valverde 2003).

Second, it abandoned the predominant focus on measurable behavior and reinvigorated the Weberian conception of social action by including analyses of the meanings and interpretive communication of social transactions (Habermas 1984, 1987, 1998). From this perspective, law is not merely an instrument or tool working on social relations, but is also a set of conceptual categories and schema that help construct, compose, communicate, and interpret social relations. The focus on actors' meanings brought into the mainstream of law and society scholarship a stronger commitment to a wider array of research methods. In particular, this new scholarship drew on anthropology and qualitative sociology, which had long been studying actors' meaning making in other domains.

Third, and perhaps most fundamentally, the turn to everyday life and the cultural meanings of social action demanded a willingness to shift from the native categories of actors as the object of study, e.g., the rules of the state, the formal institutions of law, the attitudes and opinions of actors, to an analytically conceptualized unit of analysis, the researcher's definition of the subject, legal consciousness. For most of the twentieth century, legal scholars had treated law and society as if they were two empirically distinct spheres, as if the two were conceptually as well as materially separate and singular. They are not. The law is a construct of human ingenuity; laws are material phenomena. Similarly, society is a fiction we sustain through hard work and mutual communication. People's ordinary transactions presume an objective world of facts "out there," yet close analysis of the ways people apprehend that world reveals their own collaborative social construction of those social facts (Durkheim 1982 [1895], Gurwitsch 1962, Berger & Luckman 1990 [1966], Schutz 1970, Molotch & Boden 1985). Nonetheless, we had been studying law as if it were a separate realm from society, as something that worked on social relations or was a product of social forces, as if the social experience was consonant with the linguistic distinction (e.g., Friedman 1984). We had been studying law with insufficiently theorized concepts. We were using our subject's language as the tools for our analysis and in the course finding ourselves unable to answer the questions our research generated. New theoretical materials and research methods were necessary (cf. Gordon 1984, Munger & Seron 1984, Trubek 1984). These involved more intensive study of local cultures, native texts, and interpretive hermeneutical techniques for inhabiting and representing everyday worlds to construct better accounts of how law works, or to put it another way, how legality is an ongoing structure of social action (Ewick & Silbey 1998, pp. 33–56). These also involved attention to and appropriation of the venerable traditions of European social theory that had been addressing just these questions with the concepts of consciousness, ideology, and hegemony in an effort to understand how systems of domination are not only tolerated but embraced by subordinate populations (Marx & Engels 1970 [1846], Gramsci 1999).

What became known as the constitutive perspective recaptured some of the critical tradition of law and society research. Focusing on the everyday life of citizens, scholars began to interrogate the ideals and principles that legal institutions proclaim but fail to completely enact. Both policy efforts and abstract principles were interrogated as important parts of how legal institutions create their power and authority. The ideals of law, such as open and accessible processes, rule-governed decision making, or similar cases being decided similarly, may not in practice limit the exercise of law's power; these ideals are, however, part of the popularly shared understandings that shape and mobilize support for legal institutions. They might also be part of what allows the system to be a headless tyrant. This became the study of legal consciousness.

EXPLAINING HEGEMONY BY TRACKING LEGAL IDEOLOGIES AND CONSCIOUSNESS

Scholars pursuing the constitutive paradigm turned from the study of law *and* society to the study of law *in* society, from the effectiveness of laws to law's effects. Pursuing the meanings of law among lay actors as well as professional legal actors, and reconceptualizing the unit of analysis from specific laws to legal ideologies, law and society scholars made what became known more generally as the cultural turn, an interdisciplinary discourse among the social sciences and humanities focusing attention on systems of symbols and meanings embedded in social practices (Chaney 1994). The historical moment derived from, and in its turn contributed to, a more general reconstruction of twentieth century social science scholarship that acknowledged its historicity and inescapable politics and rejected its naive realism. From studies of politics, literature, or film to explorations of the social studies of science and technology, the full spectrum of human production was re-examined to expose the layers of subjectivity and representation. Deconstruction in literary studies, the interpretive turn in social science, the culture wars in science studies, the intellectual effervescence was as noticeable in socio-legal scholarship as elsewhere. I cannot do justice in this space to the range and depth of the poststructural and postmodern critiques of knowledge that suffused academic scholarship and popular culture during the 1980s. Suffice it to say that the critique came in various flavors and was consumed in varying proportions.

Scholars adopting a constitutive perspective for the study of legal consciousness, however, took several lessons from the poststructural critique in efforts to explain how a relatively open system, continually in the making, managed nonetheless to sustain itself as a durable and powerful institution, in other words, to constitute a rule of law. Drawing from the poststructural critique, they acknowledged, "(1) the need to address the *in* determinacies of meaning and action, events and processes in history; (2) the admonition to regard culture not as an *over* determining, closed system of signs but as a set of polyvalent practices, texts, and images that may, at any time, be contested; (3) the invitation to see power as a many-sided, often elusive and diffuse force which is always implicated in culture, consciousness and representation" (Comaroff & Comaroff 1991, p. 17). Studies emphasized connections between what Goffman (1967) called the interaction order of face-to-face exchanges and social structures understood as ongoing productions of social interaction (Bourdieu 1977; Giddens 1979, 1984; Connell 1987; Sewell 1992). In these sociological theories of action and practice, culture (and legal culture as an aspect of culture) is not a coherent, logical, and autonomous system of symbols but a diverse collection of resources that are deployed in the performance of action (Swidler 1986).[2]

Although social meanings, processes, and laws are human creations, emerging from the unending contest and struggle of micro-transactions,[3] at any moment

---

[2]In the best of this work, culture is an analytical term abstracting "the meaningful aspect of human action out of the flow of concrete interactions. . .[by disentangling], for purposes of analysis, the semiotic influences on action from the other sorts of influences—demographic, geographical, biological, technological, economic, and so on—that they are necessarily mixed within any concrete sequence of behavior" (Sewell 1999, p. 4). Importantly, this conception of culture goes beyond a focus on language alone and rejects any notion that culture is uniform, static, or shared ubiquitously. In earlier formulations, the concept of culture as an aspect of social life had been invoked in diverse ways. Referring primarily to learned behavior as distinct from that which is given by nature, or biology, culture had been used to designate everything that is humanly produced (habits, beliefs, arts, and artifacts) and passed from one generation to another. In this formulation, culture is distinguished from nature and distinguishes one society from another. A narrower conception of culture refers to a specific set of social institutions that is specifically devoted to the production of signs and meanings. In this usage, cultural institutions include, for example, art, music, theater, fashion, literature, religion, media, and education. Although the first definition is overly broad, including just about all of human life, the second is too specific: The meanings produced and circulating through the other institutions and "non-cultural" spheres of life are ignored or devalued (Silbey 2001; cf. Ginzburg 1976). Contemporary cultural theory and analysis moved beyond these conceptions. Although cultural resources are often discrete, local, and intended for specific, disparate, and sometimes contradictory purposes, it is possible to observe patterns so that we are able to speak of a culture, or a cultural system. "Symbols communicate only because they have relatively structured relationships to other symbols, are part of a system. Similarly, a cultural system cannot exist independent of the succession of practices that instantiate, reproduce or, most interestingly, transform it" (Sewell 1999, p. 47).

[3]In using the phrase micro-transactions, I do not mean to suggest an overly rigid dichotomy between the micro and macro perspectives. As Bourdieu (1990, p. 130) says, "[W]hen you look too closely, you cannot see the wood for the trees." One must be aware of the social space or "point from which you see what you see."

in time and social space, their malleability and indeterminacy are constrained by history, habit, social organization, and power. "Men make their own history, but they do not make it as they please; they do not make it under self-selected circumstances, but under circumstances existing already, given and transmitted from the past" (Marx 1963 [1852]). The world, particular institutions, and practices may be socially constructed and contingent, not natural and necessary, but this does not mean that the socially constructed world is easily undone. To the defendant who goes to jail, the tenant who is evicted, the immigrant who is expelled, the woman who is denied access to an abortion, the citizen concerned about air pollution or global warming, or the consumer who is injured by a faulty product, the law is less pliable and less amenable to reinterpretation and reconstruction than poststructural critiques of determinacy seemed to suggest. Indeterminacy does not make all things possible; it means only that possibilities are not predetermined or fixed. Although they are indeterminate, events and outcomes may still be, and research has shown them to be, probabilistically predictable. Otherwise why would we keep seeing that the "haves" come out ahead (Kritzer & Silbey 2003)?

> Nowhere can anything or everything be thought or written or done or told. Most people live in a world in which many signs, and often the ones that count most, look as though they are eternally fixed. . . . While signs, social relations, and material practices are constantly open to transformation—and while meaning may indeed *become* unfixed, resisted and reconstructed—history everywhere is actively made in a dialectic of order and disorder, consensus and contest. At any particular moment, in any marked event, *a* meaning or *a* social arrangement may appear free floating, underdetermined, ambiguous. But it is often the very attempt to harness that indeterminacy, the seemingly unfixed signifier, that animates both the exercise of power and the resistance to which it may give rise. Such arguments and struggles, though, are seldom equal. They have, *pace postmodernism*, a political sociology that emerges from their place in a system of relations. And so, as the moment gives way to the medium-term, and some people and practices emerge as (or remain) dominant, their authority expresses itself in the apparently established order of things—again, in the dual sense of an edifice of command and a condition of being. What might once have seemed eventful and contingent now looks to have been part of a more regular pattern—indeed, of a structured history, a historical structure (Comaroff & Comaroff 1991, p. 18).

The concept of hegemony has been used to explain the practical determinacy of a legal system that is theoretically indeterminate and refers to just this kind of systemic power in which transactions become habituated as practices and transactional advantage becomes stabilized as privilege (Comaroff & Comaroff 1991, pp. 23–24; cf. Bourdieu 1977, p. 167). Over time, individual transactions are repeated and may become patterned. Patterns may become principled and eventually naturalized. Hegemony does not arise automatically from a particular social arrangement; instead, hegemony is produced and reproduced in everyday transactions, in which what is experienced as given is often unnoticed, uncontested, and seemingly not open to negotiation. Importantly, the cultural symbols and structures of action become over time so routinized that the distribution of influence and advantage, as well as of burdens and costs, in these transactions are relatively invisible. The institutionalization of power in this way produces commonplace transactions in which both the sources of power and the forms of subordination are buried. In these transactions, no one seems to be demanding obedience, and subordinate parties appear to be normally socialized rather than compliant. The organization of relations and resources obscures the mechanisms that systematically allocate status and privilege of diverse sorts. Social actors are thus constrained without knowing from where or whom the constraint derives.

The law is a durable and powerful human invention because a good part of legality is just this invisible constraint, suffusing and saturating our everyday life. Most of the time, legal authority, forms, and decisions go uncontested or are challenged only within the legally provided channels of contest. The American presidential election of 2000 is a perfect example of the degree to which the (social) fact of law and legal intervention, in contrast to particular legal decisions, is generally uncontested and hegemonic (Gillman 2001). There are many good reasons that the decision in *Bush v. Gore* was not disputed in the streets of American cities, nor in the U.S. Senate. The acquiescence to that decision, however, derives not solely from the specific facts of the case nor from the politics of the moment but rather from a long history of deference to the courts as both the oracles and guardians of the Constitution, the law, and justice. We need only look at the history of constitutional regimes in formation across the globe to observe the difference between taken-for-granted legality and struggles to institutionalize the rule of law (e.g., Ellman 1992, Abel 1995, McAdams 1996, Scheppele 1996, Krygier & Csarnota 1999, Klug 2000, Chanock 2001, Wilson 2001, Gibson & Gouws 2002).

Legal hegemony derives from long habituation to the legal authority that is almost imperceptibly infused into the material and social organization of ordinary life, for example, in traffic lanes, parking rules, and sales receipts, much more than in the acquiescence or capitulation to *Bush v. Gore*. In popular culture, however, the trial stands as the icon of the rule of law, whereas these routinized legal forms that constitute the law's hegemony are rendered invisible, invisible as law that is. Instead of sales receipts and traffic lanes, the trial is presented as the site of legality, a carefully orchestrated contest through which aggregations of persons, words, stories, and material are legitimately transformed into facts of intention, causality, responsibility, or property. Although we take for granted the appropriateness and legitimacy of trials for resolving conflict and for mediating and legitimating the use of force, law and society research has demonstrated that a trial is merely the tip of a giant iceberg of matters that are shaped and interpreted through law. The public focus on litigation obscures the sources of power and hegemony of law. Indeed, of the myriad activities that constitute modern life, this official, iconographic symbol of legality, the trial, is outpaced by the proliferation of expectations, norms, signs, and objects in which the traces of professional and official legal work have become indiscernible. When we speak of a rule of law, we do so because most of the iceberg of legality lies submerged within the taken-for-granted expectations of mundane life. Rather than contested and choreographed in sometimes spectacular but always statistically rare trials, law is powerful, and it rules everyday life because its constructions are uncontroversial and have become normalized and habitual. Law's mediations have been sedimented throughout the routines of daily living, helping to make things move around in more or less clear ways, without having to invoke, display, or wield its elaborate and intricate procedures, especially its ultimate, physical force.

Of course, this sedimentation and normative regulation is never complete; we do not always stay within the boundaries of legally sanctioned expectations, and the reach of law is always disputed. Thus, much of the visible iceberg of legality is about what to do in the event of breach; some of those matters of concern lead to litigation, and some, although very few, lead to trials, and then even fewer to appeals. An iceberg throws up a calf. These visible legal battles, however, are the outliers of the law's more routine activities. Ironically, the outliers are what end up constituting the textual body of legal doctrine.

More often than not, as we go about our daily lives, we rarely sense the presence of the law. Although law operates as an assembly for making things public and mediating matters of concern, most of the time it does so without fanfare, without argument, without notice. We pay our bills because they are due; we respect our neighbors' property because it is theirs. We drive on the right side of the road (in most nations) because it is prudent. We register our motor vehicles and stop at red lights. We rarely consider through which collective judgments and procedures we have defined "coming due," "their property," "prudent driving," or why automobiles must be registered and why traffic stops at red lights. If we trace the source of these expectations and meanings to some legal institution or practice, the origin is so far away in time and place that the matters of concern and circumstances of invention have been long forgotten. As a result of this distance, sales contracts, property, and traffic rules seem to be merely efficient, natural, and inevitable facts of life.

As naturalized features of modern life, the signs and objects of law are omnipresent. Through historic as well as contemporary legal decisions that are no longer actively debated, countless aspects of human life as well as matters of concern have been resolved, concretized, and objectified, literally written onto the surfaces and figuratively built into the very structures of ordinary social relations, places, and objects. Every package of food, piece of clothing, and electrical appliance contains a label warning us about its dangers, instructing us about its uses, and telling us whether (and where) we can complain if something goes wrong. Every time we park a car, dry clean clothing, or leave an umbrella in a cloak room, we are informed about limited liabilities for loss. Newspapers, television, novels, plays, magazines, and movies are saturated with legal images, although these very same objects display their claims to copyright. Although much of the time legal forms go unnoticed and cognitively disappear, they are imperfectly naturalized.

At any moment, the stabilized, historical *legalfact*[4] can reappear, perhaps becoming a matter of concern, debate, or resistance. The iceberg cracks and hits a passing ship. Hegemony is ruptured; the ideological force of law is apparent.

In the most useful formulations, the concept of hegemony is often used in conjunction with ideology, understood in a first but incomplete formulation as a process "by which meaning is produced, challenged, reproduced, transformed" (Barrett 1980, p. 87; cf. Bahktin 1981; Billig 1991; Steinberg 1991, 1999). Ideology is not, however, to be equated with culture or structure in general, or with social construction as an interactive process in general. An ideology always embodies particular arrangements of power, and it affects life chances in a manner that is different from some other ideology or arrangement of power. Meanings can be said to be ideological only insofar as they serve power; thus, ideology is not defined by its specific content but by its contextual construction and function (Silbey 1998, Ewick 2003). Ideologies vary, however, in the degree to which they are contested or conventionalized. Thus, ideology and hegemony can be understood as the ends of a continuum. At one end of the continuum are the still-visible and active struggles referred to as ideology. At the other end are the struggles that are no longer active, where power is dispersed through social structures and meanings are so embedded that representational and institutional struggles are no longer visible. We refer to this as hegemony. Although moments of resistance may be documented, in general subjects do not notice, question, or make claims against hegemony (Scott 1990, Hodson 2001, Ewick & Silbey 2003).

"What differentiates hegemony from ideology is not some existential essence. It is. . .the factor of human consciousness and the modes of representation that bear it" (Comaroff & Comaroff 1991, pp. 24, 28). Just as ideology and hegemony constitute the poles of a continuum of the seen and unseen, contest and convention, norm and deviance, so too does social knowledge and experience vary along a continuum that Comaroff and Comaroff call a "chain of consciousness," variable processes of awareness and critique of the forms and structures as well as the openings and possibilities of everyday lives. With these theoretical materials in place, Ewick & Silbey (1998) define consciousness as participation in this collective, social production of ideology and hegemony, an integral part of the production of the very same structures that are also experienced as external and constraining. In this framing, consciousness is understood to be part of a reciprocal process in which the meanings given by individuals to their world become patterned, stabilized, and objectified. These meanings, once institutionalized, become part of the material and

---

[4]Legal objects, signs, forms, rules, and decisions are understood to be a special kind of fact, a legal fact. By collapsing the distance between the words to *legalfact*, we emphasize the procedures of law that are the grounds for constructing facts, that is, *legalfacts*. In other words, jurisprudence recognizes at its core that its truths are created only through its particular procedures and that the relationship between *legalfacts* and empirical facts is at best only a specific method of approximation or invention.

discursive systems that limit and constrain future meaning making. Consciousness entails both thinking and doing, telling stories, complaining, lumping grievances, working, playing, marrying, divorcing, suing a neighbor, or refusing to call the police.

Most importantly for understanding the place of legal consciousness in socio-legal research, legal consciousness in this conceptualization is no longer something that is individual or merely ideational; consciousness is construed as a type of social practice, in the sense that it both reflects and forms social structures. Just as culture implies both practice and system, consciousness is dislodged from the mind of an individual knower, insofar as knowing always entails the invocation of collective cultural schemas and deployment of differentially available resources. Consciousness emerges out of, even as it shapes, social structures contested in ideological struggles or subsumed in hegemonic practices. The study of legal consciousness is the search for the forms of participation and interpretation through which actors construct, sustain, reproduce, or amend the circulating (contested or hegemonic) structures of meanings concerning law. Legal consciousness cannot be understood independently of its role in the collective construction of legality—how forms of consciousness combine to constitute ideological or hegemonic legality.

We should note that as the research field grew, so too did the definitions of the term consciousness. Although debate over uses of the term can be provocative and stimulating for scholars, creating a rich field in which to work their theoretical skills, it can also lead to a great deal of confusion. Authors have defined legal consciousness variously as "all the *ideas* about the nature, function, and operation of law held by anyone in society at a given time" (Trubek 1984, p. 592); as "the ways law is experienced and understood by *ordinary* citizens" (Merry 1985); as "the ways people understand and use the law. . ., the way people conceive of the 'natural' and normal way of doing things, their habitual patterns of talk and action and their commonsense understandings of the world" (Merry 1990, p. 5); as "the ongoing, dynamic process of constructing one's understanding of, and relationship to, the social world through the use of legal conventions and discourses (McCann 1994, p. 7); as interchangeable with legal ideology (Sarat 1990, p. 343); and as a concept that assumes "that the 'distributed self' continually evolves with experience, incorporating along the way multiple, sometimes contradictory elements and perspectives" (Engel & Munger 2003, p. 12). In some of these uses, ideology and consciousness are combined; in others, a method of researching consciousness is subsumed by the term without specifying the difference between a method of empirical exploration and a definition of the object of inquiry. Some add a focus on self and identity, and in many definitions the distinction between consciousness in general and legal consciousness is unspecified. Does "legal consciousness refer to consciousness in general as it focuses (perhaps fleetingly) on law and legal institutions or. . ., on the other hand, [does] it refer. . .to a particular kind of thought process that people bring to bear whenever legal matters arise" (Engel 1998, p. 119). Not all uses of legal consciousness theorize relationships to power, ideology, and the contributions of consciousness to hegemony. If understood interchangeably with ideology, how do we talk about the relationships among subjects and the collective constructions we recognize as a particular pattern of meaning? If the focus is on an evolving identity or self, what is the relationship between that self and consciousness? Often the studies of consciousness move in different directions depending on the tradition of research from which they draw and on the methods of research they employ. A similar variation plagues studies of legal culture (Silbey 2001).

Thus far, I have argued that the study of legal consciousness developed in law and society research as an explicit effort to explore the submerged iceberg, to trace this hegemonic power of law. I have suggested that this research agenda emerged directly out of the results of the first generation of empirical studies of law and society. It was pursued, however, with theoretical framing and methodological tools adopted as part of paradigm shifts in the social sciences and humanities that deconstructed scholarly claims to disinterested truth telling, reconfigured analytical practices to emphasize the ongoing struggles and instabilities in social processes buried by popular and academic master narratives, and attended to the actions, voices, and perspectives of those who had been too often overlooked in the early canon of law and society research (Seron & Silbey 2004). Such oversight was not, of course, unusual across the scholarly fields, although the relative attention to studying up and studying down was certainly not uniformly distributed across the disciplines. At the heart of this project, however, research sought to connect all these pieces: to show how the lived experiences of ordinary people produced simultaneously open yet stable systems of practice and signification; to demonstrate how the law remained rife with variation and possibility; and to explore how we the people might simultaneously be both the authors and victims of our collectively constructed history.

POPULAR UNDERSTANDINGS OF LAW

The research project around legal consciousness was further influenced by a strange contradiction in the research into people's recourse to the law. In this section, I review several genres of the empirical research from which studies of legal consciousness developed.

Surveys of Legal Use, Mobilization, and Assessment

Since the 1960s, law and society scholars had been conducting surveys of legal use: When, where, and under what circumstances do citizens turn to law? Much of the work described unequal access to law and courts with socially disadvantaged groups disproportionately excluded from access to legal remedies. This differential use of legal resources was explained by what is essentially an economic or social structural model. Citizens with greater resources of education, income, or familiarity, which is often a consequence of education or income, are more likely to use the law as a means of dispute resolution (Carlin et al. 1966, Mayhew & Reiss 1969, Silberman 1985, Goodman & Sanborne 1986). Because minority populations command and deploy disproportionately fewer social resources of education, income, status, and power, they are less likely to turn to the law or the courts with their troubles. And when they become subjects of law, their problems are often reconfigured as crimes rather than interpersonal disputes (Moulton 1969; Merry 1979, 1990; cf. Balbus 1973). Thus, race and income interacted to explain the differential use of law and courts. That differential voluntary use provided some of the evidence for Galanter's (1974) analysis of the systematic legal advantage that attaches to repeat players.

With additional research, however, the picture turned out to be somewhat more complicated. Although the research continually documented the fact that poor people make less use of lawyers (Curran 1977) and that racial and ethnic minorities are more likely to be poor and thus also less likely to use lawyers or turn to courts, it is not poverty per se, nor the interaction between poverty and race alone, that created barriers to law. Since the institution of public legal services in the 1960s, research also showed that the kinds of problems people have rather than their income, education, race, or ethnicity influenced their recourse to law (Mayhew & Reiss 1969, Miller & Sarat 1980–1981, Engel 1984, Silberman 1985). One of the most extensive examinations of disputing behavior in the United States reported that the standard demographic variables (age, income, education, ethnicity, gender) were poor predictors of rates of grievance experience, perception, or acknowledgement[5] or of the willingness to use law and courts for handling grievances, ordinary disputes, or extraordinary problems. Although demographic variables did not seem to have much impact on grievances in general, they did have consequences for some classes of grievances. It appeared that racial minorities were less likely to assert claims in consumer and tort areas than whites but were significantly more likely to assert discrimination claims (Miller & Sarat 1980–1981, p. 552). Nonetheless, researchers argued that, with the exception of torts and discrimination issues, the probability of making claims and asserting rights depends more on "problem-specific factors than on claimants' capacities" or on demographic characteristics.

If the literature described differential use of law as a function of substantive issues, it nonetheless described a generally active and assertive citizenry and a widespread, if unevenly distributed, willingness to turn to third parties, law, and courts with problems and grievances. The Civil Litigation Project reported that across all problem areas, rates of claiming and disputing were substantial. Studies of consumer complaining reported figures with a range from 70% to 80% of citizens filing complaints when they were dissatisfied with a product or service (McGuire & Edelhertz 1977, Ladinsky & Susmilch 1981, Silbey 1984). The willingness to use the law derived, Scheingold explained, from "a myth of rights [that] exercises

---

[5]Grievances are understood as the beginnings of disputes; a grievance is an individual's belief that she or he (or a group or organization) is entitled to a resource that someone else may grant or deny (Ladinsky & Susmilch 1981, p. 5).

a compelling influence. . .and provides shared ideals for the great majority. . . . Even otherwise alienated minorities are receptive to values associated with legal ordering. . . . [W]hile we may respond to the myth of rights as groups. . .most of us do respond" (Scheingold 1974, pp. 78–79). Americans participate in a shared legal discourse, collectively contributing to the construction of what would later be called legality. Thus, one answer to the orienting question of how the law sustained itself as a legitimate and governing institution suggested that citizens use and obey law because they believe in this myth of rights. Studies of public attitudes toward the U.S. Supreme Court also documented a widespread diffusion of beliefs in rights and the legitimacy of the law and courts (cf. Dolbeare 1967).

In one of the most continuously sustained research programs seeking to understand this widespread embrace of law's legitimacy usually referred to as procedural justice, another set of researchers also documented popular beliefs and attitudes, satisfactions and concerns, about the legal system. Rather than a myth of rights, this research describes Americans' attachment to particular procedures, claiming that people evaluate their legal experiences in terms of processes and forms of interaction rather than the outcomes of those interactions or abstract rights. People care, the researchers write, about having neutral, honest authorities who allow them to state their views and who treat citizens with dignity and respect, and when they find such processes, they use and defer to them (Casper et al. 1988, Lind & Tyler 1988, MacCoun & Tyler 1988, Tyler 1990, Tyler et al. 1997, Tyler & Huo 2002). The observation of a relatively homogenous and stable consensus and the lack of systematic variation in these studies, however, raised as many questions as it resolved. Why would intelligent and reflective actors willingly support a system about which, when asked, they voice skepticism concerning its capacities to deliver on the promise of that desired procedural justice? Is it possible that the image of consensus and democratic, procedural commitment emerges from the surveys because researchers inquire about only a limited number of issues, values, and institutional arrangements? It turns out that these studies often begin with a model of fairness as it is defined by existing legal processes and doctrine: the opportunity to be heard, to have professional representation, and to have access to appeal and review. The studies then measure popular agreement or disagreement with those norms. Commitments to alternative conceptions of fairness, such as loyalty, compensatory treatment, or substantive equality, are not measured. In effect, respondents are queried about their support for America's official legal ideals and myths, those aspirations repeatedly announced in public discourse and concretely enshrined in marble pediments and stone. The formulation of the questions encourages conforming answers, lest the citizen appear deviant or disloyal. The research thus reinscribes the values and institutions of legal liberalism without making them problematic for the research subject; it is possible that the research itself effaces the presence and possibilities of conflict, resistance, or attachment to alternative models as it also elides engagement with questions of power and inequality. Thus, to the extent that they are seeking access to popular culture and consciousness, the surveys often treat consciousness as a disembodied mental state, a set of

attitudes and opinions, rather than a broader set of situated practices and repertoires of action. In these studies, too little attention is paid to how people's attitudes
are produced in, through, and by social organization, ideological struggles, and
culture.

Ethnographic Studies of the Social Meanings and Uses of Law

As an alternative to surveys of citizen attitudes, knowledge, and use of law, some
researchers adopted ethnographic methods of extensive observation and intensive
interviewing to study disputes, disputing behavior, and the recourse to law. The
research sought out more contextualized understandings that had been overlooked
in many surveys of the differential mobilization and use of law. "Whether and how
people participate and use legal process results," the ethnographers argued, "in
large measure from the way law is represented in and through cultural systems in
which citizens are embedded" (Sarat 1986, p. 539). In other words, the willingness
to use law and courts includes "an ideological or normative dimension, which
may operate to inhibit participation for those otherwise seemingly capable of
participating" (Sarat 1986, p. 539). The studies specifically addressed the issues
of power and inequality that had been effaced in the broad-based survey research.

An early precursor to some of these cultural analyses on legal consciousness
was apparent in the work on "the legally competent person," a person who is both
aware and assertive, "has a sense of himself [sic] as a possessor of rights and sees
the legal system as a resource for validation of these rights" (Carlin et al. 1966,
p. 71). This sense of the self and these sets of dispositions and perceptions are
cultural products learned, shaped, and framed by interactions in specific locations.
Although these perceptions (interpretations, or forms of consciousness, as they
were later known) may be understood as matters of skill associated with social
class, they have an important and independent normative dimension. The legally
competent subject in this stream of research

> will see assertion of his [sic] interests through legal channels as desirable and
> appropriate. This is not to say that he will view law as omni-relevant, as a sort
> of all-purpose tool. He will be aware of the limits of law. But it is important
> to stress that he will not be hostile to the extension of the rule of law. When he
> believes it proper, he will make an effort to bring his interests under the aegis of
> authoritative rules. This will call for a 'creative act of influence' that will affect
> the content of official decisions. . . . It is implicit in what we have said that the
> competent subject will have a sense of himself as a possessor of rights, and
> in seeking to validate and implement rights through law he will be concerned
> with holding authorities accountable to law (Carlin et al. 1966, p. 70).

With extended fieldwork in particular social locations—a neighborhood, a housing project, a small community, a county in Illinois—ethnographers were able to
capture, in ways inaccessible to the large surveys, the variable meanings of events,
grievances, disputes, and law in the lives of citizens. Moreover, the research painted

a very different picture of citizens' responses to grievances and interpretations of law than had been captured in the surveys. The studies confirmed that all social groups experience grievances that could become claims and disputes. They also demonstrated that citizens interpret these events differently and respond to them in culturally specific and variable ways. However, the authors argued that these differences among citizen interpretations of law could not be adequately described by an economic, cost-benefit, rational calculus that had thus far characterized many of the studies of disputing (Merry & Silbey 1984). In these ethnographies, the issues that might give rise to disputes and legal claims are described as cultural events, evolving within a framework of rules about what is the normal or moral way to act, what kind of wrongs warrant action, and what kinds of remedies are acceptable and appropriate.

> Ideas about how to respond to grievances are linked with socially constructed definitions of normal behavior, respectability, responsibility, and the good person. . . . Rules about how to fight, or whether to fight, how to respond to insults and grievances, how to live with one's neighbors, are parts of elaborate and complex belief systems which may vary among social groups. . . . In other words, dispute behavior, that may give rise to legal action, or may not, reflects community evaluations, moral codes, and cultural notions, learned but not entirely chosen, of the way people of virtue and integrity live (Merry & Silbey 1984, pp. 157, 176).

Thus, researchers described the diverse cultural conditions of disputing (cf. Macaulay 1963). The work indicated that Americans prefer to handle problems by themselves, by talking with the other party, or by avoiding the problematic situation or the person altogether. In some cases, this reluctance derived from a fear of "making trouble" (Merry & Silbey 1984) or of being perceived as litigious and greedy (Engel 1984) by turning to third parties. In other communities, the reluctance to use law derived from deeply held religious principles (Greenhouse 1986). For these people, invoking the law or litigation would require an unacceptable submission to civil as opposed to religious authority. Conflict and authority were understood as evidence of sin and a fall from God's grace that could be repaired only by deference to God's authority. In another study, Bumiller (1988) described how victims of discrimination also refuse to turn to law. This group avoided litigation because they believed that courts rob them of control of their lives and isolate them from their communities at a time when they are most in need of support. Bumiller's respondents resisted what she described as a "double victimization," first in becoming an "object" of discrimination, and second, in becoming "a case" in law.[6]

---

[6]Goffman (1963) uses the term "double deviance" to refer to subjects who are stigmatized by a discredited characteristic and then fail to perform appropriately the designated deviant role. Doubling is perhaps one of the special burdens of subordinated classes. See Dubois (1999 [1903]) on the experience of dual consciousness.

When surveyed, these communities and groups registered abnormally low court usage. The courts and law were avoided not because the citizens did not know how to access legal resources or because they lacked the financial resources to invoke its agency. They would have scored well on the standard scales of knowledge of law; they were legally competent actors. They would have also claimed that they prefer processes in which they have a chance to state their case and in which they can be heard, as reported in the studies of procedural justice. However, despite or perhaps because of their knowledge of law, in these studies citizens appeared to turn to law only when their situations or their personal, community, or economic problems seemed entirely intractable, unavoidable, and intolerable. It required an extraordinary effort to overcome routine reluctance and necessitated the development of principled arguments to justify the action. Only when circumstances can be and have indeed reached the point where they are formulated as conflicts of principle do citizens feel comfortable turning to law (Merry & Silbey 1984, Merry 1990). When they get to court, however, the citizen plaintiff rapidly loses control of the process. Thus, Merry (1990) wrote, "recourse to the courts for family and neighborhood problems has paradoxical consequences. It empowers plaintiffs in relationship to neighbors and relatives, but at the same time it subjects them to the control of the court." Some plaintiffs yield to the courts' interpretations and management of their situations, but others often resist, struggling to assert their own definition of the situation (cf. Conley & O'Barr 1990, Yngvesson 1993).

A Research Agenda Emerges

Placed side by side, these studies appeared contradictory. The distinct research communities, using different theoretical resources and research methods, were producing very different accounts of the place and use of law in the lives of ordinary people. The ethnographic studies described ambivalent relationships to law and legal institutions, a much less confident embrace of law or its procedures than the survey research had provided. The ethnographies depicted variability influenced by local situations, norms, and customary ways of doing things, where the surveys had described deep, broad, normative consensus. The surveys seemed to produce generalizeable results over large populations but failed to detect the cultural variation in the meanings of events or the skepticism and resistance concerning law described in the ethnographic studies. The studies produced mixed results concerning the rates of legal use, some describing a litigious populace (Lieberman 1981) and others a legally quiescent population (Abel 1973). The most common survey methods and measures systematically excluded just those phenomena that distinguish race, ethnicity, and social class, i.e., variations in meaning systems. Although the community studies sought to investigate and understand social action in its context rather than as disaggregated component variables, measured independently and then reaggregated through statistical procedures, the results and interpretations varied from one location to another and could not be generalized beyond the locale in which each study was conducted. Surveys described consensus and support for fair and responsive processes; ethnographies described reluctance or resigned engagement and sometimes outright resistance to legal authority and processes. Neither described how the citizens' experiences, interpretations, or attitudes cumulated to produce legal ideology or hegemony. A community of scholars intent on understanding how citizens interacted with, and thus contributed to, the production of law and legal processes were generating very different results based on their research methods. When people were asked directly about the law, their relation to law appeared to be active and assertive. When people were observed in their everyday practices, their relation to law appeared to be reluctant and resistant. Here was a ripe and productive research dilemma.

HISTORICAL STUDIES OF LEGAL IDEOLOGY AND CONSCIOUSNESS

In historical studies of hegemonic law, a corresponding paradox was emerging. Although the historical record clearly revealed the law's development as an ideological tool of repression, research also uncovered spaces of freedom. It began to seem as if the law was constituted by both domination and resistance, consensus and conflict.

In the 1970s, historians working from a Marxist perspective began producing a series of closely observed studies of the eighteenth century foundations of liberal legalism. With data collected on local legal practices rather than national policies and pronouncements, British scholars revised the Enlightenment histories of the progressive march of reason that ultimately, and necessarily, produced objective science, democratic governance, and modern law. They rejected the conventional account of a consensual society "ruled within the parameters of paternalism and deference, and governed by a 'rule of law,' which attained (however imperfectly) impartiality" (Thompson 1975, p. 262). These sociologically informed histories described dialectical processes by which liberal law created spaces of real freedom for newly emergent middle classes and aspirations of citizenship for the masses, while institutionalizing legal processes that in turn contributed to the legitimacy of the developing state apparatus (Hay et al. 1975). Although these historians described "law being devised and employed, directly and instrumentally, in the imposition of class power," this law was more than simply a tool of group interests. It was simultaneously pliant, yet sturdy; it "existed in its own right, [and] as ideology" (Thompson 1975, p. 262). In the emergent rule of law of the eighteenth century, the power of the state lay not with the military, the priests, the press, or the market, Thompson argued, "but in the rituals of the...Justices of the Peace, in quarter sessions, in the pomp of Assizes, and in the theatre of Tyburn," the collective legal spectacles that deluged the cities and county seats of Britain (p. 262). Could these historical analyses provide instruction on how to study contemporary legal consciousness?

Douglas Hay (1975), for example, described the contradictory representations of legal authority in his essay, "Property, Authority and the Criminal Law." Hay observed that British law was replete with statutes mandating capital punishment, and in particular capital sanctions "to protect every conceivable kind of property from theft or malicious damage" (Hay 1975, p. 106). Not only had Parliament produced an unprecedented number of capital statues, but it had also sanctioned an increasing number of convictions under these statutes. At the same time, however, Hay observed that there was a noticeable decline in the proportion of death sentences. How and why did the legal system create this blatant and apparent disjunction between legal prescriptions and the practices of criminal law? (The proverbial gap between the law on the books and the law in action seemed to have shown up three centuries before it had been named in twentieth century scholarship.) How was this contradiction managed and what were its consequences for British society, Hay wanted to know. The contradiction was functional, he concluded, protecting the power and resources of the landed gentry exactly as it was supposed to do. The legal system as an ideological phenomenon, Hay argued, helped resolve and pacify social strains created by the emerging capitalist economy and accompanying transformations in land ownership, labor, and class relations.

The more stringent capital sanctions for violations of law, coupled with a noticeable measure of legal formalism, discretionary administration, and publicly visible mercy in the form of pardons, sustained the interests of the landed gentry by establishing not only the sanctity of property rights but the authority of law as well. The criminal law created an explicit set of obligations and materially realizable bonds of obedience and deference that legitimated the status quo by "constantly recreating the structure of authority which arose from property, and in turn protected its interests" (Hay 1975, p. 108). Here, the law served, according to Hay's analysis, to create the meaning of wealth and definitions of property by naming the actions and relationships that challenged and resisted these definitions as theft, a crime (cf. Hall 1952). At the same time, merciful pardons lessened the burden of the full weight of the law. Because ultimate power—physical strength and numbers—lay with the populace, the landed elite required a means of subjugating the strength of the populace. By strategically deploying mercy, while invoking metaphors of equality, the law served the interests of the gentry. The law provided a political, apparently consensual, solution by which the "motives of the many induce [them] to submit to the few" (William Paley, quoted in Hay 1975, p. 108). In Hay's analysis, law provided the scripts for the enactment of command and deference. The law was the means by which the power of its authors could be institutionalized, so that the authors of the script and the beneficiaries of the play became less visible. Hay is describing the invention of the discourse that contemporary subjects have been heard to speak. Returning to the metaphor of the hegemonic legality I invoked above, Hay is describing how the ice accumulates to build a glacier that later breaks off to form the submerged iceberg of modern legality.

To the propertyless Englishmen of the time, Hay writes, the law offered a majestic spectacle, twice a year in the Assizes and four times a year in Quarter sessions. Entire communities would witness "the most visible and elaborate manifestation of state power to be seen in the countryside, apart from the presence of the regiment" (Hay 1975, p. 109). In its symbolism, management of emotions, and psychic demands, the law's rituals performed much like religion (Durkheim 1965, Berger 1967). The court spectacles were like carnivals, occasions for the community to coalesce in defense of violated norms and the sanctity and deity of property. The interests and agency of the owners of property were erased by the court performance. This charade was emboldened by the "punctilious attention to forms, the dispassionate and legalistic exchanges between counsel and the judge" (Hay 1975, p. 112) that showed to all how those administering and using the laws were themselves subjugated by it and willingly submitted to its rules. As a critical coda, the majesty of law that demanded equality nowhere else available in eighteenth century Britain displayed a decorous concern for protecting the property of ordinary as well as noble Englishmen. Finally, Hay writes, the regular and consistent pardoning of convicted felons sustained the image of an independent and just legal system. "Discretion allowed a prosecutor to terrorize the petty thief and then command his gratitude, or at least the approval of his neighbors as a man of compassion. It allowed the class that passed one of the bloodiest penal codes in Europe to congratulate itself on its humanity" (Hay 1975, p. 120).

Part of a collaboration with Hay and others to map plebian culture of eighteenth century Britain, Thompson also published in 1975 his monumental account of the history of the Black Act of 1723, one of the statutes under which the judges were extending mercy in Hay's account. This act introduced the death penalty for many new offenses specifically associated with the recently enclosed common lands, offenses as trivial as deer stalking in disguise at night, cutting down young trees, and writing threatening letters. The act was a product, Thompson (1975) argues, of fierce antagonisms between the foresters who had traditionally lived off the land and those who were recently enriched through the new money economy and expanding state offices and who sought to settle themselves as landed gentlemen, deer park keepers rather than deer hunters. The Black Act was an alliance between the emerging merchant classes seeking legitimacy and security through landholding and Whig politicians and lawyers, and it provided the instruments with which to eradicate subsistence hunting and logging by turning tradition, history, and habit into criminal offenses against property (cf. Polanyi 1944).

At the conclusion of his history of the act and its enforcement, Thompson fashioned what has become one of the most compelling accounts of the hegemonic rule of law (cf. Steinberg 1997). Although eighteenth century British law could be seen, he said, "instrumentally as mediating and reinforcing existent class relations, and ideologically as offering to these a legitimation. . ., class relations were expressed, not in any way one likes, but through the forms of law; and the law, like other institutions which from time to time can be seen as mediating (and masking) existent class relations. . .has its own characteristics, its own independent history, and logic of evolution" (Thompson 1975, p. 262). For several centuries, the law was a terrain of active, bloody struggle against monarchial absolutism, not always an instrument of class rule. However, the piecemeal victories won against the crown over the centuries were inherited, Thompson argued, not by the hunters and plebian population aspiring to full citizenship but by this newly moneyed and landed gentry. Were it not for law, the legal forms, and the institutions created over those years of struggle against the sovereign, the eighteenth century gentry would face unprotected the much older, ancient heritage of unconstrained noble authority.

> Take law away, and the royal prerogative, or the presumptions of the aristocracy, might flood back upon their properties and lives; take law away and the string which tied together their lands and marriages would fall apart. But it was inherent in the very nature of the medium which they had selected for their own self-defense that it could not be reserved for the exclusive use only of their own class. The law, in its forms and traditions, entailed principles of equity and universality which, perforce, had to be extended to all sorts and degrees of men. And since this was of necessity so, ideology could turn necessity to advantage. What had been devised by men of property as a defense against arbitrary power could be turned into service as an apologia for property in the face of the propertyless. And the apologia was serviceable up to a point: for these "propertyless"...comprised multitudes of men and women who themselves enjoyed, in fact, petty property rights or agrarian use-rights whose definition was inconceivable without the forms of law. Hence, the ideology of the great struck root in a soil, however shallow, of actuality. And the courts gave substance to the ideology by the scrupulous care with which, on occasion, they adjudged petty rights, and on all occasions, preserved properties and forms.

> We reach then, not a simple conclusion (law = class power) but a complex and contradictory one. On the one hand, it is true that the law did mediate existent class relations to the advantage of the rulers.... On the other hand, the law mediated these class relations through legal forms, which imposed again and again, inhibitions upon the actions of the rulers (Thompson 1975, p. 264).

In 1980, Duncan Kennedy produced one of the earliest and most ambitious accounts of American legal consciousness that, like the British legal historians, describes a hegemonic ideology mediating class interests. Unlike the British studies, however, Kennedy confined his analysis to the interpretation of doctrinal materials and elite professionals rather than popular culture, although he built his analysis from similar theoretical concepts and resources. Like the British historians, he sought to revise a conventional history that inadequately explained how class interests came to dominate what appeared to be relatively available legal instruments and an open, democratic legal terrain (i.e., the gap in its doctrinal guise). During this period of American history (1840–1935), Kennedy writes, "treatise writers, leaders of the bar, Supreme Court Justices, and the like shared a conception of law that appeared to transcend the old conflicting schools [of jurisprudence], and to ally the profession with science against both philosophical speculation and the crudities of democratic politics" (Kennedy 1980, p. 4). Kennedy describes this synthesizing conception of law as a particular form of legal consciousness that, in his analysis, explains how the political and economic interests of the time were mediated through legal processes and institutions to produce specific case and policy outcomes.

Kennedy claims that American legal reasoning and practices divided the legal world into four distinct spheres, each of which involved a delegation of "legal powers absolute within their spheres": relations among citizens, between citizens and state, between branches of government, and between federal and state governments. These institutional boundaries were so taken for granted that the concepts and arguments that enacted them were virtually invisible, "so basic that actors rarely if ever bring them consciously to mind. Yet everyone, including actors who think they disagree profoundly about the substantive issues that matter, would dismiss without a second thought (perhaps as 'not a legal argument' or as 'simply missing the point') an approach appearing to deny" these salient features of the American legal system (Kennedy 1980, p. 6). American legal consciousness of this period, Kennedy writes, described these four institutions as specific powers delegated by the sovereign people to carry out their will, but within this delegation of sovereign power the authority was absolute. In this system of institutional spheres, the judiciary exercised a special role and commanded a peculiar legal technique: to police through objective, quasi-scientific means the relational boundaries. Each of these relational spheres was organized by qualitatively distinct bodies of law and principles: the common law, sovereignty limited by written constitutions, the equilibrium of forces between separate governmental powers, the union of sovereign states.

Classical legal consciousness, as Kennedy describes it, organized and reconciled what might otherwise appear in alternative epistemological or jurisprudential regimes as conflicts among institutions and contradictions among ideas. "Classical legal thought," as a particular form of legal consciousness,[7] "appeared to permit the resolution of the basic institutional and political conflicts between populist legislatures and private business, between legislatures and courts over the legitimacy and extent of judicial review, and between state and federal governments struggling for regulatory jurisdiction. At the level of ideas, it mediated the contradictions between natural rights theories and legal positivism, and between democratic theory of legislative supremacy and the classical economic prescriptions about the optimal role of the state in the economy" (Kennedy 1980, p. 9). Thus, Kennedy describes a body of ideas created by lawyers and through which they conceived the fundamental shape of governance and public policy. This model of American government and law was disseminated through teaching and writing so that while still the province of legal elites, it also infiltrated more popular political discourse, a point I will return to in the conclusion of this essay (cf. Kammen 1994). This emergent consciousness permitted and legitimated the judicial activism and interventionism that built the American state while simultaneously valorizing popular sovereignty and transcendent immutable law. Kennedy claims that classical legal

---

[7]Kennedy (2003) revisits the topic of legal consciousness in the context of the globalization of legal thought, 1850–1968.

consciousness wove the various strands of public discourse of law into a sturdy hegemonic fabric.

Hartog (1985, 1993) built similarly persuasive analyses with a focus on the everyday life of nineteenth century Americans. His reading of the Abigail Bailey diary (Hartog 1993) provides an apt example. Bailey's diary reveals how this woman, over the course of many years, struggled to make sense of her marriage, her husband's sexual abuse of their daughter, their separation and eventual divorce, as well as her own religious beliefs regarding her duties as a wife and mother. Hartog demonstrates that this narrative of personal tragedy and change is incomprehensible without reference to legal categories such as the prevailing law of coverture (a woman's loss of legal rights or personalty upon marriage). Abigail Bailey's perception and assessment of her situation and of her daughter's experiences were conditioned upon her understanding of the legitimacy of a husband's desires and the priority of his rights. Because the law established a husband as a virtual sovereign within his family, it was difficult to openly question or oppose her husband's actions as inappropriate. Equally important, however, the events of Abigail Bailey's narrative are incomprehensible when viewed only through the lens of formal law.

Because law is both an embedded and an emergent feature of social life, it collaborates with other social structures (in this case religion, family, and gender) to infuse meaning and constrain social action. Furthermore, because of this collaboration of structures, in many instances law may be present although subordinate. To recognize the presence of law in everyday life is not, therefore, to claim any necessarily overwhelming power. Abigail Bailey's thoughts, prayers, and arguments were filled with law; legal facts, remedies, strategies, and institutions were constantly present. Yet the nature of her consciousness was not determined by law. She bargained in the shadow of law, yet the law in whose shadow she bargained was a complex and contradictory structure, experienced as an external control and constraint, reconstructed regularly in conversations and arguments, intertwined in significant tension with religious beliefs and norms.

LEGALITY AND LEGAL CONSCIOUSNESS

In the early 1990s, these productive paradoxes came to fruition. Law was recognized simultaneously as a space of engagement, repression, and resistance. The discrepancy between generalized accounts of law and the specific experiences of actors was seen to be a source of law's power.

Ewick & Silbey (1998)[8] designed a study of legal consciousness to address the paradoxes in the previous research methods and results, hoping to reconcile the approaches of contemporary empirical research with each other and with the historical accounts. By conducting intensive, in-depth, open-ended conversational

---

[8]This discussion of legality and legal consciousness derives from work done in collaboration with Patricia Ewick in the 1990s and reported at length in Ewick & Silbey (1998).

interviews, they sought to overcome the limitations of the survey research. By interviewing over 400 people in a randomized sample of an entire state, they attempted to overcome some of the non-generalizability concerns of the anthropological ethnographies. Finally, they wanted to return to an understanding of legal consciousness that was not reduced to an individual-level variable (how people think about the law), but to analyze legal consciousness as participation in the construction of legality. The historians had shown how particular practices cumulated to produce authority, and eventually hegemony, for liberal law. The study of contemporary legal consciousness needed to address this same animating concern: to show how the diverse and sometimes contradictory legal practices nonetheless were experienced as a taken-for-granted unity. Despite an enormous variety of forms, actions, actors, and aspirations, law seems to emerge from local, particular, and discrete interactions with the ontological integrity it has claimed for itself and that legal scholars have long attributed to it. To pursue this project, it would be insufficient to map individual or group variation; it was essential to demonstrate how the variations in what people thought and did about law—that had been documented in the previous research projects—together constituted the rule of law. Ewick and Silbey produced an account not of persons but of what they called legality, defining legal consciousness as the participation in this process of constructing legality.

Ewick and Silbey use the term legality to refer to the meanings, sources of authority, and cultural practices that are commonly recognized as legal, regardless of who employs them or for what purposes. With this analytic term, they distinguish their research and theoretical focus from the institutional manifestations of legality in the laws, legal profession, forms, acts, processes, etc. The analytic construct "legality" names a structural component of society, that is, cultural schemas and resources that operate to define and pattern social life (Sewell 1992). Through repeated invocations of legal concepts and terminology, as well as through imaginative and unusual associations among schemas, legality is constituted through everyday actions and practices. In this work, legal consciousness is decentered in that the research does not document chiefly what people think and do about the law but rather how what they think and do coalesces into a recognizable, durable phenomena and institution we recognize as the law. Law and legality achieve their recognizable character as the rule of law, Ewick and Silbey argue, despite the diversity of constituent actions and experiences (forms of consciousness), because individual transactions are crafted out of a limited array of generally available cultural schemas. These few but generally circulating schemas are not themselves fixed or immutable, but are also constantly in the making through local invocations and inventions.

Several conceptual moves distinguish their work. First, Ewick and Silbey did not directly ask about law; they asked about people's lives and waited to hear when the law emerged, or did not emerge, in the accounts people provided of an enormous array of topics and events that might pose problems or become matters of concern or conflict. The conversations were analyzed to identify moments when law could have been a possible and appropriate response to a situation and was not mentioned, as well as moments when law was mentioned, appropriately or not. The conversational topics were intentionally varied and comprehensive, seeking to create rather than foreclose opportunities for people to talk about diverse experiences and interpretations. The researchers were seeking people's experience and interpretations of the law and did not want to assume its place in their lives but rather discover it as it emerged, or did not, in accounts of events. The interview was specifically designed to access the actor's interpretations of legality, not to check the quality of their legal knowledge according to some professional judgment of what constitutes the law and legality. The method did not assume the importance or centrality of law, although the object of the analysis was to create an account of hegemonic legality. It was simply the target of the research, the analysts' construction of the research problem. Thus, the work focused on everyday life, did not adopt a law-first perspective, and waited to see if, when, and how legal concepts, constructs, or interpretations emerged.

Second, Ewick and Silbey organize their work around three common schemas that ran, they say, like "a braided plait through the idiosyncratic stories people told." These schemas of legality are the researchers' constructs, abstracted from their respondents' accounts and resynthesized into narratives of legality they label "before," "with," and "against" the law.[9] Thus, in reviewing any particular respondent's interview, one encounters only pieces of the researchers' reconstructed meta-narratives, and often pieces of more than one. The researchers organize the pieces of conversations (with respect to law and legality) by identifying a common template of narrative joining social theory to everyday action and meaning. Thus, each of the common schemas of legality emphasizes a different normative value (e.g., objectivity, availability and self interest, power); it also provides an account of how social action is enabled or constrained and located in time and space within that account.[10]

The native theories of social action consonant with the dominant value (determinacy, possibility, unjust power) describe action within each meta-narrative as both institutionally constrained and enabled. These dimensions of the narrative schemas are the basic elements of social structure that are usually implicit, and only sometimes explicit, in fully developed narratives. Of course, many stories told in conversation are not fully formed with all dimensions (Bruner 1986, 1987, 1990, 1991; Polkinghorne 1988; Mumby 1993; Riessman 1993; Ewick & Silbey

---

[9]Ewick and Silbey use the term schemas following Sewell (1992) as informal, not always conscious, metaphors of communication, action, and representation. We use the term narrative (or meta-narrative) to refer to the collation of dimensions (normativity, constraint, capacity, time/space), sometimes, if appropriate, interchangeably with schemas.

[10]A similar narrative template, drawing upon the dimensions of constraint, capacity, normativity, time/space to describe social action, can be usefully constructed, we believe, for many other aspects of culture (e.g., science or sport), synthesizing the diverse accounts that have plagued the literatures over time, thus offering the possibility of significant theoretical and empirical advance for sociology (Ewick & Silbey 2002).

1995, 2003; Czarniaska 1997, 1998; Ochs & Capps 2001). Nonetheless, whenever normally competent subjects speak and hope to be understood, they draw from and contribute to a common pool of circulating signs and symbols, including aspects and understandings of social structure (Ewick & Silbey 1995, 2003). The schemas Ewick and Silbey describe as before, with, and against the law, are described as the cultural tool-kit from which popular understandings of legality are constructed. The schemas do not identify persons as having a particular, singular form of consciousness, nor are they categories naming types of action or thought that are likely to be found whole in any one account, act, or experience. One cannot easily use them as coding devices. Rather, these narrative schemas collect and organize the materials out of which people construct their accounts of law, that is, the components that constitute legality in the popular culture (the accounts of law are the native speakers' terms; the structure of legality is the analysts' conceptualization). They are abstracted and synthesized narratives that emplot the relationships among the capacities, constraints, values, and temporalities of law. More specifically for law, the narratives not only mediate alternative social theories, but they also reproduce the variety of jurisprudential conceptions of law that have for so long competed for position as *the* account of law's power and authority. Legal consciousness, in this account, consists of mobilizing, inventing, and amending pieces of these schemas.

Third, although Ewick and Silbey organize their work around the three schemas, the major import of the work is their explanation of how the ensemble of narratives work to constitute both a hegemonic legal consciousness, the rule of law, and openings for change or resistance (Ewick & Silbey 2003). After all, the study of legal consciousness was from the outset animated in large part by this concern. Analytically synthesized from myriad stories people told to the researchers, the three schemas are not three experientially separate or distinct narratives; in operation they cannot be separated, as each one constitutes and enables the other. Ewick and Silbey argue that legality's durability and strength (as a structure of social action) derives directly from this schematic complexity in popular culture and consciousness. Legality is actually strengthened by the oppositions that exist within and among the narratives.

The dialectical set of narratives of legality they develop is not simply the familiar opposition between ideal and practice, or capacity and constraint, but variation between generalized accounts of law and the specific experiences of actors. General, ahistorical truths (the objective, rational organization of legal thought and action, the availability of and access to justice, the fairness of due process) are constructed alongside, but as essentially incomparable to, particular and local practices (importance of and unequal quality of legal representation; the inaccessibility or intransigence of bureaucratic agents; the violence of police). By emphasizing the normative ideals of objectivity, rationality, and accessibility, first-hand evidence and experience—of discriminatory police, incompetent lawyers, and overworked bureaucrats—that might potentially contradict the general truth and values of rationality, accessibility, and objectivity are excluded as idiosyncratic, anecdotal, and largely irrelevant. However, a durable and hegemonic conception of the rule of law is not achieved by simply discounting everyday experiences and removing law from everyday life through abstractions or rationalized concepts and definitions. At the same time that legality is construed as existing outside of everyday life in its own professional realm and in generalized, abstracted values, it is also located securely within ordinary life and commonplace transactions. Legality is different and distinct from daily life, yet commonly present. The experiences of law in everyday life may be rendered irrelevant by an abstracted, rational, and reified conception of law as expressed in the story before the law, but the power and relevance of law to everyday life is affirmed by the story of law as a game. Any singular account of the rule of law conceals the social organization of law by effacing the connections between the concrete particular and the transcendent general. Consequently, power and privilege can be preserved through what appears to be the irreconcilability of the particular and the general.

Because legality and legal consciousness have this internal complexity, among and within the common narratives, the rule of law achieves hegemony. Any particular experience can fit within the diversity of the whole. To state the matter differently, legality is much weaker and more vulnerable where it is more singularly conceived. If legality were ideologically consistent, it would be quite fragile. For instance, if the only thing people knew about the law was its profane face of crafty lawyers and outrageous tort cases, it would be difficult to sustain the support necessary for legal authority. Conversely, a law unleavened by familiarity and even the cynicism familiarity breeds would in time become irrelevant. Either way—as solely god or entirely a gimmick—it would eventually self-destruct.

Finally, and perhaps most importantly as a contribution to interpretation and research, the schemas that Ewick and Silbey identified theoretically organized the varieties of legal consciousness that had been described in the previous research. They confirmed the observations of deep normative consensus with regard to norms of procedural fairness (Lind & Tyler 1988, Tyler 1990), while also observing tactical, sometimes cynical, sometimes earnest employment of law's devices for a variety of personal or organizational interests that so much of the literature had described. They also documented the resistance to legal processes that Bumiller (1988), Greenhouse (1986), Engel (1993), White (1990), Sarat (1990), and Katz (1988) had described in a wide range of social fields and actions. The combination of extensive data collection with intensive conversations reproduced many of the results of the existing literature, while also developing a theoretical synthesis. More recent studies have challenged some of the methods (Mezey 2001, Levine & Mellema 2001, Villegas 2003, Hertogh 2004) but have also confirmed the description of legality as multiply stranded cultural schemas (Nielsen 2000, 2002, 2004; Quinn 2000; Gilliom 2001; Steiner 2001; Engel & Munger 2003; Fleury-Steiner 2003, 2004; Hoffman 2003, 2005; Hull 2003; Kostiner 2003; Marshall 2003, 2005; Sagay 2003; Cowan 2004; Kourilsky-Augeven 2004; Pelisse 2004a,b; Albiston 2006). Researchers do not all use the same theoretical conceptualizations, especially concerning social structures of resources and schemas; nonetheless, this literature repeatedly describes heterogeneous popular conceptions of law and legal institutions.

SITUATING LEGAL CONSCIOUSNESS

Three questions animate contemporary studies of legal consciousness: how to socially situate legal consciousness in classes, genders, and racial and other status groups, as well as in organizational settings; how to resolve continuing debates about the theoretical definition, cultural meanings, and social locations of resistance to law; and how to theoretically and methodologically bridge the micro worlds of individuals and macro theories of ideology, hegemony, and the rule of law. I address the first and third questions in this and the next section, directing readers to Ewick & Silbey (2003) for an extended discussion of the second question concerning resistance to legal authority.

In a growing number of studies, scholars continue to trace the understandings of law that circulate through social relations. In much of this work, "law is understood experientially, in ways shaped by class, education, geography, and occupational position" (Cooper 1995, p. 510). The research documents how legal meanings and resources compete with and compliment other motives, needs, aspirations, and norms, demonstrating "that people make claims on the law, but not necessarily rights claims; that the law leads people to accept and acquiesce to existing social and economic arrangements without making them 'lump' their grievances; and that people may reject the formal apparatus of law even as they create viable substitutes for its power and authority" (Marshall & Barclay 2003, p. 625). Researchers attempt to map the variations in legal consciousness by associating distinct interpretations and actions with different sociological or demographic markers. Some studies begin with a particular location, such as a government office (Cowan 2004; cf. Sarat 1989; Cooper 1995) or a workplace (Hoffman 2003; Marshall 2003, 2005; Pelisse 2004a,b; Albiston 2006). Others investigate the legal consciousness of people who share social characteristics (not of space but of identity or experience) that are expected to influence their interpretations of institutions and processes including the law such as, for example, working women's experience of and responses to sexual harassment (Quinn 2000; Marshall 2003, 2005; Tinkler 2003; Sagay 2003); street women's (prostitutes' and drug users') legal and illegal income generating strategies (Levine & Mellema 2001); single sex couples' efforts to legalize or in some other way sanctify their unions (Hull 2003); or jurors' experience of capital punishment (Fleury-Steiner 2003, 2004). Because legal rights and social and cultural settings are understood in this research tradition to "mutually shape" one another (Yngvesson 1993, McCann 1994), those who enjoy constitutional or statutory protection for a categorical condition such as a physical or cognitive disability (Engel & Munger 2003) or racial (Fleury-Steiner 2004) or gender identity (Merry 2003, Sagay 2003, Nielsen 2004), and those who enjoy considerably less legal protection and command little economic or social capital, such as welfare applicants and recipients (Gilliom 2001, Cowan 2004; cf. Sarat 1989; Merry 1990; Yngvesson 1993), are expected to express differential legal consciousness.

With few exceptions, the research rarely demonstrates stable relationships between social location or status and what the researchers name as their dependent variable, variously defined, for example, as how legal *consciousness is produced* (Cowan 2004), how *law penetrates* the consciousness of ordinary people (Hull 2003), how women *understand their experience* with sexual harassment (Marshall 2003), how law *produces social change* (McCann 1994, Silverstein 1996, Kostiner 2003), *how law matters* (Levine & Mellema 2001), or how rights talk *shapes identity* (Engel & Munger 2003, Merry 2003, cf. Glendon 1991). The research more often documents how social sites (either human groups or settings) entail heterogeneous legal consciousness. Cowan (2004), for example, describes the subjective experiences of unsuccessful applicants for welfare assistance as they seek access to housing for the homeless in Britain. He describes not a singular interpretation among these particularly disadvantaged people, but rather what he thinks may be a Pandora's box of pluralistic conceptions of law in society. He describes his respondents as expressing confidence in the officials' capacities to act fairly and follow the law; they participate, Cowan says, in reifying the law on the books as more compelling than their own housing need. Here, Cowan observes exactly the hegemonic legality that Ewick and Silbey describe, valorizing the general abstract and discrediting the experiential particular. "There is," Cowan writes, "an exaggerated image of bureaucratic formal rationality whereby the officers apply clear and fixed legal rules in a simple and neutral fashion.... What our interviewees did was to distance the person they had personal contact with from the actual decision—they explained this either because the interviewer [housing officer] had to 'go by the book' or, in fact, depersonalized the interviewer within a bureaucratic hierarchy" (Cowan 2004, pp. 949, 950). However, Cowan also describes how some of the applicants recognized that the housing office needed to be played by knowledgeable gamesmen, lawyers rather than ordinary citizens, because the outcomes were not preordained by transparent rules. At the same time, Cowan also observed tactics of resistance as applicants refused to go along with the intimidating interviewers who threatened prosecution for lying on the applications that were filled out only through the intermediary of the interviewer's interpretations; applicants performed or masqueraded what they were not (calm and reasonable) in order to deny the interviewer's attribution of the applicant as out of control in the face of bureaucratic coercion and unreason. "'They think you have to wait so it calms you down, you have to calm down but it's the opposite that happens. I don't feel calm about it. When I see them, I'm certainly not, I don't even want to be polite but I know that I have to be polite because I need something off them'" (Cowan 2004, p. 946).

Almost all the research describes the double bind of experiencing constraints in the attempt to enact human agency; the studies specifically emphasize the frustrations and contradictions of empowering oneself by deploying the law's powers. "The attempt to gain power through law caused feelings of powerlessness" (Cowan

2004, p. 945; cf. Bumiller 1988). Speaking of sexual harassment, Quinn (2000, p. 1164) writes, "to take it personal, is to claim simultaneously the harm [one has experienced] and one's own disempowerment. To move beyond the local and draw on the power of law requires speaking one's pain and powerlessness to the harassers, to one's employer, and perhaps to the formal law. In so speaking, one acquires the identity of victim." Similarly, Engel (1991, 1993) expresses this double bind with regard to protection for the disabled, that one must be cast out of the world of the normal before one is afforded what should be the normal protection of the law, equal social status and respect.

The literature on legal consciousness repeatedly documents how the law's instrumentalities come with costs that are, as the early law and society research also showed, disproportionately distributed: easier to bear for those who have many forms and volumes of capital; a heavier, often disabling burden that reinscribes disadvantage for those with less. The studies describe among the disadvantaged, however, not a singular, resistant consciousness but this same complex awareness of the opportunities and constraints of legality. Thus, Sarat (1990) describes Spencer, an applicant in a New Haven welfare office, experiencing himself caught within a tightening web of law; at the same time, Spencer believed that he could use law to get what he needed. The welfare recipients Sarat observed and interviewed seem to have had a strong sense of law as an alien, corrupt, vengeful power; they did not subscribe to the myth of rights, to ideologies of legal objectivity or neutrality. Yet, they simultaneously resisted the legal agents' efforts to demean and control while they played with the legal rules and engaged with the law, hoping its power and authority could be made to work for them in this instance. Unlike most of Cowan's subjects, Sarat describes his respondents as knowledgeable players able, he says, "to resist the 'they say(s)' and 'supposed to(s)' of the welfare bureaucracy" (Sarat 1990, p. 346). Welfare recipients do not, however, normally resist the system, the law, the techniques of surveillance and control. As Gilliom (2001, p. 91) writes, they often do not even engage the law. With "few economic or political resources, little education, little solidarity, no organizational structure, no hope of putting rights to work. . .the institutional, structural, and social pressures push against the assertion of rights" or any engagement with the law. Those who do engage or resist are an anomaly.

Cooper (1995) describes government officials very much like Sarat's knowledgeable welfare recipients. They both engage and resist the law, simultaneously applicants, administrators, and supplicants, actively seeking to enlist the law's possibilities. The council agents that Cooper interviewed

> described themselves in terms remarkably similar to Sarat's informants—out of control, caught in a tightening web of law. At the same time, they deployed law where they could, challenging government ministers and departments over legislative interpretations. This was notwithstanding the fact many saw law as a ritualistic telling in which they could not be heard, other than to incite retaliation. . . . [However], not all local government actors depicted law as

oppressive, powerful, and politically significant. For others, law functioned primarily as an environmental nuisance, resource or taken-for-granted condition of local governmental activity. The range of responses to law makes it difficult to depict municipal actors as part of a single interpretive community (Cooper 1995, pp. 510–11).

Continuing the effort to situate legal consciousness within particular social spaces, Marshall has studied the construction of sexual harassment policies in workplaces and the interpretations of harassing behavior by working women. She finds that "while legal frames do provide crucial guidance to women evaluating the behavior of their colleagues and supervisors, working women deployed a number of other interpretive frames when deciding whether they had been harmed by such behavior" (Marshall 2003, p. 659; cf. Marshall 2005). Their interpretations drew from feminist ideologies about subordination and discrimination, management ideologies about efficiency and productivity, and libertarian critiques of government policies that limited sexual freedom. Marshall argues that a sense of harm does not necessarily lead to an interpretation of behavior as harassment. Interpretations of harassment and sexuality were embedded, she says, in more general interpretations of subordination, and thus consciousness of law, as measured by embrace of harassment remedies, was not unidirectional. Similarly, Nielsen's (2000, 2004) efforts to map the relationships among gender, race, and legal consciousness also produced accounts of multiple, heterogeneous interpretations of the utility, availability, and legitimacy of using law to address issues of gender or racial harassment on the public streets. Although the victims often experience themselves as diminished in freedom or status as a consequence of verbally hostile street exchanges, law is not the preferred response, with citizens offering at least four different reasons for opposing legal regulation of street harassment. Fleury-Steiner (2004) explored the legal consciousness of jurors in capital cases, expecting to find some consistent relationship between race and the responses to the crime and possible punishments. Although he sometimes finds clear differences along racial lines, these are not consistent. Race or class affinities may encourage less rather than more sympathy with a defendant, with jurors more rather than less willing to judge and condemn the defendant.

In her study of gay and lesbian couples, Hull (2003, p. 631) also challenges claims that forms of legal consciousness might be expected to correlate with social status. Although marginalized persons are hypothesized to express resistant consciousness, Hull found that her respondents, certainly among the stigmatized populations in American society, expressed some resistant consciousness but it was by no means dominant. Quite the contrary, Hull found that the same-sex couples she interviewed employed a range of schemas of legality: "At the same time that couples resist their current exclusion from official law (i.e., their lack of marriage rights), many couples also act 'with the law' by appropriating its terms and practices to define their committed relationships, and some also stand 'before the law,' awed by its perceived cultural power" (Hull 2003, pp. 631–32).

It is worth noting, perhaps, that in many of the recent studies attempting to situate legal consciousness, the object of analysis has shifted from law and legality to some other phenomena: sexual harassment, the meanings of marriage, behavior on the streets, interpretations of capital punishment, identity as a person with disabilities, social change. Thus, the research often ends up tracing not consciousness of law but of something else, e.g., race, gender, class, sexuality, identity, disability. Moreover, while much of the research claims to eschew a law-first perspective, to begin "with eyes not on law but on events and practices that seem on the face of things removed from law or at least not dominated" by law (Sarat & Kearns 1993, p. 55), nonetheless much of the research has begun with a legal probe (e.g., harassment, capital punishment). At the same time, the research has made the object of its analysis, as well as data collection, not law but something else (e.g., class, gender).

Although these variations in interpretations and discourses of legality confirm that legal consciousness of ordinary citizens is a variable phenomenon, there are good theoretical reasons why few studies have been able to produce compelling associations between legal consciousness and particular types of laws, particular social hierarchies, and the experiences of different groups with the law. First, the attempts to situate and differentiate legal consciousness among different social locations belie the processes of cultural production in contemporary, postmodern societies. Second, the analyses are too often limited to reports of data, empiricist to a fault, missing, shall we say, the forest for the trees. I take each of these concerns in turn.

Cultural Production

Given the fluidity, disembeddedness, and porousness of popular culture, we are unlikely to find unique or distinguishable cultural schemas categorically distributed among heterogeneous populations that participate in the construction of a commonly shared culture yet occupy different positions in social space (Habermas 1983, 1992, 1998; Apparadurai 1990; Bourdieu 1990; Giddens 1990; Harvey 1990; Sassen 1991; Beck 1992; Bauman 1998). In contrast to most of the studies of particular but dispersed population groups, studies of persons in highly organized, normative settings more characteristic of modern than postmodern social formations have found strong relationships between cultural interpretations, legal consciousness, and social locations. In her study of the municipal agents in Britain, Cooper (1995) suggested that two material conditions correlated with legal consciousness: party affiliation and political ideology. She believes that this differentiation, unremarked in most other studies, is a consequence of the more strongly ideological and mobilized political organizations in Britain. Seron et al. (2004) also finds that political ideology explains differences in judgments of police misconduct among New Yorkers. Thus, the association between political ideology and legal consciousness may not be primarily a British phenomenon. In another American study of two taxicab companies, companies that differed by the degree to which they incorporated worker-management cooperation or a more conventional hierarchical organizational structure, Hoffman (2003, p. 711) found significant differences in the degree to which employees expressed grievances and used grievance-handling procedures. She suggests that in the cooperative taxicab company workers' more highly developed legal consciousness did not develop by chance. The more explicit and formalized processes in the cooperative that correlated with a particular political orientation helped to habituate a more activist legal consciousness compared with the more conventional company. Thus, both the study of British civil servants and the study of American taxicab drivers suggest that legal consciousness can be developed as part of specific projects of political or workplace mobilization. These are not studies of ordinary citizens in unorganized settings or random citizens responding to standardized stimuli.

McCann's (1994) extensive study of the pay equity movement and the politics of legal mobilization also suggests that when legal consciousness is explored as a component in a political project, researchers observe strong relationships between social position and legal consciousness. McCann argues that despite the failure to win legal battles for pay equity, the litigation and other forms of legal advocacy provided reformers with legal discourse for defining and advancing their cause. The participants in the movement became more aware and active users of legal concepts and ideas, just as they became equally aware of the legal and institutional limitations and constraints on their efforts. Political mobilization and legal consciousness, that is, participation in the construction of legality, went hand in hand. Similarly, in her study of the early Civil Rights movement in the United States, Polletta (2000) suggests that adopting legal strategies and rights claims "inside and outside the courtrooms were essential to their political organizing efforts. Far from narrowing the collective aspirations to the limits of the law," as some critics of rights talk had suggested, "activists' extension of rights claims to the 'unqualified' legitimated assaults on economic inequality, governmental decision-making in poverty programs, and the Vietnam War" (Polletta 2000, p. 367). This broad-based political critique that developed in the Civil Rights movement was enabled by the multivalent character of legal rights, as well as by the institutional and organizational contexts in which they were mobilized. A more recent study of legal consciousness among social movement activists elaborates on this multivalent character of rights, specifically the contradictory ways in which activists for social change criticize the use of law. Here, as with the other mobilized populations, Kostiner (2003) observes a correlation between forms of legal consciousness and something else, in this case, the activists' particular conceptions of social change.

That social movement participation, party affiliation, and political ideology are correlated with specific expressions and forms of legal consciousness is not surprising; indeed, it is what one would expect. "Groups, such as social classes, are *to be made*.... They are not given in 'social reality'" (Bourdieu 1990, p. 129, emphasis in original).

Political work consists of producing classes and groups with similar dispositions that assemble closely in social space. Social movements and political parties are ideological fora, with expressly articulated, openly debated interpretations of social problems, resources, government action, as well as law and justice. If legal consciousness is understood to be the ways of participating in the construction of legality, these organizations are purposely, explicitly, and self-reflexively developing forms of legal consciousness.

The Empiricist-Substantialist Problem

The attempts to differentiate legal consciousness among distinct social locations commits what Cassirer (1923) and Bourdieu (1990, p. 125) call the substantialist error, "which inclines one to recognize no reality other than those that are available to direct intuition in ordinary experience.... [Yet] the visible, that which is immediately given, hides the invisible which determines it." A scholar of public opinion has succinctly explained the problem: "[I]f you ask it, they will answer. But reality or its construction...does not sit so close to the surface" (Bishop 2005, p. 187). Nonetheless, because opinions, attitudes, and interactions are tangible, because they can be observed, recorded, or filmed so that one can "reach out and touch them," they provide immediate gratification for our empiricist ambitions. Nonetheless, these empirical surfaces "mask the structures that are realized in them" (Bourdieu 1990, p. 126). Thus, when research manages to provide varying accounts of law that correlate significantly with demographic categories [e.g., as impractical, a challenge to autonomy, a set of rights and constitutional protection, or a arena of untrustworthy power (Nielsen 2004)], the authors need to show us how the different forms of consciousness or ways of participating work with each other to constitute the power of the law, or legality. In most of the studies, unfortunately, the different accounts remain as threads unwoven into the fabric of hegemony. The structure enabling and constraining these perceptions, attitudes, opinions, or, in Bourdieu's term, dispositions is absent.

The search for invariant forms of perception thus masks, according to Bourdieu, three critical processes in social construction: "firstly, that this construction [perception, attitude, or opinion about law, harassment, race, or utility of law for social change] is not carried out in a social vacuum but subjected to structural constraints; secondly, that structuring structures, cognitive structures [such as Ewick and Silbey's schemas of legality], are themselves socially structured because they have a social genesis; thirdly, that the construction of social reality is not only an individual enterprise but may become a collective enterprise" (Bourdieu 1990, p. 130).

In the laudable effort to push on the previous studies of legal consciousness, recent studies also seem to confuse the analyst's construct (legal consciousness, ideology, hegemony, legality) with the empirical measures or indicators of that construct: ordinary citizens' experiences and discourse about law. Collecting individual interpretations of the law through inquiries about capital punishment or workplace or street harassment is the beginning of an analysis of legal consciousness. Although researchers documented competing frames and interpretative schema, the aggregation of these to a cultural system or social structure of legality has given way before the task of reporting the experiences of ordinary people. Too many of the studies seem to have rested on the pixels of perception (e.g., attitudes) rather than the ground that enables perception. Legality, a theoretical construct as the object or consequence of legal consciousness, is lost as a structure of cultural production and its contribution to the production of legal ideology and hegemony unspoken. In the excavation and celebration of too often silenced voices, researchers may have inadvertently mistaken the culturally circulating terms of signification for the mechanisms by which those symbols are produced and connected so that "we the people" speak and are heard, but the orchestration and score remain invisible. In the course of this work, scholars have reinvented, without explaining, that canonical socio-legal gap, now elaborated as a gap between legal consciousness and mobilization (Marshall & Barclay 2003, p. 623).

CONCLUSIONS: THE PROFESSIONAL PRODUCTION OF LEGAL CONSCIOUSNESS

In concluding, I urge researchers to redirect studies of legal consciousness to recapture the critical sociological project of explaining the durability and ideological power of law. In doing so, it is important to acknowledge that I write at a particular historical moment: a time of war, of unprecedented political polarization, and of heavily financed and tightly organized challenges to the modern liberal state. A contemporary coalition of extraordinary concentrations of wealth and populist religion seems to be delivering the public weal almost entirely into private hands. We used to call this fascism, but I do not hear that word used very often any longer. Perhaps without the uniforms and jackboots, we do not recognize this political moment for what it is.[11]

I noted in the early sections of this review that the focus on legal consciousness developed directly from what appeared to be law's failure to realize its aspirations for equality and justice. In the 1960s and 1970s, prescient observers offered disquieting characterizations of headless tyrannies to describe the transformations of both representative democracies and communist regimes into almost homologous sclerotic bureaucracies. In 2005, we continue to live in Weberian cages, but the metaphoric iron has become silicon and electromagnetic waves, the cage itself quite purposively against Weber's prediction re-enchanted. Tyranny now seems to flow through the silicon and electromagnetic connections between our incited

---

[11] A full sociology of legal consciousness would not only focus on ideas and publications in an historic moment but would locate these in the social relations of profession, competitions for position, and the injustices of hierarchy that both animate and constrain not only the subjectivity of the persons and social locations we study, but our own positions as well. Unfortunately, space does not permit that analysis. Perhaps this review will provoke such a sociology of the knowledge of legal consciousness.

fears/desires and the apparatuses that promise to protect us from reality while satisfying us with its image (D. Goodman, personal correspondence).

Research seeking to represent the authentic voices of ordinary people belies the suffusion of everyday life by this professional, marketed cultural production. Justin Lewis (2001) describes this process, for example, showing how poll results have become a form of politically manipulated cultural representation, a means of representing the public to the public as supportive of the interests and policies of political and corporate elites. Moreover, this ability to seduce the public through mediated messages is a direct product of social scientific knowledge about human desire and cognition. A recent celebration of the one hundredth anniversary of the publication of Sigmund Freud's *Civilization and Its Discontents* focused on his nephew Edward Bernays, the reputed father of public relations in the United States. Bernays took Freud's complex ideas on people's unconscious, psychological motivations and applied them to the new field of public relations marketing. That field has prospered and with it the ability to sell anything to almost everyone. The cultural representations that suffuse the everyday life of ordinary citizens are not the consequence of a free market of ideas. In another recent account, ex-Senator Bill Bradley (2005) described in the *New York Times* the 30-year campaign of the Republican party to wrest control of the American government. At the core of the Republican strategy was the creation of research institutions, supported by the wealthiest families and foundations to train a cadre of "public intellectuals" to disseminate the party's ideas through higher education and the media. Organized to invent ideologies that would support the policies in their interests, these institutions also develop and test methods for making these ideological discourses palatable to the public whose interests they undermine.

In constructing an account of legal hegemony, it would be foolish to deny experiential, material differences in social spaces and lives. The central theoretical issue is not whether the conditions of our lives vary, but whether the cultural terms with which we understand and communicate, and with which we constitute our lives, can be correlated with concrete inequalities. Legal consciousness should not be understood in relation to external power and internal will, but in relation to the material inequality of our social life and the cultural terms of our understanding. I fear, however, that recent efforts to track legal consciousness may have inadvertently contributed to the loss of the social (Baudrillard 1983, Rose 1996, Sarat & Simon 2003), leaving us with studies of individual psychology and its accommodations to predefined policy goals. But law is not an alien power imposed upon our isolated and anarchic minds. Law is a basic, constitutive attribute of our social consciousness. It is a particular way of organizing meaning and force, and it is out of this that both law in action and law on the books proceed. The analysis of law must not be a choice between pragmatic policy recommendations of law in action or the transcendental interrogations of law on the books. Instead legal consciousness should be a tool for examining the mutually constitutive relationship between these two.

How might we move the field further? The most promising work seems to look at the middle level between citizen and the transcendent rule of law: the ground of institutional practices. In institutions cultural meaning, social inequality, and legal consciousness are forged. In institutions law both promises and fails to live up to its promises. One place to begin is the cultural industries where legal consciousness is most explicitly constructed. To describe the mechanisms by which legal schema are propagated, circulated, and received, we need institutional approaches that describe simultaneously the full range of social construction (e.g., Goodman 2005). Institutional studies of social construction, such as *Arresting Images: Crime and Policing in Front of the Television Camera* (Doyle 2003) or *Distorting the Law* (Haltom & McCann 2004), provide analyses of the production, distribution, and reception of messages about crime, litigation, and law, displaying and probing the professional production of legal ideologies.

However, it would be wrong to suppose that the cultural industries are the only producers of legal consciousness. Studies of specific institutional locations, for example medical clinics (Heimer & Staffen 1998, Heimer 1999), scientific laboratories (Silbey & Ewick 2003), insurance companies (Heimer 1985; Baker 1994, 2002; Ericson et al. 2003; Ericson & Doyle 2004), reclamation engineering (Espeland 1998), marketed rating systems (Espeland & Sauder 2004), universities (Strathern 2000), accounting (Carruthers & Espeland 1991, Power 1999, Rostain 2002), or bankruptcy regimes (Carruthers & Halliday 1998, Halliday & Carruthers 2005), can push the field further. One particularly valuable model is Larson's (2004) comparative study of security exchanges. His analysis reveals that the regulation of these industries is indeterminate because the regulation is constructed within the very field that it regulates. The formal laws and their practical applications are shaped by the types of disputes in which they are invoked, but the types of disputes in which laws are invoked are determined by the particular history of the institution. Hence, nearly identical rules result in widely divergent practices: In one case disputes might be resolved through recourse to formal rules and in another by appeal to internal norms. The temptation here is to use legal consciousness as a vague residual category and to investigate its psychological content. For Larson, however, legal consciousness is a response to the indeterminacy of law. It is not that one society has a stronger legal consciousness, but that the inherent indeterminacy of the law in action is resolved by different forms of legal consciousness, one form stressing internal norms and the other stressing formal rules.

This returns us to the tolerance for the gap between law on the books and law in action that the concept of legal consciousness was originally developed to explain. On the one hand, this gap is not simply the creation of the powerful, because indeterminacy is inherent to the application of formal laws. On the other hand, the gap is infinitely useful to the powerful, because its persistence provides an alibi for the particular form that the gap takes. Similarly, legal consciousness is not inherently hegemonic (indeed, it is the ground for the type of immanent critique favored by critical theorists); however, it is infinitely useful to hegemony. If hegemony is sustained, as I argue, by a dialectic embracing ahistorical, general accounts of law's transcendent majesty alongside pragmatic instrumental engagement with its techniques, we need to understand better the ideological struggles involved in constructing these accounts, how they provide the grounds simultaneously for valorization and critique.

ACKNOWLEDGMENTS

This essay has benefited from the insightful comments of careful readers. I am grateful for the help provided by Douglas Goodman, Tanina Rostain, Carroll Seron, Jessica Silbey, Patricia Ewick, Marc Steinberg, Jeremy Paul, Duncan Kennedy, Tom Burke, Paul Berman, Laura Dickinson, Kaaryn Gustafson, and Alexi Lahav.

The *Annual Review of Law and Social Science* is online at
http://lawsocsci.annualreviews.org

LITERATURE CITED

Abel R. 1973. A comparative theory of dispute institutions in society. *Law Soc. Rev.* 8:217–347

Abel R. 1995. *Politics by Other Means: Law in the Struggle Against Apartheid, 1980–1994.* New York: Routledge

Albiston C. 2006. Legal consciousness and workplace rights. In *New Civil Rights Research: A Constitutive Approach*, ed. B Fleury-Steiner, LB Nielsen. Burlington, VT: Dartmouth/Ashgate. In press

Apparadurai A. 1990. Disjuncture and difference in the global and cultural economy. *Public Culture* 2:1–24

Arendt H. 1972. *Crisis of the Republic.* New York: Harcourt Brace Janovich

Bahktin MM. 1981. *The Dialogic Imagination.* Austin: Univ. Tex. Press

Baker T. 1994. Constructing the insurance relationship: sales stories, claims stories and insurance contract damages. *Tex. Law Rev.* 72:1395

Baker T. 2002. Risk, insurance and the social construction of responsibility. In *Embracing Risk*, ed. T Baker, J Simon, pp. 33–51. Chicago: Univ. Chicago Press

Balbus ID. 1973. *The Dialectics of Legal Repression: Black Rebels Before the American Criminal Courts.* New York: Russell Sage Found.

Barrett M. 1980. *Women's Oppression Today: Problems in Marxist Feminist Analysis.* London: Verso

Baudrillard J. 1983. *In the Shadow of the Silent Majorities.* New York: Semiotext(e)

Bauman Z. 1998. *Globalization: The Human Condition.* New York: Columbia Univ. Press

Beck U. 1992. *Risk Society: Towards a New Modernity.* Beverly Hills: Sage

Berger PL. 1967. *Sacred Canopy: Elements of a Sociological Theory of Religion.* Garden City, NY: Doubleday

Berger PL, Luckman T. 1990 (1966). *The Social Construction of Reality: A Treatise on the Sociology of Knowledge.* Garden City, NY: Anchor Books

Billig M. 1991. *Ideology and Opinions: Studies in Rhetorical Psychology.* London: Sage

Bishop GF. 2005. *The Illusion of Public Opinion: Fact and Artifact in American Public Opinion Polls.* New York: Rowan & Littlefield

Bourdieu P. 1977. *Outline of a Theory of Practice.* Transl. R Nice. New York: Cambridge Univ. Press

Bourdieu P. 1990. *In Other Words: Essays Towards a Reflexive Sociology.* Transl. M Adamson. Stanford, CA: Stanford Univ. Press

Bradley B. 2005. A party inverted. *NY Times*, March 30, Section A, p. 17

Bruner J. 1986. *Actual Minds, Possible Worlds*. Cambridge, MA: Harvard Univ. Press

Bruner J. 1987. Life as narrative. *Soc. Res.* 54 (1):11–32

Bruner J. 1990. *Acts of Meaning*. Cambridge, MA: Harvard Univ. Press

Bruner J. 1991. The narrative construction of reality. *Crit. Inq.* 18:1–21

Bumiller K. 1988. *The Civil Rights Society: The Social Construction of Victims*. Baltimore, MD: Johns Hopkins Univ. Press

Carlin JE, Howard J, Messinger SL. 1966. Civil justice and the poor: issues for sociological research. *Law Soc. Rev.* 1(1):9–91

Carruthers BG, Espeland W. 1991. Accounting for rationality: double entry bookkeeping and the emergence of economic rationality. *Am. J. Sociol.* 97:31–69

Carruthers BG, Halliday TC. 1998. *Rescuing Business: The Making of Corporate Bankruptcy Law in England and the United States*. Oxford: Oxford Univ. Press

Cassirer E. 1923. *Substance and Function: Einstein's Theory of Relativity*. Transl. WC Swabey, MC Swabey. Chicago: Univ. Chicago Press

Casper JD, Tyler TR, Fisher B. 1988. Procedural justice in felony cases. *Law Soc. Rev.* 22: 483–507

Chaney DC. 1994. *The Cultural Turn: Scene-Setting Essays on Contemporary Cultural History*. London/New York: Routledge

Chanock M. 2001. *The Making of South African Legal Culture 1902–1936: Fear, Favor and Prejudice*. Cambridge, UK: Cambridge Univ. Press

Comaroff J, Comaroff JL. 1991. *Of Revelation and Revolution: Christianity, Colonialism, and Consciousness in South Africa*. Chicago: Univ. Chicago Press

Conley JM, O'Barr W. 1990. *Rules Versus Relationships: The Ethnography of Legal Discourse*. Chicago: Univ. Chicago Press

Connell RW. 1987. *Gender and Power: Society, the Person, and Sexual Politics*. Stanford, CA: Stanford Univ. Press

Cooper D. 1995. Local government legal consciousness in the shadow of juridification. *J. Law Soc.* 22(4):506–26

Cowan D. 2004. Legal consciousness: some observations. *Mod. Law Rev.* 67(6):928–58

Curran BA. 1977. *The Legal Needs of the Public: The Final Report of a National Survey*. Chicago: Am. Bar Found.

Czarniaska B. 1997. *Narrating the Organization*. Chicago: Univ. Chicago Press

Czarniaska B. 1998. *A Narrative Approach to Organization Studies*. Beverly Hills: Sage

Dezalay Y, Sarat A, Silbey S. 1989. D'une démarche contestaire à un savoir méritocratique. *Actes Rech. Sci Soc.* 78:79–93

Dolbeare K. 1967. *Trial Courts in Urban Politics: State Trial Court Policy Impact and Functions in a Local Political System*. New York: Wiley

Doyle A. 2003. *Arresting Images: Crime and Policing in Front of the Television Camera*. Toronto: Univ. Toronto Press

DuBois WEB. 1999 (1903). *The Souls of Black Folk*. Chicago: McClurg; New York: Bartleby.com

Durkheim E. 1965. *The Elementary Forms of Religious Life*. New York: Free Press

Durkheim E. 1982 (1895). *The Rules of Sociological Method*. New York: Free Press

Ellman S. 1992. *In a Time of Trouble: Law and Liberty in South Africa's State of Emergency*. Oxford: Clarendon

Engel D. 1984. The oven bird's song: insiders, outsiders, and personal injuries in an American community. *Law Soc. Rev.* 18(4):551–82

Engel D. 1991. Law culture and children with disabilities: educational rights and the construction of difference. *Duke Law J.* 1:166–205

Engel D. 1993. Origin myths: narratives of authority, resistance, disability, and law. *Law Soc. Rev.* 27(4):785–826

Engel D. 1998. How does law matter in the constitution of legal consciousness? In *How Does Law Matter?* ed. B Garth, A Sarat, pp. 109–44. Evanston, IL: Northwest. Univ. Press

Engel DM, Munger FW. 2003. *Rights of Inclusion: Law and Identity in the Life Stories of Americans with Disabilities*. Chicago: Univ. Chicago Press

Ericson RV, Doyle A. 2004. *Uncertain Business: Risk, Insurance, and the Limits of Knowledge*. Toronto: Univ. Toronto Press

Ericson RV, Doyle A, Barry D. 2003. *Insurance as Governance*. Toronto: Univ. Toronto Press

Erlanger H. 2005. Organizations, institutions, and the story of Shmuel: reflections on the 40th anniversary of the Law and Society Association. *Law Soc. Rev.* 39(1):1–10

Espeland WN. 1998. *Struggle for Water*. Chicago: Univ. Chicago Press

Espeland WN, Sauder M. 2004. *The reflexivity of rankings: the effects of* U.S. News *rankings on legal education*. Presented at Annu. Meet. Law Soc. Assoc., Chicago

Ewick P. 2003. Consciousness and ideology. In *The Blackwell Companion to Law and Society*, ed. A Sarat, pp. 80–94. Malden, MA: Blackwell

Ewick P, Silbey SS. 1995. Subversive stories and hegemonic tales: toward a sociology of narrative. *Law Soc. Rev.* 29(2):197–226

Ewick P, Silbey SS. 1998. *The Common Place of Law: Stories from Everyday Life*. Chicago: Univ. Chicago Press

Ewick P, Silbey SS. 2002. The structure of legality: the cultural contradictions of social institutions. In *Legality and Community: On the Intellectual Legacy of Philip Selznick*, ed. RA Kagan, M Krygier, K Winston, pp. 149–66. New York: Rowman & Littlefield

Ewick P, Silbey SS. 2003. Narrating social structure: stories of resistance to law. *Am. J. Sociol.* 108(6):1328–72

Fleury-Steiner B. 2003. Before or against the law? Citizens' legal beliefs and expectations as death penalty jurors. *Stud. Law Polit. Soc.* 27:115–37

Fleury-Steiner B. 2004. *Jurors' Stories of Death*. Ann Arbor: Univ. Mich. Press

Friedman LM. 1975. *The Legal System: A Social Science Perspective*. New York: Russell Sage Found.

Friedman LM. 1984. *American Law*. New York: W.W. Norton

Fuller LL. 1964. *The Morality of Law*. New Haven, CT: Yale Univ. Press

Galanter M. 1974. Why the 'haves' come out ahead: speculations on the limits of legal change. *Law Soc. Rev.* 9:95–160

Garcia-Villegas M. 2003. Symbolic power without symbolic violence? Critical comments on legal consciousness studies in USA. *Droit Soc.* 53:137–62

Garth B, Sterling J. 1998. From legal realism to law and society: reshaping law for the last stages of the social activist state. *Law Soc. Rev.* 32:409–71

Gibson JL, Gouws A. 2002. *Overcoming Intolerance in South Africa: Experiments in Democratic Persuasion*. Cambridge, UK: Cambridge Univ. Press

Giddens A. 1979. *Central Problems in Social Theory*. Berkeley: Univ. Calif. Press

Giddens A. 1984. *The Constitution of Society: Outline of the Theory of Structuration*. Berkeley: Univ. Calif. Press

Giddens A. 1990. *The Consequences of Modernity*. Stanford, CA: Stanford Univ. Press

Gilliom J. 2001. *Overseers of the Poor*. Chicago: Univ. Chicago Press

Gillman H. 2001. *The Votes that Counted: How the Court Decided the 2000 Presidential Election*. Chicago/London: Univ. Chicago Press. 306 pp.

Ginzburg C. 1980 (1976). *The Cheese and the Worms*. Baltimore, MD: Johns Hopkins Univ. Press

Glendon MA. 1991. *Rights Talk: The Impoverishment of Political Discourse*. New York: Free Press

Goffman E. 1963. *Stigma: Notes on the Management of Spoiled Identity*. Englewood Cliffs, NJ: Prentice Hall

Goffman E. 1967. *Interaction Ritual: Essays on Face-to-Face Behavior*. Garden City, NY: Doubleday Anchor Books

Goodman D. 2005. Approaches to law and popular culture. *Law Soc. Inq.* In press

Goodman LH, Sanborne S. 1986. *The Legal Needs of the Poor in New Jersey: A*

Preliminary Report. Washington, DC: Natl. Soc. Sci. Law Cent.

Gordon RW. 1984. Critical legal histories. *Stanford Law Rev.* 35:57

Gramsci A. 1999. *Selections from the Prison Notebooks of Antonio Gramsci.* Transl. ed. Q Hoare, G Nowell Smith. New York: Int. Publishers

Greenhouse CJ. 1986. *Praying for Justice: Faith, Order, and Community in an American Town.* Ithaca, NY: Cornell Univ. Press

Gurwitsch A. 1962. The common-sense world as social reality—a discourse on Alfred Schutz. *Soc. Res.* 29:50–72

Habermas J. 1983. Modernity: an incomplete project. In *The Anti-Aesthetic: Essays on Postmodern Culture,* ed. H Foster, pp. 3–15. Port Townsend, WA: New Press

Habermas J. 1984. *The Theory of Communicative Action.* Volume 1: *Reason and the Rationalization of Society.* Boston: Beacon

Habermas J. 1987. *The Theory of Communicative Action.* Volume 2: *Lifeworld and System.* Boston: Beacon

Habermas J. 1991. A reply. In *Communicative Action: Essays on Jürgen Habermas's* The Theory of Communicative Action, ed. A Honneth, H Joas, pp. 215–64. Cambridge, MA: MIT Press

Habermas J. 1992. *The Structural Transformation of the Public Sphere.* Transl. T Burger. Cambridge, MA: MIT Press

Habermas J. 1998. *Between Facts and Norms: Contributions to a Discourse Theory of Law and Democracy.* Cambridge, MA: MIT Press

Hall J. 1952. *Theft, Law, and Society.* Indianapolis, IN: Bobbs-Merrill. 2nd ed.

Halliday TC, Carruthers BG. 2005. The recursivity of law: global norm-making and national law-making in the globalizations of corporate insolvency regimes. *Am. J. Sociol.* In press

Haltom W, McCann M. 2004. *Distorting the Law: Politics, Media and the Litigation Crisis.* Chicago: Univ. Chicago Press

Hartog H. 1985. Pigs and positivism. *Wis. Law Rev.* 1984(4):899–935

Hartog H. 1993. Abigail Bailey's coverture: law in a married woman's consciousness. In *Law in Everyday Life,* ed. A Sarat, T Kearns. Ann Arbor: Univ. Mich. Press

Harvey D. 1990. *The Condition of Post-Modernity.* Cambridge: Basil Blackwell

Havel V. 1985. The power of the powerless. In *The Power of the Powerless,* ed. J Keane, pp. 23–96. Armonk, NY: M.E. Sharpe

Hay D. 1975. Property, authority and the criminal law. See Hay et al. 1975, pp. 17–63

Hay D, Linebaugh P, Rule JG, Thompson EP, Winclow C. 1975. *Albion's Fatal Tree: Crime and Society in Eighteenth-Century England.* New York: Pantheon Books

Heimer CA. 1985. *Reactive Risk and Rational Action: Managing Moral Hazard in Insurance Contracts.* Berkeley: Univ. Calif. Press

Heimer CA. 1999. Competing institutions: law, medicine and family in neonatal intensive care. *Law Soc. Rev.* 33(1):17–66

Heimer CA, Staffen LR. 1998. *For the Sake of the Children: The Social Organization of Responsibility in the Hospital and the Home.* Chicago: Univ. Chicago Press

Hertogh M. 2004. A 'European' conception of legal consciousness: rediscovering Eugen Ehrlich. *J. Law Soc.* 31(4):455–81

Hodson R. 2001. *Dignity at Work.* New York: Cambridge Univ. Press

Hoffman EA. 2003. Legal consciousness and dispute resolution: different disputing behavior at two similar taxicab companies. *Law Soc. Inq.* 28:691–718

Hoffman EA. 2005. Dispute resolution in a worker cooperative: formal procedures and procedural justice. *Law Soc. Rev.* 39(1):51–82

Hull KE. 2003. The cultural power of law and the cultural enactment of legality: the case of same sex marriage. *Law Soc. Inq.* 28(3):629–58

Kalman L. 1986. *Legal Realism at Yale.* Chapel Hill: Univ. N. C. Press

Kalman L. 1996. *The Strange Career of Legal Liberalism.* New Haven, CT: Yale Univ. Press

Kammen MG. 1994. *A Machine that Would Go of Itself: The Constitution in American Culture*. New York: St. Martin's

Katz J. 1988. *Seductions of Crime*. New York: Basic Books

Kennedy D. 1980. Toward an historical understanding of legal consciousness: the case of classical legal thought in America, 1850–1940. In *Research in Law and Sociology*, ed. S Spitzer, 3:3–24. Greenwich, CT: JAI

Kennedy D. 2003. Two globalizations of law and legal thought: 1850–1968. *Suffolk Law Rev.* 26:631–79

Klug H. 2000. *Constituting Democracy: Law, Globalism, and South Africa's Political Reconstruction*. New York: Cambridge Univ. Press

Kostiner I. 2003. Evaluating legality: toward a cultural approach to the study of law and social change. *Law Soc. Rev.* 37(2):323

Kourilsky-Augeven C. 2004. Images and uses of law among ordinary people. *Droit Cult.* Spec. Issue. Paris: CNRS/Soc. Legis. Comp.

Kritzer H, Silbey SS, eds. 2003. *In Litigation: Do The 'Have's' Still Come Out Ahead*. Stanford CA: Stanford Univ. Press

Krygier M, Csarnota A, eds. 1999. *The Rule of Law After Communism: Problems and Prospects in East-Central Europe*. Aldershot: Ashgate

Ladinsky J, Susmilch C. 1981. *The processing of consumer disputes in a metropolitan setting*. Presented at Meet. Midwest Polit. Sci. Assoc., Chicago

Larson E. 2004. Institutionalizing legal consciousness: regulation and the embedding of market participants in the securities industry in Ghana and Fiji. *Law Soc. Rev.* 38:737–67

Lefebvre H. 1968. *Everyday Life in the Modern World*. New York: Harper Torchbooks

Lefebvre H. 1991 (1958). *Critique of Everyday Life*. London: Verso

Levine FJ. 1990. Goose bumps and 'the search for signs of intelligence life' in sociolegal studies: after 25 years. *Law Soc. Rev.* 24:9–33

Levine K, Mellema V. 2001. The common place of law: strategizing the street: how law matters in the lives of women in the street-level drug economy. *Law Soc. Inq.* 26:169–97

Lewis J. 2001. *Constructing Public Opinion: How Political Elites Do What They Like and Why We Seem to Go Along With It*. New York: Columbia Univ. Press

Lieberman J. 1981. *The Litigious Society*. New York: Basic Books

Lind A, Tyler T. 1988. *The Social Psychology of Procedural Justice*. New York: Plenum

Lipson L, Wheeler S. 1986. *Law and the Social Sciences*. New York: Russell Sage Found.

Macaulay S. 1963. Non-contractual relations in business: a preliminary study. *Am. Sociol. Rev.* 28:55–67

MacCoun RJ, Tyler TR. 1988. The basis of citizen's preferences for different forms of criminal jury. *Law Hum. Behav.* 12:333–52

Marshall A. 2003. Injustice frames, legality, and the everyday construction of sexual harassment. *Law Soc. Inq.* 28(3):659–90

Marshall A. 2005. Idle rights: employees' rights consciousness and the construction of sexual harassment policies. *Law Soc. Rev.* 39(1):83–124

Marshall A, Barclay S. 2003. In their own words: how ordinary people construct the legal world. *Law Soc. Inq.* 28(3):617–28

Marx K. 1963 (1852). *The Eighteenth Brumaire of Louis Bonaparte*. New York: International

Marx K, Engels F. 1970 (1846). *The German Ideology*. London: Lawrence & Wishart

Mayhew L, Reiss A. 1969. The social organization of legal contacts. *Am. Sociol. Rev.* 34: 309–18

McAdams AJ. 1996. *Transitional Justice and the Rule of Law in New Democracies*. South Bend, IN: Notre Dame Univ. Press

McCann MW. 1994. *Rights at Work: Pay Equity Reform and the Politics of Legal Mobilization*. Chicago: Univ. Chicago Press

McGuire MV, Edelhertz H. 1980. Consumer abuse of older Americans: victimization and remedial action in two metropolitan areas. In *White Collar Crime: Theory and Research*, ed. G Geis, E Stotland, pp. 266–92. Beverly Hills, CA: Sage

Merry SE. 1979. Going to court: strategies of dispute management in an American urban neighborhood. *Law Soc. Rev.* 13:891–925

Merry SE. 1985. Concepts of law and justice among working class Americans. *Leg. Stud. Forum* 9:59

Merry SE. 1990. *Getting Justice and Getting Even: Legal Consciousness Among Working Class Americans.* Chicago: Univ. Chicago Press

Merry SE. 2003. Rights talk and the experiences of law: implementing women's human rights to protection from violence. *Hum. Rights Q.* 25(2):343–82

Merry SE, Silbey SS. 1984. What do plaintiffs want: reexamining the concept of dispute. *Justice Syst. J.* 9:2:151–78

Mezey N. 2001. Out of the ordinary: law, power, culture and the commonplace. *Law Soc. Inq.* 26:145–68

Miller RE, Sarat A. 1980–1981. Grievances, claims, and disputes: assessing the adversary culture. *Law Soc. Rev.* 15(3–4):525–66

Molotch HL, Boden D. 1985. Talking social structure: discourse, domination and the Watergate hearings. *Am. Sociol. Rev.* 50:273–88

Moulton B. 1969. The persecution and intimidation of the low income litigant as performed by the small claims court in California. *Stanford Law Rev.* 21:1657

Mumby DK. 1993. *Narrative and Social Control.* Beverly Hills: Sage

Munger F, Seron C. 1984. Critical legal theory versus critical legal method: a comment on method. *Law Policy* 6:257–99

Nielsen LB. 2000. Situating legal consciousness: experiences and attitudes of ordinary citizens about law and street harassment. *Law Soc. Rev.* 34(4):1055–90

Nielsen LB. 2002. Subtle, pervasive, harmful: racist and sexist remarks in public as hate speech. *J. Soc. Issues* 58(2):265–80

Nielsen LB. 2004. *License to Harass: Law, Hierarchy and Offensive Public Speech.* Princeton, NJ: Princeton Univ. Press

Ochs E, Capps L. 2001. *Living Narrative: Cre-ating Lives in Everyday Storytelling.* Cambridge, MA: Harvard Univ. Press

Pelisse J. 2004a. From negotiation to implementation: a study of the reduction of working time in France (1998–2000). *Time Soc.* 13(2/3):221–44

Pelisse J. 2004b. *Time, legal consciousness, and power: the case of France's 35-hour workweek laws.* Presented at Annu. Meet. Law Soc. Assoc., Chicago

Pitkin H. 1993. *Wittgenstein and Justice.* Berkeley: Univ. Calif. Press

Polanyi K. 1944. *The Great Transformation: The Political and Economic Origins of Our Time.* Boston: Beacon

Poletta F. 2000. The structural context of novel rights claims: southern civil rights organizing, 1961–1966. *Law Soc. Rev.* 34(2):367–406

Polkinghorne DE. 1988. *Narrative Knowing and the Human Sciences.* Albany: SUNY Press

Pound R. 1910. Law in books and law in action. *Am. Law Rev.* 44:12

Power M. 1999. *The Audit Society: Rituals of Verification.* Oxford: Oxford Univ. Press

Quinn BA. 2000. The paradox of complaining: law, humor, and harassment in the everyday work world. *Law Soc. Inq.* 25:1151–75

Rawls J. 1971. *A Theory of Justice.* Cambridge, MA: Belknap

Rawls J. 2001. *Justice as Fairness: A Restatement,* ed. E Kelly. Cambridge, MA: Harvard Univ. Press

Riessman CK. 1993. *Narrative Analysis.* Beverly Hills: Sage

Rose N. 1966. The death of the social? Refiguring the territory of government. *Econ. Soc.* 25:327–56

Rostain T. 2002. *Lawyers and accountants: the construction of professional identity.* Presented at Annu. Meet. Law Soc. Assoc., Vancouver, BC

Sagay AC. 2003. *What Is Sexual Harassment: From Capital Hill to the Sorbonne.* Berkeley: Univ. Calif. Press

Sarat A. 1985. Legal effectiveness and social studies of law. *Leg. Stud. Forum* 9:23

Sarat A. 1986. Access to justice: citizen participation and the American legal order. In *Law and the Social Sciences*, ed. L Lipson, S Wheeler, pp. 519–80. New York: Russell Sage Found.

Sarat A. 1990. '. . .The law is all over': power, resistance and the legal consciousness of the welfare poor. *Yale J. Law Humanit.* 2:343–79

Sarat A, Constable M, Engel D, Hans V, Lawrence S. 1998. *Crossing Boundaries: Traditions and Transformations in Law and Society Research*. Evanston, IL: Northwest. Univ. Press

Sarat A, Kearns T. 1993. Beyond the great divide. In *Law in Everyday Life*, ed. A Sarat, T Kearns, pp. 21–61. Ann Arbor: Univ. Mich. Press

Sarat S, Silbey SS. 1988. The pull of the policy audience. *Law Policy* 10(2–3):97–166

Sarat A, Simon J. 2003. Cultural analysis, cultural studies, and the situation of legal scholarship. In *Cultural Analysis, Cultural Studies and the Law*, ed. A Sarat, J Simon, pp. 1–36. Durham, NC: Duke Univ. Press

Sassen S. 1991. *The Global City: New York, London, Tokyo*. Princeton, NJ: Princeton Univ. Press

Scheingold SA. 1974. *The Politics of Rights*. New Haven, CT: Yale Univ. Press

Scheppele K. 1996. The history of normalcy: rethinking legal autonomy and the relative dependence of law at the end of the Soviet Empire. *Law Soc. Rev.* 30:627–50

Schlegel JH. 1995. *American Legal Realism and Empirical Social Science*. Chapel Hill: Univ. N. C. Press

Schutz A. 1962. *Collected Papers,* Volume 1. *The Problem of Social Reality*. Evanston, IL: Northwest. Univ. Press

Schutz A. 1970. *On Phenomenology and Social Relations*. Chicago: Univ. Chicago Press

Schutz A, Luchman T. 1989 (1973). *The Structures of the Life-World*. Evanston, IL: Northwest. Univ. Press

Scott JC. 1990. *Domination and the Arts of Resistance: Hidden Transcripts*. New Haven, CT: Yale Univ. Press

Selznick P. 1961. Sociology and natural law. *Nat. Law Forum* 6:84–108

Selznick P. 1969. *Law, Society, and Industrial Justice*. New Brunswick, NJ: Transaction Books

Seron C, Pereira J, Kovath J. 2004. Judging police misconduct: 'street-level' versus professional policing. *Law Soc. Rev.* 38(4):665–710

Seron C, Silbey S. 2004. Profession, science and culture: an emergent canon of law and society research. In *Blackwell Companion to Law and Society*, ed. A Sarat, pp. 30–60. Oxford: Blackwell

Sewell WH. 1992. A theory of structure: duality, agency, and transformation. *Am. J. Sociol.* 98:1–29

Sewell WH. 1999. The concepts of culture. In *Beyond the Cultural Turn: New Directions in the Study of Society and Culture*, ed. VE Bonnell, AH Hunt, R Biernacki, pp. 35–61. Berkeley: Univ. Calif. Press

Silberman M. 1985. *The Civil Justice Process*. New York: Academic

Silbey SS. 1984. Who speaks for the consumer? *Am. Bar Found. Res. J.* 1984(2):429–57

Silbey SS. 1998. Ideology, power and justice. In *Justice and Power in Sociolegal Studies*, ed. B Garth, A Sarat, pp. 272–308. Evanston, IL: Northwest. Univ. Press

Silbey SS. 2001. Legal culture and consciousness. In *International Encyclopedia of the Social and Behavioral Sciences*, ed. NJ Smelser, PB Baltes, pp. 8623–29. Amsterdam: Elsevier Sci.

Silbey SS, Bittner E. 1982. The availability of law. *Law Policy* 4(4):399–434

Silbey SS, Ewick P. 2003. Architecture of authority: the place of law in the space of science. In *The Place of Law*, ed. A Sarat, L Douglas, M Umphrey, pp. 77–108. Ann Arbor: Univ. Mich. Press

Silbey SS, Sarat A. 1987. Critical traditions in law and society research. *Law Soc. Rev.* 21:165–74

Silverstein H. 1996. *Unleashing Rights: Law,*

Meaning and the Animal Rights Movement. Ann Arbor: Univ. Mich. Press

Steinberg M. 1991. Talkin' class: discourse, ideology, and their roles in class conflicts. In *Bringing Class Back In: Contemporary and Historical Perspectives*, ed. SG McNall, R Levine, R Fantasia, pp. 261–84. Boulder, CO: Westview

Steinberg M. 1997. 'A way of struggle': reformations of affirmations of E.P. Thompson's class analysis in the light of postmodern theories of language. *Br. J. Sociol.* 48(3):471–92

Steinberg M. 1999. The talk and back talk of collective action: a dialogic analysis of repertoires of discourse among nineteenth century English cotton spinners. *Am. J. Sociol.* 105: 736–80

Steiner B. 2001. The consciousness of crime and punishment: reflections on identity politics and lawmaking in the war on drugs. *Stud. Law Polit. Soc.* 23:185–212

Strathern M. 2000. *Audit Cultures.* London: Routledge

Swidler A. 1986. Culture in action: symbols and strategies. *Am. Sociol. Rev.* 51:273–86

Swidler A. 2001. *Talk of Love.* Chicago: Univ. Chicago Press

Thompson EP. 1975. *Whigs and Hunters: The Origin of the Black Act.* New York: Random House, Pantheon Books

Tinkler JE. 2003. Defining sexual harassment: ambiguity, perceived threat, and knowledge. *Amici* 10(2):1–5

Tomlins C. 2000. Framing the field of law's disciplinary encounters: a historical narrative. *Law Soc. Rev.* 34:911–72

Trubek D. 1984. Where the action is: critical legal studies and empiricism. *Stanford Law Rev.* 26:575

Tyler TR. 1990. *Why People Obey the Law: Procedural Justice, Legitimacy and Compliance.* New Haven, CT: Yale Univ. Press

Tyler TR, Boeckmann RJ, Smith HJ, Huo YJ. 1997. *Social Justice in a Diverse Society.* Boulder, CO: Westview

Tyler TR, Huo YJ. 2002. *Trust in the Law.* New York: Russell Sage Found.

Valverde M. 2003. Which side are you on? Uses of the everyday in sociolegal scholarship. *POLAR: Polit. Leg. Anthropol. Rev.* 26(1):86–98

White L. 1990. Subordination, rhetorical survival skills and Sunday shoes: notes on the hearing of Mrs. G. *Buffalo Law Rev.* 38:1–58

Yngvesson B. 1993. *Virtuous Citizens, Disruptive Subjects: Order and Complaint in a New England Court.* New York: Routledge

Annu. Rev. Law Soc. Sci. 2005. 1:369–96
doi: 10.1146/annurev.lawsocsci.1.031805.111122
Copyright © 2005 by Annual Reviews. All rights reserved
First published online as a Review in Advance on August 19, 2005

WHY LAW, ECONOMICS, AND ORGANIZATION?

Oliver E. Williamson

*Walter A. Haas School of Business, University of California, Berkeley,
California 94720; email: owilliam@haas.berkeley.edu*

Key Words   governance, transaction costs, law school teaching

■ **Abstract**   This review shows that a combined law, economics, and organization theory approach leads to different and deeper understandings of the purposes served by complex contract and economic organization. The business firm for these purposes is described not in technological terms (as a production function) but in organizational terms (as an alternative mode of governance). Firm and market are thus examined comparatively with respect to their capacities to organize transactions, which differ in their complexity, so as to economize on transaction costs. The predictive theory of economic organization that results has numerous ramifications for public policy toward business and for teaching and research in the law schools.

INTRODUCTION

Whereas law and economics began as the application of economic reasoning to antitrust and regulation, it has since been expanded to bring economic analysis to bear (in varying degree) on every facet of the law school curriculum. Occasional dissents notwithstanding, law and economics is widely regarded as a success story.

I concur with this favorable assessment but would observe that economic analysis comes in more than one flavor. As between the two main branches—the science of choice and the science of contract—law and economics scholarship mainly works out of the science of choice tradition. All well and good for many purposes but not, I contend, for all. Specifically, those parts of the law and economics enterprise that are centrally concerned with issues of economic organization ought to be informed, additionally or instead, by the science of contract perspective.[1]

This involves, among other things, supplanting the neoclassical theory of the firm-as-production function (which is a technological construction) with the theory of the firm-as-governance structure (which is an organizational construction). A critical concession, which many law and economics scholars are loathe to make,

---

[1] Areas of the law that are most in need of a more veridical theory of economic organization include antitrust, regulation, corporations, labor law, corporate governance, agency, administrative law, property, contract, secured transactions, and torts. But the science of contract branch of economics has ramifications to the law quite generally.

is that the orthodox theory of the firm was never designed with reference to (and, hence, is often poorly suited to interpret) nonstandard and unfamiliar contractual practices and organizational structures.

I begin with a brief discussion of the sciences of choice and of contract and of the differing needs of each for a theory of the firm. I then turn in the next section to what I regard as the chief lessons of organization theory for a theory of the firm-as-governance structure. The comparative contractual approach to economic organization, of which the theory of the firm-as-governance structure is a part, is then sketched in the section on Comparative Contractual Analysis. Applications to public policy analysis are set out in the next section, and the lessons of the comparative contractual approach to economic organization for the teaching of contract law are developed in the final section. Concluding remarks follow.

CONCEPTUAL FRAMEWORKS

Choice and Contract

Although orthodox economic theory, with its emphasis on scarcity and efficient resource allocation, is widely regarded as an all-purpose theory, it is more properly regarded as the "dominant paradigm" (Reder 1999, p. 43). Plainly, dominant paradigms command more respect. Often, however, their uses are much more apt for some types of problems than they are for others.

Lionel Robbins captured the emerging consensus of what economics was all about in his description of economics as "the science which studies human behavior as a relation between ends and scarce means which have alternative uses" (Robbins 1932, p. 16)—or as Reder puts it, economics deals with "the allocation of scarce resources among alternative uses for the maximization of want satisfactions" (Reder 1999, p. 43). The theory of consumer behavior and the theory of the firm are the two key building blocks upon which this science rests: The consumer seeks to maximize utility subject to a budget constraint, and the firm is a production function that transforms inputs into outputs, with efficiency realized through the choice of optimal factor proportions. All well and good for the study of supply and demand, prices and output. The economist working out of such a setup decidedly does not, however, address himself to issues of firm and market organization except in narrowly delimited ways.[2] The firm, for all intents and purposes, is a "black box."

James Buchanan has declared this science of choice perspective as a "wrong turn" (Buchanan 1975, p. 225), but I put it somewhat differently. Economics

---

[2]As Ronald Coase has put it, in the Robbins conception of economics, the economist "does not interest himself in the internal arrangements within organizations but only in what happens on the market" (Coase 1992, p. 714).

became unduly preoccupied with the science of choice to the neglect of the science of contract. Rather than deal with contract and exchange, economics became the science of constrained optimization.

As perceived by Buchanan, the principal needs for a science of contract are found in the field of public finance and take the form of social ordering: "Politics is a structure of complex exchange among individuals, a structure within which persons seek to secure *collectively* their own privately defined objectives that cannot be efficiently secured through simple market exchanges" (Buchanan 1987, p. 296; emphasis added). By contrast, I see the needs for a science of contract primarily with reference to the field of industrial organization and in the context of private ordering.

Compared with the politics of collective action, private ordering is accomplished through the individual efforts of the immediate parties to an exchange. Out of awareness of the limitations of spot-market contracting and the impossibility of comprehensive contracting, the immediate parties to an exchange craft governance structures that permit them to realize mutual gains.

The role of the courts, for such a purpose, is very different from that projected under the science of choice perspective.

Firms

"Any standard economic theory, not just neoclassical, starts with the existence of firms. Usually, the firm is a point or at any rate a black box. . . . But firms are not points. They have internal structure. This internal structure must arise for some reason" (Arrow 1999, p. vii). The contrast between the science of choice and the science of contract in this respect is fundamental. As Harold Demsetz has put it, "It is a mistake to confuse the firm of economic theory with its real-world namesake. The chief mission of neoclassical economics is to understand how the price system coordinates the use of resources, not to understand the inner workings of real firms" (Demsetz 1983, p. 377). By contrast, the science of contract is expressly concerned with the attributes of firms, especially in relation to the attributes of alternative modes of governance, as these bear on the management of transactions. As against a technological view of the firm, the firm (and other modes of governance) are described as governance structures. John R. Commons's prescient conception of economics is broadly congruent with the science of contract perspective: "[T]he ultimate unit of activity. . . must contain in itself the three principles of conflict, mutuality, and order. This unit is a transaction" (Commons 1932, p. 4). Not only does transaction cost economics (TCE) concur that the transaction is the basic unit of analysis, but it views governance as the means by which to infuse order, thereby mitigating conflict and realizing mutual gains.

As developed below, implementing the private ordering branch of the science of contract is a much more microanalytic project than is the science of choice approach to economics. Hitherto neglected attributes of both transactions and governance structures now need to be uncovered and their ramifications worked out. In the process, a whole series of public policy differences between the choice and contract perspectives emerge.

ORGANIZATION THEORY

Organization theory is a vast field to which sociology, psychology (cognitive, social, evolutionary), aspects of political science, economics, and cultural anthropology all relate. W. Richard Scott's (1987) influential text distinguishes three main branches: rational, natural, and open systems—where the rational systems approach places primary emphasis on formal structure, the natural systems approach features informal organization, and the open systems approach examines shifting coalitions within the organization and in relation to their environment. All have a role to play in understanding complex organization. Of these three, I place primary emphasis on the contributions of rational systems theory, although provision is also made for the spontaneous forces of informal organization and the intertemporal transformations that relate thereto. Chester Barnard [1962 (1938)], Herbert Simon (1947), and March & Simon (1958) are especially prominent to the rational systems tradition. Of the many contributions that originate with this tradition, the five that I regard as most relevant to the science of contract approach to economic organization are (a) human actors, (b) adaptation, (c) intertemporal transformations, (d) choice of the unit of analysis, and (e) discrete structural features.[3]

If, as I contend, organization theory is important to the study of economic organization in these five and other respects, the puzzle is why organization theory has not been more fully incorporated within economics. The chief reasons, I think, are these: (a) organization theory has less relevance to the science of choice than to the science of contract, and most economists have been content to work out of the "dominant paradigm"; (b) organization theorists mainly deliver a negative message (the science of choice is wrongheaded) rather than relate to the opportunities opened up by the incipient science of contract; and (c) leaders of the law and economics movement, such as Richard Posner, who were votaries of orthodoxy, were dismissive of organization theory: "[O]rganization theory... [adds] nothing to...economics that the literature on information costs had not added much earlier" (Posner 1993, p. 84).

Be that as it may, my sense is that a theory of economic organization that aspires to deal with real firms and, more generally, with economic organization in an uncontrived way cannot ignore or dismiss the contributions of organization theory named above—which are not the main issues with which the "literature on information costs" has been concerned (even now, to say nothing of "much earlier").

---

[3]Other important contributions include (f) weak form selection, (g) informal organization, (h) cognitive specialization, and (i) bureaucracy.

Human Actors

Simon advised social scientists that "[n]othing is more fundamental in setting our research agenda and informing our research methods than our view of the nature of the human beings whose behavior we are studying" (Simon 1985, p. 303). The two attributes of human actors that are especially relevant to the economics of governance are cognition and self-interestedness.

Simon took early exception with the idea that human actors are supremely rational, and he proposed instead that human actors be described as boundedly rational, by which he meant that they are "intendedly rational, but only limitedly so" (Simon 1957a, p. xxiv). Human actors are thus neither nonrational nor irrational but are attempting effectively to cope.

TCE agrees that scholars' view of the human beings whose behavior they are studying has profound ramifications for the research agenda. It also concurs that human actors are subject to bounded rationality. Rather than dwell on the lessons of bounded rationality for the science of choice (where the use of maximizing apparatus was contested), however, TCE turns to the science of contract and takes the chief lesson of bounded rationality for the study of economic organization to be that all complex contracts are unavoidably incomplete.

Contractual incompleteness by itself, however, does not a serious problem of contracting make. Governance problems are posed when incomplete contracts (to include unforeseen contingencies) are combined with opportunism. The conflicts to which Commons referred now appear, especially during contract execution and at the contract renewal interval.

Note that TCE does not dispute that most people will do what they say (and some will do more) without self-consciously asking whether the effort is justified by expected discounted net gains. But while accurate descriptions of what is going on "most of the time" are important, much of what is interesting about human behavior in general and contract in particular has reference not to routines but to exceptions. Faced with unanticipated disturbances for which an incomplete contract makes inadequate or incorrect provision (by reason of gaps, errors, and omissions), such disturbances will push the parties to an incomplete contract off of the contract curve. Strategic considerations now come into play if, rather than frailty of motive, opportunism is the operative condition.[4] Contractual breakdowns by reason of defection from the spirit of cooperation and reliance on the letter of the contract are now in prospect.

Inefficiencies of all kinds nevertheless invite relief. Out of awareness of prospective hazards, parties to a contract have incentives to craft ex ante safeguards in a

---

[4]Interestingly, opportunism makes an appearance in the natural system treatment of sociologists. As Scott puts it, "there is frequently a disparity between. . .the professed or official goals that are announced and the actual or operative goals that can be observed to govern the activities of participants" (Scott 1987, p. 52). Whereas rational system theorists emphasize the normative structure of ex ante decisions, natural system theorists stress the behavioral structure of ex post outcomes (Scott 1987, p. 53).

cost-effective degree. Rather than postulate either myopia or omniscience, TCE assumes that human actors have the capacity for "feasible foresight," which is a rational spirit construction. George Schultz speaks to the point as follows: "my training in economics has had a major influence on the way I think about public policy tasks, even when they have no particular relationship to economics. Our discipline makes one think ahead, ask about indirect consequences, take note of variables that may not be directly under consideration" (Schultz 1995, p. 1). But economists do not have a lock on this. As the evolutionary biologist Richard Dawkins (1976) observes, the "capacity to simulate the future in imagination. . . [saves] us from the worst consequences of the blind replicators" (p. 200). Practitioners, consultants, and public policy analysts who possess the skills for and practice the art of feasible foresight will look ahead, discern potential hazards, and fold these into the ex ante design.

Adaptation

Interestingly, both the economist Hayek (1945) and the organization theorist Barnard [1962 (1938)] are in agreement that adaptation is the central problem of economic organization. The adaptations to which they have reference, however, differ. Hayek had reference to the adaptations of autonomous economic actors who adjust spontaneously to changes in the market (mainly as signaled by changes in relative prices). By contrast, Barnard appealed to intentionality. He featured cooperative adaptation made by economic actors with the assistance of hierarchy within firms. Although adaptation of each type is important and can be studied separately, TCE is interested in markets and hierarchies (rather than markets alone, or hierarchies alone). TCE therefore deals with adaptations of both kinds (and mixtures thereof). Specifically, TCE holds that choice of contractual mode should be derived by recognizing that the adaptive needs of transactions (in autonomous and cooperative respects) vary with the attributes of transactions and that the adaptive capacities of alternative modes of governance also differ. The upshot is that efficiency gains are realized by aligning transactions with governance structures so as to effect an economizing outcome. Pushing the logic of autonomous and cooperative adaptation to completion thereby leads to a predictive theory of comparative economic organization (Williamson 1991).

Intertemporal Transformations

That internal organization has a life of its own has been evident to sociologists of organization for a long time. There is more to it, moreover, than simply being alerted to hitherto neglected regularities. Once disclosed, the ex ante organizational design ramifications of these regularities need to be worked out.

Robert Michels' 1911 book on *Political Parties* focused on the intertemporal transformations that regularly attended democratic efforts at political organization. The most important such intertemporal transformation is summarized by the famous Iron Law of Oligarchy: "It is [hierarchical] organization which gives birth to the dominion of the elected over the electors, of the mandatories over the mandators, of the delegates over the delegators. Who says organization, say oligarchy" (Michels 1962, p. 365). Michels traced the source of these oligarchical tendencies to "the nature of the human individual,. . . the nature of the political struggle,. . . and the nature of organization" (p. 6).

Michels, moreover, had a very farsighted view of his findings: "The sociologist should aim. . . at the dispassionate exposition of tendencies and counter-operating forces, of reasons and opposing reasons, at the display, in a word, of the warp and the woof of social life" (Michels 1962, p. 6). Unless we are alert to the intertemporal propensities of organization, we will be needlessly victimized by them: "[N]othing but a serene and frank examination of the oligarchical dangers of democracy will enable us to minimize these dangers" (Michels 1962, p. 370). Thus, although the oligarchical propensities of democratic organization may have been poorly understood by academics and some practitioners until Michels clarified the issue, the lurking hazards of oligarchy should no longer come as a surprise. Today's organizational designers presumably take the Iron Law of Oligarchy into account in the initial design calculus.

Selznick characterized "Michels' theory about democratic organization. . . as a *special case* of the general recalcitrance of the human tools of action. The tendency for goals to be subverted through the creation of new centers of interest and motivation *inheres in all organizations*" (Selznick 1950, p. 162; emphasis added). The study of unanticipated consequences of all kinds—of which oligarchy is but one example—thus describes the larger research agenda.

Akin to the discussion of feasible foresight in the section on Human Actors, above, TCE responds in a three-part way. First, be alert to all the significant, unanticipated consequences and bureaucratic propensities that students of internal organization uncover. Second, take the logic to completion. For each unanticipated effect, ask from where it arises, what are the mechanisms through which it operates, what are the effects on contract and organization, and what are the ramifications for ex ante design (thereby mitigating unwanted consequences and enhancing beneficial effects). Third, upon taking a farsighted view of contract and organization, do not rely entirely on the reports by organization theorists of unanticipated consequences. Given contractual incompleteness (by reason of bounded rationality) and the possibility of defection from agreements (by reason of opportunism), practitioners of TCE look ahead to ascertain whether and when predictable contractual hazards will accrue. If and as such hazards can be projected, the governance ramifications need to be worked out. [An illustration is the Fundamental Transformation, by which a large numbers bidding competition is (sometimes) transformed into a small numbers supply relation during contract execution and at the contract renewal interval (Williamson 1985, pp. 61–63). As developed in the section on Applications to Public Policy, below, contractual safeguards and (possibly) vertical integration arise to mitigate such hazards.]

Unit of Analysis

TCE adopts the purposive perspective of John R. Commons by naming the transaction as the unit of analysis. But that is merely the first step. Naming a unit of analysis needs to be followed by providing operational content. The proponents of many would-be units of analysis never undertake this second step or founder upon reaching it.

Identifying the critical dimensions with respect to which transactions differ is facilitated by asking which attributes, among the countless ways in which transactions differ, have consequential transaction cost effects. Some transactions are simple while others are complex. What are the distinguishing features? Older style institutional economics never asked, hence never answered, this question.

The obvious place to begin is with the ideal transaction in law and economics—namely, contracts that take place between faceless economic actors, where continuity is unimportant because the identity of the parties does not matter. Then ask the question, "What attributes of transactions are responsible for the breakdown of this contractual ideal?" Relevant attributes for describing transactions between parties where identity does matter include asset specificity in its various forms (which gives rise to bilateral dependency), uncertainty (for which consciously coordinated adaptations to disturbances may be needed), and frequency (which has a bearing on the future value of preserving a continuing relation and on the incentive to incur the cost of specialized governance).

Discrete Structural

If alternative modes of organization differ in discrete structural ways, then marginal analysis can be supplanted by discrete structural analysis, which is purportedly easier to implement (Simon 1978, pp. 6–7).[5] As a comparative contractual matter, however, the real import of the proposition that moving from one generic form of organization to another is attended by discontinuities is that alternative modes of governance have different strengths and weaknesses by reason of these discontinuities. As with the transaction, moreover, there is a need to go beyond this first step to ascertain the critical attributes with respect to which governance structures differ. The question to be asked and answered here is this: How do alternative modes of governance differ in contract implementation and enforcement respects?

One device for getting at this is to pose the puzzle of selective intervention: Can a firm replicate the market mode for all state realizations for which market procurement works well and intervene always but only when expected net gains can

---

[5]Because marginal analysis is actually easy to implement, economists can be thought of as analytical satisficers: They use workable apparatus that (often) is "good enough." Also note that the use of marginal analysis and discrete structural analysis can be joined, as in Riordan & Williamson (1985), where discrete structural differences give rise to first-order effects and marginal analysis introduces second-order refinements.

be projected. If feasible, then large firms will always do as well as a collection of small firms (through replication) and will sometimes do better (by selective intervention). As I have developed elsewhere (Williamson 1985, chapter 6), such efforts are not only impossible but, if attempted, are attended by a series of unwanted effects. This is because efforts to preserve the high-powered incentives of markets within hierarchies give rise to asset dissipation losses and strategic distortions. The upshot is that the move from market to hierarchy is attended by a weakening of incentive intensity and, as a consequence, by an increase in administrative oversight and control.

A third discrete structural difference arises in contract law respects. The idea that each generic mode of governance is supported by a distinctive form of contract law can be traced to Karl Llewellyn's (1931) early distinction between contract as framework and contract as legal rules; to Ian Macneil's (1974) further distinctions among classical, neoclassical, and relational contract laws; to later treatments of private ordering (Galanter 1981, Klein & Leffler 1981); and to credible contracting (Williamson 1983, Gilson 1984).

Classical contract law of a legal rules kind applies to the ideal transaction in both law and economics, where large numbers of informed and "faceless buyers and sellers. . . [meet] for an instant to exchange standardized goods at equilibrium prices" (Ben-Porath 1980, p. 4). Such a legal rules regime gives way to contract as framework when long-term contracting with dependency relations sets in. The parties here have an interest in promoting continuity in the face of unforeseen disturbances, and hence move to a more cooperative and adaptable contracting form. Such neoclassical contracts are not, however, indefinitely elastic. When push comes to shove, the letter of the contract becomes the basis for "ultimate appeal" to the courts (Llewellyn 1931, p. 737)—wherein the written contract serves to delimit threat positions.

What then is the contract law of internal organization? As developed elsewhere (Williamson 1991), the implicit law of internal organization is that of forbearance. Thus, whereas courts routinely grant standing to interfirm disputes over prices, damages ascribed to delays, failures of quality, and the like, courts will refuse to hear disputes between one internal division and another over identical technical issues. If access to the courts is denied, hierarchy is its own court of ultimate appeal, whereupon firms have access to fiat that interfirm contracting does not.

Taken together, the lessons of organization theory for the science of contract (private ordering branch) are these:

1. All complex contracts are unavoidably incomplete (by reason of bounded rationality), and hence comprehensive contingent claims contracting is infeasible and once-and-for-all auctions (competition for the market) are often fraught with hazards.

2. Farsighted players to an incomplete contract have the incentive to look ahead, identify potential hazards, and attempt to provide ex ante relief for these hazards through the judicious choice of governance.

3. Adaptation is the central problem of economic organization, and autonomous and cooperative types of adaptation need to be distinguished and, as appropriate, provided for.

4. Because organizations have a life of their own, all significant intertemporal regularities need to be uncovered and the ramifications for economic organization worked out.

5. The key attributes of the transaction (which is taken to be the basic unit of analysis for the science of contract) need to be named and their ramifications worked out.

6. Because alternative modes of governance differ in discrete structural ways, the syndrome of attributes that defines each mode needs to be named and the comparative strengths and weaknesses of each generic form worked out.

The upshot is that, upon moving from the science of choice to the science of contract perspective, the contributions of organization theory for the study of economic organization come to life. The burgeoning study of the economics of organization thus holds that organizations matter (in the above-described way, as well as others) and that organizations are susceptible to analysis (especially when viewed through a comparative contractual lens in which economizing on transaction costs is featured).

COMPARATIVE CONTRACTUAL ANALYSIS

Discriminating Alignment

The discriminating alignment hypothesis out of which TCE works holds that transactions, which differ in their attributes, are aligned with governance structures, which differ in their costs and competence, so as to effect a (mainly) transaction cost economizing result. As indicated above, this requires that the attributes of both transactions and governance structures be identified and the relations between them worked out.

Going beyond the proposition that the transaction is the basic unit of analysis, TCE takes the next step and names asset specificity (in its various forms), uncertainty, and frequency as key attributes. Of these three, asset specificity is the most important and distinctive to the TCE enterprise.

As developed elsewhere, asset specificity is a measure of the degree to which the assets needed to produce a good or service can be redeployed to alternative uses and users without loss of productive value. Whereas identity is unimportant for generic goods and services, the identity of the immediate parties to an exchange are critical as asset specificity (of physical, human, site, dedicated, brand name, or temporal kinds) builds up. In that event, a bilateral dependency condition sets in and the parties are subject to opportunistic defection from the spirit of a contract to insist on the letter where large gains are at stake. Maladaptation costs attended by costly bargaining are the result.

Put differently, contractual hazards arise when incomplete contracts that are supported by nontrivial investments in specific assets are beset by disturbances (uncertainty). Out of awareness of these hazards, parties to such contracts have incentives to take hazard-mitigating actions, such as by devising safeguards that serve to infuse order and thereby reduce conflict and realize mutual gains.

As discussed above in conjunction with discrete structural analysis, alternative modes of governance are defined as internally consistent syndromes with respect to the following attributes: incentive intensity, administrative controls, and contract law regimes. Because different modes of governance combine these attributes differently, alternative modes differ in their capacities to implement autonomous and cooperative adaptations. The details are developed elsewhere (Williamson 1991). By way of summary, the discrete structural differences by which firm and market are distinguished are

1. incentive intensity: the high-powered incentives of markets give way to low-powered incentives in firms;
2. administrative controls: compared with markets, firms are supported by a more extensive array of administrative rules and procedures, including accounting and auditing, as well as the supports of informal organization;
3. contract law: the contract law of markets is legalistic and relies on court ordering, whereas, as described above, the contract law of internal organization is that of forbearance.

Because of these differences, markets enjoy the advantage in effecting autonomous adaptations, whereas the advantage accrues to firms in effecting cooperative adaptations.

The Simple Contractual Schema

Upon adopting a comparative contractual approach to economic organization in which (*a*) the transaction is made the basic unit of analysis, (*b*) alternative modes of organization are described as governance structures to which discrete structural differences accrue, and (*c*) economizing on transaction costs is taken to be the main case, a very different concept of the firm and of the purposes served by nonstandard and unfamiliar contractual practices and organizational structures results. Note that the firm, in this scheme of things, is not a stand-alone concept but is examined in relation to alternative modes of governance. Always and everywhere the action resides in the microanalytics of transactions and governance structures.

Thus, assume that a firm can make or buy a component and assume further that the component can be supplied by either of two technologies. One is a general-purpose technology and the other a special-purpose technology. The special-purpose technology requires greater investment in transaction-specific durable assets and is more efficient for servicing steady-state demands. Steady-state, however, is an analytical convenience: Most contracts are implemented under conditions of uncertainty for which adaptation to disturbances is needed. Because an incomplete contract between bilaterally dependent parties (that is, those for which continuity has value) is often silent on or makes incorrect or inadequate provision for some of these adaptations, contractual conflicts prospectively arise. Thus although mutual gains will always be realized upon costlessly restoring a position on the contract curve, each party may posture and make opportunistic representations over the division of gains. Costly delays and imperfect adaptations result.

Using h as a measure of contractual hazards, the transactions in Figure 1 that use the general-purpose technology are ones for which $h = 0$. Autonomous adaptation in a competitive market suffices because the parties are faceless. If instead transactions use the special-purpose technology, an $h > 0$ condition exists. Assets here are specialized, whence productive values would be sacrificed if $h > 0$ transactions were to be prematurely terminated. Such bilaterally dependent parties have incentives to promote continuity and safeguard investments. Cooperative adaptation thus comes to the fore.

Let s denote the magnitude of any such safeguards. An $s = 0$ condition is one in which no safeguards are provided; a decision to provide safeguards is reflected by an $s > 0$ result.

Safeguards can take either of two forms. One form is to provide interfirm contracts with added support: Penalties to deter breach are introduced, added information disclosure is provided, and specialized dispute settlement machinery (e.g., arbitration) is devised. This safeguard is the credible interfirm commitment option. A second form is to take transactions out of markets and organize them under unified ownership where hierarchy (to include fiat) is used to effect coordination.

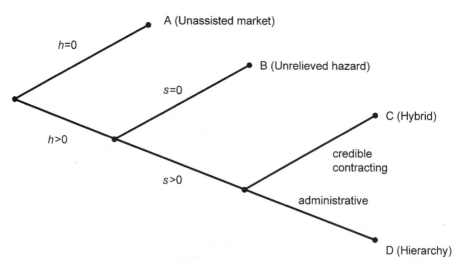

Figure 1   The simple contractual schema.

Node A corresponds to the ideal transaction in law and economics: With an absence of dependency ($h = 0$), prices are set competitively in the market (by supply and demand), and, in the event of contractual breakdown, the courts award damages. Node B poses unrelieved contractual hazards in that specialized investments are exposed ($h > 0$) for which no safeguards ($s = 0$) have been provided. Such hazards will be recognized by farsighted players, who will price out the implied risks. Nodes C and D are those for which additional contractual support has been provided ($s > 0$), either in the form of contractual safeguards (node C) or unified ownership (node D).

In the event that costly breakdowns continue in the face of best bilateral efforts to craft safeguards at node C, the transaction may be taken out of the market and organized under unified ownership (vertical integration) instead. Inasmuch, however, as added bureaucratic costs accrue upon taking a transaction out of the market and organizing it internally, internal organization is usefully thought of as the organization form of last resort: Try markets, try hybrids, and have recourse to the firm only when all else fails. Node D, the firm, thus comes in only as higher degrees of asset specificity and added uncertainty pose greater needs for cooperative adaptation.

APPLICATIONS TO PUBLIC POLICY

Node A excepted, which is the ideal transaction in law and economics to which I referred previously, the neoclassical and transaction cost approaches to firm and market organization plainly differ. These differences are due to the broader conception of economic organization out of which TCE works (where alternative modes of organization are described as governance structures, to which the lessons of organization theory apply), and these differences have ramifications for public policy toward business. Neoclassical and transaction cost interpretations of nonstandard and unfamiliar contracting practices and organizational structures are compared and contrasted here. The overarching difference is this: Orthodox economics is more imperial in that it imposes a price theoretic interpretation on the phenomena in question, whereas TCE is more curious and asks the question "What's going on here?" The TCE action is in the details of transactions on the one hand and governance structures on the other, which is closer in spirit to organization theory.

Vertical Integration/Vertical Market Restraints

Orthodox explanations for integration (backward, forward, or lateral) of the firm-as-production function kind invoke considerations of technology, inefficient factor proportions that result from double-marginalization (McKenzie 1951), and/or distortions that arise from government-imposed quotas or sales taxes.

Joe Bain's treatment of thermal economies, recently repeated by Daniel Spulber (1999, p. 270), is illustrative of technological reasoning:

[T]he cases of clear economies of integration generally involve a physical or technical aspect of the processes in a single plant. A classic case is that of integrating iron-making and steel-making to effect a saving in full costs by eliminating a reheating of iron before it is fed to a steel furnace. Where integration does not have this physical or technical aspect—as it does not, for example, in integrating the production of assorted components with the assembly of those components—the case for cost savings from integration is much less clear (Bain 1968, p. 381).

As a technological matter, however, the thermal economies to which Bain and Spulber refer actually require only that the two stages be located in close proximity to one another. That the two stages be placed under unified ownership is not implied. If, therefore, economies somehow accrue to the unified ownership of these two stages (that is, the relation between the two stages is better mediated by hierarchy rather than by market), this must be due to other, possibly transactional rather than technological, reasons.

TCE thus looks behind apparent explanations (such as price discovery or thermal economies) to see if they withstand comparative institutional scrutiny. It also asks whether outside procurement poses interfirm contractual hazards for which cost-effective relief will be realized upon taking the transaction in question into the firm (added bureaucratic costs notwithstanding). Specifically, the progressive buildup of contractual complications, as discussed in conjunction with the simple contractual schema in Figure 1, is mainly what explains successive moves from ideal market to hybrid to hierarchy.

So what about vertical market restrictions? How are these to be understood? For starters, vertical market restrictions can be interpreted as a decision to remain at node C rather than move to node D. The transaction in question is one to which hazards accrue ($h > 0$) for which cost-effective safeguards are needed ($s > 0$). If most of the hazards can be relieved at node C without incurring the added bureaucratic cost burdens (weakening of incentive intensity, added administrative costs) of unified ownership, then hybrid modes, of which franchising is an example, will be employed (provided that the contractual restrictions that accrue thereto are not treated as unlawful).

Vertical market restrictions often arise in the support of brand name capital (Klein 1980), where the concern is that such capital will be devalued by subgoal pursuit among independent or quasi-independent distributors (often franchisees), with the result that the integrity of the system is placed at risk. Depending on the particulars of the transaction, customer and territorial restrictions, exclusive dealing, or other franchise restrictions may be imposed. Absent strategic purpose, for which pre-existing monopoly power is a requisite, the choice of instruments for imposing vertical restraints will be discerned by examining where and how the contractual hazards originate.

Price theoretic explanations for nonstandard modes of contracting include the efficiency benefits that purportedly accrue to price discrimination, the benefits of efficient risk bearing in the face of differential risk aversion, and the attenuation of free-rider hazards through the use of vertical market restrictions. The allocative efficiency benefits that accrue to price discrimination in a zero transaction cost world (which can be readily displayed in price theoretic terms) are much more problematic, however, if the costs of discovering customer preferences and of preventing arbitrage are positive. Invoking risk aversion to explain contracting practices among firms, moreover, is often second order in relation to more basic concerns with contractual hazards. Finally, unspecific free-rider claims are too often used as a shibboleth. The action, always and everywhere, resides in the details.[6]

The "New Economy"

Is there really a new economy? Yes and no. On the one hand, there is nothing new under the sun: real time responsiveness, innovation, outsourcing, and predatory behavior are not novel issues. Each of these has been magnified, however, by the deployment of new information technologies, by an increasing appreciation for relational contracting, and by the races for the commercialization and control of information age and biotechnology developments. A change in kind seems to describe competition in many high technology sectors.

Orthodox microtheory bears on some of these issues, but often in limited ways. TCE makes limited yet productive contact in the following respects: (*a*) Express provision for cooperative adaptation is congruent with the need for real time responsiveness; (*b*) innovation is examined in a systems context—in which firm size, incentives, and intertemporal transformations are featured (Williamson 1975, pp. 196–207); (*c*) crafting credible commitments to support outsourcing and the bureaucratic advantages of outsourcing over internal procurement are both TCE themes; and (*d*) tests for predation that exonerate behavior directed at less efficient competitors (Posner 1976, p. 193) are too static in that they fail to make provision for contingent predation—"now it's there, now it isn't, depending on whether an entrant has appeared or vanished" (Williamson 1977, p. 339), which introduces intertemporal considerations.

To be sure, new economy issues pose strategic and knowledge creation challenges that go beyond TCE (Shapiro & Varian 1999). Also, concepts such as "disequilibrium contracting" (Williamson 1991) boggle the mind. That TCE is more responsive to many of the pressing needs of public policy in the new economy than is received price theory is noteworthy but scarcely grounds for complacency.

---

[6]Although Posner (1979) contends that "the proper lens for viewing antitrust problems is price theory" (p. 932), Alan Meese (1997) observes that, "[d]espite references by Chicagoans to 'price theory,' Chicago's approach to vertical restraints has never rested upon. . .price theory. Instead, the Chicago approach to vertical restraints is an application of [NIE/TCE reasoning]" (p. 203). Also see Joskow (1991, pp. 567–57).

Regulation/Deregulation

FRANCHISE BIDDING[7]   Posner's sanguine assessment of the efficacy of franchise bidding for natural monopoly begins with the claim that to "expound the details of particular regulations and proposals... would serve only to obscure the basic issues" (Posner 1972, p. 98). In the imperial tradition, all of the relevant action is concentrated in the ex ante bidding competition for the contract. This is consonant with Posner's dismissive view of organization theory, to which I referred at the outset, and illustrates the pitfalls of doing public policy analysis heedless of process transformations. Upon going beyond ex ante bidding competition to include ex post contract implementation, the attributes of the good or service to be franchised turn out to be crucial to an informed assessment. Specifically, if the good or service is to be supplied under conditions of uncertainty and if nontrivial investments in specific assets are involved, the efficacy of franchise bidding is highly problematic. The upshot is that franchise bidding for natural monopoly is not an all-purpose but rather a conditional solution.[8]

RESTRUCTURING ELECTRICITY SUPPLY IN CALIFORNIA   Efforts to promote efficiency by creating markets for electric power have been implemented in a number of countries with varying degrees of success. California is a recent example where the efforts to restructure have been incompletely worked through. Again, the imperial view (this is the law here) trumps the process view (what's going on here?). This shows up in two respects. First, "good theories" were naively expected to be implemented without making provision for the realities of the political and regulatory process. Failing to make ex ante provision for these realities, politics and regulation are conveniently made the ex post scapegoats for behaving in perverse or unanticipated ways that, in large measure, were foreseeable and should have been factored into the calculus (Williamson 1996, chapter 8). Such lapses in realpolitik aside, Paul Joskow (2000) observes that too much deference was given to the (assumed) efficacy of smoothly functioning markets and insufficient attention was given to potential investment and contractual hazards and appropriate governance responses thereto. As Joskow puts it:

---

[7]This subsection is elaborated in Williamson (1996, pp. 84–85).

[8]Examples in which franchise bidding for goods and services supplied under decreasing cost conditions can possibly supplant extant regulation or public ownership with expected net gains include local service airlines and, possibly, postal delivery. The winning bidder for each base plant (terminals, post office, warehouses, and so on) can be owned by the government, and other assets (planes, trucks, and the like) will have an active secondhand market. Franchise bidding is not totally lacking in merit, therefore; on the contrary, it is a very imaginative proposal. TCE maintains, however, that all contracting schemes—of which franchise bidding for natural monopoly is one—need to be examined microanalytically and assessed in a comparative institutional manner.

Many policy makers and fellow travellers have been surprised by how difficult it has been to create wholesale electricity markets.... Had policy makers viewed the restructuring challenge using a TCE framework, these potential problems are more likely to have been identified and mechanisms adopted ex ante to fix them (Joskow 2000, p. 51).

THE INSTITUTIONAL ENVIRONMENT   The New Institutional Economics operates at two interrelated levels: the institutional environment (or rules of the game) and the institutions of governance (or play of the game). The study of privatizing telecommunications by Levy & Spiller (1994, 1996) examines the institutional environment (rules of the game) in five countries through a comparative contractual lens in which contractual hazards and credible contracting, or the lack thereof, are featured. This bottom-up approach reveals that the decision to privatize and the nature of privatization vary with the condition and quality of judicial independence, the division of powers between the executive and legislative branches, the competence of the regulatory bureaucracy, and contractual safeguards. Whether and how to privatize telecommunications should therefore be made conditional on these features.

Similar considerations arise in privatizing socialist economies. The "big bang" approach pays little heed to differences among industries, whereas those who are more concerned with cultivating institutions and the mechanisms of governance advise that a more gradual program be adopted in which the "easy cases" are privatized first. Because natural monopolies pose strains on deregulation and privatization alike (Arrow 2000, Williamson 2000), these are candidates to be privatized late (if at all) and then with the support of a fall-back regulatory apparatus.

Corporate Governance/Debt and Equity[9]

Price theory was long silent on the matter of corporate governance. Firms were simply assumed to maximize profits. The idea that managers might engage in subgoal pursuit that is contrary to profit maximization was inimical to the orthodox construction [although it can be and has been addressed in nearly orthodox terms by reformulating the objective function (Baumol 1959, Williamson 1964)].

TCE interprets the board of directors mainly as a security feature that arises in support of the contract for equity finance. Specifically, debt and equity are viewed not merely as alternative modes of finance, which is the law and economics construction (Easterbrook & Fischel 1986, Posner 1986), but also as alternative modes of governance. Thus, suppose that a firm is seeking cost-effective finance for the following series of projects: general-purpose mobile equipment; a general-purpose office building located in a population center; a general-purpose plant located in a manufacturing center; distribution facilities located somewhat more

---

[9]This subsection is based on Williamson (1996, pp. 184–85).

remotely; special-purpose equipment; market and product development expenses; and the like.

Suppose further that debt is a governance structure that works almost entirely out of rules. Specifically, assume that debt financing requires the debtor to observe the following: (*a*) Stipulated interest payments will be made at regular intervals; (*b*) the business will continuously meet certain liquidity tests; (*c*) sinking funds will be set up and principal repaid at the loan-expiration date; and (*d*) in the event of default, the debt-holders will exercise preemptive claims against the assets in question. If everything goes well, interest and principal will be paid on schedule. But debt is unforgiving if things go poorly. Failure to make scheduled payments thus results in liquidation. The various debt-holders will then realize differential recovery in the degree to which the assets in question are redeployable.

Because the value of a pre-emptive claim declines as the degree of asset specificity deepens, the terms of debt financing will be adjusted adversely. Confronted with the prospect that specialized investments will be financed on adverse terms, the firm might respond by sacrificing some of the specialized investment features in favor of greater redeployability. But then a lower cost of capital comes at an added production cost. Might it be possible to relieve the trade-off by inventing a new governance structure to which suppliers of finance would attach added confidence? In the degree to which this is feasible, value-enhancing investments in specific assets could thereby be preserved.

Suppose arguendo that a financial instrument called equity is invented, and assume that equity has the following governance properties: (1) It bears a residual-claimant status to the firm in both earnings and asset-liquidation respects; (2) it contracts for the duration of the life of the firm; and (3) a board of directors is created and awarded to equity, a board of directors that (*a*) is elected by the pro rata votes of those who hold tradeable shares, (*b*) has the power to replace the management, (*c*) decides on management compensation, (*d*) has access to internal performance measures on a timely basis, (*e*) can authorize audits in depth for special follow-up purposes, (*f*) is apprised of important investment and operating proposals before they are implemented, and (*g*) in other respects bears a decision-review and monitoring relation to the firm's management (Fama & Jensen 1983).

The board of directors thus evolves as a way to reduce the cost of capital for projects that involve limited redeployability. Not only do the added controls to which equity has access have better assurance properties, but equity is more forgiving than debt. Efforts are therefore made to work things out and preserve the values of a going concern when maladaptation occurs. Thus, whereas the governance structure associated with debt is of a very market-like kind, that associated with equity is much more intrusive and is akin to administration. The correspondence to which I referred earlier between outside procurement/debt and vertical integration/equity therefore obtains. In effect, debt is the market form of finance, and equity (the administrative form) appears as contractual hazards build up. Equity is the financial instrument of last resort.

Other Variations on a Theme

TCE maintains that any issue that arises as or can be posed as a contracting problem can be examined to advantage in transaction cost economizing terms. Accordingly, the reach of transaction cost reasoning is virtually endless. I briefly sketch two additional applications here (without bothering with price theoretic explanations).

PUBLIC BUREAUS   According to Douglass North, "Political markets are. . . prone to inefficiency" (North 1990, p. 365) and "high transaction cost issues gravitate to the polity" (p. 372). That is worse than a paradox. That is perverse. Bad enough that political markets are inefficient. But surely the appropriate lesson is for high transaction cost issues to flee from rather than be attracted to the polity?

Maybe, but then again, maybe not. High transaction cost issues, after all, are ones that are inherently difficult to organize. As set out in Figure 1, such transactions are ones for which node A governance (in the market) is poorly suited compared with node D governance (in the firm). If still additional contractual hazards build up, might some of these transactions be candidates for governance in the public bureau? That is precisely the argument that I advance elsewhere (Williamson 1999). Specifically, the many disabilities of the public bureau notwithstanding—very low-powered incentives, very costly administrative procedures, very protective employment relations—there are some transactions (of which foreign affairs is an example) for which the public bureau comes off best judged, as it should be, comparatively. There is a place for each generic form of organization, yet each needs to be kept in its place.

LABOR ORGANIZATION   The organization of labor reflects many purposes, monopsony power and political purposes included. What about efficiency? Again, the action resides in the details. Those labor transactions that pose greater contractual hazards ($h > 0$) will benefit from governance efforts to mitigate the hazards ($s > 0$), whereas it will be less cost-effective to supply these same safeguards to generic labor (of a node A kind), which is a recurrent theme. As developed elsewhere (Williamson et al. 1975; Williamson 1985, chapter 10), the observed organization of labor tracks an efficiency rationale.

CONTRACT AND ECONOMIC ORGANIZATION

Alternative Approaches

If the contractual approach to economic organization has the reach that I ascribe to it, then the systematic application of TCE to legal education and to legal and economic research on contracting holds out considerable promise. This will entail going beyond the "sort of contract law that has flourished in American law schools: the law embodied n judicial decisions and studied by analyzing these decisions" (Rubin 1995, p. 109). What Edward Rubin (1995) recommends instead is that the law schools (and students of contract more generally) need a "theory of contract. . . that addresses the *contracting process itself*, rather than the judicial adjudication of that process," whereupon a "nonjudicial domain of contracting behavior" will be given prominence (p. 108, emphasis added).

In principle, law and economics could have been applied to that purpose. That project, however, took a "massive wrong turn" by the argument advanced by Posner and others that "the contract law goal [of] economic efficiency. . . [was] achieved through common-law adjudication" (Rubin 1995, p. 113). By drawing attention away from contracts and the contracting process toward judicial adjudication, "law and economics became just another tool for analyzing judicial decisions" (p. 113). Rubin is nevertheless heartened that although the "law school curriculum continues to be relatively resistant to a transactional theory of contract,. . . legal scholarship has gradually begun to shift its focus as a result of the economic and sociological analysis of transactions" (p. 114).

So what does a combined law, economics, and organizations approach to the study of contract, broadly conceived, entail? As I see it, the overarching move is to bring the lens of transaction cost economizing assiduously to bear. The examination of incomplete contracting in its entirety will be facilitated by supplanting the academic concept of contract as legal rules by that of private ordering and by inquiring into the mechanisms through which transaction cost economizing is accomplished. Interestingly, Ronald Gilson (1984) made many of these same arguments earlier in his examination of corporate finance transactions.

The Economizing Perspective

The economizing perspective holds that, subject to the remediableness criterion, inefficiency invites its own demise—where inefficiency is assessed in relation to feasible alternatives (rather than a hypothetical ideal) and provision is made for implementation costs. Because joint gains will always be realized by moving from a less to a more efficient mode, provided that implementation costs do not dissipate the gains, farsighted businessmen and their lawyers will eschew inferior outcomes (such as node B in the schema). In contrast to Machiavelli's myopic advice to "get them before they get us," the farsighted view of contracting is to "give and receive credible commitments" (Williamson 1983, 1993b)—by providing better information and added security features that serve to infuse confidence and realize mutual gains.

Gilson's (1984, p. 255) description of business lawyers as transaction cost engineers is very much in this spirit. He thus urges that transactions be examined not in a one-sided way but "from the perspective of *both* clients" (p. 245; emphasis in original), whence mutual gain is the object. He furthermore adopts a transaction cost economizing approach to private ordering (Gilson 1984, p. 255), including express reference to credible commitments (p. 281). Also, he views departures from the assumptions of the (ideal) capital asset pricing model—namely, common time horizon, identical expectations, no transaction costs, and costless information

(Gilson 1984, p. 252)—as grist for the TCE mill: "[T]he unreality of these [ideal]. . . assumptions is not cause for despair. Rather, it is the very failure of these assumptions to describe the real world that I find the *potential for value creation* by lawyers" (Gilson 1984, p. 253; emphasis added). The institutions of governance arise precisely on account of these disparities (Arrow 1963).

Private Ordering

THE CONCEPT   Marc Galanter (1981) takes exception with the usual academic/legal centralist approach to contract in which disputes purportedly "require 'access' to a forum external to the original social setting of the dispute [whereby] remedies will be provided as prescribed in some body of authoritative learning and dispensed by experts who operate under the auspices of the state" (p. 1). The facts disclose otherwise: Most disputes, including many that under current rules could be brought to a court, are resolved by avoidance, self-help, and the like (p. 2). This is because in "many instances the participants can devise more satisfactory solutions to their disputes than can professionals constrained to apply general rules on the basis of limited knowledge of the dispute" (p. 4). Gilson (1984) concurs: When business lawyers play the role of transaction cost engineer well, "the courts, and formal law generally, shrink dramatically in importance" (p. 294).

CONTRACT LAWS (PLURAL)   Karl Llewellyn's (1931) earlier dissent from the legal rules approach to contract introduces the concept of contract as framework:

> [T]he major importance of legal contract is to provide a framework for well-nigh every type of group organization and for well-nigh every type of passing or permanent relation between individuals and groups. . .—a framework highly adjustable, a framework which almost never accurately indicates real working relations, but which affords a rough indication around which such relations vary, an occasional guide in cases of doubt, and a norm of ultimate appeal when the relations cease in fact to work (Llewellyn 1931, pp. 736–37).

This last point is important in that the prospect of ultimate appeal to the courts serves to delimit threat positions.

Related ideas have been advanced by others, including Clyde Summers (1969) who distinguishes between "black letter law" (which bears a likeness to black box economics) and a more circumstantial approach to contract. The former employs the counterfactual "illusion that contract rules can be stated without reference to surrounding circumstances and are therefore generally applicable to all contractual relations" (p. 566).

The TCE argument that each generic mode of governance is supported by a distinctive form of contract law is broadly in this circumstantial spirit. The ideal (node A) transaction in both law and economics is that of spot markets to which identity is unimportant and legal rules apply (Macneil 1974). This legal rules approach gives way to Llewellyn's concept of contract-as-framework as the importance of continuity builds up and incomplete long-term contracting is adopted (node C). That in turn undergoes change when transactions are taken out of the market and organized internally (node D), where the implicit law of contract now becomes that of forbearance. As previously noted, courts routinely grant standing to firms engaged in interfirm contracting should there be disputes over prices, the damages to be ascribed to delays, failures of quality, and the like, yet courts will refuse to hear disputes between one internal division and another over identical technical issues. Access to the courts being denied, the parties must resolve their differences internally (Rubin 1995, p. 117). Accordingly, hierarchy is its own court of ultimate appeal. That firms and markets differ in their access to fiat is partly explained by these contract law differences (Williamson 1991).

Mechanisms

CORPORATE ACQUISITION TRANSACTIONS   TCE subscribes to the dictum that "explanations in the social sciences should be organized around (partial) *mechanisms* rather than general *theories*" (Elster 2000, p. 75; emphasis in original). That is evident in the way by which TCE examines the canonical make-or-buy decision and of contracting more generally. It is also evident in Gilson's (1984) examination of efforts by business lawyers to perfect the acquisition agreement in the face of "deviations" from the ideal assumptions of the capital asset pricing model:

> Earnout or contingent-pricing techniques respond to the failure of the homogeneous expectations assumption; controls over operation of the seller's business during the period in which the determinants of the contingent price are measured respond to failure of the common-time-horizon assumption; and the panoply of representations and warranties, together with provisions for indemnification and other verification techniques, respond to the failure of the costless-information (Gilson 1984, p. 293).

CONTRACT LAW DOCTRINE   A microanalytic examination of the mechanisms that arise in conjunction with contract law doctrines would also be illuminating. Ian Macneil (1974) describes the legal system's "less than total commitment to the keeping of promises" as follows:

> Contract remedies are generally among the weakest of those the legal system can deliver. But a host of doctrines and techniques lies in the way of even those remedies: impossibility, frustration, mistake, manipulative interpretation, jury discretion, consideration, illegality, duress, undue influence, unconscionability, capacity, forfeiture and penalty rules, doctrines of substantial performance, severability, bankruptcy laws, statutes of fraud, to name a few; almost any contract doctrine can and does serve to make the commitment of the legal system to promise keeping less than complete (Macneil 1974, p. 730).

The refusal by the courts to enforce stipulated damages clauses is especially puzzling. Because the parties to a contract can be presumed to know best what contractual terms serve their interests, why should the courts refuse to enforce stipulated damages in the event of breach?

One possibility is that contract is a devious thing. Thus, although such a clause may frequently be the efficient way to settle a breach, it could also serve strategic purposes, of which induced breach is one.

The issue of contrived cancellation has been addressed by Kenneth Clarkson, Roger Miller, and Timothy Muris in their discussion of refusal of the courts to enforce stipulated damage clauses where breach has been deliberately induced (Clarkson et al. 1978, pp. 366–72). Induced breach could arise when a party intentionally withholds relevant information yet complies with the letter of the contract. Or it might involve perfunctory fulfillment of obligations where more resourceful cooperation is needed (pp. 371–72). In either case, induced breach is costly to detect and/or prove (p. 371). Transaction cost considerations are plainly operative.

Ramifications for Legal Education

Gilson (1984) advises that my observation that the legal centralism approach to contract relieves "lawyers and economists... of the need to examine the variety of ways by which individual parties to exchange 'contract out of or away from' the governance structures of the state by devising private orderings" (Williamson 1983, p. 520) is too sweeping. It should be restricted to academic lawyers and economists (Gilson 1984, p. 295). That is because "business lawyers have done an awfully good job at something the law schools did not and, for the most part, still do not teach: helping people arrange their relationships in the absence of governmental intervention: facilitating *private ordering*" (Gilson 1984, p. 303; emphasis in original). But then "why have law schools done so bad a job training business lawyers?" (p. 303). Gilson's answer is that "There has been no theory... that dealt with private ordering" (p. 304) prior to the appearance of "two areas in economics—finance and transaction cost economics" (p. 305).

Twenty years later we find that the teaching of contract law has changed very little. What explains this continuing neglect?

One explanation is that mainline law and economics has remained comfortably ascendant. The relation between law and economics thus continues to be one in which textbook economic orthodoxy is the fount. The predilection to work out of a theory of the firm-as-production function setup is thus reaffirmed and the subject of organization remains disjunct. Reservations about the efficiency of common law adjudication notwithstanding, contract law teaching stays predominantly focused on legal rules and adjudication.

A second explanation is that the world of private ordering is impossibly complex. As good lawyers are quick studies, better that they learn about private ordering on the job rather than in the classroom.

The first of these arguments is a lame excuse for complacency, whereas the second overlooks the possibility that the economics of organization involves variations on a few key themes. In that event, attention can be focused on canonical cases—of which credible interfirm contracting is one and vertical integration is another. The buzzing, blooming confusion of private ordering is thereby reduced to more manageable proportions. Because the classroom is the place to lay out the intuition, merits, and mechanisms of credible contracting (node C) and to examine the comparative strengths and weaknesses of the firm-as-governance structure (node D), to relegate the study of private ordering to on-the-job training is anachronistic.

Even, moreover, if the basic law school curriculum is unmoved by these arguments, it is noteworthy that a number of leading law schools have begun to offer an elective course on complex deals, many of them modeled after the course offered by Gilson and Victor Goldberg at Columbia Law School on "Deals: The Economic Structure of Transactions and Contracting." If the demand for transaction cost engineers cannot be met by the law schools, the business schools could end up eating that lunch (Rubin 1995, p. 114).

CONCLUSIONS

There is growing agreement that "the objectives of firms, the reason for their existence and the manner of their decision taking. . . will require modes of analysis quite different from those which have dominated in this century" (Hahn 1991, p. 49). Not only does TCE hold that the way to think about contract and organization is to bring the purposive and farsighted lens of economizing to bear,[10] but the existence and governance of firms are both the key TCE issues.

As developed herein, organization theory has massive ramifications for the TCE theory of the firm. Salient contributions from organization theory include the description of human actors in more veridical terms, the importance of intertemporal process transformations, choice of the unit of analysis, and the description of alternative modes of governance as syndromes of complementary attributes. The resulting theory of the firm differs greatly from the neoclassical (Kreps 1990, p. 96). Because "[a]ny standard theory, not just neoclassical, starts from the existence of firms" (Arrow 1999, p. vii), that is very basic.

To be sure, the proximate lessons (as advanced by organization theorists) and the ultimate lessons (as viewed from an economizing perspective) often differ— and that is consequential. But the more basic point is this: Someone needed to

---

[10]Farsighted contracting is more plausible in intermediate product market contracts than in final goods markets. Still, farsighted firms that are selling to consumers who lack the relevant expertise and foresight nevertheless can and do take steps to alleviate the hazards—through branding, warranties, guarantees, and the like. I do not mean to suggest, however, that there is never an occasion to craft additional relief (possibly with the aid of public policy) against residual hazards.

step up and offer trenchant critiques and identify relevant phenomena. Organization theorists were prepared to do that when others were complacent or held back.

The theory of the firm-as-governance structure that is sketched herein is an ongoing rather than finished construction.[11] Its evolving status notwithstanding, it has already served to deepen our understanding of many complex contractual and organizational phenomena and it operates as a check against overuses and misuses of orthodoxy. In that spirit, I suggest that mainstream law and economics stands to benefit by incorporating the lessons and some of the methods of law, economics, and organization—both as these bear on public policy and in relation to the law school curriculum.[12]

ACKNOWLEDGMENTS

This paper was originally prepared for the ceremony inaugurating the Program in Law and Economics at the University of Chile in August 2000. That program is a joint effort between the Faculty of Economics and Business and the Faculty of Law to "promote and develop interdisciplinary theoretical and applied research in the area." It was subsequently presented at the opening session of the fourteenth annual conference of the International Society for New Institutional Economics in Tuebingen, Germany, at the Law and Economics Seminar at George Mason University, the Law, Economics, and Organization Seminar at the University of Southern California, and at the First Annual Symposium at the Center for Legal Dynamics of Advanced Market Societies at Kobe University. Useful questions and comments at all five sessions are gratefully acknowledged. An earlier version of this paper was published in the *Kobe University Law Review* (2004) 38:59–95.

---

[11]Full formalization is the ultimate objective. The Grossman-Hart-Moore model (Hart 1995) qualifies as a fully formal model but is lacking in plausibility (Kreps 1999). The treatment of procurement by Bajari & Tadelis (2001), which focuses on the incentive and ex post adaptation differences between fixed price and cost plus contracting, is much closer in spirit to TCE.

[12]One of the comments that I have received on this review is that the basic message has not only been heard, but that it has registered and taken effect. That is gratifying, yet other readers remark that much of this is unfamiliar terrain and needs to be more fully spelled out. I come out somewhere in between. Thus, although many of the firm-as-governance structure ideas have taken hold, private ordering remains underdeveloped and organization theory is scanted by mainline law and economics—witness the leading textbooks (Cooter & Ulen 2000, Polinsky 1989, Posner 1998). Public policy inroads notwithstanding, the basic contract law course remains immune to the arguments in this paper.

The *Annual Review of Law and Social Science* is online at
http://lawsocsci.annualreviews.org

LITERATURE CITED

Arrow KJ. 1963. Uncertainty and the welfare economics of medical care. *Am. Econ. Rev.* 53(December):941–73

Arrow KJ. 1999. Forward. In *Firms, Markets, and Hierarchies*, ed. G Carroll, D Teece, pp. vii–viii. New York: Oxford Univ. Press

Arrow KJ. 2000. Economic transition: speed and scope. *J. Inst. Theor. Econ.* 156(March): 9–18

Bain J. 1968. *Industrial Organization*. New York: Wiley. 2nd ed.

Bajari P, Tadelis S. 2001. Incentives versus transaction costs: a theory of procurement contracts. *RAND J. Econ.* 32(3):387–407

Barnard C. 1962 (1938). *The Functions of the Executive*. Cambridge: Harvard Univ. Press

Baumol WJ. 1959. *Business Behavior, Value and Growth*. New York: Macmillan

Ben-Porath Y. 1980. The F-connection: family, friends, and firms and the organization of exchange. *Popul. Dev. Rev.* 6:1–30

Buchanan JM. 1975. A contractarian paradigm for applying economic theory. *Am. Econ. Rev.* 65(2):225–30

Buchanan JM. 1987. The constitution of economic policy. *Am. Econ. Rev.* 77(3):243–50

Clarkson KW, Miller RL, Muris TJ. 1978. Liquidated damages v. penalties. *Wis. Law Rev.* 1978:351–90

Coase RH. 1992. The institutional structure of production. *Am. Econ. Rev.* 82(September): 713–19

Commons JR. 1932. The problem of correlating law, economics, and ethics. *Wis. Law Rev.* 8:3–26

Cooter R, Ulen T. 2000. *Law and Economics*. Reading, MA: Addison-Wesley. 3rd ed.

Dawkins R. 1976. *The Selfish Gene*. New York: Oxford Univ. Press

Demsetz H. 1983. The structure of ownership and the theory of the firm/comment. *J. Law Econ.* 26(June):375–93

Easterbrook F, Fischel D. 1986. Close corporations and agency costs. *Stanford Law Rev.* 38(January):271–301

Elster J. 2000. Arguing and bargaining in two constituent assemblies. *Univ. Penn. J. Const. Law* 2:345

Fama EF, Jensen MC. 1983. Separation of ownership and control. *J. Law Econ.* 26 (June):301–26

Galanter M. 1981. Justice in many rooms: courts, private ordering, and indigenous law. *J. Leg. Plur.* 19:1–47

Gilson R. 1984. Value creation by business lawyers: legal skills and asset pricing. *Yale Law J.* 94(December):239–313

Hahn F. 1991. The next hundred years. *Econ. J.* 101(January):47–50

Hart O. 1995. *Firms, Contracts, and Financial Structure*. New York: Oxford Univ. Press

Hayek F. 1945. The use of knowledge in society. *Am. Econ. Rev.* 35(September):519–30

Joskow P. 1991. The role of transaction cost economics in antitrust and public utility regulatory policies. *J. Law Econ. Org.* 7(Special Issue):53–83

Joskow PL. 2000. *Transaction cost economics and competition policy.* Work. Pap., MIT

Klein B. 1980. Transaction cost determinants of 'unfair' contractual arrangements. *Am. Econ. Rev.* 70(May):356–62

Klein B, Leffler K. 1981. The role of market forces in assuring contractual performance. *J. Polit. Econ.* 89(May):615–41

Kreps DM. 1990. Corporate culture and economic theory. In *Perspectives on Positive Political Economy*, ed. J Alt, K Shepsle, pp. 90–143. New York: Cambridge Univ. Press

Kreps DM. 1999. Markets and hierarchies and (mathematical) economic theory. In *Firms, Markets, and Hierarchies*, ed. G Carroll, D Teece, pp. 121–55. New York: Oxford Univ. Press

Levy B, Spiller P. 1994. The institutional foundations of regulatory commitment: a comparative analysis of telecommunications regulation. *J. Law Econ. Org.* 10(October):201–46

Levy B, Spiller P. 1996. *Regulations, Institutions, and Commitment: Comparative Studies of Telecommunications.* Cambridge, UK: Cambridge Univ. Press

Llewellyn KN. 1931. What price contract? An essay in perspective. *Yale Law J.* 40:704–51

Macneil IR. 1974. The many futures of contracts. *South. Calif. Law Rev.* 47(May):691–816

March JG, Simon HA. 1958. *Organizations.* New York: Wiley

McKenzie L. 1951. Ideal output and the interdependence of firms. *Econ. J.* 61(December):785–803

Meese AJ. 1997. Price theory and vertical restraints: a misunderstood relation. *UCLA Law Rev.* 45(October):143–204

Michels R. 1962. *Political Parties.* Glencoe, IL: Free

North D. 1990. A transaction cost theory of politics. *J. Theor. Polit.* 2(4):355–67

Polinsky AM. 1989. *An Introduction to Law and Economics.* Boston: Little, Brown. 2nd ed.

Posner RA. 1972. The appropriate scope of regulation in the cable television industry. *Bell J. Econ. Manag. Sci.* 3(1):98–129

Posner RA. 1976. *Antitrust Law.* Chicago: Univ. Chicago Press

Posner RA. 1979. The Chicago School of antitrust analysis. *Univ. Penn. Law Rev.* 127(April):925–48

Posner RA. 1986. *Economic Analysis of Law.* Boston: Little, Brown. 3rd ed.

Posner RA. 1993. The new institutional economics meets law and economics. *J. Inst. Theor. Econ.* 149(March):73–87

Posner RA. 1998. *Economic Analysis of Law.* New York: Aspen Law & Business. 5th ed.

Rabin M. 1998. Psychology and economics. *J. Econ. Lit.* 36(March):11–46

Reder M. 1999. *The Culture of a Controversial Science.* Chicago: Univ. Chicago Press

Riordan M, Williamson O. 1985. Asset specificity and economic organization. *Int. J. Ind. Org.* 3:365–78

Robbins L. 1932. *Essay on the Nature and Significance of Economic Science.* London: Macmillan

Rubin E. 1995. The non-judicial life of contract: beyond the shadow of the law. *Northwestern Univ. Law Rev.* 90(Fall):107–31

Schultz G. 1995. Economics in action: ideas, institutions, policies. *Am. Econ. Rev. Papers Proc.* 85(May):1–8

Scott WR. 1987. *Organizations: Rational, Natural, and Open Systems.* Upper Saddle River, NJ: Prentice Hall

Selznick P. 1950. The iron law of bureaucracy. *Modern Rev.* 3:157–65

Shapiro C, Varian HR. 1999. *Information Rules: A Strategic Guide to the Network Economy.* Boston, MA: Harvard Bus. Sch.

Simon H. 1947. *Administrative Behavior.* New York: Macmillan

Simon H. 1957a. *Administrative Behavior.* New York: Macmillan. 2nd ed.

Simon H. 1957b. *Models of Man.* New York: Wiley

Simon H. 1978. Rationality as process and as product of thought. *Am. Econ. Rev.* 68(May):1–16

Simon H. 1985. Human nature in politics: the dialogue of psychology with political science. *Am. Polit. Sci. Rev.* 79:293–304

Spulber D. 1999. *Market Microstructure: Intermediaries and the Theory of the Firm.* Cambridge, UK: Cambridge Univ. Press

Summers C. 1969. Collective agreements and the law of contracts. *Yale Law J.* 78(March):537–75

Williamson OE. 1964. *The Economics of Discretionary Behavior: Managerial Objectives in a Theory of the Firm.* Englewood Cliffs, NJ: Prentice-Hall

Williamson OE. 1975. *Markets and Hierarchies: Analysis and Antitrust Implications.* New York: Free

Williamson OE. 1977. Predatory pricing: a strategic and welfare analysis. *Yale Law J.* 87(December):284–340

Williamson OE. 1983. Credible commitments: using hostages to support exchange. *Am. Econ. Rev.* 73 (September):519–40

Williamson OE. 1985. *The Economic Institutions of Capitalism.* New York: Free

Williamson OE. 1991. Comparative economic organization: the analysis of discrete structural alternatives. *Admin. Sci. Q.* 36(June): 269–96

Williamson OE. 1993b. Calculativeness, trust, and economic organization. *J. Law Econ.* 36(April):453–86

Williamson OE. 1996. *The Mechanisms of Governance.* New York: Oxford Univ. Press

Williamson OE. 1999. Public and private bureaucracies. *J. Law Econ. Org.* 15(April): 306–42

Williamson OE. 2000. *Empirical Microeconomics: Another Perspective.* Work. Pap., Inst. Manag. Innov. Org., Univ. Calif., Berkeley

Williamson OE, Wachter ML, Harris JE. 1975. Understanding the employment relation: the analysis of idiosyncratic exchange. *Bell J. Econ.* 6(Spring):250–80

Annu. Rev. Law Soc. Sci. 2005. 1:397–421
doi: 10.1146/annurev.lawsocsci.1.041604.120006
First published online as a Review in Advance on September 15, 2005

REVERSAL OF FORTUNE: The Resurgence of Individual Risk Assessment in Criminal Justice

Jonathan Simon

*Boalt Hall Law School, University of California, Berkeley, California 94720;
email: jsimon@law.berkeley.edu*

Key Words   mentally ill, dangerousness, incapacitation, actuarial justice,
paradigm crises

■ **Abstract**   During the 1970s, the enterprise of individual risk assessment in the
criminal justice system came under sharp attack from a number of angles, including
legal, political, and empirical. A particularly acute site of this controversy was the
use of psychological expertise to make individual risk assessments of persons with
mental illness who found themselves within the criminal justice system. Successful
court challenges to the procedures under which such persons were held in custody
as dangerous were followed by empirical research on those persons released. The
result was something of a paradigm crisis in the use of individual risk assessment in
criminal justice and growing calls for its abandonment. By the 1990s, however, risk
assessment was becoming more important than ever to the criminal justice system. This
resurgence reflected the political demand for strategies to prevent violent crime and led
to significant investments in research and policy development. In the new paradigm of
risk assessment, psychological expertise is still valuable but mediated by actuarial and
quasi-actuarial methods of identifying the dangerous.

INTRODUCTION

The practice of risk assessment in criminal justice decision making, especially
in dealing with the mentally ill, experienced a dramatic reversal of fortune in
the 1990s. During the 1970s and early 1980s, powerful criticism by leading academic lawyers and social scientists led to widespread skepticism about whether
criminal justice agencies ought to engage in confinement based on the future dangerousness of individuals rather than as deserved criminal punishment and whether
these agencies were even competent to assess future dangerousness. This criticism
was supported by the Supreme Court's growing interest in the confinement of
the mentally ill, beginning with the 1966 case of *Baxstrom v. Herold*. As courts
increased the pressure on criminal justice agencies to back up their claims of dangerousness or else release mentally ill inmates, a wave of empirical analysis was
conducted (in many respects the first rigorous examinations of decision making
in institutions for the criminally insane ever done) that in the short term only

reinforced the growing skepticism about risk assessment. This downward spiral in elite support for risk assessment was further reinforced by the collapse of support among the same elites for rehabilitative penology and a rise in the prestige of philosophical arguments against preventive custody of all kinds not grounded in retributive considerations (Allen 1981, Garland 2001a). The emerging consensus in criminal justice policy appeared to be adverse to a significant role for individual predictions of dangerousness for the mentally ill as well as for the "normal" defendant.

Since the end of the 1990s, in contrast, risk assessment has become a largely uncontested aspect of a much expanded criminal process, and it has been entrusted to a range of criminal justice actors, including prosecutors, juries, judges, and administrative appointees, with little active pressure from the courts. Risk assessment has also won widespread support from leading academic scientists, including two most closely associated with the empirical part of the earlier critique (John Monahan and Henry J. Steadman). In effect, the paradigm crisis of criminal justice risk assessment that began in the 1970s has been resolved. Then, the scientific status of the field came under sustained attack (Kuhn 1996 [1962]). Today, the solidifying paradigm is not persuading all opponents, but it is effectively marginalizing them; in the words of one participant in the new sciences of risk assessment: "[T]here is no longer any serious debate about whether general criminal recidivism can be predicted among general criminal populations" (Hanson 1999, p. 8-2).

This review explores the paradigm crisis and the stabilization of a new paradigm for criminal justice risk assessment and describes the fundamental changes in how risk assessment is practiced and the resulting formation of scientific knowledge about risk factors. The kind of risk assessment that was scrutinized in the 1960s and 1970s was primarily clinical prediction by mental health experts of institutionalized persons with active mental pathologies. This was far from the only risk assessment going on in criminal justice, but it became a privileged example that influenced the broader valuation of risk assessment practice.

Since the beginning of the twentieth century, psychiatrists, psychologists, and a host of less degreed experts had played pivotal if often hidden roles in the criminal justice system and especially in release decisions over mentally ill prisoners in custody as defendants either found incompetent to stand trial, found not guilty by reason of insanity, or diverted into specialty programs for pathological sex offenders and drug addicts. Risk assessment, in this era, was primarily a process of recommendations to courts of individual experts in psychiatry and psychology, purveyors of what we might call, following Nikolas Rose (1989), psy-expertise. Epistemologically, these recommendations were anchored in the expert reading of a dossier containing, in varying quality and density, educational, psychological, medical, and criminal justice information, supplemented by narratives produced by case workers who examined the defendant and relevant witnesses.

The psy-expertise highlighted in these clinical cases was at work in a more attenuated way by the general interest in prediction and treatment choices consistent with the rehabilitative bias of almost all corrections. Although risk assessment as it was problematized in the 1970s was highly associated with the "mentally disordered"[1] among the criminal justice population, it also fit with the general posture of modern criminal justice toward individualized knowledge in the name of both social defense and rehabilitation (Harcourt 2003a,b). The indeterminate sentence and parole system operating in virtually every state by the 1960s tied the custody of most prisoners to the unreviewed decisions of administrative parole boards acting in a diagnostic and predictive mode in determining when to release prisoners on parole (Glaser 1964, Rothman 1980, Simon 1993).

During the 1970s and early 1980s, risk assessment in criminal justice remained widespread and inevitable but problematized, i.e., vulnerable to attack on legal, scientific, and political grounds. Due process decisions by courts began to create more demanding proof for continuing custody of persons held for preventive reasons. Widely cited empirical studies (some based on the releases of inmates ordered by courts) suggested that expert risk assessment was often worse than chance in predicting future dangerousness. The broader rehabilitative penology that was supporting the indeterminate sentence and the parole system also collapsed in this period for many of the same reasons, including due process pressure and empirical skepticism. Both risk assessment as an adjunct to penal control and the rehabilitative penology came under attack from a normatively libertarian perspective that questioned the authority of the state to engage in preventive custody rather than retributive punishment (Am. Friends Serv. Comm. 1971, von Hirsch 1976, Tonry 1996).

Since the 1980s, incapacitating the dangerous has come back to the fore as a justification for the massive increase in ordinary imprisonment and the creation of new forms of confinement targeted at the mentally abnormal (sexually violent predators). In both its institutional and scientific sources, criminal justice risk assessment stands in a very different posture than it did through the 1970s. Although there are exceptions, classical clinical prediction has been replaced almost everywhere with more or less structured and standardized instruments that incorporate, in style and partially in substance, the actuarially weighted and validated instruments famously used in setting insurance premiums as well as in functions like college admissions (Simon 1988).

Institutionally, risk assessment is playing a different role in the criminal justice system. Before the 1980s, it was used primarily in deciding who to release from confinement. Parole release has greatly diminished, and most Americans punished for crimes are released from prison or jail at the termination of a fixed sentence, less any general credits for good behavior, with little or no assessment of the risk either of violence or of recidivism more generally. Since 1980 risk assessment has been deployed as a mechanism for extending confinement or surveillance over persons either not yet convicted of crime or who have already served their penal sentence. Increasingly, risk assessment is being brought into the criminal justice process to

---

[1]This is itself a term of art for mentally ill persons within the criminal justice system.

select people for extended incapacitation through a variety of means ranging from registration and notification requirements attached to many sex offenders, to civil commitment, to the death penalty.

This paradigm shift in risk assessment played a significant role in the intellectual development of socio-legal studies. In the late 1970s and early 1980s, the problem of predicting violence was a pivotal site for the development of critical socio-legal knowledge about psychology and the criminal justice system. Today, the empirical science is largely aimed at finding best practices to operate a predictive system that is politically anchored but that finances the creation of technically proficient science about possible predictive factors. This epistemological hardening has followed from rather than led the widespread embrace of preventive confinement and incapacitation by political leaders as well as by the courts, including such forms as pretrial preventive detention (denial of bail), criminal sentencing in some states like Virginia (Tonry 2004), and sex offender notification programs. It has also benefited from a public discourse that merges risk and populist responses to victim status.

THE PROBLEMATIZATION OF RISK ASSESSMENT, 1975–1985

By the end of the 1970s, risk assessment in the criminal justice system seemed to be largely discredited (Monahan 1981, p. 6). This decline in standing was determined by changes in several distinct features of the organizational environment of risk assessment, including changes in the knowledge produced about risk assessment, the dominant penology shaping the criminal justice system, and the judicial standards for following clinical recommendations. The 1970s saw a steadily growing body of research assessing the success of risk assessment in criminal justice. The results suggested that violence prediction was often wrong. Many people classified as dangerous by clinicians and then released by the operation of court decisions failed to commit the predicted assaults and crimes. The revelations about mentally disordered offenders might actually have been reassuring to a public that had long believed that mental abnormality was the key to violence. But the critique of scientific risk assessment undercut its authority to justify custodial controls well beyond the boundaries of retributive justice.

For much of the twentieth century, the role of psychiatry and psychology within the criminal justice system had been a key measure of the larger cultural standing of psy-knowledge more generally. Lawyers and psy-experts seemed locked in a long-term battle for influence in criminal justice that many observers thought psy-experts would inevitably win by virtue of accumulating positive knowledge of the mind that would undermine the standing of legal culpability (Green 1995, Banner 2002). This remained the case during the 1960s and into the 1970s.

Other than a few studies of the recidivism of parolees, there was very little in the way of empirical tests of the validity of risk assessments within the criminal justice system at the beginning of the 1960s. By the end of the decade, a wave of studies had begun by a group of scholars who would devote their careers primarily to empirical studies of the problems of risk assessment and whose work remains highly influential to this day. An important starting point was the founding of the National Institute of Mental Health Center for Studies of Crime and Delinquency in 1966 (Steadman 1987, p. 83). The appointment of Dr. Saleem Shah as chief in 1967 was also important. Shah, a clinical psychologist, directed the center until 1987[2]; he was himself a leading questioner of the practice of risk assessment, publishing some of the most influential articles problematizing the field (Shah 1977). As chief of the center and as a funder, Shah supported much of the initial empirical work that defined the paradigm crisis and forged a new paradigm, including work by scholars who became both the most resolute critics of risk assessment (including Thomas Szasz and Alan Dershowitz) and the most important defenders (like John Monahan and Henry J. Steadman).

This empirical attack was an echo effect of the lawsuits brought following *Baxstrom v. Herold* (1966) challenging the confinement of mentally ill persons in criminal custody of various sorts. In *Baxstrom*, the Supreme Court held that equal protection required that state prisoners held in facilities for the criminally insane be afforded the same opportunity for a jury trial on the issue of their sanity and dangerousness as was afforded persons being civilly committed.

> For purposes of granting judicial review before a jury regarding whether a person is mentally ill and in need of institutionalization, there is no conceivable basis for distinguishing the commitment of a person who is nearing the end of a penal term from all other civil commitments (*Baxstrom v. Herold* 1966 at 111–12).

As a result of *Baxstrom* and its progeny, more than 1000 mentally ill ex-prisoners in New York alone were either transferred from high security hospitals for the criminally insane to less secure civil hospitals or released from confinement altogether when courts rejected correctional risk assessments finding them insane and dangerous (Monahan 1981). Other states followed suit. These releases provided an unprecedented natural experiment in the validity of current risk assessment practices. Each person released represented a prediction of dangerousness (one way or the other) now put to the test by a reduction in security or by full release.

The *Baxstrom* cohort in a real sense funded the formation of an empirical science of risk assessment for the mentally ill by attracting the most extensive follow-up research (Steadman 1972, Steadman & Keveles 1972, Steadman & Cocozza 1974, Cocozza & Steadman 1974). It also delivered a devastating blow to the fortunes of clinical risk prediction. The results suggested that only a small minority of those whom risk assessors had determined to be dangerous enough to require the higher security confinement of a hospital for the criminally insane proved to be in fact dangerous under the less controlled circumstances of civil hospitals or the community. Twenty percent of the total cohort transferred as a result of *Baxstrom* (either to civil hospitals or to the community) were assaultive at any time during

---

[2]Shah died in 1992.

the four years following their release, and only 3% were ultimately sent back to hospitals for the criminally insane (Monahan 1981, pp. 46–47).

This socio-legal pressure was bolstered by creation in 1972 of the Mental Health Law Project, a public interest litigation organization that both participated in a series of landmark cases dealing with the criminal justice system's treatment of the mentally ill and mobilized a broad array of young lawyers interested in pursuing such cases (Steadman 1987, p. 83). That same year, the Supreme Court widened its review of the confinement of the mentally ill to those found incompetent to stand trial, and in *Jackson v. Indiana* (1972) expanded its doctrinal grounds to include due process. The Court drastically limited the scope of confinement (from what had often been indefinite detention for life), giving rise to another wave of release studies that provided similarly negative empirical evidence about the competence of risk assessment (Cocozza & Steadman 1976).

Overall, the result of these waves of empirical research on the standing of clinical risk assessment was devastating. In Monahan's (1981) influential monograph on the state of the field, he summarizes the best research as indicating that *"psychiatrists and psychologists are accurate in no more than one out of three predictions of violent behavior over a several year period among institutionalized populations that had both committed violence in the past (and thus had high base rates for it) and who were diagnosed as mentally ill"* (Monahan 1981, pp. 48–49, italics in original).

Thus, by the end of the 1970s, much of the psy-community, as well as the legal community, believed that expert risk prediction was no better than chance in identifying which individuals should be confined as dangerous and that judges should not rely on such expertise in making decisions concerning the freedom of individuals (Diamond 1974). The American Psychological Association concluded in its 1978 task force report on the subject of "the role of psychology in the criminal justice system" that "psychologists are not professionally competent to make such judgments" (Am. Psychol. Assoc. 1978, p. 1110). The emergence of a critical empirical literature on risk assessment in the 1970s reflected in part the degree to which a set of legal presumptions in favor of expert risk prediction that had long protected experts in the criminal justice system from any serious empirical validation studies had begun to falter. The inevitability of making predictions as part of criminal justice was intrinsic to the dominant penology of individualized diagnosis and treatment, with its combination of extreme administrative discretion through parole boards (leaving judges and legislatures with little real control over custody) and appeals to a scientific, presumably psychiatric/psychological model of control. The empirical evidence against risk assessment in criminal justice would not have been as damaging had this presumption in favor of risk assessment remained unquestioned in this period.

Instead, as mentioned above, rehabilitation was facing its own empirical assault. If penal confinement was to be limited primarily by predictions as to when the prisoner was safe to release back into the community, risk assessment was inevitable and could only be improved with the involvement of psy-professionals. If, however, penal confinement was limited to that deserved by the moral culpability of the offender, confinement based on even quite reliable prediction mechanisms was presumptively unacceptable.

The 1970s saw several states formally abandon the indeterminate sentence and parole systems that had been the central organs of this dominant twentieth century penality. In the 1980s and 1990s, almost all states adopted more determinacy in their sentencing, limiting parole, requiring longer mandatory minimums, or requiring offenders to serve 85% or more of the nominal sentence. The premise of the early twentieth century that penal treatment should be individualized and remedial was reversed by the end of the century in favor of penal treatment based on the crime and on specific features of the offender's criminal record (Harcourt 2003b).

Recent decades have produced a penal ideology that is most accurately described as a volatile mix (O'Malley 1999, Tonry 2004), but in the 1970s it seemed as if a hegemonic rehabilitative penology were being replaced whole cloth by a renewed embrace of retribution. Retribution as a penal objective is grounded in the past behavior of the subject. From this perspective, prediction is anathema, an unacceptable basis for suspending the liberty of a person who does not otherwise deserve prison as punishment.

Thus, across a number of decision points in criminal justice, among both psy-professionals and lawyers, and in both legislatures and courts, risk assessment found itself on the defensive, seen as ineffective and unfair. We can take John Monahan's (1981) remarkable "statement of personal values" urging caution in rejecting a role for scientific assessment, as both a measure of how low the fortunes of risk assessment in criminal justice had become by 1981 and perhaps a rallying cry for the turn about. "Empirically," he wrote, "it is much less clear to me now than it once was that relatively accurate prediction is impossible under all circumstances" (Monahan 1981, p. 14). Not a ringing endorsement but, in the context of that moment, a significant counter to the rapid deflation of risk assessment in the criminal process. Most importantly, Monahan's careful analysis of why contemporary risk assessment seemed so difficult to defend pointed the way toward the epistemological hardening of risk assessment in the 1980s and 1990s.

This emerging optimism about risk assessment began with a clear sense of the unsustainable features of risk assessment as it had been practiced through the 1970s, especially its unguided, clinical, all-or-nothing judgment call, a technique problematized within the psychology and corrections literature since the mid-1950s (Meehl 1954). Anchoring most of these problems was the dominance of clinical prediction as the main model of risk assessment in the criminal justice system. In this model the identification of a subject as dangerous was typically made by an individual clinician on the basis of an examination of the subject's file, including as much information as was available concerning not only the subject's criminal record but also educational records, psychological testing records, and possibly also a psychological examination of the subject by the risk assessor. The identification of the subject as dangerous was not generally conditioned by any formal standards, probabilities, or weighting of factors.

The risk assessment of this period was also challenged by the lack of specification of the dimensions of risk. The status of being dangerous was subject to periodic revision, but otherwise it constituted a totalizing judgment not qualified by situational, temporal, or treatment-oriented factors. The uncertainty of prediction revealed by empirical studies clearly highlighted the inevitability of mistakes but was not by itself a reason to abandon prediction altogether. The acceptability of prediction, notwithstanding its uncertainty, might well vary depending on the specific circumstances, including the degree of harm the risk assessor believed was being prevented or the nature of the risk assessor's decision regarding prediction, such as whether the subject should be temporarily detained pending trial or whether the subject should face the death penalty.

The specific site of risk prediction problematized by *Baxstrom* (1966) and *Jackson* (1972) was also significant, although in cross-cutting ways. Because most of the subjects were either convicted of violent crimes (*Baxstrom*) or held under probable cause of having committed violent crimes (*Jackson*), they could be expected to be a relatively high-risk population, i.e., one with a high base rate of assaults. The poor success of predictions of dangerousness in this context might seem especially damning. At the same time, these subjects were mostly persons who had been institutionalized for a long period prior to the moment of risk assessment, which meant that prior history and other available risk factors might have become less relevant to the individual case. It was the shift of public attention from this problematic group to the larger population of "normal" recidivists that helped drive the reversal of fortune in the status of risk assessment.

THE RECONSTRUCTION OF CRIMINAL JUSTICE RISK ASSESSMENT

In the early 1980s, risk assessment by clinical experts remained embedded throughout the criminal justice system, but it was now deeply problematized by court decisions and a growing empirical record that threatened to unravel much of psy-expertise's hard-won respectability during the twentieth century (Borum 1996). A cycle of litigation and empirical research seemed to produce a continuous supply of bad news about the quality of risk assessment. A major professional association of the psy-community, the American Psychological Association, refused to defend the validity of clinical predictions of violence and suggested that such activity was beyond the professional capacity and even detrimental to their professional practice. Nevertheless, even as its intellectual foundations were being undermined, clinical prediction concerning mentally disordered persons within the criminal justice system continued.

Indeed, sources of a broader revival were already in motion. One source was the growing political interest in incapacitating those perceived as unreasonably dangerous to the general public. Rising crime rates and media coverage of crime had made government action against crime a potent political issue since the 1968 elections (Beckett 1997, Simon 1997, Garland 2001b). In promoting policy solutions attractive to the public, politicians shared none of the intellectuals' distrust of confinement based on risk or the science of predicting who is dangerous.[3] Proposals to fight crime with preventive detention of arrestees and long incapacitative sentences for likely recidivists emerged during the "war on crime" of the late 1960s and began to be adopted in the 1980s.

Ironically, the political demand for risk assessment comes from the community of non-governmental organizations (NGOs) supporting individual rights. Faced with increasing use of incarceration as a tool for risk management on general populations of offenders, advocates have called on the government to mandate more individualized risk assessments. One example from the periphery of the criminal justice system is the use of criminal records, including arrests as well as convictions, to exclude otherwise eligible persons from public housing. Local public housing agencies are authorized to exclude a wide variety of persons on the basis of such records, but they are provided little guidance on how to exercise this discretion. After examining practices in a number of areas, Human Rights Watch found that many people were being excluded arbitrarily with no consideration of their likely effect on the public safety of other residents. In their published report, the New York–based NGO recommended to the Department of Housing and Urban Development that it mandate "policies that require individualized consideration of each applicant with a criminal record...to determine whether he or she will pose a risk to existing housing tenants" (Human Rights Watch 2004, p. 6).

A second source of revival was the very same empirical research community that was delivering so much bad news for criminal justice risk assessment. A body of lawyers and researchers specializing in these problems had formed an extraordinary facilitative relationship in cases in which litigation drew on negative empirical findings. If the litigation was successful, it produced a new cascade of test cases for researchers. The research community, its skills sharpened on the quasi-experiments created by the release of many institutionalized people in the 1970s, began to produce for the first time a body of risk factors with a statistical basis. Their research continued, funded by the federal government and foundations. Although some continued to report relatively poor levels of success in predictions of violence among the mentally ill through the early 1990s (Lidz et al. 1993), more recent evaluations were proving optimistic (Hanson 1999).

A third source of the revival of risk assessment was court decisions, beginning with the California Supreme Court's decision in *Tarasoff v. Regents of the University of California* (1976), that held psy-professionals liable for failing to meet a standard of due professional care when they did not warn individuals of a threat from a patient. This ruling made psy-professionals' predictive powers a source of professional responsibility. Thus, there was a compounded burden of risk now placed on the risk assessor for failing to predict a patient's dangerousness:

---

[3] 95% of the public support legal intervention for a mentally ill person predicted to be violent (Monahan et al. 2000, p. 312; Pescosolido et al. 1999).

(*a*) the risk to others of becoming victims of the patient's crimes if he or she were set free or placed in a less secure hospital ward but then did turn violent; and (*b*) the risk to the risk assessor of being sued for professional negligence if the patient turned violent despite the risk assessor's predictions to the contrary (Rose 2003).

Incapacitating the Dangerous

Academic critics of rehabilitation in this period tended to emphasize retribution and deterrence as the most promising penal rationales that should guide reformed sentencing systems. But politicians in the 1980s perceived incapacitation of the dangerous as the penal rationale with the greatest public appeal (Zimring & Hawkins 1995). The public feared mentally disordered criminals even more than other criminals, and it had little skepticism about the propriety of preventively confining such persons. Since the 1980s, a steady stream of policies has expanded the role of risk identification and control as the dominant logic of the criminal justice system, many involving mentally ill or abnormal offenders, but others involving "normal" prisoners. This emphasis on incapacitating the dangerous led some, by the early 1990s, to begin speaking of a "new managerialism," (Bottoms 1983), "new penology," or "actuarial justice" anchored in risk (Feeley & Simon 1992). As officials have found themselves facing greater political demands to risk assess in a context of large caseload institutions, they have inevitably turned to risk assessment technologies that can be performed routinely through the use of readily available information, which has generally meant a turn to more actuarial instruments (Silver & Miller 2002, p. 156).

PRETRIAL DETENTION   In the 1960s, civil rights advocates and academics began arguing that many Americans were being denied their constitutional right to bail by high, judicially set financial terms that arrestees faced in order to await trial out of jail (Foote 1965). Thus, by setting a high money bail, judges were unnecessarily presuming that many cash-poor suspects were at high risk of failing to appear for their trials. At that time, the only risk recognized as being at stake in bail decisions was the risk of failing to appear for trial. In effect, this criticism paralleled the criticism of risk predictions concerning the mentally ill: Too many false positives were being produced by a prediction system based on ability to pay (as well as a few false negatives, recidivists with cash in the family). One of the most successful reform strategies, the Vera Institute's system of releasing without financial commitments arrestees with sufficient links to the community, was in its own way a much more explicit risk assessment system. The information gathered by pretrial release workers in the Vera model provided objective factors to be used in setting release conditions. Scoring each community link and requiring a threshold score for release on one's "own recognizance" created a crude but functional actuarial instrument for risk assessment, replacing the essentially clinical judgment of a judge who set financial terms on the basis of a holistic but subjective evaluation.

After debating the issue since the late 1960s, policy makers began in the 1980s to implement, at the federal level, pretrial detention based on danger to the community rather than risk of flight. Not only did the new system win acceptance from the Supreme Court in *U.S. v. Salerno* (1987), but it did so despite the fact that judges using their detention power were thus exercising the kind of clinical prediction seemingly most discredited by the paradigm crisis of the 1970s—prediction unguided by any actuarial instruments or decision trees.

PRISON SENTENCES   The passing of rehabilitation and the broader framework of individual diagnosis and treatment that had long been the master narrative of corrections and the mental health community has produced a volatile and inconsistent set of public justifications for punishment that include just deserts, incapacitation of the dangerous, and deterrence, along with a remarkably broad trend of increasing prison populations (Caplow & Simon 1999, O'Malley 1999, Tonry 2004). Nationally, the rate of imprisonment has risen from a figure of 93 prisoners for every 100,000 resident adults (not far from the lowest rates recorded in the 1920s when national statistics on imprisonment were first collected) to 482 per 100,000 in 2003 (Bur. Justice Stat. 2002, table 6.22).

At the level of sentencing, the quasi-clinical ritual of prediction associated with the indeterminate sentence and release by parole boards has been replaced by a quasi-actuarial process that generally uses a matrix or a checklist to assign a sentencing range based on objective factors of the crime and of the criminal record. Surprisingly, this has not corresponded to the development of consistent claims for predictive validity in sentencing. Although the idea of using empirically tested variables in an actuarial instrument aimed at identifying "high rate" offenders among legally similar defendants was floated by researchers in the 1980s (Greenwood 1982), only Virginia has explicitly embedded such risk assessment into its sentencing regime (Tonry 2004). But on top of the superficially retributive general sentencing schemes that dominate in most states and in the federal system, politicians and sometimes voters acting through ballot initiatives have imposed a variety of risk-based sentencing mechanisms, such as mandatory minimums and three-strikes laws that combine a certain rough actuarialism with a populist appeal to anger (Shichor & Sechrest 1996).

Inside prisons during what some sociologists have called an era of "mass imprisonment" (Garland 2001a), the experience of imprisonment with little programming aimed at treatment or education has become overwhelmingly one of custody and security (Kruttschnitt & Gartner 2005). Expertise inside the correctional system has focused on security as well. Prisoners entering most state corrections systems today are risk assessed and placed in a prison facility organized around levels of security. The most striking example of this is the rise of the supermax prisons designed to hold the "worst of the worst" prisoners who represent a threat to staff and other inmates. Risk assessors may select supermax custody on the basis of a variety of processes, ranging from misconduct inside another prison, to suspicion of having a leadership position within prison gangs (California model), to a diagnosis of "psychopathy" (Rhodes 2002).

PAROLE AND PROBATION   At the height of the rehabilitative penal regime between the 1950s and the 1970s, the importance of risk assessment to the paradigm was exemplified in probation and parole, in both their release and supervision functions (Simon 1993). As methods of avoiding prison or of obtaining early release from prison, probation and parole involved a form of risk assessment (of the prisoner's prospects for success or, in contrast, of committing a new crime once back in the community) much like the practices of clinical prediction used to regulate the release of mentally ill criminals. The recommendations of psy-professionals became a canonical part of the probation and parole file, although judges who controlled probation and administrative appointees (usually of the governor) who served on parole boards were rarely professionally trained in psychiatry, psychology, or related fields (social work, criminology, sociology). Parole field agents also had a quasi-clinical risk assessment function. In addition to actively helping the released prisoner adjust to the community, the parole agent was ideally envisioned as performing a diagnostic role to detect warning signs of criminality that warrant preventive removal from the community, such as for technical violations of the many specific commitments made by parolees in their parole release agreement (Simon 1993).

Although probation and parole were destabilized by the crises of the rehabilitative penology, the importance of both has grown prodigiously in their role as a way to protect the community through ready recourse to revocations. Sentencing reform, especially the United States Sentencing Guidelines, were largely aimed at reducing the use of probation and correspondingly increasing the use of imprisonment (Harcourt 2003a, p. 105). Probation, the most common sanction for nontraffic offenses, has grown at an even faster pace during the same period (presumably concentrating on persons who might not have gotten formal criminal justice processing at all in the past). Parole as a mode of release from prison has shrunk to about a third of total releases (from two thirds in the 1970s), but in the states where it survives, the clinical model of individualized case analysis and diagnosis has been largely repudiated, replaced by guidelines that are supposed to track risk of recidivism but that are rarely statistically validated and often allow discretion to be exercised by the parole board in the name of maximum precaution (Petersilia 2003, p. 71).

Supervision in the community follows release for most prisoners, even when they complete a fixed sentence. While on supervision, a person can be found in violation either for picking up a new arrest or for failing to satisfy technical requirements of their supervision (e.g., submitting to a drug test). New arrests and technical violations have both become major independent sources of prison admissions (Petersilia 1997, 2003). Risk assessment influences the level of supervision and conditions imposed on the released prisoner, but field supervision decisions remain very discretionary. Structured risk assessment processes usually involve a combination of actuarially determined weighted factors and individual discretion (Lynch 1998). Data are beginning to accumulate, but not with the intensity of research on the mentally ill (Gendreau et al. 1996).

CAPITAL PUNISHMENT   Although only a few states with death penalties make future dangerousness a significant factor in the jury's choice between death and life in prison, two of those states, Texas and Virginia, have among the highest death sentencing and execution rates in the country and indeed are the only states where it has begun to approximate a normal penalty in its frequency and in the relatively short time for appeals prior to execution (Zimring 2004). In both states, expert witnesses testify on the basis of clinical examination and the application of actuarial prediction instruments as to whether the defendant would be a threat to commit violence in the future if ever released. Such considerations likely influence capital jurors even in states where dangerousness is not an explicit subject of testimony.

Risk assessment in the death penalty exemplifies another feature of risk assessment in criminal justice since the 1980s, i.e., the decoupling of professional organizations from the legal importance of risk assessment. Although major psyprofessional organizations have weighed in against the use of risk assessment for capital punishment purposes, the legal system now makes the testimony of psy-professionals crucial to the battle over the death penalty in each case.

SEX OFFENSES   One of the most important sites for criminal justice risk assessment before the 1970s was in controlling the release of persons confined in special facilities under "sexual psychopath" laws adopted in the 1930s and 1940s. These laws were aimed at preventively incapacitating and treating persons with diagnosable psychopathic conditions that made them a high risk for sexual offenses, and the laws often required a specific finding of amenability to treatment. Those subject to commitment under the laws were held in special treatment facilities rather than in prisons, but those selected were often charged with relatively minor crimes or were first-time offenders who, in the absence of the civil commitment regime, probably would not have been sent to prison (Kirwin 2003). Directed at sexual psychopaths such as those depicted in popular culture at the time, the laws were frequently used against unpopular but noncriminal deviance, especially against gay men during moments of popular fear of sex crimes (Miller 2002).

When clinical risk prediction in criminal justice came under critical scrutiny in the late 1960s and 1970s, sexual psychopath laws were already falling into disuse. Concerns about the accuracy of predictions of future violence were compounded by doubts as to the initial dangerousness of people brought into the system. In the 1980s and 1990s, however, new popular concerns about sex offenses, including a wave of often bizarre prosecutions of day care workers for the sexual abuse of minors during the 1980s and a wave of concern about children stalked by sex offenders near their homes in the 1990s, produced increased use of the old laws and a wave of new ones.

Prosecutors in states that retained the old sexual psychopath laws began using them again in the early 1990s in response to popular fears of sex crimes involving children. Concerned about constitutional problems, 16 states have adopted new laws aimed at "sexually violent predators" that permit civil commitment of sex offenders deemed to pose a serious risk of recidivism. The state typically continues to have a burden of showing mental abnormality and a lack of control, but the state is no longer limited to specific diagnoses or to a showing that the offender is amenable to treatment. Although the sexual psychopath laws were generally targeted at relatively minor offenders and were imposed as an alternative to any criminal sanction, the new laws are aimed at persons convicted of serious sexual offenses who have completed often substantial prison sentences.

In place of the clinical prediction model used in the past, civil commitment under the new sexually violent predator laws almost always involves application of an actuarial instrument. Indeed, states have invested in creating their own actuarial instruments, some of which are in use in other states (English 1999, Epperson et al. 2003). For example, Minnesota created MnSOST (Minnesota Sexual Offense Screening Test) to screen imprisoned sex offenders for possible civil commitment based on the subject's history of sexual and nonsexual offenses, the number of victims, characteristics of the victim (e.g., child), paraphilias (sexual perversions), and substance abuse (Huot 1999).

Tests have also been developed by scientists aware of the strong commercial market among states for such instruments. One of the most popular and controversial is the so-called Hare Psychopathy checklist (Hare 1998; Monahan et al. 2001, p. 65), which is, in fact, a whole family of instruments aimed at screening various populations for violence potential. These instruments combined structured clinical assessment with collateral information available in official records to assess two distinct factors that the developers claim to be highly related to violence. One factor is conduct toward others reflecting "selfish, callous and remorseless use of others" (Monahan et. al. 2001, p. 66). The other factor is the status of having a "chronically unstable and antisocial lifestyle" (p. 66). Developer Robert Hare and his supporters tout the checklist as a statistically validated instrument capable of classifying mental patients and others into high and low risk groups with a significant difference in probability of violence, and one that can be readily used by officials charged with making relatively quick decisions on limited records. Critics have claimed that the checklist factors are little more than an aggregation of deviant behavioral factors that are themselves predictors of violence (Toch 1998). Monahan et al. (2001) found validation for the predictive power of the Hare checklist for assessments of patients in civil commitment proceedings but little evidence for the underlying personality structures theorized by Hare and his colleagues (Monahan et al. 2001, p. 70).

Whatever its scientific status, the success of the Hare checklist and its competitors testifies to the growing demand from a wide variety of users mandated to assess risk. The most popular style of screening process combines the results of actuarial scoring with considerable leeway for the clinician making the recommendation to rely on his or her own judgment, a process sometimes described as "adjusted actuarial" (Hanson 1999). These laws, which pose the possibility of lifetime exclusion from society even after having served a retributive prison sentence for past crimes, have been upheld against constitutional challenge in the U.S. Supreme Court, which has insisted only that treatment be a possibility [see *Kansas v. Hendricks* (1997) and *Kansas v. Crane* (2002)].

The 1990s also saw universal adoption of another kind of risk assessment aimed at preventing sex offenses. It followed the widely publicized sexual abuse and murder of seven-year-old Megan Kanka by a neighbor who had already served prison time for a sex offense against children. Congress conditioned federal criminal justice aid to states on the adoption of so-called Megan's laws, state laws requiring sex offenders to register their home address with the state and requiring notification of institutions responsible for children, including schools and day care centers as well as families, when persons deemed "high risk" are in their vicinity. Many states place all such registered offenders on websites that permit viewers to quickly view local sex offender pictures and home addresses. Most states undertake risk screening of their eligible pool of offenders required to register. As with civil commitment laws, states have actively produced their own screening instruments, often by creating a commission to evaluate the literature and produce an adequate screen. These instruments are generally related to the empirical literature but in most cases are not actuarially validated in their totality (Witt & Barone 2004).

Validating Risk

A history of risk assessment as a problem for law and social science over the past 30 years might suggest that little has changed other than the formal appearance of the risk assessment process. We see the disappearance of the model of clinical prudence, in which criminal justice borrowed on the cultural prestige of psy-experts as clairvoyants[4], and the rise of a regime of checklists and risk factors, most of them lacking in true actuarial validation but conveniently defined to meet the criminal justice system's own coding of the individual. But such an account ignores another dimension of change, one equally striking and far more optimistic, i.e., the epistemological hardening of individual risk assessment into something more like a science than it has been in the past and with some of the impulse toward self-reflexive restraint that science brings.

The formation of a new, statistically validated base for risk assessment is a product of a combination of two elements common in the recent history of social policy and social science but rarely in such a dynamic form. First, the political demand for acceptable risk assessment instruments produced by the politics of crime control made this area a zone of steady investment by government and foundations since the mid-1960s. Second, a critical mass of empirical scholars was drawn together by opportunities for research and reform that were produced by legal rights expansion. Since the 1990s, this empirical group has systematically advocated best practices standards in the risk assessment process.

The two scholars who perhaps best exemplify this generation are John Monahan of the University of Virginia Law School and Henry J. Steadman, president of

---

[4]Anthony Madden has spoken in a related context of the "clairvoyant fantasy" that technology will hand us a test capable of reliably predicting what mental patients will do in the future (Madden 2003a).

Policy Research Associates, Inc. Both Monahan and Steadman belong to a generation of social scientists (Monahan in psychology and Steadman in sociology) drawn into law and social policy by the ferment of court decisions and federal government interest in mental health during the 1960s. Both Monahan and Steadman were among the brightest of the group of young academic and state researchers funded by Saleem Shah's Center for Studies of Crime and Delinquency at the National Institutes for Mental Health in the 1970s to study the cohorts of persons released from correctional mental health facilities as a product of court decisions like *Baxstrom* (1966). Working alone, together, and with other collaborators, Monahan and Steadman have produced a continuing series of publications on risk assessment, including empirical studies, critical literature assessments, and major textbooks, culminating in the publication in 2001 in collaboration with others of *Rethinking Risk Assessment: The MacArthur Study of Mental Disorder and Violence* (Monahan et al. 2001).

The MacArthur Study was an $8 million effort funded by the MacArthur Foundation to track and monitor the risk behavior and violence of the mentally ill. The researchers tracked more than 1000 patients discharged from three general psychiatric hospitals in three U.S. cities, at a cost of around $8000 per subject, an investment that one reviewer noted as more equivalent to the norm for biomedical research than social science research (Madden 2003b). The high cost was generated by an unprecedented effort to measure behavior along multiple methodological tracks, including interviews on a regular interval and patient self-study, using both standardized instruments and open-ended questions. The results are by far the most reliable evidence ever obtained on the violence propensity of the mentally ill and ones that generally support the dominant view of the postconfinement era that mental illness by itself is not a cause of higher violence levels (although when combined with substance abuse and other factors it can be facilitative).

Perhaps more importantly, the study has provided strong confirmation for a list of factors that contemporary risk assessors have relied on for some time in structured risk assessments: previous violence, substance abuse problems, psychopathy, relationship instability, employment problems, symptoms of major mental illness, personality disorder, impulsivity, lack of social support, noncompliance with treatment, stress, and anger information about personality, previous violence, and substance abuse.

Monahan's (1981) monograph summarized the critical discussions and empirical evidence produced in the 1970s in a way that produced a baseline for future improvements. The Monahan book also laid out an agenda for a more successful research-based strategy for risk assessment concerning mentally ill violent offenders in the criminal justice system (he suggested no such role for psy-experts in the case of normal offenders). This strategy emphasized three important factors in risk assessment: (*a*) research-based factors, (*b*) a nuanced and reflexive approach to risk specification, and (*c*) greater knowledge of the patient's situation and treatment. Between Monahan's 1981 book on *Clinical Prediction of Violent Behavior* and the 2001 MacArthur Study, research into at least two of the three have advanced significantly; situational factors and treatment remain understudied. As a science with considerable authority to impose what amounts to an individualized "state of emergency" or exception, e.g., civil commitment as a violent sexual predator, risk assessment today enjoys a higher level of optimism and acceptability than at any time in its history (Mossman 1994).

THE NEW RISK ASSESSMENT

Monahan & Steadman (1996) offer a comparison that highlights both the new confidence and the circumspection that characterizes the new risk assessment: Mental health experts in the criminal justice system can be like weather forecasters. Citing the National Research Council's (NRC) Committee on Risk Perception and Communication for the proposition that weather forecasters are exemplary risk assessors, Monahan and Steadman argue that the risk assessment of mentally ill persons in the criminal justice system now approximates the practices that have made the forecasting of natural hazards, like weather, conform to expectations of a hard science.

Monahan & Steadman (1996) note five factors identified by the NRC Committee that mental health professionals doing risk assessment now share with weather forecasters: First, both have ample opportunity to test their models. Changes in the laws regulating civil commitment of the mentally ill mean that the institutionalized population has a much higher base rate of violence than in the past. Second, both enjoy significant base rate information. Weather has long been one of the most carefully recorded data sets. The wave of empirical studies of mental health risk assessment beginning in the 1960s produced by the early 1990s a range of statistically validated predictor variables. Third, both enjoy statistically constructed models that can assist in forecasting while allowing individual judgment to improve any of the fixed assumptions. Fourth, both get short-term feedback from their predictions. Even mental patients hospitalized today do not tend to stay long, meaning an opportunity to commit new acts of violence in the community are close at hand. Finally, both fields require extensive training of predictors.

According to Monahan & Steadman (1996), criminal justice system risk assessment is now operating with some of the precision that allows weather forecasting to achieve greater reliability. For example, precipitation forecasts changed from dichotomous predictions of "rain" or "no rain" to probabilistic forecasts, such as a "40% chance of rain tomorrow." Monahan (1981) criticized criminal justice risk assessment as it was practiced in the 1970s for emphasizing all-or-nothing prediction. The recent work of Monahan, Steadman, and their colleagues has deliberately pushed best practices toward using probabilities (statements about how likely a person is to become violent) versus frequencies (a statement about a particular number of violent incidents that were observed out of a total number of observations) versus a graded assessment of the risk of violence (such as low, medium, or high) and toward paying more attention to contextual and dynamic factors. In the era of the MacArthur Study, a density of data is being collected about the risk behavior of mentally ill subjects that approximates, for example, the accumulation of empirical knowledge about the body in modern medicine. The question is clearly raised as to whether something like the epistemological thaw that somatic medicine went through in the nineteenth century is taking place in the psychology of mental illness and violence at the end of the twentieth (Foucault 1977).

There are undoubtedly gaps between the model of first-class science in the MacArthur Study and average practice of state and federal criminal justice agencies, but one should not underestimate the degree to which the studies will influence best practices. The validation of a large number of variables relied upon by the practicing risk assessment community, including the elements of the psychopathy test developed by Hare and colleagues (Hare 1991, 1998), by introducing a range of complicating situational and dynamic factors not typically used, will both solidify the standing of criminal justice risk assessment and introduce the terms of scientific criticism and testing into it. One can be optimistic that heavy investment in an empirical science model will build elements of continued testing into the shape of the predictive regime in criminal justice, but concerned nonetheless that as that regime expands to meet political demands, its scientific testing culture will be irrelevant.

New Methodologies: Beyond the Actuarial/Clinical Divide

Critics of risk assessment in the 1970s noted that the typical prediction was an all-or-nothing judgment as to future violence and that a more successful approach would limit judgment to relative degree of risk. Work in the 1990s has provided evidence of scale effects by the clinician asked to assess risk. Scales that provide finer grained differentiation among small probabilities led to lower probabilities of predicted violence by forensic clinicians (Slovic & Monahan 1995, Slovic et al. 2000).

Risk assessment today is far more cautious with its predictive claims and protects itself more from accountability for failure. The question of dangerousness has been transformed into one of risk more generally. In the "new generation sex offender civil commitment laws. . .[e]valuators instead need to determine whether or not a subject is above a certain likelihood threshold for sexual reoffending, not whether he will or will not reoffend" (Doren 1998). This comes close to being irrefutable, just as the fact that I have had no accidents cannot prove that the insurance company was wrong to place me in the high-risk (high-premium) groups.

Compared with the past, more research on situational and dynamic factors has been done, including work on substance abuse, psychotic symptoms, and neighborhood characteristics. There is also a greater effort to link individual risk assessment with the growing literature on community ecology by sociologists and criminologists, much of it emphasizing the importance of concentrated poverty on the behavior of residents. For example, the MacArthur study showed that mental patients in Pittsburgh released to neighborhoods of concentrated poverty were 2.8 times more likely to commit assault than those not living in such neighborhoods, even in a model controlling for most of the leading personal characteristics associated with violence (Link et al. 1992, Silver et al. 1999).

Most of the instruments used in the study are actuarial in using regression techniques to standardize the weighting of the factors. Many of the most commonly used instruments, e.g., the Hare Psychopathy Checklist, that the sexually violent predator civil commitment laws rely on, take over an hour for a trained clinician to administer, even for the "screening version," which was expressly developed for the emerging market in faster risk assessment (Monahan et al. 2000). A goal of recent work has been to develop instruments that can be quickly assembled from documentary materials readily available in an institutional setting (Monahan et al. 2000, Steadman et al. 1994).

Many of the competitive instruments incorporate clinical assessments into the actuarial formula. They thus require expertise in scoring even if from a paper record. The instruments constrain that expertise by setting a specific weight to clinical elements' contribution toward the final assessment. There is a new consensus, supported by those whose expertise is at stake, that structured clinical and actuarial prediction can work far better than chance (Borum 1996, Slobogin 1996, Hanson & Harris 1998).

The improved status of risk assessment is due in part to the fact that risk assessment builds in more self-doubt about prediction than was true in the past. Contemporary risk assessment research is far more focused on the cognitive biases of assessors and the effects of various formatting choices in risk assessment on these biases, including whether assessors are asked to identify risk in terms of a continuous scale as opposed to discrete categories of low or high risk, whether probabilities or frequencies matter, and whether high or low scales matter (Slovic & Monahan 1995). For example, a growing body of evidence suggests that stating risk phenomena as frequencies (1 out of 10) is more alarming to both experts and the public than percentages (Kahneman & Tversky 1996).

Making Monsters

The formation of a more rigorous and methodologically sophisticated risk assessment science may turn out to be largely irrelevant when there is a political imperative to incapacitate those whom the public considers unreasonable risks, especially sex offenders whose victims are children. States that have adopted new civil commitment laws against sexually violent predators are under constant pressure to increase the level of incapacitation against a class of offenders defined as an intolerable risk. The tendency has been to admit a growing number of sex offenders who would otherwise be released from prison, and to release only a very small fraction of those admitted on an annual basis. Notwithstanding the fact that both admission and release are now regulated by a far more empirically influenced risk assessment instrument, the dynamic of expanding admissions and minimal releases is likely to make the better science irrelevant; the judgment will be administrative and guided by public interest rather than science. Treatment centers for sexually violent predators are becoming like death rows in many states.

This also raises the problem of how the risk assessment community fits into a larger correctional apparatus that has become far less oriented toward psychology, social science generally, or data-tested programming. Indeed, most correctional departments are far less open to the contributions of social science today than they were in the 1970s (although this may be changing). The sophisticated science of risk assessment that was developed in the 1990s remains highly dependent on the criminal justice system as both the producer of its major inputs and the consumer of its services.

An independent but deeply relevant factor is that state correctional systems have become a significant (perhaps the most significant) state institution responsible for dealing with the everyday needs of the severely mentally ill. This is especially true because criminal justice in the intervening decades has been anything but neutral in its own influences on the mentally ill population. Even as the body of funded research was being done on the court-ordered release cohorts of the 1970s, the mentally ill population was becoming more enmeshed in the criminal justice system itself, with more of the people released from civil mental hospitals already having criminal arrest records than had been true in the 1950s and 1960s. This criminalization of the mentally ill was also having a measurable effect on the violence rates of released mental patients in the 1970s. The reassuring statistical surprise, that researchers were able to tell the public during the first wave of court-ordered releases that mental patients had lower rates of violence than the general public, was becoming untrue (Link et al. 1992). More people were ending up in mental hospitals who already had arrests.

In the intervening decades, more mentally ill persons have ended up in jails and eventually prison because they have accumulated multiple criminal arrests that eventually assure jail and prison time, even for relatively minor property and drug crimes. With relatively strong barriers against civil commitment (which requires a finding of mental illness with danger to self or others) in most states, arrest and jail have become a common pathway for moving the mentally ill into coerced care. Shrinking welfare and wage protections for low-skilled workers may have combined to force more of the mentally ill (a population always on the margins of homelessness and abject poverty) into petty crimes and self-medication through illegal drug use.

One of the greatest concentrations of mentally ill persons in the nation is in the central jails of the largest cities, which have become in part giant mental hospitals. Prisons are also housing more people with mental illness; moreover, the promise of very long sentences served in prisons that offer no narrative of rehabilitation or hope may very well be an engine of mental illness. A large body of empirical data has documented the severe psychological effects and wide range of pathological clinical conditions that result from the extreme end of the warehousing model, the so-called supermax prisons that maintain total lockdown conditions (Haney 2003).

The same kind of feedback loop may be developing in the shift of policing and criminal sentencing of the non–mentally ill toward risk assessment and profiling. As the criminal justice system becomes more tightly coordinated, from the police to the prison system, and focused on high-risk populations, the heightened scrutiny and risk-based selection may independently increase the measurable rate of crime and risk behaviors leading to even more concentration and investment of law enforcement resources (Harcourt 2003b, p. 118). Meanwhile, the public perception that certain high-risk populations are the primary source of crime locks in the direction of future policies toward more concentration on the risk posed by these groups to the exclusion of alternative strategies for reducing criminal risk to ordinary citizens.

The weather forecasting comparison (Monahan & Steadman 1996) highlights a gaping difference between the risk assessment in criminal justice and the broader horizon of risk communication and management. In the former, the criminal justice system and specialized control institutions are the major consumers for risk assessment. In the latter, private organizations and individuals as well as the government and large insurance companies consume risk information. The one major exception is registration and notification laws that require persons convicted of certain sex offenses to register for the rest of their lives and provide for release of that information to the public under some circumstances. Some states have chosen to make the pictures and precise addresses of certain offenders available on public websites, while other states only notify specific institutions and families. The use of risk assessment has been to sort offenders into high- or low-risk groups for purposes of notification.

Ironically, little of the increasingly sophisticated body of research on the correlates of violent behavior is directed at influencing how the public, or parents of children, can reduce the risk to children of becoming victims of crimes that continue to terrify the public despite ever increasing penal severity. Recent research on the risk management of ordinary persons suggests that it reflects neither full economic rationality nor indifference to risk information, but rather a response to a field of information shaped by the availability of nearby ideas, as well as cognitive biases (Gersen 2001).

CONCLUSION

Thirty years ago, the combination of court scrutiny of the custody of the mentally ill and a wave of empirical research on how dangerousness predictions were made inside the criminal justice and mental health systems helped shatter the legitimacy of a model of clinical prediction that had anchored much of the mental health and correctional systems. Today, risk assessment has established a new scientific paradigm that is in a position to reshape much of practice. What remains to be seen is how this new expert-based knowledge will interact with a correctional system that has now grown vastly larger than it was in the 1970s (which contains a large portion of the mentally ill population once housed in civil confinement) and a public that wants to be protected from risk with none of the qualifications endemic to the current risk assessment paradigm.

The *Annual Review of Law and Social Science* is online at
http://lawsocsci.annualreviews.org

LITERATURE CITED

Allen FA. 1981. *The Decline of the Rehabilitative Ideal: Penal Policy and Social Purpose.* New Haven, CT: Yale Univ. Press

Am. Friends Serv. Comm. 1971. *Struggle for Justice: A Report on Crime and Punishment in America.* New York: Hill & Wang

Am. Psychol. Assoc. 1978. Report of the task force on the role of psychology in the criminal justice system. *Am. Psychol.* 33:1099–113

Banner S. 2002. *The Death Penalty: An American History.* Cambridge, MA: Harvard Univ. Press

Baxstrom v. Herold, 383 U.S. 107 (1966)

Beckett K. 1997. *Making Crime Pay: Law and Order in Contemporary American Politics.* New York: Oxford Univ. Press

Borum R. 1996. Improving the clinical practice of violence risk assessment: technology, guidelines, and training. *Am. Psychol.* 51:945–56

Bottoms A. 1983. Neglected features of contemporary penal systems. In *The Power to Punish*, ed. D Garland, P Young, pp. 166–202. London: Heinemann

Bur. Justice Stat. 2002. *Sourcebook of Criminal Justice Statistics.* Washington, DC: US Dep. Justice. 30th ed. http://www.albany.edu/sourcebook/index.html

Caplow T, Simon J. 1999. Understanding prison policy and population trends. In *Prisons*, ed. M Tonry, J Petersilia, 26:63–120. Chicago: Univ. Chicago Press

Cocozza J, Steadman H. 1974. Some refinements in the measurement and prediction of dangerous behavior. *Am. J. Psychiatr.* 1974:1012–20

Cocozza J, Steadman H. 1976. The failure of psychiatric predictions of dangerousness: clear and convincing evidence. *Rutgers Law Rev.* 29:1084–101

Diamond B. 1974. The psychiatric prediction of dangerousness. *Univ. Penn. Law Rev.* 123:439–52

Doren DM. 1998. Recidivism base rates, predictions of sex offender recidivism, and the sexual predator commitment laws. *Behav. Sci. Law* 16:97–114

English K. 1999. Adult sex offender risk assessment screening instrument. *Progress Rep. 1.a*, Colorado Div. Crim. Justice, Denver, CO

Epperson DL, Kaul JD, Huot SM, Goldman R, Alexander W. 2003. Minnesota sex offender screening tool—revised (MnSOST-R). In *Technical Paper: Development, Validation, and Recommended Risk Level Cut Scores.* St. Paul: Minn. Dep. Corrections

Feeley MM, Simon J. 1992. The new penology: notes on the emerging strategy of corrections and its implications. *Criminology* 30:449–70

Foote C. 1965. The coming constitutional crisis in bail. *Univ. Penn. Law Rev.* 113:959–99

Foucault M. 1977. *Discipline and Punish: The Birth of the Prison.* Transl. A Sheridan. New York: Pantheon

Garland D. 2001a. *Mass Imprisonment in the United States: Social Causes and Consequences.* London: Sage

Garland D. 2001b. *The Culture of Control: Crime and Social Order in Contemporary Society.* Chicago: Univ. Chicago Press

Gendreau P, Little T, Goggin C. 1996. A meta-analysis of adult offender recidivism: What works? *Criminology* 34:575–607

Gersen JE. 2001. *Cognition and strategy: regulating catastrophic risk.* PhD thesis. Dep. Polit. Sci., Univ. Chicago

Glaser D. 1964. *The Effectiveness of a Prison and Parole System.* Indianapolis, IN: Bobbs-Merrill

Green T. 1995. Freedom and criminal responsibility in the age of Pound: an essay in criminal justice. *Mich. Law Rev.* 93:1915–64

Greenwood P. 1982. *Selective Incapacitation.* Santa Monica, CA: Rand

Haney C. 2003. Mental health issues in long-term solitary and "supermax" confinement. *Crime Delinq.* 49:124–56

Hanson RK. 1999. What do we know about risk assessment? In *The Sexual Predator: Law, Policy, Evaluation and Treatment,* ed. AM Schlank, F Cohen, 1:8-1–8-24. Kingston, NJ: Civic Res. Inst.

Hanson RK, Thornton D. 2000. Improving risk assessment for sex offenders: a comparison of three actuarial scales. *Law Hum. Behav.* 24:119–36

Harcourt B. 2003a. From the ne'er-do-well to the criminal history category: the refinement of the actuarial model in criminal law. *Law Contemp. Probl.* 66:99–144

Harcourt B. 2003b. The shaping of chance: actuarial models and criminal profiling at the turn of the 21st century. *Univ. Chicago Law Rev.* 70:105–28

Hare R. 1991. *The Hare Psychopathy Checklist—Revised.* Toronto: Multi-Health Syst.

Hare R. 1998. The Hare PCL-R: some issues concerning its use and misuse. *Leg. Criminol. Psychol.* 3:99–119

Human Rights Watch. 2004. *No Second Chance: People with Criminal Records Denied Access to Public Housing.* New York: Human Rights Watch

Huot S. 1999. The referral process. In *The Sexual Predator: Law, Policy, Evaluation and Treatment,* ed. AM Schlank, F Cohen, pp. 6-2–6-10. Kingston, NJ: Civic Res. Inst.

Jackson v. Indiana, 406 U.S. 715 (1972)

Kahneman D, Tversky A. 1996. On the reality of cognitive illusions: a reply to Gigerenzer's critique. *Psychol. Rev.* 103:582–91

Kansas v. Crane, 534 U.S. 407 (2002)

Kansas v. Hendricks, 521 U.S. 346 (1997)

Kirwin J. 2003. One arrow in the quiver—using civil commitment as one component of a state's response to sexual violence. *William Mitchell Law Rev.* 29:1135–219

Kruttschnitt C, Gartner R. 2005. *Marking Time in the Golden State: Women's Imprisonment in California.* Cambridge, UK: Cambridge Univ. Press

Kuhn T. 1996 (1962). *The Structure of Scientific Revolutions.* Chicago: Univ. Chicago Press. 3rd ed.

Lidz C, Mulvey EP, Gardner W. 1993. The accuracy of predictions of violence to others. *JAMA* 269:1007–11

Link BG, Andrews H, Cullen FT. 1992. The violent and illegal behavior of mental patients reconsidered. *Am. Sociol. Rev.* 57:275–92

Lynch M. 1998. Waste managers? New penology, crime fighting, and the parole agent identity. *Law Soc. Rev.* 32:839–69

Madden A. 2003a. Editorial, standardised risk assessment: Why all the fuss? *Psychiatr. Bull.* 27:201–4

Madden A. 2003b. Rethinking risk assessment: the MacArthur study of mental disorder and violence. *Psychiatr. Bull.* 27:237–38

Meehl P. 1954. *Clinical Versus Statistical Prediction: A Theoretical Analysis and a Review of the Evidence.* Minneapolis: Univ. Minn. Press

Miller N. 2002. *Sex-Crime Panic: A Journey to the Paranoid Heart of the 1950s.* Los Angeles: Alyson Books

Monahan J. 1981. *The Clinical Prediction of Violent Behavior.* Rockville, MD: US Dep. Health Hum. Serv., Natl. Inst. Ment. Health

Monahan J, Steadman HJ. 1996. Violent storms and violent people: how meteorology can inform risk communication in mental health law. *Am. Psychol.* 51:931–38

Monahan J, Steadman HJ, Robbins PC, Silver E, Appelbaum PS, et al. 2000. Developing a clinically useful actuarial tool for assessing violence risk. *Brit. J. Psychiatr.* 176:312–19

Monahan J, Steadman HJ, Silver E, Appelbaum

PS, Robbins PC, et al. 2001. *Rethinking Risk Assessment: The MacArthur Study of Mental Disorder and Violence.* Oxford: Oxford Univ. Press

Mossman D. 1994. Assessing predictions of violence: being accurate about accuracy. *J. Consult. Clin. Psychol.* 62:783–92

O'Malley P. 1999. Volatile and contradictory punishment. *Theor. Criminol.* 3:175–96

Pescosolido B, Monahan J, Link B, Stueve A, Kikuzawa S. 1999. The public's view of the competence, dangerousness, and need for legal coercion among persons with mental illness. *Am. J. Public Health* 89:1339–45

Petersilia J. 1997. Probation in the United States. *Crime Justice* 22:149–200

Petersilia J. 2003. *When Prisoners Come Home: Parole and Prisoner Reentry.* New York: Oxford Univ. Press

Rhodes LA. 2002. Psychopathy and the face of control in supermax. *Ethnography* 3:442–66

Rose N. 1989. *Governing the Soul.* London: Routledge

Rose N. 2003. At risk of madness. In *Embracing Risk: The Changing Culture of Insurance and Responsibility*, ed. T Baker, J Simon, pp. 209–37. Chicago: Univ. Chicago Press

Rothman D. 1980. *Conscience and Convenience: The Asylum and Its Alternatives in Progressive America.* Boston: Little Brown

Shah S. 1977. Dangerousness: a paradigm for exploring some issues in law and psychology. *Am. Psychol.* 33:224–38

Shichor D, Sechrest D. 1996. Three strikes as public policy: future implications. In *Three Strikes and You're Out: Vengeance as Public Policy*, ed. D Shichor, D Sechrest, pp. 265–77. London: Sage

Silver E, Miller L. 2002. A cautionary note on the use of actuarial risk assessment tools for social control. *Crime Delinq.* 48:138–61

Silver E, Mulvey EP, Monahan J. 1999. Assessing violence risk among discharged psychiatric patients: toward an ecological approach. *Law Hum. Behav.* 23:237–55

Simon J. 1988. The ideological effects of actuarial practices. *Law Soc. Rev.* 22:801–30

Simon J. 1993. *Poor Discipline: Parole and the Control of the Underclass 1890–1990.* Chicago: Univ. Chicago Press

Simon J. 1997. Governing through crime. In *The Crime Conundrum: Essays on Criminal Justice*, ed. G Fisher, L Friedman, pp. 171–90. Boulder, CO: Westview

Slobogin C. 1996. Dangerousness as a criterion in the criminal process. In *Law, Mental Health and Mental Disorder*, ed. BD Sales, DW Shuman, pp. 360–83. Pacific Grove, CA: Brooks/Cole

Slovic P, Monahan J. 1995. Probability, danger, and coercion: a study in risk perception. *Law Hum. Behav.* 19:49–65

Slovic P, Monahan J, MacGregor DG. 2000. Violence risk assessment and risk communication: the effects of using actual cases, providing instruction, and employing probability versus frequency formats. *Law Hum. Behav.* 24:271–96

Steadman H. 1972. The psychiatrist as a conservative agent of social control. *Soc. Probl.* 20:263–71

Steadman HJ. 1987. Mental health law and the criminal offender: research directions for the 1990s. *Rutgers Law Rev.* 39:81–95

Steadman HJ, Cocozza J. 1974. *Careers of the Criminally Insane.* Lexington, MS: Lexington Books

Steadman HJ, Keveles C. 1972. The community adjustment and criminal activity of the Baxstrom patients: 1966–1970. *Am. J. Psychiatr.* 129:304–10

Steadman HJ, Monahan J, Appelbaum PS, Grisso T, Mulvey E, et al. 1994. Designing a new generation of risk assessment research. In *Violence and Mental Disorder: Developments in Risk Assessment*, ed. J Monahan, H Steadman, pp. 297–318. Chicago: Univ. Chicago Press

Tarasoff v. Regents of the University of California, 131 Cal.Rptr. 12 (1976)

Toch H. 1998. Psychopathy or antisocial personality in forensic settings. In *Psychopathy: Antisocial, Criminal and Violent Behavior*, ed. T Millon, E Simonsen, M Berket-Smith, R Davis, pp. 144–58. New York: Guilford

Tonry M. 1996. *Sentencing Matters.* New York: Oxford Univ. Press

Tonry M. 2004. *Thinking About Crime: Sense and Sensibility in American Penal Culture.* New York: Oxford Univ. Press

U.S. v. Salerno, 481 U.S. 739 (1987)

von Hirsch A. 1976. *Doing Justice: The Choice of Punishments.* New York: Basic Books

Webster C, Douglas K, Eeaves D, Hart SD. 1995. *HCR-20 Assessing Risk for Violence (Version 2).* Vancouver: Simon Fraser Univ.

Witt PH, Barone N. 2004. Assess sex offender risk: New Jersey's methods. *Fed. Sentencing Rep.* 16(3):170–75

Zimring FE. 2004. *The Contradictions of American Capital Punishment.* New York: Oxford Univ. Press

Zimring FE, Hawkins G. 1995. *Incapacitation: Penal Confinement and the Restraint of Crime.* New York: Oxford Univ. Press

SUBJECT INDEX

A

Admissibility
  See Expert evidence
Affirmative action, 211–16,
  223
Agency theory
  corporate governance and,
  61, 64–68
Alternative dispute resolution
  (ADR), 171, 174–78
Amnesty International, 95
Anti-apartheid movement,
  88–92
Apartheid, 88–92, 100–1

B

Bargaining
  discussion of legislation
  and contracts, 234, 236,
  251–52
  See also Plea bargaining;
  Settlement bargaining
Bell's interest convergence
  thesis, 208, 225
Bench trial, 131, 146
  See also Plea bargaining
Bilingual education, 222–23

C

Capital Jury Project, 276–77
Class action lawsuits, 50–53
Collateral estoppel and
  precedent, 47–50
Comparative law, 17, 30–32
  comparative punishment
  and, 30–32
Constitutional rights
  transnational human rights
  and, 85, 96–100
Contract theory
  lessons of organization

theory for, 377–78
See also Law, economics,
  and organization theory;
  Transaction cost
  economics
Corporate governance,
  61–80, 385–88
  agency theory and, 61,
  64–68
  best practices, 61, 72–80
  common law versus civil
  law systems, 76–79
  comparative study of,
  69–72
  family-owned business,
  70
  German model, 70–71
  government ownership,
  70
  U.S. model, 70–72
  debt and equity, 385–88
  definition, 63
  institutional model, 68–72
  labor relations and, 61,
  63–80
  property rights and, 61,
  63–80
  relations between firms and
  financial markets and, 61,
  63–80
  See also Law, economics,
  and organization theory;
  Transaction cost
  economics
Courts
  admissibility of expert
  evidence and, 105–28
  Daubert trilogy and,
  105–28
  evaluating, 114
  Federal Rules of

Evidence and,
  105, 108
Frye test, 106–108, 110,
  122
  philosophy of
  practicality and,
  111–13
  procedural
  considerations, 116–18
  social construction and
  gatekeeping, 114–16,
  118
Criminal justice
  individual risk assessment
  and, 397–418
  See also Individual risk
  assessment
Criminal punishment, 17–32
  comparative law and, 17,
  30–32
  harshness and, 25–29
  heterogeneity
  hypothesis, 26–28
  hierarchical traditions
  and, 28–29
  religious traditions and,
  27–28
  modernity and, 17–25
  Anglo-American
  penitentiary model, 19
  "new penology," 20, 25
  punishment relative to
  other social practices,
  20–25
  theory of
  individualization in
  punishment, 19
  social traditions of violence
  and, 29–30
  cultural patterns of
  personal honor and, 30

423

ANNUAL REVIEWS

Intelligent Synthesis of the Scientific Literature

Annual Reviews – Your Starting Point for Research Online
http://arjournals.annualreviews.org

- Over 900 Annual Reviews volumes—more than 25,000 critical, authoritative review articles in 32 disciplines spanning the Biomedical, Physical, and Social sciences— available online, including all Annual Reviews back volumes, dating to 1932

- Current individual subscriptions include seamless online access to full-text articles, PDFs, Reviews in Advance (as much as 6 months ahead of print publication), bibliographies, and other supplementary material in the current volume and the prior 4 years' volumes

- All articles are fully supplemented, searchable, and downloadable—
see http://lawsocsci.annualreviews.org

- Access links to the reviewed references (when available online)

- Site features include customized alerting services, citation tracking, and saved searches

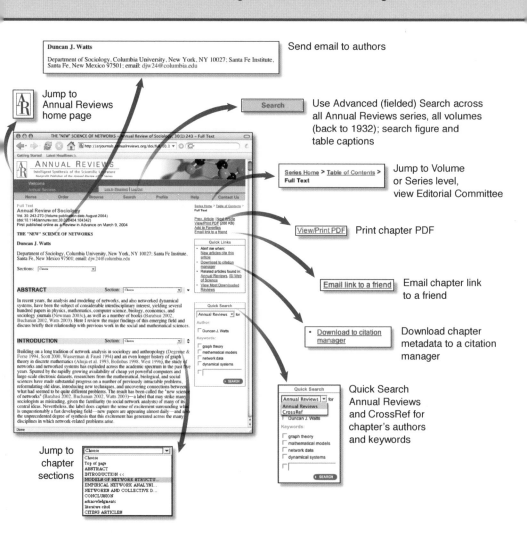